DECEPTIONS OF THE AGES

"MORMONS," FREEMASONS, AND

EXTRATERRESTRIALS

By

MATTHEW D. HEINES

Copyright © 2010 by Matthew D. Heines
All rights reserved. No part of this book may be reproduced, stored, or transmitted by any means—whether auditory, graphic, mechanical, or electronic—without written permission of both publisher and author, except in the case of brief excerpts used in critical articles and reviews. Unauthorized reproduction of any part of this work is illegal and is punishable by law.
Paperback ISBN: 978-0-615-38575-4

For my mother, my wife

And

The American People

Thank you for your all of your support.

This book is available at Heinessight.com, as well as Amazon.com, it's subsidiaries and commercial partners. It is also available at iBooks on the Apple store and eBooks in Kindle format. For more information about books by Matthew D. Heines, or the Middle East, visit www.heinessight.com.

Copyright © 2010 by Matthew D. Heines
All rights reserved. No part of this book may be reproduced, stored, or transmitted by any means—whether auditory, graphic, mechanical, or electronic—without written permission of both publisher and author, except in the case of brief excerpts used in critical articles and reviews. Unauthorized reproduction of any part of this work is illegal and is punishable by law.
Paperback ISBN: 978-1-453-87739-5

www.heinessight.com

Table of Contents

Background Check 1
Welcome to the Tree of Forbidden Knowledge 2
Controlling the Herd 29
History According to the Bible 54
Part 1 Two Histories? 81
History According to History 82
Part 2 The Ancient World 107
Rome and the Middle Ages 108
Part 3 The Modern World 133
History of the World 134
A Tale of Two Kingdoms 156
7-1 Mammon 161
7-2 The Kingdom of God 169
7-3 Mammon and the Federal Reserve Bank 173
The Kingdom of God Goes to War 180
Mammon Takes Over America 195
Mammon Goes to War 209
"Common Knowledge" 222
History According to the Latter-day Saints 244
The Book of Mormon: An Overview 263
Latter-day Saint History: The Book of Mormon 279
Rise of the Templars 309
The Secret Society 325
The Devil's in the Details 335

From Templars to Freemasons	358
Secret Societies, Getting Away With Murder	383
The Kingdoms Meet: The Latter Day Saints and the Freemasons	404
Assassination and Masonic Machinations in Nauvoo	427
Part 4 The Extraterrestrial Question	428
Homo Sapiens Science	455
Alien Science	473
Extraterrestrial Science	495
Extraterrestrial Encounters in the Scriptures	508
Back to the Past, or the Future?	537
Sources	555
More great books by Matthew D. Heines	574

1 ✪ Deceptions of the Ages

Background Check

Chapter 1

Welcome to the Tree of Forbidden Knowledge

"And I, the Lord God, commanded the man, saying: Of every tree of the garden thou mayest freely eat. But of the tree of the knowledge of good and evil, thou shalt not eat of it, nevertheless, thou mayest choose for thyself, for it is given unto thee; but, remember that I forbid it, for in the day thou eatest thereof, thou shalt surely die." (Moses 3:16-17)

This book is for that very small percentage of the human population that possesses an inquisitive nature and is willing and able to keep an open mind until all of the arguments are presented. It's kind of a tree of knowledge of the most forbidden kind. Why forbidden? Most of us have been programmed all of our lives as to how to think, speak and react to any information that has been either approved or condemned by those who control our lives and our thoughts. If you are willing to keep an open mind until the conclusion of this book, I feel that you will be rewarded with a new outlook on life that will bring you much closer to an understanding of who and what you really are and the value you possess as a human being and a member of a large and diversified group of intelligent beings that populate our universe.

If you are reading this book in order to make money refuting it, or for the purposes of ridiculing the author or the people mentioned in this book, then you will have to be careful for there are quite a few vultures in the holding pattern already. On the positive side, because of my weaknesses as a writer and a researcher, you will have lots of ammunition. Also, there will be many who will listen to what you have to say which will save them from reading this information and actually thinking about it themselves. You will, no doubt, be able to collect your twenty pieces of silver many times over.

The Best of Times

We are living in a fantastic period of history where everything that we once imagined is now becoming possible. In the age in which we live, there are, and have been dozens of earth-shattering discoveries over the course of the last decade. Every day, as we come to understand more and more about not only the world in which we live, but the universe as well, we are making discoveries and technologies that seemed like science fiction just twenty or thirty years before. Before the last decade, there were dozens of earth-shattering discoveries and the decade before that and so on and so on. If we go back a few centuries, we will find an earth-shattering discovery in almost every decade since the year 1453. So, the obvious question is what happened? Even more important, why did it happen now, and not before? Even more important than that, what mistakes have we made that got us to this place, and what can we do to keep us from making even bigger mistakes in the future? Before we attempt to answer these very broad questions, we must come to an understanding of our world and of ourselves.

In this book, I will try to give you a quick glimpse into the history of our science, economic, and belief systems. The reason for this is simple. One of the mistakes that mankind continues to make is in the assumption that these areas are somehow completely disconnected, when, in fact it is that fallacy that has led to more misunderstandings and misery than almost anything else, except for disease and starvation. We have reached the age when, as we shall see, we understand that we are not alone in the universe. Even the corporation/government/media has come to understand that they either allow the truth to be told or risk becoming a relic of the past, as the people of the world cast them aside and unite as what we are; all members of the homo sapien species with no need of a "World Order" in which the same old people with the same outdated ideas consolidate their power under the banner of "security."

And so, this book is my feeble attempt to make the average citizen of any country in the world aware of the processes that have led us to where we are today. As someone once said, "Those who don't understand History are doomed to repeat it." For that reason, I am not writing this book for the scientists, or the historians, the doctors or the lawyers or the professional "spin doctors" in the media. I am writing this book for the truck drivers, the secretaries, the high school drop outs, the janitors, the mechanics, the day care workers, the landscapers, the farmers and all the people who didn't get a chance, for whatever reason, to get a college education. I am writing it because they are the ones who always have to pay the heaviest price and they never fully understand why.

The sad fact is, to the people you vote for, and the corporations you end up giving most of your money to, you are an idiot. You are the "Joe six-packs" or the "Soccer moms" without the mental capacity to understand the schemes that are being thrown at you by the corporations, government and lawyers. Why, you don't even speak the same language as them, so when they use all those "high fluting" words, you barely understand what they are talking about and just assume they are doing what is good for you. What they are doing most of the time is taking you out of the debate and spending your money behind closed doors in return for some of that money coming back into their bank accounts.

I am what most would call an anomaly, or something that shouldn't be where it is, when it is. I come from a working class background, well, actually, "working class" to us was filthy rich. But I realized early on that in my country, if a person worked hard, they could get what they wanted, and I wanted to be a teacher. I served in the Army in order to qualify for veteran's assistance. Unfortunately for me, after obtaining a Bachelors degree in History and a Masters degree in Education, when I tried to be a teacher in our public education system, I found out they didn't want teachers, instead they wanted coaches and people who fit a certain demographic.

When my daughter was born, the woman I had been married to for all of one month after she told me she was pregnant suddenly wanted a divorce. She told me she knew, "how to use the courts," against me and I would never see my daughter. I laughed at her. This is the United States, isn't it, with justice, equality, etc.? When I saw an Oregon judge actually laugh when I asked her why we hadn't been sworn in, and then tell me that I had to, "hurry it along," because she had a, "luncheon to attend," I found out the hard way that the United States courts, especially those in the State of Oregon, don't care about the truth, they only care about lies. I found out, as most men who have been through a divorce have discovered, that men have no rights in the eyes of so-called "family courts." In spite of repeated pleas to the FBI, the Justice Department, two US attorney generals, the Governor's office and countless others, they will not help me to find my daughter and they don't enforce the law. The only people in this country who do have rights are, as an attorney once told me, the rich who can afford them or

the people that the government stipulates have rights, and that doesn't include white males. In other words, our so-called "justice" system is based upon injustice. So, if our justice system is based on lies, *what else is*?

I chose the topics for this book because of their relevance and the fact that they are the best examples of what I believe the number one problem in our world is; the lack of credible information. The "flip side" of that equation is manipulation of the public through disinformation. Those who manipulate our information know full well that we can't solve a problem unless we really understand what it is. In this book, I hope you will understand how you have been manipulated, and by whom, so that we can come together and put an end to it once and for all.

In this book, I am not saying anything new, or earth shattering. All this information is out there for you to see, study, and understand for yourself. I am only putting information together in as concise of a format as possible, so that it is presented in a manner that is easy to read, and to understand. Each chapter in this book can fill volumes of books for those that want to do further research into these topics. All I am attempting to do is to skim the surface of topics that best highlight how we are manipulated by disinformation, distorted facts and our own inability to look for the truth ourselves. We all know something is wrong with the direction we are headed, unless we are rich, of course. Unfortunately, we didn't know exactly what it is, until now.

The extraterrestrial truth

In 1985, I believe it was in the month of April, I was serving as a paratrooper in Charlie Company, of the 1/508th Airborne Infantry Battalion, a unit of the 82nd Airborne Division. We had been assigned six months of peacekeeping duty in the Sinai Desert as part of a UN Multi-National Force and Observers (MFO) contingent. Our base, called "South Camp," was situated about a mile from the modern day resort town of Sharm el Sheikh, at Naama Bay, Egypt. Myself, and five or six other members of my company had been selected for our battalion decathlon team. We trained for a week for a competition with the other members of the MFO contingent, who were located in an area in the Northern Sinai.

When we arrived at North Camp, we were assigned our rooms and, as part of our briefing, information was relayed to our squad leader that the previous night, a UFO had hovered right outside the camp perimeter fence and had sat there for about twenty minutes. The Colombian contingent had been manning the guard tower and had been given instructions not to fire upon the craft. The entire camp was alerted and weapons were being issued at arms rooms, when, suddenly, the craft began to move slowly away. When we arrived, it was the only thing that people were talking about. In the Sinai MFO publication, *The Sandpaper*, which came out during our stay there, an article was printed in which all of the above information was repeated, and in the closing paragraphs, it simply stated that the Sinai desert had a long history of UFO sightings.

At this point, let me say, that I have never seen anything that can be described as a UFO. As an avid camper, I, of course see lights in the sky that I could not explain due to their incredible speed, or height, or both, but I personally have never seen anything that I would ever describe as an extraterrestrial craft. Now, why is it so important that I say that? Because, for whatever reasons, the subject of extra-terrestrials has become, not a subject of scientific study, at least on the popular level. Instead, it has become a belief system.

The question is hardly ever asked, "Do you *think* there are UFO's?" The question is always asked, "Do you *believe in* UFOs?" It is a simple game of semantics, people *believe in* God, Santa Claus, Manifest Destiny, lower taxes, and the Easter Bunny, because if we phrase the question like that, then we automatically categorize the noun, or UFOs or extraterrestrials as intangible objects that cannot necessarily be seen or proven, much like lower taxes. It is a subtle mind trick, but how many times have we heard the phrase, "*He believes in UFOs,*" to describe someone in a derogatory fashion? How many times have you heard someone say, "*He thinks that there are UFO's*," especially in the popular media? If you *think that*, as opposed to *believe in*, then there is the implication that there has been some kind of reasoning involved and then there might be follow-up questions, either intended, or accidental, such as, "why?" or "Why do you *think that* there are extraterrestrials?" Maybe we don't want to hear the answer, so we don't ask any questions that involve the word "think" because it can just get too messy. Someone who *believes in* something is much easier to discredit than someone who, *thinks that*.

The" Balloon Boy," "UFO nuts" and Science

For example, as recently as 2009, when the news channels around the world were covering the Richard Heele so-called "Balloon Boy" scandal in Colorado in the United States, the UFO shaped balloon that his son was supposed to be riding in, was on millions of television screens when I heard a Fox News commentator ask about the father's credibility.

"Is he one of these people who *believes in* UFOs?"

Not to take anything away from the cerebral and well thought out commentary of the Fox News people, but the insinuation was clear; they were looking for anything they could use to assassinate the character of UFO balloon builder, and *Balloon Boy* father, Richard Heele. The fact that his son was supposedly aboard a UFO shaped craft was something that even the people on Fox News could figure out by themselves. If Richard Heele was a "UFO nut," then he was obviously, in the eyes of the corporate/government/media, someone who was mentally unstable and someone whom the corporate/government/media didn't have to spend a lot of time investigating in order to gather enough information to destroy the credibility and the life of a man who dared to venture into the realm of science on his own. We will talk about the influence of the corporate/government/media later on in the book, but for now, it is important to be aware that the corporate/government/media has its own system of language that is used to control the way we all think. Like magic, once you learn the trick, it seems easy, but if you don't know the trick, you don't how you are being fooled.

Richard Heele is also a fine example for another aspect of our study, the field of science. Richard Heele had an interest in science, anti-gravity, electromagnetism and the study of the weather. In an interview, his neighbor said he was a nice guy. He was just, "different." He was "different" because he was interested in science? Was he like Dr. Emmitt Brown in the Steven Spielberg, *Back to the Future* movies? Unfortunately, for the common man, or woman, there has been such a disconnect when it comes to dissemination of our wonderful advances in science, that the only connection most of us have to advances in technology and biology happen when we buy something or we have to visit the doctor. People who we actually call "scientists" have become "different" than the rest of us.

In the next few decades, in a world where we have calculated that our knowledge doubles exponentially every five years, there will undoubtedly be discoveries in science, history, archeology and psychology that will most likely change, in some degree our biological and spiritual evolutionary paths. In other words, who we are now and what we will be for the next two hundred thousand years could significantly change over the course of the next few years, and there is a very real chance that most of us won't even know it when it happens. Why is that? What is so intrinsically wrong with us as a species that we cannot be honest with one another anymore? Why can't we all have access to science, at least in a simple, uncomplicated way?

I wrote this book for a number of reasons. I am not a scientist, but I love science. I am not a historian but I love history. I am not a philosopher, but I love philosophy. I am not religious, but I love religion. I am here to tell you that **it is okay to be interested in something that makes you more aware of the world and the universe than you were before**. In fact, as I have discovered, and you will soon discover, the universe is, as someone once said, "not only stranger than we can imagine, it is stranger than we can possibly imagine." In the modern age, the fields, of religion, science, philosophy and history are, as tango dancers who, having parted in the apogee of their dance for the last four hundred years, are coming back together to form a single body out of two very distinct, graceful figures.

In this book, I would like to give you an understanding of where we have been and why the world is the way it is, so that you may at least have a chance to help to determine the way the world of the future will be. But you cannot know, as Dr. James Burke once said, where you are going until you understand where you have been.

Before we begin to look into our past, let us look at a topic that later we will be discussing in much more depth as we continue through our investigation of some of the key mysteries of our time. Let us conduct what Albert Einstein would call a, "thought experiment." This will serve two purposes. First, it will familiarize you with the topic we will discuss in the last sections of this book. Second, it will give us an introduction into what this book is really about, and that is the subject of information and how it is altered, withheld, spun, distorted and exaggerated until what we would classify as the truth is nowhere near what actually happened. Are you ready? Good, on with our though experiment!

An imaginary encounter

Imagine one summer day that you and your kids are having a barbecue in the backyard of your lovely suburban home. Your backyard is of medium size and on either side of you is a family of similar size and make-up. They are also enjoying what has turned out to be a wonderful summer day. The sun is shining and a cool breeze is blowing, keeping the temperature just like your delicious burgers, not too hot and not too cold. Your children, ages nine and eleven, are playing lawn darts with the children from the house next door. Your spouse is setting the table and your stomach is growling from hunger and the delicious smell of hamburgers on the barbecue.

Suddenly, you realize that you are not standing in the warmth of the sun any longer. Instead, a shadow has made its way across the yard and stopped. You, with your spatula in hand, continue to flip the burgers, but, as you do, you begin to recall that just a few moments ago, there was not a cloud in the blue sky. You get the feeling that something is not exactly right, but you continue with your burger flipping as the thought of a summer rain shower fills your mind. Suddenly, your daughter looks up in the sky.

"What's that?"

Instinctively, you look up towards the sky without looking at your daughter. You expect to see a cloud, but instead there is a strange object hovering over your house. It appears to be round and silver like a giant hubcap. The other thing you notice is that the object is huge. It's big enough to cover your entire block. Instantly, your brain begins to process information as it matches the known images you have stored with what appears to be hovering over your house. There doesn't appear to be any stored information in your brain that matches your past experiences with that object. In milliseconds, your brain then sifts through your brain's database and as it does, you hear your neighbor Frank say, "What the hell is that?" But no one seems to answer.

"I dunno," you say, without thinking.

Your brain has sifted and combed until it arrived at a possible explanation.

"It looks like one of them flying saucers," you hear someone say.

Faced with the unfamiliar, your heart begins to race, and you feel the hair stand up on the back of your neck. As the strange object continues to hover, your curiosity changes to fear of the unknown and you are afraid for your children.

"Alright, everybody get inside."

But you don't take your eyes off of the object as it hovers quietly above your house.

"Frank, you're seeing this, right?" you ask.

On the other side of your house, you hear commotion as the Martinez family spills out into the yard. "It's a UFO!!" You hear one of their children say.

A UFO... A UFO...

"Yeah, I see it," Frank says.

He yells at his children in your yard to get inside the house. Still, the object hovers, motionless. You guess it is a hundred feet above your house, and nobody appears to be moving. At the Martinez house, you hear Mrs. Martinez talking to her children.

11 ✪ Deceptions of the Ages

"Quick, go get the camera."

Her apparently calm voice and the mention of such a common item as a camera reassures you that there is nothing to fear. And still, you stand motionless, unable to move. Then, the round, silver object appears to be getting smaller as it climbs slowly higher and you realize it's going away. You feel yourself consciously breathing again, and for the first time, you look down and across the yard at your children. You hear someone at the Martinez house say, "Here mom," and then she says something but you don't hear what it is she is saying because your children have just begun to release themselves from their hypnotic state.

"What was it?" Was it a space ship?" they ask, but you don't hear them.

And then, the silvery object speeds off faster than anything you have ever seen. You become more aware of your surroundings as the smell of burning meat fills your nostrils and you become aware of what you consider to be your normal life. You look at the hamburgers on the grill and try to flip them over in order to prevent irreparable damage. Your spouse, unaware of the strange visitors, returns outside.

"What's going on out here?"

You hear your children's voices again.

"What was that?"

And at the same time, next door, you hear your neighbor Frank.

"You shoulda seen it honey, it was huge!"

In the Martinez yard, you hear one of the kids talking to his mother.

"I saw people on it, little people."

You didn't see any people.

"Did you get a picture?" you say, looking over at Mrs. Martinez.

"I think so," she says, "but it probably isn't very good, it was flying away by the time I got it in focus."

Your children's voices become more distinct as they continue to ask you questions.

"What was it?"

"It was a flying saucer. I read about them in school. It was a flying saucer, right?" you hear your son say.

You look at your neighbor, Mrs. Martinez. Her husband is a policeman and works on the weekends. She and her children are looking at the images on the small digital camera. You look over the other way at your neighbor Frank, who seems to be staring at the sky, as if the strange craft may return. Suddenly you hear your son's voice.

"…right? It was a UFO, wasn't it?"

Your daughter keeps telling you she is scared, but only now, are you aware of it. She isn't the only one.

"It was a UFO right!?" Your son shouts again.

You don't know what to say. You need confirmation from someone before you say anything. Finally, you answer.

"I'm not sure, take your sister inside."

Your son looks at you for a second, and then grabs his sister by the hand. You throw what's left of your burnt hamburgers on the side of the grill and stroll across the yard to where Frank and his children are now standing motionless, looking at the sky.

"Frank, can I talk to you?" you say while looking at the children.

He stops looking at the sky and focuses his gaze upon you.

"Oh, sure. "You kids go in the house," he says.

The children stop looking at the sky, say nothing and begin walking to their house.

"Whaddya think?" you ask.

13 ✪ Deceptions of the Ages

"I don't know," he replies. "Looks like a flying saucer."

Frank works as a sales representative for a local beer distributor. His wife died a few years ago and he is single, raising two children.

"I know," you agree. "What I mean is, what are we going to say?"

Frank looks back up at the sky, and then at you.

"Oh, I see, well, I ain't saying anything I didn't see anything. I can't afford to lose my job, I need the insurance and I'm ten years from retirement."

"Okay," you agree. You remember seeing stories of how people who come forward with stories about UFOs and abductions are ridiculed and humiliated, not to mention unemployed.

"I sure don't want to be the "UFO nut" at the office. I would never hear the end of it."

Suddenly, you become aware of some commotion coming from the Martinez' yard.

"I got it," she yells in your direction as if it is some kind of great news. She begins the journey across your yard with her children in tow.

"Great," you hear Frank mutter under his breath, "just what we need."

She walks up to where you are standing with Frank and holds up the camera. In the display window, you can see what looks like the silvery object, but it is a little blurred.

"You see," she says, "I got it just before it started going really fast. The other pictures are too blurry to make out.

"What are you planning to do with it?" Frank asks.

"Put it on my computer, let my kids take it to school," she replies. "I'll send it to your email," she says.

You, being the more diplomatic of the two, ask the next question.

"Do you think that is a good idea, I mean to send your kids to school with that picture?"

"Sure, why not, their friends will think it's cool. Maybe they can do a report on it in their science class."

There is silence for a few moments as both you and Frank look at her, thinking.

Finally, Frank speaks.

"Well, you can do what you want, but don't get us involved, and don't ask us to support your *story*." The way Frank says *story*, with an edge on the word, makes it obvious he is getting upset.

Suddenly, her expression changes as she looks at Frank and then back at you.

"Why not? Mrs. Martinez asks, "It's the truth. Are you going to lie and say you didn't see it?"

"That's exactly what we're going to do," Frank says, "If you insist on making a fool of yourself in public, don't get us involved."

Mrs. Martinez suddenly becomes angry.

"A fool? For telling the truth? I would rather be an honest fool, than a liar. What are you going to say to your children?"

"I guess I'll tell them that's how the world works," Frank says.

You try to reason with her, to make her understand the reality of UFO's and what happens to people who see them.

"Maybe you should talk this over with your husband when he gets home. He might be able to explain this a little bit better."

"I will have a talk with my husband," she says as her hand with the camera drops to her side.

"And, we will do what is right. This is important. That was a real spaceship with little people on it and we need to help people to understand that. I am not going to lie to my children or anyone."

As she walks out of hearing distance, you hear Frank mutter.

"Those crazy Mormons…"

There was a heated discussion that night in the Martinez household that you could hear as you sat in your yard, wondering if possibly, that strange craft might return. For a few days nobody said anything again about the flying saucer. As the days went by however, the story, or the picture of the UFO, made its way first, to the local junior high school internet server, and ended up on the first page of the local newspaper, under the caption, "Mormon woman "photographs" flying saucer.""

The story in the paper explains how the wife of a local Mormon patrolman claims to have photographed the saucer from her back yard. Her neighbors, who denied seeing the flying saucer, or having any knowledge of it, suggested that her children liked to play Frisbee with an old hubcap and that was probably what she saw and photographed. Neighbors declined to comment when asked if the woman had a history of irrational behavior. Local Air Force officials confirmed the hubcap theory as the most plausible. Her husband, Sergeant Martinez, the story continued, is now known on the police force as "Martian-ez" and according to department officials, is slated to receive the first, Galactic Officer of the Year Award next spring. It is also noted that Sergeant Martinez did not see the UFO and agrees that the picture is most likely what the neighbors and Air Force said it was.

Of course this account, or thought experiment, has no basis in reality per se, but the elements in the story probably have a familiar ring to the reader. It is a well-known fact that people who claim to have seen or have been abducted by extraterrestrial craft are often ridiculed, are denounced as liars, frauds and depicted as emotionally unstable. They have their professional licenses revoked. They are dubbed "UFO nuts" by the community and are generally ostracized for their 'outlandish' claims. Of course, the media will automatically look for any obvious clues, such as divorce, financial instability, drinking habits and, as in our case, association with groups that the media has previously manipulated the public into thinking about in derogatory fashion, such as members of the Church of Jesus Christ of Latter-day Saints whom they have dubbed, "Mormons" in a derogatory manner since the beginnings of the Church in the early 1800's.

Of course, that is not to say that there aren't some individuals with questionable reliability and credentials that do make outlandish claims of encounters with extraterrestrials. I can remember a certain individual, a gentleman well along in years, that almost every month, stood up in Fast and Testimony meeting and told the members of the church that, while he was walking his dog near the school grounds, a space ship landed and the spacemen got out and started telling him certain things. I do not recall what it was that he claimed that he told them, because my friends and I were trying desperately not to start laughing in the middle of the church service. In fact, we spent the time inflicting pain on ourselves, trying to avoid the giggling faces of our compatriots and sudden outbursts of laughter. Whether this individual actually had encounters with extraterrestrial beings on our school grounds is not something that I would spend a lot of time dwelling about. However, when airline and military pilots, ground controllers, policemen and people in our aerospace engineering industries come forward with claims of encounters with extraterrestrial craft, I am not so programmed that I will dismiss them out of hand.

"Brainwashing" and the media

Programmed you say? As in *brainwashed*? This is the United States and not the Soviet Union. The corporation/government doesn't use the media to brainwash people, *or does it*? If you think the government does not brainwash people in the sense that it gives its citizens common visual images in which to associate with ideas, concepts or people it likes or doesn't like, let us try another thought experiment.

For example, when I say John F. Kennedy, what is the first thing that comes to your mind? Do you see a black and white image of President Kennedy standing in front of a podium? Do you hear, "Ich bin ein Berliner?" or do you hear, "Ask not what your country can do for you…?" What about Richard Nixon? Do you see a portly, balding gentleman with a dark suit waving two *peace* signs from the door of the Presidential helicopter? How about Ronald Reagan? "Well…"Albert Einstein? Frizzies.

Mahatma Gandhi? Good tan, old sheet, bad spectacles. Saddam Hussein? Burt Reynolds moustache and hand held out in the "Queen" style wave. D-Day? You see dead Americans lying on a black and white beach. What about Russia? You see missiles in Red Square. Joe Stalin? You see beady eyes, bushy moustache, and bad cap. Italy? The Coliseum. Germany is Adolf Hitler, and on it goes.

So, what if I say extraterrestrials? You think of a little gray or green man with big eyes. If I say UFO, you say…"Nut?"

What if I say Mormons? You think, "*Joe Smith*," six wives, a golden bible and funny underwear.

What if I were to say, Freemasons? What do you think? You think of nothing? You don't think of anything when I say, "Freemasons?" Why would you know more about a group as obtuse as the, Mormons than the very men whose ideas founded this country? It's not the why in this case that is important. What is important is that you recognize this programming you have had all of your life.

In this book, we are going to talk about topics that you have already been programmed over and over again to visualize, and we are going to re-examine them in an objective fashion. Why? Because all of your life, you have heard that **Mormons, Freemasons and extraterrestrials** are things that people, possibly even you, "believe in." Now we are going to throw out the "believe in" tag and we are going to look at them as something that people think are true and have merit, so much so that they have staked their careers, their financial well-being and in some cases, their lives on the fact that these ideas, or the reality that they represent are not something to be "believed in," but that they are as real as the light that comes from the sun.

As I said in the beginning of this book, the world is changing so fast, that it is very hard to keep up. Because of our advances in technology, even the corporation/government knows that in order to maintain at least some of its credibility, it must begin to come to terms with and release this information because their credibility has eroded to almost zero because of their insistence on feeding misinformation to the public on a day-to day basis.

Knowledge and the Information Age

Therefore, knowledge, the way we know and disseminate it in our day and age when we want everything quickly and painlessly is by its own nature, at a disadvantage. Let's take the idea of DNA, for example. DNA is a chemical blueprint for every cell in every living thing on earth. How it works is not easy to explain, and not the subject of this book, so I will forego the Biology 101 lecture and get to the point. You cannot reduce how DNA works into a cliché, or a catch phrase. Therefore, it is not likely that any more than twenty per-cent of the people whom you pass on the street will be able to adequately explain what it is and what it does. If we want people to know what it is and what it does, we have to sit them in a classroom or lecture hall, probably charge them fees, and expect them to sit through a rather dull, lifeless presentation. Nobody is going to watch a sit-com about DNA. Let's face it, amino acids are just not that funny, therefore there is no need for people to want to learn about it, unless it has some financial reward behind it, or people can be made to think that it is some kind of threat.

But, that is just one concept. What about the breakthroughs we have made in quantum physics and mechanics? Can we explain those in a cliché or a catch phrase? What about the Unified Field Theory? What happened when the glaciers receded eleven thousand years ago? What science explains those things? How do they come to their conclusions? Unless we come to a fundamental change in ourselves, our systems of education and why it is important that people are constantly involved in the process of learning new things, then our brains, with the limited capacity they possess, will never be able to keep up with the ever-changing field of knowledge that is around us.

The technology that we have developed can be used as the tools to increase the knowledge level of each human being. Through the internet, the use of CGI, and our teachers, our government and our corporations can, instead of encouraging us to waste our lives playing video games, and watching mindless chatter on TV, take us on a journey through the cell, the universe, a blood vessel, a hydrogen powered vehicle or economic theory.

Think of it this way; we have made the advances we have made in science and technology because of less than one percent of our population. What kind of amazing innovations and technology would be available to us if that number were to increase to five or ten or twenty percent? We need to change our fundamental attitudes towards learning and science, but before we do, we must understand a few things about the relationship between science, and what, for thousands of years, mankind has mistaken for science, or what we call religion. We must understand that it is the very opposition of these two schools of thought that has created the world in which we live today. If we cannot learn to reconcile these two areas of human thought, it will not be possible for us to progress as a species very much farther than we already have, and we will succumb to the many problems that science and religion have created for us, and if that happens, there will be very few of us left to understand or to explain to future generations what exactly went wrong.

Science vs. Religion

When it comes to science and technology, religion and philosophy we see the same limitations as we do with the rest of our knowledge. The problem stems from the ancient idea that science and knowledge need to be, for lack of a better term, compartmentalized. The most obvious compartmentalization is that a scientist cannot profess a belief in religion and vice versa. For reasons that we will soon see, any archeologist who finds evidence of a biblical account being accurate, soon becomes a pseudo-archeologist, and their funding is revoked until someone with a more "rational" mindset comes along. In the scientific world, any mention of or allusion to religion in research is forbidden. Similarly, in the religious world, any mention of Evolution, or the possibility of the Bible not being accurate to the last crossed '*t*' will, in most religions, meet with a rather hostile reaction from those who use the Bible to make a living.

But the compartmentalization of science goes beyond its age-old struggle with religion. Even among scientists themselves, the limitations of specialization in one field may severely limit our understanding of our own world. For example, an archeologist studying why the movements of northern tribes to southern regions, might suggest that overpopulation was a key factor, when a climatologist could have told them it was due to what we know as a "mini" ice age. The climatologist might not ask an astronomer if there were sunspots occurring at that time, although it was the sunspots that ultimately caused the mini ice age, which in turn caused the migration. A historian might not understand the biological and hereditary effects of slavery on African nations. An economist might not take into account a border skirmish that affected a country's trade and arable farmland during a period of years in which the country seemed to have descended into ruin.

Lastly, there is the need or desire to protect information for monetary, social or political reasons (*"Mormons," Freemasons and Extraterrestrials*) that might keep the knowledge of some great discovery in the closet for years after its, well, discovery. I could go on, but I think you get the point. In other words, there are ways to either prove or disprove theories these days simply by calling on other fields of science, but sometimes, for whatever reason, science doesn't make itself available to do so. In some cases, as in the cases of, *"Mormons," Freemasons and Extra-terrestrials*, science absolutely refuses to even discuss them, which would be like a witch-doctor telling his patients the new neurosurgeon in town doesn't exist.

In our culture where everything is, "dumbed down," because of a fear of a loss of Neilson ratings, it is going to be very difficult for the majority of people to have any say whatsoever about the changes in the future for their lives and the lives of their descendants when they are neither aware, nor do they understand the issues that are facing us. Therefore, we are at a crossroads, we can either educate ourselves or we can allow everything to be decided by technocrats and the rich. There is no middle road, and most leaders already feel that letting common people make their own decisions is inherently dangerous in our technologically advanced world.

No matter what your level of understanding, I think the issues in this book are of paramount importance for the future of mankind. I think the issue of extraterrestrials is as important as looking at the claims made by both the Freemasons and the Church of Jesus Christ of Latter-day Saints. If you scoff, I applaud you, as I want this book to look at these issues objectively and, with some degree of skepticism without the programmed bias we have already been programmed to have.

Those Crazy "Mormons"

To begin with, the LDS Church has, since its very early days, made some rather remarkable claims regarding everything from having knowledge and the writings of ancient civilizations, to visitations from otherworldly visitors. Among those claims, are no less than the visit of God and Jesus Christ who, the LDS Church claims appeared to Joseph Smith in the year 1820? In other words, if what Joseph Smith has said is true, the one event that the entire Christian world has been waiting for has already happened. Why hasn't the world been informed of this? Even better, why doesn't science take an objective view of these claims and refute them once and for all for the benefit of the thirteen million members of the fastest growing Church in Christianity, and anyone who may be misled in the future?

We know that there are plenty of people who have taken up the cross of attempting to discredit Joseph Smith, the LDS Church and sometimes even its members. As we will soon see, no one has come forth and proved that Joseph

Smith, a poor, uneducated laborer from upstate New York was the fraud that many claim. Nor, have they proven that the claims of the Church in regard to its doctrine or history are false. On the contrary, many of the advances we have made in science recently, serve to support the claims of the LDS Church. This brings up the final question, if the claims of the LDS Church are true, shouldn't we start paying attention to what they are saying? Even more, what is the motivation of the people who would want this knowledge kept from the rest of the world, who are these people and why is it so important for them to destroy the LDS Church?

No more miracles

I think if you will only bare with me for a few chapters while I present evidence, you will come to understand that because of our understanding of the universe, there really are no "miracles" any more. Science and the research and work of the greatest minds in history has brought many of the great mysteries of life nearer to the point of being solved than ever before. Unfortunately, because of our very nature, this moment will pass us by because, on the one hand, the truth of who we are and why we are here would cost the rich and powerful the two things they have that the rest of us don't; money and power. There are also a lot of people who either would "flip out" because the world wasn't what they thought it was or there are those who would say, *"I guess I don't have to go to work tomorrow, I think I'll go on a killing spree."* In any case, any new revelations about our existence would be better if left to those who are rationale enough to handle them. I would assume you are one of them and that is why you are still reading this book.

Before we actually jump in, I would like to come clean about my own viewpoint. Personally, I don't trust religious people and furthermore, I don't trust people who are not religious. I trust the people who are somewhere in the middle. I trust the people who believe in God and act like it, but don't try to push their beliefs on other people. I was raised in the LDS Church, and don't *believe in* it, but I *know that* there is nothing in the teachings of the Church, that is not philosophically and morally sound. Whether I believe that Jesus Christ appeared to Joseph Smith, or not, is a matter of faith and not science and therefore is my own personal business.

Unlike most, I love philosophy and good philosophy is good enough for me. Joseph Smith said that Jesus Christ and God, and a lot of other people appeared to him and told him how to form the new and final Kingdom of God on this planet. As long as his philosophy was correct, I would have known he was telling the truth then as surely as I know now, by looking at the evidence of how the Church of Jesus Christ of Latter-day Saints has grown to encompass the world with teachings of honesty, love and charity, that he was serious about what he said and what he did.

On the outside looking in

For those of who would claim that I am writing this because I am a "Mormon," you are only half right. I seldom attended church after high school. I joined the Army, went to college, and spent the years after either teaching or trying to get a teaching job all the way from Seattle to Alaska. I have experience as Joni Mitchell once said, of looking at, "life from both sides." Whatever you may have done in your life, I have probably done as well. I have spent the years since September 11, 2001, outside of the United States, working as a teacher in Arabian countries. I haven't attended an LDS Church service since I sat in an Oregon Courtroom in the year 2000 and watched the mother of my daughter, who also happened to be a member of the LDS Church, lie and perjure herself in front of a woman judge. She lied on court documents and what was more she lied after swearing on the Bible and promising to tell the truth. Needless to say, that experience really damaged my faith in people and in the institutions that we so inaccurately describe as our justice system. But the actions of one person who somehow manages to hide behind the cover of Latter-day Saint Church, does not mean that I blame the LDS Church, as some would.

Having spent most of my life outside of the Church, I have always been aware that there was never one thing that was taught or preached that was untrue, or even more important, unsound, or bad for me. So, that, plus my understanding of history and my love of learning, has given me a unique perspective on life that few have had. However, that experience in an Oregon courtroom did ruin any chance of me ever walking in to an LDS Church for the rest of my life without reliving the fact that because of my association in the Church, I will never have a normal family life and because of my association with the Church, I have a daughter somewhere that I have never seen and may never see, at least until we meet in the world in which there are no lies. But, as Jesus once said, "I have drunk from the bitter cup my father gave me." Like Jesus Christ, I don't blame my Heavenly Father for what human beings have done. I believe that when life hands you the bitter cup, the real test is whether or not you can drink from it and keep on smiling.

The Devil Worshippers

Be that as it may, my first, rather shocking experience of the hatred that people feel for members of the LDS Church happened when I was in the 7th grade. Until that time, I knew very little about the world, and because of the rosy picture that had been painted of the world and its people by the LDS Church, I had a pretty good outlook on both the world and my prospects within it.

So, let me take you back to a clear, crisp autumn morning in 1976. I was in the seventh grade then, and was making my way down the white and black checkerboard hallways of my school. To the right and left were lockers, some occupied by students talking, or getting books, or putting the last touches on their Farah Fawcett hairdos. I reached my locker and kicked it on the bottom, since it opened a lot faster that way, and pulled it open. I was rummaging through the mess looking for my math book, when I heard some commotion behind me. I turned around and saw a group of eighth graders looking at me.

"What?" I asked. I hadn't stolen anything of theirs or made fun of them, so I didn't know what they wanted with me.

"You worship Satan," one of them announced.

In our little town, we had more churches than people, and not only had I known my accusers most of my life, I also knew that they didn't go to my church.

"Okay, ha ha!" I said. I figured it was some kind of joke. No one ever talked about church in school. They didn't start laughing, or go away, so I began to feel a little uneasy.

"No joke, you *Morons* worship Satan!" One of the other guys said as if it was important enough for the hallway to hear.

I turned around and looked at the three. They looked deadly serious.

"Who said that?" I asked.

One of them, the leader of the group answered.

"Our pastor. We learned about it in church. We even watched a movie."

That was a surprise.

"They told you that in Church?" I asked.

"Yeah, we know all about Joe Smith and that Mormon Bible," the shorter of the three answered.

"Who?"

"Joe Smith, the guy who wrote the Mormon Bible."

I really didn't know what to say. I was cross checking my facts as fast as possible. I had never heard of anybody worshipping or even mentioning old Beelzebub in any but a none-too-flattering context in church. I didn't know anything about a, "Mormon Bible," as far as I knew. Our Bible was the same as everyone else's. Lastly, I had never heard of Joseph Smith referred to as, "Joe Smith." I wasn't angry. I was confused.

"Do you mean the Book of Mormon?" I asked. "It was *translated* by Joseph Smith, but we use the same Bible you do."

There were a lot of firsts in that particular junior high school encounter. It was the first time anyone had made the association with the name *Mormon* and *moron*, which, I thought was somewhat clever and therefore, something that I should have said. The second thing that surprised me was that another church was actually discussing our Church while they were in church. We had to sit in church for three hours on Sunday listening to stories about Jesus, listening to people give talks, singing and attending one meeting after another, while their church was sitting around talking about us and how we worshipped Satan? I thought then that if I had to sit in a meeting and listen to someone trash-talking the Catholics or the Jehovah's Witnesses, to escape the boredom I would have hung myself with my clip-on tie.

I knew that none of the things these kids said were true, and were so far from what I knew to be true, the fact that my friends so adamantly believed it made my worldview change forever. I still wasn't sure if it was a joke, but the serious looks they were giving me made me think it wasn't.

"Well, have you read the Book of Mormon?" I asked.

"No, I don't have to read it, it's a book of the devil," the leader announced.

I was surprised by that response. "How can you say that if you never read it?" I asked.

"I would never read the book of the devil," he answered.

And so, that morning, I also learned that people will hate someone simply because it is easier to hate because of an easy lie than to find out a difficult truth. I learned that people believe what they want to believe. What I couldn't understand was, why they would hate the Latter-day Saints. There were other people who definitely deserved hating more than us. Take the Jehovah's Witnesses, for example. They didn't even have to go to public school and they were always passing out those pamphlets. Then there were the Seventh-Day Adventists, they didn't attend public school *and* they went to church on Saturday, which meant they got to shop on Sunday when the store (we only had one) was empty. There were the Presbyterians, whose name it was so difficult to spell. But, why pick on us? We went to public school, we went to Church on Sunday and our name, "Mormon" or LDS, was really easy to spell.

Well, there was something else. It was the fact that LDS Church has temples that are not open to anyone outside of the Church. Even from within the Church, there are strict guidelines that must be met in order to enter a temple. So, it was the secrecy, the goings-on-behind-closed-doors, that got people in a huff, or so I thought. As I went through life, I began to notice, that unless you lived in Utah, you never heard of the LDS Church at all, unless some polygamist in southern Utah was being locked up for marrying his wife's thirteen-year-old sister. Similarly, I have had lots of friends outside the church that knew three things about the, "Mormons." First, they had five wives. Second, they wore funny underwear. Third, they hated them. When I would explain that I was a

"Mormon," they would simply say, "Really? Well, you sure don't act like a "Mormon.""

"How does a "Mormon" act?" I would ask.

"I don't know." They would answer. "You're the only Mormon I know."

Before we continue, let me point out, if it is not already obvious, I am not endorsing the LDS Church, nor am I endorsing anything but the right for people to make their own decisions and the right everyone has to correct information in order to make those decisions. Other than that, I will endeavor to look at claims and evidence. Faith is something that goes beyond the scientific inquiry, and is usually based on the belief in a being or beings that exist outside our natural world, and who have the ability to control the events of our world beyond its own physical laws. Furthermore, the being or beings cannot be called to manifest themselves or provide proof of them without usually incurring the wrath of said Being or beings. In other words, you can't prove that there is a God, and you can't prove that there isn't.

Semantics and definitions of the terms in this book

I would just like to examine the subjects that we know in popular culture as The LDS Church, the Society of Freemasons and finally the phenomenon of visitors from other planets. Before we do however, I would like to make it clearly understood that I am talking about, in the case of the LDS Church, the main branch of the Church whose head is in Salt Lake City, in Utah. There are other branches of the LDS Church that have broken away from the main body for various reasons. Therefore, I am not referring to the RLDS (Re-organized Church of Jesus Christ of Latter-day Saints). Nor am I referring to a group of polygamists who moved to southern Utah or Arizona to live outside the laws and doctrines of the main Church.

Although members of the Church of Jesus Christ of Latter-day Saints are commonly referred to as "Mormons" and have even begun referring to themselves as such because that is how non-members refer to them. In this book, unless I am attributing a quote to a non-member or a piece of information put forward by a non-member, I will refer to members of the Church of Jesus Christ of Latter-day Saints as "LDS" or in some cases as "The Saints." The term

"Mormons" denotes a worship of Mormon, a Book of Mormon military leader, historian and prophet and is therefore a misnomer and a tool of slander against the Church so that people can say that members of the Church of Jesus Christ of Latter-day Saints are not "Christians." Members of the LDS Church do not worship anyone but God and Jesus Christ. Therefore I am not going to use the misnomer "Mormons" except where it is necessary.

In a similar note, when I refer to the Society of Freemasons, I am referring mostly to the Scottish Rite Order of Freemasonry, but these are not the only Orders of Freemasonry and I would like to make it clear to the reader that there is a distinction, which I will do later in the book. Unless it is necessary due to the context, I will not refer to *"aliens"* or *"UFOs."* I will refer to them as exactly what they are, and that is extraterrestrial beings. In other words, beings that are not originally from this planet.

Now, I should also like to detail my usage of terms just a little bit further. There are two kinds of extra-terrestrials (I won't call them E.T.'s because that might encourage the reader to drift off into Steven Spielberg's movie and completely forget what you are reading about). The first kind, are those who have physical bodies, or, what the government refers to as extra-terrestrial biological entities (EBE). The second kind are those who do not share our same physical characteristics and appear to be able to move between dimensions. We may call them angels, or ghosts, but not in this book. Since they appear to be lacking in substance and at times, according to people who claim to have seen them, sometimes give off excessive amounts of light, we will refer to these as extraterrestrial non-biological entities or extra-dimensional beings. (Hold on, don't close the book yet!)

Finally, as a student of history, I know it can be confusing for people who do not read history to read a phrase like, "in the twentieth century" when the writer means something that happened somewhere between 1900-1999. Since this book is not written specifically for historians or archeologists, but common every day working people, I will not use this kind of phraseology. For example, if something happened over an extended period between 1100 AD and 1199 AD I will say "in the 1100's" to keep the confusion of the reader to a bare minimum.

As you read this book, please forgive my shortcomings when it comes to my understanding of science. My background is in history. However, I am interested in all fields of learning, which, I believe allows me at least the motivation to write this book. In order to make this book "readable" I have tried my best to stick to the subject, present my evidence and then allow you to come to your own conclusions. For that reason, where it is possible, I try to use the words of the sources I am quoting in the fullness of their context, which sometimes requires some lengthy reading. I do this simply because I believe you are intelligent enough to understand what someone or something says, without me putting some kind of "spin" upon the text. In order to make this book appealing to as many people as possible, I will spend time explaining concepts and ideas as I would to someone who has no prior knowledge. If you have prior knowledge about any subject and wish to skip ahead, please do so. If you feel I have made grievous errors, please let me know.

Now, with all of that said, let's jump right into to some of the great Deceptions of the Ages!

Chapter 2

Controlling the Herd

"And he beheld Satan, and he had a great chain in his hand, and it veiled the

whole earth with darkness; and he looked up and laughed, and his angels rejoiced."

(Book of Moses 7:26)

An introductory overview (whatever that means)

Albert Einstein once said, "Everything is a miracle, or it isn't." With apologies to Dr. Einstein for this rather simplified explanation of his statement, what he meant was that everything can be explained scientifically, or else nothing can. In the early history of man, most things, such as the sun coming up in the morning, the plants that grew out of the ground and the changes in the weather, could simply be explained as the work of the gods, or God, and that was sufficient enough to allow people a reasonable amount of comfort and security in their lives. It was a simple equation. Keep the gods (or God) happy and the sun will shine, the plants will grow and the rains will come every spring. If the gods (or God) get angry, the sun will not shine, the plants will not grow and the rains will not come.

Since the 1600's, thanks to the Philosophes and the ancient Greeks, who gave us the Scientific Method, or the idea that knowledge should be based on observations, we in the West have been able to understand that the planet we inhabit orbits a medium sized star and twirls around in a full circle every twenty four hours. Our planet makes a big circle or orbit around our medium-sized star every 364.3 days. In modern times, we also understand that certain plants grow from certain seeds, and those seeds can be interbred with other plants that have desirable characteristics to make better plants. Crops can be rotated to make healthier soil. Rain comes more often than not in the spring as the earth's orbit and tilt allows the northern hemisphere more exposure to direct sunlight. This is all pretty elementary stuff that even a school child can explain in our time, but a few hundred years ago would have been considered the ideas of the Devil.

Once people like Galileo, Copernicus, and Newton figured out the big answers to the big questions, the questions began to change. Some began to ask, about the nature of God. For the next two hundred years, God evolved from the supreme all present and powerful Being who controlled our lives and the universe on a day-to-day moment-to-moment basis of the Old Testament until the late 1700's when He took on the form of a divine watchmaker. God made the universe and then left it to run itself. In our time, Dr. Stephen Hawking, the world famous astrophysicist, began his exploration of the universe by asking if there was a God at all and whether or not He was limited by the physical characteristics of this universe. Hawking came to the conclusion that there was not a God, or at least that God was not necessary to create the universe that we see (Hawking 4). However, the study of the infinitely big universe coincided with the study of the infinitely small atom, and in the discoveries we have made, we have discovered, that in fact, the universe is not only stranger than we imagined, it is stranger than we could have possibly imagined four hundred years ago before God got into the watch making business.

I must apologize here, for I have left out one option, for I am begging the question as the philosopher Thomas Aquinas once did when he asked if there was a being so great that He could create an object which even He, who was omnipotent, could not move. Like Aquinas, I am begging the question, or assuming automatically that there is a God, or an omnipresent intelligence. There are, in a bastardized version of Einstein's statement about miracles, two possibilities to this whole discussion. Either there is something there (a greater intelligence or Being) whereby things can be explained or there is not and everything is just a miracle or a random set of possibilities that worked out well for us.

The easiest route to take will be to simply dismiss it all as nonsense. If this is the course the reader chooses to follow, then I applaud the reader for exercising the free choice that is available to us all. If, however, the reader instead chooses to continue reading in order to make a more informed decision, after hearing the information I will present, I applaud that choice as well. Finally, I hope that the reader will forgive what may be considered blasphemy by some in order to explain, using the Scientific Method of observation, a new understanding of who and what God, or the gods that have been written about since the beginning of mankind may actually be. I hope to do so in an explainable and rationale way that will not alarm people and result in my being burned at the stake by the dogmatists in the corporation/government/media of our time.

In the last chapters we will see the testimonial evidence that the universe is stranger than we can possibly imagine, but it is a universe that is so strange, we are not allowed to imagine it, or at least talk about it without serious repercussions. We will read the testimonies of people who served in the military, intelligence and government communities who know that there is plenty of physical evidence available to show extraterrestrial phenomenon is real. I will explain why people who report sightings, and abductions, especially credible witnesses such as pilots, policemen and military personnel who are naive enough to file reports, are discredited and in some cases, have their lives and their careers ruined by simply telling the truth. We will see just whom it is that has the power to keep this information from the general public, destroy lives and sometimes the people themselves.

Personally, I do not feel that a race of beings like the human race that kills, hates, maims, steals and threatens others, not for food or survival like other animals, but simply for pleasure, or the intangible concept we call security, has any right to know what is really going on with regard to the extraterrestrial beings who apparently pose no threat to us. However, this is not a book about my own feelings, nor is it about extraterrestrials other than as a case in point. This is a book about information and how and why it is manipulated as well as by whom. Both the corporation/government/media and I can rest assured that most of those who are given this knowledge will continue grazing like sheep in a field. Hopefully, there are those few out there, who once they realize they have been taken in by the illusion, much like the audience at a magic show, that will have the intelligence to step back and say, "Oh, I see what's going on," and once they are able to see, will be able to use the technology we now understand to develop new ways of making energy and new ways of viewing the human race.

The LDS Candidate, the UFO Phenomenon and the "thought offensive"

In the 2008 presidential campaign, candidate Dennis Kucinich was asked if he had ever seen a UFO. The question stemmed from Kucinich's prior admission that he had, in fact seen a UFO. Once the laughter in the room subsided, LDS

Presidential candidate Mitt Romney was asked whether or not he believed in extraterrestrials. Mitt Romney's answer was based not so much on what he believed, rather, his answer was based upon what would hurt the chances of his candidacy after he had spent millions of his own money on his campaign. Romney declared, "No, I don't believe extraterrestrials have ever visited the earth." (Naymik)

The fact that sixty years after an extra-terrestrial craft, or crafts, crashed at Roswell New Mexico, that a presidential candidate like Romney, already at a disadvantage as the "Mormon" candidate would not tell his true beliefs about extra-terrestrials in a public forum, testifies to the effectiveness of the campaign to destroy lives and careers of people for even discussing the subject. Also, it shows the ongoing extraterrestrial "thought offensive" that began in the 1950's is even greater than the "thought offensive" carried out against the Church of Jesus Christ of Latter-day Saints since the1820's.

Managing the "thinking" herd

How does the "thought offensive" work? At the most basic levels of understanding, humans, like most other animals, operate in groups or what I will call "herds" hence the term, "herd mentality." The number one goal of the herd is the survival of the herd. Therefore, each individual's stake in the survival of the herd is based on a simple relationship: the herd's survival = the individual's survival. Throughout human history, primarily the males have protected the herd, and most often, the dominant males assumed a role of leadership in the herd. Domination of the herd was, more often than not, based not only upon brute strength, but also upon the ability to make beneficial decisions and an ability to make sure those decisions were carried out.

As human herds began to group together, there were sometimes struggles as to which herd's leaders would become the dominant decision makers, and unfortunately, more often than not, it was not intelligence, or moral virtue, but brute strength and deviousness that allowed some members of the herd to rise to leadership within the bigger and bigger herds. Regardless of who became the leader or how they assumed leadership, for thousands of years the herd followed the decisions of the dominant males, whether the decision was to move to new hunting grounds, build cities or go to war against another herd.

During the Renaissance, philosophers like Thomas Hobbes, Rene Rousseau and John Locke described this relationship between rulers and ruled in what they referred to as the "social contract." Individual members of the herd gave up the right to make decisions, redress grievances, and protect them to what we today call the government. In days gone by, it was to a warlord, as in Europe or Japan, or sometimes to religious leaders, as in Islamic, Native American and Hindu Cultures. Most often there is a relationship between warlords and religious leaders, as in ancient Egypt, Babylon and Medieval Europe whereby the religion gives legitimacy to the warlord and vice-versa.

However, the key element of the social contract was a quid pro quo relationship; the individual gave up certain rights, such as the right to make decisions for the herd, in return for food, shelter, security and a reasonable chance of finding a mate. Americans see this as "Life, Liberty and the Pursuit of Happiness." Should one of these elements be eliminated for enough of the sub-dominant males within the herd, depending on the circumstances, the herd would search for a new leader, although, very rarely would they search for a different form of government.

For millions, or thousands of years, depending upon your philosophical beliefs, humans have survived and evolved by belonging to herds of one form or another. In pre-history, our herds were family, bands or tribes. In the modern day, we may call them unions, or communes, congregations, gangs, lodges, political parties, cities, states and nations. We choose to belong to herds, because, as in the hunter-gatherer years, there was safety and security in a herd. In the herd, there is more of a chance of reproducing and seeing your offspring themselves mature to reproduce. In the herd there is food. In the herd there is shelter. On the most basic level of all, within the herd there is more chance that an enemy or a predator will kill another member of the herd before they get to you, giving you more warning to escape. In summary, in the herd there is safety, whether real or imagined. Outside of the herd, there is loneliness, danger and a lot more work.

Modern man and technological society has taken the herd to levels undreamed of before the twentieth century. You are reading a book (hopefully) that took literally thousands of people and hundreds of herds to make. Someone had to write it. Someone had to make the computer it was written on. Someone had to make the software for the computer. Someone had to cut the trees to make the paper. Someone had to stock it on the shelves, or make sure it was shipped to the right address. Someone had to make sure the money you paid was deducted from your credit or debit card, and so on and so on. We exist in religious herds and family herds. There are herds where we work. There are herds where we learn, such as our college sororities or fraternities, teams, clubs and student governments. Our educators belong to herds. We have sports herds, car herds, political herds, religious herds, chat room herds, drinking herds, job herds, TV or movie star herds, and organized crime herds.

A hundred years ago, a person may have belonged to five herds at most, but we belong to dozens and sometimes hundreds of herds throughout our lifetime. So, what influences our decision to join a particular herd? Basically, there are two reasons we join a particular herd. First, we join the herds that our family is associated with, such as a trade or a religion. Second, the more selfish of the two reasons is we join a herd that we think will improve our abilities to get things. In that respect, we haven't evolved too far from the hunter-gather stages of our evolution. For example, people join a union herd to counteract the basic instincts of the greed of the company they work for. People join the Lions, or Rotary, or Freemasons in an effort to get more affluence. People join religious groups to get to heaven. People join charitable groups to get a good feeling for helping others.

As in the hunter-gatherer stages, there is always the desire to belong to the dominant herd. When our sports team wins, we didn't do anything, but we feel good. When our candidate or party wins an election we feel good because we voted for the right herd. When we go to war and our side wins a battle, we feel good as long as we weren't killed or maimed. It is a basic survival instinct for us to desire to be in the winning herd because the winning herd gets more things. However, there must be a dominant herd on top of all of these herds and that herd is called the government. In the days of the warlord, the warlord had a herd upon which he depended to control everybody else. In the twentieth century, there were some radical ideas about controlling the herd, but, as we have seen, it was the same kind of herd with a new vocabulary.

The Communist model

In Russia, for example, they traded the warlord-religion power model for what is known as the Bolshevik or Communist state. The idea that was sold to the people of Russia was that "the people" knew better how to run things. They sold this idea by saying that the state was based upon rule by "the collective will" and was superior to the previous model of rule based upon the ownership of land, church etc. However, the system had flaws from the start. The most obvious flaw being that the new organization was exactly the same as the old one, there were just new names. Once the Bolsheviks seized power, there was to be no more talk about the collective will and all that nonsense within the circles of ruling elite. People like Leon Trotsky who wanted free elections, were to find that out the hard way when he was hunted down in Mexico and executed in 1925.

The ruling herd, especially one that wants to stay in power, understands that the people it rules will always outnumber it. Therefore, it always needs an outside threat to remind its people that no matter how lousy the ruling herd is, they are doing everything in order to keep the outside threat, outside. Using the West as a threat to their grand experiment, the Bolsheviks established a number of secret police organizations to weed out undesirables within the country or, in other words, anyone who questioned the legitimacy of the Communist government. Anyone who objected was hunted down and "disappeared." They were either sent to work in slave labor camps or simply killed publicly so that they could be associated with the outside threat and therefore deserving of their punishment.

Thugs like Lenin and Stalin who gained control in Russia understood the herd mentality very well. They understood that what motivated people even more than self-interest was fear of death or a life in prison. In the

Soviet Union of Nikolai Lenin, Joseph Stalin, Nikita Khrushchev and the rest, no one was safe except for the leaders themselves. Everyone below them was subject to purges, random imprisonment, torture and execution. It is estimated that Joseph Stalin killed more than twenty million Soviet citizens, but nobody knows for sure and the number is likely to be even higher than that. As Joe Stalin himself famously said, "One death is a tragedy, one million deaths is a statistic." No one can argue that the idea of random terror was effective in controlling the Soviet herd. In a country where the most loyal, hard working citizens could simply one day disappear, even his top aides were too terrified to ever consider smashing his head with a blunt object and seizing control for themselves.

The National Socialist model

The Germans, masters of efficiency as they are, also traded in the warlord-religion model for their own brand of totalitarian one-man rule called National Socialism. National Socialism was not Communism, because the landowners and the corporations, for the most part, were able to hold on to their property. They saw Adolf Hitler as a man who would make them more money and power as the nation became more powerful than Germany had ever been before. But it didn't stop there. In Nazi Germany there was something for everyone in the herd. The National Socialists offered food when there was no food and security when there was no security. The Nazis gave employment to the unemployed. The Nazis gave a powerful military to the Prussian military class. To women, the Nazis gave the glorification of German motherhood. To children and students, the Nazis gave health and sports clubs like the Hitler Youth. For scholars and researchers the Nazis gave grants and scholarships as long as it was the "correct" research.

Unlike the communists, who cared little about the plight of the common man, Hitler and his thugs sold the common man a bill of goods that would be hard to meet even on Madison Avenue. The common German man, whether a taxi driver, a waiter, an engineer or a common thief, was, according to the Nazi mythology, from the bloodline of the Aryans, god-like beings who were destined to rule the earth. In a country that had only been united as a single entity since the 1800's, with no common culture, heroes or leaders, Hitler offered an identity to the identity-less. Along with bread and security, he offered the Germans self-esteem. According to

Hitler, the German people were the dominant herd and their destiny was to rule all other herds.

There was only one catch to the whole Nazi deal and that was Herr Hitler himself. He was an insane megalomaniac who existed in a fairy tale world. But, he was a man with a plan, in the right place at the right time, so, he was able to sell his fairy tales to a lot of people simply by playing upon their own fears and feelings of inferiority and betrayal that stemmed from the German surrender at Versailles in World War I. His plans, which he outlined in his book, Mein Kampf, squarely put the blame of all of Germany's ills upon outsiders such as Jews and Communists.

The threat to the German herd was the threat posed by these "inferior" races. They had somehow snuck into Germany and polluted the Aryan herd's bloodline, betrayed them to the allies during World War I, and were set on betraying them to the Russian Bolsheviks. People didn't realize at the time (or now), how close to home this "threat" had struck. Hitler's own grandfather, Alois Shickelgruber had been a Jew who had "polluted" Hitler's own bloodline!

Under Hitler and the Nazi crazies, Germany had a destiny to fulfill and there was work to be done. The first item of business was to identify and isolate the weaker elements in German society. To do that, the Germans would need a secret police organization that could spy on and detain anyone it wanted felt might pose a threat. The Germans, like most herds, were eager to give up their own freedoms and privacy for the sake of security. So, the roundups began, Jews, intellectuals, students, Catholics, even Freemasons.

Then they needed to cull the herd of any undesirable genes that might degrade the master race, should they somehow mix with persons of pure Aryan blood. They also needed to weed out any thinkers, who may at any time, come out and say that the Nazis were clinically insane. The concentration camps began to fill, and there needed to be a solution as to what to do with all of Germany's, and then Europe's "riff raff."

Next, the German herd needed to address their external threat, and get back the land stolen from them by England and France. This was most important; the "master race" was going to need a place to live, and

Germany was not big enough. What they needed was "lebensraum" or, "living room" for the Germans. That could easily be found in the East in places like Russia, Poland and in the South, in Austria and Czechoslovakia, which was full of Germans anyway. Yes, it was a grand plan and would take a few years of hardship as the mighty German war machine rolled through the countries it wanted to make into a "greater" Germany, and there would be some costs, but in the end, the "master race" would fulfill its destiny. (Shirer)

Of course things did not go as planned. In fact, most Germans who bought into Hitler's insane notions thought the war with England, Germany's only real threat, would be over by the summer of 1940. But it wasn't and a year later, in 1941, millions of German men were in Russia where by 1943, they were being slaughtered by the thousands or starved or they froze to death. During all that time, right up until the bitter end, very few complained, and those who did, or tried to stop Hitler, saw not only themselves, but all of their friends, families and associates wiped out by the Gestapo, Hitler's Secret Police. Hitler and his bullies controlled the German herd with German efficiency; they knew that a person might risk his own life, but would almost never risk the safety of his own herd. That would be anti-evolutionary.

The democratic model

Next, there is the third "modern" model of controlling the herd, that of the "democracy," as it is called in the West. Like Communism or National Socialism, it is a catchy phrase with very little to do with the reality of the type of government by which "democracies" are ruled. "Democracy" means literally, "people rule," and comes from the Athenian city-state where people who voted in the Aeropaus, or town council, were called "demes" and the Greek word for rule, which is "craci" (actually, I just made that last part up). They were landowners, male and the heads of their respective clans. Although it was a far cry from one man, one vote, it was still much closer than our own "democracy."

As we will see, in 1787, when the United States Constitution was actually ratified, there were all kinds of ideas about the kind of government we should have. It was decided that the best government was that in which the herd was allowed to participate in the decision making process as much as possible, as in ancient Athens. However, because that was impossible with the former colonies being so far flung and so varied in background and common interests, the best idea was to compromise and form a republic, as in, "to the republic for which it stands" in the Pledge of Allegiance. The republic that was formed was based on the idea that men are good. Government is bad.

In order to ensure that a totalitarian government would not take hold in the new nation, three safeguards were put in place. First, the new government was "hamstrung" so to speak from the beginning, because it was made of two houses of delegates from each state. In order to get anything done, there would have to be a consensus vote in one house, an almost impossible task, and then a consensus vote in the other house, which would have to agree with the first. Finally, the presiding officer of the government, or President, would have to agree with both houses and sign the bill into law. Unless the Congress passed a law, the Constitution could not be changed. Second, there were three offsetting branches of government, one of which, the court, was dedicated to ensuring that the other two branches followed the Constitution or rules which governed the governing bodies.

Finally, in case all else failed, ordinary citizens, unlike any other country in the world at the time, were allowed to keep and bear arms. At the time, it was entirely possible for a foreign power to march on the capitol, as the British would in 1812 and capture the government. Fortunately, in 1812, the British were caught in a freak hurricane and were forced to abandon the city, but I think you get my point. American citizens were guaranteed protection from prosecution for resisting foreign threats to the government and the Constitution by the Constitution. Therefore, for over one hundred years, the United States Government got very little done, and the people were free to pursue their lives, liberties and happiness.

The Corporation State

We will see what happened to the US government in the twentieth century soon enough but for now, we find ourselves citizens of a government that is best described as a corporation-run republic or what I call a "Corpican" form of government. This odd state of events happened because there were unforeseen movements afoot at the time the United

States was founded. The corporation as we know it today hardly existed in 1787. The founding fathers had little idea that in the next one hundred and thirty years, there would be telephones, automobiles, and airplanes. They also had no idea that a "printing money for nothing scheme," would be implemented. All they could do, and what they did do, was to set up a government that, more or less, didn't actually work very well. By constraining the government to three offsetting branches and dividing the elective branch into two distinct houses with distinct interests, they created a government that would hardly ever get anything done, which, in theory, would leave the people of the United States to govern them.

We will see in the upcoming chapters of this book how the ideas of limited government that were agreed upon by the founding fathers were subverted by the influence of money, personal greed and the self interest of corporations and wealthy individuals. However, the United States, or at least the corporations of the United States, in order to perpetuate themselves into greater markets around the world, still needed to portray some semblance of rule by the people of the country in order to open other countries and their people to similar forms of government, that, in turn could be controlled by the same money interests that controlled the United States and Europe.

Once in power, the first thing that needed to happen was to maintain control and consolidate the power of the ruling classes in the U.S. In other words, the herd of the United States needed to be fed and placated so that the herds around the world could look upon the United States and its form of government as something to aspire towards, and in many cases, to die for or against.

In the United States of America, we have "free speech," "free elections," "the right to bear arms," and so on and so forth. So, how does the corporation/government in such a "free" society as ours control a people who can say anything they wish? How does the corporation/government control a people where "anyone can be president" and the right to overthrow a corrupt government is basically spelled out in the Constitution?

The government of the United States rules at the behest of the corporations who contribute to election campaigns, control the media and the law making and enforcing bodies from Washington all the way to your local city council. If there is any doubt about this, please look at the amount of money your state senator, or representative spent on their last election and find out which corporations paid for them. In reality, we do not elect people; we elect corporations to rule us. Of course, the people make the ultimate choice at the ballot box, but the success or failure of an election campaign is little different than the decision to buy Pepsi or Coke, and usually, the campaigns are run by the same advertising agencies. Therefore, the government in the U.S. is more accurately referred to as the corporation/government. Of course, the corporations own the television and radio stations, the movie industries, the music industries and the software companies that surround you day in and day out and bombard you with advertising, opinions and their own view of reality. Therefore, I will hereby refer to this body as the corporation/government/media.

Rule by Psychology: The Poll

How does the corporation/government maintain control of such an obviously "free" people? They do it because they understand the mentality of the human herd, and they have a number of psychological tools in their bag of tricks. One if the tricks being the corporation/government/media's use of a psychological tool known as the "poll." Understanding the herd mentality of the people of the

United States, the corporation/government/media cites "polls" on issues and candidates so that the people of the U.S. will know how to think and vote. Contrary to a popular misconception, the majority of Americans don't think for themselves. Thanks to their sandbagging of the public schools for the last fifty years, Americans just don't know that much about, well, anything that isn't on TV. They don't have the historical, technical, political, or scientific knowledge necessary to make decisions on most issues. They prefer instead to simply go along with the rest of the herd (TV). Most Americans don't want to be seen on the unpopular side of an issue or candidate, because then they will be seen as losers, or even worse, politically incorrect. This kind of poor decision-making may result in them being looked upon unfavorably in their own herds. Simply put, nobody wants to suggest their opinion is any different than the acceptable opinions on TV.

In the early stages of presidential campaigns, for example, the "polls" are the indicators of who is "ahead" and who isn't. What they never tell you is how they conduct the polls. In other words whom did they ask and how did they ask the question? You can get pretty much any answer you want from a poll simply by calling the right people and asking the wrong question the right way. Political action committees, corporations and candidates spend a lot of money on polls. They aren't likely to hire a polling agency that is going to come back to them with results that they don't want to hear.

Likewise, there is also a strong correlation between who is seen on TV (in favorable news reports) and who is ahead in the polls. As we said, the people who manage political campaigns are, more often than not, the same people who created advertising campaigns to sell you cars and soda pop. So, if you want to know who is going to win any given presidential election, you just have to count how many times a candidate appears in favorable news reports over a given period. Who decides who will be given favorable news reports? Corporations like General Electric, Sony, Disney and other powerful corporate interests who own or control networks decide who will win elections. They direct television station owners, who direct their news editors, who direct the reporters that bring you the information you need to decide on the next candidate. Whether you like it or not, that is the way every president has been elected since John F. Kennedy. Prior to that, it was the newspapers that decided elections.

But don't be discouraged. If you will recall, there is still a "social contract" that exists between the ruler(s) and the ruled in any society or, in our simplified example, our American herd. The ruler(s) are providing for the basic needs of the herd (us), and the herd, in turn gives them (the corporation/government) the right to make decisions for the herd. In our "free society," in theory at least, the members of the herd are allowed to speak up, and to revoke the contract between the ruled and the ruler(s) if the ruler(s) are found to be incompetent or, in some cases guilty of actually doing damage to the herd, at least in theory.

In the, "best of all possible worlds", as Erasmus might say in his book *The Praise of Folly*, the media might bring to the public awareness the fact that the ruler (s) are not looking out for the best interest of the herd, and sometimes they do, but only enough to give the corporation/government/media some semblance of credibility. They rarely, however, follow up on a story unless there is some financial reward, or political agenda that they want to put forward to the American people. In other words, the corporation/government/media gives you the information it wants you to have, and it keeps the information away from you that it doesn't want you to have. For example, watch a news program on any TV station. The lead story is always about some tragedy, or as they say in the editing room, "If it bleeds, it leads." Notice as you watch, that the first stories are about doom, mayhem, and sometimes even corruption and scandal. But as the show progresses towards the end, the broadcast always winds up with a story about pets, or some common citizen doing their part to help the community. Why?

Because the corporation/government/media wants you to watch their show, in the first place, by making you afraid of something so the corporation can use you to get advertising revenues. Since all the news is the same from station to station, they have attractive people reading the teleprompter who match demographic interest polls. Usually, that amounts to a few young blondes or exotic Asians with some token men scattered here and there so the station doesn't look like it is "pimping" the news. By the time the news show is over, and you realize the Apocalypse is not around the corner, you will have a good enough feeling through a catchy phrase or joke by the newsreader about the world, that you will be able to sleep, and more importantly, you will feel secure enough to go out buy the products you saw advertised during the broadcast. In other words, the corporation/government/media wants the herd to be alarmed and concerned, yet confident enough in the future to buy that new car or boat.

They also want the herd to have a feeling of being "well informed" to ensure their own credibility. The corporation/government also wants the herd to be reassured that the corporation/government is doing everything possible to maintain the security of the herd. While the corporation/government is doing its job to maintain the "American way of life," the job of every citizen is to stay in the herd, not raise the alarm about impending danger, pay taxes and not make any trouble for the corporation/government. In other words, they don't want the herd to feel a need to get involved, because that just makes more work for them.

Rule By Misdirection: The "Spin"

Have you ever seen a magic show where the magician is able to make a Ping-Pong ball appear to float in the air? You sit mesmerized while the ball floats back and forth between the magician's fingers. It is a fascinating trick if you don't know he has two pieces of thread tied to his fingers. Once you know that, the trick seems kind of silly. The magician uses misdirection by making you focus your concentration on something instead of what he is doing to make the trick appear to be magic. The corporation/government/media uses this idea of misdirection to pull some rabbits out of its own hat when there is damaging information about the government or a corporation that just can't be kept quiet. For that, there is another psychological tool available to the corporation/government/media.

It's called, "the spin." The spin is a way to treat information that can't be covered up or denied because it is right there in plain sight for everyone to see. This kind of information is not a problem, as long as the common citizenry doesn't actually think about it in a common sense fashion. Unfortunately, the most glaring and easily understood example of a "spin" occurred on September 11, 2001, when the twin towers of the World Trade Center were attacked by terrorists, killing over three thousand innocent people.

Did any news anchors, reporters, or government officials call for the immediate resignation of the Director of the CIA, FBI or Immigration and Naturalization, whose reason for being was to stop such attacks? To give you an idea about how much things have changed in America, when the Japanese attacked Pearl Harbor, Admiral Kimmel, the Navy Commander at Pearl Harbor, who did what he could based upon the information that was supplied to him by Naval Intelligence, was hauled before Congress, and vilified.

In 2001, nobody even asked how known Al Qaeda operatives had been allowed into the US in the first place. Instead, we were given ludicrous stories about how they failed to "connect the dots," as if our lives were no more important than a child's game. In the subsequent investigations, it was revealed that FBI agents had warned the President in August 6, 2001 about a domestic threat but somehow failed to notify United States Attorney General John Ashcroft. (Shennon, Bergmann). That same day, the German ambassador informed President Bush of the time and place of the attack. Bush reportedly thanked him and told him he was aware of it.

(Makow) Mysteriously, during the same time period, Ashcroft stopped flying on commercial airliners (Shennon, Bergmann). Four years before the attacks, the Taliban had been invited to the U.S. as guests of Unocal Oil. Working on behalf of British Petroleum, who were also heavily involved in the deal was George Bush senior's Secretary of State James Baker (Gonsalves).

In 1942, following Pearl Harbor, thousands of American citizens of Japanese descent were sent to internment camps. In 2001, the relatives of Osama bin Laden and hundreds of other wealthy Saudis were allowed to fly out of the country twenty-four hours after the attack, even though former President George W. Bush had himself been grounded. Later, the Director of the CIA, George Tenant was given the Medal of Freedom for his role in both the September 11th attacks and the subsequent attacks on Iraq after he lied and said there were "weapons of mass destruction" in Saddam Hussein's arsenal. And nobody dared ask why any of this happened.

Why? Because the attacks were to divert attention away from the fact that the corporation/government/media was stripping the American people of whatever rights they had left in the form of the Patriot Act. This is not possible to do during peacetime. They wanted a lead story to put into the news media for the next ten years while they allowed millions of illegal aliens, drug lords and a number of other assorted thugs to move into the United States. At the same time, they created unprecedented military and intelligence apparatus and siphoned trillions of dollars from the U.S. Treasury. If there really were a threat, wouldn't it have come across the U.S. Mexican border? George W. Bush said it most eloquently when he said, "This is no time for conspiracy theories."

Just like the Communists in Russia and the Nazis in Germany, those who took control of the government after the "elections" of 2000 produced an enemy that was never going to go away. For years, every network ran an "alert threat level" with their broadcasts and every story was about the next potential target. The Patriot Act was passed specifying that any American could be detained for any reason. In other words, in the analogy of the herd, the good shepherd had abandoned the flock and the wolves had made it clear to the sheep that they would come for anyone who asked questions, but with all the danger and threats, who had time for questions?

Rule by Herd Mentality: "The Mainstream"

Finally, the corporation/government/media even has its own word for people in the herd that don't ask questions and agree with their "spins" no matter how bizarre. It is a clever term called, "Mainstream America." Mainstream means exactly what is says. The "mainstream" is the place in the stream where most of the herd lives, eats, consumes and dies. It is the center of the herd. The mainstream is the commonly accepted view of the culture, of the world and most importantly, of thought. The Communists had a mainstream, and a lot of them froze to death in Siberia. The Nazis had a mainstream and they froze to death in Russia. People who get up and go to work, pay taxes, fight in wars, don't break the law (unless they are part of the government) and don't make trouble, or ask too many difficult questions, are considered mainstream. We like mainstream people because they are just like us. They think like us, they dress like us, they listen to the right music, they drive the right cars and they have mainstream kids.

But, the use of the "spin" and trying to keep people in the "mainstream" has created some problems of its own. The problem with the modern herd or, the "mainstream" in America is that it is so hard to keep up with. The corporation/government/media keeps changing its ideas about what we should wear; eat, like, watch, drive, think, and, most importantly, who its enemies are. But we can all be assured that the corporation/government/media, like any government in the twentieth century, has convinced us, as members of the herd, that those enemies are right in the herd with us and they are doing everything they can to "weed them out."

In the 1950's, being an anti-communist was mainstream and that was good, because there were so many communists in so many places, they had to have Senate hearings just to dig them out. In the 1960's, anti-communism was out and "free-thinking" was in. Unless you were freethinking it was okay to burn your draft card and avoid killing communists in Southeast Asia. The "counter-culture" movement in the 1960's occurred because young people knew what the corporation/government/media was up to and they tried to do something about it, or they tried to escape from it. They knew that the Vietnamese were not as much of a threat to us as the corporation/government/media and so the corporation/government/media had to find a better one, a little closer to home.

During the years between 1965 and 1972, the corporation/government/media almost lost control, so they had to make sure that political and social thought remained within the correct boundaries. The assassinations of John Kennedy in 1963 and then Bobby Kennedy and Dr. Martin Luther King and, finally Nixon's election in 1968 had begun to swing the "mainstream" away from the "Kennedy-ish" notions that the government was for the people. The government for the corporations by the corporations was here to stay.

In the 1970's, freethinking was out. Nixon ended the draft in 1972 and the protests suddenly died as the protesters realized they wouldn't have to go to Vietnam and they had to get jobs-in the corporations. By the mid 1970's people realized they had to get in line. The corporation/government/media was going to consolidate its hold on the mainstream by using the adage of "divide and conquer." Suddenly, the "Great Melting Pot" was transformed into a house divided as the herd began to feed on itself and the fears brought on by the corporation/government/media.

Feminists were given a public voice, and oppressive men and the traditional family became the enemy. The legal system was restructured so that children were taken away from their fathers, as well as the father's income and belongings. The public schools began the first in a series of steps to "dumb down" American students while lawyers and parents began using the public schools as targets of frivolous lawsuits. African Americans were placated with their own TV shows, which depicted them as a poor, separate cultural entity. Freemasons took the reins of African American leadership and, as opposed to Dr.

King's message of love and unity used their relationship with Dr. King as an excuse to arrive at the scene of any racial controversy involving members of the African American community and whites, which stirred up the "racial pot" even more. Movies like *The Godfather* showed Italian Americans as Mafioso types. And so it went: women vs. men, black against white, liberal vs. conservative. In the realm of law and education, preference was given by race and sex quotas, which divide the poor, working classes even more. Even if you were white and middle class, the enemy was the traditional thinking, church going, hard working American, or "squares" like Archie Bunker who faced off against liberal "Meatheads." Nobody paid attention to the corporation/government/media's encroachment into American life. They were too busy keeping an eye on their neighbors.

By the 1980's, the social order based upon greed, corporations and materialism, as well as living on credit were in and were here to stay. Where did those "free-thinkers" from the 1960's go? They were making millions from their albums and concert tours, or they had gone to work for Apple, Microsoft or were practicing corporate law.

The War on Drugs: the first War on America

The constant changes in what is considered mainstream left everyone glued to the television for the latest cultural handouts so we would know what was, "mainstream" and what was not. Drugs, by the 1980's became "mainstream," but they were not the same drugs of the 1960's. The corporation/government/media went on a literal blitzkrieg to promote the use of cocaine. Everyone from politicians, celebrities and sports stars, to waitresses, students and truck drivers were consuming tons of the drug, which suddenly became "available" through massive sophisticated distribution operations that rivaled MacDonald's and Texaco for their ability to get the drugs to the marketplace. (Phenomenon Archives)

At the same time, even though the drug trade was funding secret armies in Central and South America, the corporation/government/media had to appear to be against drugs. Even though her colleagues out in Hollywood were endorsing and using them by the ton, First Lady, Nancy Reagan began telling kids to, "Just say no to drugs." Mandatory sentencing laws were passed at the federal level making a conviction for the distribution of any drug punishable by five years in prison. The prisons became so crowded with young, middle class kids that they had to let the murderers and rapists out early. Children were encouraged to call the police if they found their parents using drugs. The War on Drugs was the first War on the American People. (Phenomenon Archives)

Then there were the communists. During the Cold War, we hated the communists in Russia and China, and we swore, "Better dead than red." By 2000 we loved the communists. The Chinese for example, with their lack of human rights, slave labor camps, censorship and no rights for their workers, became our best friends. They could provide us with cheap manufactured goods because they didn't have to pay for their labor, and they have no environmental laws, which means today, the corporation/government/media is making more money than ever before. Well, the government isn't making money because the mainstream has been put out of work as high paying jobs manufacturing jobs went overseas, but they are borrowing on a grander scale than ever, and the mainstream is on the hook to pay back the banks who own shares in the Federal Reserve.

The Never Ending War and the Brave New World (War on America Part II)

Since September 11th 2001, there is a new threat to our herd called Islamic Fundamentalism. The corporation/government began importing Muslims in the 1980's, and continues to import them on a massive scale today. At the same time the corporation/government is attacking their home countries. Because of this new "threat," and the multi-billion dollar government agencies who seem to be helpless in stopping them (wink, wink) the corporation/government has asked us to give up our rights, privacy, liberty, and most of all, our money, to protect the corporation/government from the Islamic Fundamentalists they are letting into the country. These terrorists openly admit they have no "beef" with the American people, only the corporation/government/media. Therefore, the herd, or we, or the mainstream, must sacrifice, and sometimes even be sacrificed, to keep the corporation/government/media safe and the profits rolling in. We are literally their human shields.

During it all, we were all safe in the mainstream as long as we stayed in the mainstream. Sure, there were some hiccups along the way, John and Bobby Kennedy were assassinated, but they weren't "mainstream" because they dared to speak out against the Vietnam War, the Mafia and the secret government. Dr. Martin Luther King spoke out against the injustice of the social order, so the US government took care of him as an example to African Americans who were getting out of the mainstream. In the 1970's we saw Richard Nixon's secret organization openly commit crimes with the purpose of destroying the lives of Americans who were getting out of Richard Nixon's corporation/government mainstream. He went after people like Alan Ginsburg, who said Vietnam was a bad idea and people like the Black Panthers who said that violence was the only way African Americans would ever get justice. And of course, there were the hippies in the Democratic Party who had stolen his election in the 1960.

By the 1980's, the government, the corporations and the media had become synchronized and have stayed so ever since. With such a relationship, the corporations could ship American jobs overseas, and the media would tell the public how good that was for us, while the politicians took the corporation's campaign contributions and said nothing as their constituents went on welfare and unemployment. They could all get behind wars that were engineered by the intelligence community and even though a lot of people died, suffered, were maimed or homeless, the ratings went up, the deficit went up, the profits went up and the campaign contributions kept coming.

Today, there are new words to describe those who may commit the crime of thinking outside of the mainstream. In the late 1980's the term "political correctness" hit the mainstream culture of the United States. It was the first hint that ideas that did not originate within the corporate/government/media were not going to be tolerated. Anyone who questions the corporation/government/media explanation of anything, are branded either "politically incorrect" which carries with it an automatic "get out of the herd free" card. People who complain about what the corporation/government/media are actually up to are labeled "conspiracy theorists." The corporation/government/media has its own hired thugs and lawyers, journalists, newsreaders, authors, filmmakers, producers and investigators in the "mainstream" media who are paid and rewarded handsomely for towing the corporation/government/media line and attacking anyone who doesn't conform to their way of thinking.

Outside of the Mainstream-JFK, Conspiracy Theorists, UFO Nuts and the C.G.M. attack dogs

Historically, the term "conspiracy theorist" came out of the Kennedy assassination, and the subsequent Warren Commission report that pointed to Lee Harvey Oswald as the lone gunman. Because more than one person committing a crime constitutes a "conspiracy," and since nothing was ever admitted by the government regarding anyone being involved except Oswald, the "theory" of more than one person involved constituted a "conspiracy" therefore, the term "conspiracy theorist." The term 'theorist' also has the handy connotation of implying a "theory" which makes it sound like it isn't true, or more importantly, has never been proven. As we will see, when a certain group commits crimes, there is always a mysterious lack of evidence due to it being mishandled, or, in some cases, the evidence just "disappears." "Conspiracy theorist" was a handy term that had the same connotations as "nut" and "wacko." After all, most of the people who were at Dealy Plaza were mysteriously dead within a few years, so there were few live witnesses alive or willing to challenge the corporation/government/media's version of the story.

As far as John F. Kennedy's assassination went, the "conspiracy theorist" label worked pretty well, and most of the herd didn't pay much attention to them until 1988, when Oliver Stone's movie *JFK* was released and the Zapruder tape was displayed in public. For the first time, it was obvious to a horrified country that the President of the United States had been shot in the head from the front. Before the movie was even released, the corporation/government/media put its "spin" machine in high gear to discredit Stone as a "conspiracy theorist" so that anyone who watched the movie would already have been told what to think about it. The same thing happened again when Michael Moore debuted his movie *Fahrenheit 911*. Even though every bit of the movie had been documented in newspapers and TV news reports, the American public saw the movie only after they were conditioned to think that Michael Moore was a socialist and a "conspiracy theorist," thanks to the "spin doctors" and attack dogs in the corporation/government/media. Adolf Hitler once said, "A lie becomes the truth if you tell it enough" and the corporation/government/media learned that lesson well.

The fact that the Bush government had been warned about 9/11 Al Qaeda, and did absolutely nothing to prevent it and then hurried the bin Laden family and prominent Saudi Arabians out of the country didn't even phase the American people. After all, there was danger afoot and they didn't want to be outside of the herd during an "orange" alert, especially when the FBI was tapping phones and reading emails of every person in the country they thought might be a threat. It is always best just to stay quiet and hope they don't come looking for you.

The best way to sum up the relationship between the corporation/government/media and the citizens of the United States is that certain thoughts are acceptable, for example, spending more than you make, driving a gas guzzling SUV, and invading countries that have never threatened us. What is not acceptable is to question anything the corporation/government/media says or tells you to think. If you do, you are most likely, as in the days of the Puritans, to be put in the stockade of public opinion where the uneducated, ill-informed, highly paid people the corporation/government/media will throw tomatoes and cabbage in the form of insults and innuendos, and you, in the stockade, will never have a chance to answer them back because you don't own a TV station. Then of course there are the other consequences of thinking wrong thoughts or saying wrong things; loss of job and career, divorce, friends, family, respect. In the worst cases, it's jail, or an accidental death. Sometimes, you just seem to disappear, Joe Vogler style. It's always better to just shut up and hope they don't come for you.

The corporation/government/media's magic trick: the disappearance of credibility

There was only one drawback to the corporation/government/media's assault on people who questioned the corporation/government. Like the boy who cried wolf, the attacks on investigators, the disinformation and the fact that evidence was later introduced, as in the *JFK* film that showed the corporation/government/media had deceived the American people, began to have two unintended consequences. The first was that the government began to lose more and more credibility. The second consequence was that anyone who claimed that there was, in fact a conspiracy in everything from fluoride in the drinking water to the moon landings, began to gain more and more credibility in the eyes of the American people. In fact, when the September 11th attacks happened, it was really "lucky" that so many corporation/government/media film cameras were out in the streets to show the world that the airliners crashing into the World Trade Center were not just another corporation/government/media deception. Well, let's just say it was lucky the cameras were there rolling when it happened, otherwise people would claim it didn't happen at all.

So, the question is, how did we get here? It would be easy to say things like "they" and "them" but who are, "they" and "them?" In order to understand why the world is the way it is, we really have to go back, all the way to the beginning, because as sophisticated as we think we may be, we have changed little since the early days of civilization. What is happening now has happened before and, in spite of our best efforts, will most likely happen again.

So, with that, we will now undertake a journey into the realms of history, theology, science, economics and political thought. We will focus on three seemingly unrelated topics for our quest: "Mormons," Freemasons and extraterrestrials, because in understanding them, it is my belief the reader will better understand more about the world today than through the study of any other subjects. Fasten your seat belts. We are going to embark on an amazing journey from which you will hopefully emerge unscathed, enlightened and a little more hopeful about the future.

Chapter 3

History According to the Bible

What is history?

Whether you like history or not, the fact is, everything in this world has a history. Everything and everyone comes from somewhere. One of the most unfortunate misconceptions that human beings make of the world is the assumption that everything as it is in the present is the way things have always been. If there were no such thing as history, or the act of passing down important events to future generations, people in their natural state would just assume that the world stays basically the same. For example, once on a history exam, I asked some high school students to describe their life colonial America in the 1760's. One student wrote a very creative letter to her landlord complaining that her electricity had been off for days along with fact that the plumbing in her apartment never seemed to work. I hope her inattentiveness in class and the fact that she never opened her textbook is not a widespread phenomenon, but it does highlight people's ignorance of what history actually is. As people grow older however, they have no choice but to reference changes in their lives and their surroundings that make them aware that things do change, sometimes for the better and sometimes for the worse. With age, humans feel it is important that younger generations are aware of how things were when they were young. Usually the information centers on the difficulty of life "back then" and often contains a reference to a ten-mile walk to school. In fact, I suppose the first old man, or woman who sat their grandchildren around the cave fire and related the stories of their youth, while the younger ones tried desperately to stay awake, could be considered the first historian.

55 ✪ Deceptions of the Ages

In modern times, there are as many histories as there are people and things. Since there are a lot of people and a lot of things, there are a lot of histories. As stated earlier, everything has a history. In this book, which is about the relationship between the, Latter-day Saint Church, the organization known as the Freemasons and the idea of extraterrestrial beings, we have to make sure that we understand that there is a separate history for each of our subjects of study and that there are reasons why there are separate histories. It may sound complicated at first, but it really isn't.

Imagine that you are going to write a history of your own family. What would you write? Would you write the good things only? What if your great-great-great grandfather was the famous outlaw Jesse James? The fact that he was a bank robber is not necessarily good, but the fact that he was famous makes it more than likely that you will write about him because his notoriety makes people more able to identify with your family, especially if they are still in the bank robbing business. But, what if your family doesn't want people to know about your infamous, six-shooter-toting, bank robbing, murdering ancestor? You would have two options according to the "unwritten rules" of writing history. One option is, you could leave him out of your family history altogether and hope no one ever researched your family and found out the truth. The other option you have would be to "spin" the story around and point out how evil the banks were and how they and the people that Jesse and the rest of his gang murdered, were deserving of what they got.

So, what else would you write? The first thing you would probably want to do is find out all of the good things your family did in the past. If you were a good historian, you would also try to find out the key events in your family's history that brought them to be the people they are today.

Now, let's say that your neighbors, the Joneses, are engaged in a similar project. Will the Joneses have any information about your family in their history? We would guess that they would not, unless something happened between your two families that changed the course of history for both families. So, will your family history be completely different from the Jones family history? Before we can answer that, we need to think of the things that have happened in the world that may have affected both of your families. For instance, let's say your grandfather and the Jones' grandfather served in Vietnam. Though they may not have known each other, the Vietnam War had an effect on both of your families, if nothing more than the fact that both of your relatives served in that conflict.

There are many things besides wars that change people's lives and that affect where and how they live. An invention, such as the telephone, may have made it possible for your family to make a lot of money selling telephone services. Maybe it was your father's ability to communicate with your mother without your grandfather knowing, that may
have resulted in them falling in love. The automobile made it possible for the Jones' father to commute from his family's farm to the college where he studied engineering. The computer gave you the skills and ability to find work in the IT field. So, each of these inventions had an effect on the lives of your families. There are social movements, medical breakthroughs, fads, music, and even food that all affected the world in which you live, and are a part of, by a seemingly unbelievably random set of circumstances and events that had to happen just for you to be sitting where you are reading this book.

In school, you probably were taught that history is a series of events that happen along what your teacher described as a timeline. With the understanding that you were taught this way because you were supposed to know a certain number of names and dates in a limited amount of time, we will forgive your teachers for this completely inaccurate description of how history actually happens. History does occur on a line, and that line is time and it goes in one direction, which is something we will talk about in more detail much later on. However, there is not just one line that makes up history, rather there are an almost infinite number of lines that intersected with each other that make up what we call "history." There are also different events, ideas and people that change history and the people they affect. Therefore, history is more like a woven fabric, than a line. Confused?

Think about your grandfather as a young man. Now think about old grandfather Jones, also as a young man. Now imagine them as they were at the age of eighteen. They are just out of school, driving around town looking at the pretty girls without a care in the world. Now, think of each of them on a starting line, like sprinters ready to start a race. This starting point is one point of reference on their timeline. Of course, their timeline at that point is pretty short, and you can see that ahead of them, there are nothing except possibilities. Your grandfather at that point is interested in music and would like to start a band. Grandpa Jones was a star baseball player and was getting ready to try out for the major leagues. They were getting ready to run a race called life and they were at the starting line with only the faint lines that make up a sort of tree laid out in front of them. That faint tree is, all the possible futures that they might have.

Now, on the same starting line, let's make a new line and that line we will call United States (or Vietnamese) History. Behind the racers are the past events that put them on the same starting line. When the gun sounds, the United States (or Vietnamese) government needs young men to fight in the war. So, your grandfather and Grandpa Jones and the United States do not have a separate timeline anymore. At the starting gun, they are drafted and go to the timeline of the history of the United States (or Vietnam) and they stay there until they either end the race by being killed, or they leave the service of the United States and begin their own time lines once again. They are still a part of the history of the United States, but, for the most part, their history is not as intertwined with the decisions of the U.S. Government as it is when they are in the military service.

The Vietnam War did not begin one day when the leaders of the two opposing sides randomly decided to have a war with each other. If we think about the events that led to the Vietnam War in which Grandpa Jones and your grandfather were involved, we would have to understand the conflict between the two opposing philosophies of capitalism and communism. These ideas began in the 1800's as possible alternatives to the land ownership-based system of power in Europe. Therefore, if a historian argues that the Vietnam War was based upon two opposing ideologies, the War actually began one hundred years before it was fought. Of course, there were many more reasons that Grandpa Jones and your grandfather ended up in Vietnam as young men, but hopefully you will understand that history is very complicated and it does not occur in a straight line with a random set of unrelated events.

One idea or occurrence such as Christianity, Islam, inventions like the gun, the printing press and the discovery of electricity, changed entire societies. Therefore, it is not just important to know that the Wright Brothers flew the first airplane in 1903. It is just as important to understand the effect that event had on the lives we lead today. In other words, it is important that we, as human beings divorce ourselves of the idea that knowledge is two-dimensional and occurs on a straight line. We must begin to understand history, as well as our other knowledge in the third and fourth dimensions, which we will discuss later.

Of course, this may be an oversimplified explanation, or it may be confusing to some, but looking at history is just like looking at an object with a microscope. The more intensely we focus, the more there is to see. If the reader understands that no event, from you having cereal for breakfast to the launch of the Space Shuttle stands alone, the reader understands enough to know why it is necessary to explain the history of each of our topics.

With the understanding that things usually don't "just happen," we can better understand the topics we are going to cover if we understand not only how they came to be in the first place but how each seems to cross paths, much like the example of yours and the Jones' grandfathers, and how their future has been affected by that crossing. In this book, we will be talking about the history of the LDS Church, the Freemasons and extraterrestrials. But, before we can start to look at their histories, which will give us a better idea of who and what they are, we need to establish some kind of common ground as to which history we want to study. That will help us to create the most accurate picture. In your family history, there was the idea of what actually qualifies as history according to your particular family. So, it would therefore be necessary to look at each one of our topics of as a separate history of its own or, the history of the LDS Church, the history of the Freemasons and the history of extraterrestrials. There is, as in the case of the Vietnam War, the history of countries that correspond with the histories of separate groups, as in the example of how your family and the Jones family were affected by the Vietnam War. Therefore, it is necessary to establish histories that all can agree upon. If we can establish more details, and those historical details are accurate, then we can get a more accurate picture of what it is that we are studying

Is the Bible really History?

The first "common" history we will look at is the history that people have used for thousands of years as the last word in history, the Bible. After we discuss a brief overview of the Bible, we will familiarize ourselves with what we call history or, "popular history," "secular history," or "recorded history" because we, with some exceptions, agree that what we accept as the history of the world, based upon input from written records, historical texts, archeological excavations and scientific analysis, accept this information as the most accurate description of the experience of mankind that we have so far. This is the history you may remember from high school or college survey course texts. We will also, unfortunately see, that the Bible does not qualify as the last word in the history that people for the last five thousand years, have claimed it to represent. However, the Bible is essential for the study of our chosen topics, so it is imperative for the reader to have a basic idea of its concepts.

Once we have familiarized ourselves with Biblical and historical records, we will be much better able to understand the world of our subjects of study. To neglect to understand what is called the "historical context" of our subjects of study would be similar to you mentioning that your grandfather served in an artillery unit in Vietnam to a group of five year olds without explaining what "artillery" is, what it was used for, and why it was so important. Because The LDS Church, the Society of Freemasons and extraterrestrials either appear, or in fact, have their origins in both of these versions of historical accounts or records, it is necessary for the author to make the reader at least partially familiar with these two histories.

Our task is not an altogether easy one, simply because the histories of modern scholarship and the histories as they are recounted in the Holy Scriptures don't always agree. There are a number of reasons they don't agree, but two very obvious reasons stand out. The first reason the histories don't agree is that each is looking at the world for different reasons and therefore, some events, such as the return of the Children of Israel to Palestine, was one of the most important events in the history of the three religions. However, in ancient Egypt, where they kept pretty good records, there is little mention of the Hebrews. In other words, what was important to one culture was not important to the other and therefore, did not make it into their history books or papyrus manuscripts, as it were, with the same amount of importance placed upon the event as it may have been by the culture that considered the event a high point, or victory. This is an idea that we must keep in mind, if we are to keep an open mind.

Our second reason, that histories sometimes do not agree at all, makes somewhat of problem, but sometimes the first reason is the explanation. In other cases, say for example, the theory of creation, the three Western Faiths, Judaism, Christianity (to include the LDS Church) and Islam say that the world began about seven thousand years ago. Science, on the other hand, dates the beginning of the world back a little farther than that at four and half billion years. Because this is just the nature of history, we will have to make sure we understand what history we are talking about and we will have to keep track of the time.

As we will also see, there are times when these histories are mutually supportive of each other. In the book of Daniel, for example, in the Old Testament, it is prophesied to Darius of Babylon about a great king that will emerge.

"And now, I will shew thee the truth. Behold, there shall yet stand up three kings in Persia; and the fourth shall be far richer than they all: and by his strength, through his riches he shall stir up all against the realm of Grecia. And a mighty king shall stand up, that shall rule with great dominion, and do, according to his will. And when he shall stand up, his kingdom shall be broken, and shall be divided toward the four winds of heaven; and not to his posterity, nor according to his dominion which he ruled: for his kingdom shall be plucked up, even for others besides those." (Daniel 11:2-4)

In this prophecy, of Daniel, Darius, the King of Persia, is told that a great king shall emerge, although Daniel avoids an unpleasant scene by failing to make it clear that king will come out of Greece. We all know now that this king was Alexander. After his bodyguards killed Darius III, Alexander died and his kingdom was divided into four parts by his generals. It is the rare times such as this, when separate histories confirm an event, a person, or an achievement that we can be at least slightly confident that the thing or person happened as the histories say it did. Of course, there are times when those telling the story are not fulfilling their responsibilities of being objective. At those times it is necessary to remember the old saying that there are two sides to every coin and, where it is possible, to try to look for facts someplace else

Historical Jesus

At the risk of offending some, I would like to use Jesus Christ as an example of the discrepancies between history and Bible or, scriptural history. Every book in the New Testament refers to Jesus Christ, except for the Book of Revelations. Jesus gets nothing but good press in the Gospels and we come away from reading them with an understanding that he was the Son of God. Whether or not he was the Son of God has been a source of conflict, hatred and wars ever since Jesus lived. Be that as it may, there are few records of Jesus outside the small group of followers he had while he was alive. Thanks to the discovery of biblical texts, such as the Dead Sea scrolls and the Gnostic gospels that were found in Egypt, many of the things that were written about him were not chosen to be included in the Gospels of the New Testament. The information that is in the Gospels, according to modern scholars, was not even written down until many years after Jesus' death and resurrection.

Aside from his followers, there are no tax records, public registries or other documents that may confirm what is written in the Gospels. In other words, Jesus got a lot of great P.R. from his friends, but when it came to other evidence that Jesus even existed, there is not much to go on. The Jewish historian Josephus, who documented the Roman destruction of the kingdom of Judah about forty years after the Crucifixion of Jesus, is the only contemporary "non-Christian" writer to make any mention of Jesus. Because of the scant facts and the supporting details of the life of Jesus, there are some who could and would argue that Jesus was merely a literary character, at best. We can all be thankful for Josephus and for the work and the sacrifices made by the first Christians to keep Jesus' teachings and name alive. We can also be thankful that he wasn't taken up in a spaceship…

When looking at the Holy Scriptures as a source of history, there are a number of very obvious drawbacks when it comes to complete understanding of what has been written and passed on as the literal "Word of God." Modern scholars have concluded that the first five books of the Old Testament, which make up the Hebrew Torah, were not written until the reign of Solomon. In fact, it is believed that two separate authors wrote what is known as the Septuagint, the first five books of the Bible. One author is called "E" because this author refers to God as "Elohim." Another author is called "J" because he refers to God as "Yahweh" the Hebrew form of Jehovah. Books from the Northern Kingdom of Israel and the Southern Kingdom of Judah were later merged into one account. According to Daniel Smith-Christopher of Hebrew Bible at Loyal Marymount, "We think that the J material was first gathered together under King Solomon. It represents Solomon's attempt to gather up the stories of the people, to knit them together into a coherent narrative. To tell the story of how the people of Israel came to be a people. And so it became a kind of national epic. In response, the people in the north begin to do the same thing." (Who Wrote the Bible?) Furthermore, the Dead Sea Scrolls contain books from every book in the Bible, with the exception of the Book of Esther. Within the Scrolls are differing versions of the same books. (Who Wrote the Bible?) So, the obvious question is: how could the "Word of God" vary from one book the next?

Then, there is the limitation presented by language and translations. The language in which the Old Testament was originally written was Hebrew. As we know, over the years languages evolve so that it is sometimes hard to pinpoint the exact meaning of some words because meanings change over time. Add to that, the Old Testament was transcribed or copied many times, and then it was translated into many other languages. The Old Testament that appears in the King James Bible was translated from Hebrew to Greek, to Latin, and then to German and finally into English. These transcriptions and translations took place over thousands of years.

There are other problems, such as credibility, embellishments, conflicting facts and so on and so forth. All of these obvious problems and shortcomings aside, it is important for the reader to understand the historical context in which we are making these judgments. In our time, we have carbon 14 dating, archeology, a multitude of ancient texts, geology, satellite imagery, electron microscopy, etc. in which to aid us in verifying or disproving stories from ancient accounts. But, since we are the first generation to have access to these tools, everyone up until our time believed these accounts to be true exactly as they were written, translated and transcribed, and so they have not only survived, they have been the very foundation for Western thought, culture and law for almost two thousand years.

So, there we have another of the great dichotomies of history. Just because someone says something is true, does not make it true, and vice versa. We could get into that dull philosophical discussion of what truth is, but we will not. For this book, there is no truth. There is only what has been written and there is physically provable science. To put it bluntly, either something happened, like World War II, or someone says that it happened, and whether or not you choose to believe something happened because someone says that it happened is up to the reader.

On that note, I would like to save time by not beginning every sentence with, "according to," especially in cases where there is a general consensus on the subject. For example, we all know that there are things called airplanes, so I would just say "airplane" instead of, "according to the NTSA, there are airplanes." However in the case of Noah's Ark, I would have to qualify that statement by saying "according to the Old Testament a man named Noah built a big ship that is called an Ark."

Now that the reader understands the way in which material will be presented, we will start with the History of the World according to the three Western monotheistic religions.

I do apologize to those who feel I am treating the topic too lightly, or skimming over some detail while including others. It is my purpose in this book to demonstrate that there are claims made by the LDS Church, the Society of Freemasons and those who have studied the phenomenon of extraterrestrials that are actually supported by science and both versions of history. Therefore where those areas overlap upon which I will concentrate, while leaving other details out. Once again, this book is written to be entertaining enough so as to keep the reader interested. If the reader is already an expert on religion, or throws the word "blasphemy" about like snowballs in January, I encourage you to continue on to the next chapter.

History according to the Bible…sort of

According to the Holy Scriptures of each religion, God created the world in seven days, around seven thousand years ago. After He created the world, God created the animals, the fish, birds and sometime after that, God created man. He saw that man was happy, so he put a stop to that by creating a woman by ripping out one of Adam's ribs (There is still some debate as to which was more painful). Almost immediately, things began to go wrong for Adam. Eve began telling him to pick up his socks and to put the lid back on the toothpaste when he was finished with it.

Adam was of course confused. Eve was great to look at, and sometimes even made good company, at least until she started asking him where he was all the time and who he was with on bowling nights. To make matters even worse for the somewhat confused Adam, Eve started shopping at God Mart, the Lord's all-in-one shopping warehouse. At the behest of Satan, who was posing in the guise of a serpent working as the store produce clerk, Eve overdrew the checking account while buying the apples the serpent was actively promoting. She came home that night and insisted Adam wear a pink and white striped cardigan she had picked up on sale, and to make matters even worse, Eve insisted that Adam try one of the apples she had picked up at seventy-nine cents a pound. Adam was incensed when he found out about the checking account, but that was just the beginning of his problems. Along with the effeminate looking sweater, the Lord became even angrier when He found out about the apples (they weren't supposed to go on sale until the next week). When God saw Adam in the cardigan, eating an apple and looking somewhat ridiculous, He also noticed that they were once again overdrawn on their checking account. Citing their status as a poor credit risk, The Lord of Hosts foreclosed on their "Paradise Estates" property immediately and sent them packing into the world, whereby they ended up in the projects somewhere in southern New Jersey.

God and Adam had a falling out of sorts, but, after Adam blamed everything on the woman, and said he was sorry, God forgave Adam and Eve. He gave them the order to "be fruitful and multiply," a wish to which Adam readily complied after the debacle in the Garden of Eden. The first sons of Adam and Eve were known as Cain and Abel. Abel was a hardworking lad, most likely a Republican, while Cain was a lay-about. Jealous of his brother, Cain slew Abel at the behest of Satan and that wily serpent. When God found out about that, Satan was rebuffed and the serpent was sentenced to slithering along the ground for eternity, although the Bible never specifies exactly which area of law he began practicing.

After that, there was a lot of what is known in the Bible as "begat-ing." Methuselah begat Enoch and Enoch begat someone and someone begat someone and so on and so on… The list goes on and on until we find ourselves with Noah during the onset of the rainy season. In what seems to be a recurring theme, God becomes angry at the ne-r-do-wells he has created (man) and He tells Noah to build a huge boat and put every animal on earth upon it. Once that is accomplished, God destroys the world with a flood, and forty days and forty nights later, the boat, or "ark" comes to rest on the Mountains of Ararat. The sons of Noah, after being confined with the family and the smell of the ark and all those animals, see fit to leave and populate the rest of the world.

After the population of the world recovers, they become civilized and build a great city called Babel. In Babel, they come up with the idea to build a tower that will reach to heaven. God is not happy with prospect of drop-in visitors from earth and decides the best way to keep us humans on the farm so to speak, is to confound our language. Once again, man is forced back to a primitive state, where he resides for many years.

The birth of Israel

Sometime later, we come across an elderly Abraham, the patriarch of modern Hebrews and Arabs, who is about to become a father for the first time. At the time of the baby shower, Abraham, much to his chagrin, is instructed by God to sacrifice his only
son Isaac, to which, he complies rather reluctantly. Abraham and his wife were well into their nineties by that time and it didn't seem likely they would have

another chance at a little Abe junior. At the last minute, the Lord sends a reprieve before the joke gets completely out of hand and Isaac is spared while an unsuspecting nearby goat is the unfortunate and unwitting "pinch-hitter" sacrifice to the Lord of Hosts.

Isaac then creates a mess of things by marrying two wives who bare him two sons, one son per wife. The sons are as different as night and day. Esau, the oldest, is an outdoor type who enjoys hunting and helping his father, while Jacob is a momma's boy who spends most of his time dawdling in the family tent. Isaac loves Esau because he knows where to score the best vittles. Therefore Jacob makes plans to pass on the family estate to his favorite hunter and gatherer. When the big day finally comes, at the behest of his mother, Jacob tricks Isaac into giving him the blessing that was supposed to go to his firstborn son. Esau is understandably put out.

Jacob seems to have been forgiven by God for the dirty trick he played on his father and Esau. At some later point, Jacob, possibly as part of an ancient witness protection program, changes his name to Israel. He is promised that he will be the father of a great nation. Not wanting to waste any time, Israel begins to be fruitful and multiplies himself by twelve. Of his twelve sons, one becomes the Minister of Agriculture for the Pharaoh in Egypt after his jealous brothers sell him into slavery. They say, "What comes around goes around," and nowhere else does that seem to be true than in the affairs of the Hebrews. Years later, there is a famine in Palestine and there is neither a bagel nor a mitzvah ball to be found.

Israel (formerly Jacob) sends his eleven sons to Egypt to buy wheat. There they find their own brother, whom they had previously beaten, thrown into a hole and then sold into slavery. Joseph by that time had made his way out of the slave pits and was running the Pharaoh's most important enterprise, the food stores. When he sees his brothers, Joseph doesn't let on at first (who would?) but eventually he reveals himself as the guy who they left for dead so many years ago. Joseph seems to have forgiven his brothers and invited them all down to Egypt to enjoy the good times and abundance of the Land of Egypt.

Sometime afterwards, about half a million children of Israel later, Pharaoh, distrusting of this nation within his nation, decides he can save himself a lot of paperwork and political trouble if he just enslaves the whole lot. Hearing their cries of despair, the Lord sends a man by the name of Moses to convince Pharaoh that He is not happy with the plight of his Chosen people. Moses advises Pharaoh to either send them on their way or suffer a few plagues, famines and pestilences of, shall, I say, Biblical proportions.

Pharaoh displeases the Lord of Hosts by not only refusing Moses, but by cracking the whip on his Hebrew slaves, who are becoming somewhat "uppity" now that Moses has been sent by God to give the Pharaoh what for. God then unleashes flies, toads, locusts, turns the Nile red with blood and generally turns Egypt into what we would identify with as eastern Texas in our own time. However, it isn't until the Lord releases the Avenging Angel, who subsequently kills the first born of all those who do not have a lamb carcass on their door, that Pharaoh gives his famous command, which, translated into Canadian means, "Hey! Take off, you hosers!"

The children of Israel (as they are now known) did, "take off." They took off with the gold and jewelry and anything they could get their hands on when they left. Pharaoh was not happy to see all that free labor get away, not to mention the loot the Israelites had promised to return in a week. He had a change of heart and went after the Children of Israel equipped with his army and a foul temperament. He caught up to the Children of Israel at the Red Sea and made ready to unleash the fury of his army on the whole lot. Moses, knowing that if he didn't do something quick, the future of the gold shops in Israel would be in peril, raised his staff and parted the sea. The Israelites escaped through the parted waters and, once they had crossed, Moses brought the Red Sea crashing back together again on the army of Pharaoh, which became the first Egyptian submarine force. The Israelites then escaped into the Sinai Desert, safe from the Pharaoh, who was, as they say in the mafia, "swimming with the fishes."

Unfortunately for the Children of Israel, Moses had a lot of neat tricks up his sleeves but it turned out that he was a much better liberator than navigator. They got lost, all half million of them and ended up wandering around the Sinai Desert for forty years looking for Palestine. In his defense, there are unconfirmed accounts that a gas station attendant gave Moses the wrong directions, but these accounts could never be corroborated. During their "whirlwind" tour of the Sinai, Moses received a series of Ten Commandments from the Lord that were to be the cornerstone of not only Jewish, but Western ethical and legal thought until the eighteenth century. The Children of Israel were also instructed to make a box out of gold and wood and other fancy stuff, in which to keep the stone tablets on which the Ten Commandments were written. The gold box was called the "Ark of the Covenant" and to keep it protected from the elements, the Lord commanded that a sort of "mobile temple" be built in the form of an elaborate tent in which the Lord of Hosts could travel from time to time on their forty-year camping trip.

The forty years that the Children of Israel wandered in the Sinai Desert were a sort of "boot camp" for the entire nation. During that time, the Lord fed them in the form of manna, which was a kind of bread that they found at their camp every morning. He provided them with water, and in a rather subtle way, the Lord kept them in the Sinai until most of them were dead, and a new generation was allowed to mature. It was an entire generation that had been dependent on the will of their God for even the most basic necessities of life. The new generation knew nothing of the ways of the Egyptians. They only knew that if they didn't do exactly what the Lord told them, they would die of hunger, thirst or have their heads smashed in by the Levites. The new generation was lean, and hungry, much like Sylvester Stallone in the first *Rocky* movie. They knew that the time would come when they would get their big fight in the land of Palestine, as the Lord had promised that he would give the land to them in exchange for their obedience to his laws. God, so it seems, planned on making a literal killing in real estate.

When the children of Israel did finally enter Palestine, they did so, according to the Old Testament accounts as ruthless invaders smiting the kingdoms of the region with reluctance in some cases and great zeal in others. In little time, the Children of Israel, formerly known in Egypt as "brick backs" "Red Sea pedestrians" and "Sinai Sojourners," were the masters of some of the most fertile land, strategic locations and the best sunbathing beaches in the Middle East. During their stay in Egypt, the Children of Israel had divided themselves into tribes that went back to the original sons of Jacob, a.k.a. Israel. When they returned, they divided the land according to the tribes of the House of Israel, eventually breaking up into a Northern and a Southern Kingdom.

The new kids on the Palestine block, the Israelites who left the Sinai, were little more than sheep and goat herders. Once they possessed the land of Palestine, they found themselves situated between the most powerful kingdoms and empires of the time. In the north, there were the seafaring Hittites and Phoenicians. The Philistines ruled in the east, the Egyptians ruled to the south. Further east were the Assyrians and the Babylonians. All of these kingdoms were in possession of knowledge and technology that either the Israelites did not know about, understand or at least initially, possess. According to the Bible, the Israelites had access to the only thing they needed to keep them from being dominated by their numerically and technologically advanced enemies. They possessed the knowledge that they were God's "Chosen People." They also had one other little gem in their bag of tricks, the Ark of the Covenant.

Until the time of Jesus Christ, the History of Israel, as it is recounted in the Old Testament, is a history of a people with an identity crisis, hostile neighbors and a harsh schoolmaster. The Israelites were initially ruled by a series of judges, but they gave in to the pressure to have an absolute monarch going against the better wishes of the prophet Elias, who warned of the consequences of a having a king when they already had one (God). Saul, David and Solomon were the greatest kings of Israel. But, it is Solomon who is the king we will be concerned with in later chapters. Solomon is the most important king because it was Solomon who built the Temple in Jerusalem. While other minor kings were able, at least for a while, to hold off the armies of their surrounding enemies, in the end, the Children of Israel will be conquered by the Assyrians and then the Babylonians, as the Old Testament explains, as retribution for their failure to follow God's commandments.

The harsh lessons visited upon the Children of Israel were not forgotten, and served to bring the people closer to each other in their religion and in their desire to be independent of outside powers. By the time that the events that make up of the Gospels of the New Testament took place, the Israelites had seen the Assyrians, the Babylonians, the Persians, Alexander the Great and the Romans come and go, well, except for the Romans. The Romans had developed a foreign policy two centuries before Christ that, simply put, said, "Get them before they get you." In other words, the Romans probably couldn't care less about the Jews or Israel or their single God. They were interested in the gold and the resources of Palestine, Egypt and modern day Iraq and Syria. To the Roman Empire, Palestine was simply a jumping off point to better places. It was important to them only as a way to keep their supply lines and their marching routes secure. Because of the vast amount of wealth available by anyone who controlled the trade routes through Palestine, the Romans were determined to hold on to that land, no matter what the cost.

Jesus, Israel and the Kingdom of God

Jesus Christ was born in the insignificant town of Nazareth at the beginning of the Roman Empire, just a few decades after the death of the first emperor, Julius Caesar. Jesus started preaching a lot of things that neither the Romans, nor the Jews wanted to hear. The Israelites on the one hand, saw the Romans as they had seen the Assyrians and the Babylonians. They saw the Romans as another affliction given to them by their God for their unwillingness to follow His laws. What they wanted was another military hero, like David, to come and smite the Romans and free them. According to their own history, the formula for the Children of Israel was a simple one. If they all followed the commandments, as well as the multitude of laws that were laid out in the book of Leviticus, then God, in turn would fulfill his end of the bargain by liberating, or helping them to liberate themselves from their oppressors, no matter who they were, nor how powerful they appeared to be. It was what we may call in our time, "a no-brainer."

From the Roman perspective, the Jews represented a rebellious group of zealots who placed religion ahead of anything else, including the Roman's rule. The Romans themselves had religion, a pantheon of gods they had inherited from the Greeks, but their real god was money, women, power and conquest. Their gods took little notice of what they did, unless they failed to pay them the proper respect, which usually amounted to a donation to the local temple every now and then. The Romans could not begin to understand the Jew's fanaticism for their One God, but they did have enough sense to understand that the Jews were much more willing to comply with Roman laws and tax policy if Jewish religious leaders were placed in positions of power. To put it simply, the Romans didn't care much for the Jews, unless the Jews began to revolt, which was a constant threat. Putting down revolts cost money and that money had to come from Rome, therefore any governor who might ask for aid in putting down a revolt would be deemed incompetent. Roman governors of Palestine governed on the edge of a razor.

So, I hope it is understandable to the reader what a huge problem Jesus was for both the Jews and the Romans. In the first place, the Jews were only trying to make the God who had brought their ancestors out of Egypt, had fed their ancestors in the Sinai and made a promise to their ancestors that the land of Palestine was theirs if they would obey Him, happy. He had laid down the law and the Jews were going to follow it. In return, He
would reward their obedience with a deliverer along the lines of David or Moses.

Instead, a man appeared from the lineage of David, who began to heal people and to teach peace and forgiveness. When asked what loyalty they, as Jews owed to the Romans, He simply held up a coin with a head on it, asked whose head it was and then replied, "Give unto Caesar what belongs to Caesar." His answer was as non-committal and non-confrontational as one could be. He didn't even seem to care about the Romans at all. Jesus was not the military commander that was promised by the covenant the Jews had made with their God. What was worse for the Jews, Jesus preached that in Him, (Jesus) the Law of Moses (Ten Commandments, Leviticus and Deuteronomy) was fulfilled.

What was worse was that people began to believe Jesus and his disciples and they in turn, repeated His words to their friends. In very little time, Jesus had a following of hundreds, if not thousands of people who believed in loving their neighbors, forgiving their enemies and helping the poor and the sick. Jesus was literally turning potential rebel fighters into peace-niks. This did not go unnoticed by the Jewish leadership. In their eyes, Jesus was going to bring either the wrath of God or the wrath of the Romans down upon their heads. The last act that was committed by Jesus was to pick up a whip and start beating the moneychangers who had turned Solomon's Temple into a foreign currency exchange. For the Jewish leadership, this act was the "last straw" as far as they were concerned. Jesus of Nazareth had to go.

On the Roman side of things, they didn't care much about Jesus one-way or the other. In fact, He had Roman soldiers in his following. If anything, the teachings of Jesus were good news to the Romans and they probably wished there were more Jews like him. But, by claiming to be the king of the Jews, he was guilty of sedition and He was convicted by the Roman governor, Pilate at the behest of the Sanhedrin, a religious sect of the Jewish leadership who feared he was a challenge to their authority. He was also an affront to the God who had promised to deliver them and a threat to their upcoming revolt. It was more to please the Jewish leadership, and make it appear to the Jews that the Sanhedrin and the Pharisees were in charge than any fear the Romans had of one Jew who went around preaching peace and love.

In the end, Jesus was crucified by nailing his wrists and feet to a cross. It was a horribly painful yet popular punishment of the Romans. It was a public example for all
who violated the law of contesting their authority. According to the Gospels, Jesus died and was laid to rest in a tomb, where he was resurrected on the third day. Also, according to the Gospels, he returned to Earth in his glorified form and instructed his disciples in the formation of a new religion based upon his teachings.

Enter the Gentiles

Following his death, Jesus disciples ventured out and preached his unorthodox message of love and forgiveness, compassion and mercy to the Mediterranean World. The writings of the apostle Paul make up the first intellectual arguments of the Christian Church and lay out in more detail what is and is not acceptable for the followers of the new faith. It was Paul's teachings that started the rift between the followers of the Jewish-Christian school of thought and the new non-Jewish Christian school of thought. It was through the teachings and writings of Paul that the idea of non-Jews being allowed into the Christian faith became acceptable in the doctrines of the new religion. For the Jewish-Christians in Palestine and elsewhere, the idea of the unclean "gentiles" being allowed into the Church was a source of serious contentment. Jesus was a Jew who followed all of the Jewish traditions. To them, the only way a non-Jew could be allowed into the faith was through conversion to Judaism and then baptism into the Church. It was the first of a never-ending series of controversies that would plague the early Church for the next two hundred years.

For the Jews in Palestine, they scarcely noticed what was happening as far as the new sect was concerned. They had gotten rid of the troublemaker Jesus and they were going to have their rebellion no matter what. They were too busy preparing themselves for the upcoming revolt to give the new movement any thought as a potential threat. In fact, they could hardly care less about the peace loving and non-committal Christians who officially chose to "render unto Caesar" than risk their wonderful new church being stamped out. The Jews finally got their revolt and succeeded in throwing the Romans out in 67 AD. Three years later, the Romans returned and the Jews felt the full brunt of the Roman wrath as they destroyed Jerusalem and left few that they found alive.

Who is to blame for the Crucifixion of Jesus?

For the next two thousand years, the Christian world would use the crucifixion of Jesus Christ as an excuse to persecute the people of the Jewish faith. This speaks more to the ignorance and hypocrisy of the people who practice Christianity than almost anything, except for all the wars and atrocities committed in the name of Christianity. Jesus Christ knew exactly what was going to happen to him when He began preaching. He would have had to be completely ignorant of his own people's history, doctrines and the covenant that they held with their God not to understand the implications of His teachings and the subsequent backlash that both He and his followers would feel. I think there are few people, Christian or non-Christian, who would claim that a man with Jesus' wisdom was not aware of the political realities of the Roman World. In other words, Jesus knew exactly what He was doing when he incited the Jewish leadership in Jerusalem. To put it simply, Jesus was responsible for His own death.

For their part, the Jews were simply following what they had been taught over the course of a thousand years of some very harsh lessons. They feared God and they feared the Romans. God had promised to send them someone to deliver them and very few of them (as would very few of us) understood that their deliverance would come in the form of a spiritual liberation from the horrors of this life. They cannot be blamed for following God's will, as they knew it. What would have happened if they had chosen to accept Jesus as their King? He never would have been crucified for our sins and His mission would never have been accomplished. If common sense tells us anything, Christians should embrace the Jewish people for their adherence to their faith and their culture and for allowing the Will of God to be done on the earth. In other words, if there were no Jews, there would be no Christians.

After their rather unsuccessful revolt, those Jews that could flee to all known parts of Europe, Africa and Asia, did. The Christians, on the other hand, found themselves accepted in, of all places, the Greek world, where the educated classes were schooled in the writings of Plato. In fact, there was little difference in the philosophies of Jesus and Socrates, Plato and Aristotle. The stories of Jesus rising from the dead and promising eternal life coincided with the Greek religions as well as the religions of Rome (also Greek) and Egypt.

Because of the willingness of the Old (Greek) World, which had been conquered centuries before by Alexander, which then consisted of modern day Turkey, parts of Syria, Egypt and parts of Iraq, to accept the teaching of Jesus and his Apostles, the Christian Church, in all its varied forms soon was in competition with all of the religions
In the Middle East, Africa and the West.

And, there is the history of the world according to the Bible, more or less. In summary, in case it is not blatantly obvious, the History of the World, at least according to the Old and New Testament, seems to be more or less the history of the descendants of the twelve children of a prolific sheepherder who wasn't afraid to use guile to get what he wanted, and who had no qualms about cheating his own blood (Esau, the "father" of the Arabs) to do it. Why was this book, which leaves out nearly every major people and culture in history, accepted for nearly sixteen hundred years as the explanation for everything from our laws to our own origins with no questions asked? There is no simple reason, as we will see in the next chapter, why the Bible came to be the last word on everything. For now, the simple reason is that it was the best explanation anybody had to offer. Other people had ideas and explanations about why things were they way they were, but they couldn't put the "Word of God" tag upon them, so, for over almost two thousand years a person had a choice of either accepting the Bible as the exact words spoken by God, or else suffer some very serious consequences.

Of course, one could fall back on the issue of morality to explain the success of the Bible, Torah and Koran over all these years. In these Holy Books, we see the same theme over and over again which seems to be that all people have a choice in life. They can either obey the Lord or they can suffer really harsh consequences (remember Cain, Pharaoh, Sodom and Gomorrah?) in this life and the next. The Bible, or at least the Old Testament, is full of stories that are meant to inspire fear. There is the fear of God, fear of wickedness, fear of non-believers and non-conformers. There is the fear of punishment for not obeying the word of God. Why does the Lord seem to be pre-occupied with threatening people all of the time? The answer to that has more to do with the human psyche and condition than what the Bible actually tells us. The Lord, in fact, does not threaten anyone in the Bible, He only makes promises of what will be the outcome of not listening to His counsel, as would any parent. Unfortunately, the people who have used the Bible to maintain control of people's minds all of these years, specify the threats and punishments, while seeming to skim over the promises God makes if people follow the teachings of the Bible.

In the world that existed prior to the foundation of the United States of America, it was much easier to control people living under these circumstances by describing a God that they could relate to, instead of a God who loved them and was going to watch over them. As we shall soon see, the social system was not set up with the best interest of the common man in mind. It was set up to exploit the poor and the weak. Control was maintained by fear, so fear appeared to be the main theme of the Bible to many illiterate, uneducated peasants who served as chattel slaves to their local warlord. It also didn't hurt if, from time to time, the use of torture was used to inspire, if not a fear of God, then a fear of the local political system that claimed its source of power was that same God. Under these circumstances, a merciful God was a little bit hard to sell in a system that had no mercy. For most people who have lived throughout history, the only hope they had was the hope that there was a better life in the next world if they obeyed God's and later Jesus' commandments in this one. If they did, they could escape the barbarity and injustice of this world upon their passage into the next, and if not, there was a similar system waiting for them on the other side.

The Bible as History?

So we see, as a philosophical record, the Bible has been misinterpreted throughout History. As a historical record, the Bible has even more shortcomings. The Bible was written to outline the relationship between God and man. Unfortunately, it was not for all men, as only a very small proportion of the world's population is even mentioned in the Bible, yet it somehow became a historic text for almost half of the world, which was never its intended use. The problem with the Bible as History is that, even today, few people, especially religious ones, understand that the majority of the Old Testament was written during the reign of the Kings of Israel between 900 and 600 BCE. Yet, it portends to explain events, like the creation of man, which occurred according to the Bible, at least four thousand years before that time, if a person is inclined to accept the Biblical account of Creation.

To give you an idea of how much time four thousand years is, think back a mere two thousand years to the time of the New Testament. What do you know about the world two thousand years ago? What do you know about life two thousand years ago? Even more importantly, how do you know the things that you do know? If we want to come as close to the facts as possible about life two thousand years ago, we have no choice but to
rely on people who wrote at the time, and we have to trust that they and those that passed on that information had no ulterior motive other than to write the truth. We are also limited by language, changing social customs and traditions as well as geographic locations. In other words, to write about life two thousand years ago

would be extremely difficult, especially if you didn't have access to written records that you could actually read and understand.

If you were to travel back in time to join the writers of the first five books of the Old Testament around the time of Solomon, they would most likely explain to you that they were going to document the history of the world, all the way back to the "beginning of time." When they announced to you that the beginning of time was five thousand years ago, you might ask them how they came to that figure. They would say that so-and-so told so-and-so and so-and-so told so-and-so and the process might take a couple of days to cover the entire four thousand years. You, remembering your days trying to stay awake in World History class in high school, might suddenly shout out, "Aha, that's not true! Modern man, or homo sapiens, is at least one hundred and fifty thousand years old!"

Your Old Testament scribe friends might look at you for a moment, maybe do some calculations on an abacus and then reply, "Says who?" You would say you read about it in a book in high school. Since they would not know what a "book" or a "high school" was, they would laugh at you for a few minutes, realizing that you were talking about some "fairy-tale" you may have heard as a child. If you tried to reason with the scribes of Solomon, you might ask them, "Where is your proof that the world began four thousand years ago?" They would reply, "Our proof is in the words of so-and-so who told so-and-so who told so-and-so…" Once that was finished, they would humor you by asking, "Where is your proof?"

The entire point here is that it would have been impossible to have an accurate accounting of the last four thousand years when the writers of the first five books of the Old Testament sat down to write the history of man. However, the reader should also understand that oral traditions were the only way to pass on knowledge in illiterate cultures. There was little motive to embellish, or change oral tradition, but there was the human element of sometimes getting details of the story wrong, which would explain why there were different versions of Biblical texts found in 1947, which are known, to us as the Dead Sea Scrolls. By our standards, the Bible is not history. But does that mean
that the events described in the Bible never took place?

The Bible as Science?

The Bible as a scientific text in the modern world has the same shortcomings that it has as a historical text. Since the age of the Enlightenment, when people began to actually observe nature and compare it to biblical accounts, it was obvious that the Bible didn't stand up as a scientific text either, though it had been considered the last word in science until then, and in some circles, is still considered the last word in science even today. The first questions began to arise when the advocates of what is called uniformitarianism, or the idea that earth changes occur slowly over time, so much time that it would be impossible for the earth to be seven thousand years old, asked, "If the flood killed all the land animals, why were there so many fossils of extinct fish?" In the 1830's Charles Lyell wrote *Principles of Geology* based on his own and earlier proponents of the idea that earth changes occurred much more slowly than anyone could have anticipated.

In fact, at about that same time in History, scientists and religious leaders both began to scramble to explain all of the seeming discrepancies in the Bible. The age of the earth could be explained by rationalizing that the six days that it took God to create the earth were actually calculated in, "God's time." In fact, so much rationalizing was done, that in the period from the early 1700's to the middle 1800's, God himself changed. In the late 1800's many people got tired of trying to explain God at all and said that, in fact, there was no God. As we shall see in the next few chapters our presence on this planet can simply be explained by Darwin's ideas about evolution.

Today, many Christians, Muslims and Jews cling to the Old Testament as the last word on where we came from and what we are doing here. We have seen that science has, in fact refuted many of the claims made by the Bible, but did science refute all of the claims? Is there any evidence to support the historic claims made in the Bible about events that occurred in the Bible, like catastrophic floods, the cataclysm at Sodom and Gomorrah and the destruction of the town of Jericho?

The flood story is not a story that is limited to the Judeo-Christian tradition, either. It is also corroborated in the Epic of Gilgamesh, found in the ruins of the ancient Assyrian capital. Gilgamesh, according to the legend, also survived a cataclysmic flood by building a large wooden vessel. The flood story is a story that is found on nearly every continent on earth, in nearly every culture, to include the Chinese, Egyptian, Native American and Greek Cultures. Unfortunately, science and religion make strange bedfellows and their historic hatred, or fear of each other, has made us like the child of the divorced parents who are constantly trying to win our affection by constantly attacking the credibility of the opposite parent.

Physical and scientific evidence uncovered in the last twenty to thirty years does support the idea that there was a catastrophic flood that occurred not at the time the Bible says, but much, much earlier in 11,700 BC, and again in places like the Northwestern and Northeastern United States some ten thousand years ago as great glacial dams gave way and their contents flowed into the oceans. Furthermore, an expedition to the area around Mt. Ararat in modern day Turkey led by the late Ron Wyatt, in which a deposit of stone in the shape of a very large ship was found in the 1980's, gives us at least some evidence that there was at least one very large ship that is much older than previously thought possible. Wyatt, through a series of seismographic tests proved that there is a colossal boat that matches the descriptions of the dimensions of Noah's Ark sitting in a petrified state below the mountain.

Furthermore, Wyatt claimed to have found evidence of petrified wood, and the chemical deposits that are consistent with huge steel beams that served as reinforcement for the internal structure of the ship. For his efforts, and his claims that this structure is possibly the Ark mentioned in the Bible, the late Ron Wyatt continues to be scandalized by the scientific community for his theories. This is a common pattern of the relationship between science and religion that continues to this day. Claims that support the Bible, or other Holy Scriptures, as well as claims of the existence of extraterrestrial life are tirelessly refuted by the scientific community which, as we shall see, has changed from the searchers of the truth, to the purveyors of the truth as those who control their funding wish that truth to be.

So what does the average person do? Accept the Bible on blind faith? Discount the Bible because a professor makes money and gets a prestigious appointment for discounting the claims of Wyatt and those who claim the Bible does contain some elements of historic fact? Does the fact that one story about a big petrified boat, an

Assyrian text and theories about climate change mean that the Bible is in fact accurate? Of course it does not. The best thing that a person can do is to try to come to an understanding of the conflict between science and religion as a parent would when refereeing a fight between two stubborn children. It is a conflict that is peculiar to the Western tradition, where, as we shall see, religion once dominated, and then was forced to give way to science, which in turn, has become the new religion, in every sense of the word.

Ever since Charles Darwin published his Origin of Species in 1859, the world has divided itself into two camps. Those who relied on science and observation to explain the physical world were quite small in number at the beginning of the twentieth century. One only has to go back to 1925 to the Scopes Monkey Trial and see the passion it aroused to understand the gap that was growing between organized religion and science. Ever since that time, both fields have put up barriers to each other. A respected scientist could not believe in Creationism and a respected churchgoer could not believe in the theory of Evolution. The fact that today, most of us think that the idea that a teacher would be fired and imprisoned for teaching the Theory of Evolution, even in Tennessee, as incredible, shows just how far attitudes have swung to the side of science at the expense of organized religion. Are we going to need to go back and rethink everything we once "knew" about the world and then threw out in favor of science?

So, maybe this is an oversimplified explanation, but the answer to the question is not as important as the fact that it can be a question at all. Something happened, sometime, somewhere, that broke the stranglehold of those that used the Bible to explain not only the world but also, their justification for being the masters of it. Therefore, we must step out of the confines of the Church and find out what other history we seem to have missed.

PART 1

TWO HISTORIES?

Chapter 4

History According to History

Before we begin a brief overview of what is known as "popular history," let me acknowledge that popular or not, people either love history, or they hate it. With this in mind, I will try to give the reader a general overview of what is commonly known as "world history" by concentrating on important ideas and cultures that will be relevant to the rest of the book. I do apologize to readers outside of the realm of the Western World for neglecting your fantastic histories, but since they are not relevant to the subject matter of this book, they must, unfortunately be left to people like yourselves to write. That being said, History, as complicated as it may seem, is really not that complicated at all if you understand that there are basic forces involved when it comes to history.

"Popular" history?

History is generally the study of peoples who live together as a society and who do things for the purpose of self-interest. As bleak and as skeptical as it may sound, all of history can be more easily understood if you "follow the money," as they say. Why did the Greeks attack Troy? According to the story, it was for the honor of Greece, getting back Helen and all that, but how many people in reality are going to risk their necks against the most feared city in the world for some indecisive tart? Unless, that is, there is a lot to be gained (trade, money, land) from its destruction? Why did the English colonists in America vote to have a war with the most powerful empire on earth? Freedom and democracy sound good in the history texts, but the colonists understood that they could get rich must faster if they didn't have to pay taxes to the English. If you look at nearly any event in history, from the crucifixion of Christ to the discovery of America, you only have to look at who stood to make money or, get or maintain their power, and then you will find it much easier to understand the events and the people involved.

"Popular history" then, is a political study of how the wealthy and powerful maintained their wealth and power by manipulating the lower classes through fear, superstition and misinformation. In fact, what we call history is basically a continual chain of events from which someone came out ahead by killing a lot of other people, in most cases, or taking control of them and their possessions in some other less-than fatal way. The "story" in history occurs in the way events are "spun" by the winners to make sure that people remember how they did what they did in the most noble and flattering fashion and why mankind was better off because of their efforts. As one of history's biggest scalawags, Adolf Hitler once said, "The victors write the history books." Unfortunately for him, he wasn't a victor and his brutal crimes became known for what they were. These two basic principles of history go as far back as Sumer and ancient Egypt and were as true then as they are in our time and most likely will not change anytime soon.

Of course, not all history is as a dark and bleary as an evening with an insurance salesman. To make history come alive, instead of looking at it as a dull and boring exercise in remembering names and dates, look at history as a sort of criminal investigation of events and people that took place sometime in the past. Sometimes you will find that history, since it is real, is much more fascinating and incredible than any fiction you could ever imagine. You will also find that sometimes, though not often, men and women don't always behave as perfect scoundrels.

In the beginning...

The history of the world, according to the people we call scientists, physicists, astronomers, geologists, archeologists, anthropologists and historians, really began twelve to fifteen billion years ago with what has come to be known as the "Big Bang." The Big Bang is a rather simplified name for a rather complex process that we still do not fully understand. I would prefer to call it "From Nothing to Something," because that is a more accurate description of what happened, according to science. Of course, "From Nothing to Something," is not as exciting as "The Big Bang." "From Nothing to Something" also leaves the theory open to the obvious; it violates the basic laws of the people who proposed it, the physicists themselves who say that you can't create something out of nothing. We will discuss physics, or the laws that govern the universe, in a later chapter, so, suffice it to say that before, "From Nothing to Something" (or The Big Bang), there was nothing. In other words, it would not have been possible for anyone or anything to observe the universe then, because there was no space, no time, no light, no atoms, no planets, no stars, not even a chili dog.

Then, for reasons that are still unknown, there was a violent explosion that was so powerful it can scarcely be imagined. At that one millionth of a millionth of a second, there was something. If it were possible to witness that moment, it could only be described as "all hell" breaking loose or "free hat night" at a Cleveland Indians game. That something that emerged from nothing, according to scientists, consisted in the first few millionths of a second where energy in the form of subatomic particles combined to form the first matter. Later, the subatomic particles attracted to more particles and thus became what we call the nuclei (plural of nucleus) that made up the first atoms. That nuclei gained energy as fields of negative and positive charged particles came together, or, more accurately, slammed into one another as they sped away from the explosion and left what we call space behind them.

The end result of all this explosive power and subatomic chemistry was a substance we call matter, which, more or less at that time meant gas. The first gas was hydrogen, followed by helium and so on and so on. We will go into much more detail about atoms later, so for now, suffice it to say, the gas coalesced into larger and large bodies, creating gravity, which created stars and, after about ten billion years and the collapse of the star from which our present solar system was formed, created the beginnings of our planet some four and a half billion years ago.

Four billion years was a long time, during which the earth underwent many changes as life began and evolved into creepy things that would eventually become the dinosaurs, the birds, the fish and a little rat that would develop over millions of years into what scientists call homo sapiens, or man (and woman).

It is important to note that science has many theories about how life actually came to exist on our planet, but none of them have yet been proven. It is also important to note that science in the last few decades has discovered life in places in the earth that were thought too hot, cold, or devoid of oxygen and the appropriate materials we previously believed were necessary to support life. Based on these discoveries and observations, we now know that somehow life is able to exist in the most unexpected places. Therefore, our ideas that places in our own solar system could not possibly support life have had to be re-evaluated as mankind is actively searching the solar system for forms of primitive life that may explain, in a scientific way, how life formed on our planet.

According to science, the first Homo sapiens (that's us) evolved in Africa around 195,000 years ago. Homo Sapiens are the last apes in a long chain of an evolutionary process that was begun around four million years ago. The scientific evidence that supports that theory was an ape-like creature dubbed "Lucy" by her discoverer, Dr. Richard Leaky, who found her bones in the Olduvai Gorge in East Africa in the late 1960's.

You say you want an Evolution

If you do not understand the process that put us at the far end of a chain of apes that begins with an ape, which appeared to walk upright four million years ago, I will try to explain. The theory that man, or Homo sapiens, could not just come out of nowhere, originated out of the work of Charles Darwin in his work, *The Origin of Species*, which was published in 1859. According to science, where "Deux ex machina," the intervention of the gods, is not allowed, man had to have evolve, just like every other creature on the earth. Therefore, if he (or she) had to evolve, man must have evolved from the creatures he most resembled, and of course, that leads us to the family of monkeys, apes and chimpanzees. If you don't believe me, take a good hard look around at your next family reunion. The only problem with the theory is that there are huge gaps in the fossil record between these ape-like creatures and our closest evolutionary relation, a knuckle-dragging cousin known as Neanderthal. Neanderthal was so named because the remains of these humanoid creatures were first found in the Neanderthal region of France.

Before we get ahead of ourselves, let us review what happened between the formation of the solar system and our planet earth that led to the rise of the species known as homo sapiens According to the scientific theory, the earth formed along with the sun and other planets in our solar system after the collapse of a star many times larger than our sun. Life began to evolve when the earth was between two and three billion years old. For hundreds of millions of years, reptiles that evolved in steps and became increasingly larger and more complex until the age of the dinosaurs ruled the earth. Sixty five million years ago, the dinosaurs died, leaving mammals (warm blooded creatures who gave birth to live offspring as opposed to eggs) to develop in size and complexity. Finally, according to the latest discoveries published in Nature Magazine, a mere one hundred and ninety-five thousand years ago, which is not even a hiccup in the context of the age of our planet, Homo sapiens began to roam the plains of Africa and eventually spread across the globe.

The Civilization Gap

Continuing on, the oldest civilizations, according to the scientific crowd, date back around five thousand years to **Mesopotamia** and **The Indus River Valley**. I will say that one more time because it is a key element in our story. The Mesopotamian and the Indus River Valley civilizations date back five thousand years, to roughly three thousand five hundred B.C.E., whereby, as we have already said, scientists date Homo sapiens back 195,000 years. If you are one of those people who likes to ask a lot of annoying questions, at some point you may ask yourself, why do we not have anything to show for one hundred and ninety thousand years except for some pointed sticks, cave paintings and sharpened rocks? It took almost two hundred thousand years for we Homo sapiens to learn to read and write, build cities and create civilizations?

If that is true, what was it that motivated mankind five thousand years ago to start reading, writing, discover mathematics, science, economics, and law? That process that began with people writing with a stick and pressing it onto wet clay has resulted in this writer, around one hundred and thirty generations later, writing by using electrons that are manipulated by the touch of a key on a keyboard. Could we have missed something?

When it comes to the age of what we call civilization, we find one of those rare occasions when science and religion actually agree. As we have seen, religion has an easier "out" when it comes to explaining the age of man and the subsequent rise of civilization because religion does not leave a gap where one hundred and ninety thousand years are unaccounted. As we have already said, the Bible puts the age of the earth at around seven thousand years. If we start in Sumer at 3,500 B.C.E and backtrack, that only leaves a two thousand year gap between man's hasty exodus from the Garden of Eden and the rise of civilization. In that time, there *could have been* a flood that wiped out all of mankind, except for the Noah family. They would have had at least a thousand years of fruitfully multiplying and eventually arrive at our civilizations in **Sumer** and the **Indus River Valley** in 3,500 BC. Before we give the advantage to the Bible and the religious crowd when it comes to the actual history of man however, let us revisit science one more time for a possible explanation from which they can exhume themselves from the mire of the "Origins of Man" argument.

The earth, in term of its climate is relatively stable. It was this stability, which allowed the evolution of complex organisms, such as you and me to take place. However, the earth is sometimes a harsh and cruel place for the life that it supports. One thing that we do know for sure, thanks to the scientists who examine glacial ice cores that go back 250,000 years is that nearly twelve thousand years ago, the northern hemisphere was covered in great sheets of ice. Sheets of ice covered Cities like London, New York and Moscow two miles thick. We are also pretty sure that because the earth's climate is stable, one day, London, New York and Moscow will be covered by ice again. Knowing that, what would have happened (or what will happen) to everything that was (or will be) covered by the ice? It will be frozen, smashed and regurgitated by a glacier and end up as sand or rock. In other words, if we were to digress back to our primitive state, within ten thousand years or less, there will be no evidence that we even existed except for all the mysterious bare spots where we buried our radioactive waste.

So, should it choose to, science could explain the "civilization gap" by citing the continual spreading and receding of the ice sheets and the subsequent rising and lowering of sea level which would have destroyed any evidence of a civilization that may have existed in the regions that are covered by the ice or the higher sea level at fairly regular intervals. But what if there were remnants of a civilization that existed before or during the ice age? How would science explain that? After all, it was such a long time ago and any proof of that civilization, either physical or historical, would have long since vanished, wouldn't it? What if there were civilizations before the last ice age or in the ice age before the last ice age, or the ice age before that?

We will return to this line of questioning later, but for now, it is sufficient to say that science doesn't bother trying to explain anything older than the "Holy Grail" of civilizations in Mesopotamia and India because it isn't necessary. Science and archeology, much like religion, tell us that there is no evidence of any civilization that existed before Mesopotamia and the Indus Valley civilizations that began around 3,500 BC. If anybody presents evidence, such as incredibly large rocks that were quarried and somehow moved, or pyramids that appear to be much older than any known civilization, science simply says there is no evidence at all. Anybody who tries to speculate about older civilizations, are immediately put on the list of people who see, "little green men." We will come back to this idea later.

Civilization at Last, or at First…

So, we first arrive in Mesopotamia, specifically at the city of **Sumer**, which lies in southern Iraq between the Tigris and Euphrates rivers in 3,500 B.C.E. Here, there is a thriving metropolis that is based upon agriculture and trade. The people are ruled by king, who, are supported by a large bureaucracy of what we refer to as priests. The term "priest" is applied to anyone in the ancient world who is not engaged in farming, building or the military. A priest in ancient cultures is not the same as what we would think of when we attend Mass or a wedding. In ancient times, the priests were also concerned with the day to day running of the bureaucracy.

To ensure their employment and convince the general public that they were in fact a necessary evil, they appeased the gods during temple ceremonies with sacrifices and rituals. More importantly, the priests were the educated class. They were lawyers and scientists, teachers, writers, accountants, tax collectors and so on. In those days, and ours, it is much easier to classify ancient white-collar labor as "priests" than it was (or is) to make up specific titles and expect people to remember them. This system of power has remained in effect to the present day in one form or another and is the key element in making up what we call "civilization."

At the same exact time that the people of Sumer were building their cities, irrigating their fields, charting the heavens and inventing their own written language, a similar culture was evolving in the **Indus River Valley** in modern day India and Pakistan. Excavations of the **Indus River Valley Civilization** show that the Indus River peoples were proficient in architecture; agriculture, engineering and their houses were the first in the world to have indoor plumbing. It has long been believed that the cultures of **Sumer** and the **Indus River** grew up independently of each other, but evidence along the ancient sea-trade routes offer evidence that they may have interacted and even competed with each other for trade in the Persian Gulf and on the Arabian Peninsula. (*Heines 244*)

Both of these civilizations would become attractive to peoples living as nomads and raiders on the outskirts of the limits of their small empires. Over time, these outsiders would become conquerors and they, in turn would be conquered by other outside forces, hoping to live the good life that was available to those who possessed the cities. In fact, once the first cities began, a flurry of activity began for the next thousand years as the skills of metallurgy, engineering and building, irrigation and the military arts spread throughout the region. Peoples of all different backgrounds and regions in the Middle East began to build cities. The more cities that were built, the more their rival cities coveted them and so, within a thousand years, the first of the ancient empires, the Assyrian and the Babylonian, began to vie for control of the fertile lands between the Tigris and the Euphrates in modern Iraq.

Walk like an Egyptian

Plodding on as we were through our brief jaunt through world history, we leave the first civilizations in Iraq and India around 2700 B.C.E and move south and west to ancient **Egypt**, where the ever-dependable Nile River floods every year and deposits tons of nutrient- rich soil that it carries downstream from the mountains of Sudan and Ethiopia. Because of the regular flooding and the annual deposit of mineral rich sediments, crops in Egypt grew in abundance, which contributed to an ever-increasing population. The region that started as a collection of farmers and independent tribes and communities at the same time as the cities in Mesopotamia and India, had, by 2,700 B.C.E. organized itself into an empire that stretched from the mouth of the Nile in the north, southward for over a thousand miles to its headwaters.

The government of Egypt was based upon a government that was centered upon a religion that was centered upon the king, or Pharaoh, who was no less than a god in human form. The very act of the sun rising each day was dependent upon the Pharaoh. Every night, the sun god Ra rode his chariot through the underworld and, if his journey was successful, the sun would rise again in the east the following morning. It was the responsibility of the Pharaoh-god to ensure the sun god was able to make the journey every night through offerings and ceremonies. In order to keep the Pharaoh-god happy, priests performed the ceremonies and rituals that ensured the sun god would appear every morning and would also ensure the continuing cycle of annual flooding by the Nile. They also made sure to collect enough food, gold, labor, soldiers, boats, houses, minerals etc. to keep the Pharaoh happy.

Another way of looking at the **Egyptian Civilization** was to see it in terms of the negative. If there were no sun god, or if someone did something to interrupt his journey, the sun would not rise. If there were no Pharaoh-god, there would be no one to communicate with the sun god. In other words, if there were no Pharaoh, there would be no sun. If there were no priests to perform the required rituals (and collect taxes) to ensure the safety of the Pharaoh-god, there would be no sun. If the people did not comply with the wishes of the Pharaoh-god, or his priests, there would be no sun. If there were no sun, there was no life. Obviously, the Pharaoh-god system, like most religions, was a pretty good racket. It allowed the Pharaoh-god and his priests, complete control over the kingdom and only depended on the continued ignorance and superstition of the general population, who believed the sun rising every day and the Nile flooding every year depended upon the general population doing exactly as they were told.

Other than that, the ruling classes had little to worry about as far as peasant revolts and invasion from outside. Egypt was just too isolated and spread out to get to with an army intact enough to fight. The stability of the region allowed the Pharaoh-god, through his priests, to command workers to build his temples, farmers to pay their taxes and soldiers to conquer his enemies. Due to an absence of newspapers, or news papyrus, the Pharaohs advertised their deeds on the walls of temples they had erected in their honor. That way, the common peasants could see a multi-media slide show of sorts. They could see pictures of the Pharaohs as they slew their enemies and rubbed shoulders with gods like Osiris, Isis and of course, Ra. The whole society lived in a world of fantasy that was as far from reality as it was possible to get in the ancient world.

The Egyptian Civilization with the Pharaoh-god at its center lasted in various forms until the Muslim conquests in 622 AD. In other words, the Pharaoh-god system, a totalitarian state that was centered on an absolute monarch who, in turn, was supported by an educated class of scholars, engineers, economists, scientists and scribes, who, in turn kept the masses of people ignorant of any knowledge above what they needed to know to keep them in line, lasted virtually unchallenged for three thousand years. Based in reality or not, the Egyptians were able to last longer than any civilization in Western history, so maybe there is something to the old saying that "ignorance is bliss."

At the center of the Egyptian Civilization an enigma was left that still puzzles, fascinates and inspires us to this day. As we all know, there were people in Egypt (and other parts of the world) who had a skill in working with large stones that we still cannot replicate. Because we cannot explain how the Pyramids of Giza were built, there are almost as many theories as to how they were built, as there are stones in the Great Pyramid. So far, none has been proven conclusive, practical or, in the case of science, capable of being repeated. The only thing we can say for sure about the construction of the Pyramids of Giza is that somehow someone in Egypt was able to move large rocks for hundreds of miles in some cases, and place them with a precision that modern men were capable of only after the advent of global positioning satellites. In later chapters we will return to Egypt to look into this fascinating mystery, but for now, we must move on to our next important empire.

Hanging around Babylon

Leaving the luxury of Egypt, we will meander back over to the cradle of civilization and see what is going on in the Fertile Crescent, or the area between the Tigris and the Euphrates Rivers in what is modern day Iraq. As we said earlier, the ancient city of **Sumer** had spread its techniques of engineering, writing, accounting, agriculture and government throughout the region. A new city was beginning to dominate the region around 2,500 BC. The city was called **Babylon** and its rulers began a series of conquests that would lead it into confrontations with every empire and kingdom until Alexander the Great would finally conquer it in 323 BC.

Babylon, reported to be the most beautiful city of the ancient world, sported terraced gardens, zoos and marvelous palaces. The city's schools were repositories of learning, science and engineering. Scholars, engineers, astronomers, artists, linguists, botanists, painters, sculptures and architects were recruited to work in Babylon from the territories that were conquered by its ambitious rulers. Others were invited to Babylon to practice their craft as well as teach. Unlike Egypt, the civilization in Babylon was not pre-occupied with moving large rocks around. Surrounded by the Persians to the East, the Assyrians to the Northwest, the Egyptians to the South and any number of smaller kingdoms and peoples such as the Philistines in Palestine, the Hittites in Turkey and later the Dorians in Greece, most of Babylon's endeavors were concentrated on conquering its enemies, securing its frontiers and maintaining its place as the pre-eminent power in the Fertile Crescent.

What made the **Babylonian** and later the **Persian Empire** great, also greatly influenced its downfall. Its location in the center of all the cities and states, kingdoms and empires that emerged with the rise of civilization gave it access by warfare, trade or treaty, to all of the best ideas of the known civilized world, with the exception of China. It could draw on intellectual advances in all fields from Egypt, Palestine, India, Pakistan, Mesopotamia, Arabia, and even Europe. However, its proximity to these empires and peoples made Babylon the most desirable of all the city-states and empires to the would-be conquerors that ruled these kingdoms and who were always looking to expand their own territory.

The only way Babylon could survive was to maintain a constant state of military preparedness, or active warfare, which meant that men whose main purpose in life was battle could only rule Babylon. In other words, the citizens of Babylon and her client states were mere subjects whose primary purpose was to support Babylon when the ruler went to war. As we will see, the average soldier in the Babylonian army had no personal stake in the outcome of any battle, other than self-preservation. They fought and died as conquered people serving their own conqueror. Although they were lacking in motivation, the fact that the Babylonian king could field armies that were usually larger than the entire population of the enemies he meant to vanquish meant that battles were usually quick, and decided by weight of sheer numbers.

The Babylonian rulers were known for the brutality they inflicted upon those who opposed them. But, as in the case of the **Greeks** in the later years of their Empire, the Babylonian and then Persian rulers were just as content to receive submission in the form of a symbolic handful of dirt from its client cities and states as a symbol of their submission. The brutality of a Babylonian conquest was usually enough to influence any would-be combatants to submit to the generally light yoke of Babylonian rule. However, there were some exceptions, one of them being the Southern Kingdom of Israel, which fell to the Babylonians around 600 BC. Living up to their reputation, entire cities of the Israelites were evacuated and their populations sent to Babylon to work as slaves.

Meanwhile around 2,000 B.C.E., on the island of Crete off the Greek Coast in the Mediterranean, the **Minoan Civilization** was flourishing. The **Minoans** were traders whose ships sailed the Mediterranean in search of trade and commerce. Their empire extended to Greece, the coast of Turkey, Palestine and even Egypt. According to the evidence left behind, which includes elaborate palaces that included such things as indoor plumbing, the Minoans were advanced engineers, architects and of course, sailors and shipbuilders. The excavated palace at Knossos shows their interest in art and is covered with dazzling pictures of beautiful, athletic men and women performing various acrobatic feats.

The End of the Ancient World

Around fifteen hundred years before the birth of Jesus Christ, social as well as geologic upheaval was beginning to disrupt the somewhat stable world of the first civilizations. First, the island of Thira exploded around fourteen hundred B.C.E. It destroyed many of the cities and ports that had been the trading centers of not only the Minoan, but the numerous other empires of the Mediterranean as well. Around twelve hundred years before the birth of Jesus Christ, the Hebrews invaded and took control of Palestine. Though good for readers and writers of the Bible, the Hebrew invasions were disastrous for the local inhabitants.

At the same time, the Dorians, a Germanic race from Europe, overran Greece and the surrounding islands, as well as the western coast of Turkey. The Dorians became the ancestors of what would come to be known as the Classical Greek Civilization and their tales and battles would be recounted in the works of poets like Homer and Hesiod. The famed Trojan War was more than likely an account of how the Dorian-Greeks forced their way into power in the eastern Mediterranean by subduing cultures and cities such as **Troy**, which had long dominated Mediterranean trade and politics.

As for the Minoans, nobody is sure what exactly happened to them, but their demise was both quick and total. The archeological record shows that civilizations like the Minoan display evidence of fire and destruction. From the looks of things, the thousand years before Christ was going to be a time of violence and upheaval that ushered in an age unlike the relative peace and stability of the previous two thousand years. The Old Empires, such as Egypt and Babylon that were based upon a world order which had been accepted for two millennia struggled against the new upstarts on the scene, the Greeks and then later on, the Romans.

The Greeks

The Greeks are important to our story for many more reasons than I care to recount at this time or that you probably wish to read. Later, in the book, we will revisit Greece, but for now, we must look at ancient Greece because of the influence they have had in shaping the world around us. The first reason the Greeks are important is that they served as a kind of bridge or catalyst between the Old World (Babylon and Egypt) and the new (Rome and Western Europe). Unlike the totalitarian states of Egypt and Babylon, the Greeks formed governments based upon the idea that free people create a more enriched culture and stable government than oppressed people do. In other words, the Greeks ideas of government resembled their military operations.

Debates and speeches preceded votes that were held in the Areopagus, a town meeting open to the landholding males. Its decisions were binding and final. Therefore the art of rhetorical oratory, or public speaking ability, was a talent valued as much as military prowess. This is a theme we will see again and again in the study of later Western European and American culture.

In Greek society, no one man was to be seen as more important than any other. Leaders, who were seen as a necessary evil, were never given more power than they needed and never longer than was necessary to get the job done. The Athenians, the leaders of the Greek world until the time of Philip and Alexander, went so far as to vote to *ostracize*, or send into exile, one man every year that the rest of the town felt had become too rich or too important for the good of the rest of the city.

For a thousand years, the Greeks existed on the outskirts of both the Persian and the Egyptian spheres of influence. They called themselves **"Hellenes"** and considered themselves, their culture, their learning, their poetry, drama, music, religion, military prowess and so on and so on, far superior to anything around them. In today's terms, the Greeks were an extremely "cocky" bunch similar to the English of the 19th century or Americans of the modern age. The Greeks thought little of the people who existed outside their realm of influence. They considered non-Greeks to be subhuman slaves and lackeys. They called them "bar-bar" which was a derogatory way of classifying any language that was not Greek and was the original term for the word "barbarian."

In the Greek mind, the barbarians, or anyone who was not a Greek, was hardly deserving of the freedom that the Greeks enjoyed. Many times, first at Troy and then later as their colonies on the coasts of Asia Minor rebelled against the Persians, the Greeks fought the Persians and their allies. Over the course of hundreds of years the Greeks never learned the respect, or fear, for the Persians that the Persians would someday learn to have for the Greeks.

West vs. East: the beginnings of the conflict

And so, the stage was set for the ultimate confrontation that would begin in 490 BCE when the Persian king Xerxes decided he had enough of the Greeks. Xerxes hated the arrogant Greeks, especially the Athenians who had repeatedly incited and supported revolts in the Greek cities of Asia Minor, the western border of the Persian Empire. Battles like Thermopylae, Marathon, Plataea, and the naval battle of Salamis outside of Athens, gave rise to stories and legends that are still taught in schools, universities and military colleges throughout the world. In the eyes of the people of the West, it was the victorious Greeks who kept totalitarianism out of Europe. It was a victory of democracy and self-rule over despotism. It was Western culture and free thought over the corrupt and immoral cultures of the East.

In the eyes of the people of the East, or today's Middle East however, the Greek victories were the beginning of a series of incursions, invasions and inflictions upon their peoples that continue to this day. Whatever view one takes, the fact of the matter, the Persians tried twice to conquer the miniscule city-states of Greece and failed. Not only did they bring upon themselves the sense of their own inferiority, they also instilled in the Greeks a lust for revenge that would take one hundred years, a murdered king and a Macedonian prince to come to fruition.

If it were not for the Greeks, many of the modern institutions that we see in the West, such as universities, governments, churches, schools, theater, sports, attitudes about health and the individual's role in the state might be completely different. Were it possible to bring an ancient Greek such as Plato, Themistocles, Aristophanes or Alcibiades into the modern world, once they understood English and how to operate our machines, they would feel almost at home. No other culture in the ancient world, with the exception of Rome could claim that same familiarity with our world as it is today.

We can also thank the Greek's for our outlook on life, business and our preoccupation with youth, fitness and beauty. We can thank the Greeks for their love of the mind and the fact that they believed that strength was good, but being clever was better. We see in the tales of Homer, author of the Odyssey and the Iliad, the two books that served as texts for educated Greek children for almost a thousand years, that brute force alone could not solve all problems. We also see in the Odyssey a narrative not only about one man's life, but also about the trials and tribulations that all men must endure in the narrative in their own lives.

The Greeks though self assured, were pious men who relied on the favor of their gods and feared incurring their wrath, jealousy and anger more than they feared their own enemies. The most famous example of Greek piety was the battle of Marathon, where the Spartans refused to assist the Athenians until their religious festivals were complete. Their piety forced the Athenians and their allies to face the Persians alone. In the aftermath of the battle, the victorious Athenians never publicly begrudged the Spartans and attributed their victory in part, to the Spartan's devotion to their gods.

The Greeks are important to this story not only for laying the groundwork of Western Civilization. They are also important, as we stated earlier, as the link between the Ancient World and the world of today. Specifically, it is their stories, legends and understanding of the universe that will bring us back to visit them in later chapters. Most of us are aware of the fact that they were quite skilled in building with stone. We can see hints of Masonic beliefs and practices in their rituals and in their temples such as the Parthenon and its show piece, the temple of Athena. But for now, we must forge on ahead with Alexander and his Companion Cavalry into the heart of the Persian Empire and beyond to the limits of the known world.

What is Freedom?

Before we continue, we must pause at this juncture in history to more closely examine two factors that allowed Greece, the puny little peninsula on the Mediterranean Coast, to not only defeat, but also eventually conquer all of the Persian Empire, Egypt, and all the kingdoms and cities between Greece and the Indus River.

First, the Greeks fought, lived and prided themselves upon being "free" men. Today, in the countries of the West, the term "freedom" is batted around more often than a tennis ball at Wimbledon, especially around election time. Therefore, in order to have a more complete understanding of the periods and places of history that we are about to visit, the one idea that is used to unite, divide, conquer and inspire people in the West; the idea of "freedom" must be understood. Fortunately, "freedom" can best be discussed in the context of ancient Greece, because it was their ideas of freedom that were eventually passed on to our culture.

As we stated, the Greeks considered themselves to be "free" men, and the Persians, their client states, allies and so on, were considered by the Greeks to be barbarians, or slaves who needed to be and deserved to be ruled by the superior Greeks. It was Aristotle who put it into Alexander's head that, the barbarians of the world, should be ruled by the Greeks because the Greeks were superior in all things (is this beginning to sound familiar?) because they were free men.

So, all of the Greeks were free? We cannot begin to answer that question until we come to a definition of what "free" actually means. The best answer we can come up with, one that covers the broadest range of the human experience is that "free" in the context of all civilizations means that an individual can neither be bought, nor sold. Therefore, when we are speaking of "freedom," it is within the context that a person is either free, or the property of someone else, or what we would call a slave.

In Greek, and later Roman society, there were an abundance of slaves. In fact, most people have an erroneous notion that the Americans were the only country to practice slavery. The fact is; the idea that a person could be bought and sold as property was and has been a common practice in every country on earth from the beginning of recorded history to this day. The European colonists in the Americas who owned slaves initially bought them from Arabs and Muslims who raided along the African coasts for slaves for their own markets. All cities and civilizations in the ancient world used warfare in order to keep a steady supply of slaves in their local economies. When slaves were needed, the city or kingdom attacked the neighboring city or kingdom and, if they won, they brought back the soldiers and anyone else they could grab as to work as forced labor. Slaves did the backbreaking work of raising, harvesting, transporting and selling crops. Slaves were used as interpreters, scribes, teamsters, carpenters, miners, landscapers and so on.

If you think of the things you do during the day, imagine life without a stove, a shower, a telephone, a car, a toilet, a washing machine, a plow, a clothing store, a supermarket, a hairdresser etc. Everything that you can do today in minutes thanks to technology required a slave in the ancient world. If you were one of the very few and fortunate that was not a slave, the one thing that you would be most concerned about was that neither you, your wife, your children, your cousins aunts and uncles, ever be one of those people who were worked to death, beaten, maimed and raped just to provide you with the basic comforts of life. As horrifying as it sounds, this is the condition in which ninety percent of the world's population has lived and died once human beings began to be "civilized." If you understand what slavery meant to the Greeks, who knew quite well what the fate of the slave was, it is easier to understand why they preferred death to submitting to the will of the Persian kings.

Cold steel "Greek style" and the rise of technology

The second aspect of the Greek's success was not an idea or a legal status. Instead, it was as tangible as the hard, cold steel they used for their armor and weapons. In fact, it *was* the hard, cold steel they used for their armor and weapons that allowed the Greeks to not only beat the Persian armies sent to attack them, but which allowed the Greeks to annihilate the Persian soldiers by the thousands, while suffering only minor losses.

If you will recall, the order of battle for the kings of the empires of Egypt and Babylon (Persia) was to put an overwhelming number of soldiers, chariots and cavalry into the field. It was the first psychological warfare ever practiced. The idea was that the enemy forces, seeing such an overwhelming number of soldiers would start to think that a battle with such forces would more than likely result in defeat and death or capture for all who didn't run away at the commencement of the battle. In other words, the Empires were used to fighting battles that were decided psychologically before they were decided militarily. Most of the time the battle was never fought, or if it was, the outcome was decided long before the first soldiers began sticking each other with swords and spears.

When Xerxes attacked the Greeks at the narrow pass at Thermopylae, the age-old Persian tactic of using an overwhelming number of soldiers to force the issue before the battle was fought was put into play. In fact, to stack the deck in his favor, Xerxes, according to Herodotus, is reported to have brought one million men to the campaign in Greece. Of course, this is likely an exaggeration but an army even half that size would nearly equal half the population of Greece. One million men to not however, the Persians were in for a big surprise. They didn't know it yet, but for the first time in their history, they were up against an enemy that not only knew how to fight, but in fact, were actually born and bred for little else.

The Spartans

At Thermopylae, the Persians found themselves opposite the Spartan army of King Leonidas and his group of fanatic Spartan warriors who knew not only how to fight, but who also knew what it meant to be a slave. The Spartans had, for hundreds of years, enslaved the people called the **Helots**, from a neighboring town to do their work, while the Spartans themselves lived every day in anticipation of a great battle. They trained continuously. Spartan men (and women) boxed, wrestled, lifted weights, ran, and threw javelins. From the time they were seven, Spartan boys joined and spent their entire life with the squad in which they would fight in battle. The Spartans suffered a horrible and cruel existence by our standards, just so that they would never end up like their slaves, the Helots. In fact, the Athenians made fun of the Spartans by saying that their eagerness to go to war was not because of their bravery, instead, they went to war because it was the only holiday they ever got. Athenian humor aside, Spartan women told their sons and husbands, "Come back with your shield, or on it." Which meant die, but don't dishonor me by running away.

The Spartans and the rest of the Greeks knew battle because they had spent hundreds of years in constant warfare with their rival city-states. Because of their pre-occupation with war, they were the first to treat the battlefield as a scientific laboratory. Successful tactics and weapons were studied and improved upon over hundreds of years. They learned from their mistakes and the mistakes of their enemies. In other words, warfare was as much of a sport to the Greeks, as sports are to us. In fact the modern Olympics are based upon Greek games that were designed to improve the military skills of Greek soldiers.

In modern times, we have a misconception of the ancient battlefield as a bunch of guys slugging it out with swords, trading blow for blow until one of the two dropped dead. One thing the Greeks did understand was that the "front line" of the battle, where the two forces met, was the key to success or failure. To give the reader a more realistic picture, think of a rock concert, or any place where a crowd is moving in one direction. At a rock concert, the people in the front are literally pinned by the force of the people behind them, and are basically helpless to go in any direction except forward. Within the crowd, it is impossible to move backwards as well. When people die in these situations, it is usually because they cannot breathe due of the pressure exerted on their chests and lungs from the front and the back and they collapse and are either suffocated from lack of oxygen, or they are trampled to death.

The ancient battlefield was no different and the Greeks understood this better than most. It was at the front that the battle was decided and it was usually decided within the first ten minutes of the engagement. "The press" as it was known, occurred as hundreds and sometimes thousands of men, pushed the men in front of them in a continual motion that started from the back of the formation and squeezed each man against the man in front of him, all the way to the front line. Just like in a modern American football or rugby match, it was the front line that could push the opposing front line back upon its own formation, thus suffocating the soldiers in the first ranks, which usually won the battle.

Knowing that the men on the front line could not move, nor swing a sword around, and that an undisciplined army on the opposite side would be pushing its own soldiers from the back, instead of giving them room to breathe, the Greeks held a long wooden spear with a metal tip to aid in the suffocating process. The Greeks held a large metal shield in their left arm that was positioned to protect the man on their right, thus interlocking each man to the man beside him. When the enemy soldiers advanced, or were pushed onto the front lines, the spears penetrated the flesh where the shields did not protect the body of the soldier.

The Greeks, understanding the realities of the battlefield, carried a bronze shield and developed full-face armor, metal shin guards called "greaves" and a breastplate. When it came to Greek against Greek battles, where two sides were fighting in similar armor, victory was most often determined by the ability of one side to stay in formation and, using sheer brute strength, push the opposite line back upon its own troops, break up their formation and kill them with swords. There is a famous story in Plato's Dialogues where Socrates describes how, in a battle with the Thebans, the Athenian line was "broken" in just such a manner. Socrates held his shield over the future Greek general Alcibiades, protecting him, while the Thebans were desperately trying to kill them both.

This was what happened when the Greeks fought each other. The Persians who arrived at Thermopylae had no idea that the little army in front of them was about to form up into what amounted to a steel wall with iron spears and knives sticking out in front of it. Nor did they realize that the men behind the round shields were as hard as the bronze of their shields and were eagerly waiting to carve the Persians into little pieces. As they had done in all their battles, the Persians rushed the Greek wall expecting an easy victory. The Persians didn't have steel shields, armor or anything but a spear with a metal tip and a wicker shield. Imagine their horror when the men in the second and then third ranks of the Persian lines saw the blood dripping tips of the Greek spears as they emerged from the backs of the men in front of them one millisecond before they themselves were pushed from behind onto the very same spear. With the first, second and third line of Persians dead, the fourth and fifth lines behind them would have tried to escape the same fate by instinctively turning around to flee and in turn, were pushed past the dead bodies of their comrades onto the waiting spears of the second line of Greeks. It was surely the most horrifying scene ever witnessed by the overconfident Persian army and one they would repeat over and over in every battle they fought with the Greeks for the next one hundred and fifty years.

Greek technology and Greek power

It is not my intent to regale the reader with the horrors of ancient warfare. Rather, it is my intent to demonstrate to the reader another key aspect of understanding history. Technological innovation, whether it is the use of bronze over copper, the stirrup, bronze shields, Viking long ships, gunpowder, tanks, planes and so on, that often determines the course that history takes. Likewise, it is the failure of cultures to adapt to new advances, ideas and technologies that either leads to their extinction or their decline into the "also-rans" of the history books. In the case of the Greeks, their technological advances in weaponry and armor, their advances in physical training, and their reduction of the battlefield to a scientific study allowed the tiny collection of city-states to briefly obtain the predominant position in the world in the last few centuries before Christ.

Alexander the Great

The culmination of Greek civilization was Alexander the Great. Though Alexander was not actually Greek, his father, Philip had long held ambitious plans of conquering the constantly bickering and quarreling Greeks. From his mountain kingdom in Macedonia, just north of Greece, Philip had sent Alexander to study under Aristotle. Aristotle, a student of Plato, who in turn was a student of Socrates, instilled in Alexander not only the idea of the supremacy of Hellenistic culture, but a burning desire to spread that culture to the corners of the earth. In his youth, Aristotle taught Alexander the ideas passed on to him from Plato and Socrates regarding the perfect society and government. Aristotle had impressed upon the young Alexander that the world had reached a stage of maturity that made it possible for a new leader to put aside the superstitions of the old world and establish a new order based upon science, reason, observation and philosophy.

Young Alexander could hardly wait to get started. All he needed was his own army. Luckily, the convenient murder of his father by an assassin in 333 B.C.E. gave him just the tools he needed. Alexander, some might say, was an enigma of history. More than any person before or since, it almost appeared that the entire history of Greece had been a centuries' long preparation for the coming of the young and fearless leader. For 500 years, the writings of Homer and Hesiod had instilled in the hearts of Greek children a sense of fearlessness and a longing to travel and conquer and, if necessary, to die gloriously in a desperate battle. The Greek victories over the Persians a hundred and fifty years before had given them confidence that there was no foreign army in the world that could match the Greek formations.

At Alexander's disposal were battle-hardened, heavily armored infantry who had spent years fighting each other until they had become united under Philip just prior to Alexander's ascension to his father's throne. The Greek army had evolved since the campaigns against the Persians. By the time of Alexander, the Greek infantry carried twenty-foot long spears before them called *sarissas* that were meant to shish-kabob four or five lines of front row troops before the Greeks pulled out their short swords and began hacking the men to pieces who were foolish enough to stand in their way. As his counselors, Alexander had men who were arguably the best generals in the world at that time. They had been with Philip fighting and conquering the Greeks while Alexander was still in school. They knew their men personally. Most importantly, they knew what they were and were not capable of doing.

Alexander's "ace-in-the-hole" was his "**Companion**" cavalry. His father, Philip had introduced "wings" of cavalry to get behind enemy formations and exploit any weak points in their lines. The Companions had smashed through the Greek lines with Alexander at the lead in the battle that brought all of Greece to its knees, the **Battle of Chaeronea**. It was Alexander's belief that his army of Greek infantry and Macedonian cavalry could beat any army, no matter how large. It was Alexander's idea that he and his cavalry could finish any engagement successfully with a pell-mell charge through the gaps in the stagnant lines to surround and finish off any army faster than they knew what hit them.

After years of training at Aristotle's Academy, where he had learned hatred of the Persians, Alexander was instilled with a sense that he was the one chosen to spread Hellenistic culture into the lands of the barbarians. His mother had raised him constantly insisting that he, Alexander, was no less than the son of Zeus, the greatest of the Greek gods. Suspecting the Persian king of complicity in the murder of his father, Alexander marched his army eastward in search of the Persian King Darius III. The Greek's subsequent defeat of the Persian king Darius at Issus and again at Gaugamela in modern day Iraq left him in control of an empire that had existed for over two thousand years.

Alexander's New World Order

Alexander, fulfilling his teacher's wishes, would finally put to rest the Babylonian civilization, which had been inherited by the Persian Empire, which had long been a source of trouble for the Greeks and vice versa. In its place, he set up a government where the conquered people were treated as equals in a new empire that was based upon Greek learning and culture. Of course, the Greeks knew what was better for mankind than anyone else. So, logically, the Greeks would be the first leaders in the new world order until the conquered peoples were "up to speed" on Hellenistic culture. This idea was unlike any ruler before him, in that Alexander did not conquer for power or glory only (though some might argue this). As a student of the great philosophers, Alexander conquered for knowledge and unification. With his army marched scholars, geographers, mathematicians, teachers, mapmakers, architects, engineers and builders. His soldiers were just the first tools in his construction of the new world order.

Absolute Power Absolutely Corrupts Alexander

At some point, Alexander's grand scheme of making the world a place of tolerance, commerce and learning took a turn for the worst. Some say it happened at the tiny Oasis of Siwa where, following his entry into Egypt, Alexander had left his army and traveled with a small contingent to the temple of Zeus (who could easily be replaced in the written record as the Egyptian god of the sun, Ammon Ra). The journey through the desert was long and perilous, but at the end, Alexander got what he was looking for.

The priest of the temple told Alexander that he, in fact, was no less than the son of Zeus. From that point on, things went sour for the visions of the great philosophers as their most successful student tossed aside logic and reason and took on the trappings of every Eastern ruler and despot that had gone before him. Believing himself a god, Alexander pushed his Army east into Afghanistan where Alexander one day announced to his troops that from then on, he should be treated as a god. His troops grumbled, but they had no choice. It wasn't like they could just quit and start walking home. Alexander led them into India on an expedition of bloodletting and conquest that has not been equaled since.

Though he was largely successful in his Indian conquests, Alexander's troops told him there that they had enough of fighting and bleeding and dying. They wished to return home and so, following the omens of the gods, which foretold disaster for Alexander, they began the long journey homeward. In a battle that year, Alexander had been wounded with an arrow that pierced his lung, and lay dying for almost a week. It was said that he never fully recovered from that wound, and it was sometime then that possibly Alexander realized that he was not the immortal he had been duped into believing he was. Alexander survived long enough to return to Babylon where his mother, the first person who had convinced him of the divinity of his birth, met him. Ironically, she would see her immortal son breathe his last breaths as the greatest conqueror the world had ever seen.

When Alexander died three hundred years and twenty-three years before the birth of Christ, the dreams of the great Greek philosophers almost died with him. Following his death, his empire was split into four pieces between his four best generals. The division of Eastern and Western Europe, the Middle East and Egypt into separate principalities was the only legacy Alexander left to the world he had tried so desperately to unite. In other words, his new world order based upon science, reason and philosophy fell victim to the same superstitions, beliefs and petty squabbling that he had sought to destroy, but they ended up eventually destroying him. All Alexander had really achieved was the weakening and consolidation of ancient empires that would make it easier for the next major player on the world scene, Rome, to conquer and devour them all.

Part 2

The Ancient World

Chapter 5

Rome and the Middle Ages

The Republic

Rome got its start, according to the historian Plutarch, as a collection of criminals and vagabonds who settled the easily defensible Palatine Hills in central Italy. To offset the bad publicity of being founded by cutthroats and thieves, the myth of Romulus and Remus, two brothers raised by a she-wolf came to replace the seamy historical facts behind Rome's dubious founding fathers. Either way, the Roman's first claim to fame was the conquest of their neighbors, the Etruscans. Like two people on an escalator going in opposite directions, the Romans, during their rise to power ran into the Greeks on the Island of Sicily during the declining stages of the Greek, or Athenian Empire. The Greeks were on Sicily as part of an ill-fated all-for-nothing gamble to secure the wheat fields of Sicily and the treasure of the tyrant of Syracuse as a source of income and food for the city of Athens which was under siege by their arch rivals, the Spartans.

The Greek general Pyrrhus, who barely managed to squeak out a victory that day, saw that the soldiers who had opposed him and who lay dead on the battlefield, to a man, had wounds in the front of their bodies as opposed to their backs. In other words, even though the battle had been lost, the Roman soldiers chose to fight and die where they stood rather than the resorting to the commonly accepted practice of leaving the field in haste if things weren't going according to plan. Pyrrhus noted correctly that these soldiers from Rome were going to cause a lot of trouble for the Greek world. With the Greeks constantly squabbling and pre-occupied with their own wealth and self-interest, Pyrrhus proved to be correct. A hundred years after the death of Alexander, the Romans began to be the rising star of Europe.

So far in history, we have seen two types of government, or rule, and it was the Romans who will offer us the third form of government, of which every government since, in spite of claims to the contrary, is some derivative thereof. A government is either a totalitarian state, or "kingdom" as in Babylon and Egypt, a democracy, as in Greece, or controlled by powerful interests, as in the case of Rome, at least for half of the life of the later Empire. This form of government is known as "Republican" and, as is obvious, is somewhere between the democracy of Greece and the totalitarian states of the kingdoms of Egypt and Rome.

All in the Family

There is a saying in the world of engineering that, "form follows function," which means, use the design that works best for the circumstances. In the case of Rome, the citizens did not meet one day and vote for a Republican form of government. The circumstances in which Rome was founded, as a coalition of families and tribes that were intensely jealous of each other's power was the reason that Rome did not initially decline into a kingdom nor evolve into a democracy where the larger families could dominate the vote. These ideas would be revived two thousand years after Rome was founded by the men who decided upon the Constitution of the United States of America, therefore, it is important to understand what went right and wrong in Rome.

The simplest way to describe the government in Rome, at least in its initial stages, would be to compare it to the Cosa Nostra, or mafia families of the twentieth century. The family head, called a "Patrician" from the Latin word for father, like Marlon Brando and Al Pacino in the movie *The Godfather,* had complete and absolute authority over the members of their clan. Fathers retained the right over life and death of their own children and made the major decisions that affected the entire family, and this included punishments. In the early years, it was these heads of the most powerful families, or "patrician class" who met and formed what we would call the Roman Senate. As in the Greek city councils, actions were proposed, debated and then voted upon. All decisions were made by vote and all decisions of the Senate were binding and final. If you were not under the protection of a "patrician" you were of the lower "plebe" class and didn't enjoy much respect in Roman society.

What motivated the Romans to maintain the balance of power between the families? The answer was simple, the Romans were a paranoid lot, and rightly so. After their destruction of the Etruscans in their early days, their neighbors on the Latin Peninsula did not look upon the Romans favorably and they were fearful that someone might sneak up on them and return the favor. They also had foreign enemies like the Gauls, a ferocious Celtic tribe from France who, early on in their history, overran the city and left the Romans hiding in their last standing citadel.

They eventually paid the Gauls to go away, and then raised an army to deal with them once and for all. As it turned out, they dealt with them once, but not for all. The Romans, for the rest of their history, feared the return of the fierce tribe from France more than any other enemy.

A lot of Gaul: the Carthaginians 265-146 B.C.E

After their experience with the Gauls, the Roman Senate decided that the best defense was a good offense. The Romans began a campaign to take over influence of Sicily in the south and Spain in the east, which would give them ample supplies of wheat and deprive the Gauls of a direct and easy access route via the Mediterranean Coast into Italy. From Spain, the Romans could wage war against the Gauls away from the Italian Peninsula. Control of southeastern Spain also gave them the added benefit of having a direct access route to the towns and villages of the Gauls via the Mediterranean Coast.

In Sicily and then in Spain, however, the Romans found out the hard way that the Gauls had made an alliance with the city of Carthage, which lay across the Mediterranean Sea on the coast of North Africa, almost due south of Rome. Carthage, according to the *Iliad* by Homer, the famous Greek poet who wrote of the Trojan War, describes Carthage as a city founded by the defeated Trojans. In the years that Greece was finding its place of prominence on the world stage, and Rome was carving out bits and pieces of farmland from its neighbors, Carthage had been establishing a naval trade empire and a city that rivaled any city in the Western Mediterranean.

A comparison between Rome and Carthage in the period prior to the Punic Wars, as the wars between Rome and Carthage would come to be known, would be like comparing New York City to Trenton, New Jersey. In fact, when the Greek general Pyrrhus whom we spoke of earlier, described his ill-gotten victory against the Roman soldiers he had run into, the Romans were in fact, on one of their first military outings to secure the wheat fields of Sicily for the growing city of Rome.

Nearly two hundred years later, they still had not conquered Sicily thanks, in part, to a Carthaginian general named Hasdrubal who had defeated the Romans on Sicily and was continuing to give them a lot of trouble in Spain. Well, at least until the Roman legions finally killed him. However, before he died, Hasdrubal made his son Hannibal promise to revenge his death and defeat the Romans once and for all. Hannibal, true to his promise, had plans of paying Rome back in kind; the kind that is known as killing as many Romans as he could, burning the city and selling anyone left as slaves. As most of us know, Hannibal took his army through the Pyrenees Mountains of Northern Italy and broke out into the Italian Peninsula. Hannibal knew that most of the cities on the peninsula hated Rome as much as Carthage hated Rome. He therefore gambled on the fact that they would join him in his campaign. Hannibal turned out to be only half right. Some cities did join him as he waged a campaign of attrition against Rome by annihilating every army that came out of Rome to defeat him. However, for every army that he defeated, another showed up to take its place.

The Baggage of War

The Punic Wars raged for almost one hundred years. But, in the end, Rome beat Hannibal, sacked Carthage and in doing so, became the superpower of the West. Once again, the Punic Wars though bloody and as full of derring-do as any military campaign in history, are not important themselves as are the emotional and psychological scars they left upon Rome. The Romans had come close many times to being defeated, invaded and sold as slaves in the market places of Carthage. They had spent most of their money raising armies and buying equipment. They had seen their neighbors turn against them in hope of cashing in on the spoils that would come with the sacking of their city. Most of all, they had lost a large portion of their young men to the spears and swords of Hannibal's army. That was just the psychological effect.

By winning the war, there was another effect, a financial one, which would lead to Rome's ultimate triumph as the ruler of the Mediterranean, the Middle East, Europe and Africa for the next six hundred years. The

Romans, who, up to that time, had been content to secure parcels of land here and there for their growing population, had discovered that war was big business, especially if they won.

The war with the Carthaginians had changed Rome from a collection of farming families to a full-time military encampment. In other words, Rome had become a society that was almost entirely based upon war, conquest and tribute from its captured territories. With the emotional scars still fresh, slaves and treasure began pouring in from Carthage and her conquered allies. Millions of acres of liberated land became available for settlement and, of course, there were still scores the Romans were eager to settle with their neighbors. In what we may call the ultimate "Faustian compromise," Rome traded the simple, peaceful life for the much more lucrative life of conquest, murder and terrorizing entire populations. With the powerful families in Rome even more powerful and richer than ever, no one was going to object to the new way of doing business in the greatest city in the Mediterranean world. In fact Plutarch, the Greek historian, noted in his book, *The Lives*, that during the entire history of the Rome, the doors of the Temple of Jupiter, which remained open during a time of war, had been closed for a total of eleven years.

Julius Gaius Caesar and the Empire

As we have seen in the histories of Babylon, Egypt and Greece, societies that base their purpose for being upon conquest and justify it by proclaiming their own desire for freedom are like a dog chasing its own tail. Ultimately their societies lose that freedom because of the ill will they have sewn by their actions. Ultimately, that freedom they valued so much has to be turned over to a totalitarian leader who will promise them security and safety, but in the end, only gives them brutality, death and slavery. And so it was with Rome when an ambitious Julius Caesar, who sought to protect Rome from the corruptions of its own Senate, took on the role and the crown of Emperor forty-four years before the birth of Jesus Christ. Thereafter, the balance of power between the powerful families of Rome was destroyed, as were many of the families that opposed the clan of Gaius, Julius Caesar's family. After Julius Caesar was assassinated, the history of Rome's government became first, a collection of competing factions and families who sought the imperial crown and second, a long line of emperors who ruled at the whim of the military on which Rome's success and ultimate survival was based.

Rome's one advantage was that its sheer size and its system of military order allowed it the luxury of not being taken lightly by its enemies. Its liberal attitudes towards citizenship for the prominent members of its client states meant that the conquered provinces were full of people who had a stake in the dominance of Rome, and therefore were more than likely to choose loyalty to the world power over loyalty to their own "backwards" countries, cities and people.

It was about one hundred years before the birth of Christ, or shortly thereafter, that the Western World became intertwined with affairs in the Middle East, to include the Kingdom of Israel. Up until that time, the Romans did not care as much about religion as their predecessors, the Babylonians, the Egyptians and the newly conquered Israelites. In fact, lacking any real educational system of their own, the wealthier Romans had been sending their children to study in the newly conquered territories of Greece for hundreds of years. In Greek schools, the Roman kids adopted the Greek language, philosophy, religion, and, they adopted the Greek gods as their own Because of these rich and powerful "Greekophiles," Greek religion and culture was spread throughout the Roman world, which would present few problems in the conquered territories until the Romans entered Palestine.

The Cantankerous Hebrews and the rise of Christianity

The Jews, most of who refused to give up the worship of their single God and the laws He had laid down for them, were a pain in the backside of the Romans. As we have already discussed, the Hebrew people had learned some hard lessons that dated all the way back to their flight from Egypt. After the captivity in Babylon around 600 B.C.E, or five hundred years before the Romans, they were pretty much convinced that any deviation from the path their God had laid out for them was going to have dire consequences. They, just like the Greeks before them, had learned to fear their God more than any army of men.

Of course, the Romans were not aware of the paranoia of the Jews, and why should they be? They had conquered countless kingdoms and cities in the previous two centuries. Most of the conquered cities and territories had chosen the safe track and sacrificed to the Roman gods, with no ill effects. But the Jews were different. They not only refused to sacrifice to the Roman gods, they openly defied Roman laws and customs, such as bathing in public baths and attending the gymnasiums for nude exercises. Worst of all, they continued to worship their single God, who they seemed to fear more than the wrath of the Romans.

For a hundred years, the Romans fought a never-ending guerrilla campaign against hardline Jews who refused to submit to anything Roman. Of course, there were "practical" Jews who sided with the Romans and adopted their customs. There were enough of these "quislings," especially in the ranks of the Jewish leadership and ruling families to give the Romans the illusion that the troublesome Jews were slowly coming over to the side of Roman progress. However, this turned out to be quite far from the truth; even the "quisling" Jews were just biding their time until God sent them a new Moses or David to lead them in a final battle against the Roman occupiers.

The Prince of Peace and bloody revolt

Instead of a conquering hero, the Hebrews (and the Romans) began to hear stories about a teacher who preached forgiveness and tolerance, healed the sick, and gave hope to the poor by talking about eternal life and the Kingdom of God. Worst of all, for the Jews anyway, this strange teacher told his followers, who appeared to be growing in leaps and bounds, to "render unto Caesar what belongs to Caesar." He was the absolute antithesis of the conquering hero the Jews were expecting. They were more than happy to turn over this "troublemaker" to the Romans who killed him by their favorite method of execution, crucifixion.

But crucifying Jesus had two unintended effects. The militant Israelites began to think the conquering hero they were expecting was not going to come at all, so in 67 AD, the Jews in Jerusalem began to take matters into their own hands. Thirty-three years after the death of Jesus, the entire nation rose up and began slaughtering the Romans and their collaborators wherever they found them. The Romans retaliated in kind three years later by sending its most ruthless legions into Palestine to kill the Jews wherever they could find them. The only Jews, who survived, did so by fleeing their promised land altogether. To put it simply, the Jew's plan to rid themselves of the Romans backfired on a colossal scale. But, in an ironic twist of fate, the Roman plan of ridding themselves of the Jews backfired on them also.

The first effect, unintended as it was, was to spread the Jewish faith throughout Western Europe and Africa. The other unintended effect was that the Jew they had crucified in 33 A.D. seemed to have gathered quite a following. His followers even claimed that once Jesus died, he had arisen from his tomb and returned to them as a glorified personage. To make matters worse, his followers claimed that Jesus would return again, and when that happened, there was going to be "hell to pay" and they meant it literally. Most of Jesus' followers took this to mean that he would be returning shortly, so they just had to wait it out until he returned. But, Jesus didn't return. By the time they realized this, his followers had grown old and feared that they would die before they saw the return of the "Son of God" as they claimed him to be.

The "Christians," as they came to be known, began to write down the important events of Jesus' life and his teachings in case he didn't return while they were alive. They even sent missionaries to the major cities of the Roman Empire to convert non-Jews to their new religion. The missionary effort began to pay off in earnest. Christianity seemed almost tailor made for the Greek world that had been conquered and expanded by Alexander and then inherited by the Romans.

The Early Church

The first Christians met in secret, but as their numbers began to increase, they began to be more open, as well as affluent. Within a hundred years of the death of Jesus, the first Churches began to be built as centers for worship for the growing numbers of the new faith. However, there were some problems. The Early Christian Church had the same difficulties with doctrine as the Christian Churches of today. When discussing things you have never seen for yourself, such as God, heaven, what Jesus meant when he said such-and-such, etc. etc., it is hard to agree on anything. The fact was, there were a number of books in circulation at the time, written by various saints or followers of the new religion and some of them were inconsistent with other works. To add to that, there were controversies over what God was made of, whether Jesus was God, whether Jesus and God were spirit, or flesh, whether there should be pictures of Jesus and so on and so on.

Bishops in large cities such as Cairo, Antioch, Rome and Jerusalem were in constant competition for supremacy over their counterparts over issues of doctrine and policy. To add to that, there were a lot of people known as "pagani" or pagans, who wanted nothing to do with the Christians and who continued to worship as their ancestors had done. In Rome, which was suffering calamitous defeat after calamitous defeat on the battlefield, thanks to their unwise policy of trying to "civilize" the tribes in Germany, Christians were blamed for everything from the outbreak of disease to barbarian incursions and the fire that burned down the center of Rome.

Nearly three hundred years after the Crucifixion of Jesus, the Emperor Constantine finally took two actions that would have repercussions to this day. First, he split the Empire into Western and Eastern provinces. Second, Constantine, who was not a Christian until the day he died, but a savvy politician trying to hold onto a crumbling empire, recognized the value of the loyalty of the Christians. From 318-325 AD Constantine called a series of councils and summoned bishops and representatives from throughout the empire to meet in order to standardize Christian doctrine. There and then, Constantine cleaned up the Christian Church.

The Council of Nicaea and the Roman Catholic Church

In the year 325, the final decisions of the Councils were announced. The Bishop in Rome was named as supreme leader of the new Roman Catholic (Universal) Church by citing the scripture that Jesus said to Peter, *"On this rock I will build my Church."* The logic being that Peter (Petra means "rock" in Latin) ended up dying in Rome at the hands of the people he was trying to convert. Since it was in Rome that he was buried, logic stated that the "rock" of which the pun-loving Jesus spoke, must be the place where Peter died and rested, Rome.

The Council of Nicaea chose from a list of books that had been handed down from the Jews as well as the early Christians, keeping some and discarding others. They assembled the books they had chosen into one book with the books of the Jews at the beginning that they called the Old Testament and the writings of the four gospels of Jesus and the letters of the Apostles as the New Testament. Together, they dubbed the book, "The Holy Bible" (Byblos is Greek for book).

This logic worked to sort out most of the problems of the Early Church, but not all of them. Though the council of Nicaea did bring some order out of the chaos, it created a rift with the Bishop of Constantine's capitol, Constantinople, which lies on the shores of the Bosporus in modern day Turkey. The newly named capitol contained enough wealth to buy the decaying city of Rome many times over. The Bishop of Constantinople begrudgingly accepted the supremacy of Rome but he and those who would serve after him didn't like it. Likewise, the Bishops of the great cities of the Eastern Empire such as Jerusalem, Cairo and Antioch also resented the supremacy of Rome, but they saw an official imperial endorsement as the best thing that had happened to the Church and were not about to make any kind of waves that would put their position and necks on the line.

To placate those who were not Christians, since most members of the Empire were not, the new church incorporated things like Christmas on December 25th which had always been the day set aside for worshipping Amen-Ra, the Egyptian sun god. It was originally a holiday, which was celebrated by decorating a tree, and putting wrapped presents underneath. The Council also added "Amen" to the end of the Christian prayers, invoking the name of the Egyptian sun god, which seemed to keep the Egyptian pagans happy and thus, the Christian Church in Egypt flourished. To placate the Greek pagans, the festival of Demeter was changed to Easter and instead of Demeter rising from the dead and giving out colored eggs, Jesus would be remembered rising from the dead to give eternal life to his followers. Pretty nifty huh? Well, actually no, there were a lot of problems with the early church, but through it all, there were enough people who sincerely believed it represented the church of Jesus Christ that it spread and flourished throughout Europe, the Middle East and Africa.

The End of Rome and the New World Order: Chaos and the mounted thug

Almost one hundred years later, the Roman Empire in the West ceased to exist when the Germans showed up at the gates. The Christian Visigoth King, Alaric, head of one of the many Germanic tribes the Romans had made the mistake of civilizing, entered Rome in 410 AD. It may be hard for us to imagine, but the world, from the vantage point of those living at the time, virtually descended into chaos. There were no more civil engineers to build and maintain buildings and aqueducts for water. There were no more schools, police, local governments, and even the roads that had allowed the Romans the ability to move troops, supplies, trade goods and officials, fell into disrepair and were infested with thieves waiting to rob, kill and rape anyone who used them. Those who had the means, retreated to manor houses where they built walls to keep the other marauding Germanic barbarians like the Vandals, Goths, and Franks out as best they could.

It was the barbarian tribes, drawn like iron to a magnet that would move into the lands vacated by the Romans and their armies. Once again, technology and political necessity set the stage for the next thousand years of social and political life in Europe. Sometime in the late stages of the Roman Empire, the stirrup was introduced into the ensemble of the barbarian fighter. It may seem odd that such a simple and obvious piece of riding equipment could have such a far-reaching impact, but it did. With a stirrup with which to maintain his balance, a mounted warrior could suffer direct blows from an oncoming horseman and have more of a chance to remain on his own horse. From this more stable platform, a mounted warrior could deploy a long spear, a sword, axe, bow and arrow or the ever-popular mace. In addition to the stirrup, chain mail, which was made from thousands of tiny links of steel and then made into a shirt and leggings, made barbarian fighters less vulnerable to direct blows from arrows and sword thrusts.

But best of all, on horseback, a group of a few dozen of these warriors could move farther, faster and wreak more havoc than hundreds of legionnaires on foot. The mounted warrior soon took the place of the once invincible Roman square of the legions as warfare changed for the first time in over a thousand years when the Persians had run up against the Spartans at Thermopylae.

In order to maintain power, barbarian chiefs and later, kings would need to provide each member of their armed forces with enough land to support a good supply of horses and a forge from which to hammer out mail armor and weapons. In order to keep their comrades in arms in good fighting order, peasants were needed to grow food, build buildings, shoe horses, forage for iron etc. While the peasants were taking care of the day-to-day necessities of the apportioned piece of land, the local man-in-arms practiced for whatever upcoming battles the chief or king had in store.

The new social order was a simple one. The peasants, a nicer and more rustic sounding name than slaves, were those people who survived the onslaught of a barbarian attack and who were willing to maintain a contract with the new warlord. In return, for their lives and loyalty, peasants were initially allowed to work a certain portion of the land in return for a certain percentage of their labor and crops being given to the local warlord. For the peasant, one warlord was as good as the next, so their loyalty was questionable at best. As time wore on and the political situation became more stable, lands began to pass from one warlord or landowner, to his descendants. This arrangement would eventually evolve into the legal title of "landlord." Likewise, the peasants and their offspring, like the land, were passed from one owner to the next. So there were peasants and there were land-warlords, but there was one more addition to the social structure that was evolving into what history has dubbed the Middle or Dark Ages.

The vacuum left by the collapse of the Roman Empire was not absolute. As the barbarians moved south and West from places like Germany, Sweden and Russia, they met missionaries from the Roman Catholic Church who converted them to the new Christian religion. The newly converted barbarians allowed the Catholic Church to build schools, monasteries and churches on their newly conquered lands so that, in some respects, the Catholic Church took over where the Roman Empire left off. The result of their arrangement was that, for the next thousand years, the Catholic Church became the center of local government in thousands of little chunks of land across Europe. This also meant that the Catholic Church was the pre-eminent authority in education, learning and science. In other words, their Bible was the last word on everything that was knowable, and if it wasn't in the Bible, it wasn't worth knowing. The Catholic Church also maintained its monopoly on learning by keeping the Bible out of the hands of the common man. They did this by insisting it not be translated from Latin, which was the language only the rich and educated could read and write.

With a monopoly on eternal salvation, education, and as a proponent of the social order in the context of the eternal order of things, the question would soon arise, "Where does the Church lie on the social ladder?" The Church maintained that, as God's representative organization on earth, it sat above what was termed "the nobility," a term which sounded nicer than "the landowning warlords." Of course, the landowning warlords took issue with this arrangement and this seemingly trivial question created a bit of a squabble that would not be resolved for hundreds of years, and even then, it would only be resolved temporarily.

The Muslim Threat

In 632, just when it appeared things were beginning to settle down in Europe and the Middle East, there was a new movement afoot that would have the same far-reaching consequences as the Christian Church itself. It came out of the Arabian Peninsula like a sandstorm. The Muslims, followers of the Prophet Mohammed, broke out of the deserts of Arabia and conquered from India in the East to Spain in the West. The Roman Empire, which had been kept alive in the East, had long maintained its existence like a man in traction. The rulers of Constantine's city (or Constantinople) had sucked the landowners in the Eastern Empire dry for hundreds of years through increasing taxes and military campaigns undertaken to maintain the predominance of the city and its emperors Faced with the Muslim onslaught, the great cities such as Cairo in Egypt, Jerusalem, Baghdad, and Damascus fell with ease.

The Muslims conquered all the way across North Africa and crossed over into Spain, where they threatened to overrun France and then the rest of Christendom. It was in hinterlands between France and Spain that they met the armies of Charles Martel (The Hammer) who stopped them in their tracks. An uneasy truce existed between Christians and Muslims until Charles Martel's grandson; Charlemagne (Charles the Great) drove the Muslims from Spain. To put it bluntly, the Muslims terrified the whole of Europe. Any look at a contemporary map would show that they threatened the Byzantine Empire in the East and the whole of Western Europe from the West through Spain. Christendom, or Europe, which had existed as a loose collection of lands and warlords for over three hundred years, needed to be unified to face the new danger.

The Holy Roman Empire

For his efforts in defending Christianity, the Pope crowned Charlemagne *Holy Roman Emperor* in 800. With one single gesture, the Pope settled the hundreds of years of debate about the supremacy of the Church by crowning the single greatest leader Europe had seen since the age of the Caesars. In other words, the Pope not only justified and endorsed the rule of an Emperor to which all of the landholders of Europe owed allegiance. The Pope, in placing the crown on Charlemagne's head, signified that the Emperor of Europe owed his allegiance to the Pope as he took his vow as "defender of Christendom." To put it simply, lesser warlords, such as counts, dukes, earls, princes and kings answered to the Emperor, the Emperor answered to the Pope, the Pope answered to God, but since God didn't write letters or show up at policy meetings, the Pope answered to no one. And so, the Holy Roman Empire was formed.

There was no time for Charlemagne or the Pope to dwell on their laurels, however. Because, just when it appeared that Charlemagne would unite Europe, a new threat to stability arrived from the North. Almost overnight, Europe began to be the shopping mall for a group of cutthroats, thieves, murderers and assorted ne-er-do-wells from Scandinavia who didn't believe in paying for things they wanted. At first they came in ships in small bands. They would raid and plunder, maybe smash a few heads, rape a few village women, but then they would go away, as was the case in the first Viking raid at Lindesfarne, Ireland in 732. By the time of Charlemagne's coronation by the Pope, the raiders from the Denmark, Norway, Sweden and Finland had begun to run a highly sophisticated operation. By the 900's they were arriving by the thousands in fleets of long ships and terrorizing all the way from London and Moscow to Paris and Constantinople. As the years went by, the "Normans," as they were called, stopped murdering and stealing and instead, began to settle along the coasts of England, Ireland, Scotland, France, Italy and Spain.

When Charlemagne died, he ensured the division of Europe that would remain until the present day by dividing his kingdom between his two sons, Lothair and Pepin. Lothair received modern day Germany as his kingdom while his other son, Pepin, received France. In turn, each son would divide his kingdom into smaller principalities so that Europe was back to the same place it had been in 800 AD. But, there was no time to lament the newly divided Europe as the wave of migrations of Northmen began to disrupt the balance of power once again.

The New Power in Europe

By the 1066, when William the Conqueror crossed the English Channel to invade England, the Vikings, a name that had its roots in the Norwegian word for the act of piracy, had, thanks to their penchant for skullduggery and deception, become well entrenched throughout the castles and strongholds of Europe. As in the case of William, the illegitimate son of a Viking chief one generation removed from Scandinavia, the raiders from the North had given up the practice of robbing and looting along the seacoast and instead chose to rule the lands their forefathers had plundered.

The Swedish family of Roos had taken power in Russia, while the French King had bought off the Normans by awarding them the Province of Normandy on the southwestern coast of France to keep them from sailing up the Seine to raid Paris. They ruled Scotland, Italy, and Holland and worked as bodyguards for the Eastern Emperor. The Normans adopted the language and customs of their conquered lands and were the power brokers in their new domains. In England, for example, the ruling Norman class spoke French and Latin, while the defeated Saxons and Celts spoke a form of Old English; a combination of German and the older Gaelic languages.

Old habits die hard however, and the Vikings did not bring peace. The ambitious sons and grandsons of the Viking raiders were always on the lookout for new lands to conquer, even if it meant at the expense of their neighbors and relatives. By the end of the eleventh century, medieval Europe had become a running battlefield. Something had to be done to get the "noble" classes to stop killing and plundering at their own pleasure.

Fortunately for the Catholic Church, the barbarians from the north accepted Christianity as well as the Church's supremacy over matters of religion, education, and, should the need arise, as an arbiter of disputes. In an attempt to quell the violence of the ruling classes, the church introduced codes of chivalry, which further increased the Church's power by including in the code that all who were deemed worthy to carry arms were automatically required to defend the Christian faith. This meant they owed their ultimate loyalty to the Pope; and the Pope had plans for them.

The Crusades

The "defender of the faith" clause in the code of chivalry worked even further to the advantage of the Church when the Seljuk Turks came out of the mountains of southern Russia and began to threaten the Eastern Empire. If you will recall, when the council of Nicaea declared the leader of the Church of Rome supreme over all of the Catholic Church in 325, the wealthy Bishops in Constantinople had been forced to serve as underlings of the Roman Bishop for the next seven centuries. During these intervening centuries, in spite of the Muslim incursions into the major cities and provinces of the empire, the Eastern Empire had enjoyed relative stability. But the greed and corruption of the Eastern Emperors had taken its toll. When the Islamic movement had spread into Palestine, Iraq and Syria and deprived the Emperor of much needed revenue, the Byzantine Emperor as he was then known, had little in the way of money or the number of men they needed to reclaim their lands.

The Seljuk Turks, ferocious fighters who had migrated out of Russia a few hundred years before and who had stopped just long enough to convert to Islam, had overrun most of Western Turkey by the time the Byzantine Emperor got out his quill pen and parchment and begged the Pope in Rome for a few hundred mercenaries. What the emperor was looking for, according to the wording of his letter, were a few hundred rough and ready Normans like the ones the Byzantine Empire had been using for the past hundred years as personal bodyguards of the Emperor. What he got was something quite different.

While the Pope in Rome had been given absolute power over the church in the West, in reality he was in control of little more than vast forests full of ignorant and filthy peasants, homicidal landlords and very little in the way of financial compensation. In contrast, the Eastern Church and Empire had been relatively stable and had become rich and prosperous, at least right up to the point that the Turks began arriving en masse. The timing could not have been worse. One year before the Emperor made his request, the Bishop of Byzantium and the Bishop of Rome had formally excommunicated each other. In the Eastern Empire, the Catholic Church became the "Orthodox" Catholic Church and the division between the two became permanent.

A Call to Arms

For whatever reason, common sense would say to get half of his church back, the Pope in Rome, Urban II, seems to have totally gotten the Byzantine Emperor's cry for help all wrong. Instead of posting a want ad on the walls of some of the local castles asking for a few hundred adventurous mercenaries, the Pope went to the abbey in Clermont, France and claimed the holy city of Jerusalem, had been overrun by the Muslims (this had actually happened one hundred and fifty years before). The Pope also added that it was the duty of every Christian, be he a nobleman, a peasant or a criminal, to enlist to free the holy city from the grasp of the heathen infidel.

The Pope also threw in the clause that any man who took up arms to free Jerusalem would be absolved of all debts, crimes and sins that they had committed prior to their answering the call to free Jerusalem. In other words, no matter what sadistic, barbaric and unsavory things a person had done in the past, if they were lucky enough to die on the journey or in battle, they would immediately be granted passage into paradise. In Europe, it had been hard to make an honest living for six hundred years. The Crusades offered the lure of booty if successful, and a quick passage to heaven if not. It was a strong enough enticement to convince thousands of landless, property-less men, thieves, murderers, rapists and other anti-social types to undertake the Great Crusade.

It was not only the poor who saw the Crusades as a way out of their sorry lot in life. Many nobles, the second and third offspring of landholders throughout Europe who were not going to get much in the way of land when their fathers died, saw these Crusades as a way to obtain new lands through conquest. Considering that these men were the sons, grandsons and great-great grandsons of the original Viking raiders, the fact that they would be venturing out into lands unknown where all sorts of perils and dangers may lie was nothing new to men whose ancestors had left the freezing shores of Scandinavia just a few generations before.

All across Europe, men, women and even children, gathered in groups that grew in size like giant herds of cattle on the Chisholm Trail. The long and seemingly endless train of people, horses, cows, wagons, goats and sheep clogged the roads of Western Europe from the Baltic in Northern Germany to Italy and the Mediterranean. There, thousands waited for passage to the Holy Land. Others, coming from Germany and Poland chose the overland route through central Europe to finally converge on the Constantinople.

The Big Surprise

What a surprise for the Eastern Emperor, Alexis that morning in the year 1097 when he looked over the parapets of the walls of Byzantium and, instead of a few hundred armored knights, found the rabble of Europe in the thousands camped out in his front yard. It must have looked like Woodstock, but with filthy people, cows and swords. What a bigger surprise he must have had when he found out they weren't there to help him with his Turk problem at all. Instead, they were on their way to Jerusalem. This led to a brief, embarrassing incident when Alexis ordered his soldiers to drive the riff-raff of Europe off the grounds, which resulted in the riff-raff trying to sack Constantinople. After the loss of much life on both sides, the Crusaders settled for safe passage aboard ferries across the Bosporus and continued on their journey of horror, depravity and death.

The Crusades ended up being more or less a flop, but there were positive outcomes from all the fighting and killing. For almost two hundred years, Europe was able to divulge itself of its least desirable elements, to include the landless nobles who had been causing so much trouble before the Crusades. The Middle East had become a safety valve of sorts, where the most depraved; disreputable and downtrodden could find either glory, or an ignominious death. Either way, the Crusades freed the decent folks of Europe of their unwanted presence.

During the Crusades, the Europeans were also able to see cultures much more advanced than their own, as well as discover that there was in fact, a world of learning outside of the Old and New Testament. They were able to open up trade routes to Africa, the Middle East and Eastern Europe. The Knights of the Temple or, the Templars, had introduced the idea of banking and finance. The Knights of the Hospital had opened up a series of clinics to nurse sick pilgrims back to health and began the first organized medical treatment in Europe. As we shall see, there were many technologies and ideas that were brought back from the Middle East to Europe that they would soon change the way Europe looked.

The Medieval Period; doubt, plague and famine

The Middle East adventure had lasted almost 200 years, but the fortunes of Europe were about to change, and not for the better. In the late 1200's, after almost two hundred years of Crusades, explorations, advances in technology and learning, things began to unravel. First, the Crusader armies were wiped out by Saleh al-din (Saladin) at the horns of Hattin in modern day Syria. Jerusalem fell a few months later. In spite of a half-hearted attempt by Richard of England and Phillip of France, the Crusaders never made it past the city of Acre, north of modern day Tel-Aviv.

The very organizations that grew in power during the Crusades, namely the Church and the Templars, began to lose political and economic credibility after their failure to retake Jerusalem. But the failure of the Crusades was just an opening act for the end of the 1200's and beginning of the 1300's. There were a few other nasty surprises in store for the Christians of Europe. In the first part of the century, the minister of France and a small band of thugs beat the Pope so badly he died of his wounds within days. In the middle of the century, the Papacy was split in two, and the Pope in France excommunicated the Pope in Rome and vice-versa. Known as the **Great Schism**, it left the population of Europe doubting the Church's relationship with the Divine Being.

As they say, "When it rains, it pours," only in Europe's case, it didn't rain, it snowed. What scientists now call the "Mini Ice-Age" struck in the middle of the century. The rain and freezing temperatures destroyed crops and killed or weakened millions through disease and starvation, just in time for the next calamity (Oerlemans 675-677). In 1347, a ship arrived in Genoa, Italy and with it, came rats carrying the Black Plague. The disease spread through Europe in just months, decimating almost two thirds of the already starving population. It was no wonder that the population of Europe began to question just how effective the Church was at interceding on their behalf.

The loss of the Holy Land, the mini-ice age and the Black Plague, which had killed a large percentage of the doctors, teachers, engineers, scholars and priests of Europe, left Europeans wondering if God was inflicting retribution in biblical proportions upon them for something someone had done. Rather than suffer the population of Europe to begin pointing their collective fingers at the Church for the corruption that surrounded the Papacy, the Church pointed its finger at the non-believers in Europe whom the Christians had suffered to live within their presence. In an age of receding faith, the best solution the Church could come up with was to revive the Inquisition it had begun in the middle of the 1200's in southern France. Doubters of the Church's authority were tortured into submission, which either revived their faith, or they died a horrible death. Jews, Muslims and those practicing the Black Arts, or suspected of practicing the Black Arts, were mercilessly beaten and tortured until they confessed and then they were killed. Jews and Muslims were forced to convert to Catholicism or die in the most painful ways practitioners of medieval torture could devise.

The 1400's: Gunpowder and the beginning of the rebirth

By the 1400's, however, just a few generations after the Plague, things in southern Europe were going swimmingly once again. The banking families in Italy, like the **De Medici's** had successfully convinced the Church that usury, or loaning money for interest was not really what the Bible was referring to when it forbade the practice of loaning money for interest. As a result, the banking families prospered, the Church prospered and Italy began to prosper on a scale unseen for over a thousand years. Suddenly, Italian cities like Venice and Genoa became flushed with cash from trade and banking. They became so rich that their power and wealth rivaled that of many European countries. It was this new way of looking at money along with a technological invention that would change the face of society once again.

Italian merchants, who had, since the Crusades, been importing goods from the Orient and the Middle East to the otherwise bland dining tables and homes of the European nobility, had come across a nifty substance while traveling through China. That nifty invention was called gunpowder, and was something the Chinese, for whatever reason, had not seen a potential use for, outside of the occasional fireworks display. In Europe, where landowners, princes and kings were always on the lookout for new lands to take by force from their neighbors, the Italian merchants saw a potential market for a new device that used the explosive powder to propel a ball of steel through a castle wall or a suit of armor and the unfortunate chest of an adversary.

The Europeans did not pick up on the implications of the cannon until 1453 when the city of Constantinople finally fell to the Turks after the Turkish Sultan brought monstrously huge cannons up to smash down the walls of the city that had stood impregnable for over a thousand years. The fall of Constantinople was to have two major implications for all of Europe. The first of course being that all the courts of Europe were to put their local bell makers to work fashioning the new cannon which they could use on the walls of their enemies. Creative minds in Europe then began producing a smaller version of the cannon that could be held by a foot soldier. Used in a group, the volley of fire produced by the new weapons was deadly, terrifying and highly effective. The new gadget was going to change the world forever, but not quite yet.

The second effect of the fall of Constantinople was the massive influx of the art, books and scientific learning of the past two thousand years, which became instantly available on the streets of Rome, Venice and Paris. Manuscript copiers worked night and day to reproduce the "new" old learning. To the amazement of the Europeans, it appeared that there had once been a very highly evolved state of learning in the days preceding Christianity, and they couldn't seem to get enough of it. A butcher with the writings of Aristophanes and Plato on his shelf was more than just a cutter of meat. He was a man in touch with Classical Greece. A lady who could converse with other ladies about the histories of Herodotus was more than just another boor at the local beauty salons.

The discovery of the "new" old learning began what was known as the **Renaissance**, or "Rebirth." What was even more important for our story was that people began to realize that the Bible was not the end-all of knowledge. The Church responded as it usually did when threatened by logic and reason, with a re-invigorated Inquisition. Of course, they didn't add to their popularity when they began selling indulgences, which were pardons for sinful acts obtained at a price.

The Printing Press, Martin Luther and the Reformation

By 1517, Northern Europe was back in full swing and people there appeared to have had their fill of the influence and corruption of the Roman Catholic Church and the de Medici Popes who appeared to all to have bought the Papacy. At least that is, those people the Church's agents couldn't immediately get at who were far away in Germany, Holland, England and Scotland. That same year, a priest named Martin Luther nailed his 95 Theses (complaints) to the Monastery door in Wurms, Germany.

Instead of admitting its own mistakes, the Church went on the offensive. It declared Martin Luther a heretic and stepped up its public relations campaign to win the ignorant back to the fold. Michelangelo had painted the ceiling of the Sistine Chapel by 1512 and the Church commissioned him to paint other works, such as the *Last Judgment* as a none-too subtle warning to the heretics of the day. Suddenly, the Old Testament was back in fashion, almost. Back in Germany, Martin Luther was supported by a large number of powerful German nobles who resented sending their fortunes to the de Medici Popes of Rome, never to be seen again. In 1534, Henry VIII of England threw the Catholic Church out altogether and named himself the head of the new Anglican Church.

Once the "cat" was out of the preverbal bag, just like in the days of the Early Church, there was no end of people's interpretation and ideas as to what the Christian Church should be. Calvinists said that everyone was pre-ordained to either heaven or hell and there was nothing to do to change that. Lutherans believed in a simple church and a simple life. There were Shakers, Quakers and candlestick makers. The recently discovered New World offered refuge to those seeking freedom from the oppression of the church or the next town's competing sect. First, the Puritans arrived in Massachusetts Colony and then came the Calvinists, Lutherans, Mennonites and Anglicans. In the New World, new ideas spawned new sects with new ideas. Over the next two hundred years, Baptists, Methodists, Jehovah's witnesses, "Mormons" and Seventh-Day Adventists would get their starts in the New World and then venture out to find converts in the old.

These broad interpretations of the Christian Gospel, which started, with Martin Luther's Reformation became possible because of another piece of technology that the Europeans borrowed from China. It, like the gun, was to change the world forever in ways that could hardly have been foreseen. The first victim of the printing press was the Catholic Church, which, for over a thousand years, had kept its followers basically ignorant of their own religion by printing the bible only in Latin. They educated only the rich and the clergy in Latin, so that there was no motivation to disrupt the status quo. The common rabble, or people if you prefer, depended on whatever their local priest said was the way to salvation. Thanks to the introduction of the printing press in 1519 the Gutenberg Bible became the first Bible printed in German. Soon to follow were Bibles in English, French and Spanish. A hundred years later, the King James Version, which was translated from Hebrew and Greek texts, became the final version of the Bible in the English-speaking world.

The return of science

The printing of Bibles was a lucrative business indeed, but there began to be an even greater demand for knowledge outside the realm of the Ecclesiastical. While the Bible was spreading throughout Europe in languages that people could actually read, the translators and printing presses were going non-stop to fill a thousand year old void in the mental appetites of the Europeans. Soon, people like Copernicus, Kepler and Galileo were formulating theories about the solar system based on observations, as the Greeks had done, instead of explaining everything away as God's Will or quoting scriptures from the Bible. They were coming up with some amazing conclusions about the world that began to fly in the face of the religious dogma of the day.

Before we continue any farther, we must remember that what seems common and everyday knowledge to us was incomprehensible to the common man of the Medieval Period. The Bible said God created man in His own image. Therefore, man, according to the Bible was second only to God in the natural order of things. Therefore, logic stated (it doesn't actually say so in the Bible, we must blame Aristotle for this) that man was the center of the universe, the earth was the center of the solar system and everything revolved around the earth, from the perfectly circular planets, to the far off heavens. The Greek philosophers had proposed a universe where all bodies in the heaven moved in orbits of perfect circles and the Catholic Church adopted this theory. It all made perfect sense, so nobody bothered to test it until Galileo pointed his new-fangled telescope at the planets in the 1500's.

Probably the most important observation of the time was Galileo's claim that the Sun does not revolve around the earth. He reported seeing craters on the supposedly spherical moon and saw the rings around Saturn for the first time. Later, based upon the prior works of Tycho Brahe, Johann Kepler, and Nicolai Copernicus, who had worked out the orbits of the planets, once again, it seemed the "perfect universe" was not perfect at all. There were no perfect circles, as had been believed since the days of Aristotle. Flying in the face of two thousand years of accepted knowledge and putting God's favorite creation out of the center of the solar system and universe and onto a rather minor planet was a hard pill to swallow for most. It was especially hard for the Catholic Church. They warned Galileo not to point his telescope at the sky, and he did. (Burke) They told him not to publish his findings, and he did.

Galileo was also the first to test the known laws of gravity. What he found was that, contrary to popular belief, objects fall at the same rate, no matter what their weight. That meant that there was some kind of universal force at work that was the same, no matter where a person conducted the experiment. He called it gravity. When Galileo proposed that the earth was revolving around the Sun, and there were much larger planets than the earth, the Church had a medieval tizzy fit, excommunicated him (until 1977) and put him under house arrest.

Suddenly there began to be whispers throughout Christendom that if the Church had been wrong about something as basic as gravity and the nature of our own solar system, what else were they wrong about? The ideas that had been circulating with the ancient manuscripts around Europe, one of which stated, that the world could be understood by observation (and not religion) was by no means limited to the discipline of Astronomy. It seemed that everything that was considered as knowledge needed to be re-checked and either confirmed through the scientific method, or thrown onto the refuse heap of time.

In the new universities and colleges that began to spring up all over Europe, there came to be new ideas about disease and medicine, farming and agriculture, architecture and engineering, banking and even the notion of government itself. The ideas that came off those printing presses made their way into the hands of people like Sir Thomas More, Sir Isaac Newton, John Locke, Rene Descartes, Diderot and Rene Rousseau. They in turn wrote works that ended up in the hands of Thomas Paine, Benjamin Franklin, Thomas Jefferson and George Washington, to name a few. Using the new (old) ideas, they formed a government based upon the principles of natural law and the writings of people like Plato and Aristotle, Sir Thomas More, Voltaire and John Locke.

The Reformation of Martin Luther was the catalyst that led, at least in Northwestern Europe and England to the introduction of many news ideas about everything from rotating crops to the Nature of God. However, the change did not come about overnight. Those who had the most to lose did not easily accept the new knowledge. The first of course being the Church, and the second being those governments, which established their authority, based on the power of the Church. In fact, from the time the first books from Greece, Rome and the Arab World started showing up to Charles Darwin's *Origin of Species* in 1859 was over four hundred years. During that time, ideas of knowledge by observation, hypotheses and testing, the nature of government or the idea that disease was not the result of an angry God, but caused by viruses and bacteria could get a person either killed or put into very unpleasant circumstances.

Part 3

The modern World

CHAPTER 6

HISTORY OF THE MODERN WORLD

Religion and Science

By 1618, the division between Protestants and Catholics in Europe had come to a head, splitting Europe into two factions. In the northern countries as well as England, Wales and Scotland, the fear of the countries doing the Pope's bidding, such as Spain and France, had resulted in alliances between the countries who considered themselves predominantly "Protestant" and those that considered themselves predominantly Catholic. In 1588, the most powerful country in Europe, Spain, which had enriched itself with stolen gold and silver taken from the Aztec and Incan Empires in the New World, failed in a disastrous naval campaign in its attempt to invade England. The Spanish fleet was routed by English ships under Sir Francis Drake and then blown into the North Sea by a hurricane.

However, the divisions between Catholics and Protestants were not so neatly divided by territorial boundaries as one might think. In England, Ireland and Scotland, there were still factions loyal to the Pope. The same situation was true in France, where the Protestant Huguenots were seen as a possible threat to the Catholic Monarchy. Similarly, Germany, which was not Germany, but a loose alliance of principalities, was alternatively Protestant and Catholic.

If you will recall, in the last chapter, we discussed a bit of technology from China called gunpowder, which led to the cannon that broke up the walls of Byzantium or Constantinople. By the time, in 1618, that the representatives of the Catholic royalty were thrown out of the window into a pile of manure at a conference in Prague, Czechoslovakia, the smaller, hand held use of a clumsy artifice called a "musket," the predecessor to the rifle, had been used haphazardly in skirmishes and other armed confrontations. With what would become known as the "Defenestration of Prague," the Thirty Years War was officially "on."

As we have said already, old ways die hard and the fighting styles of Europe, with mounted horsemen in armor charging into enemy formations, was still the military order of the day for the first part of the war. Then, in 1631, at the battle of Breitenfield, the Swedish King Gustavus Adolfus was the first military leader in history to field an entire army equipped with cannons and heavy, awkward, unreliable and mostly inaccurate firearms. The battle was a route, as the opposing army, terrified of the horrific wounds, sounds and smoke from the Swedish Army's guns, were sent scampering for the hills. The news quickly spread about the effectiveness of the new weapons and suddenly, everyone seemed to want one.

The Thirty Years War and the beginning of the New Order

We must pause here to consider the social, political and economic implications of the newly introduced gun. If the reader will recall, it was the stirrup and armor, introduced at the end of the Roman Empire, which changed the social, political and economic nature of Europe. The forces that supported the local chief, warlord or king, needed land on which to raise the horses the armored fighters or "knights" used on the battlefield. Along with the land came peasants who performed all the agricultural and building activities, which allowed the local warlord time to practice, train and perform service to their higher-ups. It was a system known as "Chivalry" that had, over the years, developed its own laws, legends and codes of conduct. Economically, socially and spiritually, it was supported whole-heartedly by European society, who, over the millennia had come to accept it as the natural order of things.

The day Gustavus Adolfus and his army of musket and cannon bearing troops routed their opposition, the entire social structure of Europe was, or at least soon would be, put on its tin-plated head. The soldiers in the Swedish King's Army were not highly trained, expensively equipped, landowning knights. The people who represented the old order of things on the other side of the battlefield were made up of the usual assortment of knights and peasants. For the first time since the fall of the Roman Empire, the mounted warrior was no longer indestructible. In fact, mounted on a horse and burdened with armored plating, the landowning knight was just as easily destroyed as the peasants with whom he surrounded himself.

On that day in 1631, it became clear to competent military strategists, and later to the ruling classes, that the era of Chivalry was over. The battle of the future would be won by thousands of men armed with muskets facing off against each other. Whichever side could sustain the most horrors, wounds, dismemberments, decapitations, noise, smoke, and inclement weather, and still repel an enemy onslaught would be the victor of the battle of the future.

The Thirty Years War, that began in 1618 ended, if my arithmetic serves me correctly, in 1648. Most of what today is modern Germany had been raped, burned, starved, pillaged and looted. Disease and malnutrition was rampant. The results of the Thirty Years War were even more alarming. After vast fortunes had been spent, entire village and towns, along with their populations were wiped out and hatred and bitterness was left seething in the hearts of the survivors, nothing had been accomplished. At the peace conference, it was decided that the local ruler would determine the religion of the province he ruled. This is exactly how things had been before the war started. Human beings in the name of religion, I should add, were responsible for all of the depravity. This is an important point to remember because it was a point not lost on the thinking men of the day.

The greatest result of the Thirty Years War was, as we have already stated, the beginnings of the erosion of the power of the landowning classes. To put it bluntly, the kings in each country no longer needed their services, other than as local magistrates and keepers of the social status quo. What the new kings needed was money for the guns and troops that would become their new source of power. They also needed ways to collect that money in the form of taxes. Members of the nobility, who had long since given up spending their days training for, or involved in some form of combat or other, needed places for their children to be educated in things like mathematics, theology, literature, languages and the new science. In other words, they needed to find another job.

The Philosophers and the Age of Revolution

As the 1600's turned into the 1700's, more graduates from more universities were making more discoveries, proposing new theories and taking knowledge and learning to undreamed of heights. The European monarchs, whose financial officials made clear to them that more tax revenue could be gained when the citizenry was allowed to prosper, started all kinds of new initiatives for trade, technological innovation, and the establishment of colonies throughout their empires. These innovations occurred in countries that had devolved themselves of the influence of the Church, such as England, Scotland, and parts of Germany, Scandinavia and Holland, where, along with the new learning, entirely new ideas about the social structure were being written about and learned and debated. As we shall see, it was at this point in time that a secret society of men who had remained in the shadows, literally sometimes, of Europe's castles and power structure came out into the light.

Up until the time of the early 1700's, discussing or writing about the nature of government, the role of the Church or even nature itself was not exactly lucrative nor a safe occupation. Societies of educated men formed to discuss such questions throughout Europe and America. By the end of the 1700's, many of the inhabitants in the English colonies in America, English, Dutch, German, Scotch and Irish settlers had readily accepted the ideas of the philosophers of Europe. Men like Benjamin Franklin, Thomas Jefferson, Alexander Hamilton, Patrick Henry, Samuel Adams and Thomas Paine used those ideas to form a government based on the laws they had observed in the natural universe.

In 1781, near the small town of Yorktown on Chesapeake Bay in the soon-to-be former British colonies of North America, the British band played, "*The World Turned Upside Down.*" There, the American Commanding General, George Washington, accepted the surrender (by proxy) of Lord Cornwallis, effectively ending the colonial rule of the largest British Colony in North America. The United States was the first colony to establish itself as a nation based on the ideas of Natural Law and reinforces it with armies of common citizens using the firearm and cannon to repel the landholding system of Europe.

By 1798, the ideas that had been imported to the American Colonies took hold in France when Louis the XVI (sixteenth), King of France, who had almost gone broke financing the American Revolution, found his head at the bottom of a wicker basket as the first French Republic was born. The Revolution in France was the first revolt of the peasant classes that Europe had seen and the landholding classes in neighboring countries did not take it lightly. Until 1815, with Napoleon at the helm, France had been embroiled in a series of campaigns with the landholding or "aristocratic" sponsored armies throughout Europe. The French Revolution ended with the restoration of the French Monarchy, but the landholding classes in Europe had seen the writing on the wall.

The invention of the gun had been the catalyst for the new societies in Europe that otherwise would have been nothing more than a philosophical discussion at a tavern. But, the victory by the Royalist forces at Waterloo, Belgium, could not stop the effects the new science was having upon society that had nothing to do with observations and hypotheses. The underlying grievances that had sparked the French Revolution had been quelled but not silenced. The problem itself was in the iron-fisted grip the landholding classes insisted on maintaining upon their societies. The new systems of learning, trade and technology had produced men of immense wealth, such as the Rothschilds of Europe, but who, because of their status as landless merchants or businessmen, were not acceptable as "respectable" society. They still remained in theory, as deprived of the legal rights as the poorest and most uncouth peasants of Europe.

In the early 1800's, factories began to spring up in the coastal cities of England, the Netherlands, Germany and the new United States. Landlords throughout Western Europe and Britain suddenly began to see their work forces diminished as their peasants made their way to the cities to try to find work. The steam engine, invented by James Watt in the middle of the 1800's, changed almost overnight the way man had lived and worked since the beginning of history. With the invention of the steam engine, men no longer needed to rely on the wind to sail across the globe. Machines could make products such as cloth and linen so fast that the only limitation was the ability of the market to provide raw materials and absorb the finished products. However, because there had been no plan as to where and how the new factory workers would live, slums and shantytowns appeared in all the large port cities. Diseases, such as cholera struck hard in the filthy conditions created by the new slums. This unforeseen and unplanned change in the social fabric gave a rather bleak outlook on what the new science would do for the common man. On the other hand, for the factory owners, bankers and merchants who made loans, manufactured and sold the new factory goods, life couldn't have been better.

The European nobility during the eighteen hundreds, especially those who did not see the writing on the wall and who failed to become involved in trade and industry, found themselves mere paupers compared to the bankers and industrialists, some of whose wealth began to be used to buy the very titles that assured their preferential treatment in society. Those that did not adapt, soon found themselves broke and landless or both. In Northern European countries, the ruling classes saw the new technology and rise of industry as a two-fold threat to their own power. First, should they allow their neighbors to gain any sort of technological advantage over their ability to produce the latest in technologically advanced armaments and navies, they would soon be conquered. Internally, as advancements in medicine and treatment, diet, sanitation and hygiene (Europeans started bathing) eradicated the diseases that once kept their populations small, the ruling classes feared sheer numbers would soon overwhelm them. For other countries, such as Russia, Turkey, Spain and Portugal, who were more interested in holding on to their far-flung empires through force and repression rather than taking advantage of the technological innovations of the time, the clock was ticking.

Evolution and the Super Ape

When Charles Darwin published the *Origin of Species* in 1859, there were two initial reactions. The first reaction came from the majority of the population in Europe and America who had come to terms with the benefits the advances in technology and medicine had brought to their lives, but who still found the story of the Creation as told in the Book of Genesis to be the quintessential reason not only for our being, but the reason for our existence. The Genesis account also determined the nature of our relationship with our fellow creatures and gave us instructions as to populating the planet. To put it simply, the new science hadn't come up with any real evidence to prove the Bible wrong. Then as now, understanding the claims that science made required an education in science that most people didn't have. Most people at the time had grown up reading the Bible and not scientific journals and the Bible's answers seemed the most convenient, after all, they were the "Word of God."

The second group, the group that made up the fields of biology, medicine, archeology and anthropology, in other words the world of science, breathed a collective sigh of relief. Finally, someone (Charles Darwin) had been able to put into words all the ideas that had been floating around concerning the nature of life and how and why we, and the rest of the forms of life that exist, do exist, while things that men had been digging up for hundreds of years like dinosaurs and mammoths did not. For the first time in two thousand years, Noah was out and Darwin and his theories of natural selection were in.

The Industrial Revolution that began at the same time as Darwin's *Origin of Species* began to circulate, coupled with advances in the field of medicine sparked exponential growth in the populations of the Western countries. Less women dying in childbirth meant that they could reproduce more and more children and there was a much greater chance that those children would grow to reach adulthood and, in turn, spend more years producing more children than ever before. The United States, with its vast areas of land, undeveloped resources and factories in need of workers became the release valve for the excess populations of Europe. There, Darwin's theories were almost immediately accepted by the scientific and the not-so-scientific world as well.

Social Darwinism

Darwin said that organisms compete in their respective environments for finite resources like food, water and space. He said that nature favored those mutations which allowed the organism to survive and produce successful offspring, so, what about mankind? Did not nature favor some individuals or even races over their counterparts? Were some forms of government better adapted to survive than others? By the turn of the century, these theories were used to defend and explain the ascendancy of industrialists and bankers like Andrew Carnegie, Henry Ford and Nelson Rockefeller. The idea of the "White Man's Burden" to civilize the rest of the world began to be used as an excuse for the exploitation of populations in China, India, and the countries of Africa and the Middle East.

In the early part of the century, the science of Eugenics, or the science of producing healthy populations and societies became the rage in Western culture. It was argued that the Industrial Revolution with its medicine, clean water, sanitation and healthy food, was having the undesired effect of allowing undesirable people, who, in the natural world would not have survived and reproduced, to do just that. In America and England, people with inferior traits, criminal behavior and mental illness were forcibly sterilized. "Social Darwinism" would reach its climax in the sterilization and euthanasia chambers of National Socialist Germany, but not quite yet.

By the end of the first decade of the 1900s, the old questions that had been fought over in Europe by the armies of Napoleon had still not been settled. The landowning aristocracy still maintained prominence on the top of the social ladder, which meant that they made the major decisions when it came to things like government investments and foreign policy. Most European countries had made concessions in government to the "lower" classes by forming parliamentary bodies, but they were mostly token in nature. The aristocracy easily overruled the lower bodies. In Central Europe, from Austria to Italy, the Holy Roman Empire, an outdated relic from the days of knights in armor, was seen as a major obstacle by many, to the ideas of democracy and self-rule for millions of Europeans. In Russia, the iron grip of the Czars and the aristocracy on the peasant classes had forced them to live in abject poverty while their counterparts in Europe were enjoying all the benefits of industrialized life. The people of Central Europe and Russia were looking for a catalyst to throw out the Czars, the Hapsburgs and their wasteful and inefficient aristocratic government altogether.

Political Darwinism

Economically, the European merchant classes sought greater influence around the world where they wished to open markets for their manufactured goods, obtain cheap land labor and resources and send their excess populations. It was called "colonialism" and had grown in popularity in Europe ever since Christopher Columbus had sailed into the New World. The corporations and political leaders of the democracies in the West were making a grab for as much land as they could find, conquer and then defend from the other Western powers. Germany, England, and France wanted control of the Middle East, where early explorations had discovered the food for the modern industrial machine, oil. Finally, seventy years of industrialization had created a population explosion that even the United States was reluctant to absorb. The best solution for all of these problems was of course, World War I, or the Great War, as it is known in Europe.

The War itself began with the assassination of Archduke Ferdinand, heir to the Holy Roman Empire in 1914. Due to Europe being divided by a system of alliances France allied with England and Russia, Germany joined its Holy Roman counterparts in Austria and the fracas was on. At the start of the conflict, the German Army simply walked around the French Army by marching through Belgium. The whole German circus was well on its way to Paris, when, for some odd reason, the German commander stopped. Using the excuse that he was worried about being outflanked, he spread his lines out to the West, which allowed the French and British time to regroup and counterattack. The Germans dug trenches and slaughtered the counter-attacking French and British with their latest in technological innovations, the machine gun.

The War to Begin all Wars

Realizing that they had better start hiding from the German machine guns or be annihilated, the French and British dug in as well. The trench war then dragged on for the next four years. The horror was unspeakable. During the 1916 Battle of the Somme for instance, 250,000 British and French soldiers (mostly British) were sent against the German trenches. In the end, most of the British soldiers ended up dead, wounded or captured and the lines remained roughly in the same place.

By 1917, all of the countries involved were nearly bled dry. There was talk of an armistice until two things happened. First, the Bolsheviks took over in Russia and pulled themselves out of the war. Second, the Americans entered the war on the side of England and France. Suddenly, it was a whole new ball game as fresh American troops entered the fray and German troops, freed up by Russia's capitulation entered the war on the Western Front. The death and carnage would continue for two more years.

For the monarchies of Europe, most of whom were first and second cousins, the Great War was great for some and not so great for others. The Kaiser of Germany and the Hapsburgs of Austria were dethroned, the Czar was shot and the landowning aristocracies retreated to their manor houses to await the next chain of events. The monarchies in the victorious countries, such as England, the Netherlands, Italy, Sweden, Norway and Denmark, enjoyed even greater popularity after the war as they laid wreaths at the tombs of those millions of citizens who died, were maimed or suffered privations for the sake of keeping them warm, cozy and in control. For the common citizenry of Europe, the outcome was ghastly at best. There is no accurate number, but at least fifty million died of wounds, starvation and disease while millions more were left homeless, orphaned, fatherless and destitute.

As we will see, the people who really made out well during the First World War were the bankers and the makers of the machinery of war. For four years, the front lines had been like a giant garbage dump for all the weapons, food, gasoline, ammunition and men the opposing armies and their governments could buy (or borrow for) and then dump into the abyss of the trench systems of Europe.

At the end of the war, Germany was devastated not only by the actual war itself, but also by the reparations it was forced to pay to England and France. President Woodrow Wilson tried to bring the United States into the newly formed League of Nations, but was rebuffed at home. In the end, the U.S. chose not to participate, as France and England carved up what was left of the Ottoman Empire and divided the Middle East and Far East between themselves. "The War to End All Wars," as it had been cleverly called in the American press, was, in reality, the war to begin the next war.

After the War, there was prosperity in the West as new industries sprang up, the population grew and technologies like the radio and the telephone began to unite people across vast distances. Unfortunately, the new prosperity didn't last as long as people thought it would. Ten years after the war's end, the economies of the world collapsed. In response, governments stepped in and expanded on scales that were never thought possible a few decades before.

Adolf Hitler in Germany promised a dissolute population in Germany that his brand of socialism and Darwinian "racial purity," would bring back the dignity of the German people. In the U.S., Franklin Delano Roosevelt promised a "New Deal" for the destitute masses in America. In Russia, Nikolai Lenin and then his successor, Joseph Stalin, promised the prosperity that would come with the victory of the World Worker's Party and the Soviet Union's triumph over capitalism in the West. What the people of the world got was ten years of massive government programs designed to modernize their infrastructures for industry and another, even more expensive World War.

At the end of World War II, with a few atomic bombs in its arsenal, the United States sat unopposed as the greatest superpower on earth. With the factories of the industrialized nations of Europe, Russia and Japan in heaps of rubble across their respective landscapes, the United States was easily able to convert war production into the production of toasters, dishwashers, Chevrolets and refrigerators. With no markets to compete with per se, along with an educated, ambitious population, and with an abundance of oil, the United States had all it needed to dominate the world economically for the next forty years. Unlike the end of World War I, the United States, which had refused to join the League of Nations, eagerly adopted resolutions to join the newly formed United Nations, to be headquartered in New York on land donated by one of the great benefactors of the wars, the oil-rich Rockefeller family.

In the aftermath of the Second World War, many thousands of Jews, victims of the Adolf's Hitler's racial purity campaigns had been flooding to their ancient homeland in Palestine. In 1947, representatives of the newly formed State of Israel stood before the world body of the United Nations and announced its existence as a state separate from the Arab peoples it had displaced through mutual campaigns of terrorism, murder and assassinations. The United States and Russia, as well as England and France immediately recognized the new state.

The Wars of the Future

War, which had concentrated vast amounts of the world's economic resources in the hands of the world's banks and industrialists was too good of a racket to give up. What they needed to keep their balance sheets in the red were wars that, unlike the first two world wars, would never end. The Palestinian-Israeli Conflict or "Arab-Israeli Conflict" as it would come to be known, would be just one of many conflicts in the world that emerged from the ashes of Europe and the Islands of the Pacific in 1945.

The Soviet Union, using the excuse that it had been attacked by the Germans in World War II and the U.S. and Britain during World I, refused to give back any of the territory it had liberated from the Germans, citing the need for "buffer" states between the "Workers Paradise" and the "Capitalist West." The occupied countries suffered under the brutal puppet regimes of the Soviets. Their horrible crimes and atrocities made front-page news in the US and Europe as the Cold War got under way. In 1956, with U.S. encouragement, Hungary revolted and suffered brutal reprisals from the Soviet Union, while the U.S. stood by and did nothing. In 1968, the same process was repeated in Czechoslovakia.

Blood money and the shadow government

From 1947 to 1991, the Western countries spent vast amounts of money to counter the Soviet threat. The money was funneled into projects and technological development that created a world that was unimaginable one hundred years before. Under the cloak of National Security, an entire governmental apparatus was created and agencies such as the Central Intelligence Agency, the National Security Agency, the Federal Bureau of Investigation, the Defense Intelligence Agency, and the Drug Enforcement Agency were created or massively expanded. By the end of the 1950's a shooting war had broken out, with CIA provocation, on the Korean Peninsula. By 1965, the US had taken over France's role in suppressing the Vietnamese War of Liberation. These conflicts, unlike the conflicts in the first part of the century, were fought in a completely new manner of warfare that would continue for the next fifty years.

Death: Protecting our way of life

To better understand how and why the new kind of warfare was necessary, just imagine a worker at the Boeing plant in Seattle, Washington, during World War II. For four years that worker worked as many shifts as was possible without collapsing physically. The money the worker made from building the planes used in Europe and Japan had been, although not fantastic, steady. Overtime was available and during the four years, the steady income allowed the worker to make a down payment on a house, a car, and a boat for cruising around Puget Sound on the odd sunny day in Seattle. Enough had been put aside to start a college fund for the worker's teen-age son.

Now, imagine the Boeing plant in January of 1944. The War in Europe appears to be coming to a close, the aircraft from there can be transferred to Japan and the Army has stopped buying airplanes. Boeing is handing out lay-off notices by the thousands. Suddenly, the apparent bonanza has come to a screeching halt. The loss of jobs means a loss of tax revenue and a drain on the local government's budget for schools and roads, not to mention social assistance like unemployment and welfare. The end of the war, as wonderful as it might sound, has caused a major financial crises on the workers and the major corporations like Boeing, MacDonnell Douglass, General Motors and Ford, just to name a few.

As cruel, heartless and selfish as it might sound, in the worker's minds, things would be better if the war would continue indefinitely. And why should they care? They aren't slugging through the snow in some god-forsaken forest in Germany. They aren't being attacked by a kamikaze bent on destroying the carrier they are serving on in the Pacific. But none of that concerns the workers, the plant managers and most important, the owners and stockholders of the war industries corporations and of course, the banks.

What the economy needs is a small war against a primitive country that goes on indefinitely. This small-scale war will allow the continued influx of government dollars to the corporations for years and years. War is good for business and good for national morale, unless someone finds out the truth about it. These small wars are good for the media, good for employment, good for technological development, good for political officials, good for career military officers, good for intelligence agencies and best of all, small wars against people who can't fight back is good for national prestige. The only people a war is not good for are the ones silly enough, or in the days of the draft, unfortunate enough to be selected to fight it. But, this is such a small percentage of the total population that they can be swept under the carpet with a few medals, a song, a few movies, and a memorial service or a rock in a park in Washington D.C. Of course there are those poor people from the country being attacked who will die in the millions, but, as long as you keep them "over there," what are they going to do, attack you?

Psychological Warfare

Of course, just coming out and telling the population that the country needs to go and kill, mutilate and destroy the homes and livelihoods of a lot of innocent people so that the corporations can expand into the unfortunate country and make gains on the stock market, while local economies thrive and generals can get shiny new medals, would be met with rioting in the streets and a disaffected population, at least in the areas where the economy didn't depend on the war.

What really gets people motivated is to scare them with the true stories of millions of peasants starved or worked to death by their oppressive government. The population needs to be shown pictures of hundreds of people waiting in line for a loaf of bread while missiles and tanks are paraded down the main street of the country's capitol. The media needs to make a movie or two about the hapless plight of the people, or "heroes," who are trying to help themselves by helping you and your war against them. The general public needs to be personally and physically involved by educating them about such things as "The Hun" (WWI), the "Yellow Menace" (WWII) or the "Red Menace" (Cold War). Making them do atomic blast drills while at school should frighten even the kids. Writers and television stations (that you own) should run daily stories about the threat the enemy poses to you and your children. The one thing the people who mastermind these wars don't do, at least until the statute of limitations is up, or they are on their death beds, is announce that you started the war in the first place.

As we shall soon see, in one of the greatest cons in the history of the world, the people of the United States feared the threat of the Soviet Union and the spread of Communism more than they feared the encroachment of the secret government and apparatus that took control of their government while they stood by and watched. The Truman Doctrine of 1947 gave the U.S. Government, its military and intelligence agencies carte blanche to fight the communists and communism (or anybody who wasn't friendly to American business interests) wherever it reared its "ugly head." It was the fear and paranoia of the Communists that decided every presidential contest from 1948 to 1988. It got the U.S. involved in two wars that ended up in stalemates, cost hundreds of billions of dollars and killed, wounded or maimed, millions of Koreans, Vietnamese, Cubans, Hondurans,

Nicaraguans, Chileans, Peruvians, and Argentineans, not to mention the loss of thousands of young American men and women.

The never-ending war and the American decline

The United State's willingness to defend the rest of the "Free World" from attacks by aggressors, allowed its benefactors, such as Germany and Japan, the freedom to invest in or copy the techniques for producing consumer goods more cheaply than the U.S. By the 1970's, America had used up most of its oil. The Japanese had successfully copied American production techniques and revolutionized manufacturing by using robots instead of factory workers in its assembly plants. The Germans and the Japanese were pioneering new technological advances in micro-circuitry and plastics, while the industrial capacity and technological supremacy of the U.S. was slowly eroding away.

By the 1980's, the U.S. had become dependent on all things foreign. Foreign cars, consumer goods, and most importantly, oil, as the U.S. began running trade deficits every year and every year the American dollar was becoming worth less and less. To get the U.S. out of its economic slump, which was brought on by the closing factories and higher oil prices, the U.S. needed another war. In 1986, after years of setting up an infrastructure to import cocaine onto the streets of the US, the country declared a "War on Drugs," and suddenly, billions of (borrowed) tax dollars were available to combat, or at least to wrest control, of the cocaine empire in Colombia and Peru.

On the home front, policemen went into the public schools to arrest students and encourage them to turn in their parents. The supply of cocaine, imported through places like Bill Clinton's Arkansas by ex-CIA pilots and operatives like Barry Seal, skyrocketed, as did its use, as the media glorified it in movies and song, lamented its abuse and made it more popular than Pepsi. The War on Drugs gave the government unprecedented power over the private and confidential lives of Americans. It also gave them billions in unaccounted-for dollars. Suddenly, the secret agencies had a cash cow that was not dependent on the sometimes fickle funding of the American Congress. But the U.S. still needed a "real" war.

Lessons learned: War is good for everyone

President Ronald Reagan had begun a new arms race that essentially bankrupted the Soviet Union. But with all the new equipment, what were we to do with all the old equipment? For one, we sold it to the Afghan rebels who had been invaded by the Soviets in 1979. In 1981, Iraq declared war on Iran, so there was plenty to be made selling weapons, technology, and offering expertise in return for Saddam Hussein's oil money. Israel, who always had good credit because of their connections with international banking, could "buy" some of our equipment and then pay for it with U.S. loans, foreign aid and subsidies. That way, Israel would have enough equipment to go after the Palestinian Liberation Organization in Beirut in 1982.

But, the people in the secret government began to get greedy and nearly blew the lid on the whole operation when, in 1986, it was discovered that the National Security Agency was supplying missiles to Iran, in an attempt to free C.I.A. station chief William Casey, who had been taken prisoner and was a hostage in Beirut (where he was killed). The Iraqis (our allies) were furious, Congress was furious and, in the Congressional Hearings, Ronald Reagan became famous for saying, "I don't recall."

Iran-Contra or no, the 1980's were a bonanza for the war industries, international bankers, drug dealers and manufacturers, lawyers and police forces all over America. Once again, the victims were the American taxpayers and those who were "mandatorily sentenced" to five years in prison and were forced to spend time with rapists, murderers and other violent criminals in places like Attica, Sing Sing and Folsom for possession with intent to sell the drugs the U.S. government was importing.

The naked capitalists and the return to feudalism

In 1991, when the secret government of the United States had wrested enough control of the United States from its own people, the Union of Soviet Socialist Republics officially "collapsed." Its satellite states were given their own autonomy and that opened the door to animosities that had been brewing for fifty years in places like Yugoslavia, where the Serbian minority sought its own national identity at the expense of the Croatians and the Muslims. Once again, war was business and business was good.

In the United States, where the corporations and banking interests no longer needed the loyalty and support of the American people as they had in the past, thanks to the shadow government's military machine, a massive political, economic and propaganda operation began. The goal of the American corporations was to shift their operations overseas where they could take advantage of the cheap, sometimes slave labor of developing countries like China, Malaysia, Vietnam, Mexico, Honduras and so on and so on. The loss of American jobs was downplayed, while the rise in corporate profits was highlighted in the media. The North American Free Trade Agreement (NAFTA) and the General Agreement on Tariffs and Trade (GATT), which were rubberstamped by the US Congress under the watchful eyes of the Clinton Administration, virtually assuring the economic destruction of the United States. When Ross Perot, an independent Presidential candidate told the American voters that the "sucking" sound they were going to hear was the sound of their jobs leaving for Mexico, he was made a national joke by the news media.

The massive profits made by corporations which added money to the 401(k) plans the workers of the United States through investments on the rising stock market, left everyone with a sense of security. People assumed that what was happening was just the natural order of things as the forty and fifty dollar an hour construction and manufacturing jobs were eliminated and millions of middle-class workers, shop-owners, and the millions more who provided their dental care, day care, pizza delivery, auto repair, plumbing, etc. were also put on the ranks of the unemployed and forced to work for a fraction of their wages.

Except for documentary filmmakers like Michael Moore, the corporate-owned news media wanted the destitution and misery caused by the corporate world out of the spotlight and out of the public consciousness. What they needed was something big to put on the TV screens of the American workers who were going from shop owners to clerks at the local Wal-Mart. They needed something to make Americans feel good again. America needed another war.

The Mother of all Battles

In 1991, the U.S. armed and financed leader of Iraq, Saddam Hussein, sent his armies into Kuwait after asking the Americans if they had any objection and received no response. President George H.W. Bush, with the newly equipped, state of the art, American military at his disposal, drew his "line in the sand" and rallied the nations of the "New World Order" in the deserts of Saudi Arabia where they routed the Iraqi Army in only one hundred hours, and then stopped fighting. Oddly enough, after Korea, Vietnam, and the War on Drugs, we didn't see that one coming. In the eighties, the only wars we won were against Grenada and Panama, each of which was like invading Terre Haute, Indiana. Luckily, the US media announced that we had, in fact won the war. Saddam had been removed from Kuwait and the Emir had been restored to power. No one seemed to question the fact that we started out fighting kings in the 1700's but by the 1990's we were restoring them to power. In fact, no one seemed to question anything anymore.

But it turns out we hadn't really won. Saddam went after his enemies, the Christian Kurds in the north and we needed a military operation to keep them from dying of starvation or being gassed with the chemicals we had supplied to him in the 1980's. It was necessary to station thousands of troops, planes, tanks and aircraft carriers off the coast of Iraq in the Persian Gulf just to keep Saddam in "check." We didn't win the war in the old context of the term winning a war. In the new context, we had won a major victory.

The United States had found another never-ending war to fight. The Iraq standoff would keep the "defense" corporations rolling in U.S. taxpayer money in what seemed to be a never-ending game of cat-and-mouse with Saddam Hussein. In an ironic twist of fate, after hearing that his armies had been obliterated and that the American troops and planes were on the road to Baghdad but, that they had actually stopped and proposed a peace conference and the cessation of hostilities, Saddam announced, "I won!" The United Nations imposed sanctions that allowed Saddam to sell his oil at below market prices to his neighbors and keep most of the profits. His antagonism toward the State of Israel did not win him any points, nor did the assassin he sent to kill George H.W. Bush. But what he did do was give the U.S. news media something to throw on the television screen and the newspaper headlines to pre-empt bad news about the American economy and the loss of jobs for the next fourteen years.

The Never Ending War: Israeli Style

In 2001, not a year after the secret government apparatus had given George Bush Jr. the White House, twelve men, nine of them from the Kingdom of Saudi Arabia, hijacked four airliners and crashed two of them into the World Trade Center and another into the Pentagon. The fourth plane, after an unsuccessful attempt by the passengers to seize the plane, crashed into a field in Pennsylvania killing all aboard. The United States then declared war on a group of militant Muslims known as Al Qaeda who claimed responsibility, through their leader, Osama bin Laden of the World Trade Center attacks. The only problem was that Al Qaeda lived in Afghanistan, which didn't require much to bomb them into the Stone Age. A never-ending war could be fought, but it wouldn't make the big profits for the war machine makers and the banks that were making a pretty penny from the interest on the deficits required for financing the war. However, they could make even more money if the United States attacked a country that actually had an army.

In 2003, the United States led a much smaller "coalition of nations" into Iraq to depose Saddam Hussein once and for all. Eight years after the September 11th attacks, Osama bin Laden remains free. Saddam Hussein and his sons along with possibly hundreds of thousands of Iraqis, and four thousand U.S. Servicemen are dead. And there is no end in sight to these wars.

Running on empty

In 2005, after Hurricane Katrina destroyed major sections of New Orleans, in a Senate Budget Committee meeting televised on C-Span, the Budget Director announced to the committee members that the biggest threat America was not Al-Qaeda or any other Islamic terrorists. The biggest threat to America was the fact that the American economy was based on real estate. He told the members of the Senate that were present that they needed to immediately cut spending. In answer, every member of that committee acknowledged the "fine work" the Director had done and then insisted that they were going to keep spending. In effect, the United States was a Cadillac that was running on empty and our Senators voted unanimously to step on the gas.

In 2007, the price of gasoline hit 4.50 cents a gallon in response to the Federal Reserve announcement that it was going to cut interest rates, in effect, to start printing money that was essentially worthless. The domino effect that followed saw the housing market collapse as companies and consumers had to cut back to pay for more expensive fuel. The major banks either collapsed or were on the verge of collapse. In a matter of months, the unemployment rate jumped from six to eight and then settled at ten percent. The actual unemployment rate is closer in 2010 to twenty per cent, but the government has a way of skewing statistics in favor of the current administration. In response, the government announced that it was going to spend more money than ever before in order to stimulate an economy that had already been razed and pillaged by the corporations and the United States government. It was like a robber taking all of a person's possessions and then forcing them to sign for a loan.

And so, how did we come to this horrible place in history? Was it by accident? Was it by some sinister plan? In order to answer those questions, we must look again at certain aspects of history, of people and events that are never included in "popular history." Once we find out those answers, we will be better able to understand how we arrived at this place at this time. Understanding how we got where we are does not guarantee that we will ever be able to change the future. But not understanding how we got into this mess will guarantee our future will be much, much worse than our past.

Lessons learned?

From our brief overview of history we have hopefully learned some basic things about ourselves. One of the ideas that are predominant throughout the history of what we refer to, as "civilization," is that governments use information along with force to maintain their own power. In ancient Egypt we saw the absolute power of the Pharaoh and the class of priests who were able to maintain a world order based upon the idea that the Pharaoh was solely responsible for maintaining the cycles of life, from the rising of the sun to the annual flooding of the Nile from year to year. Should someone have come along and suggested that the flooding was due to the cycle of rains that occurred further south in the mountains of Sudan and Ethiopia, that person would have had a very limited time allotted to him or her amongst the society of the living.

In the totalitarian regimes of Assyria, Babylon and Persia, an absolute monarch in one form or another encouraged learning and study, but the knowledge that was discovered was not for the betterment of the people. The information they learned was for the use of the king and his advisers, and therefore, when the king or the empire collapsed, the knowledge they had was usually lost.

It wasn't until the Greeks, that our modern ideas of science for the good and betterment of the condition of man was introduced and, had Alexander the Great not "flipped out" and gone the way of most of the absolute rulers before him, we may have had two thousand years of advances in all the sciences. If we ponder at how much we have achieved in the past two hundred years in the ways of science and technology, just think how advanced we might be now if that were *two thousand* years. As we have seen, that did not happen. The Romans were not a sophisticated lot and were interested in what men are always interested in, power, money and conquest. A Church that claimed absolute authority over all areas of learning and that set man back a thousand years, for a thousand years until the Renaissance, supplanted the order that they were able to maintain.

So, can we blame our current state of affairs on the Romans and then the Catholic Church? Of course we cannot. They both contributed to the world by keeping some kind of order in the midst of chaos. It is not the institutions that are to blame. Men will always be men, and if the present state of things is any indication, it is quite possible that we may have eradicated ourselves from the planet a long time ago were it not for their suppression of the development of science and technology.

Be that as it may, we are at a crossroads. Because of our endeavors in the fields of science, we are discovering daily that what was myth is now fact and vice versa. Our government and other institutions are no better or worse than those that have gone before. We still have powerful people who want to maintain their power at whatever cost. We still have governments that look for any ideas or innovations that might be dangerous to their power and who will try to control the way common people think and react to any knowledge or circumstances that might threaten their own control of their populations.

Deceptions of the Ages

It is with that understanding about history and about the nature of men and power that we will proceed with our inquiry into how we arrived at this place...

Chapter 7

A Tale of Two Kingdoms

"For it must needs be, that there is an opposition in all things..." (2 Nephi 2:11)

Before we begin: Moving the flashlight of history.

What you have seen so far is the "story" that those who write "history" want you to know. Some of it, they would prefer you forget, but, it is commonly accepted because the events that we have described have been published in textbooks, newspapers, magazines, aired on news broadcasts and therefore constitute what is known as popular history. Now, we will look at history from a completely different perspective. But, before we do, imagine yourself entering a large dark room, or, a large, dark caves as Plato would say. Imagine that inside that room the only person present is a woman (or man) with a flashlight. Because the room is so large and dark, it is impossible for you to make out anything except the very objects upon which the woman focuses the beam of light. The room, in case you haven't figured it out yet, represents the past. The woman represents whomever it is that brings that past out for you to see. Of course you can't see all of the past, so whatever you do see, you see for a reason and that reason usually has to do with what someone, somewhere has decided that you should know, while other things it has been decided that you shouldn't know. You watch as the woman shines her light on a grand piano here, and a large dining table over there. So, you make an assumption that because of the two objects you have seen, you are in the house of a rich or great family.

Naturally, being in such a large and luxurious place, you lose your fear of the dark space as you assume after looking at objects you associate with luxury and comfort that it is a place of safety and there is no harm that could come from the dark. And so it is with history. Popular history, or what was covered in the last chapters, is nothing more than the very narrow beam of a flashlight shone upon events, places and people, in order to give you a brief glimpse into things that happened in the past so that you have some kind of understanding of where you stand today. Suppose then, that the woman was to shine the beam on another object, say, a crouching lion and yell, "It's a lion!" Based on the alarm in her voice and the image of a lion in the beam of light, your fears would return, and you may even lose control of some bodily functions, at least until you come to realize the crouching lion was stuffed.

However, what if it was a real lion and the woman began laughing hysterically instead of warning you of the danger? Possibly, because of her laughter, you would feel confused. A lion represents danger, but because the woman (or man) is laughing, you are not sure how to interpret the new information. You want to trust the woman, so you wouldn't feel there was much of a threat until it actually pounced on you and tore out your jugular vein.

The ability to focus your attention and assign feelings to objects in the room as threats or benign objects, gives the woman incredible power over you as you constantly assess the figures in the beam of light. But what about the things in the dark you cannot see? Are they less harmful to you? Of course not, but you are not going to be afraid or alarmed of anything you cannot see, hear, smell or taste, unless you are instructed to be afraid, alarmed, happy, sad, etc. The ability to focus your attention on history, and upon events that occur in your world that make up history gives those with the flashlight an incredible power over not only you, but whole societies as well. Therefore, in the next section of this book we will look at two aspects of history that are certainly not secret, but that have remained hidden in the shadows, so to speak for hundreds of years.

What is History again?

With apologies then, for the purposes of keeping the reader interested, it is going to be necessary to jump around on our timeline of history for the next few chapters. As we discussed in the last chapter, history is not a linear process. Time, as we said, is linear, but time does not occur on the two dimensional graph that you may recall from your days in history classes in junior high school. As we said in a previous chapter, time is a fabric woven at the same rate in which trends, inventions, occurrences and movements intersect with people as they move across the loom towards the finished product. These trends, inventions, occurrences and movements add a specific color to the fabric we call time.

For example, in the 1950's, rock music became popular with a new generation of teen-agers. That music by the 1960's became a mouthpiece for rebellion against the established order and the war in Vietnam. If we were to give "Rock and Roll" music a color, say, a nice "Purple Haze," we would have to tie in various shades of colors that make up the color purple. The importation of African Americans in the 1700's and 1800's, who developed the style of music called "Rock and Roll," might give us a nice red. The discovery of electrical current might be indigo, the phonograph violet, the freedom to travel created by automobile a nice navy, and the commercial marketing techniques developed by the music industry a nice black. The end result would be that the young people coming across that piece of fabric of time would be tinted a beautiful color of purple because of all the previous threads that had been woven into the fabric as they met the warp and the woof.

In order to understand the different colors or threads of what brought us to the place we are now, which would probably be a nice bright red, we must understand some of the significant threads that have crossed the warp of time in the past. Possibly, these threads you may not be aware of because they don't show up in very many history books. It is the very fact that they don't show up in the history books, but have had such far-reaching effects on the history of the world for the past two hundred years that should automatically make the seriously inquisitive person wonder why the world of academia and the media prefer to keep such things hidden from view.

I will caution the reader at this point. This is a serious inquiry based on facts as they are known and have been written down in various historical and religious texts. Most people in the modern world have been mentally conditioned like a person in a room with someone holding a flashlight to dismiss these subjects and issues as nonsense and not worth consideration at all. For that reason, we can tell a lot about who is holding the flashlight if we know what it is that they don't want us to see, consider or to be alarmed about. If the reader at this point, due to previous mental conditioning, feels uncomfortable learning about the truth behind the restoration of the Church of Jesus Christ (of Latter-day Saints), or the cover-up regarding extraterrestrial beings that are and have been visiting our planet from not only other planets, but from other dimensions as well, please put this book down at this point. You may feel more than confident that, as you relate to your friends and colleagues how utterly ridiculous this book and the subject matter are that you will have lots of well-respected company. In fact, depending upon your occupation, you may even be able to gain some substantial financial and career rewards for your condemnation of this book and its subjects. You will not be the first, nor will you be the last to throw the beam of light in another direction, in order to keep the general populace of the world "in the dark," so to speak. If this is your decision, I wish you all the luck in the world.

If you are one of the small percentage of people in this world who is curious to find out at least some basic truths about the world is and why things are they way that they are, then we must come to some kind of an understanding. As we discuss the issue of The Church of Jesus Christ of Latter-day Saints, there are two, possibly three options open to us:

Option 1: (The easy option) the "founder" of the Church of Jesus Christ of Latter-day Saints; Joseph Smith Jr. was a liar and a fraud. He liked to tell stories and was only looking for a way to make money as his critics and critics of the Church of Jesus Christ of Latter-day Saints still claim.

Option 2: (The more difficult option) Joseph Smith Jr. was not a liar and a fraud. He was visited by God, Jesus Christ, the angel Moroni, John the Baptist and various other Old Testament prophets who bestowed upon himself and his assistants, the keys to the Priesthood of God that had been passed on through the tribes of Israel since the days of Adam, but was taken from the earth at the time of the Resurrection of Jesus Christ. He was given a record of the inhabitants of the American Continent that migrated from the Middle East at various times in ancient history. He translated the record, along with other ancient texts with abilities that were given him through powers that we are only beginning to understand scientifically. In the record known as the Book of Mormon, Jesus Christ appeared after His resurrection and taught the ancient culture we know as the Maya, about the workings of the Holy Priesthood, baptism and other things that were not mentioned in the record but that allowed their culture to flourish.

Option 3: (The not as difficult option as number 2) I am not sure, but I will continue to read with an open mind and make a decision about these subjects once I have read the material in this book and, if I am still not convinced, I may possibly even read the books mentioned in this text before I make a decision.

Are you still here? Great! The first matter we must address then is the matter of who would have the power to mentally condition you to have the attitudes you possess about these subjects (Latter-day Saints and extraterrestrials). I am going to give you evidence so that you can come to your own conclusions about why these powerful entities would find it so important to condition you about the most important events in the history of mankind. It is not the writer's intent to endorse any belief system, only to lie out facts as they are and as they have taken place so that the reader can make their own informed judgment concerning these matters.

I will further caution the reader, that the information in this book is at times both frightening and at other times depressing. Sometimes it frightfully depressing and other times depressingly frightful. However, there is information in this book that is also exciting and uplifting and will give the reader a true and hopeful sense that human beings have as much potential for love, thought, advancement and technological, spiritual and philosophical breakthroughs as we can dare to imagine. It is for that reason that the author has put the frightening and depressing information at the beginning of the book and saved the inspiring, hopeful and uplifting information for the last. All we must do as a species is break free of the chains of our mental, spiritual and physical bondage or, in other words, the history that we read about in the last three chapters. We must learn not to fear the unknown. We must learn to open our minds and our thoughts to new ideas and new ways of doing things. Most importantly for now, we must learn to open our minds and accept facts as they have happened, no matter how disturbing or different from what we have been "taught" as they may seem. Finally, we must all become racists, human race-ists, that is. We must come together as one particular class of "intelligent" beings and show the rest of the universe that we are, in fact, ready to join them in their community.

7-1

MAMMON

No man can serve two masters: for either he will hate the one, and love the other; or else he will hold to the one and despise the other. Ye cannot serve God and Mammon. (Matthew 6:24)

<u>Mayer Amschel Bauer</u>

On September 19, 1812, an old man lay dying on his bed in a sparse ghetto apartment in Frankfort, Germany. The old man who lay on his deathbed had started life in rather humble circumstances, but through skill, planning and an incredible amount of good luck, had obtained more wealth over the space of his lifetime than any single person, and in some cases, entire countries within Europe. The dying man's wishes were simple ones. First, only immediate family members were to hold key posts in the family business. Second, the family was to intermarry. Only first and second cousins would be acceptable in order to keep the family fortune within the family. Third, there should never be a public inventory or announcement made of the family's holdings. Fourth, female members of the family were to have no part in running the family business. Furthermore, all family business was to be done in secret and all business transactions were to be done ruthlessly.

Taken out of context, the austere measures invoked by the dying man may seem the machinations of a delusional paranoid. However, within the historical context of what was Germany in the early 1800's, the measures may seem at least understandable given that Jews, like the dying man, had not been allowed to leave, or live anywhere else in the city and were looked upon as common vermin by German society. The dying man was named **Mayer Amschel Bauer**, but history knows him by his adopted name, **Rothschild**. For good or ill, it was this man whose ultimate legacy is the modern state of Israel and the release from bondage, if you will, of the Jewish people from pogroms, racism and the persecutions that have been carried out against the Jews in Europe and Russia since the Romans sacked the city of Jerusalem. The feelings that the Jews, especially the Rothschilds have had towards so-called Christians because of the Christians' repeated displays of their own ignorance and depravity throughout history is integral to understanding the malevolent feelings of the Rothschilds and the Jews towards Christians in general. To tell the Rothschild's story without explaining this aspect of history would be leaving out a very important part of the Rothschild story.

In case you are not aware of who the Rothschilds are, as most Americans are not, they are the single wealthiest family in the world. They have financed wars, arms races, and revolutions. They control governments and the fate of billions of people. They have manipulated economies, monopolized industries and driven millions of people to destitution and death. The funny thing is, of the billions of people whose lives they control, maybe a few million even know their name. How could one family control so much and so many yet seem so obscure in the pages of the history that they themselves have created? The answer lies in the words of Mayer's son, Nathan, who said:

""I care not what puppet is placed upon the throne of England to rule the Empire on which the sun never set. The man that controls Britain's money supply controls the British Empire, and I control the British money supply."

Control the money supply of the greatest nation on earth? How did a Jewish coin dealer who grew up in the ghettos of Frankfort, ever come to have a son who could make such a boast? How could the same family come to control the money supply in not only the United Kingdom, but the United States and the nations of Europe as well? It is a complicated question with no easy answer because the answer is difficult to understand unless you know how a situation where a single family could gain access to the money supply of any country. Even more, the story of how such a situation came about reads better than any fictional tale and is just about as hard to believe. With that understanding, let's "give it a go," as they say in jolly old England.

Young Mayer

Mayer Amschel Rothschild started life as the son of an itinerant moneylender and goldsmith named Moses Amschel Bauer who opened a shop on Judenstrasse (Jew Street) in the Jewish ghetto of Frankfort after the birth of his son, Mayer. Moses Amschel Bauer had tired of wandering in Eastern Europe and saw Frankfort as having potential as a stable environment for the upbringing of his son. Hanging above his shop was a sign in the shape of a red shield.

As he grew, son Mayer was notably a gifted and highly intelligent young man. After the death of his father, who had instructed Mayer in all the trade secrets of money lending and the gold trade, Mayer went to work in a bank owned by the **Oppenheimer** family in Hannover, Germany. Mayer's understanding of the banking world earned him a reputation early on and he was able to move up to the position of junior partner. By the 1760's, Mayer was able to return to Frankfort and buy his father's shop. The red shield that his father hung above the door or "rot schilde" in German became the inspiration for Mayer's new family name, which he officially changed to Rothschild.

The Prince and Mayer

Through his friendship with a German general, for whom he had run errands in Hannover, Mayer was able to meet Prince William of Hanau. Because of the Prince's fondness for rare coins and Meyer's ability to acquire such coins, over time he gained enough favor to be able to obtain permission to post on his red shield, the fact that he was a "court factor" or, in other words, that his shop was officially sanctioned and recognized by Prince William himself.

Before we continue further, let us pause for a second and see if we can't recall what is happening around the world in the 1760's. In America, the colonists had just concluded a rather costly war with the French and their Indian allies known as the Seven Year's War. The treaty that was signed prompted the Proclamation of 1763, which stated that the English colonists in North America could not pass a proclamation line west of the Appalachian Mountains.

The British Parliament also felt that the Americans should pay their fair share of the war and initiated the Stamp Tax. Both of these measures set the American colonists and the British Parliament on a collision course that would come to a head ten years later. In 1760, a new English king, George III was seated on the English throne. King George had family ties throughout Europe and especially in Germany, one of those family ties being George's cousin, Prince William of Hanau. This connection would come to benefit the newly named Mayer Rothschild immensely in the years to come.

What would also come to benefit Mayer and his princely counterpart was the social system in Europe that had not changed for over a thousand years. In spite of the technological innovations and scientific knowledge that were spreading across Europe, European landowners and holders of royal titles still held firm to the belief that there were landowners and there were slaves, or, serfs, or peasants as it were. If you had no land, no title, and no royal bloodline, you had no rights aside from what was specifically granted to you by your landowning master. The idea that humans were nothing more than bonded slaves, would also come to benefit Mayer and the Prince in the years to come as the peoples of France and America began to rise up to throw off their chains of bondage.

Prince William of Hanau and Mayer Rothschild had a beautiful symbiotic relationship. Mayer Rothschild was good with money, and Prince William within a few years was going to have more than he knew what to do with. For the time being, that time being the 1770's, Prince William was involved in human trafficking, with a twist. He rented out his peasants as mercenaries to rough up the enemies of any royal court who could afford his fees. One of those courts happened to be that of his cousin, King George III of England. King George was busy in the mid-1770's trying to quash a rebellion in his colonies in America known as the American Revolution. Prince William and Mayer were not only able to profit from the use of William's peasants as cannon fodder. Mayer was also able to increase William's profits by not paying returning soldiers what they had been promised. What were they going to do, sue him?

As we all hopefully will recall, King George's army, Hessians or no, did in fact lose their struggle with the peasant armies in America. In 1781, the British General Cornwallis surrendered at Yorktown in Maryland, and two years later, a peace-treaty was signed in Versailles, France. For our two heroes, however, things were good and were just about to get better. They had made handsome sums off of King George's War. The beautiful thing was, in these new wars, it didn't matter whose side won, because the financiers got paid either way. Mayer Rothschild probably took note of this fact and watched events unfold in the brewing social cauldron that was Europe at the end of the 1700's.

Prince William's father died in 1785 and left his son a vast fortune, a fancy title and more land than you could shake a scepter at. As his right hand man in all dealings financial, Mayer Rothschild became involved in tax collection and property management for some of William's princely properties. He worked in this capacity for fifteen years until he was designated overseer in 1801.

Things had begun to heat up in France a few years earlier, as the peasants suffering from starvation due to consecutive freezing winters, began to turn on their king, Louis XVI. King Louis was in dire straits, because he needed soldiers, such as those supplied by Prince William. The problem was, King Louis had loaned vast amounts to the Americans and they hadn't paid him back. Louis was not only broke he was a poor credit risk as well. Without soldiers loyal to his cause, and his army made up of the peasants he and the nobility had been brutalizing for centuries, King Louis and his noble entourage were destined for the guillotine.

When, five years later, Napoleon, the new Emperor of France and champion of the peasant cause, came waltzing into Frankfort, Mayer "hid" William's money for him, while William high-tailed it out of Germany and off to stay with his wife's relatives in Denmark until things settled down a bit. He entrusted to Mayer the princely amount of 600,000 pounds, an amount estimated to be between three and five million dollars in today's money. While William was in exile, Mayer made out quite well schmoozing it up with the opposition, in particular with Prince Dahlberg, Napoleon's political appointee. In 1810 Mayer was appointed to the Electoral College of Darmstadt. In spite of all of his civic obligations, Mayer was still in the business of making money. Fortunately for him, he had Prince William's cash, which the Prince would not be in need of in the foreseeable future with which he could "play the market," literally.

Nathan corners the London currency market

In the years between taking over his father's business and being appointed to various official capacities of his major sponsor and benefactor, Mayer Rothschild had married and raised five sons. It was his most promising son Nathan, whom he had sent to London, England to open a branch office for the *Rothschild and Sons* money lending institution that was going to be essential in the continuing good fortunes of the Rothschild clan. Mayer sent the Prince's money to Nathan, who, in turn used it to buy 800,000 pounds of gold from the East India Company. That gold was then borrowed by the British Crown to finance Wellington's campaign at Waterloo, Belgium.

Well, in the world of international finance, nothing is simple when there are profits to be made and so it is true with the money that Nathan used to buy East India gold. First, Wellington needed money to pay for his war with Napoleon. Since Wellington didn't have access to the princely sums that Nathan had, he had to buy the gold from Nathan, which he did by the use of promissory notes, a fancy name for an "I.O.U." Nathan then sold the promissory notes to investors, took the cash and bought back his gold back from Wellington. Nathan made a nice profit converting the I.O.U.'s to ready cash and then buying his gold. Nathan then took the gold and sent it to Portugal, where it would be used as the basis for future *Rothschild and Sons* loans. When all was said and done, on the basis of his loans to the British Crown (Wellington), the Rothschilds had amassed a fortune far greater than the fortune of original Rothschild backer and unwitting loan maker, Prince William had left with Mayer for safe-keeping. But that was just the beginning.

The *Rothschild and Sons*, money loaning business occupied offices in London, Paris and Naples. They used their connections in the relatively new Freemason lodges to establish a keen intelligence network throughout Europe, which provided them with information on anything that might have economic, or political repercussions on their current or future investments. In 1815, there was no more looming economic and political event than the upcoming battle of Waterloo in Belgium, upon which no less than England's very existence was at stake.

On the eve of the battle, the Rothschild's spies had sent a special courier to Nathan, who was a key member of the London Stock Exchange. During the three-day battle, Nathan signaled for his agents on the floor to sell all the consuls (English currency) they had in their possession. With the stake of England itself at risk, the traders on the exchange took this as a signal that Nathan's agents had tipped him off about the outcome of the battle, and apparently, things didn't look good for England.

Soon, the value of the consuls depreciated to almost nothing as traders tried to unload them for whatever they could get. Nathan was then able to buy them up for fractions of what he had sold them. It is estimated that he had quadrupled his fortune with the sale of his East India gold to the Crown and then he had made that amount twenty times over in English consuls, of which he was the majority holder. And so, this is why a slightly inebriated Nathan was able to boast that it didn't matter who ruled England, because he owned all the currency. But the Rothschild boys were just getting started.

The French, Italians and the Catholic Banks

The Rothschilds, landless, title-less and Jewish to boot, had been snubbed by the monarchy of France. Once Napoleon was out and the nobility was firmly back in place, they decided to make their financial moves. With the money they made from their success on the British gold and currency markets, they bought as much of the French treasury bonds as they could get their hands on starting in 1817. Because they were buying it in such large quantities, the value of the currency increased year to year until 1818 when the Rothschilds decided to dump it on the market-all at once. Due to the massive inundation of the French currency market with notes payable, the French currency became worthless almost overnight. Subsequently, the French throne, desperately in need of a loan, welcomed the Rothschilds with open arms. Their subsequent takeover of the Italian currency left them the masters of European finance. In 1823, the Rothschilds took over the financial dealings of the Catholic Church and then, with all of European Christendom on their balance sheets, they set their eyes on the biggest prize, and their biggest continuing problem, the new United States

7-2

THE KINGDOM OF GOD

"For I remember the word of God which saith by their works ye shall know them; for if their works be good, then they are good also." (Moroni 7:5)

<u>The Return of the Father and His Son, Jesus Christ</u>

Just as the first, or money kingdom began with the son of a poor, simple man trying to make a better life for his family, so the second Kingdom began in the frontier regions of the early United States. In upstate New York, in the year 1820, at the same time that the banking empire of the Rothschilds was consolidating its hold upon Europe, a young fourteen year-old boy, the son of a poor farmer, found a quiet grove in which to pray.

If the reader will recall, the Protestant Revolution of the early 1500's and the subsequent printing of the Bible into the common languages of Europe had the unforeseen effect of spawning a variety of religious movements as well as a variety of convictions and creeds and all with one common denominator; the unflinching belief that their particular way of worship, of praying, and of God himself were correct, while other beliefs were misguided and their followers were doomed to an eternity of hellfire unless they somehow came to see the light.

At that particular time, in the newly found United States, according to the later accounts of the young boy, there was a religious revival sweeping through the region. Competing for the hearts and minds of the local farmers were Presbyterians, Methodists and Baptists, each promising heaven for their followers and eternal damnation for the followers of the competing sects. Carrying such a heavy burden as the eternal damnation of his soul should he choose the wrong religion, the young boy had been fervently searching the Bible for clues as to which of the local sects was the correct one. According to his account, he read in the Book of James:

"If any of you lack wisdom, let him ask of God, that giveth to all men liberally, and upbraideth not; and it shall be given him." (James 1:5)

Armed with this advice from the Holy Scriptures, the young boy got on his knees in the dense grove of trees. According to his own words, as he began to pray:

"...thick darkness gathered around me and it seemed to me for a time, as if I was doomed to destruction...But exerting all my powers to call upon God to deliver me out of the power of this enemy which had seized upon me, and at that very moment when I was ready to sink into despair and abandon myself to destruction-not to an imaginary ruin, but to the power of some actual being from the unseen world, who had such marvelous power as I had never before felt in any being-just at this moment of great alarm, I saw a pillar of light exactly over my head, above the brightness of the sun, which descended gradually until it fell upon me.

"It no sooner appeared than I found myself delivered from the enemy which held me bound. When the light rested upon me I saw two Personages, whose brightness and glory defy all description, standing above me in the air. One of them spake unto me calling me by name and said, pointing to the other-This is My beloved Son, hear him!

"My object in going to inquire of the Lord was to know which of all sects was right, that I might know which to join. No sooner, therefore, did I get possession of myself, so as to be able to speak, than I asked the Personages who stood above me in the light, which of all the sects was right (for at this time it had never entered into my head that they were all wrong)-and which I should join.

"I was answered that I must join none of them, for they were all wrong; and the personage who addressed me said that all their creeds were an abomination in his sight; that those professors were all corrupt; that: they draw near to me with their lips, but their hearts are far from me, they teach for doctrines the commandments of men, having a form of godliness, but they deny the power thereof."

(JS History 15-19)

Three years later, in the year 1823, the same year the Rothschilds took over financial operations of the Catholic Church, the same young boy began to pray at his bedside in the humble cabin where he lived with his father, mother and three brothers. He later related the following occurrence:

"A personage appeared by my bedside, standing in the air, for his feet did not touch the floor."

Joseph Smith goes on to describe the figure as being clothed in a robe of; "most exquisite whiteness, it was a whiteness beyond anything earthly I had ever seen nor do I believe any earthly thing could be made to appear so exceedingly white and brilliant. He called me by name, and said that he was sent from the presence of God to me and that his name was Moroni; that God had a work for me to do, and that my name should be had for good and evil among all nations, kindreds and tongues or that it should be both good and evil spoken of among all people. He said there was a book deposited, written upon gold plates, giving an account of the former inhabitants of this continent and the source from which they sprang. He also said the fullness of the everlasting gospel was contained in it, as delivered by the Savior to the ancient inhabitants, also that there were two stones in silver bows-and these stones, fastened to a breastplate, which constituted what is called the Urim and Thummim-deposited with the plates and the possession and use of these stones constituted Seers in ancient of former times; and that God had prepared them for the purpose of translating the book." (Testimony of the Prophet Joseph Smith)

The Golden Plates

Four years after his initial visitations, Joseph Smith received the Golden Plates. On September, 22, 1827, "the same heavenly messenger delivered them up to me with this charge: that I should be responsible for them, that if I should let them go carelessly, or through any neglect of mine, that I should be cut off, but that if I should use all of my endeavors to preserve them, until he, the messenger should call for them, they should be protected." Joseph Smith goes on to recount the various efforts that were made to get the plates from him. "For no sooner was it known that I had them, then the most strenuous exertions were used to get them from me. Every stratagem that could be invented was resorted to for that purpose.

The persecution became more bitter than before, and multitudes were on the alert continually to get them from me if possible."

So where are the plates? Joseph Smith explains that, "Once the translation was completed, the plates were given back to the Angel Moroni who possesses them to this day."

7-3

MAMMON AND THE FEDERAL RESERVE BANK

"The government should create, issue and circulate all the currency, creating and issuing money is the supreme prerogative of government. Adopting these principles will save the taxpayers immense sums of interest"

-Thomas Jefferson

Money for nothing: the Rothschild bankers and the United States

While the impoverished Joseph Smith was struggling against the persecution and the stratagems of those who wished to obtain the ancient records for themselves, the agents of international finance were hard at work against their own sworn enemy, President Andrew Jackson, who refused to renew the charter of the Bank of the United States.

What Bank of the United States? In order to sum up a somewhat complicated sidelight to our story, we must jump back a few years in time to the conclusion of the American Revolution. The new country, known as the United States of America, had emerged from the Revolution heavily indebted to countries such as France, as well as to its own citizens and soldiers. Because the Congress had issued millions of notes called "colonials," thanks to the printing press, all of the "colonial" notes would be due to be redeemed for gold or silver in 1791.

Unfortunately, because the United States had no money to meet its financial obligations, Secretary of the Treasury Alexander Hamilton proposed a "United States Bank." The bank was a clever scheme to create the illusion of a solid currency backed by gold, silver and foreign currency that was actually worth something. Basically, the new "bank" would sell ten million dollars worth of stock. The U.S. Government would buy two million dollars worth of the stock and sell the other eight million to private investors. The private investors would have to buy one quarter of their shares in either gold or silver and the rest in acceptable notes. President George Washington was extremely hesitant to grant the charter, most likely because it was in direct conflict with the newly ratified Constitution of the United States, which specifically states:

"Congress shall have the power...To coin Money, to regulate the value thereof, and of foreign coin..." (Article 8, Section 5 U.S. Constitution).

Political wrangling however, along with an agreement to place the new U.S. capitol in the Southern State of Washington's Virginia, and name it after him, finally swayed Washington to endorse and sign the charter.

The United States had no gold, silver or acceptable notes of its own (if you will recall, virtually the only acceptable notes in Europe would be controlled by the Rothschilds within the next twenty-five years). The only gold or silver the bank owned was that which was used to pay for one quarter of each private investor's share. This ultimately meant that *the bank had the power to create money out of nothing*, with the exception of the two million in gold, silver and acceptable currency it had garnered from its private investors. In turn, the bank could loan the money it printed, at interest.

The first problem with the newly established "government" bank was that the U.S. Government didn't have two million dollars to buy their shares. Thanks to the clever Alexander Hamilton, that problem could be easily remedied. To solve the government's cash-flow problem, the bank would "loan" the money to the government to buy its shares. Things worked out fairly well for the new bank until 1795, when the bank's directors became nervous about the two million dollars owed it by the U.S. Government. With no way to come up with the cash, the government was forced to sell its shares to private investors, whereby the First Bank of the United States became a privately owned bank, in direct violation of the Constitution.

Money for nothing?

If I may interrupt here for one second to point out, in case it is not obvious to the reader, the sheer malfeasance of this whole money printing scheme. It is important to do so here because it will become a continuing trend in this ongoing argument between the international financiers and their few opponents until 1913, when the financiers will ultimately triumph by their creation of the United States Federal Reserve Bank. Because the First Bank of the United States was able to print money for nothing and then sell it for an added percentage of its value, the stockholders in the bank, in exchange for depositing their gold and silver as the price for their shares (which could be sold at any time at no loss to the shareholder) stood to make as much money as they could possibly print and sell to member banks.

A more easily understood analogy of how this works is if you were to go to your back yard and pick up a bunch of rocks, write "U.S." on them and then give them to someone with the promise that they would return those rocks to you, plus a few more "U.S." rocks, which you call "interest." You would explain to your cohorts that they in turn could give out those rocks under the same conditions, but could charge whatever "interest" they felt like charging.

Then you would make a law in the town that nobody could buy or sell anything without the use of the rocks with the "U.S." stamp. If someone were to ask you why this rock is worth anything, you could reply, "Because the government says it is." The only limit to how much money you could make would be the number of rocks that you put into the market and the interest you were charging for those rocks. The only limit to your fortune would be the number of people to whom you could sell your rocks and the number of rocks you had access to. Since rocks are slightly harder to come by than paper (remember the printing press) and harder to carry, if you could use paper as a substitute, you would have a fortune in no time.

Even better, is the fact that in order to pay that interest on your free money, someone, somewhere, has to actually work to make or sell something to get more rocks to pay for the rocks they borrowed. Once you have enough money, or rocks, you can buy those companies or at least controlling interest in them and tell those workers exactly what you are willing to pay them. If they don't like it, or the company refuses your advances, you can buy the competitor's company, undercut the first company's prices and throw the lot of them out of work. Even better than that, is that the same thing works with entire countries, especially democracies.

Why would democracies be so vulnerable to your scheme? In democracies, where people vote for their leaders, they vote for those leaders for three reasons. The first reason is that the people agree with what the politician says, or stands for. The second reason the people vote for a politician is that they vote for whoever will provide the most benefits for the local population. Third, people vote for the politician that they hear the most favorable stories about. Therefore, for two of the three reasons, the politician is dependent upon you and your vast financial resources you have garnered from your money, or rock-printing scheme. The politicians need to get their message out, and because of your rock scheme where everyone is working for you, over time you either own or control through stock or advertising, quite a few newspapers, TV stations, radio stations and magazines (not to mention book publishers!). The politicians also need to have favorable stories told about them in the press. As luck would have it, you can help them out in that regard as well. Finally, the zinger is in the fact that a politician who gets into office and starts suggesting raising taxes and/or cutting spending and the resulting bacon they have been bringing home, will be committing political suicide.

Instead, they will come up with all kinds of crazy schemes to borrow money from you, once they have spent all they have taken in. And what if they don't? You just put more rocks out on the market by charging less rocks in return, the resulting inflation will mean that all prices will need to be adjusted upwards, which means the government will need more money. Once you are collecting interest from the government on a national scale, it is only a matter of time before you control the government, the nation and the people, which I think is what Nathan Rothschild was alluding to.

Of course, at some point in time, people are going to realize that because of your clever scheme, your financial holdings and your control of all aspects of the economy to include the government, you are beginning to accumulate all of the wealth and power. As the poet John Donne once said, "No man is an island." So, what you need are people working for you who are loyal to your cause (becoming richer and more powerful) and who will deny that they have any involvement with you. But that is a matter we will discuss sometime down the road, so let us continue with our story.

Thomas Jefferson, the U.S. Bank and the Louisiana Purchase

In 1803, the French Revolution was making great progress. Napoleon Bonaparte had taken on the title of Emperor of France, which kind of went against the reasons for having the revolution in the first place, but those who may have protested, like the famous philosopher Robespierre, had already contributed their heads to the guillotine bucket. Like every civilization that had gone before, when faced with outside or inside threats, the strong man is always the People's choice. Napoleon was not so much a strong man, but a man who understood modern warfare, at least as far as the early 1800's was concerned. His philosophy was best summed up in his saying, "God is on the side of the big battalions."

In the 16 year-old United States, President Thomas Jefferson saw a potential threat from the "Little Corporal" should he decide to string the English lines thin with another war in North America. The fledgling country and its Declaration-of-Independence-writing-President had to do something to avoid this eventuality which would prove disastrous should such a thing occur. The United States Government still had not made good on its commitments with its own bank. When the federal government had tried to raise the funds to make good on its bargain with the bank by taxing the one pleasure available to the poor rural farmers of the nation, whiskey and property, a rebellion had broken out in Pennsylvania and another in New Hampshire. Quelling the rebellions had cost the government even more money so that, with no credit from its own bank, the U.S. could not possibly afford to take sides in such a war.

President Jefferson and his advisors saw a way out in a win-win situation for both sides. He sent emissaries to France to convince Napoleon to sell France's claim to the Louisiana Territory. Luckily for the Americans, Napoleon did not trust the international financiers of Europe and did not want his future staked upon their willingness to provide him with loans. Instead of borrowing for his planned campaigns in Europe, Napoleon saw his own and the salvation of his Revolution through the sale of the Louisiana Territory to the Americans. It was the perfect way to add gold to his coffers while staying out of debt to the financiers of Europe. Using the vast tract of land that occupied nearly a third of what is now the continental United States as collateral the U.S. government bought the Louisiana Territory while the Bank of the United States was tasked with overseeing the purchase.

In the end, the Louisiana Territory was not actually sold to France. Instead it was sold to the Baring Bank in England, who financed the transaction through the sale of bonds to European investors. Baring then transferred the gold to Napoleon's account for eighty eight cents on the dollar while the Americans (the U.S. Bank) were liable for the total amount of fifteen million dollars, plus the interest that was accruing on the bonds (I.O.U.'s) that had been issued to investors. In more simple terms, the U.S. government had actually pawned land that it didn't even own to the bonds traders in England.

Nearly ten years later in 1811, the charter of the First Bank of the United States ran out and failed to be renewed by one vote in the House of Representatives and in the Senate. The Vice President's deciding vote killed the First Bank of the United States. The following year, the furious Rothschild controlled England declared war on the United States, sailed up the Potomac and burned the White House. With no money to finance the War or the peace, currency was being printed once again by state governments with no limit, and inflation was threatening the country as it had done after the Revolution. President Madison and Secretary of the Treasury Albert Gallatin pushed a bill through Congress for the formation of the Second Bank of the United States. They had been working since 1808, prior to the First Bank's charter being up for renewal, in order to avoid the unpleasant consequences that seemed to befall the United States whenever it was lacking a nationally endorsed, foreign financed money printing industry.

In 1816, a charter was granted to the Second Bank of the United States, which was doing a booming business. The sale of the new land acquired from the Louisiana Purchase had created a bubble in the real estate market. Borrowing with little, and sometimes no money down, speculators were making money hand over fist, while the price of land doubled in the new territories and sometimes tripled. The land bubble finally burst when European investors, who had bought the bonds issued to the Baring brothers by the First Bank of the U.S. to finance the Louisiana Purchase, demanded payment of four million dollars in interest payments, not in the paper they had issued, but in gold and silver.

The Second Bank of the United States, which had "forgotten" to make its payments to the Louisiana investors during the boom, in turn were forced to call in the loans they had made, not in paper currency but also in gold and silver. The immediate contraction of credit caused many land speculators, like future President of the United States, Andrew Jackson, the hero of New Orleans, to suffer near financial devastation and ruin as they lost their property and still owed money on their loans.

Jackson Takes Action

When Andrew Jackson became President in 1828, he refused to have anything to do with the Second Bank of the United States and its Director Nicholas Biddle, who had begun applying for a renewal of its charter in 1832, four years before it was due to expire. Jackson vetoed the bill extending the charter, which began a conflict between Jackson and the pro-bank forces. In 1833, Jackson ordered his Secretary of the Treasury to pull government money out of the bank and distribute it to state banks. When his Treasury Secretary refused to comply, Jackson re-appointed him as Secretary of State. His replacement, who also appeared to be dragging his heels, was fired and was replaced with Attorney General Roger B. Taney, who complied with Jackson's wishes. To fight back, Biddle tightened the nation's money supply once again in an effort to force Jackson to renew the charter. Raising the price of the free money caused another financial crises but Jackson remained steadfast.

On January 30, 1835, one year before the charter of the bank was set to expire, Richard Lawrence, an unemployed house painter from England, attempted to assassinate Jackson by firing first one and then another pistol at Jackson, both of which misfired. Lawrence blamed Jackson for his economic woes, stating, that with the President dead, "money would be more plenty." There were some attempts to keep the Second Bank of the United States alive, including the "Panic of 1837" but, having lost its biggest depositor, the bank was doomed to fail, which it did in 1841.

CHAPTER 8

THE KINGDOM OF GOD GOES TO WAR

"And it shall come in a day when the blood of the saints shall cry unto the Lord because of secret combinations and works of darkness." (Mormon 8:27)

The Gathering

In 1830, while Andrew Jackson was beginning his fight against the United States Bank and the international financiers in Washington, the Church of Jesus Christ of Latter-day Saints was officially formed in a simple log cabin in upstate New York, subsequent to the printing of the first edition of the Book of Mormon. Once the Church was officially founded, new members were immediately ordained to the Priesthood and encouraged to leave their homes and farms to serve as missionaries in order to teach and recruit new members in the U.S., Europe, the Pacific Islands and Central and South America. Most of the new converts, convinced that they were laying the foundation for the literal Kingdom of God on earth, which would be arriving at some point in the not-too-distant future, willingly complied. With little more than the clothes on their backs, and copies of the Bible and the Book of Mormon in their knapsacks, they left their families behind to face unknown hardships in unfamiliar lands and territories.

The missionaries preached a gospel that was centered on these fundamental beliefs of the new church, or what are known as the *Articles of Faith*:

1) We believe in God the Eternal Father and in His Son Jesus Christ, and in the Holy Ghost.

2) We believe that all men will be punished for their own sins and not for Adam's transgression.

3) We believe that through the Atonement of Christ, all mankind may be saved, by obedience to the laws and ordinances of the gospel.

4) We believe that the first principles and ordinances of the gospel are: first, Faith in the Lord Jesus Christ; second, Repentance; third, Baptism by immersion for the remission of their sins; Fourth, Laying on of hands for the gift of the Holy Ghost.

5) We believe that a man must be called of God, by prophecy, and by the laying on of hands, by those who are in authority, to preach the gospel and administer the ordinances thereof.

6) We believe in the same organization that existed in the Primitive Church, namely, apostles, prophets, pastors, teachers, evangelists and so forth.

7) We believe in the gift of tongues, prophecy, revelation, visions, healing, interpretation of tongues and so forth.

8) We believe the Bible to be the Word of God, as far as it is translated correctly. We also believe the Book of Mormon to be the Word of God.

9) We believe all that God has revealed, all that God does now reveal and we believe the He will yet reveal many great and important things pertaining to the Kingdom of God.

10) We believe in the literal gathering of Israel and in the Restoration of the Ten Tribes; that Zion (The New Jerusalem) will be built upon this, the American Continent; that Christ will reign personally upon the earth, and, that the earth will be renewed and receive its paradisiacal glory.

11) We claim the privilege of worshipping the Almighty God according to the dictates of our own conscience, and allow all men the same privilege, let them worship how, where, or what they may.

12) We believe in being subjects to kings, presidents, rulers and magistrates, in obeying, honoring and sustaining the law.

13) We believe in being honest, true, chaste, benevolent, and virtuous and in doing good to all men; indeed, we may say we follow the admonition of Paul-We believe all things, we hope all things, we have endured many things and we hope to be able to endure all things. If there is anything virtuous, lovely, or of good report or praiseworthy, we seek after these things. (*History of the Church*)

In the Protestant countries of Northern Europe, the news that God and Jesus Christ had returned and with them, they had returned the fullness of the gospel of Jesus Christ to the young son of an American farmer was big news in the sprawling cities of the industrializing countries of England, Scotland, Sweden, Germany, Norway Finland and Denmark. Curious people flocked to hear the messages of the LDS missionaries in private homes, town halls and even churches, where they were asked to preach by local ministers. It was not long however, before local religious leaders began to see a massive migration of their flocks as thousands sold livestock, homes and possessions in order to partake in the building of the New Zion in America. Once the ministers of the Anglican, Presbyterian and Methodist Churches realized the threat the message from the Church had upon their congregations and livelihoods, their receptiveness to the Church began to change. In the Pacific Islands of Hawaii and Samoa, the LDS missionaries were able to convert entire villages. Even in Mexico and South America, where the Catholic Church was dominant, the news that a record of their ancestors and their covenants with the ancient White God had been found, led to thousands of conversions among the Latin American peoples.

From the 1830's to the 1860's, thousands of European immigrants began to flood into the eastern seaport cities of Boston and New York on their way west to join their brothers and sisters in the Latter-Day Saint Church in the West in the frontier regions of Ohio, Illinois and Missouri. As we have seen in the Latter-day Saint Articles of Faith, the reason for the movement westward towards Missouri was because of the LDS belief that the New Jerusalem would be built upon the American continent, or, to be more specific, it would be built in Jackson County, Missouri.

The First "Mormon War" Misery in Missouri

In the early days of the United States and the LDS Church, the State of Missouri still constituted a sparsely settled territory. It was populated mainly with immigrants from the Southern States. Many who planned on extending plantation society with its accompanying slavery into the new territory. The new anti-slavery Latter-day Saints were as welcome in Missouri as ants at a picnic.

There were a few attempts at starting colonies in the counties surrounding Caldwell County, Missouri, where the LDS Church had received a charter. But the attempts at starting new colonies outside of Caldwell County went against the recommendations of the leadership of the LDS Church particularly Joseph Smith. In the outlying regions, the new LDS settlers were met with violent opposition from the local residents, who had long feared "Mormon" expansion from Caldwell County where they had assured the local residents that they would remain.

Fearing that their expansion would not only dominate local commerce but politics as well, the first conflict to erupt occurred at the polling station in Gallatin, in Daviess County, just south of Caldwell County. The Latter-day Saints who showed up at the polling station to vote were immediately confronted by a group of locals who told them their right to vote was, "no more than Negroes." A fight broke out in which the outnumbered Mormons appear to have gained the upper hand. This was the first in a series of running battles between members of the LDS Church and local mobs, militias and vigilantes.

The violence against the Latter-day Saints prompted Missouri Governor Lilliburn Boggs to issue his now infamous "Extermination Order" against members of the LDS Church. The violence of the vigilante mobs culminated in the "Haun's Mill Massacre," where eighteen LDS men and boys were killed in a gun battle after they had taken cover in a workshop that afforded them little protection against the bullets of their assailants.

Following the incident at Haun's Mill on October 29, 1838, Joseph Smith and the rest of the outnumbered Missouri LDS group fought a few skirmishes, but with little success against the Missouri State Militia, they retreated to Far West, Missouri where the State militia surrounded them. The Saints asked for the terms of their surrender and were told that the only acceptable conditions were; the confiscation of their property, their removal from the state and the arrest of Joseph Smith. Smith was incarcerated overnight and the order was given that he be executed the following morning. The man given the order to execute Joseph Smith, General Alexander William Doniphan, refused to carry it out and Joseph Smith escaped with the rest of the Mormon Militia.

Nauvoo

The Saints left Missouri and gathered on the eastern bank of the Mississippi River in the town of Commerce, which they promptly renamed Nauvoo, Illinois. In contrast to the debacle in Missouri, the new settlement of Nauvoo became a thriving metropolis almost overnight as the members arrived from Missouri as well as the new converts from Europe. In Nauvoo, they once again set out to build their "New Zion."

Many of the new members were from Europe's working classes. They were tradesmen, carpenters, masons, wheelwrights and blacksmiths. Once established in Nauvoo, they set to work plying their trades and doing a brisk business with the people moving up and down the Mississippi River. Soon, penniless immigrants found themselves wealthier than they could have ever imagined in their home countries.

Almost immediately, construction began on a temple, or, a House of the Lord, as Joseph Smith and his young assistant, Brigham Young called it. To understand the LDS Church, either then or now, it is imperative to understand that, in the minds and hearts of the members of the newly founded church, they had individually been chosen by God, to do no less than what the Children of Israel three thousand years ago had done when they entered Palestine carrying their God in an ark before them. The new Saints would carry that same powerful God with them and He would dwell in their temples wherever they settled. Even more importantly, the President of the Church, or Joseph Smith, was no less than a new Moses, who received direct instructions from God for the building of his Kingdom. In no time, the new settlement at Nauvoo was the envy of all cities up and down the river and, with the new wealth, came new suspicions from their neighbors.

At the time, the western regions were mostly unsettled and those that chose to live there did so for their own independence, or to get a fresh start in the new country. To the non-LDS residents, the Mormon city in Nauvoo had three strikes against it. The first strike was that Nauvoo had grown so fast, its population would soon dominate politics in Illinois (Joseph Smith, in a desperate attempt to save the Saints from corrupt politicians and vigilantes would run for president of the United States in 1844). The second strike was the power and wealth that seemed to be concentrating itself into the hands of the Church leaders. The outsiders failed to see the distinction between the Church and Joseph Smith, who seemed to control every aspect of the Saint's lives.

The third strike or reason people were suspicious, had to do with the Latter-day Saint religion itself. If you will recall, Joseph Smith's saga began when he started to doubt the sincerity of the other churches that were then in existence. His claim that Jesus Christ had told him the other churches were an, "abomination," whether true or not was not a claim that would win him favor with the local Baptist, Methodist and Presbyterian clergy. This admission alone would probably cost Joseph Smith some popularity votes, if not his life. But, to add to the disparity was Joseph Smith's claim that he had translated golden plates that no one else could see but his two assistants, and that they had been given back to the angel who gave them to him. Finally, all of this was done in order to organize a Church that Joseph Smith claimed was the "true" church of Jesus Christ. It is at least understandable that skeptics, as well as the preachers and pastors of the day might have had a few words to say to their congregations about the "Mormons" as they began to be called, that most likely were less than flattering.

The Assassination and the Exodus

Joseph Smith was murdered in 1844 while he was incarcerated in the jail in Carthage, Illinois, the county seat. He had been lured out of Nauvoo to answer charges and post bail for the insidious charge of "inciting a riot." But the forces of darkness and the people of Illinois would conspire to commit a crime that could never be fully covered up, though we will soon see that every attempt was made to do so. Following the assassination of the Latter-day Saint Prophet Joseph Smith, Brigham Young was named President of the Church. The animosity towards "the Mormons" did not subside, nor did the Latter-day Saint Church, as many had hoped. The new Latter-day Saint Prophet, Brigham Young, a hardworking carpenter and

Freemason, was completely unlike his predecessor. Where Joseph Smith had been soft-spoken and an intellectual in his approach, Brigham Young was a from a working class background who was forceful and direct when it came to the leadership of the Church. He ran the Latter-day Saint Church as a foreman would run a construction site.

When the non-Mormon communities around Nauvoo realized the death of Joseph Smith would not break up the church, the various mobs and other groups hostile to the Church decided their best plan of action was an all-out war against the Saints. An arms race began in which both sides acquired guns, powder, ammunition and cannon for the war. Shortly after the dedication of the Nauvoo Temple in 1846, Brigham Young, realized they would never have peace in Illinois. He advised the Saints to pack everything they could fit on wagons and carts. They would go to the West to find a new place to build their Zion where their enemies could not burn their homes and farms and murder their sons, fathers, mothers and daughters.

In the freezing cold in the winter of 1846, the entire community of Saints left the comfort of their homes in Nauvoo and headed across the prairie to a place that Brigham Young had told them existed out in the Rocky Mountains where they would be safe from the mobs. After many deaths, hardships and starvation, the Saints reached the Salt Lake Valley in August of 1847.

Immediately, the Latter-day Saints went to work planting and irrigating the Valley. Brigham Young and the leaders of the Church began the business of setting up the community. They surveyed and partitioned land. They appointed work parties to build houses and places for storage. To make the journey easier for the Saints who would follow, they sent work parties back along the route to construct dwellings and shelters, and plant crops for the Saints that would soon be making the journey from the Eastern United States, Great Britain and Europe. Until the railroad was finally completed at Promontory Point in 1869, thousands of converts from the United States and Europe would pass along what came to be known as "the Mormon trail."

First, they would come in wagons pulled by oxen and later; they would come by handcart, pulling all of their worldly possessions across the plains and then up and down the treacherous passes through the Rocky Mountains. Many died along that trail, but many more would make the passage and come to the very spot in Immigrant Canyon just outside of Salt Lake City where, Brigham Young had once declared, "This is the place where we will make Saints."

The Mexican War, the Nauvoo Legion and the '49ers

The United States Government was in a precarious position when it came to the Latter-day Saint movement. First of all, it was political suicide to appear to be on the side of the Saints when it came to their conflicts with local inhabitants. The Church's official adoption of the Old Testament policy of plural marriage had outraged the majority of the country, who believed whatever outlandish stories about the "Mormons" and their practice of polygamy that came their way. Second, the control that both Joseph Smith and Brigham Young had over the Saints, who had shown themselves not only willing but capable of defending themselves, meant that where ever they went, they were a traveling economic, political and military machine who appeared to outsiders to be loyal to their "Prophet" first and the government second.

Unfortunately, in 1847, the U.S. government had bigger fish to fry. After the fiasco at **the Alamo** in Mexican territory, the U.S. was more worried about a conflict with Mexico than a seemingly bizarre religious sect that no one seemed to know anything about. Mexico was threatening to exert a four hundred year old Spanish claim from Mexico to Alaska to thwart the white settlers who were claiming the Western territories, like Texas and California, for the United States.

The U.S. government, under the cry of "Manifest Destiny," realized the need of ready troops to exert the United States claims to the land in the West. Unfortunately, the government was in no condition to mobilize for the war that had been thrust upon it by a few zealous frontiersmen who had gone to Mexican Territory and picked a fight with the Mexican government. The United States government knew there were troops available in the highly disciplined Latter-day Saint **Nauvoo Legion** who were already trained and experienced under fire. After the Saints had successfully crossed the Mississippi, Army leaders had approached

Brigham Young and asked for five thousand men for whom they would pay the Church directly.

After all that they had suffered at the hands of the United States and its "legal" system, Brigham Young, who was also desperately in need of cash for the journey, made a brief speech to a the men of the Legion. Shortly after discussions with wives, fathers and mothers, five thousand young LDS men fell out for duty with the United States Army. They marched to Texas, but by the time they reached there, the Mexican General, **Santa Ana**, had already been defeated and the terms of the peace were being ironed out.

With Texas secured, the "**Mormon Battalion**," as they were known, marched onward to California in order to garrison forts in the newly won territory. Some of them made it all the way to San Francisco, California, where, upon their release from service, they elected to find work in the local economy. Some of the members of the Mormon Battalion took jobs cutting lumber at a place called Sutter's Mill. It was their discovery of gold there in 1849 that began the California Gold rush. In turn, the massive westward migration of "49ers" was to be a major boon to the Latter-day Saints in the Salt Lake Valley, who were able to sell cattle, tools, wood and food to the prospectors on their way across the Rocky Mountains.

The Second "Mormon War"

The occupation of the Salt Lake Valley was, like the LDS Church itself, a two-edged sword as far as the US government was concerned. On the one hand, it meant that the wastelands of Utah, southern Idaho and Arizona, where Brigham Young had ordered the Saints to start settlements, would be occupied and therefore in need of territorial government. Territorial governments would secure and establish order in the land for the United States' expansion westward, which had begun on a massive scale in the 1840's. The well-organized, industrious Latter-day Saints had already established order in the territories in which they had begun to build communities. They had good relations with the Native Americans, whom they called their "Lamanite brothers," and provided the government with accurate geographic knowledge of the land. If the Saints would submit to federal control, their settlement of the Utah Territory would be advantageous for the United States.

From the Latter-day Saint perspective, the Saints had suffered at the hands of the territorial governors like Ford of Illinois and Boggs of Missouri. There, they had issued repeated pleas for help on the local and national level against the mob, militia and vigilante atrocities committed by their Christian brethren with no avail. Under the "protection" of the Illinois governor, Joseph Smith had been murdered. The protection of the government was tantamount to a death sentence to the LDS Church. Therefore, the Latter-day Saints had no intention of settling the new territory only to have a repeat of the Missouri and Illinois calamities befall them. In simple terms, the Latter-day Saints were not about to surrender their lives and homes again to another corrupt governor on behalf of the United States Government. In the Salt Lake Valley, if it came to that point, the Latter-day Saints were determined to make their last stand.

By 1857, the Latter-day Saints had struggled for ten years in the arid regions of the Great Salt Lake, irrigating, farming and building. Memories of their treatment at the hands of "non-believers" were still fresh in their minds, as was the brutal crossing they had made in the dead of winter in 1846-47. Thousands of Saints had made the crossing in the following years and thousands more were arriving every month. In the Salt Lake Valley, the Saints were beginning to prosper. Surprisingly, it was this prosperity, next to mob violence and the encroachment of non-believers on the territory, which was one of the biggest fears of Church President Brigham Young. Young felt that economic success would distract the Saints from their mission of building up a place where the Saints could live in peace apart from the temptations of the outside world. After the disasters in Missouri and Illinois, in which they had worked so hard to build homes and farms, Young had no intention of once again giving up the ground they believed God had chosen for them to either external, or internal threats.

Oddly enough, it was the politics of slavery in the 1850's that were going to have adverse effects on the destiny of the Saints in the Salt Lake Valley. The **Compromise of 1850** and the **Kansas Nebraska Act** were attempts to settle the issue of slavery in the newly settled territories. The Compromise of 1850 gave individual states the right to determine, by popular vote, whether or not they would allow the practice of slavery. Though the legislation had been passed with the institution of slavery in mind, anti-slavery Republicans in Congress argued that under the new laws, the "Mormons," who abhorred slavery, but practiced polygamy, were protected under the new laws. The practice of polygamy was seen as repugnant to the rest of the nation and was one more political tool to incite the United States citizenry against both the "Mormons" and the advocates of slavery.

Brigham Young's Reformation

In 1856, ten years after their departure from Nauvoo and the East, more and more emigrant trains were pushing through to the Oregon and California territories. Brigham Young, fearing the complacency of the Saints and a tendency towards "backsliding" to their days before they had taken on the LDS covenants of baptism, began to take measures to secure their spiritual and temporal safety. To secure their "stake," President Brigham Young announced a Reformation in an attempt to re-instill and remind the Latter-day Saints of the reasons they had left Nauvoo in the first place. The reaction on the part of the Saints was a re-invigoration of faith in their God, their leaders and in their status as the "Chosen People" of the latter days. The other result of Brigham Young's Reformation was a deep-seated mistrust of outsiders and non-believers. In January of 1857, the

Nauvoo Legion was reformed and a "siege mentality" once again began to instill the old fears of violence and persecution of Missouri and Illinois.

Confrontation of the Kingdoms

Fearing the new militarism in the Salt Lake Valley, three federal officials, a US Marshall, a disreputable judge and a federally appointed surveyor fled the territory. They brought to U.S. President and Freemason, James Buchanan, news of harassment, fraud, theft and the destruction of court records. Buchanan's friend and substantial campaign contributor was August Belmont, a German Jew, who immigrated to the U.S. during the Panic of 1837 to iron out the Rothschild's business interests. Through donations to both parties and candidates, Belmont had managed to secure an appointment as a U.S. representative to The Hague in Holland where he had befriended Buchanan. While at The Hague, the Rothschild agent had recommended annexing Cuba as a slave state, which led to his being denied the post of Ambassador to Spain (Spain still owned Cuba) upon

Buchanan's election. Still, August Belmont carried influence with the newly inaugurated President Buchanan both politically and financially.

Buchanan's response to the anti-slavery Latter-day Saints was quick and decisive. Based upon the exaggerated accounts of the three officials, President Buchanan's first act in office on March 4, 1857 was to mobilize 2,500 federal troops and send them West against the Latter-day Saints in Utah. President Buchanan gave orders that the Army install the new, federally appointed governor, Alfred Cumming, by force if necessary. The Army was also ordered to establish an outpost near Salt Lake City, whereby the Federal Government via the U.S. Army, would enforce law in the territory. The Latter-day Saints in the Salt Lake Valley, already bristling as a by-product of Brigham Young's Reformation, knew only what they read in the exaggerated reports in newspapers that came out of the East. Buchanan's failure to communicate his intentions directly to Brigham Young reaffirmed both Young's and the Latter-day Saints' conviction that the army was coming with orders to wipe them out once and for all.

Act 1: The Fancher Party, Wrong People, Wrong Place, Wrong Time

In April of 1857, just three months after the marching orders for the Army had been issued, a party of 140 emigrants consisting of men, women and children, known as the **Fancher Party**, left western Arkansas heading for California. They set out on the southern trail, which would make it necessary for to cross through southern Utah. In the same month, an outraged husband murdered one of the Church's Apostles, a man by the name of Parley P. Pratt, in Arkansas after his wife ran off with Pratt. In June, news of Pratt's murder reached Utah where the Saints were busy preparing for a war with the forces of the United States Army. The murder of a Church leader, no matter what the circumstances, served to refresh in the minds of the Latter-day Saints the murder of their first Prophet, Joseph Smith in Illinois. Pratt's murder seemed to raise the intensity level of the conflict significantly.

A month later, in July of 1857, the US Army left Kansas in their march westward toward the Salt Lake Valley. Brigham Young was tipped off by Joseph Smith's former bodyguard, a hard drinking gunfighter named **Porter Rockwell** about the movements of the soldiers from Kansas.

Brigham Young, upon hearing the news, immediately declared martial law. In the minds of the Latter-day Saints, the war with the United States had officially begun. One of the stipulations of the order of martial law was that no emigrant trains would be allowed to pass through the territory without Young's permission. Brigham Young's pronouncement would lead to events and accusations regarding a tragedy that remains unsettled to this day.

In September, after five months on the trail, the Fancher party from Arkansas reached **Cedar City**, some 250 miles south of Salt Lake City. Unaware of Young's declaration of martial law, members of the party made the mistake of trying to goad the Latter-day Saints in Cedar City by claiming to have the pistol that killed Joseph Smith. Local elements of the Nauvoo Legion were unsure what to do with them. Some feared they might be scouting a southern route for the Army.

Whatever was the case, they were the wrong people saying the wrong things in the wrong place at the wrong time. The members of the Nauvoo Legion in Cedar City, according to the Church, took the matter into their own hands and assaulted the party disguised as their accomplices, some members of the local Paiute Indian tribe. The skirmish led to a stand-off that was broken when the two of the party, attempting to steal horses, were discovered and shot at, resulting in the death of one of the young men. The survivor of the skirmish made his way back to the siege and informed the rest of the party that their assailants were "Mormons" and not Indians as they had assumed.

Fearing the backlash of an enraged nation once the word got out, the decision was made to kill the entire party with the exception of the young children. A truce was negotiated, whereby the LDS Militia would allow the party to walk out of the Territory, but members of the party would have to leave their wagons and livestock behind. The party was then divided into columns and told to march. Once they reached a place called **Mountain Meadows**, the members of the militia, as well as their Native American co-conspirators, turned and fired into the line of settlers. Of the 140 of the original Fancher party who started the journey, 120 died that tragic day.

There is no way to prove or disprove the exact version of what exactly happened that led to the **Mountain Meadows Massacre** in September of

1857. All emigrant trains were supposed to get direct permission from Brigham Young before being allowed into the territory, therefore, many claim that Young did know about the Fancher Party and ordered their execution. Church officials claim to this day that what happened at Mountain Meadows was a direct violation of church law and was the result of overzealous local commanders. Whatever the truth of the matter is went to the grave with Brigham Young.

Buchanan's Blunder

The military campaign, later dubbed "Buchanan's Blunder," was fraught with disaster. The Mormons had fortified Echo Canyon, which they assumed would be the most likely place for the Army to pass through to gain access to the Salt Lake Valley. Meanwhile, the Army quartermaster, an Army captain by the name of Van Vliet, was sent into the Territory with a letter stating that the Captain was to be provided with provisions for the Army from the Saints.

Captain Van Vliet was sympathetic to the "Mormons," and was in turn respected by them. While delivering his message to Brigham Young, he told the LDS Prophet, "The Mormons have been lied about worse than any people I ever saw." Brigham Young, in turn, wanted information about the Army. Specifically he wanted to know if the Army was preparing an assault on the valley and if they were coming for him personally. When Van Vliet replied that the Army was merely there to install the new governor, the LDS leader breathed a brief sigh of relief and sent Van Vliet back to the Army-with no provisions.

Denied of provisions, the Army began to undergo a series of hardships. The expedition had started out just a few months before the onset of the harsh Rocky Mountain winter and had arrived to find that Fort Bridger (the property of the LDS Church) had been burned to the ground. Captain Van Vliet had informed the Army commanders that the Latter-day Saints had fortified Echo Canyon and an assault there would lead to the loss of many lives.

Members of the Nauvoo Legion, mostly teen-agers who were sent to defend Echo Canyon, set the grass on fire in front of the approaching army, which served to stampede the army's cattle, thus leaving them with little food. Later, a party under Lot Smith burned fifty-seven supply wagons. The army with no other choice, and fearing Van Vliet's descriptions of the assault that awaited them in Echo Canyon, instead chose to retreat and find a way south from the northern approaches through Montana. The U.S. Army force spent the winter freezing in the mountains of Montana until emissaries could communicate with President Buchanan directly.

Back in Washington D.C.

President Buchanan, who had never adequately explained his intentions to Brigham Young, was suffering scathing criticism, some of the most vocal coming from his political enemies and men such as Sam Houston of Texas, who believed the Latter-day Saints had been wronged and who also believed any Army that made its way into the Territory would almost surely die there. While the slow negotiations were taking place, the Bannock Tribe ruled out their first option, the Bitterroot Mountains of Idaho and Montana, the Mormons were looking for other territory in which to flee, after an attack on a Mormon outpost. Instead, during the winter of 1858, the Saints began migrating south.

Meanwhile, negotiations between the federal government and the leadership of the LDS Church were undertaken. In April of 1858, sixteen months after Buchanan ordered the Army to Utah, Territorial Governor Cummings and his escort were received and welcomed by Brigham Young and leaders of the Church and the civil government. A Proclamation of Buchanan, who granted amnesty to those involved in the rebellion on the condition they take op their duties and responsibilities as citizens of the United States, called off hostilities officially. Although somewhat inaccurate, a reporter for the New York Herald wrote, "Thus ended the Mormon War, killed none, wounded none, fooled everybody."

Chapter 9

Mammon takes over America

"Give me control of a nation's monetary system, and I care not who writes their laws."

Nathan Rothschild 1820

"If the American people ever allow the banks to control the issuance of their currency, the banks and corporations that will grow up around them will deprive the people of all property, until their children will wake up homeless on the continent their forefathers occupied."

Thomas Jefferson

The Bankers and the American Civil War

The crises in the Utah Territory came to an end and faded out of the public consciousness with the start of the American Civil War in 1861. If the reader will recall, thanks to President Andrew Jackson, the Second Bank of the United States had ceased to exist three decades earlier. However, the financiers of Europe such as the Rothschilds had not given up hope that a private bank could either be set up in the U.S., or in its absence, the country could be split into two opposing factions which would leave it unable to exist without the financing of the major European banks. To accomplish this goal, British agents throughout the American South used various tactics to goad the secessionist leaders into an open conflict with the North.

The South, heavily dependent on selling cotton to England for its textile mills, could not risk an extended war with the North because of the latter's ability to cut off or disrupt the shipping lanes, which would economically devastate the region in a very short time. Neither could the South suffer the North to force the abolition of slavery through Congressional action. The quickest solution for the European bankers and the Confederacy would come in the form of a rapid advance on Washington by Southern troops. When, on December 29th 1860, the State of South Carolina officially seceded from the Union, President Buchanan (possibly still smarting from the Mormon War) did little to oppose it. When the Republicans and Abraham Lincoln took power in January of 1861, Lincoln's first act was to choke the trade of the Confederate States who had chosen to follow secessionist South Carolina's lead with a naval blockade.

Trouble South of the Border

Twelve months later, with the Civil War in a stalemate, the government of Mexico found itself in bankruptcy, whereby the Mexican government announced it would cease making payments to the international bankers of Europe. To secure their loans, British, French and Spanish troops began arriving in Mexico, a direct violation of the Monroe Doctrine, in order to seize the government and make sure those payments were made on time.

The presence of foreign troops in Mexico was a very real threat to the Union, which, up to that point had lost almost every battle in which they had engaged. In the Northern capitol, there was a growing concern that either France, under Emperor Napoleon III, or Britain was going to enter the war on the side of the South. In reality at that point in time, they had little to fear. The European bankers still saw immense profits in funding both sides of the war. In 1862, Abraham Lincoln, stovepipe hat in hand, had approached the international financiers for loans. They demanded an interest rate of 36 per cent, which Lincoln refused to pay. Instead, he followed the Constitution and began issuing Union "greenbacks," at no interest to the American government.

Abraham Lincoln also appealed to England's enemy, Czar Alexander II of Russia for help. According to those present when Czar Alexander II received Lincoln's message, the Czar held Lincoln's letter in his hand unopened and said, "Before we open this paper or know of its contents, we will grant any request it may contain." In September of 1863, the Russian Fleet sailed into New York Harbor, while the Pacific Fleet sailed into San Francisco Bay.

England, which had recently brutally suppressed a rebellion in India by hanging the children of one of the rebel leaders from the gates of a Delhi fort, could not afford a repeat of the costly Crimean conflict against Russia ten years earlier. Slowly, England pulled out its support for the South, while at the same time Union victories in the North began to grow in number. On May 5th of 1862, Mexican forces had handily defeated the French and momentarily stalled the plans of Napoleon III. A year later, the French returned and occupied Mexico, but the presence of the Russian fleet and the victory of the Union at Gettysburg meant that the South was no longer a viable investment for the bankers and governments of Europe.

The assassins and the bankers

The decision to snub the financiers of Europe would ultimately cost Abraham Lincoln his life when actor John Wilkes Boothe shot him in the back of the head at Ford's theater in 1865. The granddaughter of Boothe, Izola Forrester, wrote in her book, *One Mad Act* (1937) that her grandfather had been in close contact with mysterious Europeans prior to the assassination and had even traveled to Europe. She claims that after the assassination, John Wilkes Booth was secreted away by the Knights of the Golden Circle, a Masonic organization dedicated to establishing a new nation that incorporated the American South as well as those portions of Mexico bordering the Gulf of Mexico. According to Boothe's granddaughter, Boothe lived for many years following his disappearance.

Whether this is true or not, another man implicated in the murder of President Lincoln was a man by the name of **George Nicholas Sanders**. Sanders had been appointed to the office of consul in London in the 1850's by then Secretary of War **Jefferson Davis**, who would later be named as the President of the Confederacy. While in London, Sanders became active with revolutionary groups whose aim was the assassination of heads of state in order to bring about democratic reform. The idea of abolishing monarchies was left over from the supposedly banned and defunct Illuminati organization, which had hidden itself within the lodges of the European Freemasons in the late 1700's.

When his revolutionary activities in London became known, Sanders was forced to return to the United States, and was unheard of again until he is implicated with John Wilkes Boothe, along with the other conspirators and the Knights of the Golden Circle in the assassination of President Lincoln. The question still remains as to whether the financiers of France and England, who had invaded Mexico to secure their loans, who attempted to split the United States by their support of the Southern cause and, who also attempted to force Abraham Lincoln to accept their loans at over thirty-six per cent interest, also financed the clandestine group who killed Lincoln in Ford's Theater.

Whatever the case, and whatever those who write "history" claim, the facts are clear. Along with Andrew Jackson, Lincoln became the second U.S. President to oppose the European bankers. Unlike Andrew Jackson, he was the first U.S. President to be the victim of a successful assassination attempt. Unfortunately, Abraham Lincoln would not be the last US President to oppose the banks and die of a gunshot to the head.

European capital, robber barons and the Federal Reserve Bank

At the end of the Civil War, the banking interests of Europe still did not have what they wanted; a private bank in the United States that would make money from nothing and loan it out at interest. However, conditions in the United States made the country as ripe as a Georgia peach for the picking. The Civil War had momentarily halted the expansion westward, where deposits of silver and gold, iron, and later oil, were waiting to be discovered. The invention of barbed wire, the extinction of the buffalo and the subjugation of the last Native American tribes, closed off what had been open rangeland and allowed a new breed of cattlemen to consolidate massive herds of cattle from the Canadian border to the Rio Grande.

In the cities of the North, industrial enterprises that had received a kick-start from lucrative government contracts awarded during the Civil War were being merged into corporations. Companies like Colt, Procter & Gamble and Oscar Meyer were just a few of the corporations that switched from providing their wares to the Union Army and began providing consumer goods on a massive scale to the growing cities and towns of the United States. The transcontinental railroad was nearing completion and, when finished, would allow its owners and investors a monopoly which would allow them to charge whatever they wished for anyone wishing to transport goods or people across the vast nation. What the enterprising Americans needed desperately was European capital to fund their expansion and their new corporations. What a stroke of luck it was that the banking interests in Europe needed someone to marry their finances with the "right kind" of energetic Americans, and marry they did.

With the defeat of Napoleon and the return of the landowning aristocracies to power in the early part of the 1800's, the Rothschild sons and then grandsons had been consolidating their own power in Europe. Since the beginning of t the Industrial Revolution in the middle part of the 1800's, European financiers like the **Rothschilds, Schiffs, Oppenheimers** and **Warburgs** saw their old game of currency manipulation and the profits from the sale and guarantee of government bonds and currency as enterprises not nearly as profitable as investment in the burgeoning new industries like railroads and textile manufactures.

Through ready-made loans to European monarchs from Prussia to Naples, the Rothschild sons were cementing their royal connections and in return were being granted political favors and titles. The Rothschilds also continued to use their connections as prominent members of the Society of Freemasons as well as allies in the royal postal services as their eyes and ears on the world. But they still needed a foothold in the United States.

In 1875, a seemingly obscure trading firm from Lafayette, Indiana; **Kuhn, Loeb and Co**. set up shop in New York as bankers. They invited the Rothschild backed **Jacob Henry Schiff**, the son of a family who had once lived in the same apartment house as Mayer Rothschild in Frankfort, to join their company as a partner. That same year, Jacob married Teresa Loeb, his partner's daughter. Within ten years, the German immigrant was the head of the firm.

Jacob Schiff was not only connected to the Rothschilds, he was also connected to British and French capitalists. He made loans to the railroads, AT&T and Westinghouse. Jacob Schiff also sat on the board of directors for such companies as Central Trust, Western Union and Wells Fargo. Using Rothschild capital, they were able to finance **John D. Rockefeller** (Standard Oil), **Andrew Carnegie** (U.S. Steel) and **Edward Harriman** (Union Pacific, Southern Pacific Railroads, etc.).

JP Morgan: Monopoly Man

Another ally of the European financiers was none other than **J. P. Morgan**. Morgan's father, **Junius**, had been appointed as the successor to George Peabody, an American financier who set up shop in London in 1837. Junius Morgan and George Peabody, originator of the "tax-exempt foundation," was so highly regarded in London for his charity work that his statue was erected across the street from the **Bank of England**. Peabody's most notable achievement was his philanthropy towards London's poor, as well as the foundation of the Peabody Institute. During the Civil War, George Peabody and the somewhat less philanthropic Junius Morgan were suspected of playing both sides of the conflict. George loaned money to the North while Junius was shipping goods to the South.

George Peabody left the firm five years before his death in 1869 and Junius took over, renaming the company ***J.S. Morgan and Co***. That same year, Junius' son, J.P. was named as a partner for the firm and left for New York to manage its operations there. In 1869, J.P. returned to London where he met with the Rothschilds, who gave him instructions regarding the Rothschild banking firm, **Northern Securities**. In 1871, J.P. Morgan merged with Tony Drexel, heir to the Philadelphia Bank. ***Drexel, Morgan and Co.*** bought a building on Wall Street and the ground was once again secure in the United States for Rothschild capital.

Once J.P. Morgan, Paul Warburg and Jacob Schiff had secured the lines of investment for Rothschild and their consortium of European financiers, capital was made available to the new technological industries coming out of the United States (and Europe). Through their connections with European and Rothschild money, investment capital was made available to Freemason Society members in the manufacturing industries like, **Henry Ford**, **Walter Chrysler**, **Ransom Olds** (automobiles), the **Du Ponts** (General Motors and chemicals) and **Samuel Colt** (armaments).

With the influx of capital, they were able to squeeze out competitors until only the "right" businesses and companies survived. In the 1920's and 1930's the American movie industry came to be dominated by Freemasons **Louis B. Mayer** at MGM, **Jack Warner** at **Warner Brothers** and **Daryl Zanuck** at 20th Century Fox. Even today, Americans are polarized by Rupert Murdoch's Fox Television Network against the "liberal" media at

NBC, CBS, and ABC, all of which are, like Fox, owned, run and managed by prominent members of the Society of Freemasons.

The Big Money Squeeze: The Panic of 1907

By the turn of the century, the Rothschilds, though heavily invested in the country, still did not have control of the United States Treasury. To speed things along, in 1902 Paul Warburg arrived in New York from Hamburg, Germany and went to work for *Kuhn, Loeb and Co.* In 1907, While J.P. Morgan, head of *J.P. Morgan & Co.* was in Europe, presumably meeting again with the Rothschilds, Jacob Schiff said in a speech to the New York Chamber of Commerce that, "unless we have a central bank with adequate control of credit resources, this country is going to undergo the most severe and far reaching money panic in its history." This not-so-veiled threat was followed seven months later by the most severe and far reaching money panic in US history.

There were many reasons for the instability of the market in 1907. The San Francisco earthquake had required massive amounts of capital from the East Coast for repair and reconstruction. *The Hepburn Act* had given the government the ability to set maximum prices the railroads could charge for shipping goods. As a result, railroad stocks dropped, taking the stock market with them. The government, accusing them of anti-trust violations subsequently sued Standard Oil Company, under Nelson Rockefeller, taking the market down even further.

First, there had been a drop of 7.7 percent in late 1906. In the first months of 1907, there was a further drop of almost ten percent. The influx and outflow of money as harvests were purchased in the fall, forced banks to increase interest rates in order to bring that capital back to the city's banks. It was at the time of the higher rates that European investors made capital available in order to make more money from the higher rates. At the end of 1906, the Bank of England raised its interest rates, making capital even scarcer. By September of 1907, the stock market had lost 24 percent of its value. Then things went from bad to worse.

The money men "catch-up" to the Heinzes

The **Panic of 1907** arose from the unsuccessful attempt of millionaire and majority shareowner Augustus Heinze and his brother Otto, to corner the market on shares of their own United Copper Company stock, where Augustus had made his fortune. The Heinze brothers began aggressively buying the stock, hoping to force the hapless investors who had bought the stock on borrowed money hoping to "short sell" it when the price dropped, to be forced to pay whatever price the Heinze brothers demanded. The Heinze brothers somehow "miscalculated" the amount of shares available as the stock went from $39 dollars to $52 and almost hit sixty dollars per share during their buying spree.

The next day, Otto called in the shares of borrowed stock, expecting to make a fortune due to the inflated price. The miscalculation became apparent and suddenly, instead of owning all the stock, the hapless Heinze brothers became aware that there were plenty of shares available to the short-selling investors. Sensing the Heinze brother's attempt to squeeze them, shareholders began to sell at a frenzied pace until the price of the stock plummeted to ten dollars in one day.

The Heinze brothers, as well as their brokerage house, the Knickerbocker Bank were bankrupt. The shares they had used for collateral in other banks caused those banks to fail or fueled rumors that they were also going to fail. Officially the panic began as bankers called in loans for any shares sold on margin. The result was a run on the banks as people tried to withdraw savings to pay off their stocks, or simply get hold of their savings fearing their bank would shut its doors. Soon, the banks had no cash to give and the whole Wall Street financial system was close to collapsing.

Rothschild backed J.P. Morgan, who had studied banking in Germany and who had made his initial fortune through buying outdated Civil War rifles, refashioning them and then selling them back to the Army (even though the guns were known to blow the thumbs off of their users when they backfired) averted the crises. He became a hero to millions for bringing the New York bankers to meetings where they were literally held captive until they came up with millions to keep the banks in cash and prevent them from closing their doors and spreading the panic nationwide. Morgan himself had lost twenty one million dollars but came out ahead when he convinced Andrew Carnegie to buy Tennessee Coal, Iron and Railroad Company and incorporate it into **U.S. Steel**, which Morgan later purchased from Carnegie for four hundred million dollars on a handshake.

The "Hide" at Jekyll Island

The Panic of 1907 had been the result of higher bank interest rates, the government's attempt at reigning in the monopolies of Rothschild financed Rockefeller and Harriman and some unscrupulous dealings on Wall Street. As a result of the malfeasance of the big money men, in 1908, Congress passed the ***Aldrich-Vreeland Act*** that established the **National Monetary System**, which would draw up the blue prints for the **Federal Reserve System**. **Senator Nelson Aldrich**, the committee chairman, then took a trip to Europe to study the European banking system. In 1909, the newly "educated" Aldrich introduced a bill in Congress to establish a **national income tax**.

In November of 1910, a top-secret meeting was held at **Jekyll Island** off the coast of Georgia. In attendance were the heavy-hitters and their lackeys who were representing the Rothschild backed financiers: Nelson Aldrich, Chairman of the Senate Finance Committee, A.P. Andrew; undersecretary of the Treasury, Paul Warburg: Kuhn, Loeb & Co., Frank A. Vanderlip, National City Bank of

New York, (Citibank), Henry Davison; J.P Morgan, Charles Norton; First National Bank of New York (J.P. Morgan) and Benjamin Strong; (J.P. Morgan).

B.C. Forbes was to later write:

"Picture a party of the nation's greatest bankers stealing out of New York on a private railroad car under cover of darkness, stealthily riding hundreds of miles South, embarking on a mysterious launch, sneaking onto an island deserted by all but a few servants, living there a full week under such rigid secrecy the names of not one of them was mentioned, lest the servants learn the identity and disclose to the world this strangest, most secret expedition in the history of American Finance. I am not romancing; I am giving to the world, for the first time, the real story of how the famous Aldrich Currency report was written."

If you can't beat 'em, split 'em in two

On January 11, the National Monetary Commission published its report. The **Aldrich Bill**, which took two years to pass, was *initially defeated* in

1912 by Congress during the Taft Administration. According to author William Still, "once the Aldrich Bill flopped, the bankers immediately moved to Plan B. It didn't work trying to push it through with Republicans, so they tried to push it through with Democrats." (Monopoly Men)

A friend of JP Morgan called Teddy Roosevelt out of retirement, in order to form the Bull Moose Party, splitting the Republican Party. Woodrow Wilson defeated incumbent President William Howard Taft and "Bull Moose" Party Candidate, Teddy Roosevelt. One of Wilson's first acts was to sign the **16th Amendment** to the Constitution, the personal and corporate income tax.

On December 22, 1913, after many senators and congressmen had gone home for the Christmas holiday, the Congress passed, and newly elected President Woodrow Wilson signed, the ***Federal Reserve Act*** into law. European banker Paul Warburg, after a brief stint of a little over ten years of residency in the United States, resigned as President of Wells Fargo in order to serve on the Federal Reserve board, under former Undersecretary of the Treasury, Charles Hamlin, while J.P. Morgan's deputy, Benjamin Strong served as the first president of the New York Federal Reserve. There were some, but not many who made their voices heard when the Federal Reserve Act was passed. Senator Charles Lindbergh Sr., father of the famous aviator said upon its signing into law:

"This (Federal Reserve Act) establishes the most gigantic trust on earth. When the President (Woodrow Wilson) signs this bill, the invisible government of the monetary power will be legalized…the worst legislative crime of the ages is perpetrated by this banking and currency bill."
-Congressman Charles A. Lindbergh Sr. 1913

"From now on, depressions will be scientifically created."

-Congressman Charles Lindbergh Sr. 1913

Congressman Lindbergh was not the only one who saw the future of the American people and democracy itself in peril with the passage of the *Federal Reserve Act.*

"The (Federal Reserve Act) as it stands seems to me to open the way to a vast inflation of the currency…I do not like to think that any law can be passed that will make it possible to submerge the gold standard in a flood of irredeemable paper currency."

-Henry Cabot Lodge Sr. 1913

Ironically, the person who lamented the passage of the Federal Reserve Act the most was the very man who signed the bill into law.

"The growth of the nation and all our activities are in the hands of a few men."

-President Woodrow Wilson 1916

"I have unwittingly ruined my government."

-President Woodrow Wilson on his deathbed

To many "conspiracy theorists" (as the lackeys of the conspirators like to refer to them), who blame the Federal Reserve and the Rothschilds and their extensive international banking empire, the Federal Reserve, is but half of the equation. What really allowed the Rothschilds and the international banking cartels their control over the United States was the 1909 law pushed through by Nelson Aldrich that would allow the United States government the ability to tax the income of each and every working American, company and corporation. Why this is so often missed is that, to even begin to understand who profits from the system, it is necessary to find out who owns the member banks that are shareholders in the privately owned Federal Reserve Bank. Because the Federal Reserve is such a complicated system, it is easy to forget the other components of the laws that allowed the bankers their real power. Before we get to that, should the reader be interested, here is a brief overview of the Federal Reserve System:

The Federal Reserve System

The Federal Reserve is a corporation that has twelve component branches. Each branch has the power to print and issue money, at interest, to commercial banks. Each branch, such as the New York Federal Reserve, has shareholders who purchase stock in the Federal Reserve Bank. Shareholders may not sell their shares and, at the end of the year, they receive a return of 6% profit for their investment. The rest of the profits are returned to the United States Treasury.

According to the Federal Reserve website, this six percent return is a minimal sum. However, the year in which they calculated the return was 1995, which was one of the few years in recent memory that the federal budget was close to being balanced. Since that time, the government has done everything possible to run up the national debt. Can you imagine what the profits are at 6% on a multi-trillion-dollar loan? Furthermore, the Chairman of the Federal Reserve is a political appointee, but the decisions they make are based upon simple physical laws, or, what goes up must come down. When the economy is booming, the Federal Reserve increases the amount it charges for the money it prints out of nothing. When the economy is stagnant, interest rates are lowered, in order to encourage spending and borrowing. The key is to know when the interest rates are going up and when they are going down. It doesn't hurt that appointees to the Federal Reserve are former employees of banks like Goldman Sachs etc.

Either way, the shareholders of the Federal Reserve and those with access to inside information win. And who are the shareholders? According to Eustice Mullins author of, *The Secrets of the Federal Reserve*, "The City of London set the whole thing up. The New York Federal Reserve, the most powerful of the Federal Reserve banks, is owned by five merchant banks in London chartered by the Bank of England." (Remember the Rothschilds?). As to who owns the other individual shareholding banks throughout the country that own Federal Reserve

stock, requires more time and space than the author is willing to devote to this book however, there is a website listed in the bibliography where this information can be obtained. A quick overview of the corporations and banks that control the reserve is more or less a who's who in the world of corporate America and European finance.

The most important point here is that the Federal Reserve Bank, whether you like it or hate it, is in strict violation of the Constitution of the United States, Section 8 Article 5, yet never has it been so much as challenged in the Supreme Court or any other court in this country. The Federal Reserve Bank is a private bank. A simple web search for the

Federal Reserve will yield only the bank's governors under the address ".gov" while the member banks are all listed ".org" which means they have nothing to do the United States government.

Americans on the hook; the War to Finance all Wars

So, that leaves us with the real issue of how the banks could be so powerful. How would the passage of the national income tax law have more repercussions than the law that allowed the Federal Reserve to print money from nothing and then loan it out for interest?[1] If you will recall, the First Bank of the United States was allowed to borrow the money to pay for its twenty percent stake. But what Alexander Hamilton found out, and we all know too well, is that in a democracy, talk about raising taxes is political suicide.

What happened to the First Bank of the United States was that its intention to pay its debts through taxes on imported and domestic liquor consumption was never enough to pay the nation's debts. In fact it could probably be argued that just collecting the taxes and bringing to justice the offenders who didn't pay them probably took more out of the treasury than it brought in. When the board of the bank demanded that the government pay up for the shares it had borrowed to become a member in 1819, the government didn't have enough money to pay and was forced to sell its shares and then the First Bank of the United States was, just what the Federal Reserve is today, a privately owned bank.

With the passage of the **National Income Tax Act**, it became possible to put every American "on the hook" for any money the Congress spent beyond what it took in, plus interest. In the words of Chief Justice John Marshall in the opinion given in the Supreme Court ruling regarding the first Bank of the United States, Chief Justice Marshall ironically wrote, "The power to tax is the power to destroy" (*McCulloch v Maryland* 1819). Even the Federal Reserve admits that its profits are distributed amongst its shareholders. In other words, the profits it makes from creating something

---

[1] This is a rather simplified view. Until the Nixon Administration, the United States adhered to first the gold and then silver standard. U.S. currency was accepted because in theory it could be redeemed for gold or silver. This is no longer the case. Now, U.S. currency is just, as Ben Bernanke the Federal Reserve Chairman says, a "paper product.

out of nothing and then loaning it at interest to private as well as government concerns. If anyone had ever proposed a law forbidding the government from spending more than it took in, people would have cried, "What about the Depression?" Only in 1913, there hadn't been a Depression yet, so nobody could propose a limit on government spending, nor justify it if they did. The Federal Reserve Act was passed, not to save the common man from the horrors of a constricted money supply. The Federal Reserve Act and the National Income Tax were passed, coincidentally, just in time for the world's most expensive war. Well, at least until that point in time.

Chapter 10

Mammon Goes to War

"Generals gathered in their masses, just like witches at Black masses. Evil minds that plot destruction, sorcerer of deaths construction. In the fields the bodies burning. As the war machine keeps turning. Death and hatred to mankind, poisoning their brainwashed minds."

Black Sabbath; War pigs

The war to begin all wars

In August of 1914, Lord Cunliffe, governor of the Bank of England remarked, "There will be no war. The Germans haven't got the credits." The reason the Rothschilds and other European financiers would not loan the German government money for the war was due to the fact that the governments of Europe had taken over the business of selling their own treasury bonds, through which their banks and major contributors were making a hefty sum overseeing and servicing the transactions.

Because they were making so much money "financing" their own debt, the countries of Europe had loaned themselves into oblivion. Once the Federal Reserve Act and the Sixteenth Amendment to the Constitution were passed with Paul Warburg on the Federal Reserve board and his brother Max serving as the head of the German Secret police, the Germans suddenly had enough credit to go to war. The citizens of the United States were ultimately liable for any loans made by the government (through the financiers) to belligerent countries. A mere seven months after the Federal Reserve Act was passed, World War I broke out in Europe.

Stalemate and the Wall Street intervention

By 1917, the belligerents in the conflict: Germany, France, England, Russia and Italy were in a stalemate that appeared unbreakable. The United States had been leasing and loaning to the Allied powers, through Morgan Trust and Paul Warburg, Kuhn Loeb & Co. while Warburg's brother, Max, president of M.M. Warburg in Hamburg was funneling Rothschild money to the Germans.

But in 1917, there was the very real danger of the countries suing for peace before the United States; the only country in the world left with good credit, was able to enter the War. The only questions were how to get the US involved in the war as quickly as possible and how to keep Germany and its allies from capitulating. To answer the first question, the sinking of the munitions carrying (?) *Lusitania* passenger liner by a German submarine in April of that year with over one hundred Americans on board was great copy for the nation's newspapers. Woodrow Wilson, who had campaigned and won on the slogan, "He kept us out of war," used the Lusitania incident to get the U.S. into the war by declaring war on Germany and its allies.

In Russia, **Leon Trotsky** and **Nikolai Lenin** whose ideals were suspiciously similar to those of the Illuminati of the late 1700's, were making secret deals with their connections in Germany and the Rothschilds banking empire to foment a revolution and overthrow the Czar. Ultimately, the Rothschilds and the Wall Street financiers would provide the Communist Revolution billions of dollars worth of credit and gold bullion. With Germany no longer fighting a two front war, they could concentrate their forces on the Western Front.

How lucky it was for the international bankers that Paul Warburg, on the board of the United States Federal Reserve Bank, had a brother who was serving as the head of Germany's secret police and who was actively funneling money to the Communists in Russia! With the United States sending fresh troops and financing new weapons and supplies for England and France, the war could continue until one side had literally bled the other dry.

At the end of the First World War, Europe was in a shambles. England and France were in so much debt from the First World War that they had depleted their gold reserves. In order to get more gold, they insisted in the Versailles Treaty (written in part by the Rothschild bankers) that Germany pay its reparations in gold and silver. Of course Germany didn't have any gold or silver either, so they bought it from the United States. Only they didn't really have anything backing up their money (like gold or silver) so, they printed money, as it was needed. The more gold the German government bought from the U.S., meant the more money they needed to print. Pretty soon, Germans citizens were wheeling wheelbarrows full of Deutschmarks to pay for loaves of bread and the country was ripe for revolution.

The Federal Reserve's first victory: The Great Depression

In the 1920's, business in America was booming. In fact, it was booming so much that President Calvin Coolidge's famous saying that, "The business of America is business," became a slogan we still remember today. The Federal Reserve which was created to prevent anything like the Panic of 1907 by raising and lowering interest rates on its free money, had lowered interest rates and freed up credit to banks while average Americans went on a credit binge. People were buying stocks on margin, which meant paying one dollar for a ten-dollar stock and then selling it when the stock increased and, after paying off the bank, pocketing a nice little sum. The banks were making money, corporations were making money, farmers were making money, railroads were making money and everyone was happy. Probably nobody was happier than the banks and the agents of the Rothschilds in America whose money scheme was loaning out paper at interest on a colossal scale.

The Great Depression started in 1929 exactly as the Panic of 1907 started. The only difference between the two was that J.P. Morgan was not there to influence his banking associates to put cash into banks where people, fearing their bank may go out of business, were standing in line trying to get their money. Instead, of the kind-hearted J.P. Morgan, there was the Federal Reserve Bank that had been signed into law in 1913 to prevent such things like the Panic of 1907 from happening again. Only the Federal Reserve, controlled by the masters of international finance, had no intention of staving off a panic in 1929.

According to Dr. Larry Bates, author of *The New Economic Disorder*, "Sixteen months prior to the Crash of '29, *the Federal Reserve increased the money supply by 62%*...people were buying, pledging, selling, thinking the good times would never end. And, then, at the time of the crash, they pulled the plug.

People lost their stocks, their bonds, their homes, their cars, everything. They pledged their savings accounts and they lost it all."

Nobel Prize winning economist **Milton Friedman** explained it this way: "Depositors all were worried about the safety of their funds and rushed to withdraw them. There were runs and failures of banks by the droves. And all the time, the Federal Reserve System stood idly by when it had the power and the duty and the responsibility to provide the cash that would have enabled the banks to meet the insistent demands of their depositors without closing their doors." In other words, the Federal Reserve, which had been created in order to ensure that banks were capitalized during times of economic crises, refused to do the very thing they had been created to do.

"Gee, no G.E., I'm broke!"

To understand what went wrong, take the example of G.E. stock. In 1920, G.E. stock was valued at $5 per share. In 1929, before the crash, G.E. stock, thanks to easy credit and the demand for shares, reached a whopping $60 dollars a share. Anyone who had purchased G.E. at any time during that boom period, would have, at a minimum, doubled their money right up until the point the stock reached thirty-one dollars. However, if you were a member of the board at G.E., Ford, GM, Westinghouse, AT&T etc. and had friends at the Federal Reserve, you knew when the "Fed" was going to hike up interest rates, so you could sell your stock before that happened.

So what happened in the crash of 1929? The Fed increased interest rates to "cool" the economy and, at the same time, people like the Fords, Rockefellers, and Kennedys and so on, began to sell their shares. Common investors, who had purchased their stock on borrowed money, panicked as they saw the big money men selling (remember Nathan Rothschild at the London Stock exchange during the Battle of Waterloo?). Common investors had to pay off loans for stock purchased on borrowed money whose value was plummeting. The banks called in their loans on one hand and then closed their doors, because they didn't have enough cash on hand to give to their depositors. Whereas in 1907 when JP Morgan had influenced his banking friends to put cash into banks where people were lining up to withdraw their savings, to keep the panic limited to New York, in 1929, the Federal Reserve refused to loan money to the banks to pay off their depositors.

When all was said and done, hundreds of banks had failed, GE stock was back where it started at five dollars and thousands of businesses went bankrupt. If a person had been tipped off about the rising interest rates, they could have sold (for example) G.E. at sixty and then bought twelve shares for the price of one when it hit five dollars. Or, they could have just pocketed a nifty fifty-five dollars per share profit. Out of the Crash of 1929 emerged Citibank, JP Morgan, Chase Manhattan and Wells Fargo and they were stronger than ever. A lot of people went broke, but others, like Joseph Kennedy, founder of the famous Kennedy clan, made millions of dollars from the crash. Once again our well paid for members of Congress sat on their thumbs and watched the crises unfold. Some, like Louis McFadden expressed outrage, but he was in the minority:

"We have in this country, one of the most corrupt institutions the world has ever known. I refer to the Federal Reserve Board. This evil institution has impoverished the people of the United States and has practically bankrupted our government. It has done this through the corrupt practices of the moneyed vultures who control it."

Congressman Louis T. McFadden 1932

"The Federal Reserve banks are one of the most corrupt institutions the world has ever seen. There is not a man within the sound of my voice who does not know that this nation is run by the international bankers."

Congressman Louis T. McFadden 1932

"Some people think the Federal Reserve Banks are the United States government's institutions. They are not government institutions. They are private credit monopolies that prey upon the people of the United States for the benefit of themselves and their foreign swindlers-

Congressional Record 12595-12603

Louis T. Mc Fadden, Twelve years as the Chairman of the Committee on Banking and Currency June 10, 1932

Social Insecurity

In the Depression Years, the federal government began to deficit spend (borrowing money at interest from the Federal Reserve) to get people to work and get money in their pockets and food on their tables, which is why today there is no law against the government spending more than it takes in. Massive federal programs were created and new ways were thought up to get at the money in the pockets of working class Americans, such as the Social Security Administration, which assigned all Americans a number for the purpose of identifying them to the federal government. We all know now that money was used, much like the "pension funds" of the mafia run unions, as the piggy banks of the politicians, so they didn't have to raise taxes, but back then, the government saving money for the common man, and not the untrustworthy banks, seemed like such a good idea.

"I have never seen more Senators express discontent with their jobs…I think the major cause is that, deep down in our hearts, we have been accomplices in doing something terrible and unforgivable to our wonderful country. Deep down in our heart, we know that we have given our children a legacy of bankruptcy. We have defrauded our country to get ourselves elected."

John Danforth (R-Mo)

One Sour Kraut

Meanwhile, back in Germany, where the economy was in shambles and with no foreseeable way to ever extricate itself from its debt, a new rising star in the form of Adolf Hitler and his National Socialists began to emerge on the German political scene. Like anyone else, the Nazis needed money and they got it from the same place everyone else did, the Rothschilds.

It may seem odd that someone who was as anti-Jewish as Hitler (who was actually one quarter Jewish) would go to a Jewish banker to get money, but, since they were the only act in town, the Nazis had no choice.

If you will recall, Mayer Rothschild had his start in Germany and the connections between the Rothschilds and the likes of the German Krupps (steel), IG Farben (chemicals), Mercedes (automobiles) etc. ran quite deep. Their support for Hitler was enough to get the ball, or tanks, rolling across Europe. The connections between the Fords, JP Morgan's Bank, Citibank and the Nazis, all of whom stood to profit from their German businesses, didn't hurt either.

The Nazi Business Model: Murder Slavery and Theft for Profit

The financial officials in Hitler's Third Reich had a very unique, yet effective business plan to sell to their financiers. They were going to murder and enslave millions of people and steal everything they could get their hands on. Hitler's business proposal was put down on paper while he was serving time for the Nazi's unsuccessful Beer Hall Putsch in Bavaria in 1924. It was his book entitled *Mein Kampf*. The Nazis, in their campaign of genocide, financed the war through the theft of lands, money, art, factories, bank accounts, houses and the use of slave labor. The gold, which was used to repay loans to banks in Switzerland, was made from melted down wedding rings, watches and of course, the gold teeth of millions of Holocaust victims. Whatever one said about the Nazis, they paid their bills on time.

Further east, in Stalin's Russia, millions of peasants had been forced into labor camps as the Soviet Union embarked on massive projects in an effort to industrialize an agrarian economy that had changed little since the days of Peter the Great. Stalin also needed financing for these projects and, fortunately for him, the international bankers of Europe and the United States were always willing to jump in and lend an interest-bearing dollar wherever they could.

We all know, or at least I hope we all know, that, at the end of World War II, England, France, Russia (now the Union of Soviet Socialist Republics) and the United States emerged from the war victorious, while the losers, Italy, Japan and Germany were in ruins. Hundreds of millions of people were dead, homeless, maimed, psychologically scarred, orphaned, and on the verge of starvation. But, the world was not looking back to what went wrong. The world was intent on making sure that the same things, like economic collapse, the rise of brutal dictators and sneak attacks, never happened again, unless it was to advantage of the bankers. The United States, which had been attacked by the Japanese government before a formal declaration of war, vowed never to let anybody "sneak up" (at least militarily) on her again. But who would want to sneak up on the United States?

The big con is on

Do you remember how the financiers on Wall Street funded Lenin and the Bolsheviks? That was the best billion-dollar investment in the history of the world. The bankers knew that before anybody got wise to them, and started asking a lot of questions, they would need a new enemy that would scare the Americans into agreeing to any amount of money, loss of liberties and blood, if need be. That new enemy was, of course, the Wall Street and Rothschild financed Soviet Union.

Under Joseph Stalin, at least twenty million people had been murdered or died in labor camps. No American wanted to live under the heel of the Soviet boot and, from their actions after the war, which made front page news on an almost daily basis, it was apparent that nothing more than world domination was their intent. The United States began spending more and more money on "defense" than it had spent in all the wars it had fought combined. In spite of all the security surrounding the Manhattan Project, which produced the first atomic bomb, somehow the Soviets got a hold of the plans, which meant that the US would have to spend even more taxpayer money to counter the threat. In the late 1940's, when the Soviet Union exploded their first atomic bomb, the American media made scapegoats of the Jewish couple, Carl and Ethyl Rosenberg, who the American public was gullible enough to believe was somehow capable of leaking the elaborate plans. The Rosenbergs were simply a diversion to keep attention away from the man in charge of the project, J. Robert Oppenheimer, whose family connections with the Rothschilds went back almost two hundred years. The Rosenbergs went to their deaths before a firing squad pleading their innocence.

The Holocaust, the Rothschilds and the State of Israel

So what about Hitler and the Jews? He killed, according to the historical records, over six million of them in concentration camps. How could the

Jewish Rothschilds tolerate this and a monster like Hitler? There are boundless theories, but I would prefer to stick to historical facts. During World War I, the Ottoman Empire controlled the Middle East from Egypt to Iraq and all of Asia Minor (modern day Turkey) and had done so ever since the 1400's. When Germany lost the war, the Ottoman Empire lost everything. They had borrowed heavily from the Rothschilds and had nothing with which to pay back their debts. The Rothschilds, who had loaned money to both sides, and whose representatives were present when the terms of the armistice were written, demanded the rights to the railway leading into Palestine.

Anybody who has seen Lawrence of Arabia, knows the betrayal of King Faisal of Saudi Arabia when he found out that his reward for helping the British liberate the Holy Land was to see all of the Arab Lands divided into small independent countries and the land of Palestine turned over to a British Protectorate under the Balfour Agreement of 1917. To further secure the northern section of railway, France was given control of Lebanon and Beirut. This would ensure that travelers or settlers traveling on the railway would be unmolested on their way to the Palestine. Of course, with the exception of some smelly, freewheeling Europeans, nobody would be traveling to Palestine except Jews seeking to return to their historical homeland.

Prior to World War II and the extermination of six million Jews, nobody in the world would have agreed to allow millions of people who were basically Europeans to settle and displace the historical occupants of an entire nation. After World War II, public opinion and sympathy rested with the Jewish people and they wasted no time relocating to Palestine. The Arabs living in the region became alarmed as each passing month brought boatloads and trainloads of Jewish settlers into the region.

Inevitably, violence broke out as forces of the *Irgun*, the militant arm of the Zionist movement, began to assassinate Arab leaders and the Arabs began to retaliate. In 1947, the I*rgun* blew up the King David Hotel, the headquarters of the British peacekeeping efforts. The British announced their intent to withdraw, while at the same time, the United Nations was formed and located on land donated by the Rothschilds agents, the Rockefellers in New York. In 1947, before the world body, the nation of Israel announced its existence and was immediately recognized by the

United States and the Soviet Union, along with Britain and France; all members of the UN Security council.

A couple of other things happened in 1947 of note. President Harry Truman, fearing he may lose the upcoming election, was advised to "scare the hell" out of the American people, which he did. Communists in Greece had begun an armed conflict and Truman used the conflict to demonstrate how tough he was. He pledged to fight communism, "wherever it rears its ugly head." The Truman doctrine gave every president until Bill Clinton the right and the power to ship money, arms and equipment to any country that asked for it, without the approval (and many times knowledge of Congress). The result, as we all know, was fifty years of people like Pinochet in Argentina, Batista in Cuba, the Shah of Iran, the Ba'athists in Iraq, etc. And, in 1947, the same year that the UN, the CIA, the State of Israel and the Cold War officially got underway, reports emerged in the press about a crashed flying saucer in a place called Roswell New Mexico.

Meanwhile in the Kingdom of God...

And, far away in the State of Utah, the tiny Kingdom of God announced that its worldwide membership, which had started out with six original members in 1830, had reached one million.

The Rise of the Secret Government

Subsequent to 1947, the Central Intelligence Agency, and a long list of shadowy intelligence gathering agencies were formed, and in many cases, staffed with ex-Nazi intelligence officials. The Federal Bureau of Investigation was given broad funding and powers to spy on the lives of Americans and in many cases, simply for the amusement of its director, J. Edgar Hoover. Entire military programs were given "classified" status so that their budgets and activities would remain secret for decades until the Freedom of Information Act was passed in the 1970's and even then only some of the government's operations were brought into the public light.

In effect, the United States had become an armed camp, controlled and policed by agencies over which there was no apparent oversight and certainly were not allowed in the United States Constitution. President Dwight D. Eisenhower, former five-star general and commander of Allied Forces in Europe, upon leaving office in 1961, gave the citizens of the

United States a stern warning. He cautioned against giving up our freedoms to the "military-industrial complex."

The rise of television, as well as the movie and recording industries was to give the government, the international bankers and the rising military-industrial complex opportunities for control that they never had enjoyed before. With only three television networks and all of their content controlled by the banks that financed their operations as well as the government through the Federal Communications Commission, only the ideas and information the corporations wanted aired were to be were allowed on the national airwaves.

US Presidents, beginning with John F. Kennedy were elected based upon their television appearances. Ronald Reagan, who began acting in the 1940's in "B" rated Hollywood movies, was to rise to become the governor of California and the President of the United States in 1980.

Since President Eisenhower's stern warning, The U.S. government, in the name of "security," has sent troops to the Dominican Republic, Vietnam, Grenada, Panama, Kuwait, Lebanon, Iraq, Bosnia and Afghanistan to engage in expensive public military campaigns. The U.S. has also been involved in secret wars and the murder of foreign rulers. In that time we have seen one of our Presidents assassinated, and another forced to resign when he was caught with his hand in the Secret Government cookie jar. We sold arms and provided millions of taxpayer dollars to Saddam Hussein and then invaded his country in the name of a New World Order.

So why do we just sit by and let it happen? As we all know today, even with the advent of cable TV, "news" is the same on every channel. Reporters who challenge political leaders lose privileges and access to politicians so that the news we hear is the news the corporation/government wants us to hear. The source of the news, especially internationally, comes from the White House through the State Department and the CIA. Corporations, whose boards of directors are more concerned with the profitability of the news broadcast and advertising revenue, than they are with reporting news, often own news organizations themselves.

John F. Kennedy Warns about Secret Societies

All too often, the leaders, such as Harry Truman, J. Edgar Hoover, CIA Directors, Directors of federal agencies, banks, owners of movie studios, television stations, newspapers and members of Congress belong to the same fraternity that has made the money kingdom the most powerful kingdom in the history of the world. In the fifty years since the end of the Second World War, using the pretext of the Cold War, that kingdom has managed to gain control of the world's population, resources and finances.

In a society where technology, industry, science, and finance are intermarried, where members of the same fraternity serve as board members that make the decisions for corporations, government, foreign policy and scientific research, could it be possible for a secret fraternity to infiltrate into these positions of power?

President John F. Kennedy thought so and he felt so strongly against it he said so in a speech in 1961, a year after President Eisenhower warned of the growing military industrial complex:

"The very word 'secrecy' is repugnant in a free and open society. And, we are as a people, inherently and historically, opposed to secret societies, to secret oaths and to secret proceedings.

For, we are opposed around the world, by a monolithic and ruthless conspiracy that relies primarily on covert means for expanding its sphere of influence, on infiltration instead of invasion, on subversion, instead of elections, on intimidation, instead of free choice. It is a system, which has conscripted vast human and material resources into the building of a tightly knit, highly efficient machine that combines military, diplomatic, intelligence, economic, scientific and political operations.

Its preparations are concealed, not published. Its mistakes are buried, not headlined. Its dissenters are silenced not praised. No expenditure is questioned, no secret is revealed. That is why the Athenian lawmaker Solon decreed it a crime for any citizen to shrink from controversy. I am asking your help in the tremendous task of informing and alerting the American people. Confident with your help, man will be what he was born to be; free and independent."

John F. Kennedy and the Federal Reserve Bank

Furthermore, on June 4, 1963, President Kennedy signed Executive Order 11110, which stripped the Federal Reserve of the power to loan money to the United States Government at interest. On November 22, of that same year, Kennedy suffered the same fate as President Abraham Lincoln; death by a gunshot wound to the head. The following is a list of prominent Freemasons who held positions of power on November 22, 1963 and who served as head of the CIA, the FBI and on the Warren Commission, which "investigated" his assassination.

John McCone- Director of the Central Intelligence Agency (Knights of Malta)

J. Edgar Hoover-Director of the Federal Bureau of Investigations (Freemason)

Lyndon Baines Johnson-Vice President of the United States (took over the Presidency) (Freemason)

Chief Justice Earl Warren-Head of the Warren Commission (Freemason)

(Former CIA Director fired by Kennedy) Allen Dulles -Warren Commission member (Bilderberger-Rothschild agent)

Gerald R. Ford-Warren Commission member (Freemason)

Earl Boggs-Warren Commission member (Knights of Columbus) (Boggs objected to Warren Commission findings. He "disappeared" in an airplane somewhere in Alaska.)

John Sherman Cooper -Warren Commission member (Skull and Bones)

Arlen Spectre-Warren Commission member (Freemason)

Hubert Humphrey-Warren Commission member (Freemason)

Robert S. McNamara-Warren Commission member (Freemason)

Meanwhile in the Kingdom of God...

The same year that John F. Kennedy was assassinated, 1963, the tiny Kingdom of God announced that its worldwide membership had reached two million members.

Chapter 11

"Common Knowledge"

Myths, Lies and Half-Truths About the Church of Jesus Christ of Latter-day Saints

"And he became Satan, yea even the devil, the father of all lies, to deceive and to blind men, and to lead them captive at his will, even as many as would not hearken unto my voice." (Moses 4:4)

(Author's note: The following chapters contain summaries of the Latter-day Saint Scriptures. In effect, I am putting the "cart before the horse." This is done of necessity to, "disprove the disprovers," because of the plethora of distorted information regarding the LDS Church. By arranging the text in this fashion, the reader will have the luxury of knowing that no credible refutation of the Book of Mormon or LDS Doctrine exists, *before* the reader is able to read a summary of these scriptures.)

So far, the purpose of this book has been to lay the groundwork for the foundation of the greatest deceptions of people in the modern world, excluding Geraldo Rivera's *Al Capone's Secret Vault* TV special. One of the greatest of the three great deceptions this book is concerned with is the spread of lies and disinformation about the Church of Jesus Christ of Latter-day Saints. If the reader will recall the words of Captain Stewart Van Vliet who, during the "Utah War" told Church President Brigham Young that the people known as the members of the Church of Jesus Christ of Latter-day Saints "…have been lied about the worst of any people I ever saw." This chapter then, is to bring forth some of those lies and examine them for their accuracy.

Before we continue any further, for the benefit of the non-LDS reader, I would like to bring forth just some of the lies and the half-truths that have served as the basis for people's opinions and "knowledge" throughout the world about the Latter-day Saint Church. Most of these lies began right from the Church's inception and continue to this day. I would also like to clear up some of the misconceptions that seem to be believed simply because they are much easier to accept than to honestly investigate the facts and go against the common knowledge of "the herd." Where these lies and deceptions come from, it is up to the reader to decide.

Common knowledge: the Church of Jesus Christ of Latter-day Saints.

1) True or False-Mormons have many wives.

2) True or False-Mormons where funny underwear.

3) True or False-Mormons have bizarre sexual relations in their temples.

4) True or False-Joseph Smith wrote the Book of Mormon.

5) True or False-The Book of Mormon is the Mormon Bible.

6) True or False-Mormons are racist white supremacists i.e.; Mormons hate black people and don't allow them in their church.

7) True or False-Mormons worship Satan.

8) True or False-Mormons are a branch of the Freemasons.

9) True or False-Mormons hate homosexuals.

10) True or False-You can't be a Mormon if you smoke, drink, use drugs or listen to rock and roll.

11) Finished? Let's see how well you did.

1) *True or False*-Latter-day Saint men have many wives.

False. Sometime after the LDS Church was founded, Latter-day Saint Prophet Joseph Smith instituted the idea of plural marriage as an eternal practice based upon revelations given to him by Jesus Christ. Plural marriage was an accepted practice in the Old Testament and is still practiced in Islamic societies today for the same reason. During the early days of the restored Church, there were also practical reasons for plural marriage; there were simply more women who wanted to convert to the Latter-day Saint religion than men. It is LDS Doctrine that families on earth will be sealed (in the temple) for all time and eternity. Women desired to be sealed to a husband in this life so that their family could continue in the next. It is also believed that there will be many more women in heaven than there are men (I'm not sure if you can actually call that "heaven"). However, in the 1870's, when the U.S. government took issue with the Latter-day Saint practice of polygamy, the Church, which is obliged to "uphold and sustain the law of the land" forbade it and gave notice that anyone not obeying the law, would be excommunicated. Since then, some groups that follow LDS Doctrine continue the practice and are promptly excommunicated for doing so.

2) *Latter-day Saints wear "funny" underwear.*

True. Members of the LDS Church, who have been to the temple or are married in a temple ceremony, wear what are called "temple garments." The purpose of which is to remind the wearer that they have made covenants to Jesus Christ in the temple and that they must maintain the purity of their minds and bodies. The garments are also meant for protection of the individual.

3) *Latter-day Saints have bizarre sexual relations in their temples.*

False. LDS Temples are considered pure and sacred. In effect they are, according to LDS Doctrine, conduits to the Kingdom of God and Jesus Christ. Nothing impure may enter or occur in the temple, and that includes sexual relations of any kind. It also includes those who do not uphold their vows of chastity and their covenants of marriage.

4) *Joseph Smith wrote the Book of Mormon.*

False-Joseph Smith translated a set of gold plates written in a form of Egyptian Hieroglyphics, the end result of which was named, *The Book of*

Mormon. "Mormon" comes from the name of one of the last authors. Mormon was a general and a historian who was one of the last survivors of a civilization that was wiped out by the Native Americans around 400 AD. His son Moroni was given the plates to hide in a hillside in New York. It was Moroni who came to Joseph Smith and revealed to him where the plates were hidden. Moroni is the golden angel on all Latter-day Saint temples calling upon the nations of the world to repent.

5) *The Book of Mormon is the Mormon Bible.*

False. The King James Bible is the Mormon Bible. There were some errors in translation that were corrected by Joseph Smith, but they were minor.

6) *Mormons are racist white supremacists i.e.; Mormons hate black people and don't allow them in their church.*

False. When Joseph Smith was a candidate for President of the United States in 1844, he promised to free all slaves and reimburse their owners with the sale of public lands. For obvious reasons, members of the Church were not well thought of in slave-holding states like Missouri, or in Illinois where Smith was martyred that same year. It is true that African Americans were not allowed to hold the priesthood until 1977 when the ban was lifted. Today, there are many Africans and African Americans who hold the Priesthood and who are upstanding members of the LDS Church, to include a prominent former member of the 1960's Black Panther movement. The ban itself was due to the curse that was brought upon the descendants of Ham, the son of Noah, which was repealed by revelation. Members of all cultures, races and nations are welcome to investigate and become members of the Church of Jesus Christ of Latter-day Saints and take upon their families, their communities and their nations the blessings of the Most High God. Today, Africa, and South America represent the fastest growing LDS Communities in the world. Spanish is the predominant language of the Latter-day Saint Church.

7) *True or False-Mormons worship Satan.*

False. LDS Doctrine recognizes Lucifer, or Satan as a contemporary of Jesus Christ who presented a plan to God that all spirits that came to the earth to inhabit bodies would be forced to obey God's commandments.

Jesus presented an alternative plan where all would be able to choose to obey God if they wished. Lucifer was not happy when God chose the plan that Jesus presented and took a third of the angels with him to the earth to deceive mankind through lies, discontent, fear and hatred. The belief in "free agency" is the cornerstone of the LDS faith and one of the reasons the LDS Church considers the Constitution of the United States as a document inspired by Jesus Christ, and is therefore, sacred. To put it another way: Satan bad, Jesus good.

8) *True or False-Mormons are a branch of the Freemasons.*

False. We will talk about this issue in much more detail later therefore I will keep the reader trembling with suspense.

9) *True or False-Mormons hate homosexuals.*

False. The LDS Church does not advocate hatred of anybody. However, sexual relations of any kind outside the covenant of marriage between a man and a woman (or any variable thereof) are absolutely forbidden. The punishment for homosexuality with regards to members of the Church is the same as for committing adultery where one or both of the guilty parties are married; immediate excommunication. The Church recognizes upholds and defends the family as an eternal institution, which means that families are the cornerstones of life throughout the universe.

10) *True or False-You can't be a Mormon if you smoke, drink, use drugs or listen to rock and roll.*

False. The LDS Church abides by section of 89 of the Doctrine and Covenants, which is a rule of general health. Tobacco, alcohol or any substance, which might be mind altering, or habit forming is discouraged. However, the penalty for using these substances is not assessed by the Church, with exception that it is not possible to enter a temple if one is a user of any of these substances, nor is it possible to hold an office in the Church that would be designated as of "leadership capacity." The Word of Wisdom as it is known is a general rule for health and includes eating meat "sparingly" while sustaining oneself on fruits, breads and vegetables and moderate exercise. The body, according to Church doctrine, is a similar to a temple where unclean substances, ideas and thoughts should be kept out at all cost.

Why hide the truth?

So, how did you do? If you were honest in your answers and are not a member or former member of the LDS Church, you most likely scored anywhere between one and two correctly. It is not my intent to make you feel ignorant rather, I want to point out to the reader that what you know about the Church of Jesus Christ of Latter-day Saints, or in other words, what you *thought* you knew about the LDS Church is based on what you have been told by the popular media, or someone else who does not want you to investigate the LDS Church for yourself.

The fact is, you most likely know more about the 1960's sitcom *The Munsters* than you do about the LDS Church. From what we have seen in the previous chapters there is a logical explanation for this. If everybody were to become members of the LDS Church, there would be little need for government, as it exists today. There would be no need for the churches who disparage the Church for fear of losing their congregations. There would be an understanding, at least philosophically and spiritually that we are all here on the earth to accomplish something that will determine what we will do in the next life. Can you imagine what kind of chaos that kind of radical thinking would cause? We wouldn't need armies and navies, we wouldn't need to spend so much of our state and federal budgets on police forces, and we could trust our government leaders.

Let me put it another way. Alcohol is a major part of our social activities. In movies, we see beautiful people "relaxing," "socializing," and "partying" to celebrate significant occasions. We see alcohol in advertisements in all of our magazines, on television and in places where people gather. However, what happens if a person has too much to drink and gets behind the wheel of a car? Sometimes, they kill people. Other times, they are arrested and taken to jail. They lose their jobs, and sometimes their families. People who use alcohol commit violent crimes like assault, and through the use of alcohol, they bring violence into their own homes. But you rarely see that on TV (except on *Cops*) or in the movies.

Why is something that is so harmful, so encouraged in societies around the globe? The answer is money. There is a multi-billion dollar a year industry that exists simply because people see drinking alcohol as glamorous because it is portrayed as glamorous in the media. In "monkey-see-monkey-do," fashion, people copy what they see such as rich, beautiful, popular and famous people doing. The industry that thrives on alcohol use includes, lawyers, judges, law enforcement, probation officials, jails and prisons, rehabilitation programs, impound lots, bars, restaurants, and on it goes.

The alcohol industry, knowing of the evil that it causes in society, encourages people to, "drink responsibly" which is a paradox. People drink so they have an excuse not to act responsibly. What would happen to all those people if one day, people just stopped drinking? Hundreds of thousands of people who feed off human weakness would be out of work. But that is not going to happen because they and the companies that produce alcohol are so powerful that, barring some drastic change in individual behavior, they will spend whatever it takes to keep the uneducated in the system. No other country in the world spends so much to criminalize an activity that is perfectly legal!

Of course there are many other things that are harmful in our society that are encouraged. There are drugs that are illegal, such as marijuana and cocaine, both of which were legal until the 1920's. They are glamorized in movies and on TV in order to support another multi-billion dollar a year industry of law enforcement, courts, border patrols, drug testing companies, and other government funded programs. If you have sex with many partners, you have a very good chance of getting a disease that may cost your life. If you smoke cigarettes, you will get cancer, and so on and so on. All of these multi-billion dollar a year industries are dependent upon one thing, that the general populace is too stupid to make its own decisions, or as P.T. Barnum once said, "There is a sucker born every minute." It would seem that if governments around the world were really concerned about the well-being of the citizens of their countries, they would at least try to promote the lifestyle that is promoted by the LDS Church, whose members enjoy some of the healthiest and longest lives of any group in an industrial society in the world. Instead governments promote unhealthy lifestyles through allowing the advertisement of unhealthy habits. Sick people need to be taken care of.

The Latter-day Saints: The Kingdom within a kingdom

So, that is where we stand, in a society that seems to feed us false or untrue information and that seems to be pre-occupied with our failures, rather than our successes. But, whether you like it or not, there is a whole other culture that has developed at exactly the same time as the culture of Mammon that you see around you. Although many people may not be aware of that fact, the Church of Jesus Christ of Latter-day Saints does exist and has so ever since the 1830's. Furthermore, as opposed to most Christian Churches in the twentieth and twenty-first centuries, who have seen a massive decline in their memberships, the Church of Jesus Christ of Latter-day Saints continues to grow, gaining thousands of converts all over the world every month.

What is probably the most astonishing thing about the Church of Jesus Christ of Latter-day Saints is the fact that the Church makes some rather extraordinary claims. The fact that those claims are believed by millions of people is, if nothing else, of some sociological, if not psychological significance. Why has there not been some closer scrutiny of the claims the Church has made, especially regarding the history that is recounted in the Book of Mormon? I am not talking about the pseudo-science of well-funded detractors that we will soon see, but actual scientific inquiries into the claims of the Church? Why have the detractors of the Church placed their focus in dissemination of lies and distortions that can easily be disproven? The answer to that is, of course, obvious. As we will soon see, the incredible claims of the Church are beginning to hold up to the scrutiny of history and science. If that reality is ever allowed into the "spotlight" of history, the story of mankind will need of a lot of revision, and the idea of who we are and why we are here will take on a whole new meaning.

"I cannot read a sealed book," the Harris/Anthon Controversy

From the time that Joseph Smith Jr. first made it public that he had in his possession, "golden plates," every lie, and as he says, "every stratagem" was used against him. First, the idea was to get the plates out of his possession. Secondly, his enemies sought to challenge his translation of the plates. Finally, with the publication of the *Book of Mormon* in 1830, every effort was made to discredit both the book, Joseph Smith and the Latter-day Saint Church. Those efforts are still ongoing, but, as we will see, not one of them has been successful. What has been successful is that though these attempts have been thwarted and refuted in every way, they *continue* to re-surface in popular culture as "evidence" that the Book of Mormon and Joseph Smith are frauds.

The first attempt to establish the correctness of Joseph Smith's translations is still ringing with controversy and has been since 1828. In what is known as the **Harris/Anthon Controversy**-an incident that is used by both supporters and detractors of the Book of Mormon.

The controversy originated when Joseph Smith sent his financial benefactor, **Martin Harris**, an uneducated farmer of modest means, to New York with a list of characters he had transcribed from the Golden Plates. It was the intent of Joseph Smith and his assistant **Oliver Cowdery**, to get some kind of verification that their translation of the Golden Plates was correct.

What kind of characters was he bringing to Dr. Anthon? In the beginning of the Book of Mormon, the book's first author, Nephi, makes this statement:

"Yea, I make a record in the language of my father, which consists of the learning of the Jews and the language of the Egyptians." (1 Nephi 1:2)

In other words, the subjects of Nephi's writings are about the Hebrew's relationship with the God of the Jews. Nephi is explaining that he is writing in the language of the Egyptians or hieroglyphics, or a variation thereof.

In New York City, Joseph Smith's emissary, Martin Harris, first visited with **Dr. Samuel L. Mitchill**, vice president of Rutgers Medical College, who had the reputation, according to LDS detractor **Dale Lowell Morgan**, of being "a living encyclopedia." Mitchill could not decipher the characters on the paper, so he sent Harris on to **Dr. Charles Anthon** of Columbia University. Later on, Dr. Anthon described the characters on the paper as:

"All kinds of crooked characters disposed in columns and had evidently been prepared by some person who had before him at the time a book containing various alphabets. Greek and Hebrew letters, crosses and flourishes, Roman letters inverted or placed sideways, were arranged in perpendicular columns, and the whole ended in a rude delineation of a circle divided into various compartments, decked with very strange marks, and evidently copied from the Mexican calendar by Humboldt." (Letter to E.D. Howe, February 17, 1834)

Later, detractor Dale Lowell Morgan recounted the meeting between Harris and Dr. Anthon as Anthon described it in a letter after the Book of Mormon was published. At the same time, the LDS Church was publicizing the meeting as the fulfillment of the Old Testament Book of Isaiah as well as the book of Second Nephi in the Book of Mormon.

"And the vision of all is become unto you as the words of a book that is sealed, which men deliver unto one who is learned, saying, Read this, I pray thee: and he saith, I cannot, for it is sealed: And the book is delivered unto him that is not learned, saying, Read this, I pray thee: and he saith, I am not learned." (Isaiah 29:11-12)

"And it shall come to pass that the Lord God shall bring forth unto you the words of a book, and they shall be the words of them which have slumbered. And behold, the book shall be sealed; and in the book shall be a revelation from God, from the beginning of the world to the ending thereof. Wherefore, because of the things which are sealed up, the things which are sealed shall not be delivered in the day of the wickedness and abominations of the people. Wherefore the book shall be kept from them. But the book shall be delivered unto a man, and he shall deliver the words of the book, which are the words of those who have slumbered in the dust, and he shall deliver the words unto another; But the words which are sealed he shall not deliver, neither shall he deliver the book. For the book shall be sealed by the power of God, and the revelation which was sealed shall be kept in the book until the own due time of the Lord, that they may come forth; for behold, they reveal all things from the foundation of the world unto the end thereof. (2 Nephi 27:6-10)

"But behold it shall come to pass that the Lord God shall say unto him to whom he shall deliver the book: Take the words which are not sealed and deliver them to another, that he may show them unto the learned, saying: Read this, I pray thee. And the learned shall say: Bring hither the book and I will read them. And now, because of the glory of the world and to get gain will they say this, and not for the glory of God. And the man shall say: I cannot bring the book, for it is sealed. Then shall the learned say: I cannot read it. Wherefore it shall come to pass, the Lord God will

deliver again the book and the words therof to him that is not learned; and the man that is not learned shall say: I am not learned. Then shall the Lord God say unto him: The learned shall not read them, for they have rejected them, and I am able to do mine own work; wherefore thou shalt read the words which I shall give unto thee.   (2 Nephi 27:15-20)

These claims by the Church did not sit well with Dr. Anthon. In the letter, Dr. Anthon recounts:

"Some years ago, a plain and apparently simple hearted farmer, called upon me with a note from Dr. Mitchell of our city, now deceased, requesting me to decipher, if possible, a paper which the farmer would hand me...Upon examining the paper in question, I soon came to the conclusion that it was all a trick-perhaps a hoax. When I asked the person, who brought it, how he obtained the writing, he gave me the following account: A "gold book" consisting of a number of plates of gold, fastened together...by wires of the same metal, had been dug up in the northern part of the state of New York, and along with it, an enormous pair of "gold spectacles."...Not a word, however was said about the plates being deciphered "by the gift of God." The large spectacles deciphered everything in this way. The farmer added, that he had been requested to give a large sum of money toward the publication of "the golden book," the contents of which would, as he had been assured, produce an entire change in the world and save it from ruin"...on hearing this odd story, I changed my opinion about the paper, and instead of viewing it any longer as a hoax upon the learned, I began to regard it as part of a scheme to cheat the farmer of his money, and I communicated my suspicions to him, warning him to beware of rogues. He requested an opinion from me in writing, which I declined giving him, and he then took his leave, carrying his paper with him. (Howe, Mormonism unveiled pp. 270-271)

According to Dale Lowell Morgan, the LDS account of the meeting is somewhat different:

"Precisely what took place between Harris and Anthon has vexed Mormon history from the moment Anthon showed his visitor (Martin Harris) to the door. The substance of the discussion, as first given out among Joseph Smith's followers, was that Anthon thought the characters very curious, but admitted his inability to decipher them, so that Harris came home with the joyful intelligence that none but Joseph himself was "learned enough to English them."

Harris' version, as later related second-hand by Joseph Smith fourteen years later, was that Anthon pronounced the letters to be "Egyptian, Chaldaic, Assyric and Arabic," and stated that the translation was correct, "more so than any he had before seen translated from the Egyptian," after which he wrote out a certificate "certifying to the people of Palmyra that they were true characters, and that the translation of such of them that had been translated was also correct."

The lack of any third witnesses and the diversity of claims make the whole account comical, at best. There was no translation offered by Martin Harris, only characters, and even had a translation been offered, it would have been of no use, because the French linguist Champollion had not yet worked out the grammar of the Rosetta stone and Anthon therefore, would not have been able to translate them anyway. As Harris was leaving, according to Joseph Smith's account, Anthon bethought himself to inquire how the young man who wrought this translation had found the golden plates. On being informed that an angel of God had made known their existence, Anthon tore up the certificate, saying there was no longer such thing as the ministering by angels. He then told Harris to bring in the plates and he would translate them himself. When Harris replied that part of the plates were sealed, and that he was forbidden to bring them, Anthon put an end to the interview, saying shortly, I cannot read a sealed book."

Because there is no account of the interview by Martin Harris himself, the discrepancy in the claims by both Joseph Smith and Professor Anthon left the Book of Mormon open to controversy even before it was published. Whatever took place at the meeting, Martin Harris did not return and declare Joseph Smith a fraud as Professor Anthon had supposedly advised him. Instead, Martin Harris returned with a renewed faith in what Joseph Smith was doing, and did in fact finance the publication of the Book of Mormon.

The Solomon Spaulding Saga

Even today, the controversy lingers on, as "scholars" on one side try to disprove the authenticity of the Book of Mormon, using circumstance, conjecture and pseudo-research while scholars from the LDS community try to reaffirm their faith through archeological research and historical study. One modern example that, like the Anthon Controversy, began with the early detractors of the Book of Mormon and though disproven is still cited as "evidence" that the Book of Mormon is a forgery.

In what is known as the "**Spaulding Saga**," a project that is financed by the Methodist Church, detractors of the Book of Mormon, such as Spaulding Saga researcher Dale R. Broadhurst, who is one of not a few ex-Latter-day Saints who have, over the years, sought to add some silver to their coffers by exposing Joseph Smith as a fraud. Other ex-Latter-day Saints go so far as to claim the Church of Jesus Christ of Latter-day Saints is a devil-worshipping cult that enslaves women and performs unspeakable sexual acts in their temples. Unspeakable sexual acts aside, I will provide the reader with a brief overview of the *Solomon Spaulding Controversy*, as well as the reaction of the Church. As it is neither the author's intent to endorse, nor detract from the LDS Church, I will leave it up to the reader's curiosity to further explore the matter, which can be done on the internet, or through reading Mr. Broadhurst's Books.

Mo-town madness: Prelude to the Spaulding Saga

Dale Broadhurst claims that the Book of Mormon is a plagiarized version of a book that was written and turned in for publication by **Solomon Spaulding** (1761-1816), a Calvinist preacher and land speculator who wrote books as a pastime. In 1823, years before the publication of the Book of Mormon and before the Solomon Spaulding Controversy, according to "researcher" William Moore, a controversy began surrounding a manuscript that was found in the foundation of a house in Detroit. The manuscript was found by persons "indirectly associated with Joseph Smith," according to Moore, particularly, one Colonel Abraham Edwards. The mysterious paper was sent to the same Dr. Mitchill of Rutgers Medical College that was later visited by Martin Harris, who referred him to Dr. Anthon of Columbia University with Joseph Smith's hieroglyphics. It was later discovered according to Moore, that the mysterious writing was a kind of shorthand used by Catholic monks who had come from Ireland in the 1500's to convert the Native Americans to Christianity.

So, what was the connection of the mysterious transcript finder, Colonel Abraham Edwards and founder of the LDS Church, Joseph Smith? According to Moore, Colonel Edwards was an, "occasional business partner" of Joseph Smith's maternal uncle, Stephen Mack, who was a cousin of Oliver Cowdery, the same person who helped Joseph Smith translate the Golden Plates into the Book of Mormon. According to Moore, who admits, "…there is no proof to this conclusion," Oliver Cowdery left Vermont with his cousin Stephen Mack in 1822. They passed through Palmyra, New York, where they allegedly stopped to see Stephen Mack's sister, Lucy, who was the wife of Joseph Smith Sr. and the mother of Joseph Smith Jr. Moore hypothesizes that the 17 year-old Joseph Smith then accompanied the party west to Buffalo, where they meet with Baptist Preacher Sidney Rigdon.

Who is Sidney Rigdon? According to William L. Moore in his article, *The Great Book of Mormon Sham*, Solomon Spaulding turned in his manuscript entitled, *A Manuscript Found* in 1816 to **R & J Publishing** in Pittsburgh where Sidney Rigdon, a Baptist preacher, "…took a great interest in it, or obtained a copy of the story." Later, in 1827, according to the article, Rigdon met with Oliver Cowdery and twenty-two year old Joseph Smith and together, they conjured up the Church of Jesus Christ of Latter-day Saints. According to Moore, and Broadhurst, the whole basis for the Solomon Spaulding controversy is this:

"Nobody now knows what finally became of Spaulding's original manuscript, but one this is certain: when the so-called Mormon Bible was published in 1830, its narrative followed precisely the outline of Spaulding's story. The plot was essentially the same and the proper nouns Mormon, Lehi and Lamanites were the same."

Thanks to the dedicated research of Mr. Moore, it would appear that, indeed, the Book of Mormon is a complete sham, a plagiarized version of a story left in a print shop where the unscrupulous preacher, Sidney Rigdon was able to get his sticky fingers on it whereby he either copied it or stole it. He then conspired with Joseph Smith Jr. and Oliver Cowdery to concoct an entire belief system based upon the work of a hapless deceased author who would never receive credit for his literary efforts, were it not for the research skills of William Moore, who published his work in *Far Out* magazine, a publication owned by none other than *Hustler* magazine's own Larry Flint.

There are only a few minor problems with the claims made by Mr. Moore in his article. The most obvious problem was that the manuscript, entitled, *A Manuscript Found* was in fact, a manuscript found. In a rather bizarre chain of events, one publisher and editor, Mr. L.L. Rice, found Solomon Spaulding's manuscript sometime in the latter 1800's. Mr. Rice had purchased the shop where *Mormonism Unveiled*, one of the first books written to officially denounce the Latter-day Saint Church, was printed. The author of *Mormonism Unveiled* was E.D. Howe, whom we have already seen in relation to his describing the events that transpired between Martin Harris and Dr. Anthon of Columbia University in regards to Joseph Smith's translation of the hieroglyphics.

E.D. Howe had obtained the manuscript of Spaulding's *A Manuscript Found* from a man by the name of D.P. Hurlbut, who had been excommunicated from the LDS Church for sexual improprieties and who had subsequently sworn to destroy the church. Hurlbut had approached the widow of Solomon Spaulding and asked to borrow the manuscript, which he did and failed to return it. It was the intent of both Mr. Hurlbut and E.D. Howe to use the manuscript, like Mr. Moore, Mr. Broadhurst and many others to discredit the LDS Church as well as Joseph Smith and the Book of Mormon as a fraud and a "sham." Unfortunately for all involved, when L.L. Rice purchased the shop, he had also inadvertently taken possession of the Spaulding manuscript, "without even knowing what it was for some forty years," according to the account related by later Church President Joseph Fielding Smith.

The manuscript found

The bizarre story unfolded in 1885 when the President of Oberlin College of Ohio contacted an Elder of the LDS Church in Honolulu, Hawaii. The Elder in turn, sent the college president's correspondence and a newspaper clipping to Joseph Fielding Smith, who was serving a mission in the Sandwich Islands for the LDS Church. The letter was in fact, a letter sent to the Church in Honolulu from James A. Fairchild, the President of Oberlin College in Ohio. In the letter, Fairchild recounts how he had requested anti-slavery and Civil War articles and correspondence from Mr.

Rice that might be of historical significance for the library of Oberlin College. During his search, Mr. Rice had stumbled upon a manuscript by Solomon Spaulding. In his letter, James A. Fairchild explains:

> "There seems to be no doubt this is the long lost story. Mr. Rice, myself and others compared it with the Book of Mormon, and could detect no resemblance between the two, in general or in detail. There seems to be no name nor incident common to the two. The solemn style of the Book of Mormon, in imitation of the English scriptures, does not appear in the manuscript. The only resemblance is in the fact that both profess to set forth the history of the lost tribes. Some other explanation of the origin of the Book of Mormon must be found, if any explanation is required."
>
> (Letter from Dr. Fairchild to the LDS Church)

Mr. Rice allowed Joseph F. Smith to examine the transcript, and, in fact, to obtain a copy of the version that Mr. Rice copied himself. That the LDS Church under the strict conditions published manuscript in the Deseret News, which Mr. Rice had insisted upon, allowing no error, crossed out, or erased word to be taken from the text. As for the story itself, according to Smith, the story concerned a group of people who left Rome in the times of the Empire destined for England. However, they were carried away by a storm and ended up somewhere in the region of the Great Lakes. The characters, contrary to the popular version of the story, had Roman names, or names that would be associated with Native Americans. They were not Jews, nor did they claim to come from Jerusalem.

However, those who had used the manuscript to defame the Book of Mormon had already had their say for forty years. If you recall, *R & J Patterson Printing* in Pittsburgh is where Dale Broadhurst claims that Sidney Rigdon pilfered or copied the manuscript. In his book, *Who Wrote the Book of Mormon?* Robert Patterson makes the following claim:

> "In this discussion there are manifestly but two points to be considered. The first is to establish the fact that the historical portions of the Book of Mormon are certainly derived from Spaulding's Manuscript Found; and the second to show, if practicable, in what way and by whom the plagiarism was probably effected.(sic) Of these, the first is the only vitally

important one. If the identity can be determined, imposture can be proved even though it may not be possible to demonstrate absolutely how the fraud was perpetrated."

In other words, Mr. Patterson was sure that the Book of Mormon was "certainly derived" from Spaulding's manuscript and that was the only important issue. How Joseph Smith may have come across the manuscript and subsequently copied it was not important. Mr. Patterson's *a priori* logic is more than likely based on the fact that at the time, he knew the manuscript was sitting in his office. Should someone somehow ever question how it could be in his office and in the hands of the plagiarizing Joseph Smith was not important (hence the "pilfering Sydney Rigdon" Theory). It is obvious someone making such claims was also quite confident that *Manuscript Found* would never be found. In reality, the only thing that we can be sure of as far as Mr. Patterson's testimony is, that based on the findings of James A. Fairchild, the President of Oberlin College, Mr. L.L. Rice, a distinguished former newspaper editor and publisher, and future President of the Church, Joseph Fielding Smith, that the manuscript had nothing to do with the Book of Mormon. Patterson was confident therefore, that his statements would never be verified. Other than claiming it was stolen or copied by Sydney Rigdon, he had no way of demonstrating how it may have gotten into the hands of Joseph Smith. How the manuscript was ultimately left in the shop to be discovered deserves further investigation.

In light of the fact that the only persons known to have physically handled the manuscript were Solomon Spaulding himself, Mr. Patterson's father, who had returned it to Spaulding with the instructions to, "polish it up, finish it, you will make money out of it," Spaulding's widow, who turned it over to Mr. Jerome

Clark in order to have it delivered to D.B. Hurlbut. D.B. Hurlbut then turned the manuscript with attested signatures over to D.E. Howe for use in his book *Mormonism Unveiled* (1835).

Because of the manuscript finally and inadvertently ending up in the possession of editor and publisher L.L. Rice, we can only assume that Mr. Patterson published his book, *Who Really Wrote the Book of Mormon?* relatively sure that the manuscript for *A Manuscript Found* would never actually be found. But Mr. Patterson, son of the owner of the Pittsburgh print shop was not the only person willing to stake their reputation on the dastardly theft of Mr. Spaulding's manuscript by the unscrupulous "Mormons."

Along with the testimony of Mr. Patterson, there were a number of signatures with the manuscript attesting to the fact that both the Book of Mormon and *A Manuscript Found* were indeed the work of Solomon Spaulding and their signatures were attested by none other than LDS excommunicate and vowed enemy of the Church, D. B. Hurlbut. Those witnesses are, Aaron Wright, Oliver Smith, John M. Miller and five others. Solomon Spaulding's own brother, John, claims that Mr. Spaulding read to him "many passages" from the book. John Spaulding described the book his brother wrote this way:

"It was an historical romance of the first settlers of America, endeavoring to show that the American Indians are descendants of the Jews, or the Lost Tribes. It gave a detailed account of their journey from Jerusalem by land and sea, till they arrived in America under the command of Nephi and Lehi…"

Along with John Spaulding's testimony is the testimony of his wife Martha, who states:

"I was personally acquainted with Solomon Spaulding some twenty years ago. The lapse of time which has intervened prevents my recollecting but a few of the incidents of his writings, but the name of Lehi and Nephi are yet fresh in my memory as being the principal heroes of the tale…"

Henry Lake, a former partner of Spaulding recounts his partner's literary piece in this fashion:

"He (Spaulding) very frequently read to me from a manuscript which he was writing…Some months ago I borrowed the Golden Bible (Book of Mormon), put it into my pocket, carried it home, and thought no more of it. About a week after, my wife found the book in my coat pocket as it hung up and commenced reading aloud as I lay on the bed. She had not read twenty minutes till I was astonished to find the same passages in it that Spaulding had read to me more than twenty years before in *A Manuscript Found*."

John N. Miller attested to the authenticity of the manuscript and exposed the fraud perpetuated by Joseph Smith this way:

"…I have recently examined the Book of Mormon and find in it the writings of Solomon Spaulding from beginning to end, but mixed up with scripture and other religious matter which I did not meet with in *Manuscript Found*. Many of the passages are verbatim from Spaulding, and others, in part. The names of Nephi, Lehi, Moroni, and in fact all the principal names are brought fresh to my collection by the Golden Bible…"

Aaron Wright, who also attested to the authenticity of the manuscript said:

"The historical part of the Book of Mormon I knew to be the same as I read and heard read from the writing of Spaulding more than twenty years ago: the names are more especially the same without any alteration…"

Oliver Smith, with whom Spaulding boarded while selling tracts of land he had purchased, recollects how Mr. Spaulding spent his leisure hours:

"All his leisure hours were occupied in writing an historical novel founded upon the first settlers of this country. He said he intended to trace their journey from Jerusalem, by land and sea, till their arrival in America; give an account of their arts, sciences, civilizations, wars and contentions…"

According to Joseph Fielding Smith, in a series of articles that were published in the LDS magazine *Improvement Era,* in 1900, there were a number of other similar witnesses that attested to the same facts. When the news that the manuscript had been found became public, a number of persons who were either descendants of Solomon Spaulding or descendents of those who had made these spurious claims immediately clamored for the manuscript. Once their fraud had been made public, their only recourse was to seize the manuscript and claim that it was not the manuscript written by Solomon Spaulding at all. This was the second attempt to do so. The first attempt came from Mr. Hurlbut himself who had his agent obtain the manuscript from Spaulding's widow under the guise as a representative of the LDS Church. It was then that Hurlbut was going to insist that it was, "sold to the Mormons and destroyed by them."

It was somewhat fortunate therefore, for the LDS Church that Mr. D.P. Hurlbut possessed the foresight to get the signatures from the witnesses prior to the publication of *Mormonism Unveiled* by D.E. Howe in 1835. Smith himself writes that Oberlin College President, James A. Fairchild, "had originally been convinced that the "Manuscript Story" was indeed the origin of the Book of Mormon, and while, perhaps as eager as anybody to demonstrate that fact was greatly disappointed as was also Mr. L.L. Rice..."

Why would these people so adamantly state what they knew to be false in such a brazen attempt to discredit the Book of Mormon? First of all, there is always the possibility the D.P. Hurlbut, in his zeal to destroy the Church, simply forged the testimonies of the witnesses as they appeared in Howe's book. If they actually did provide testimony, it is interesting that each one points out that their testimonies are based upon what they "heard" Solomon Spaulding read from his manuscript, rather than what they actually read. Also important to note is that most of the witnesses claim that the names and the history are identical. Since it is obvious that in neither case are these statements accurate, could it be possible that these people were actually illiterate and poor, and their motivation to cooperate with Messrs. Hurlbut and Howe, if, in fact that is the case, was most likely the same reason for the lies and slander that have been, and continue to be perpetuated against a group of people who have, in their history, harmed no one (except in self defense) slandered no one, and have been foremost in advocating the rights of all groups to be able to practice the religion of their choosing? Most likely, the three main reasons were then and are now, money, money and money. Even today, slandering the LDS Church is a very lucrative enterprise. Former members of the Church, competing religions and people who hate what the LDS Church stands for, such as Larry Flint, publisher of *Hustler* and *Far Out* magazine in which the Moore article first appeared, make a lot of money writing expository books, producing paraphernalia and selling videos about the Church.

Those darn "Mormons!"

Why would a group of people like the completely uninteresting members of the Latter-day Saint Church be of such interest to the rest of society? The answer requires looking briefly into our own psychological make-up. Simply put, members of the LDS Church are different. It is basic human nature to single out and destroy anything and anyone who is too different from the rest of the primeval herd. They believe in an entire world system based upon the rather bizarre claims of a farm boy and a few of his associates, a visitation from God and Jesus Christ, an ancient book that no one has seen since and a church that bases all of its decisions upon what it claims to be the revelations of God. No one can be blamed for their skepticism, because the history of the human race, unfortunately, is peppered with the spice of charlatans. American history is fraught with "snake oil" salesmen, carpetbaggers and get-rich-quick aficionados, who made and continue to make a living bilking the poor and unsuspecting out of their money. So would we be wrong to suspect Joseph Smith?

Next, we have to look at our own development as a species. We credit our survival, in part, to our ability to maintain a sense of normalcy within our social groups. The "Mormons" are themselves to blame for fostering their identity as being different. Their intolerance for behavior that is against their system of beliefs and their version of morality is yet another source of antagonism and a visible differentiation or gap between themselves and the rest of society. Their seeming unwillingness to be open to alternative points of view, especially those that are deemed "politically correct" also tends to set them apart from the rest of the world, particularly those whose thoughts and ideas are fashioned by the rulers of the money kingdom.

Members of the LDS Church are also human beings. Human beings are human beings and as such are constantly making mistakes. Like the people populating the large building in Lehi's vision (which we will see shortly), society laughs and applauds when a member of the LDS Church is found to fall short of the high expectations of the Church. Members of the Church, like any religious institution, tend to judge and compare their counterparts, while failing, as Jesus once said, to "remove the mote" from their own eye. This leads many members of the Church to leave the Church for reasons as trifling as a poorly spoken comment, or a feeling that they are not being appreciated as they feel they should be. When people do leave the Church, there are many waiting to applaud their decision and so they receive comfort for their bruised feelings and egos but find that comfort only serves as fertilizer as the bruised egos and feelings continue to grow and to dominate their feelings about the Church.

The next reason that people have for their antagonism for the Church is the least flattering for us as human beings. Quite simply, many people are just mean and ignorant. Many people have a need to hate someone or something in order to feel better about themselves. People who hate "Mormons" also probably have a list that contains Jews, blacks, Catholics, Christians, Muslims, whites, Mexicans, Italians, Democrats, Republicans, gays, men, women, the government, Barney the Dinosaur, etc. If you were to ask these people why they hate "Mormons" or some other group, most likely they would start blurting out a list of facts that you would most likely know to be false. If you were to try to point out the errors in their reasoning they would insist upon your own ignorance or accuse you of being, "one of them."

Finally, there is one other factor that sparks a psychological and philosophical interest in the LDS Church that makes us all afraid. It is the fear that they may in fact, be right. When Galileo pointed his telescope at the planets five hundred years ago, he moved man from the center of the universe, which was a place where Western Civilization had been quite comfortable for twenty-five hundred years. All of a sudden, we had to rethink everything. That process has taken hundreds of years and it was not a transition that has been easily accomplished. If, what the things that the Church of Jesus Christ of Latter-day Saints claim are true, then once again, we as a society are pushed into another realm of consciousness for which many of us are not prepared.

The first Christians, Muslims and Jews would easily recognize the antagonism of the outside world toward their groups, as do the Latter-day Saints of today. Their entire belief systems as well were ridiculed and they underwent political, economic and sometimes violent persecution because of the unorthodox claims of the founders of their religions. Yet they persevered over the centuries and the God that they worshipped appears to have protected them and has allowed them to prosper and multiply throughout the world. In the modern world, there is one fact that cannot be denied, the world has been mentally conditioned through the popular media to have a negative opinion of the Church of Jesus Christ of Latter-day Saints. We know who has the power to do this. Now it is time to give a "rebel yell" of sorts and take a serious look into exactly what is that they don't want us to see.

Chapter 12

History According to the Latter-day Saints

"And then the Lord said: Let us go down. And they went down at the beginning, and they, that is the Gods, organized and formed the heavens and the earth." (Abraham 4:1)

The visitors

Let me begin this chapter by saying, once again, that it is not my intent to promote the beliefs of the Church of Jesus Christ of Latter-day Saints. The Church of Jesus Christ of Latter-day Saints is important to this book because of their relationship with the Freemasons and some of the similarities in their belief systems. The LDS Church is also important because of the evidence, coincidental or otherwise, of Christian and Masonic influence within the Mayan, Incan, Aztec and other Latin American cultures, as well as Masonic influence in the Egyptian, Greek and Hebrew cultures which in turn are also present in LDS belief systems. Last of all, and probably most important, every one of the millions of members of the Church of Jesus Christ of Latter-day Saints believes that God the Father, Jesus Christ, John the Baptist, the apostles; Matthew, Mark and John as well as the angel Moroni, appeared to Joseph Smith, and other members of the Church at various times. Their leader or prophet is, according to their beliefs, in direct communication with the Creator of the known Universe.

Like the extraterrestrial phenomenon, every person on the face of this planet should be concerned about these claims. Furthermore real scientific inquiry should be undertaken, if for no other reason, than to disprove and dismiss these claims once and for all. Unlike the extraterrestrial phenomenon (as we shall see later), no official study or panel was ever assembled to decide on a course of action regarding the claims of the Latter-day Saint Church. Instead, the only answer that we have seen is the spread of disinformation. Why won't science and archeology honestly and objectively investigate the claims of the LDS Church? Hopefully, the reader will be able to arrive at his or her own conclusions based upon the information that follows.

There are similarities in the beliefs of the Freemasons and the Latter-day Saint Church regarding extraterrestrial visitors. The above-mentioned personages who visited Joseph Smith and other Church leaders arrived here from both a world and a dimension that is not of this planet therefore, they must be classified scientifically as "extraterrestrials." Later, we will discuss the need for the term EBE, or "Extraterrestrial Biological Entity," as opposed to just calling the visitors found at crash sites, "extraterrestrials." In order to understand the Freemason and LDS beliefs regarding these entities, it is important to understand how members of the Latter-day Saint Church view the world and its history before we can develop any kind of possible connection between the three.

Finally, the LDS Church, like the extraterrestrial phenomenon, is another example of a belief system that the organizations who control the media, the government and financial institutions have attempted to defame, slander and, as we have seen and will see, sometimes to destroy. In order to save a lot of unnecessary writing on my part and reading on yours, please understand the information that follows in this chapter is preceded with the phrase, "According to LDS doctrine..." which will save the reader a whole lot of time and the writer and publisher the same amount of space.

In order to understand history according to LDS beliefs, it is important to understand that Church history, doctrine and beliefs are one in the same according to the LDS Church. The reason for this has more to do with semantics than anything else. First of all, we can't call the LDS version of what happened in the Americas during the centuries preceding and following the Common Era "history" because the ideas accepted as fact by the Latter-day Saints are not accepted as fact by anyone other than church members (at least not yet). Therefore, there are versions of LDS history that are actually "history" if you accept them (LDS members) and "beliefs" (non-LDS members) if you don't. Second, doctrine is also intertwined with LDS history and is therefore classified as a belief, but LDS doctrine also delves beyond history into spiritualism, procedure, and protocol and, in some cases, promises held out to the obedient by Jesus Christ, as they are told in the New Testament, the Book of Mormon and the Doctrine and Covenants.

The Latter-day Saint scriptures: the Books of Moses and Abraham

The history of the world, according to the LDS Church, fairly coincides with that history we see in both the Old and New Testament in the Christian Bible. In spite of popular beliefs, the LDS Church reveres the Bible, like all other Christian faiths, as the Word of God. However, the LDS Church holds three other books in equal reverence to the Bible. Those books are, *The Pearl of Great Price*, which contains the Book of Moses, revealed to Joseph Smith by Jesus Christ, the Book of Abraham, which is a translation of hieroglyphs that came into the hands of Joseph Smith in the way of Egyptian papyrus in the 1830's, as well translations of certain hieroglyphic tables that also appeared on the papyrus. *The Pearl of Great Price* also contains Joseph Smith's translation of the Gospel of Matthew, a brief history of Joseph Smith and the *Articles of Faith*, which we saw in a previous chapter.

Briefly, the Book of Moses contains a much more detailed account of the story of the creation of universe, the earth and man than does the Book of Genesis. In the Book of Moses, Moses speaks with God, who reveals how and why the world was created. Also, in the Book of Moses we see two very important pieces of information that have been left out of the Old Testament. One is the identity of and the mission of Jesus Christ and the idea that there are other worlds besides our own over which God has dominion, which will become important later in this book.

"And worlds without number have I created; and also I created them for my own purpose; and by the Son I created them, which is my Only Begotten." (Moses 1:33)

The Book of Moses relates the account of Adam and his transgression when he and Eve partook of the Tree of Knowledge of good and evil.

However, Adam, realizing his mistake, repents and is forgiven. Thereafter, Adam develops a close relationship with God. Adam also receives the fullness of the Gospel of Jesus Christ as well as the holy order of the Priesthoods that will be passed on to Melchezidek and Aaron.

"And thus the Gospel began to be preached, from the beginning, being declared by holy angels sent forth from the presence of God, and by his own voice, and by the gift of the Holy Ghost. And thus all things were confirmed unto Adam, by an holy ordinance, and the Gospel preached, and a decree sent forth, that it should be in the world, until the end thereof, and thus it was. Amen." (Moses 5:58-59)

But, alas, it was Adam's offspring, in one sense, that were to be the source of both his and God's woes. The first murder to get gain would be committed by his son, Cain. Cain's descendents would initiate and pass on a chain of secret masters who would use murder to gain power and wealth and use oaths to keep their works secret. Cain's descendant Lamech, who killed his great-grandfather for revealing the secret oaths, would commit the first murder for an oath:

"Wherefore Lamech, being angry, slew him, not like unto Cain, his brother Abel, for the sake of getting gain, but he slew him for the oath's sake. For, from the days of Cain, there was a secret combination, and their works were in the dark, and they knew every man his brother." (Moses 5:50-51)

We will discuss these secret societies in more depth in a later chapter. Suffice it to say, that the descendants of Cain led the descendants of Adam down the primrose path to hell, with a few exceptions. One of those exceptions was Adam's son Seth, who, like his father, administered and taught the Gospel to the descendants of Adam. Seth and his descendants in turn, preached the gospel and created a community of righteous people who lived the Gospel of Jesus Christ as it had been passed down from Adam. The patriarchs in the line of Seth that are discussed in the Book of Moses were Enoch and his son Methuselah, the grandfather of Noah.

Enoch, like Moses, spoke face to face with God. One of the common themes throughout the Bible, the Book of Mormon and the Doctrine and Covenants is also present in the Pearl of Great Price. God and Jesus Christ never seem to make social calls. They only show up when they want someone to do something for them and Enoch was no exception. Enoch, to his credit, would try to use the same excuse that Moses would use a thousand or so years later, but it didn't seem to have much effect in either case.

"And he heard a voice from heaven, saying: Enoch my son, prophecy unto this people, and say unto them-Repent, for thus saith the Lord: I am angry with this people, and my fierce anger is kindled against them; for their hearts have waxed hard, and their ears are dull of hearing, and their eyes cannot see afar off." (Moses 6:27)

"And when Enoch had heard these words, he bowed himself to the earth, before the Lord, and spake before the Lord, saying; Why is it that I have found favor in thy sight, and am but a lad, all the people hate me; for I am slow of speech; wherefore am I thy servant?" (Moses 6:31)

The Lord didn't, as it turned out, care much for Enoch's excuses. Subsequently, through his preaching, Enoch was able to convince many people that the warning of the Lord, *"Repent, lest I come out and smite them with a curse and they die,"* (Moses 7:10) is advice better heeded than not. Through his preaching, Enoch was able to gain enough of a following to establish a city:

"And the Lord called his people Zion, because they were of one heart and one mind, and dwelt in righteousness; and there was no poor among them. And Enoch continued his preaching in righteousness unto the people of God. And it came to pass in his days, that he built a city, that was called the City of Holiness, even Zion."
(Moses 7:18-19)

Later, we will talk about the fate of the city of Zion. For now, to finish up our brief summary of the Book of Moses, his son Methuselah carries on with his father's work of preaching the gospel. By the time of Noah, the Lord is angry as all-get-out at how evil men have become. Noah and his sons try in vain to warn the population that mankind will be destroyed unless they repent, but, as we know, Noah's efforts were wasted and finally, in desperation God instructs him to build an ark.

"And God said unto Noah,; The end of all flesh is come before me, for the earth is filled with violence, and behold, I will destroy all flesh from off the earth." (Moses 8:30)

The Book of Abraham

The Book of Abraham, one of the other major works in the *Pearl of Great Price,* is an account of the biblical patriarch of the same name. The account of Abraham describes his abduction by Egyptian Priests who attempt to sacrifice him to the Gods of Egypt. Fortunately for Abraham, God interferes. He kills the priest, destroys the temple of Elkenah and allows Abraham to escape. Abraham then describes his own lineage, and his possession of the holy priesthood that went on board the ark with Noah. Abraham also describes the origins of the Egyptians as descendants of the Canaanites, who are in turn, descendants of the son of Ham, one of the three sons of Noah. The Egyptians claim the priesthood of Noah, though Abraham is quick to point out that they are pretenders and not entitled to the priesthood or, as he says, *"the pharaohs would fain claim it from Noah,"* (Abraham 1:27) because of the cursing Noah put upon Ham and his descendants.

Abraham is promised the land of Canaan as an inheritance for himself and his generations. In the latter books of Abraham, the creation of the earth and the heavens is recounted. This version more closely resembles the creation stories of Mesopotamia than that of Genesis. For example, it is not God, but *"the Gods,"* who create heaven and earth. Also of note in the Book of Abraham is the use of the Urim and Thummim, a device that would later be used by Joseph Smith to translate the Book of Mormon. Abraham uses the Urim and Thummim in order to communicate directly with God. God explains to Abraham about the nature of planets, stars, moons, and explains that the greatest planet of all is called Kolob and it is Kolob that is the closest planet to God.

"And thus shall be the reckoning of the time of one planet above another, until thou come nigh unto Kolob, which Kolob is after the reckoning of the Lord's time, which Kolob is set nigh unto the throne of God, to govern all those planets which belong to the same order as that upon which thou standest." (Abraham 3:9)

Abraham is shown that all beings possess intelligences that are eternal, which is an idea that we will see again in the writings of Plato.

"Howbeit that he made the greater star; as, also, if there be two spirits, and one shall be more intelligent than the other, yet these two spirits, notwithstanding one is more intelligent than the other, have no beginning; they existed before, they shall have no end, they shall exist after, for they are gnolaum, or eternal." (Abraham 3:18)

And so, these are some of the major points of Book of Abraham and the Book of Moses that serve to fill in some of the gaps left in the Bible through thousands of years of trying to recount everything from memory or transcribing faded parchments and doing so in a variety of religious and political climates. Of note, is the absence of the mission of Jesus Christ in the books of the Old Testament, the presence of the Priesthood and the basic ordinances of the Gospel, which are based upon the principals of faith, repentance, baptism and the gift of the Holy Spirit.

In these accounts, there is no digression from the spirit and the message of the Old and New Testament. Many will argue, as there are entire faiths based upon the Old Testament version of history, that these books have no valid place in religious doctrine. Many have argued and many continue to argue that all of this information is nonsense, and the product of an overactive imagination. However, in spite of all of their attempts, no person, church, government or organization has been able to destroy the Church, nor conclusively prove that the teachings, scriptures and ideas of the Church of Jesus Christ of Latter-days are anything but consistent with the Old and New Testaments. The only thing they can conclude is that their own beliefs differ from those of the Latter-day Saint Church.

The Book of Mormon: An Overview

Latter-day Saints also uphold the Book of Mormon as the Word of God. It contains two histories of peoples that inhabited the Americas in two different time periods. Before the reader becomes confused, please be reassured, in this chapter we are only concerned with the Book of Mormon and the accounts of the two cultures that it describes. The book that describes the older of the two cultures is contained within the Book of Mormon as a separate book and is called the **Book of Ether** (ee-ther).

The Book of Ether is about a people or culture known as **"Jaredites"** who came out of the Middle East at the time of the **Tower of Babel** and resided in the Americas until they destroyed themselves because of their corruption and hatred for each other. A family, who crossed the ocean in vessels, that more or less sound like they were constructed, using a submarine for a blue print, founded the Jaredite civilization. The Book of Ether describes these vessels in the following manner:

"And they were built after a manner that were exceedingly tight, even that they would hold water like unto a dish; and the sides thereof were tight like unto a dish; and the ends therof were peaked; and the top therof was tight like unto a dish; and the length thereof was the length of a tree; and the door therof, when it was shut, was tight like unto a dish." (Ether 2:17)

The Book of Ether is based upon twenty-four plates that were discovered by the second peoples of the Book of Mormon, the **Nephites** (nee-fites). The Nephite Prophet-King Mosiah by means of the Urim and Thummim translated these plates. The Jaredite civilization that is described in the twenty-four plates is much older, lasted much longer and was most likely much more technologically advanced than the Nephites and their counterparts, the **Lamanites** (lay-man-ites) whose history makes up the bulk of the Book of Mormon. The Nephites and Lamanites (modern Native Americans) were Jews that left Jerusalem prior to 600 BCE, just before the city was attacked and many of the inhabitants were taken as slaves in what is known as the Babylonian Captivity.

When Moroni and his father Mormon, some of the last survivors of the Nephite Civilization, were preparing to hide the Golden Plates, Moroni wrote a condensed version of the Jaredite's history. Therefore, what is in the possession of the LDS Church is actually a translated, abbreviated version of a much older and more elaborate record. In other words, it is a translation (Joseph Smith's) of a condensed version (Moroni's) of the original translation by the Nephite King, Mosiah.

"Therefore, he took the records which were engraven upon the plates of brass, and also the plates of Nephi, and all the things which he had kept and preserved according to the commandments of God, after having translated and caused to be written the records which were on the plates of gold which had been found by the people of Limhi, which were delivered

to him by the hand of Limhi; And this he did because of the great anxiety of his people; for they were desirous beyond measure to know concerning those people who had been destroyed."

"Now after Mosiah had finished translating these records, behold, it gave an account of the people who were destroyed, from the time that they were destroyed back to the time of the building of the great tower, at the time the Lord confounded the language of the people and they were scattered abroad upon the face of the earth, yea, and even from that time, back to the creation of Adam." (Mosiah 28:11-12,17)

Moroni explains in the Book of Ether that the entire record of the Jaredites begins at the time of Adam and continues through to the tower of Babel. Moroni explains in the Book of Ether that since the Jews, as well as his own people already possess the records between the time of Adam and the Tower of Babel, he chose to save time by starting his abbreviated version at the Tower of Babel. His account details the Jaredite's ocean crossing, some of their accomplishments, wars and finally, their destruction.

The Jaredites: Back to the Flood and the Tower of Babel

Since we have previously discussed the history of the Bible, as well as the history of the world, it should not be too difficult for the reader to understand some of the differences in the Latter-day Saint belief system, from those that are present in the Holy Bible. What may surprise the reader is that some of the beliefs in LDS doctrine are also present in the belief systems of pre-Christian cultures, such as the Mayan, Greek, Mesopotamian and Egyptian. Although the first reaction might be to scoff at such outlandish claims, and this writer encourages the reader to scoff wherever scoffing might seem appropriate, in this chapter we will look at some recent discoveries that make the story of the Jaredites, the Nephites and the Lamanites begin to seem almost plausible.

Trying to pin down specific dates in the Bible is like trying to get an honest answer out of a politician. It is extremely difficult, if not impossible to do. Biblical dates are based upon personal prejudices as well as the range of flexibility within an individual regarding how much information is to be taken literally. If the reader will recall, in the previous chapter when we were discussing the popular history of the world according to scientists, historians and the rest of the "ivory tower" crowd, science has recently discovered that 11,700 years ago, there was a massive melting of the glaciers in the northern and southern hemispheres, followed by a catastrophic flood that resulted as the ice turned to water and filled in the ocean basins and flooded what had been land for thousands of years.

For some unexplained reason, at that time, 11,700 years ago, the earth, which had been in a cold cycle for thousands of years, began to warm, which is a trend that has continued to the present day. Evidence recently uncovered and published in *Cosmos* magazine describes yet another cataclysmic flood that occurred around 8,000 years ago as water trapped under the ice sheet in North America melted. It escaped at the rate of "fifteen times the rate of the Amazon," into the Atlantic Ocean, raising sea level by estimates of up to fourteen meters, or forty-two feet.

If the reader will also recall that in the Bible, there is a story of a catastrophic flood in which a man named Noah and his family, along with two of everything, were able to survive in a large boat. As we stated earlier, not only is the flood story present in the Bible, it is also present in almost every culture around the world. The conflict between science and religion as far as the Biblical flood story is obvious. The considerable gap in time between the catastrophic floods of the glacial break-up and the Biblical account being one of the most blatant of the many conflicts associated with the Biblical flood story. Biblical scholars, who claim the age of the earth is seven thousand years, begin to box themselves in when they place the flood of the Book of Genesis within that time period. This would mean the earth was created in 5,000 B.C.E. That would leave around 1,500 years from the Creation, to the cities of Sumer and the Indus River. If we take in to account all of the "begat-ing" we spoke of earlier, then a flood, then another series of fruitful multiplying, it is really cutting things close. Furthermore, there is no record in any of the existing civilizations of the time (Sumer, Indus River) of a concurrent flood that wiped out all of mankind except for Noah's family, so we have to push things back toward the Beginning. The farther back we push the flood toward the Creation, the less time we have for "begat-ing" and fruitful multiplication, making the story even more and more difficult to put into the given time period of the staunch Biblical crowd. However, a few thousand years later, the

Assyrians, contemporaries of the Babylonians, recount how their mythical hero Gilgamesh, survived a flood similar to the Biblical accounts. Later, a similar story shows up in the Old Testament of the Hebrews, so, there must be something to flood, which will work if we just push the Creation just a teensy weensy bit further back.

The predominance of the account of a catastrophic flood in most of the world's cultures cannot be ignored outright as a coincidence, especially since there are many similarities in the names assigned to the man in the story by various and distinct cultures. Could there have been civilizations that were ultimately destroyed when their preference for building cities near water ultimately led to their destruction when the floods came as the ice melted? The Noah story seems implausible unless we put him back in time to the melting of the ice sheets, and then, it becomes not only possible, but also highly likely.

So, what does this conflict between geologists and historians and the proponents of the Bible story of the flood have to do with the Jaredite civilization in the Book of Mormon? According to the Book of Mormon account, the Jaredites were a small collection of families that existed somewhere near the city where the Tower of Babel was built. Do we have any historical references today that refer to the Tower of Babel? Unfortunately, as with the flood, we come up "dry" as we are lacking in concurrent references outside of the Bible that would corroborate the story. Therefore, for the moment, let us swallow a gulp or two of our "humble pie" with a glass of milk and see if there is further evidence that might later corroborate the Tower of Babel with the Bible, the Jaredites and Moroni's account. If the reader will recall, at the time of the Tower of Babel, God confounded the language of mankind:

"And the whole earth was of one language, and of one speech. And it came to pass, as they journeyed from the east, that they found a plain in the land of Shinar; and they dwelt there. And they said to one another, Go to, let us make brick, and burn them thoroughly. And they had brick for stone and slime had they for mortar. And they said, Go to, let us build us a city and a tower, whose top may reach unto heaven; and let us make a name, lest we be scattered upon the face of the earth. And the Lord said, Behold the people is one, and they have all one language; and this they begin to do: and now nothing will be restrained from them, which they have

imagined to do. Go to, let us go down, and there confound their language, that they may not understand one another's speech."

(Genesis 11:1-6)

According to the Jaredite record, at the time of the destruction of the Tower, the group known as the "Jaredites" pleaded with God so that he would not confound their language, to which He complied. The group then left what some scholars believe was the Fertile Crescent and, according to some LDS researchers like George Potter, author of *Lehi in the Wilderness* and *Nephi in the Promised Land*, the group made their way south to the ancient city of Khor Rori near the modern day city of Salalah in the Sultanate of Oman. There, they built their ocean-going vessels and crossed to America, landing, according to Potter, on the coast of Peru. Scientists, historians and researchers may argue that a far-fetched tale and the historically unreliable account in Genesis does not a plausible theory make, but, there are many new details that have come to light that may, if not confirm this story, then at least mark it as an amazing coincidence.

The Jaredites who crossed the ocean were originally twenty-two in number, but it was a journey that took many years and, since they had children along the way, they had a population arriving in the Americas somewhere between twenty two and one hundred. If the reign of each king in the Book of Ether is given an average reign of forty years, from the time they arrived in America until they had completely killed each other off, would have allowed somewhere between two and three thousand years to pass (according to the record, many kings ruled for much longer than forty years). In their final battles, the accounts in the Book of Ether suggests upwards of two million people being slain in a series of campaigns that raged all over the continent over the space of ten to twenty years. For the population to grow that large in a pre-industrial society that was continually at war would have required a very long time for the population to reach those levels.

In the Book of Mormon, one of the last Jaredites is discovered somewhere between 400 and 200 BCE. If we count backwards from that time, the Jaredite Civilization must have arrived in the Americas between two thousand B.C.E. at the latest and three thousand B.C.E., (the beginning of the Pharonic Dynasties) give or take a few hundred years. Is there any evidence of a civilization that existed in that time period in either North or South America? Is there any evidence of a people with cultural similarities to the people of the regions of the Middle East at the time period to support this crazy theory? Does science give us any corroborative evidence, or can we conveniently dismiss them as mere "Babel-ing?"

According to LDS archeologists working on the Nephi Project, as well as many others in the "legitimate" field of archeology and history, there are some amazing correlations between the Jaredite accounts and the city of Caral, which was discovered in Peru in 1994. But, before we continue, let us make sure we are not getting confused.

First, there was a great Flood, which Biblical scholars (and no one else) claim took place somewhere between 3,000 and 4,000 BCE, or 5,000 to 6,000 years before our time. Generations later (we aren't sure exactly how many) a civilization that was concurrent to the first civilization at Sumer or another began to build a great tower that was of enough significance to anger God, who confounded their language. The Jaredites, with their language intact, then left the region known as Mesopotamia and ultimately, according to the archeologists working on the Nephi Project, ended up on the coast of Peru. If we push the dates of the biblical flood to 5,000 BCE, there are 1000, to 1500 years between the time of the flood (of which we have no written or archeological evidence outside of the Bible) to the rise of what we call "civilization" in Sumer in modern day Iraq between 4,000 and 3,500 BCE. Therefore, if the Jaredite Civilization, if it existed, would have left the Fertile Crescent around 3,500 B.C.E

Caral, Peru: The Archeological Evidence

If the records in the Book of Mormon are correct, there would also be a corresponding civilization in the Americas at roughly the same time as those of Sumer and the Indus River Valley. If there is no such civilization that remotely matches the civilization in Sumer, then we can almost be sure that the Book of Mormon is nonsense. So, once again, we are back in the year 1994 on the coastal plains of Peru at the archeological site of Caral. Here, I shall to defer to George Potter, who writes:

"It was quickly apparent that Caral was a very ancient city. Jonathan Hass, an archeologist for the Field Museum of Natural History in Chicago and his wife Winifred Creamer, an archeologist at Northern Illinois University, established in 2000 that Caral was founded around 2,600 BCE. That was just the beginning of the discoveries at Norte Chico where, the ruins of twenty-four more ancient cities have been discovered. From what we presently know, Norte Chico is the site of the New World's first urban complex. Charles Mann writes in his bestselling book, *1491:* "The oldest date securely associated with a city was about 3,500 B.C. at Huaricanga. Other urban sites followed apace: Caballete in 3100 B.C.E., Porvenir and Upaca in 2,700 B.C.E. Taken individually, none of the twenty-five Norte Chico cities rivaled Sumer's cities in size, but the totality was bigger than Sumer's. Egypt's pyramids were larger, but they were built much later."

So there you have it, solid evidence that people from the tower of Babel got into boats on the southern Arabian coast in what is now the modern country of Oman and sailed the ocean to Peru and settled on the coast of South America. Well, not quite. In order for this to be any more than just coincidence, we would need more proof. Are there any other similarities between the cultures of Mesopotamia and Caral? The first similarity, or coincidence, depending upon your point of view, is the "creation myth" of each group of people, as well as their views about the world around them. Of course, the Jaredites would explain their Creation story the same way as it is written in Genesis. Regarding the peoples of ancient Caral, I will defer once again to an article written by George Potter, who quotes Harvard Professor Gary Urton in his description of the Peruvian Creation story:

"…they (the Incas) hand an ample account of the deluge. They say that in it perished all races of men and created things insomuch that the waters rose above the highest mountain peaks in the world. No living thing survived except a man and a woman who remained in a box and, when the waters subsided, the wind carried them…to Tiahuanaco (where) the creator began to raise up the people and the nations that are in that region."

With the exception of the "Mexo-centric" final landing place of the boat and the number of passengers, the Incan story is almost completely identical to the flood story in Genesis. It is remarkable in its similarity considering the fact that the Incan Empire began in 900 and ended in 1570, separating from the actual event by at least five thousand years. However, you may have noticed that in the Incan story, there is no mention of long tube-shaped barges crossing the ocean from the Middle East to land on the coast of Peru. This lack of an account of how the ancestors of the Incas actually arrived in Peru leaves everything open to question, or does it? According to George Potter:

"The Incas believed that the first people who arrived in their land called it *Pirua* (corrupted by the Spanish into Peru). Earlier Spanish chroniclers were told by the Indians that the name Pirua was derived from the name "Ophir," the same name as the famous Biblical sailor (Genesis 10:29; 1 Kings 10:11,22). The seamanship skills of Ophir might even explain how in antiquity commerce took place between the Old and New Worlds." This is evident by the New World plants of coca and tobacco having been found in the graves of Egyptian mummies starting in 1070 B.C.

Potter goes on to say that, "Book of Mormon scholar J.M. Sjodahl cites, "Fernando Montesinos is one of the early writers on Peruvian history, but he is not considered an authority except as far as he copies other writers, especially Blas Valera, which he is said to do frequently. He records the theory that Ophir, a 'grandson of Noah' settled 'Hamerica' as he spells the name, 340 years after the deluge, and that 'Peru,' the name, is derived from "Ophir."

According to George Potter, "Why is Ophir a clue for understanding where the Jaredites landed in the New World? The answer lies in the fact that Ophir was the brother of Jerah. Jerah fled Mesopotamia with Ophir and his other brothers at the time of the confounding of the languages. The family initially migrated to Southern Arabia (Genesis 10:26-30). The leader of the family was Jerah, who appears to be the family leader named Jared in the Book of Ether. Rev. Charles Forster, a former preacher in the Cathedral of Christ, Canterbury, provides these variant spellings for Jerah, Jarah, (Arabia Felics), Jarach, Jare (St. Jerome), Jehra (with umlauts) by modern Arabs. Smith's Bible Dictionary (London 1863, 1:964) states the "Jared" is the Jered of 1 Chronicles 1:2. According to Smith and Sjodahl's commentary on the Book of Ether, some early Bible translations spelled Jerah, "Jared." Their parallel stories in the books of Genesis and Ether make it probable that Jerah of the Bible and Jared of the Book of Mormon are the same person (Genesis 10:25-30, 11:1-9). One element of those stories is that the brother of Jerah, (Ophir) and the brother of Jared and Moriancumer were also the same person. That said, we are left with the distinct possibility that Peru is actually named after the great Book of Mormon colonizer, known to us as the "brother of Jared."

Evidence of a match between the Book of Mormon Jaredite Civilization that existed around Caral, Peru, goes even further when it comes to their abilities in the art of metallurgy, or the ability to create various types of implements, be they tools or weapons, from iron, copper, gold and silver ore, which is abundant in the mountains surrounding coastal Peru. Potter goes on to explain that the common

LDS belief that the Jaredites are actually members of the Olmec civilization that dates around 400-200 B.C.E. are lacking in the support of physical evidence because there is no evidence that Mesoamerican civilizations were involved in metal working until around 900 A.D., according to Book of Mormon scholar John Sorenson. However, the Andean Culture that Potter describes is, as they are depicted in the Book of Mormon account of the Jaredites, proficient in metallurgy.

According to Potter, "Although nearly all the popular LDS literature on the Jaredites places them in Mesoamerica, usually associating them with the Olmec Civilization, such Mesoamerican models are problematic. First, the record of the Jaredites was inscribed on golden plates (Mosiah 8,9) and early Jaredite warriors fashioned swords out of some form of steel (Ether 7:9). However, no archeological evidence of metalworking has been shown to exist in Mesoamerica until the first century BC, long after the fall of the Olmec civilization. There is only scant evidence of any metalwork in Mesoamerica before 900 A.D.

"Book of Mormon scholar John Sorenson notes that the only significant evidence for metalwork in Mesoamerica dates back to only 900 A. D. On one hand, the Jaredites were working metal since their earliest years in the New World. On the other hand, archeologists have uncovered extensive Peruvian metalwork dating back to almost the dawn of the Jaredite Age. Sorenson summarizes it this way:

"Archeologists only recently learned that metal was being worked in Peru as early as 1900 B.C., and was being traded in Ecuador before 1000 B.C. At the same time, all Mesoamerican scholars agree that intercommunication with Peru and Ecuador occurred over a period of a thousand years. Some definitely believe that it was via these voyages that metalworking reached Mexico and Guatemala. At the same time, we are asked to suppose that something as valuable as metal waited to be carried north until 900 A.D. then, suddenly, the metal connection finally "took."

In the Book of Mormon account, there is also the description by Moroni that suggests the Jaredites possessed skills in metalworking that surpassed that of the later Nephite culture. In the tenth chapter of the Book of Ether, we read:

"And they (the Jaredites) did work in all manner of ore, and they did make gold and silver, iron and brass and all manner of metals and they did dig it out of the earth; wherefore, they did cast up mighty heaps of earth to get ore, of gold and of silver, and of iron and of copper. And they did work all manner of fine work." (Ether 10:23)

Furthermore, Moroni goes on to explain that either he does not exactly understand what kind of metals they made, and, or, for what purpose they were making them.

"...and they did work all manner of fine work, even of exceedingly curious workmanship." (Ether 10:27)

The phrase "curious workmanship" appears in two other places in the Book of Mormon. The first time the phrase is mentioned occurs when the Nephites have left Jerusalem and are, for all intents and purposes, lost in the wilderness. At that time, they found a ball made of brass one morning, just lying on the ground outside of Lehi's tent. Nephi describes the brass ball, which he called "Liahona," as being of, "curious workmanship."

"And it came to pass that as my father arose in the morning, and went forth to the tent door, to his great astonishment he beheld upon the ground a round ball of curious workmanship; and it was of fine brass. And within the ball were two spindles; and the one pointed the way whither we should go in the wilderness." (1 Nephi 16:10)

The ball was in fact, a compass, which showed them the correct direction of travel. It was an unusual compass in that it only seemed to work when Nephi's older brothers, who thought it was insane to give up the good life in Jerusalem to go scraping around on their father's desert adventure, weren't trying to kill him. Later, when Nephi was involved in building a boat to cross the ocean somewhere in Oman, according to George Potter's book *Lehi in the Wilderness*, Nephi again uses the phrase.

"...and we did work timbers of curious workmanship." (1 Nephi 18:1)

I think it worth pausing for a moment to at least try to understand the phrase, "curious workmanship" because it highlights the technical achievements of the Jaredite culture and the technology they possessed that we are just beginning to understand. In the account written by Nephi, he is writing in the first person. Then Joseph Smith, who, if we assume translated correctly, was implying that Nephi didn't understand how the brass compass, or Liahona was made, translated Nephi's account into English. By using the term "curious" we can assume that Nephi was curious about how the compass was made, but had no idea as to how to explain it. Later, when Nephi used the phrase to describe how he was forming timbers for his ship, we can guess that Nephi was forming them in a way with which he was unfamiliar. The only alternative being that the timbers had already been formed in a way that he didn't understand. We may picture a person standing there, scratching his head and saying, "How did they do that?"

When we look at Moroni's description of Jaredite metal working technology, we know he would have been familiar with Mosiah's translation and phraseology because he and his father had been lugging the plates around for some time, but Moroni could not explain what the Jaredites were making because they had no words to describe it in their written language, as Moroni laments:

"Thou has made our words powerful and great, even that we cannot write them; wherefore, when we write we behold our weakness, and stumble because of the placing of our words..." (Ether 12:25)

In modern terms, if we were fortunate enough to find a pristine culture that did not possess cell phones, they would probably describe them using the same phrase (but probably not in English) because they wouldn't have the words to describe an electrically powered device that translates magnetic signals into radio waves in order to communicate with other similar devices. Even greater than the lack of accurate nouns and verbs, would be the pristine culture's inability to understand how the cell phone was made. If the culture was to describe the cell phone in their own pristine language as being of "exceedingly curious workmanship" we can infer some things from the accounts of Moroni and Nephi.

If a brass compass suddenly shows up on the ground one morning outside of Lehi's tent and points in the right direction only when Nephi's brothers aren't trying to kill him and Nephi describes it as being of "curious workmanship," while Moroni describes the technology of the Jaredites as "exceedingly curious," it is quite possible that the Jaredite civilization possessed technology that far surpassed the understanding and the vocabulary of the Nephites.

In summary, the information we have seen does not give us the easiest way out, which would be simply dismissing the Jaredite accounts in the Book of Mormon as mere fantasy or the delusions of Joseph Smith. Of course, it would be irresponsible of us to conclude that because of the work of Hass, Creamer, Mann, Potter, Sorenson and others that we can definitely match the accounts of the Jaredites to those of the Caral Civilization in Peru, but like the rest of the Latter-day Saint version of history, neither can we refute it.

Chapter 13

Latter-day Saint History
The Book of Mormon

"For the time shall speedily come that all churches which are built up to get gain, and all those who are built up to get power over the flesh, and those who are built up to become popular in the eyes of the world, and those who seek the lusts of the flesh, and the things of the world, and to do all manner of iniquity; yea, in fine all those who belong to the kingdom of the devil are they who need fear, and tremble and quake; they are those who must be brought low in the dust; they are those who must be consumed as stubble; and this according to the words of the prophet." (1 Nephi 22:23)

Now that we have seen some evidence that the Book of Mormon does correlate with at least one ancient American culture, and looks more and more to be what Joseph Smith claimed it was; an ancient record of the Hebrews and the Jaredite peoples who populated the Americas in the centuries prior to the coming of Jesus Christ, we can make a closer examination of the substance and the purpose of the Book of Mormon itself. Because it would be better for the reader to actually read the Book of Mormon for themselves, than listen to my dry and often uninteresting descriptions, I have included what I feel are the two most important parts of the Book of Mormon. If the reader will read these two passages, I feel that they will have more of an understanding of why it is so important to so many that people do not read the Book of Mormon at all.

Chronologically, the Book of Mormon begins in Jerusalem around 600 B.C.E. during the reign of Zedekiah in the Hebrew Kingdom of Judah. The Book of Mormon, with the exception of the account of the Jaredites, is a narrative written over the space of between six and eight hundred years by a number of different authors. Most of the authors were rulers, while at other times the authors were prophets and sometimes the authors were both. It is an account of the descendants of a family that left Jerusalem at the prompting of God and who, like the Jaredites, sailed across the ocean to settle in the Americas.

In the beginning of the book, which is a narrative written by Nephi, there are five main characters. The father, Lehi (lee-hi), is a reasonably successful merchant. He is described by his wife Sariah, as a "visionary man," which probably means the same thing as someone who has their "head in the clouds" in modern terminology. In other words, she sometimes suspects that his mind is elsewhere. In spite of her personal feelings, Sariah dutifully follows Lehi wherever he leads. Lehi has four sons, Laman, (lay-mun) Lemuel (lem-ule) Nephi and Samuel. Laman and Lemuel view their father pretty much in the same way as his wife does. In contrast, his younger son, Nephi, appears to be cut from the same cloth as his father and believes whatever his father, Lehi tells him.

One day, when Lehi is praying, he receives a vision that becomes the key to the Book of Mormon.

"Wherefore it came to pass that my father, Lehi, as he went forth prayed unto the Lord, yea, even with all his heart, in behalf of his people. And it came to pass as he prayed unto the Lord, there came a pillar of fire and dwelt upon a rock before him; and he saw and heard much; and because of the things which he saw and heard he did quake and tremble exceedingly. And it came to pass that he returned to his own house at Jerusalem; and cast himself upon his bed, being overcome with the Spirit and the things he had seen. And thus being overcome with the Spirit, he was carried away in a vision, even that he saw the heavens open, and he thought he saw God sitting upon His throne, surrounded by numberless concourses of angels in the attitude of singing and praising their God. And it came to pass that he saw One descending out of the midst of heaven, and he beheld his luster was above that at noon-day. And he also saw twelve others following him, and their brightness did exceed the stars in the firmament. And they came down and went forth upon the face of the earth; and the first came and stood before my father, and gave unto him a book, and bade him that he should read. And it came to pass that as he read, he

was filled with the Spirit of the Lord. And he read, saying: Wo, Wo unto Jerusalem, for I have seen thy abominations! Yea, and many things did my father read concerning Jerusalem-that it should be destroyed, and the inhabitants thereof; many should perish by the sword, and many should be taken captive into Babylon." 1 Nephi (5:13)

Shortly thereafter, Lehi announces that the family will be packing up and moving out of the doomed city, posthaste. Understandably, there is a revolt amongst his oldest sons, who suspect that their father has finally cracked up. His younger sons, Sam and Nephi, along with Lehi's wife, outvote his oldest sons. The family agrees to high tail it out of Jerusalem before the Babylonians show up. They flee into what is described as the wilderness, which, according to George Potter in his book, *Lehi in the Wilderness,* means the inhospitable deserts of the interior of Saudi Arabia. Nephi's account in the first Book of Nephi covers their departure from Jerusalem, their struggles in "the wilderness," and a vision of the future rise of Christianity that is seen by his father. This vision is also key to not only Lehi and his family, but to the world in general.

> "And it came to pass that while my father tarried in the wilderness he spake unto us, saying: Behold, I have dreamed a dream; or, in other words, I have seen a vision. And because of the thing which I have seen, I have reason to rejoice in the Lord because of Nephi and Sam; for I have reason to suppose that they, and also many of their seed, will be saved. But behold, Laman and Lemuel, I fear exceedingly because of you; for, behold, methought I saw in my dream a dark and dreary wilderness. And it came to pass that I saw a man, and he was dressed in a white robe; and he came and stood before me. And it came to pass that he spake unto me, and bade me follow him. And it came to pass that as I followed him, I beheld myself in a dark and dreary waste. And after I had traveled for the space of many hours in darkness, I began to pray unto the Lord that He would have mercy on me according to the multitude of his tender mercies. And it came to pass that after I had prayed unto the Lord, I beheld a large and spacious field. And it came to pass that I beheld a tree, whose fruit was desirable to make one happy. And it came to pass that I did go forth and partake of the fruit thereof, and beheld that it was most sweet,

above all that I ever before tasted. Yea, and I beheld the fruit thereof was white, to exceed all the whiteness that I had ever seen. And as I partook of the fruit thereof it filled my soul with exceedingly great joy; wherefore, I began to be desirous that my family should partake of it also, for I knew that it was desirable above all other fruit. And as I cast my eyes roundabout, that perhaps I might discover my family also, I beheld a river of water; and it ran along and it was near the tree of which I was partaking fruit. And I looked to behold from whence it came; and I saw the head thereof a little way off; and at the head, I beheld your mother, Sariah, and Sam and Nephi, and they stood as if they knew not whether they should go. And it came to pass that I beckoned unto them; and I did also say unto them with a loud voice that they should come unto me, and partake of the fruit, which was desirable above all other fruit. And it came to pass that they did come unto me and partake of the fruit also. And it came to pass that I was desirous that Laman and Lemuel should come unto me and partake of the fruit also; wherefore, I cast mine eyes towards the head of the river, that perhaps I might see them. And it came to pass that I saw them, but they would not come and partake of the fruit. And I beheld a rod of iron that it extended along the bank of the river, and led to the tree by which I stood. And I also beheld a straight and narrow path, which came along by the rod of iron, even to the tree by which I stood; and it also led by the head of the fountain, unto the large and spacious field, as if it had been a world. And I saw numberless concourses of people, many of whom were pressing forward, that they might obtain the path which led unto the tree by which I stood. And it came to pass that they did come forth, and commence in the path which led to the tree. And it came to pass that there arose a mist of darkness; yea, even an exceedingly great mist of darkness, insomuch that they who had commenced in the path did lose their way, that they wandered off and were lost. And it came to pass that I beheld others pressing forward, and they came forth and caught hold of the rod of iron; and they did press forward through the mist of darkness, clinging to the rod of iron, even until they did come forth and partake of the fruit of the tree. And after they had partaken of the fruit, they cast their eyes roundabout as if they were ashamed. And I also cast my eyes roundabout, and beheld, on the other side of the river of water, a great and spacious building; and it stood as if it were in the air, high above the earth. And it was filled with people, both old and young, both male and female; and their manner of dress was exceedingly fine; and they were in the attitude of mocking and pointing their fingers towards those who had come and were partaking of the fruit. And after they had tasted of the fruit, they were ashamed, because of those that were scoffing at them; and they fell away into forbidden paths and were lost. And now I, Nephi, do not speak all the words of my father. But, to be short in writing, behold, he saw other multitudes pressing forward; and they came and caught hold of the end of the rod of iron; and they did press forward, continually holding fast to the rod of iron, until they came forth and fell down and partook of the fruit of the tree. And he also saw other multitudes feeling their way toward that great and spacious building. And it came to pass that many were drowned in the depths of the fountain; and many were lost from his view, wandering in strange roads. And great was the multitude that did enter that strange building. And after they did enter that building they did point the finger of scorn at me and those that were partaking of the fruit also; but we heeded them not. (1 Nephi 8:2-33)

Following his father's vision of what would become the allegorical spiritual future of mankind, Lehi's son Nephi, is instructed by God to build a ship. When the ship is finally finished, the family embarks to their new home in what God tells them is the "Promised Land." They arrive in what is most likely Central America and they begin to build a new civilization.

In their initial days in their new home in the Americas, Nephi, his brother Sam, and later his father's last son, Benjamin, who was born in the wilderness, serve as his father's allies in a never-ending struggle between Nephi and his two brothers, Laman and Lemuel. The reluctant sons eventually rebel against their goody-two shoes brothers and leave the family to make their own way in the New World. At some point, either because of their unfaithfulness, or their penchant for sunbathing, the skins of their rebellious brothers turned brown. From that time onward, they would forever be marked as "Lamanites," different from their white cousins, the "Nephites."

The Book of Mormon is the account of people who were waiting for the same Son of God who had previously appeared in Lehi's visions in Jerusalem, and in the wilderness to come to teach them, and to fulfill the Law of Moses, which, they, being Jews, still practiced. Both the Nephites and the Lamanites populated the land, built cities and enjoyed the abundance of the New World. The Book of Mormon itself was written mainly to record the spiritual affairs of the people, but there is enough in the way of political, social, economic, jurisprudence and military information to paint a pretty detailed picture of the culture that existed during that period.

Along with their great prosperity, the Nephite civilization was plagued throughout its existence by the threat of their Lamanite cousins who chose to live outside the control of the Nephites and their cities. The Book of Mormon describes accounts of horrific battles, suffering and torture inflicted by both sides. They have extremely righteous leaders, like King Mosiah, and extremely evil ones as well. There are marked periods of peace that coincide with being obedient to God between the two cultures. Missionary work is carried out and non-believers on both sides are converted to the Gospel of Jesus Christ. Prophecies concerning the Nephites, the Lamanites and the people who will someday inhabit the Americas, known as the Gentiles are recorded. However, because of secret societies and combinations, there are times when the Nephite culture falls into disrepute, only to be saved by their faithful Lamanite cousins.

Jesus Christ appears in America

By the time Jesus Christ is born in Bethlehem, both cultures have fallen into vile lifestyles. They are combined by their secret societies, murders, and assassinations. Because of these secret combinations, they are involved in a seemingly never-ending war of attrition with each other. Prophets, such as Samuel the Lamanite, testify to the people that Jesus is alive in Jerusalem, and that the prophecies about Him (and God's upcoming wrath) are about to be fulfilled, but few believe Samuel.

Upon the death of Jesus in the year 33, there is a calamity that occurs in the Americas that has not been seen before or since. Entire cities are swallowed and valleys are pushed into mountaintops. The wind blows in hurricane force for three days and then, suddenly, everything stops and the land is quiet. In the dead silence, Jesus Christ appears in the clouds and descends to teach the Nephites and the Lamanites the Sermon on the Mount. Jesus anoints Twelve Disciples and He teaches the people about baptism and about His Gospel of repentance and forgiveness. Over the course of three days Jesus teaches the Lamanites and the Nephites many other things of which we unfortunately have no record.

"And now it came to pass that there were a great multitude gathered together, of the people of Nephi, round about the temple which was in the land Bountiful; and they were marveling and wondering, one with another, and were showing one to another the great and marvelous change which had taken place. And they were also conversing about this Jesus Christ, of whom the sign had been given concerning his death. And it came to pass that while they were conversing one with another, they heard a voice as if it came out of heaven; and they cast their eyes round about, for they understood not the voice they had heard; and it was not a harsh voice, neither was it a loud voice; nevertheless, and notwithstanding it being a small voice it did pierce them that did hear to the center, insomuch that there was no part of their frame that it did not cause to quake; yea it did pierce them to the very center and did cause their hearts to burn. And it came to pass that again they heard the voice and they understood it not. And again the third time they did hear the voice, and did open their ears to hear it; and their eyes were towards the sound thereof, and they did look steadfastly toward heaven, from whence the sound came. And behold, the third time they did understand the voice which they heard; and it said unto them: Behold, this is my Beloved Son in whom I am well pleased, in whom I have glorified my name-hear ye Him.

And it came to pass, as they understood they cast their eyes up again towards heaven; and behold, they saw a Man descending out of heaven; and he was clothed in a white robe; and he came down and stood in the midst of them; and the eyes of the whole multitude were turned upon him, and they durst not open their mouths, even one to another, and wist not what it meant, for they thought that an angel that had appeared unto them.

And it came to pass that he stretched forth his hand and spake unto the people, saying,

Behold, I am Jesus Christ whom the prophets testified shall come into the world. And behold, I am the light and the life of the world; and I have drunk out of the bitter cup which the Father hath given me, and have glorified the Father in taking upon me the sins of the world, in the which I have suffered the will of the Father in all things from the beginning.

And it came to pass that when Jesus had spoken these words the whole multitude fell to the earth; for they remembered that it had been prophesied among them that Christ should show himself unto them after his ascension into heaven.

And it came to pass that the Lord spake unto them saying:

Arise and come forth, that ye may thrust your hands into my side, and also that ye may feel the prints of the nails in my hands and in my feet, that ye may know that I am the God of Israel, and the God of the whole earth, and have been slain for the sins of the world.

And it came to pass that the multitude went forth, and thrust their hands into his side, and did feel the prints of the nails in his hands and in his feet, and this they did do, going forth one by one until they had all gone forth, and did see with their eyes and feel with their hands and did know of a surety and did bear record, that it was he, of whom it was written by the prophets, that should come. And when they had all gone forth and had witnessed for themselves, did cry with one accord, saying: Hosanna! Blessed be the name of the Most High God! And they did fall down at the feet of Jesus and did worship him.

And it came to pass that he spake unto Nephi (for Nephi was among the multitude)[2] and he commanded him that he should come forth. And Nephi arose and went forth, and bowed himself before the Lord and did kiss his feet.

And the Lord commanded him that he should arise. And he arose and stood before him.

---

[2] Not the same Nephi who wrote the first part of the Book of Mormon.

And the Lord said unto him: I give unto you power that ye shall baptize this people when I am again ascended into heaven.

And again the Lord called others, and said unto them likewise; and he gave unto them power to baptize. And he said unto them: On this wise shall ye baptize; and there shall be no disputations among you.

Verily I say unto you, that whoso repenteth of his sins through your words, and desireth to be baptized in my name, on this wise shall ye baptize them-Behold ye shall go down and stand in the water, and in my name shall ye baptize them.

And now behold, these are the words which ye shall say, ye shall call them by name, saying:

Having authority given my by Jesus Christ, I baptize you in the name of the Father, the Son and the Holy Ghost. Amen.

Then ye shall immerse them in the water, and come forth again out of the water.

And after this manner shall ye baptize in my name, for behold, verily I say unto you, that the Father, and the Son and the Holy Ghost are one; and I am in the Father and the Father in me and the Father and I are one.

And according as I have commanded you, thus shall ye baptize. And there shall be no disputations among you concerning the points of my doctrine, as there have hitherto been.

For he that hath the spirit of contention is not of me, but of the devil, who is the father of contention, and he stirreth up the hearts of men to contend with anger, one with another.

Behold, this is not my doctrine, to stir up the hearts of men with anger, one with another; but this is my doctrine that such things should be done away.

Behold, verily, verily, I say unto you, I will declare unto you my doctrine.

And this is my doctrine, and it is the doctrine which the Father hath given unto me; and I bear record of the Father and the Father beareth record of me, and the Holy Ghost beareth record of the Father and me; and I bear record that the Father commandeth all men, everywhere, to repent and believe in me.

And whoso believeth in me, and is baptized, the same shall be saved; and they are they who shall inherit the kingdom of God.

And whoso believeth not in me, and is not saved, shall be damned.

Verily, verily, I say unto you, this is my doctrine, and I bear record of it from the Father, and whoso believeth in me, believeth in the Father also; and unto him will the father bear record of me, for he will visit him with fire and with the Holy Ghost.

And thus will the Father bear record of me, and the Holy Ghost will bear record unto him of the Father and me; for the Father, and I, and the Holy Ghost are one.

And again I say unto you, ye must repent, and become as a little child, and be baptized in my name, or ye can in nowise receive these things.

And again, I say unto you, ye must repent, and become as a little child, and be baptized in my name, or ye can nowise receive these things.

And again, I say unto you, ye must repent, and be baptized in my name, and become as a little child, or ye can nowise inherit the kingdom of God.

Verily, verily, I say unto you, that this is my doctrine, and whoso buildeth upon this, buildeth upon my rock, and the gates of hell shall not prevail against them."

And whoso shall declare more or less than this, and establish it for my doctrine, the same cometh of evil, and is not built upon my rock; but he buildeth upon a sandy foundation, and the gates of hell stand open to receive such when the floods come and the winds beat upon them.

Therefore, go forth unto this people, and declare the words which I have spoken, unto the ends of the earth."

This fantastic account of the words and the teachings of Jesus Christ to the peoples of the Americas is the main reason of and for the Book of Mormon. We see in the words of Jesus the beginnings of wisdom, of peace and a way for men (and women) to live together in harmony. Most importantly, we see the basic principles of His gospel: love and forgiveness of all men, no matter what, and the importance of repentance and baptism. When He leaves, Jesus promises the people that he will return someday.

Following the appearance of Jesus Christ, there was a period of peace that lasted around two hundred years. At the end of the two hundred years, the two civilizations resumed their conflict again, and the remnants of the Nephites venture, or rather fled to the north where they fought numerous battles with the Lamanites. Nothing remained in the hearts of the majority of the Nephites and the Lamanites except for hatred and vengeance. They crossed the land fighting horrifying battles involving thousands of people and the dead were piled high in mounds. In the end, the Nephites were ultimately defeated and hunted to extinction by the Lamanites.

The last two Nephites to possess the records of the people are Moroni and his father, the Nephite General, Mormon. Mormon wrote his last entries into the books and entrusted his son Moroni to hide them. Moroni added his commentary as well as the abbreviation of the Jaredite account and then hid the plates in a concrete box in upstate New York where, they were shown by Moroni to Joseph Smith in the 1800's.

And so, there, in a nutshell, is the gist of the Book of Mormon. The Book of Mormon as a literary work is highly entertaining. As a historical account, The Book of Mormon is highly descriptive and informative and actually allows the reader to see the old cities and people as well as to feel the emotions of its long dead authors. As the Word of God, it contains the wisdom of thousands of years of human thought and is remarkable for its clarity.

In the words of Le Grande Richards, the Book of Mormon is "A marvelous work and a wonder." So much so that his authoritative book about the Book of Mormon and the Latter-day Saint Church carries the same name. Whether the reader remains skeptical or not, it is the cornerstone of belief for millions of people around the world, and the number of people who accept the Book of Mormon as the Word of God continues to grow. It is this author's sincere hope that the reader will, at some point, skim at least a chapter or two of the Book of Mormon and make the final judgment as to whether it is worth reading and investigating for themselves. I think that those who do will find its wisdom and its information, worth the time. Best of all, if you get it from the LDS Missionaries, it's free!

Archeology and the Book of Mormon

Many things that Jesus taught the Nephites and the Lamanites were not included in the Book of Mormon. Are there clues in Mexico and Central America that a white, bearded God appeared out of the heavens and taught the people? Are the clues as to what else He, or the beings with which he came, may have taught? We left off in the last chapter, looking for actual scientific evidence of the Book of Mormon account of the Jaredites. According to archeology, during the two hundred year time period following the Book of Mormon account of the appearance of Jesus Christ in the Americas, there was a flourishing of culture, building, astronomy and mathematics. What could have possibly happened to inspire the people in Mexico and Central America to such great accomplishments? Are there any accounts in the cultures of Central America of a "God" appearing to teach them?

The first thing we should look for is a civilization that experienced a sudden change, if not a cultural, political and spiritual revolution at the time of the death of Jesus Christ. Was there a civilization living in Central America at the time that the Book of Mormon claims Jesus returned? Was there a culture that experienced a drastic change in their knowledge of building, mathematics, science and, most important of all, wisdom? Was there a period of peace that lasted long enough to create lasting reminders of a great culture? Was there a culture in Central America that also possesses a history of a visitor or a "god' who taught them? If there wasn't, then we can easily dismiss the account.

However, we need look no farther than the city of **Teotihuacan** in Mexico, whose dates of construction are somewhere between 100 B.C.E. and 200. The Mayan civilization at Teotihuacan, for some reason and, around the same time of Christ's birth and death, exploded with knowledge regarding, mathematics, geometry, and the solar system. Even more mysteriously, they seemed to possess a remarkable understanding of the universe itself. The city of Teotihuacan is laid out precisely according to astronomical principals and contains on one end the Pyramid of the Sun and at the other, the Pyramid of the Moon. The name Teotihuacan means, "Place of those who have a road of the Gods," according to Thelma Sullivan, an expert in Mesoamerican mythology. A broad thoroughfare called the Avenue of the Dead connects all of the temples within the Teotihuacan complex. Along the Avenue of the Dead lies the Temple of the Feathered Serpent. Who is the Feathered Serpent and why is he so important to the Mayan understanding of the universe?

The Feathered Serpent is the Mayan supreme god (Kukalcan) to whom the Maya attributed many functions. Not only was he the god of the four elements, he was also the creator god and the god of resurrection and reincarnation. The Mayan god Kukalcan also appears in other cultures. In the Inca culture (the descendants of the suspected Jaredite culture we spoke of in the last chapter), Kukalcan is known as Viracocha, the bearded white god. In the Aztec culture, which came to prominence in Mexico around 1000, Kukalcan is known as Quetzalcoatl (feathered serpent) and he shares some interesting attributes with Jesus Christ. Quetzalcoatl was born of a virgin birth. He is the Aztec god of the priesthood and learning. He gave the Aztecs (Maya) the calendar, books and learning, which may possibly explain what Jesus was doing those three days that weren't written about in the Book of Mormon. Furthermore, when the Spanish arrived in 1517, they found the Aztecs immersed in the ritual of human sacrifice. Could it be possible that over time, they somehow misconstrued the idea of the "blood sacrifice" of Jesus Christ?

It all sounds pretty convincing, but did the god Kukalcan appear during the time in question? In all of my research, barring commentary by noted "UFOlogist" and non-LDS researcher Erich Von Daniken, who insists that Kukalcan did appear at the exact spot where the temple of Kukalcan, or "El Castillo" was constructed around the year 100 and taught the Maya many great things, I could find nothing in the annals of "legitimate" science and archeology suggesting an actual visitor from space. However, the fact that most of the information we have is from the Aztecs, who arrived on the scene a thousand years later, yet still attribute the same qualities of the mysterious being known as Kukalcan to the Maya and later Quetzalcoatl to the Aztecs, also correspond suspiciously to the Book of Mormon account of Jesus Christ. Modern scholars ignore the possibility altogether and suggest that it merely some amazing coincidence that Kukalcan, Quetzalcoatl and Jesus Christ all seem to share the same characteristics. Scholars suggest that it is all coincidence because they have good reason for doing so, which we will see in a moment. However, what is the truth? Is there any more evidence that Jesus Christ may have appeared to the people of Central America two thousand years ago?

Evidence of Circumstance

In the Book of Mormon account, the people of Central America are left believing that at some point, the Son of God will return to them. As further evidence, there is the claim by many that the ease with which Hernan Cortez and his conquistadors were able to subdue an empire as vast and as complex as the Aztecs was due to Cortez being mistaken for the white bearded god Quetzalcoatl, who left and promised to return to the Maya. Many, especially members of the LDS church, cite this fact, as further evidence that Jesus did visit the inhabitants of Central America and did promise them that he would return. However, "legitimate" scholars have always denied the authenticity of that claim. Others, especially the Hopi Indians of Arizona, refer to Kukalcan as "Pahana." Pahana is the lost White Brother who left for the east but promised to return in the fifth age (Coulander 31). The Hopis continue to claim that the story of the Aztecs mistaking Cortez for Quetzalcoatl was, in fact the reason for the submission of the Aztecs. (Locke 139-140)

And what does the Latter-day Saint Church say about the unusual correlation between the Mayan and Aztec Cultures and the Book of Mormon accounts? According to President John Taylor of the LDS Church, "The story of the life of the Mexican divinity, Quetzalcoatl, closely resembles that of the Savior; so closely, indeed that we can come to no other conclusion than that Quetzalcoatl and Christ are the same being. But the history of the former has been handed down to us through an impure Lamantish source, which has sadly disfigured and perverted the incidents of the Savior's life and ministry." (Taylor 201) So, let us continue onward to try to discover an explanation as to why such important knowledge as that possessed by the Church of Jesus Christ of Latter-day Saints must be hidden from the world.

The burden of "proof"

There are two basic problems when it comes to what is known as the burden of proof for any archeologist or historian. The first problem is that archeologists and historians are looking into a window of time sometimes so far in the past that many conclusions based upon scant evidence are left open to subjective interpretation that is extrapolated from our own culture. For example, in ten thousand years, if society is based upon some form of religion, our own toilets, because they appear to be in every house in Western countries, archeologists may conclude they had significant religious connotations for Western Civilization. Whereas in other countries, of the same time period, the different type of commode, such as the ones common in Asian and Middle Eastern countries, may influence some scholars to associate the Western style commode with Christianity and the other style with Islam or Hinduism. If society in ten thousand years is not based upon religion then there will need to be some other more, secular explanation for the humble commode. Unless of course, someone were to come along and provide significant proof to the contrary, such as a pipe connected to a sewer it would be hard to "flush" this theory, no matter how incorrect, down the drain of historical correctness.

Correct interpretations, funding and tenure

The other limitation to archeologists and historians is that their entire livelihoods are based upon "correct" interpretations. Correct interpretations, such as in the case of the commode theory, cannot differ significantly from what has already been determined as correct in the eyes of the world of academics. For an archeologist to say that the civilization at Caral is the same as the one in the Book of Mormon account, would be tantamount to claiming the pyramids were built by aliens in the eyes of modern, "legitimate" scholars. Anyone making such a claim would soon find their funding and grant pool as dry as a ten thousand year old commode. In the cases of independent researchers like Ron Wyatt (Noah's Ark), Potter and Sorenson whose funding is supplied from sources associated with the LDS Church, they do not have the burden of seeing their names blacklisted from the peer review publications of universities and research grant organizations.

One of the best examples of what happens to scholars who publish information outside of the scientific "mainstream" is Dr. Paul Laviollette. In an interview with the astronomer, physicist and author of many "legitimate" scientific papers on astrophysics as well as books such as, *Secrets of Anti-Gravity Propulsion: Tesla UFOs and Classified Aerospace Technology*, Dr. LaViolette was asked the question, "Why haven't I read about this in the newspaper?" Here is Dr. LaViolette's answer:

"…another group of people, and I'm one of them, have been blacklisted by Cornell University's physics archives. When our name comes up our papers are uniformly rejected, even though we've been published in refereed journals. Why? Because some of our ideas are not fitting the paradigm…this goes on. I mean people lose their jobs from government positions because, let's say, they might talk about cold fusion and they get kicked out."

Funding for scientific and historical research is funneled through university grants and government funding sources, such as the National Science Foundation. Faculty positions on college and university campuses across America are dependent upon the ability to publish and withstand the scrutiny of the stringent peer review process. Any scientist, academician or researcher whose livelihood is dependent upon the ability to be published in peer review journals is not going to risk being blacklisted by universities, such as Cornell University, for publishing, or publicly supporting and discussing anything that might fall outside of what Dr. Laviollette describes as the "paradigm" of what those who control our information want us to know. With this kind of power over the world of academics, it is fairly easy to steer the world of education and knowledge in the direction that a group with enough power and influence may wish it to go. Sound kooky? Just wait, it gets even kookier.

Chapter 14

The Rise of the Templars

Hugh Payen and Solomon's Temple

Because Freemasons claim that they are not a secret society, rather, they claim to be "a society with secrets," there are two aspects of Freemasonry that we will examine in this book. The first aspect is Freemasonry as a society or organized social institution. This will include their history, the rituals, which they themselves have made public, and their evolution over the years. The second aspect of Freemasonry has to do with their existence as a secret society, or, pardon me, a, "society with secrets." However since, by their very nature as a "society with secrets," it is not possible to claim to know what secrets they hold, and since there is ample information available from other sources regarding that subject, I will simply give an overview of what is known about secret societies in various historic or religious records. If the reader wishes to infer that there is a connection between secret societies of the past and the Society of Freemasons, please, let me make it clear to the reader, that my opinion regarding the Society of Freemasons is one of complete neutrality. If the reader chooses to form an opinion about the Society of Freemasons based upon my writings, the reader is at liberty to do as he or she pleases, but I would like to recommend further study of more authoritative works than this general overview in order for the reader to make a more qualified judgment.

Before I begin, I would like to detract a little, as teachers of History so often do, and take the reader through what was once my own journey of inquiry and discovery regarding the Freemasons. The author's anticipated benefit will be to allow the reader to understand my own interest in the subject and to create a framework for our later field of inquiry. Hopefully, this method of relating the information will allow the reader the added benefit of being able to "browse" the subject in a broad context before we delve into specifics. Then again, it may also have the undesired effect of putting the reader into a state of fitful slumber.

Risking that, like the knights of old, let us throw caution to the wind and charge into a rather interesting chapter of history.

A visit to modern day Jerusalem

To begin, I must confess to the reader, if it is not already obvious, that I am a lover of history although let me point out I mean that figuratively and not literally. Once I learned how to read, while other kids were reading about Dick, Jane and Spot, I was devouring everything I could get my hands on. This included reading Reader's Digest from page to page, newspapers, and my first interest; adult level books about the American Indians, biographies of Lincoln, George Washington and Buffalo Bill, just to name a few. I was the terror of the local library system. By the time I was in the 7th grade I was reading at the level of a college freshman. In fact, I never completed one homework assignment the whole time I was in high school and somehow managed to maintain a 'C' average (+ or – a + or -). I was completely fascinated by history and the thought that people were actually able to live and survive outside the context of what we call, modern civilization. Ever since then, I have read almost nothing but books about history and I watch little but TV shows and movies about history. Of course, this is to the detriment of my poor wife, relatives and friends who find me somewhat of a boor. I would say my interest in history is due to my own personal interest in what some would call the truth. In other words, if it didn't happen and doesn't offer an insight into the way the world is today, I just don't care that much about it.

Harking back, once again to my halcyon years in the U.S. Army, my battalion was assigned peacekeeping duty in the Sinai Peninsula, near the modern town of Sharm el Sheikh, Egypt. During that six-month tour of dirt, heat and sand, we were offered weekend passes to Israel every so often. During my first visit to Israel, I remember standing in the Old City of Jerusalem, near the Church of the Holy Sepulcher, where I saw a small white sign on a post at the intersection of two streets. On the sign was the red cross of the Templars. Underneath the symbol of the Templars, the sign read:

"On this spot during the first Crusade, the blood from the victims of the slaughter reached the shanks of the Crusader's horses."

At that moment, the sounds of passing vehicles ceased in my ears, and in my mind's eye, the intersection where I was standing became flooded with crimson gore. I heard screaming and yelling while sweating men draped in scorching hot mail carrying long swords, rushed down the hill from the street above and ran past me. In the narrow alleyways there were heaps of mangled flesh and dirty clothes leaking blood into the street that ran downhill and collected where I stood. It was a scene of horror that, thankfully, only lasted a millisecond. Just as quickly as the scene appeared, it disappeared and the sounds of traffic and tourists and children selling cheap jewelry filled my ears. I became aware once again of the hot sun beating down on the shoulders of my dark blue t-shirt with Israeli jump wings on the front. I stood there thinking to myself, *"What is a shank?"*

Mysteries in Stone

Coming from a small town in Washington State, I had never heard of Freemasons. However, during my college years, as I worked toward my bachelor's degree and my dream of someday becoming a teacher of history, I was able to study European history. Because of my experiences in the Middle East, I was particularly fascinated by the history of the Middle Ages. As, I began to read and study, I began to notice some peculiar things. The first thing I noticed, was that, prior to the Crusades, the castles in Europe, barring those remnants of Roman forts that remained occupied and therefore stayed in some semblance of repair, were not made of stone.

Instead, the castles of pre-Crusade Europe were basically high patches of land, or a hill if one were available, with large wide ditches dug in a circle towards the bottom, with the earth thrown out onto the inside of the circle. The ditch, which was sometimes filled with water, was known as the "motte," or moat. On top of the dirt were wooden poles, or stakes, which created a wall that surrounded the hill. The construction of the moat and the palisade on the dirt was meant to be an obstacle to attackers and a line of defense for defenders. On the top of the hill was a wooden structure of either one or two stories. This building was the home of the local warlord, or thug, as either description is probably accurate. It was called the "bailey." This style of castle is called the Motte and Bailey and it was prevalent from Ireland to Moscow. However, during and after the Crusades, the technology of building fortresses changed dramatically. The days of wood were out and stone was in. If one looks at the progression of building from the 1100's onwards, it is more than obvious that people were bringing back more from the Crusades than sunburns and stab wounds.

A modern detective story

Long before the current craze that resulted from books like the *Da Vinci Code,* I wasn't sure what had changed between the years of the Crusades until I began to read about two military orders of monks whose origins could be traced back to the Crusades. One was the Knights Hospitaller, who once occupied the famous *Crac de Chevalier* Castle in Syria and the other were the Templars, or the Knights of the Temple. Actually, it wasn't the Knights of the Temple themselves that sparked my interest, so much as the name of the last leader of the Knights of the Temple, a man by the name of Jacque De Molay.

When I heard the name, "De Molay" I remembered when I was in school, that some of my friends from time to time, attended meetings for an organization called, "Demolay." Naturally, I wondered if there was a connection and *Shazaam!* It turned out that the Demolay meetings my friends were attending were associated with a group called Freemasons. But that didn't make sense. The Templars were wiped out, according to the history books, so why would the Freemasons have an organization named after their last leader? It didn't take me long to solve the puzzle, and, years before anyone ever heard of the *Da Vinci Code*, I had formulated a theory.

The Enemy of My Enemy

From my studies of the Crusades, both in and outside of college, I became aware of the fact that when the Crusaders arrived in the Middle East, they happened upon a group of local principalities that were, like the small principalities of Europe, run by local warlords. More often than not (also like Europe) the neighboring warlords were often at war with each other. One of the reasons the Europeans were able to gain a foothold in the Middle East and hold on to their land for as long as they did, was due to the factional strife that existed between neighboring principalities and their warlords.

In spite of their dispensation to cleanse the Holy Land of the Infidel, the Crusaders, who were outnumbered by a thousand to one, had to make deals with the local rulers. The deal was, once they had overthrown a Muslim warlord and taken over his principality, they would make an alliance with his former enemies and neighbors. The Christian Crusaders would agree to defend against that ruler's enemies. In turn, the Crusaders would receive a guarantee that they would not be attacked and would receive help from their Muslim allies in case such a thing should happen. Of course, had the fact that the "Holy" Crusades were nothing more than a mish-mash of easily broken alliances with Muslim warlords ever found its way back to Europe, the whole thing would have been a disaster, and so, the reality of the European occupation was played off as a glorious victory for Christendom, and the money and reinforcements kept coming.

It may seem a little confusing, so I will re-state it like this. In order for the Europeans to maintain their landholdings in the Middle East, they had to throw their religious convictions out of the chapel window, or at least swallow them before they swallowed the bitter pill of an organized Muslim revolt. Nobody apparently realized this more than the Knights of the Temple. In doing so, they were able to move about freely, and, more important, they were able to learn many things from the Muslims and the Jews who occupied the Middle East.

We have already seen evidence that they learned the art of constructing forts and buildings using stone, but what else did they learn? It is at this juncture that we can leave my personal digression and odd theories behind and begin a more thorough and fact based study of the predecessor of the Freemasons, the Poor Knights of the Temple of Solomon (The Templars) their history their myths and their scandals.

The Knights of the Temple and the Freemasons

What exactly are Freemasons? In order to begin to answer this question, we must answer many questions. First of all, from where does the idea of a "Freemason," originate? Why do they associate themselves with the

Crusades and a Holy Order called the Templars? Well, let's begin with the basics and see if we can't just complicate things from there.

Freemasons are masons. Masons are craftsmen who build structures out of brick and stone. Masons, but not necessarily "Freemasons" probably constructed many buildings in your town. Why? Simply put, the term "Freemason" comes from the Middle Ages. Back then, it was a term used to describe a member of the Masonic guild who had the legal authority, by virtue of his status as a master of his craft, to cross borders without the permission of a landlord, hence the term, "free" mason. Later on, rich and influential members of English, French and other European societies would begin to join a different kind of organization with the same name, but with a whole new approach to life. What exactly made that chain of events happen is the next part of our story.

According to the Freemasons, their organization dates back to the time of building of the temple of Solomon, which was completed around nine hundred and fifty years before the birth of Christ. The Temple of Solomon was later destroyed by the Babylonians around 600 BCE, rebuilt and then destroyed again by the Romans after the crucifixion of Jesus. However, we shall soon see that some of the knowledge used to build the Temple of Solomon originated much earlier in Egypt, and that explains why the Freemasons also date their knowledge and rituals back to the ancient Egyptians and even before.

The Freemasons, as we pointed out earlier, are a society with secrets. Having secrets leads people to speculate about what those secrets might be, so now is as good of time as any to point out that some people suspect, and have suspected the Freemasons, and their predecessors, the Knights of the Temple, of being privy to information that is not shared with anyone but those who are initiated into the Order, or group. According to Jim Marrs author of *Rule by Secrecy,* "Freemasonry is the latest incarnation of what is known as the underground stream. This is a hidden stream of knowledge that has been passed down since the dawn of human history." What this knowledge is and whether it is knowledge of good, evil, or simply the claims of a club who likes to make boasts that they know more than anybody else, is anybody's guess. The Freemasons are also a society, which constantly reminds their members of two aspects of their order, their ties with the past, and their oath to keep their knowledge secret.

Ritual murder or the murder ritual of Solomon's master builder

According to the Freemason's history and ritual, during the time of the building of the temple in Jerusalem, the master builder, men seeking a secret password, which, according to one of the many Freemason re-enactments, he refused to reveal, murdered a man by the name of Hiram Abiff. During the Freemason ritual which was aired on the History Channel documentary, *Freemasonry Revealed*, Hiram Abiff is accosted three times by nefarious characters known as Jubalah, who slashes or stabs Hiram with a ruler, Jubalo, who slashes Hiram with a mason's square and finally Hiram is fatally whacked in the forehead with a mallet by Jubalom, the apparent ringleader of the three brothers. In the ritual, Hiram Abiff dies without revealing the secret word, and is then brought back to life by Solomon himself.

The Freemasons have made this ritual, which is undertaken for members seeking admittance into the 3rd degree of Freemasonry, public, so this is not secret knowledge. Besides being a fun way to spend a Friday night, there is something of a moral to this re-enactment. Take the secrets of the Order to the grave or else suffer very serious consequences. Kevin McNeil-Smith editor of *Freemasonry Watch* tells us, "According to Masonic ritual, if you break your oath, you will be murdered. That is the basis of the oath." Furthermore, according to the documentary, *Freemasonry Revealed*, "The Masonic oath guarantees a gruesome death for those who reveal the secrets. They pledge, I do promise and swear under no less penalty than to have my breast torn open, my heart and vitals taken from thence and exposed to rot on the dunghill."

Now that the reader has at least a basic understanding of the beginnings and the nature of the Order of Freemasons, and hopefully a little bit of interest, we can discuss the history of the Freemasons and their predecessors the Knights of the Temple in order to gain a greater understanding of their organization. In case the reader is wondering, this understanding of the Freemasons penchant for secrecy will be of great importance later, in relation to the Latter-day Saint Church and the Extraterrestrial Phenomenon.

The history of the Order of Freemasons, at least for non-initiates and those who occupy the lower echelons of the organization, is surrounded in myth and mystery, conspiracy and intrigue. Some of this is due of course to the secret nature of the Freemason organization and some is due to the myths propagated by the Freemasons themselves. Further yet, some of the myth and mystery, conspiracy and intrigue is due to the work of so-called "conspiracy theorists" and some is due to the very facts that surround the history of the Freemason organization. One thing is for sure, the history of the Freemasons is not only interesting, it is also enlightening, literally.

Thanks to the work of scholars, researchers and historians, we have at least a sketchy understanding of the Freemasons and their European predecessors, the Poor Knights of the Temple, or the Knights Templar. What follows then is the information that is generally considered common knowledge about the Freemasons and their history as it pertains to the Knights of the Temple, along with some of their myths and a small amount of necessary speculation on the part of the author. In the spirit of Ockham's razor, which says, "The simplest solution is probably the best," I would like to lay aside the myth and mystery and look at the practical reasons for the Templars, their rise to glory, their subsequent fall from grace and their apparent disappearance.

Origins of the legend of the Knights of the Temple

If the reader will recall from the previous chapter on the History of the World, in 1095, Pope Urban II responded to Byzantine Emperor's request for a few hundred mercenaries by calling for an all-out, no-holds-barred war against the infidel Muslims who had occupied Jerusalem, while leaving out the fact that Muslims had been in control of the city for a hundred and fifty years. The response throughout Europe was overwhelming and in no time, a mass migration of over a hundred thousand armed and semi-armed adventurers, holy men, knights, landless nobles criminals, and assorted riff-raff made their way to the Holy Land.

The story of the Poor Knights of the Temple began sometime after the fall of Jerusalem in 1099. According to the popular version of the Templar story, in the year 1119, nineteen years after the fall of Jerusalem, two of the original Crusaders returned to Jerusalem and asked permission of Baldwin II, the second French king of Jerusalem, for permission to form a holy order in which to protect pilgrims journeying to the Holy Land. One of the knights was Hugh De Payens whom, it is believed had distinguished himself as one of the best knights of the Crusades, and his cousin Godfrey de St. Omer, both of whom, according to the legend, had accompanied Godfrey of Bouillon on the original crusade as vassals (soldiers) of Godfrey, who would ultimately be crowned the first French king of Jerusalem in 1099. Baldwin II conceded to the request of Hugh de Payens and Godfrey de St. Omer and gave them space near the Muslim Al Aqsa Mosque, which was believed to be the original site of Solomon's Temple, thus they became the Knights of the Temple.

From these beginnings, mystery surrounds the Knights of the Temple. Why did Baldwin II grant them accommodations at the Temple mount? Was Hugh de Payens granted that particular spot because he was looking for ancient secrets? The fact is, we don't really know why he was granted that particular spot. What we do know is, as Sean Martin, author of *Knights Templar: History and Myths,* tells us, "Once Jerusalem was captured, most people wanted to go home." The fact of the matter was, at the time, many people thought that the capture of Jerusalem would result in the second coming of Christ. Once the city was captured and Christ failed to return, the Crusaders were faced with some stark realities. Enemies surrounded them and they occupied the second most holy site in Islam. The only way they could maintain their position was to keep support coming from the West.

The rise of tourism in the Middle East

In a land with no gold, silver, or anything worth shipping back to Europe (Europe already had its own share of lunatics), there was only one way to keep money coming into the Crusader effort and that was tourism. Once Jerusalem was captured, European Christians wanted to travel to the Holy Land to see the sites and places they learned about in their local churches. These travelers were called pilgrims and, like today, some were very rich and some were very poor. These traveling civilians were considered easy targets by the Muslims and down-and-out Christians they met along the way. Tourists then, presented another huge headache to the rulers of Jerusalem and the principalities along the route who not only had the Muslims to contend with; they were also charged, according to their vows of chivalry and defenders of Christendom, with protecting and accommodating their European visitors. The cost in trained men and equipment was mounting.

The facts surrounding Templar beginnings

The circumstances surrounding the foundation of the Holy Order of the Knights of the Temple are themselves shrouded in mystery, conflicting information, rumors and unverifiable claims. One of the first clarifications we must make is that the founder of the Templar order was a man whom we initially referred to by his French name, Hugues, or Hugh de Payan, and whose name we shall, with the stroke of a few keys, change to the English translation and more easily remembered name, Hugh the Pagan. Let the author point out, "de Payen" (the Pagan) signifies Hugh's place of birth, not necessarily his religious affiliations. The confusion surrounding Hugh the Pagan stems from the fact that he was a vassal or an armed underling of Count Hugh of Champagne. It is possible that this "blending of Hughs" has been the cause of some historical error as pertaining to the story of the founder of the Templars.

To recount the events that led up to the founding of the Templar order, we *do not know for sure* that Hugh the Pagan and his boss, Count Hugh, fought in the initial Crusades, which culminated in the capture of Jerusalem in the year 1099. We can only assume that Count Hugh accompanied his boss and the soon-to-be first French ruler of Jerusalem, Godfrey of Bouillon on the first Crusade. We do know that Count Hugh (Pagan's boss) did make a pilgrimage to the Holy Land in the years 1104-1107. Count Hugh returned to Jerusalem in the years 1114 and returned home in 1116. We can only assume that Hugh the Pagan returned to Jerusalem in 1114 with his boss, Count Hugh, and stayed. In 1120 and 1123, "Hugues de Payens" appears on a witness list on Jerusalem documents. In 1125, Hugh de Payen's name appears on a charter and his title appears as "Magister Militium Templi (Master of the Temple Force). (Wallace-Murphy 17)

According to the popular history surrounding the Templar myth, Hugh the Pagan, was accompanied by eight other knights. The group was given permission to take up residence near the Al-Aqsa Mosque, which was believed to be the site of Solomon's Temple. Who were these nine knights? Dr. Karen Ralls, author of *The Templars and the Grail*, tells us, "The first nine nights were very much a family affair." These knights who made up Hugh the Pagan's temple force were, according to Marilyn Hopkins, co-author of *Templars in America*, "…all related by blood or by marriage."

What we can probably assume then, is that twenty odd years after the fall of Jerusalem, the occupiers of the Holy Land, to include Hugh the Pagan, saw a need for a regular military force to occupy Jerusalem. He simply proposed what we would today call a business model to Baldwin II and Baldwin agreed. Why? The climate was hostile, politically, militarily and in terms of the, well, climate. Nobody but a real fanatic would want to spend more time there than was necessary to pick up a few war stories to tell the young ladies back home. That was what Hugh the Pagan and his entourage needed, real fanatics. So, how does a person recruit fanatics? Well, that is the next part of the story. It is also the next part of the mystery surrounding the Templars.

In fact, the Hugh the Pagan and his Templars who are listed as the "Temple Force" in a Jerusalem document seemed to be somewhat neglectful of their duties from the very beginning. Alan Butler co-author of, *The Warriors and the Bankers* tells us that, "The original idea of the Templars was to protect pilgrims traveling from the coast to the Holy Land." However, according to Butler, "There doesn't seem to be a single account of anyone who ascribes guarding the road to the Templars."

What were these relatives of Pagan, who Dr. Tim Wallace-Murphy, co-author of *Custodians of Truth* describes as; "Nine middle-aged knights (who) were hardly in a position to protect very much," actually doing in Jerusalem? According to popular history, the small group of Templars was busy excavating beneath the remains of the Temple. Suddenly, ten years after their order was established, they made like gangbusters back to Europe and began recruiting for their order. What was it that they found? Was it treasure? Was it secret knowledge? Was it all just a hoax? Or could it have been all three?

Recruiting for God's Army

What we do know is that Hugh the Pagan appeared in Scotland in 1128 on a recruiting campaign. George Smart, author of *The Knights Templar Chronology* tells us that they met with the Sinclair family, who will later be instrumental in the story of the Freemasons. As Smart tells us, "The Sinclair family has long been associated with the Templars because they are one of the first families to give land grants to the Templars when they came back from the Holy Land." Much speculation has surrounded the alleged marriage of one of the Sinclairs to Hugh the Pagan, but written documentation has never been produced that attests to this fact and it was never put forward until 1967.[3]

In 1129, yet another myth was born when the Catholic Church officially sanctioned the Templars as a holy order of monks in Troyes, France. We also know that Hugh the Pagan's second in command, Godfrey de St. Omer had family ties to Viking rulers who had set themselves up in Scotland, England and on the Northwestern coast of Europe in what is known today as The Netherlands. Dr. Tim Wallace-Murphy tells us, "Suddenly with marginal publicity, they start to get grants of land in every part of Europe. They are able to send 300 mounted knights to the holy land within 8 months. With each knight there would have been a squire, horses, there were ferriers, there were trades people and armorers to go with them and all the transport had to be organized."

The new order was distinguished from other monastic orders in that they vowed to fight for the cause of Christ and they renounced all personal possessions except for their swords. In other words, these new "Knights of the Temple" were completely different than your usual run-of-the-mill monks who wore brown tunics, prayed and read the Bible all day. These monks were heavily armed and looking for a fight. Knights who joined their order swore a life of poverty, but the order itself did not, which will be a cause of some concern later in their clouded history. Since the Templars only recruited from the sons of the wealthy classes, the new recruits were expected to donate their wealth, lands, gold, horses, etc. to the order. The order also had key connections in France to endorse their cause, one being Hugh's De Payen's nephew, the future Saint Bernard of Clairevaux, who served as their public relations man in France. In a tract written in 1135, he wrote:

"(A Templar Knight) is truly a fearless knight, and secure on every side, for his soul is protected by the armor of faith, just as his body is protected by the armor of steel. He is thus doubly armed, and need fear neither demons nor men."

From defenders to bankers: the Immaculate Exemption

---

[3] *Les Dossiers Secrets d'Henri Lobineau* (1967)

To put it bluntly, the Templars found not only the fanatics they needed, they found the "cream" of the fanatic crop. As a military and monastic order whose mission was to protect pilgrims on the way to Jerusalem, they were given contributions in the way of money, land and recruits from the best families in Europe. Hugh the Pagan and his relatives, with their grants of land, knights and even a holy sanction, were truly "in business" as they say. In 1139, the Pope declared the Templars *exempt* from all laws except the Pope himself. This worked out quite well for the Templars, who began loaning money to monarchies around Europe, a practice forbidden in the Bible, in the year 1150.

The Templars also developed a system whereby they took deposits from pilgrims in Europe on their way to the Holy Land and who, in turn, issued coded documents that were used in lieu of cash. The documents were the world's first ATM cards. Should the pilgrim fail to return, the money, lands, or the Templars kept valuables left in the safekeeping of the Templars. Dr. Tim Wallace-Murphy, explain what they really were.

"They became bankers in a very big way. They lent to emperors, priests, bishops, and kings. There was a church law against charging interest, so they didn't charge interest they charged rent. It was a neat little euphemism to get around it (the law)."

What made the Knights so powerful-the mystery of the Temple?

Until the year 1200, the Knights of the Temple were a relatively small order, but by that time, the Knights of the Temple had become extremely wealthy. So they must have found something that would lead to their official sanction by the Church, right? George Smart author of *The Templar Chronology* explains it this way:

"The Templars got an extraordinary package of perks from the Catholic Church. They were allowed to cross borders, which was a big deal back then. They were absolved from taxes. They were under no one's authority, except the Pope himself, which was really an exceptional arrangement for the time. The most reasonable explanation for all these perks was simply as a thank you, if you will, for protecting the pilgrims. But, I'm skeptical as to whether that was really the true purpose. There were many possibilities for why this sweetheart deal was struck. It could have been that the church didn't want information to get out. The first theory for why this would have happened was that the Templars found extraordinary items and relics and scrolls underneath the temple of Solomon. Scrolls that were not quite along the lines of Catholic Orthodoxy that suggested, for instance, the possibility of a more significant relationship between Jesus and Mary Magdalene. A different account of what happened between Jesus and the apostles or anything that was a variation of what was in the approved canons of the Bible."

Although the claim that many make, that Hugh the Pagan and his band of knights found something of great interest to the Catholic Church makes great literature and fuels the imaginations of many, the simplest explanation, whether accurate or not, is evident in the route that Hugh the Pagan and Godfrey took on their recruiting effort. Contrary to the myth, they did not immediately approach the Catholic Church and gain an official sanction. By the time they approached the Church, they had already been given land grants in Scotland and in northwestern Europe. When they approached the Church at Troyes and later the Pope himself, they most likely presented themselves as an answer to a long standing problem the Church had been trying to address for forty years; the need for a steady flow of money and recruits to secure the Holy Land. Who would not have agreed to that proposal? As we shall see, it would be an agreement the Church would later regret.

It may be hard for us to comprehend the extent of the power the Templars gained during their almost two hundred years of existence. If the reader will recall, Europe at that time was a very loose collection of alliances between warlords who, in turn owed loyalty up a chain of warlords that ended with the king of each particular nation. However, the idea of a nation as we may think of it did not exist then. In the days before the Internal Revenue Service, each landlord was dependent upon oftentimes, unreliable vassals for service and money. In turn, the king was forced to rely upon them all for his own keeping.

The Magna Carta, which was signed in 1215, limited the rights of the King of England. It was the first in a series of social contracts in England that emphasized how dependent the King was upon his underlings for their support. For the Church, which was dependent upon the money and the soldiers that were provided by the individual kingdoms for its own security and its foreign enterprises, the European system was a huge headache. By declaring the Templars exempt from all laws and under the direct control of the Pope, Europe and the Church had what it had been in need of since the days of Charlemagne; a European army. Not only were the Templars a European army, because of their banking enterprises and landholdings, they were a well-financed, self-supporting European army as well.

The Templars as a military force

As a military force in the Middle East, the Templars were a great asset to the Crusader army. They were feared by their Muslim enemies and were often used by the conventional Crusading forces in the way modern tanks would be used on the battlefield today. These highly trained professional soldiers were fearless, heavily armored and they rode large warhorses. They charged through and broke up enemy formations of cavalry and foot soldiers. Simply put, the Templar formations were basically suicide squads. Their Muslim counterparts were well aware of the fact that the Templars on the battlefield were all business. Templars did not take prisoners. Templars asked for and gave no quarter. Templars who were captured were immediately executed rather than ransomed. As a strategic force, however, the Templars were lukewarm at best. The height of the Templar legend was the Battle of Montisgard in 1187. The so-called victory however, was not so much a victory as a comedy of errors on behalf of the Muslim and Christian commanders.

Montisgard and the Horns of Hattin

The **Battle of Montisgard** began when a contingent of five hundred Crusader knights were blocked by a much larger force on the coast of Palestine by the Egyptian Mamaluke leader, Saladin (Saleh-al-din) and an overwhelming force of Muslims. Instead of annihilating the Crusader Army while he had the chance, Saladin left them pinned on the coast by a part of his army and went on to re-take Jerusalem. Eighty Templars broke through the lines of the blocking Muslim force, which allowed the Crusader knights and their small contingent of Templar reinforcements to escape to the north, traveling along the coast. By chance, the Crusader knights and their Templar contingent happened upon Saladin's personal bodyguard along the way and slaughtered them, which forced Saladin to retreat back to Egypt.

The "victory" was not wasted on their chief public relations man in France, Hugh the Pagan's nephew, St. Bernard of Clairevaux, who soon announced:

"A handful of righteous warriors can vanquish the most overwhelming hoarde."

Believing their own publicity was to prove their downfall ten years later when the battlefield success of the Templars at Montisgard was tempered by their colossal blunder at the **Battle of Hattin** in 1197. There, the poor decision making of the Grand Master of the Templar Order led to the defeat and capture of nearly the entire Crusader army, including the majority of the Templars serving in the Jerusalem.

The debacle at Hattin began when, instead of staying put in their fortified city, the Grand Master of the Templar Order insisted the Crusader army march out into the desert in the middle of summer and meet the Muslims head on in open battle. The "battle" was nothing more than a slaughter of the Christian forces, that were, by the time of the battle, near death from thirst and fatigue from the long march. To make things worse for the Templars, the Grand Master allowed himself to be ransomed, or his freedom bought for a price, which was against the rules of the order. Meanwhile, the rest of the Templars were beheaded on the spot. After the loss of the Crusader army, the days of the Christian occupation of Jerusalem were numbered. Dr. Karen Ralls sums up the feelings in Europe about the Templars when she says, "After that, the reason for the Templar's existence was not as acute as it was before. From that point on, some felt, well maybe God didn't bless the Templars as well as we had thought."

Did the Templars really find something in the Temple of Solomon?

In order to satisfy the insatiable curiosity of those who point at the Templars and the Freemasons as a grand conspiracy to hide secret knowledge, we must address some of the questions that surround their mystique. First and foremost is the lingering question of what "secrets" did the Order of the Poor Knights of the Temple possess which made it necessary to maintain their high level of secrecy? Did they actually find something during their excavations, such as treasure, or a "hidden stream of knowledge" as author Jim Marrs insists? Or, were the Templars just putting out misinformation to gain support for their Order? Like everything that seems to be associated with Freemasons, in order to begin to address that question, we must first find the answers to a number of other questions. So, let us address these questions first, and then see if we can find any clues that would indicate what possibly the Templars could have found lying hidden underneath the famed temple of Solomon.

Probably the best place to start is at the beginning, where, we shall see that the organization that contains so many "mysteries" itself begins with a mystery.

Question 1: How would Hugh the Pagan have known there was anything worth digging for under the temple of Solomon?

As any tourist knows, it is hard enough making your way around a foreign city, especially when you don't speak the language. The Crusaders had one more strike against them; they had killed many of the inhabitants of Jerusalem upon their arrival. There must have been a certain amount of hostility toward the Christians that would have been hard to overcome. The idea that somehow Hugh and his French-speaking band of knights "magically" knew not only that there was something to dig for under the Al-Aqsa Mosque but exactly where to dig makes the story seem highly implausible. However, Templar researcher Margaret Odrowaz-Sypniewska tells us that, "Hugh and many Templars learned to speak Arabic and other local languages, making them easy diplomats." The fact that Hugh and his boys knew how to speak the local language at least gives the story a little more credibility. Although Margaret Odrowaz-Sypniewska does not specify it, we can assume the other local language the Templars learned to speak was Hebrew.

The Islamic and Jewish religions and traditions give the story even more credibility. Had the Muslim or Hebrew inhabitants of Jerusalem suspected that there was, in fact, something of value hidden underneath the Al Aqsa Mosque on the Old Temple Mount, digging for it would have meant defiling the very spot where Mohammed descended into heaven, making it the second holiest site in Islam. For the Jews, the same spot was where Abraham had once almost sacrificed his only son Isaac. Probing the area with picks and shovels would have been sacrilege of the most lethal and likely most painful kind, not to mention the guarantee of hell-fire once the perpetrators reached the other side. Therefore, no Muslim or Jew living in a Muslim controlled city would undertake such a blasphemous and potentially lethal enterprise. However, once the Christians we in control of the city, well, that was another story entirely. They didn't have any sentimental attachment to the site. As far as the local inhabitants would be concerned, the bloodthirsty Christians were all going to hell anyway. What did one more sin matter to them? Whoever might have told Hugh and Godfrey there was something of interest beneath Solomon's Temple may have made some kind of business arrangement with the Templars.

Conclusion: We do know that the Templars would have had the ability to communicate with the local inhabitants of Jerusalem. We can assume that if there were some kind of financial reward involved, it may have been motivation enough to tell the Templars where to dig. This aspect of the story at least merits the *possibility* of being accurate.

Question 2: Is there any evidence of the Crusaders actually digging in the area where Solomon's Temple once stood?

In 1867 a British archeological dig uncovered tunnels that began at the site of the Templar headquarters and the southeastern side of the Temple Mount. The tunnels extended downwards twenty-five meters and then extended horizontally underneath the Al Aqsa Mosque, which many believe to be built on the site of Solomon's Temple. Whoever dug the tunnels knew exactly how deep to dig and in which direction to go. According to Tim Wallace-Murphy, co-author of *Custodians of Truth*, "The tunnels were re-excavated in the early 1900's by Lieutenant Warren of the British Royal Engineers." According to Wallace-Murphy, Lieutenant Warren's excavation found Templar artifacts, "…such as spurs, and various pieces of armament." Therefore, there is actual evidence that the Templars did in fact either excavate or occupy the area underneath the old site known as the Temple Mount. This of course leads to our next important question.

Question 3: What did the Templars find?

This question has been unanswered for a thousand years. If we knew what the Templars found, if anything at all, there would be no point in this part of the book, or the hundreds of books and other works that have been produced speculating about what was found under the Temple of Solomon. If anybody does know that something was in fact uncovered, they have been keeping the secret for a very long time. The lack of any substantial evidence regarding what lay hidden under the Temple of Solomon has been the inspiration for volumes of works starting with the writings of Chretien de Troyes in 1180 that wrote about the Templar's discovery of the Holy Grail to Dan Brown's *Da Vinci Code* in our own time.

In addition the Templar's own claims, that they are in possession of religious artifacts, such as a piece of the Tue Cross, only adds the Templar mystique. Freemasons like George Lucas with his Jedi Knights (*Star Wars*) and Stephen Spielberg's and Lucas' *Indiana Jones* series also keeps the Templar mystique alive in the public consciousness. (Deceased Freemason) Walt Disney's *National Treasure* movies also serve to keep the mystery of Templars and their Freemason descendants alive. So, with all the hype, they must have found something, right?

Theory 1: the Templars found the Treasures of Solomon's Temple

According to the Dead Sea scrolls, when the Romans destroyed Jerusalem, vast amounts of gold were hidden in a secret location. In fact, one document, called the *Copper scroll* that was found with the Dead Sea scrolls, actually contains an inventory of the treasure that was hidden from the oncoming Roman army. Could the Templars have excavated and found this treasure, or the clues to where it was hidden? According to the History Channel documentary *The Templar Code,* "The (treasure theory) gains credence in 1952 when one of the Dead Sea scrolls known as the copper scroll is unearthed. Incised on sheets of hammered copper it seems to list an inventory of treasure, itemizing some 200 tons of gold and silver."

Of course it is *possible* that the Templars uncovered this treasure, but at the time, the entire force of the Templars amounted to nine men. We know that at the same time as their alleged grand discovery, Hugh the Pagan went back to Scotland with Godfrey to recruit for the Order. What did they do with all that treasure? Did they take it back with them? How could they possibly have handled such a large amount (two hundred tons) of gold and silver? How could they transport it and guard it all by themselves without anyone finding out what it was? Did they leave it in Jerusalem? How would their colleagues have been able to keep such an important find a secret?

The fact is, there were people and there are people who like to exaggerate their own importance by spreading stories. Were the Templars and are the Freemasons guilty of this flaw of human nature? Chretien of Troyes wrote in 1187 that the Templars possessed the Holy Grail, no treasure, just a Holy Grail. Okay, where is this Holy Grail? The more down-to-earth and somewhat less interesting and marketable truth probably lies in the fact that the Templars became rich because of the massive donations the Order received along with the stipulation that the new members of the Order come from the wealthiest classes and they must surrender their belongings to the Templars while they themselves swore vows of poverty and chastity.

According to author Sean Martin, "The King of Argonne for instance, when he died in the mid-1130's, left large chunks of Spain to the order. All of sudden they had this vast tract of land." The fact that they recruited and sought donations from the wealthiest families in Europe, and then went into the business of loaning money for interest, probably made the Templars far richer than a mere two hundred tons of gold and silver that they found stashed in the ground under the Temple of Solomon.

Conclusion: There are other reasons to doubt the claim that the Templars found a vast cache of gold and silver, which we will discuss later. For now, such an unsubstantiated rumor as a vast treasure, or the discovery of religious artifacts would certainly raise the "stock" of the Templars in the highly superstitious and gullible society of Medieval Europe as well as our own society. Lacking any physical proof, the theory is once again possible, but considering the difficulty of concealing and transporting such a find, is highly unlikely.

Theory 2: The Templars found evidence of the bloodline of Christ

The trail of the Templars and the modern Freemasons becomes even more bizarre when claims of Jesus' bloodline, a rather odd theory which most of us became aware of when author Dan Brown's book and the movie *Da Vinci Code* hit the bookshelves and the movies screens. While some have cited the fact that the Sinclair family, owners and guardians of

Rosslyn Castle and its famous chapel had nothing to do with the Templars and even testified against them in English court, others say there is a link between the Sinclairs and the Templars-in-hiding, and a rather bizarre one at that. Christopher Knight and Robert Lomas claim it in their book *The Second Messiah*:

"The original Knights Templar of whom little is known, are believed to have been representatives of the ruling families of Champagne (De Payens), Anjou, Gisor and Flanders. The leader of the Templars was Hugh de Payens, a middle aged ranking nobleman who married Catherine St. Clair, the niece of his crusading partner, Baron Henri St. Clair of Roslyn."

According to Barry Chamish, in his online book *Who Murdered Yitzhak Rabin*, the modern Sinclair connection and the order of the Society of Freemasons, connects the Templars, the Freemasons and a somewhat outrageous claim that the bloodline of Jesus Christ lies within the Sinclairs themselves:

"The Sinclairs are recognized as "hereditary Grand Masters of Scottish Freemasonry" and rank high among the "sacred" Merovingian families deemed worthy to assume the throne of Jerusalem. These deluded power elites base their fabricated claim on the blasphemy that Jesus Christ sired children whose descendants intermarried with the bloodlines of the thrones of Europe, infusing them with the holy blood of Christ."

Blasphemy or no, since the Scottish Rite Freemasons claim no connection to Jesus, only to an obscure god that takes on many names and forms and a god that suspiciously resembles Jesus' opposite in heaven, any person they would support to claim the throne of Jerusalem with any kind of connection to Jesus, since there was only one of him, could only fall into the category of "anti-Christ." The modern claims that the Templars possessed some secret knowledge that was the "source of the Church's power on earth," as was written about in *Da Vinci Code*, make for good literature, but fail to bear out under scrutiny. The claim that the offspring of Jesus and Mary Magdalene is somehow the predecessor of the Merovingian Kings of France has no more evidence to support it than the claims, made by the Merovingian kings themselves that they were born of sea serpents. According to researcher Lisa Shea:

"To reiterate, there is no documentation linking Mary to anyone. The Merovingians claimed that they came from Mary's bloodline - but they also claimed they came from Atlantis and from sea creatures at other times. The earliest known Merovingian king was back in the 400s - nothing at all is known or documented about his parentage. Like all the other theories, it is very difficult to prove without any real evidence."

The stand of the Catholic Church that Jesus could not have married and produced offspring, along with the argument that if Jesus did produce children, Jesus was not who he claimed to be is neither based in logic, nor reason. If it were to come to light that Jesus had a wife and a child, it would simply mean he was a human being like the rest of us. Since Jesus died upon the cross, it stands to reason that he was, in fact, human. It was what he taught us before he was crucified and what happened after he died that should be of importance to people of faith.

The idea that if the Catholic Church's version of the life and death of Jesus is not correct, then no version of the life of Jesus is correct is ludicrous. The Catholic Church came into existence three centuries after the life of Jesus and their (and most of Christianity's) version of Jesus' life is based upon four written gospels of which there were most likely dozens from which they could have chosen. This would be similar to choosing four people as witnesses to a murder based upon the fact their stories all sounded the most similar to each other.

Furthermore, should it somehow be proven that Jesus did have children and his descendants were to be discovered, the idea that they somehow are infused with "holy blood" is similar in logic to claims of the hunters and dealers of religious relics and artifacts of the Middle Ages. A cup that Jesus drank from is still a cup. A piece of the cross is still a piece of old rotten wood. Except for the type, the blood that was in the veins of Jesus was no different than the blood of anyone else. It is true that these artifacts may hold intrinsic and historic value, but to claim that a cup, a piece of wood or someone's blood is any different chemically or biologically because Jesus had something to do with them is absurd and only perpetuates superstitions and the age-old claims of the ruling classes of Europe that their lineage and position was due to anything but the fact that one of their ancestors was a violent criminal who happened to be more successful than the rest of the violent criminals in his neighborhood. It is this kind of illogic and superstition that the world could readily do without.

Conclusion: The story that the Templars uncovered Jesus' bloodline, like the mythical Templar treasure is made with no evidence whatsoever and therefore, has absolutely no basis in the realm of facts. The claim that the Templars guarded "the source of the Catholic Church's power on earth" is more accurately stated as, "the Templars were the Catholic Church's standing army and the real source of their power on earth." Furthermore, considering the religious and political climate at the time, were the early Templars to make such an outrageous announcement to the leadership of the Catholic Church, their whole order would have been immediately declared heretical and their fate would have been immediate torture and an invitation to a rather unpleasant barbecue.

Theory 3: The Templars found ancient documents pertaining to the occult and called them "The Secrets of Solomon."

In order to prove, disprove or measure the merits of this theory, it would be necessary to know something of King Solomon himself. It would also be necessary to look for clues as to what kind of knowledge he may have possessed and the possible sources from where the knowledge came. Furthermore, it would be necessary to take a look into the known practices of the descendants of the Templars, the Freemasons, and see if there are any similarities either real or claimed between biblical Solomon, and the Freemasons. Due to the absence of concurrent written accounts of the period, the logical place to begin to look for evidence of King Solomon is the only source available to us in the English language, the Old Testament Book of Kings.

"*Then sat Solomon upon the throne of David his father; and his kingdom was established greatly.*" (1Kings 2:12)

As we have already seen, recent Biblical scholarship and research has discovered that it was during the time of King Solomon that many of the books of the Old Testament were either written, or compiled in the Hebrew *Torah.* This fact is fortunate for our inquest because it allows us a more contemporary and detailed view of Solomon than any other Biblical character until Jesus. Because of Solomon's father David's lifelong campaigning against the enemies of Israel, Solomon inherited a kingdom that was at peace with its neighbors and which had been strengthened from within. The Bible describes Solomon in his early years this way:

"And Solomon loved the Lord, walking in the statutes of David his father. Only he sacrificed and burnt incense in high places." (1 Kings 3:3)

Solomon gained a reputation as a wise ruler. He received gifts and tribute from Israel's traditional enemies. In later years, The Queen of Sheba would arrive in Israel to give gifts of treasure and wealth to the charismatic ruler of Israel. His judgments were considered the wisest in the land, and so, he became loved by his people. It is while he was at the height of his political popularity that Solomon decided it was time for Israel to have a resting place for the Ten Commandments and the Ark of the Covenant. It would be a place where the Levites, the high priests of the Israelites could perform sacrifices and administer the holy ordinances of their priesthood. With his grand scheme in mind, the Bible tells us:

"And Solomon sent to Hiram, saying, Thou knowest how that David my father could not build an house unto the name of the Lord his God for the wars which were about him on every side, until the Lord put them under the soles of his feet. But now the Lord my God hath given me rest on every side, so that their neither adversary nor evil occurent. And behold, I purpose to build an house unto the name of the Lord my God, as the Lord spake unto David my father, saying, Thy son, whom I will set upon the throne in thy room, he shall build an house unto my name."
(1 Kings 5:2-5)

To finish his House of the Lord, Solomon seeks the help of the second of two Hiram's who appear in relation to the building of the Temple. The second Hiram, "the widow's son, will be important to our story a little later.

"And King Solomon sent and fetched Hiram out of Tyre. He was a widow's son of the tribe of Naphtali, and his father was a man of Tyre, a worker in brass: and he was filled with wisdom, and understanding, and cunning to all works in brass. And he came to King Solomon, and wrought his work."
(1Kings 7:13-14)

Here we begin to see some strange irregularities in the story. Hiram, "the widow's son," was filled with wisdom? What wisdom did Hiram, the widow's son, possess that the chroniclers of the book of the wisest of the Israelite kings felt it necessary to describe, since the second Hiram is more or less a "common" workman? We could easily say that the writer of the book of Kings meant to describe the skill that Hiram of Tyre possessed, however, the writer makes that apparent when he specifically states that Hiram was, in addition to his "wisdom and understanding," also, "cunning to all works in brass."

To further emphasize the mystery of Hiram of Tyre, if the reader will recall, the Freemason ceremony for initiates into the third degree of Freemasonry is a reenactment of the murder of a builder of Solomon's Temple named Hiram Abiff who is killed in the ceremony because he will not reveal a secret word. In his death throes, he cries out, "Will no one help a widow's son?" The Freemasons claim that their Hiram Abiff is a fictional character. However, if this were a modern day crime scene, this Hiram of Tyre, the "widow's son" would definitely be noted as a person of interest. In our inquiry into the Freemason mystery, we shall call this Hiram back later for further questioning.

Solomon's ties to the occult

Why would Hiram of Tyre be a person who may hold a key to the mystery of the contents of the secret chamber underneath the Temple Mount? The evidence is circumstantial at best, but from the time of the building of the Temple to his death, Solomon the great king begins sliding into a world of worshipping false gods, even as far as to receive a personal warning from God.

> *"But if ye shall turn at all from following me, ye or your children, and will not keep my commandments and my statutes which I have set before you, but go and serve other gods and worship them: Then will I cut off Israel out of the land which I have given them; and this house, which I have hallowed for my name, will I cast out of my sight; and Israel shall be a proverb and a byword among all the people."* (1 Kings 9:6-7)

We can say that from Solomon's behavior following this admonishment from the Lord that someone somehow influenced him in a way that was far more effective than the harsh warnings he received from the Lord of Hosts. After the Queen of Sheba's visit, Solomon seems to have gone off the deep end. He takes many foreign wives and he begins to worship the false gods of Israel's enemies.

> *"But King Solomon loved many strange women, together with the daughter of Pharaoh, women of the Moabites, Ammonites, Edomites, Zidonians and Hittites."* (1 Kings 11: 1)

The first foreign wife of Solomon was Phillo, Pharaoh's daughter. (1 Kings 9:16) Since the Freemasons claim their knowledge dates back to ancient Egypt, yet they also claim to have their origins in the time of Solomon, what was the connection between Solomon and the Egyptians? Pharaoh gave Solomon the land of Gezer as a dowry for Phillo. Was it possible that Pharaoh also provided Solomon with more than the land of Gezer for his wise ally and the father of his grandchildren? We saw in the Book of Abraham that the Pharaohs were pretenders to the holy priesthood, though they had no right to it as descendants of Ham. Did the Pharaohs also possess an alternative form of the priesthood? We know that the Egyptians were a storehouse for ancient knowledge. Whatever was the knowledge that the Egyptians, or the wise and understanding Hiram of Tyre may have passed on to Solomon is anybody's guess. But if the Book of Kings is to be believed, then something happened that changed Solomon from a man of virtue to something else. The Book of Kings tells us:

> *"For it came to pass, when Solomon was old, that his wives turned away his heart after other gods: and his heart was not perfect with the Lord his God, as was the heart of David his father. For Solomon went after Ashtoreth the goddess of the Zidonians, after Milcom the abomination of the Amonites. Then Solomon did build an high place for Chemosh, the abomination of Moab, in the hill that is before Jerusalem, and for Molech, the abomination of the children of Ammon."* (1Kings 11:4-5, 7)

It is these three verses that provide us with clues about the knowledge that King Solomon may have possessed and, that subsequently show up again in the litany, rituals and the practices of the Freemasons. Ashtoreth, according to historical sources, is the Egyptian goddess Astarte who is associated with the Sphinx and the planet Venus. Milcom**,** Chemosh and Molech are generally agreed by historians to be one and the same person.

He was worshipped in the ancient city of Carthage. According to a Jewish rabbi who wrote in the 1100's, "Tophet is Moloch, which was made of brass; and they heated him from his lower parts; and his hands being stretched out, and made hot, they put the child between his hands, and it was burnt; when it vehemently cried out; but the priests beat a drum, that the father might not hear the voice of his son, and his heart might not be moved."

If the reader will recall, Hiram, the architect who King Solomon employed to work on the Temple was filled with wisdom, understanding, and was, "cunning to all works in brass." Again, it is pure speculation, but is the seventh verse of the eleventh chapter of the Book of Kings a clue? Did Solomon, or Hiram, "the widow's son," build something underneath the Temple of Solomon that was an "abomination?" Did the Templars discover this secret chamber and its hidden knowledge and possible artifacts?

Another piece of circumstantial evidence is the attitude that Jesus (who was a carpenter, not a mason) himself had toward the Temple when he cleansed it of the moneychangers. In three of the four gospels, Jesus refers to the Temple of Solomon as, "a den of thieves." An expert in Aramaic, the language of Jesus, would be better able to put across this argument, but in the English language, a den is a quiet room, and is usually secluded from other rooms in order to allow its occupants to be able to read, work, or study in relative piece. A den is also a cave or place of shelter for wild animals to keep their young. Yet, Jesus cleared the public, noisy part of the temple. Why did he use the term "den" or its equivalent in Aramaic? Did he know about the secret chamber underneath the temple? Is this the "den of thieves" to which Jesus was referring?

Conclusion: The theory that the Templars uncovered the hidden Wisdom of Solomon, which is based on at least some evidence, circumstantial though it might be, begins to lend more credence to what the Templars may have discovered, based upon the evidence offered by the Freemasons themselves. They do associate themselves with Astarte who is also Venus, and Lucifer, the son of the morning as he was referred to in the Masonic text Morals and Dogma, written in the 1870's by Grand Master Mason Albert Pike. Still, though slightly more circumstantial is the association with Moloch, the Moabite god of brass, who is also associated with Saturn, the Roman god of War. Both Hiram, the builder of the temple and another figure we will look at more closely when we discuss the history of secret societies have a connection with those who are experts in the working of brass.

Theory 4: The Templars found scientific documents and knowledge that dated back to the ancient Egypt and the beginnings of human civilization.

The Freemason organization itself is the best evidence to support this theory. They admit, or at least claim that they possess knowledge and "mysteries" that date back to the origins of man. This is a topic we will discuss in more detail in the last chapters of this book. At this juncture, however, it is sufficient to say that, at the time, the charge of heresy by the Catholic Church was a crime that made torture in order to get a confession perfectly legal by Papal Edict.

What crimes would merit the charge of heresy? Having any other belief about the world than that espoused by the Catholic Church was one. If the reader will recall, the Catholic Church had, since the Council of Nicaea in 325, the last word on everything. In more simple terms, the Templars with their language skills, their ability to build stone forts, concoct indecipherable codes and who had an excellent grasp of geometry, geology, mathematics and possibly even physics and chemistry, were delving into the realms of what the Catholic Church would classify as witchcraft. The Catholic Church had a monopoly on learning for a thousand years by the time of the demise of the Templars. Conspiracies aside, if the source of Templar power came from the learning of infidels like Muslims and Jews, the logic of the day said that they were cavorting with anti-Christians. Even without references to mysterious secret knowledge and the accusations of being dabblers in the occult, according to the power vested in Inquisitors by the Catholic Church, they had every right to accuse the Templars of being "anti-Christ."

Theory 5: The Templars found nothing. They may have simply come across old tunnels that had been dug for some other purpose and used them for storage.

We can never know for sure unless we know what it was that Hugh the Pagan and the Templars uncovered underneath the Temple. As we have seen, one of the most popular legends associated with the Templars is that they dug under the temple until they found something of significance, whereupon they returned to the Vatican and met secretly with the Pope. In popular movies like the *Da Vinci Code*, it is stated that they found evidence that would destroy the power of the Catholic Church. The Pope then granted them a dispensation and immunity to any laws but his own. Since we do not know exactly what motivated Pope Innocent II to grant the dispensation, we must look for a more practical explanation.

In reality, the dispensation was not granted until twenty years after the Templar's occupation of the Temple site in the year 1139. By that time, Hugh the Pagan was dead. He and his cousin, Godfrey had been recruiting amongst the wealthy of Europe for ten years. A more reasonable explanation would be that the Templars, who were charged with safeguarding pilgrims from the beginning of the establishment of their order ten years prior, thought the pilgrims would be a less tempting target if they carried no cash or valuables. The immunity granted by the Pope was no different than the immunity granted to any monastic order that the Church didn't want to see used as an easy source of wealth for local nobles. Between the time of their founding in 1119 by Hugh the Pagan and the execution of Grand Master Jacques De Molay in 1314, the Templars had amassed more wealth than any individual state in Europe. They had lands, offices, and estates in almost every city in Europe and owned the island of Cyprus. After their defeat at Hattin, their attempts to regain control of the Holy Land ended in one failure after another.

The Templars, as the Pope's private army and banking establishment, left many of the local rulers in Europe in a state of uneasiness, and debt. Their freedom to move about Europe, the secrecy of their organization and most importantly, their continued military blunders, left many questioning their legitimacy as soldiers of God. Finally, the French King, Philip IV pulled the plug. He declared them redundant and had them arrested on October 13, 1307. The members of the order, only ten percent of whom were actually combatants, were charged with heresy, worshipping the devil and practicing homosexuality. They were tortured until they confessed and many of them were burned at the stake. It was then possible for the Church and Philip IV to confiscate their wealth. In 1314 Jacques de Molay, who had confessed under torture and then later recounted his confession, was burned at the stake, where, according to contemporary accounts, he uttered the word "Baphomet" before he succumbed. Jacque de Molay also prophesied that the Pope and Philip would join him before the year was finished. It was a prophecy that turned out to be an accurate one.

So, for now, in spite of our efforts, we can only rely on our previous speculations as to what it was that the Templars found underneath the remnants of Solomon's Temple. Possibly the only clue we have as to what the Templars found can be found in the words of 33rd degree Freemason Steven Spielberg's movie character Indiana Jones in the movie, *The Kingdom of the Crystal Skull,* when Indiana Jones says, "Their treasure was knowledge." Later in this book we will look at some of the knowledge that they may have uncovered. For now we must leave aside our speculations and return to the world of historical facts.

Chapter 15

The Secret Society

Practical secrecy

If we look at the modern organization of Freemasons, whose members are inducted into a society where they swear not to reveal the secrets of the Order upon the pain of a rather ignominious death, we can see how it may have been possible for the Templars to conceal their identity, their knowledge and their trade secrets until the time was right for them to reveal themselves in the light of day. Secrecy was the key to the Templar's power and their ability to exist as an organization. During the height of their power in the years of the Crusades, the Templars used secret codes in order to provide travelers with a system of "money on demand" which would be useless to any bandits or thieves unfamiliar with the code. For a Templar to betray those codes would have been a disaster, not only for the particular Templar, but also for the reputation of the order. We could see a modern parallel in the attorney client privilege in the United States. If lawyers began revealing their client's secrets, there would be little reason for lawyers.

In order to better understand the fate of the Templars and even more reasons for the mystique associated with their descendants, the Freemasons, it is important to understand the situation in which the men and the institutions behind the demise of the Poor Knights of the Temple found themselves at the beginning of the 1300's. The key historical figure associated with the destruction of the Templar Order was none other than **Philip IV** of France, also known as Philip the Fair who ruled from 1285-1314. Philip the Fair got his nickname due to his complexion rather than his business dealings, which we shall soon see.

Philip the Fair

King Philip acquired the throne at the age of seventeen in the year 1285. As soon as he ascended to the throne, he became aware of his need for two things, power and money, but especially money. According to *The Warriors and the Bankers* author Alan Butler, "France was very poor during the reign of Philip IV. His father had spent tremendous amounts of money on war. He had inherited a very poverty stricken nation." To make matters worse, Philip's economic plans weren't exactly sound either. In order to restock his coffers with gold, he had done what most rulers at the time did, which was to declare war on anyone with money. This didn't work out quite so well for Philip either. The only people willing to loan him the money on the scale that he demanded, considering has status as a poor credit risk, were of course, the Poor Knights of the Temple, who by the 1300's, were neither poor, nor any longer of the Temple. George Smart, author of *The Knights Templar Chronology* explains how Philip's economic plans got him even further into economic hock than before, "He owed the Templars an enormous amount of money for a variety of failed military operations..." In other words, Philip's economic strategy, and his credit rating went sour on him every time his army felt the need to run away from the battlefield.

Philip the Fair had more than just an empty treasury and a huge debt to the Templars weighing on his regal mind. There were other, political issues that were testing the king's patience as well. The question of who was really the ultimate power in Europe had been a hotly contested item and had been since the crowning of Charlemagne in 800 by the Pope. Since that time, the Pope in Italy claimed to be the supreme law of the land by virtue of his being God's representative on earth. Over the years, the Pope had never attempted to back up the claim by force. Popes simply excommunicated whoever didn't see things their way. Excommunication was a way of peaceful, legal wrangling and of keeping the princes and potentates of Europe in line. Since all knights were defenders of Christendom, according to their sworn oath, once excommunicated, a king, a count or a prince, having lost his status as a Christian, could no longer call upon his subordinates to fulfill their oaths of loyalty towards him. The threat of excommunication was usually enough to get compliance from European rulers and so, the system had worked right up until the time Philip IV's economic woes began to affect his relationship with the Church in the late 1200's.

The Pope and King Philip

By the time Philip had been in power for nine years, the power struggle between Church and State, (particularly the economic "state" of France) was coming to a head, as the Italian influenced church elected an Italian, **Boniface VIII** as Pope. Philip, still needing money, declared church lands in France liable for state taxes, to which Boniface responded by issuing an edict, exempting church properties from taxes. Needless to say, Philip IV was furious as well as deprived of revenues he had counted on to get himself out of debt to his bankers, the Templars. Philip, in response, stopped all tithing payments to the Church from leaving the kingdom, which forced Boniface to compromise with yet another edict in 1302 stating that a king could tax in times of emergency, while at the same time, Boniface claimed that "God made Popes to rule over kings." Thus rebuked, Philip turned to confiscating the properties of Jews and the money of Italian bankers to raise money.

However, the matter was not completely settled to the satisfaction of the French throne. In response to the Pope's edict, Philip's chief minister, Guillaume de Nogaret, not a man to take a personal affront lightly, accused the Pope of being a criminal, as well as a heretic before the French Clergy. De Nogaret and Philip also accused the Pope of sodomy, a charge which would become a favorite of Philip when the time came to deal with the Templars. A year later, Nogaret and a private army surprised Boniface at his retreat and demanded that he resign as Pope. Boniface refused and was beaten by de Nogaret and his thugs. Boniface never recovered from the thrashing and died a month later. With Europe short of a Pope, Philip consolidated his power and his northwestern flank by making peace with Edward I of England. After the unfortunate demise of Pope Boniface, Philip installed **Clement V** as Pope in 1305, and moved the Vatican from Italy to Avignon, France.

Philip moves against the Templars

With the Pope and the Church now under his direct authority and his rear literally covered and secure from an invasion by the English, Philip initiated his second economic initiative to get himself out of the royal poor house. Another noble method of ridding oneself of debt, besides stealing money from people under the guise of "war" in Medieval Europe was to throw your creditors in jail. Of course, Philip didn't make his intentions so obvious with a group as powerful and numerous as the Templars. Instead, he thought it might be better to trick them into getting their leaders to meet in one place, and then spring his trap. His first move was to announce that the two military orders which had arisen from the Crusades, the Hospitallers and the Templars, were to be combined under his leadership. As their leader, Philip naturally would have access to their bank accounts. The Templar leadership under Grand Master Jacques Demolay refused Philip's rather unfair offer.

By 1307, the Templars were not the same organization that had charged the ranks of the Muslim cavalry with suicidal fervor a hundred years earlier. The Templars had long since withdrawn from the battlefields of the Middle East and had established, what was as Dr. Karen Ralls describes, "the world's first multinational corporation."

Thanks to the privileges granted to them by the Vatican, the Templars had accumulated more power and influence in all aspects of life in the Medieval World than any other institution but the Church itself. They began building churches and castles. They bought farms and vineyards. They were into manufacturing, importing and exporting trade goods from countries in Europe and the Middle East. They maintained a fleet of ships that were used to transport pilgrims and combatants to the Middle East and back, along with a variety of trade goods. The Templar organization had its own leadership, which was independent of the ruler of the country, county or city in which they presided. Each country had its own Templar Master and overseeing them all was the Templar Grand Master, who was elected for life. It was he who controlled the military movements in the East and oversaw the Templar holdings in the West.

Author Sean Martin describes the extent of the Templar holdings throughout Europe, "Every town had a Templar presence. Everyone knew who they were. A lot of people did business with them because they were working on Templar farms or Templar vineyards or keeping their life savings in a Templar account so they were really a part of the fabric of life for that period."

But the Templar Order had seemed to outlive its usefulness. According to Tim Wallace-Murphy, "After the loss of the Holy Land, they were literally at a loss themselves, because everything was geared up to maintain an army in the field and protect the Holy Land, and the Holy Land was gone. Jacques De Molay went around to the crowned heads of Europe in an attempt to create a wave of enthusiasm for a new crusade, and found there were no takers."

It was in this political, religious and economic climate that Philip decided to make his move against the Templars with his childhood friend, Pope Clement V supporting his claims. Templar leaders of France were summoned to Paris to meet with Philip IV believing they were there to discuss a possible merger with other military orders. Jacques Demolay, apparently not wanting there to be any doubt as to the power and the influence of the Templars, "…came and brought a large number of knights and a large treasure train," according to Dr. Tim Wallace-Murphy. The next morning, on October 13, 1307, in Paris and in Templar commanderies all around France, Templar leaders were rounded up and charged with high crimes. They were renounced throughout Europe. They were subjected to ruthless tortures and imprisonment until they confessed to charges of heresy, devil worship, witchcraft and the seeming favorite of the French Royal Court, the charge of sodomy. Subsequently, many of the Templar leaders were tortured and then burned at the stake.

The end of the Templars: the beginning of the mysteries

And so, upon their exit from the world scene, the Templars left us pretty much in the same fashion as they had begun; with still more mysteries and myths and very little in the way of verifiable answers. Of course, the first mystery surrounding their demise has to do with all that gold and treasure they supposedly found and the wealth they accrued in all of their banking and commercial enterprises. Where did it go? The second mystery has to do with the fact that the entire order just seems to have disappeared from the pages of history. Where did they go? Finally, the last mystery revolves around whether or not there was any evidence to support the allegations of the crimes for which they were charged. What were they up to in those secret meetings? With apologies to the hundreds of people who have come up with as many fantastic theories regarding the Templar's seeming disappearance, along with the disappearance of their fantastic wealth and their mysterious secret knowledge, as unexciting as it may be, let us stick to the known facts that were taken from people actually writing during the time period, or from "legitimate" scholars and finally, from the Freemasons themselves.

Mystery 1: Where is the Templar Treasure?

First and foremost, Philip wanted two things: the Templar's wealth and the forgiveness of his debts to the Order. He achieved the latter, but when it came to the former, the wealth of the Templars seemed as elusive as the facts surrounding them. Alan Butler, co-author of *The Warriors and the Bankers*, explains it this way, "The most interesting thing about what happened when Philip's men broke into all the Templar offices throughout France was how little they found there, not just in terms of personnel but in terms of goods. They found virtually no money. The records of the Order seem to have disappeared. An incredibly small percentage of the Knights Templar, both knights and everybody else within the organization was captured in 1307, probably not even a tenth." Dr. Tim Wallace-Murphy further adds, "King Philip didn't benefit as much as he thought he might have done. Obviously his considerable debt to the Knights of the Temple was wiped out. It certainly didn't solve his financial problem." So, where did all that money go?

Like many other mysteries surrounding the Templars, the lack of any credible evidence forces us to look once again for the simplest explanations that are at least supported by reasonable circumstantial evidence. When looking for an answer to the question of the final disposition of their wealth, we must first assume that there were people to carry it with them in their flight from France. In that regard, there are a few theories that seem to have more basis in reality than UFO's, Oak Island or an old chapel on Wall Street.

How many Templars were there on that fateful day in October in 1307, and how many escaped the wrath of King Philip? Dr. Karen Ralls tells us, "There were up to 15,000 Templar houses at one time at their peak." And, during the roundup of Templars in France, author George Smart suggests, "In France only 620 of 3,000 were captured." In fact, it was only in France and England where the brunt of Philip and his new ally, Edward I of England, were pressing any Templars they could seize into jail and put their confiscated wealth into their coffers. However, the Templars were spread throughout Europe. Clearly, thousands of members of the Order were never tried and never imprisoned. Did they just throw away their Templar memorabilia and blend back in to normal medieval society? Maybe some did. Maybe some did not.

If the reader will recall, early in their history, the king of Argonne donated a large tract of land in the modern country of Spain to the Templars. After they were denounced, the Templars living in the modern country of Portugal simply changed their name to the **Knights of the Cross** and went on with business as usual. Other Templars joined the **Knights of Malta** and engaged in campaigns against the encroaching Turks. Some speculate that the Knights of Malta later emerged as the **Skull and Bones Society** of Yale University. So, does this

explain the seeming disappearance of the Templar Order, their treasure and their secret knowledge?

The Templars in Switzerland

In his book, *The Warriors and the Bankers,* author Alan Butler suggests that based upon events of the time period, Switzerland may have been the final resting place of not only the Templars but possibly a portion of their wealth as well. Butler cites the fact that the trade routes through eastern France went directly through the Alps that border and geographically divide France, Italy and Austria. According to Butler, "The Templars knew this region extremely well. They'd been using it for well over a hundred years, but it was almost impassable, with many hiding places and little isolated communities where normal armies would not be able to operate. Nowhere would have been better for hiding what remained of the Templar treasure than in that region." Butler also cites the attempt by Austrian Emperor Leopold I to secure the routes through what is now Switzerland in order to have a direct route to Italy. "Leopold sent 5,000 knights on the operation and they were soundly beaten by farmers with no military experience." Butler recounts that legends and folktales from the time period recall, "armed white knights" that came to help the people of the villages.,

Butler also cites the fact that almost overnight, the Swiss became known as legendary fighters. One example to support the notoriety of the Swiss soldiers of medieval Europe is the fact that even today, mercenary soldiers recruited from the ranks of the Swiss Army guard the Vatican. Furthermore, Butler notes the fact that almost immediately after the fall of the Templars; the Swiss suddenly took up banking. As he points out, "One of the things that really set Switzerland apart right from its conception is how secret it is. The banking systems that were set up in Switzerland are not like those in other parts of the Western World. They are as pathologically secretive now as they were, which makes them exactly the same as the Templars." One last clue that may support Butler's theory is the very flag of Switzerland. It is a white cross on a red field, exactly the opposite of the Red Cross the Templars emblazoned on the chests of their white tunics.

So, have we found the final resting place of the Templars in the Swiss Alps, where they continued their practices of banking and providing mercenaries to foreign governments? We can only say that the evidence, circumstantial as it is, does provide a nearby geographic location, a suspicious rise of militarism among a class of former farmers who seemingly turned overnight into the highly secretive bankers of Europe that we know today. So, have we solved the age-old mystery regarding the wealth of the Templars? Possibly, yet there is another contemporary account from the time period that lends credence to the possibility that the Templars and their wealth did not all end up in the land of great chocolate and reliable watches.

The Templars in Scotland?

According to Sean Martin, a contemporary account of the time period tells us that on October 12, 1307, there were eighteen Templar ships at anchor off the coast of La Rochelle, France. On October 13, the day of the Templar arrests, they were gone. Where did they go? What was their cargo? This account, if factual, is probably the catalyst for most of the theories, outlandish or not, as to the fate of the Templars and their treasure. The most likely destination for the ships and their cargo, if in fact the account is correct, was the land of bagpipes, kilts, William Wallace and Robert the Bruce. The very political and economic circumstances that led to the arrest of the Templar leadership in France, also assured that those very same Templars who were seeking refuge from the rack and the medieval version of a "hot night" on the town would be not only safe, but also welcome in Scotland.

As we have seen, the relationship between the Templar Order and the Scots went back almost two hundred years to Hugh the Pagan's first recruiting efforts in Europe. According to historian Margaret Odrowaz-Sypniewska, "In 1128, Hugh de Payens met with King David I of Scotland, soon after the Council of Troyes. King David granted Hugues and his knights the lands of Ballantradoch, by the Firth of Forth. William the Lion promoted and encouraged the knights and they received lands around the Lothians and Aberdeen. They had deeds to property in Ayr and western Scotland."

So, the Templars obviously had no shortage of places in Scotland where they could seek refuge until things cooled down. But, would the Scottish King respect their land titles, or would he enforce the denouncement and toss them into prison as his hated counterpart, Edward I was doing in England? As luck would have it, King Robert the Bruce, his counts and, in fact all of Scotland at the time were in the status of "excommunicate" from the Catholic Church by decree of the Pope. It seemed that a year earlier, Robert the Bruce had killed a man in the Church. Not, a man belonging to the Church, he killed a man inside the walls of a church, which went against some decree or other that said killing must be done outside of the Church, even in Scotland.

Incensed by this seeming disrespect for Church property, not to mention the cost of cleaning up the mess, Pope Clement used the power of excommunication to bring King Robert back into line. Excommunication was not what it once had been or at least it wasn't in Scotland because King Robert's counts and dukes continued to maintain their loyalty to their king. Therefore, Pope Clement excommunicated them in the hopes that the God-fearing Catholics of Scotland would rise up and depose their disrespectful king, their leaders and bring Scotland back into the Catholic fold. Well, of course, Scotland being Scotland, nothing of the sort happened. Enraged, Clement excommunicated the whole lot of them.

And so it was, that at the time of the Templar trials, imprisonments and executions, there was one entire country that had little loyalty to the Church, and a long history of ties to the Order of the Poor Knights of the Temple. The relationship between the Templars and Scottish Crown seems to blend the two entities into three legends that have to do with a castle, a battle, and a church constructed a hundred years after the last Templars went to the grave. These legends also give us more circumstantial evidence as to what may have happened, if not to the treasure, to the knowledge the Templars possessed.

The Secrets of Rosslyn

Rosslyn Castle was built in the 1100's on land owned by the Sinclair (St. Clair) clan who, we have seen, had connections from the very beginning with the Templars, along with an unsubstantiated claim that Hugh the Pagan married Catherine Sinclair. The castle was used as a repository for medieval knowledge, or, as Dr. Karen Ralls describes it, "It was called a scriptorium in ancient times, which was a place where books were copied by monks. Rosslyn was the center of learning and in that sense it would be like a very important college or library today." So, the castle at Rosslyn had a dual purpose as an archive, or library. What kinds of records it may have contained was kept secret thanks to the historic events that were about to unfold in Scotland, where, in 1314, Robert the Bruce declared war on England.

According to legend, and historians like Dr. Tim Wallace-Murphy, the Templars were a deciding factor in the **Battle of Bannockburn** in 1314. As Dr. Wallace-Murphy describes it, "There is a long standing legend, which I think is a reflection of fact. That at the Battle of Bannockburn, the charge that saved the day for Robert the Bruce was the charge of the Knights Templar. And if one does not believe that, then one has some explaining to do, because the English Army outnumbered the Scots by about 3 to 1." As a result of their victory, the Scots were able to gain independence, at least long enough so that those who sought the Templars and their knowledge (or treasure) were long since in their graves, and the secrets of the Templars and whatever lay inside Rosslyn Castle were able to remain so.

Over two hundred years after the last Templar had gone to his grave, in the year 1546, Mary of Gees the Queen Regent of Scotland and mother of Mary, Queen of Scots, wrote a mysterious letter to William Sinclair of Rosslyn. In the letter she referred to a great secret within Rosslyn. Whatever this "secret" is, it has been used as a plot device by authors, historians and conspiracy theorists to support the idea that Rosslyn contains religious relics and Templar treasure from the holy land. Most of the speculation centers not on Rosslyn Castle, but on an adjoining structure commissioned in 1446 known as Rosslyn Chapel, the last stop in our search for the Templar Treasure.

In plain sight-where are those elusive Templar secrets?

Like the myths that surrounded the Templars then, such as their supposed possession of the Holy Grail, ancient relics, secret knowledge and so on and so on, their descendants, the Freemasons, in their movies like Steven Spielberg's and George Lucas' Indiana Jones as well as the (deceased) Freemason, Walt Disney's National Treasure movies, continue to bend impressionable minds in the modern day with the argument that, if nobody found the treasure of the Templars, which no one ever claimed existed with any credible evidence, then it must be hidden somewhere in some secret location. That would be as logical as saying that unicorns exist because no one has ever seen one. Does the same argument hold true for the secret knowledge they claimed to have possessed? What secrets are hidden in Rosslyn Castle or Rosslyn Chapel? The best answer lies in the words of author George Smart, who said, in response to an unsuccessful effort to attempt to tunnel underneath the chapel in 1991.

"Tunneling into Rosslyn chapel is a lose-lose situation for the chapel. If nothing is found, then it will destroy the tourism industry that surrounds the Rosslyn myth. If something is found, the increase in tourists will destroy the chapel itself."

In other words, it is better to let the simple-minded believe in the myths rather than the facts. This is certainly a solution that has worked for authors like Dan Brown, writer of the *Da Vinci Code*. But could there be something hidden, like the Swiss flag, in plain sight? What about all those mysterious images in Rosslyn chapel? What about the only written inscription in the chapel that says, "Wine, is strong, women are stronger, kings are stronger yet, but truth is the strongest of them all." What truth could the builders of the chapel have been referring to? Since the inscription is in Latin, is there a possibility that by truth, the workers who left that inscription may have meant, "knowledge" or "facts?" Because the builders are long since dead, we can never really know what they meant, but what we can know is how knowledge and facts were to kick European society out of the medieval age, and it would be the descendants of the Templars, the Society of Freemasons, who were wearing the boot.

Who is this Baphomet?

Before we don our hose and powder our wigs, we cannot leave this discussion without addressing the issues of whether or not there was any basis in fact for the charges against the Templars. Did they possess some kind of occult knowledge or were they were somehow anti-Christ (against Christ). In order to address the issue objectively, it is important to define knowledge in its historical context, which, at the time, was fairly easy to do. If it was in the Bible, it was knowledge. If it was not in the Bible, it was not knowledge and anyone who professed to possess knowledge that did not come from the Bible, often ran the risk of being accused of witchcraft.

In our highly technological society, this sequestration of knowledge may seem a rather bizarre notion. However, if the reader will recall from the earlier reading, until about a hundred and fifty years ago, intellectual thought for ninety-five percent of the population of the planet revolved around having enough food to eat, staying warm and staying alive, none of which was an easy thing to do. Under those circumstances, the lessons of the Bible were sufficiently intellectual. Obey God, obey the Ten Commandments, have mercy on the poor and remember that Jesus died for all of our sins. If a person were to do that, then God promised to keep his promise of giving eternal life to the obedient. It was a pretty simple deal all around. Nobody was asking any difficult questions because there was no time. Life was full of death, disease, hunger, brutality and other reminders that tenure in this world was precarious. It was just better to spend your time worrying about what was going to happen to you after you died, because, in the days before taxes, it was the only thing of which people could be sure.

Were the Templars then guilty of possessing knowledge that was not in the Bible and therefore, by definition, witchcraft? They absolutely were guilty as charged. There is nothing in the Bible that describes how to cut a stone, how to find the area of a triangle or how to determine what kind of ore to use to make steel. There is nothing in the Bible that tells how much water a man in armor and a horse will need to perform combat operations in the scorching deserts of the Middle East. There is nothing in the Bible to describe how to treat a broken bone or a stab wound. There is nothing in the Bible that explains why the earth is cooler during one part of the year than another. All of this knowledge had to be obtained from either studying works other than the Bible, or by observation and experimentation. Once out of Europe and the iron grasp of the Catholic Church, it was not difficult for the intellectually curious to see how wrong things had gone in the world of Christianity.

An aspect of Freemasonry as it is practiced today is the idea of religious tolerance. Similarly, the Templars were known for having respect for their Muslim enemies, which was probably the reason, along with their Arabic speaking skills, that they were often used as diplomats. Freemasons today are members of not only the Christian faith, but include Jews, Hindus, Buddhists and Muslims as well. The Christian invaders who entered the Levant quickly learned the adage that "the enemy of my enemy is my friend."

Based upon these utilitarian principles and throwing out the old, 'kill them all, let God sort them out,' mentality, we must ask the question; did the tolerance of non-believers allow the very same non-believers that the Templars had vowed to destroy, the opportunity to instruct the Christian Templars in the art of stonemasonry, medicine, geometry, algebra, engineering, metallurgy, accounting and finance? It is fairly obvious they didn't get this knowledge from Europe. Was this religious tolerance the source of at least one of the accusations against the Templars for heresy? Furthermore, was it possible that the Templars, like many intellectual thinkers that came after them, held the Catholic Church responsible for the ignorance and superstition that pervaded Christian Europe for the next six hundred years? Could it also be possible that the Templars did not hate Jesus, they simply saw Jesus as the hammer the Church used to smash intellectual thought in Europe? Was it necessary then, in order to destroy the world of ignorance, to destroy Jesus as well? Or, were the Templars simply guilty of being worshippers of Satan as they were charged? Of course, because both the Freemasons and the Templars are "societies with secrets," we cannot know, but as we shall see, it is an argument that begins to make more sense over time.

What do secrets and religious tolerance have to with the disappearance of the Templars? Conspiracies aside, it is only common sense that, in order for the society of Templars to continue to exist in whatever form they may have following the events of 1307, they had to be able to keep their organization secret, especially from the church and their Inquisition. As foreboding as it may sound, the oath taken by the members of the Masonic Order to keep the secrets of the Order upon the threat of a rather unpleasant death, does not sound so foreboding and mysterious if one considers the punishments inflicted upon the Templars or anyone thought to be associated with their banned society.

Fortunately for the Templars and the Freemasons, their whole existence had and has been based upon secret codes, symbols and handshakes that would easily escape thieves, the uninitiated and later, the wandering gaze of the spies of the Church. Add to that, the protection of local lords who needed the Freemason's skills to build fortresses in which to hide and the protection of the Church as it embarked on a building spree during the period from 1300 to 1700 and you have all the trappings of the one organization that might be able to outlast the Inquisition and quite possibly, the Church itself. In the world of Medieval Europe such an organization might have continued on to the present as it was; an organization familiar only to its members. But events in Europe were to change the political and intellectual environment to one more conducive to alternate ideas of thinking. But before we can put on our tri-cornered hats and begin to shout, "Liberty, Equality, Fraternity," we must complete our inquiry into whether or not the Templars were, in fact, guilty of a more serious form of heresy, that of blasphemy and worship of the occult.

Goat's head soup

According to contemporary records, of the 138 Templars questioned in Paris:

> 105 admit they denied Christ during their secret Templar initiations.

> 103 confessed that an obscene kiss was part of the ceremony.

> 123 say the spat on the cross.

Admittedly, "questioning" during the times of the inquisition involved much more than the "good cop, bad cop" routine we may be familiar with today. It involved excruciatingly painful tortures designed to jog one's memory, as well as bone structure. According to the interrogation routines of the day, the painful treatment was applied until the questioned was willing to admit, or confess to the charges, at which time the inquisitor would determine if repentance was appropriate or, in the worst cases, a bonfire was the best solution for the accused. Suffice it to say, that no relevant information would have been gained from the tortures and their subsequent confessions. However, there was one charge that tells us more about the Templars than their actual confessions. Unlike others accused of the time period of the normal charges of spitting on the cross, denying Jesus, homosexuality and the Catholic Church's favorite; sodomy, one charge was unique to the Templars only. It was the charge of worshipping a head. Author Sean Martin tells us that the head-worshipping charge "was something that was unique to the Templars, which suggests there was something there."

In fact, according to historical accounts, the last word of Jacques Demolay, as he was being roasted alive, was the word, "Baphomet." And who is this Baphomet? For one, he, or it does not seem to appear in historical documents until the time of the Crusades, The name Baphomet first appears around 1195 in the Occitan poem, "*Senhors, per los nostres peccatz*" by the troubadour Gavaudan. Around 1250, in a poem bewailing the defeat of the Seventh Crusade, Austorc d'Aorlhac refers to "Bafomet." De Bafometic is also the title of one of the four surviving chapters of an Occitan translation of Ramon Llull's earliest known work, the *Libre de la doctrinal pueril*. After Baphomet's brief, periodic entrances into the world of medieval literature, this mysterious Baphoment seems to disappear until the middle of the 1850's.

In our own time, Philip Gardner, author of *Gnosis*, describes a modern initiation ceremony that he allegedly underwent to become a member of a particular Freemason lodge. He describes the ceremony this way:

"In the room was a very large curtain. Through the curtain was a big head, a goat's head, all dripping, it was quite disgusting, and they called it the head of Baphomet, the head that the Knights Templar were supposed to have worshipped. During the initiation, the Grand Master would say to you, go and kiss the backside of Baphomet, which means, I've got to go through the curtain, do as I'm told... go through this curtain, kiss the backside of this disgusting looking goat, so I did. When you get through there it's actually a naked woman, or her buttocks, so the backside of Baphomet is a reward if you do as you're told."

Dripping goat's head? Kissing naked women's buttocks? What exactly is this Baphomet all about besides being a detriment to certain farm animals and a possible hygiene hazard? The English mystic, master of the occult and legendary Satan worshipper, Alistair Crowley wrote of this same Baphomet at the beginning of the 1900's:

The Devil does not exist. It is a false name invented by the Black Brothers to imply a unity in their ignorant muddle of dispersions. A devil who had unity would be a God…'The Devil' is, historically, the god of any people that one personally dislikes…This serpent, Satan, is not the enemy of Man, but He who made Gods of our race, knowing Good and Evil; He bade 'Know Thyself!' and taught initiation. He is the Devil of the Book of Thoth, and His emblem is Baphomet, the Androgyne who is the Hieroglyph of arcane perfection. He is therefore Life, and Love. But moreover his letter is ayin, the EYE, so that he is Light; and his Zodiacal image is Capricorn, that leaping goat whose attribute is Liberty."

Holy Toledo! Suddenly our seemingly innocent inquiry has descended into the very depths of Hades itself, all thanks to the reported last word of the Templar Grand Master Jacques Demolay! Was this the hidden knowledge that the Templars found and later passed on through their descendants, the Freemasons? We cannot know for sure, because the Freemasons are a self-proclaimed, "society with secrets." What we can say is that regardless of our own beliefs, what is important is that there are people who believe in these ideas, and they do have interesting similarities and correspond quite coincidentally with the Freemason mythology and litany. However, before we begin to dissect and analyze this information like a frog in a high school Biology lab, let's get the entire creature, or goat, or sea monster (leviathan) as it were, on the dissection table.

CHAPTER 16

THE DEVIL'S IN THE DETAILS

(A PHILOSOPHICAL INTERLUDE)

Baphomet: the goat man and the star

In an interview, Satan worshipping high priest Peter H. Gilmore described the meaning of the Baphomet symbol:

"The goat face represents carnality. In ancient Egypt goats were considered representations as god symbols of lust, and we think lust is an important factor of biology that keeps humanity going so we value that. The five-pointed star really comes from the Pythagoreans. That is the one figure in which every element is within the golden mean of each other (more about the 'golden mean' later). It's this wonderful mathematical symbol of perfection, organic perfection specifically. Since we are organic life and enjoy the idea of perfecting ourselves that star is right for us and it perfectly fits the goat head inside. Now around it are two circles, one at the tip of the points of the star and one outside. In that are Hebrew characters starting at the bottom and going counter-clockwise spelling Leviathan. In Hebrew mythology Leviathan was the great dragon of the abyss, this powerful earthly figure that even Yahweh was afraid of. So, all these things taken together create a symbol that Anton Le Vey identified with Satanism, specifically. When he started the Church of Satan, usually upside down crosses were considered Satanic, and he saw that these different elements and felt that this was a positive symbol you could tie to the Satanism he was creating."

Who would have ever associated a dragon of the abyss, lusting goats, Greek geometry clubs (Pythagoreans) and Hebrew characters with the devil? Apparently, somebody did, because before our Baphomet character became a goat, he was a sea serpent of some sort. If the reader will recall, the Merovingian kings, who some perpetuators of Templar myths claim to have the blood of Christ in their genetic make-up, claimed to be descendants of sea serpents as well. In the Old Testament Book of Psalms we read that this same Leviathan was actually killed by Yahweh, the Hebrew God and served to His followers with pita bread and hummus.

"For God is my King of old, working salvation in the midst of the earth. Thou did divide the sea by thy strength: thou breakest the heads of the dragon in the waters. Thou breakest the head of leviathan in pieces and gavest him to be meat to the people inhabiting the wilderness." (Psalms 74:12-14)

Furthermore, in the Book of Isaiah, we see that Leviathan the serpent has a rather ill fated future in store for him.

"In that day, the Lord with his great and strong sword shall punish leviathan the piercing serpent, even leviathan that crooked serpent; and he shall slay the dragon that is in the sea." (Isaiah 27:1)

In the Old Testament accounts, we see two forms of Leviathan the serpent. In one, he is the "guest of honor" at the Lord's banquet for his people and in the other, he is still out there, somewhere, waiting for the Lord to slay both him and the dragon. With all that "heat" on him, it is no wonder Leviathan changed into a goat. Of course, in a world of supersonic airplanes, cell phones, space shuttles and GPS, all of this talk of androgynous goats, sea serpents and geometrical figures may seem just a little bit silly. However, if the reader will bear with me for just a few more paragraphs, I will attempt to explain a belief system that will present a little more understandable argument, whether actual or philosophical, that has been taking place for the entire history of mankind, no matter which history you might believe in. To begin, we must go back to the beginning, literally, as we consult the Book of Moses once again.

And I, the Lord God, spake unto Moses, saying: That Satan, whom thou hast commanded in the name of my Only Begotten, is the same which was from the beginning, and he came before me saying-Behold, here am I, send me, I will be thy son, and I will redeem all mankind, that not one soul shall be lost, and surely, I will do it, wherefore give me thine honor. But behold, my Beloved Son, which was my Beloved and Chosen from the beginning, said unto me-Father, Thy will be done, and the glory be thine forever. Wherefore because that Satan rebelled against me, and sought to destroy the agency of man, which I, the Lord God, had given him, also that I should give unto him mine own power; by the power of mine only Begotten, I caused that he should be cast down; **and he became Satan, yea, even the devil, the father of all lies, to deceive and to blind men, and to lead them captive at his will, even as many as would not hearken unto my voice.** *And now the serpent was more subtle than any beast of the field which I, the Lord God had made. And Satan put it into the heart of the serpent, (for he had drawn many away after him) and he also sought to beguile Eve, for he knew not the mind of God, for he sought to destroy the world."* (Moses 4:1-6)

Let us tie this hodge-podge of Satan, Capricorn, Venus the all-seeing eye, goats and sea serpents together for the modern, somewhat enlightened individual according to the three Western religious traditions of Islam, Judaism and Christianity. First, God created the world. Why He created it, is up to you to decide, but, after He created it Eve and then Adam became aware of the Tree of Good and Evil or Knowledge. The barrier separating heaven (or the other dimension) was opened and it was possible for more spirits to cross over and obtain physical bodies. However, before Adam and Eve were created and before any apple pilfering actually occurred, God asked his leaders for some kind of plan to allow his spirit children to cross into a dimension of physical matter and carry on the process of bringing more spirits into this dimension. God wanted his spirit children to enter this dimension.

God did not want his spirit children to be slaves, which was what Satan proposed. God wanted to see how we would behave in a world where we had no memory of the place from which we had come. He thought that being his children, some would come and try to make a heaven on the earth, while others may not. Either way, God and Jesus wanted it to be up to the individual to decide. Well, of course, Satan got mad and left the council. He took his followers with him and he became the negative force which must accompany the positive force in order for it to be a complete system. In physics, Satan is a negative charge and Jesus is a positive one. It's not exactly rocket science. Satan, Lucifer, Venus, Capricorn, Molech, Astarte, the all-seeing eye or the prancing Baphomet is present in all cultures and is obviously represented in the symbolism of Freemasonry. If a person chooses to serve the negative forces of the universe and furthermore, to perpetuate them through lying, stealing, cheating, killing and trying to control the lives of others, then the reward or result for those actions cannot, according to the laws of the universe, be positive.

Knowledge vs. Religion and the Philosophy of Good and Evil

For the benefit of the reader who does not understand or believe in the concepts of the Christian religion, I would like to make one small philosophical point before we continue onward in our inquiry. For thousands of years, people have been and continue to be misled by confusing religion, at least in the Christian tradition, with knowledge. The knowledge that the Old Testament as well as Jesus Christ imparted was a moral philosophy along with certain practices and procedures that pertained to the world from which we came and where we will someday return. Some religions however, used the moral teachings, practices and procedures of the scriptures as a tool to gain power and wealth for themselves. They even changed scriptures to justify their actions. For example, if you compare the words of Jesus from the Book of Matthew to the words that Jesus taught the Nephites, you come across a very obvious discrepancy in both the spirit and meaning of Jesus' message.

"But I say unto you, That whosoever is angry with his brother, without a cause shall be in danger of the judgment..." (Matthew 5:22)

"But I say unto you, that whosoever is angry with his brother shall be in danger of the judgment..."

(3 Nephi 12:22)

By inserting the phrase, "without a cause," it suddenly becomes acceptable to be angry with someone (all men are brothers in the eyes of God) as long as there is a cause for the anger. Are we ever angry with someone without a cause? Is the statement in Matthew really consistent with the teachings of Jesus? How many times have wars and crimes against humanity been justified by people using religion as their motive for their dark acts? How many wars have been fought because they were a "just cause?" As a somewhat cruel joke, the United States even called the invasion of Panama in 1989 under Skull and Bones man, President George W. Bush to remove their puppet cocaine dealer and dictator, Manuel Noriega, "Operation Just Cause."

The vision of Lehi in the Wilderness

If the reader will recall, in the earlier chapter entitled *History According to the Book of Mormon,* Lehi, the patriarch of the family that would ultimately come to be known as the Nephites and the Lamanites had a vision in which he followed Jesus Christ to the Tree of Life where he partook of the fruit. Please note that Adam did not partake of the fruit of the Tree of Life, or the gospel of Jesus Christ until after he and Eve had partaken of the Tree of Knowledge of Good and Evil. It was not possible to repent, which is the fruit of the Tree of Life, and the gospel of Jesus Christ, until Adam and Eve had actually sinned. That was the plan that God and Jesus had dreamed up between themselves. Satan or no, they knew men would commit sin. Jesus would give up his life, which would allow those who followed Him to sin and to repent. Those who sinned, acknowledged their mistakes, made amends and stopped whatever malfeasance they were involved in, went through the process of repentance. They could follow Jesus by obeying His teachings, helping others and living the simple life that He lived. If they followed Jesus, they could then literally follow Jesus back into the dimension that was reserved for those who chose positive lives here on the earth.

According to Satanists like Alistair Crowley, Peter Gilmore as well as Morals and Dogma author and Freemason Grand Master, Albert Pike, Satan, Baphomet, the all-seeing eye, Venus, Lucifer, Leviathan, Astarte, and whatever else the dark one calls himself (he must have a hard time ordering out for pizza) should be appreciated and acknowledged for showing mankind the knowledge of good and evil. It is a plausible argument that they make, except for one thing. In true Luciferian fashion, their argument is fraught with deception. While they are applauding Satan for tempting Eve, they seem to forget the whole part about the possibility made available to us to repent and be forgiven, thanks to the plan and the sacrifice of Jesus Christ, which He made on our behalf. It is that kind of deception which is based on a half-truth about Satan while he lies and spreads lies about Jesus and those that sincerely follow Him that make Satan such a slippery and ultimately unsavory character.

In Nephi's account, the only way to reach the Tree of Life in Lehi's vision is to hold fast to the iron rod. What that literally means is that in this life you can choose to hold fast to the iron rod, which are the teachings of Jesus, or you can take any number of paths, to include going in search of the Tree of Knowledge.

But if you search for and partake of the Tree of Knowledge, especially knowledge that is approved by those whose loyalties are highly suspect, there is a high risk that you will put yourself in peril. But it does not have to be this way. Knowledge is great. Knowledge is what brings us closer to our God and allows us the opportunity to improve ourselves, our world, and, the conditions in which we live. It is only when those who wish to control our thoughts by controlling the truth can use that knowledge to lead us into the "mists of darkness" of Lehi's vision that it becomes the Knowledge of Good and Evil. Usually, it's just evil.

Why is it that we must make a choice between the Tree of Knowledge and the Tree of Life? After all, the simple gospel of Jesus Christ tells us (roughly),

1) Believe in me, know who I am, know what I taught. Try to do what I did. Hopefully the Cross thing won't be necessary but sometimes it, or other "bitter cups" are just in your cards.

2) Get baptized and get the Holy Spirit to guide you through life.

3) Repent of the mistakes you make. You will make mistakes. You are engineered to make mistakes. Mistakes are no big deal. Know you made them stop making them and say you are sorry.

Basically, that's it. There is nothing complicated about that. There is no secret lengthy dogma, no symbols, no mysteries, no secret handshakes and no hidden knowledge. Anyone can partake of the gospel of Jesus Christ. Old, young, rich, poor, black, white, green, gray, smart, stupid, funny serious, handsome, homely, large, small, handicapped-it doesn't matter because in the gospel of Jesus Christ, one size fits all. Sadly, many who partake or wish to partake of the fruit of the Tree of Life are laughed at and humiliated, just as in Lehi's vision, by the people across the hypothetical river in the large and spacious building.

Those who wish to partake of the Tree of Knowledge, are in turn, scorned by those who claim to have access to the Tree of Life. So, to get away from being looked down upon all the time by people who claim to know everything because they read the Bible (etc.), they rent a two-bedroom condo in the large and spacious building of Lehi's vision. In other words, because of the actions and words of the "Tree of Lifers," many who could partake of the fruit of the Tree of Life choose to forego spiritual awareness for knowledge and the approval of those in the high-rent building.

If we are ever going to leave the zoo and take up residence with the greater intelligences that populate our universe, it will be necessary for the religious crowd or the "Tree of Lifers" to show the people in that large building (those darn secularists) the way to the path that leads to the iron rod, and the Tree of the precious fruit, without judging and ridiculing them in the process. Likewise, it is necessary for those in the field of science and academics to come down out of their ivory towers and embrace and acknowledge the sound moral concepts and philosophies of the teachings of Jesus Christ as well as the other great teachers who have come to us from time to time over the course of history. The modern world is proof that both schools of thought can no longer exist separately from one another. Religion is not science and science is not and never will be a sound moral philosophy.

The Human Dilemma Freedom: vs. Slavery

The same conflict exists today, whether real or philosophical as it always has; the choice between our two gods. One God is, of course the God of the Jews, the Muslims, and the Christians and the other is the god of the opposite, who, as we will see, managed to get the wonderful world of science and learning into his camp, thanks to the ignorance and corruption of organized religion. Now that science has become the religion of many, with the opposite lurking in the background waiting to use our knowledge against us, we are confronted with the same dilemmas that confronted us before the advent of time and during the entire period that we, as mankind have counted ourselves "civilized." I speak of the choice between freedom and slavery.

Philosophically speaking, Jesus represented forgiveness, sacrifice, tolerance, and helping others. In fact, to prove his point, Jesus goaded the established order of the Old World with his great ideas until they killed him for it. In a hypothetical world where we all are free to use our time as we wish, if we all chose to live our lives to help our brothers and sisters, to care for the sick, to love and cherish the beautiful earth that God gave us, and to use our talents to make the world a better place for all who inhabit it, we wouldn't need to pay people to do it for us. If we used our knowledge of science and mathematics to find ways to cure diseases and make free energy that would be available to everyone, we would live in a world that would not need, police, government, armies, navies, spies, weapons and secret societies.

But we don't live in that world. We live in the world of the adversary, or, the world whose plan was suggested by Satan himself at the beginning. Because of that, we are told we must live our lives in fear. We live with the fear of the government, fear of terrorists, fear of disease, fear of nuclear war, fear of economic instability, fear of criminals and fear that our underarm deodorant or mouthwash will stop working halfway through the work day. We will soon arrive at the day when the corporation/government will propose to solve all of the world's problems by planting a chip in our bodies so that they can make us obey because they have the ability to watch us with their Freemason style all-seeing eyes.

Accepting the Hard Truth

The problem with mankind has always been our own inability to face up to the fact that most of the things we do, or wish we could do, are based upon our own selfish interests. We are, to some degree and whether you like it or not (The Bible says God created Man out of the dust, it doesn't say how) products of an evolutionary process that allowed us to survive in the wild as a species by being lustful, selfish, greedy and dishonest, just like that old Billy goat, Baphomet. Those attributes helped us to survive in our primeval state as hunters and gatherers.

However, we also possess another nature, one that is not of the natural world. Our other nature allows us to reason and to put others before ourselves. It compels us to help the weak and the sick. It compels us to sacrifice our lives sometimes for people we never met. It allows us to think about the future, the past and our reason for being. It was this nature that, for some reason, compelled us to leave hunting and gathering because we found safety in larger and larger herds.

Using our higher natures we were able to build cities, and once we did, we no longer needed to be selfish, greedy and lustful to survive. The whole community would only survive if we put our natural instincts aside and were governed by our higher thoughts. Our immediate reward was peace within the community. If the community survived, we survived. The question was, in the first communities and now, whether or not we would choose to remain free in our communities by following our higher natures and doing what is good for everyone, or whether we would choose slavery by doing only things that benefit ourselves and therefore make it necessary for a strong government to impose its idea of good, upon us. As our history shows, it is our own nature that leads every time to slavery and despotism. Does it always have to be this way?

Illogical logic-Jesus never gave a history lesson

One of the great deceptions of the ages is the foolish belief that religion is science. According to that argument, if the science of religion is not correct, such as the earth being 7,000 years old, man is the center of the universe, etc. then religion is not correct. If religion is not correct, then science is the only correct belief system. If science is the only belief system, then we are at a dark point in our history because science does not have all the answers. More accurately, with every question that science answers, it only gets more questions that need to be answered. Science, especially in the hands of the adversary as it has been, is never going to lead us anywhere but back to moral, philosophical, spiritual and physical slavery. In the past century, science has brought us murder on an industrial scale, starvation, shortages and fear. If we are going to truly advance as a species, the moral teachings and the basic doctrines of the gospel of Jesus Christ, whether a person accepts them as a "religion" or not, must be included in the base of what we call knowledge for the centuries to come. Otherwise, our descendants will suffer the same fate as the people of this century have suffered through wars, famines, depressions and the erosion of their lives and their liberties. And who is responsible for keeping Jesus and his teachings out of the debate?

Stephen Tsoukalis, author of *Masonic Rites and Wrongs,* sums it up best when he says, "Jesus himself said, '*I am the way, the truth and the life, no one comes to the father except through me.*' What is Freemasonry doing giving these lessons of salvation to those who would reject Jesus Christ? Therein lies the rub with Christianity." We are long since passed the days of Inquisition, so why must the Freemason organization, descendants of the "secret society" that went underground after the denouncement of the Knights of the Temple, feel a need to continue as a "society with secrets?"

It appears that we are ultimately left, after all of our efforts of investigating the facts surrounding the fate of the Templars, with what some may call myths and mysteries, and others would simply call lies and half-truths. Through it all, there is no vast heap of lost treasure, there is no "holy grail," and there is no big mystery waiting to be solved. This vast web of conjecture, confusing evidence and goat's head soup will go a long way to explain the motivation for the modern claim that the Templars possessed knowledge which proved that Jesus Christ was a man, and therefore not the Son of God. All of this makes for interesting literature and hypothetical arguments and is certainly effective in casting doubt on impressionable minds, but, with no proof, just like the Templar's mythical treasure, it adds up to nothing more than a myth that is little different than the existence of leprechauns, the boogey man or the rumor that "The Beaver" was killed in Vietnam.

Chapter 17

From Templars to Freemason

A Society with Secrets

From swords to squares

In modern times, it has become quite clear that the Templars never really disappeared from History. As we have also seen, what became of the Templars is the subject of much speculation but we can say that most of the evidence points to the fact that the Templars simply evolved into something else. That evidence, if the reader will recall, adorns the countryside of Europe. As we discussed at the beginning of the chapter about the Templars, the introduction of stone fortresses and cathedrals throughout Europe began during the period of history known as the Crusades.

During and after the Crusades and the denouncement of the Templars as a Holy Order, castle and cathedral building in Europe began on a frenzied scale. Is it simply enough to say that the Templars went underground and gave up their swords for mortar, trowel and brick? Probably not, but, for the sake of the reader, since there has been so much work done by other experts on this subject, it would be easier to just point out some of the odd coincidences that have been pointed out by not only historians but the Freemasons themselves that support that very conclusion, instead of building some kind of sleep-inducing legal case for the theory.

1) The technology of stonemasonry and the ability to build large structures out of stone, to include arches, turrets, stairs, vaulted ceilings, etc. did not

exist in Europe prior to the Crusades at the level that is evident after the Crusades.

2) The technology the stonemasons of Medieval Europe possessed either evolved suddenly in Europe, or it was imported from another part of the world.

3) The Templars built extravagant stone fortresses during their tenure in the Middle East. Their contemporaries, the Hospitallers, built *Crac de Chevalier* in modern Syria, which is possibly the most, sophisticated stone fortification ever built.

4) The Templars, as we have seen, spoke languages other than their native Italian, French, English or German. The Templars also served as ambassadors to Muslim courts. Therefore, they would have had exposure to building techniques (among other disciplines of knowledge) from Palestine, Mesopotamia and Egypt.

4) The very term "Freemason" describes the legal status of the highest level of stonemason. A "Freemason" was able to travel across borders without the permission of the local ruler, which is similar to the legal status of the Templars prior to their denouncement.

5) The guild of stonemasons had a pantheon of secret handshakes, codes and knowledge, as did the Templars.

The Oath: Plus and Minus

The Chapel at Rosslyn, which the Freemasons themselves claim contains the secrets and learning of the Templars, was finished in 1484. After that, there is no more mention of them, at least publicly until 1718. So what happened? How were they able to keep themselves both organized and undiscovered for that length of time? Clearly they had become a secret society. The very fact that the Freemasons are a society whereby members swear oaths to keep the lodge's secrets under threat of a rather horrific death makes it a very useful and advantageous organization in political and religious environments where free thought, discussion and debate are forbidden by the power elite. Western Civilization, with its free and open societies, liberal ideas and religious tolerance, owe a grand debt to the

Society of Freemasons who took many risks over the years to bring us out of the days of oppression, ignorance and superstition.

In the modern world, the fact that the very ideas that were so secretly guarded in the early Masonic meeting places seem so commonplace may make it hard for the reader to comprehend how dangerous and sometimes reactionary these ideas were considered when they were discussed in places like the Goose and Gridiron Tavern in England or the Green Dragon in Boston. The very fact that those new ideas, which were discussed in quiet whispers, all seem commonplace in our own time is a testament to the successful struggle of the Society of Freemasons. Ideas such as the freedom to say whatever you wanted, the freedom to worship in the manner of your own choosing, the freedom to associate with whom you wanted and assemble where you wanted were not discussed at the time the Freemasons became a "public society" without bringing imminent danger to the speaker and his or her audience.

However, there is also a dark side to the arrangement that Freemasonry shares with its members. A vow of secrecy also serves to protect those who do not have the best interest of mankind and society at heart. Throughout history and in the world today, there are and have been a number of "secret societies" such as the Italian and Sicilian mafia. Though they are not associated officially with Freemasonry, they do swear similar oaths of death for the revelation of secrets. In the case of the mafia, their legacy in ruined and destroyed lives, murder, drug trafficking and other nefarious activities, is all kept hidden by the nature of their oath of silence.

The Italians and Sicilians have received so much publicity in this century that any organization involved in illegal activities and whose members are more afraid of the reprisals of their own colleagues than law enforcement authorities, have been dubbed with the suffix "mafia." As a result, there are dozens of these secret societies such as the "Cuban Mafia," "Jamaican Mafia," "Jewish Mafia," "Chinese Mafia" and so on and so on. Why does the word carry such an air of fear and foreboding? Simply, because the term *mafia* represents a ruthless secret society whose ways and means are always linked to evil.

Like the various mafias, the Freemasons are a powerful, well-known society whose inner workings have remained secret until the present century when "conspiracy theorists," writers and filmmakers have attempted to expose them as Satanists, occultists, and a secret elite who control world events through a common agenda, the control of international finance and sometimes even murder. Like the mafia, they warrant suspicion in the eyes of the general non-Freemason public because of their apparent wealth, influence and their ability to protect their secrets by the threat of death.

Freemasons Good, Freemasons Bad

In this chapter, we are going to examine both sides of this issue of the benefits and the drawbacks of secret societies like the Society of Freemasons, starting with the philosophers of the 1600's and 1700's, who used the cover of the Freemason lodges of Europe and America to discuss and debate ideas that would have landed them in jail if their words had fallen on the wrong ears. These men and their ideas laid the groundwork, and in many cases were responsible for the success of the American Revolution, the U.S. Constitution and its government of checks and balances. We will also discuss and examine specific examples of how a secret society can quickly change from a beneficial organization to one that can easily threaten the very freedoms and rule of law that it professes to protect.

Furthermore, we will examine corresponding secret societies that have existed with the same governing principles and ceremonies throughout the history of the human race. Once again, this information is available in public documents, historic research and Holy Scriptures and in no way reflects the opinions of the author. If the reader is able to identify the similarities in these organizations and wishes to come to some kind of conclusion, whether good or bad, about the Society of Freemasons, once again, the author encourages further study in these subject areas, as the information in this books is, once again, little more that a brief overview.

The Stonemasons-hiding in plain sight

If you will recall from the chapter on the history of the world, there was a marked difference between Europe before the Crusades and Europe after the Crusades. Europe before the Crusades was a collection of petty states and fiefdoms that were ruled by mounted knights or ruffians as it were, who were obliged under oaths of fealty to the landholder who granted them their land. The oath of fealty or service meant that the landholder owed his lord forty days of military service each year. This meant that for forty days a year (not necessarily the same ones), all around Europe, knights, counts, earls, dukes, squires, vassals and peasants were involved in some kind of work project or military action against any person whom the lord deemed forfeit of his lands.

If you happened to be one of those ruffians, the only thing that kept you safe from some other ruffian, or band of ruffians, was your fort (before the Crusades) or castle (after the Crusades). During and after the Crusades, the construction of stone castles across Europe was undertaken at a frenzied pace. The question still remains, where and how did the technology to build complex stone structures such as castles and later on, cathedrals come to Europe? If it came by way of the Templars, how did the Freemasons transform themselves from the villains of the failed Crusades to the champions of castle construction? Logic and common sense tell us that it had something to do with power.

Medieval Europe in the years between 1314 and 1718 was teeming with threats to the local landlord; unhappy peasants, neighboring landlords who were always on the lookout for more land, invading armies, not to mention plagues, highwaymen and ambitious relatives. The best place for the landlord to be was inside a castle with walls made of stone. The best friend of any landholder in the period would probably be the local Freemason, or, in our case, the local Freemason guild. For example, let's just say you, the reader, are a member of the Templar Order and you were lucky enough to escape to the nether regions of Europe before the Inquisition tortured you and then burned you at the stake.

What kind of employment can you get once your employer is declared heretical? Earlier, we mentioned that only ten percent of the Templars were actually combatants. What did the rest of them do?

As we saw in the previous chapter, many of them were at work building…castles. We know that some were bankers, and bankers needed a secure building to keep their wealth. A building made of wood and straw? Most likely not, in fact, up until the end of World War II, banks were based on designs that signified strength, permanence, and most important, impregnability or in other words, a veritable fort or castle, if you will. The Templar buildings, forts and banks were constructed of stone, and therefore it is logical that sufficient members of the order were well enough versed in the art of stonemasonry, that they could, in turn, train other members of the Order (like yourself) in the art of stonemasonry which would keep you and the members of the Order in porridge and kidney pie during the dark years.

If the Freemasons had funny handshakes, convened in private houses, seemed a little secretive, and were rumored to be remnants of the outlawed Templars, what did the landlord, or local priest or cardinal care as long as they finished their projects before more ruffians or the Pope's representatives showed up? The stonemasons then, were ideally suited to hide their identities as former Templars. So, then, what kind of secrets did they possess?? According to S. Brent Morris, author of *An Idiot's Guide to Freemasonry*,

"There were the trade secrets-how to cut a stone or build an arch, or most important, how to make a stone square."

Then of course, there was always the problem of identifying who is a mason and at what level of experience and knowledge he is coming to your worksite possessing. In the Middle Ages, when everyone was poor and looking for work, or on the lamb from an overbearing landlord, Robert Cooper, Curator of the Grand Lodge of Scotland, describes the simple solution. "The stone mason who is traveling from one building site to another, maybe between countries even, over hundreds of miles who can't read and write, how is he going to identify himself to someone who is a stonemason? Well, he's got a handshake and only shows this to another stonemason, that they are stonemasons. We still like to use our handshake instead of a piece of plastic or a piece of paper."

As we know from our chapter on the *History of the World*, the 1300's was a century where it seemed as if one disaster followed another. In 1347, the Black Plague swept through Europe. At the same time, what is known as the "Little Ice Age" brought unusually cold temperatures to northern Europe. Millions of people died of disease or the starvation that accompanied the failure of crops and the loss of livestock. In 1378, the Italians elected their own Pope at the same time the French elected a Pope of their own in what is known as the Great Schism. Suddenly, Christendom had two Popes who declared the Papacy of the other, null and void. Northern Europe, still reeling from the freezing temperatures and the loss of its population, became a mere afterthought as the countries of Italy and Spain, where the Catholic Church had its strongest grip, became centers of commerce. The city-states of Italy such as Venice and Genoa produced wealthy merchant families who competed with each other for power, commerce and control of the Catholic Church.

The "new" old learning

If you will recall, in the 1453, the city of Constantinople fell to the Ottoman Turks. The vast stores of art, literature, scientific writings and philosophy from the pre-Christian and the Islamic world, made their way to Italy and from there, were passed on, thanks to the Chinese and their printing press, to all parts of Europe. Most notably, in the 1500's they found their way to a scientist and inventor in Italy by the name of Galileo, who began to read the ancient texts and, in turn, who began to come up with some ideas of his own. Of course, the Catholic Church did not tolerate any of his ideas about planets, gravity, nor the earth orbiting the sun. Subsequently, he was called before the Inquisition for his heretical beliefs. His subsequent imprisonment was to set the precedent as a warning for would-be scholars for the next one hundred years.

By the 1500's, countries in northern Europe had recovered from the decimation of the 1300's. In 1517, Martin Luther tacked his 95 Theses to the Monastery at Wurms and the Catholic Church went on the offensive against anyone who challenged her supreme authority in Europe. As a result, Europe became divided between north and south, between Protestant and Catholic, between nationalists and those who supported the supremacy of the Popes, between rulers like Henry VIII of England and Gustav of Sweden. This stalemate ended one hundred years later. In 1618, the uneasy truce between Protestants and Catholics was broken when a representative of the church was thrown out of a window in Prague and the Thirty Years War was on. The conclusion of the war in 1648, which left most of Germany and its neighbors in ruins as well as missing almost two thirds of its population left people as disillusioned with religion as they had been during the days of the 1300's with its Great Schism and the Bubonic Plague.

The first underground societies

During the intervening time period following the Thirty Years War and the foundation of the first Masonic lodges, the new learning that had emerged from Constantinople again went underground and could only be discussed in secret societies, like those of the Freemasons, to whom the new learning was probably not new at all. As we saw earlier, the end result of thirty years of horror and bloodshed between Protestants and Catholics was an agreement that the religion of the local ruler would be the religion of the people governed by that ruler. In short, after all the starvation, depravity and bloodshed, things would go back to the way they had been before. The disillusionment with organized religion was at an all-time high and left people looking elsewhere for answers to the big questions about life and man and our place and purpose in the universe.

Rethinking the thinkers

The period known as the Enlightenment really got into full swing as the result of the brutal Thirty Years War. It was a period where all knowledge was suspect. Earlier in our chapter about the *History of the Modern World*, we discussed how, in the middle of the 1600's and early 1700's, a group of people emerged in France and England known as the Philosophes. The Philosophes had a lot more explanations to offer about the world and why things were they way they were than a scripture or a passage in the Bible. These Philosophes included great thinkers like John Locke, Rene Rousseau, Rene Descartes, Thomas Paine, Sir Isaac Newton, Benjamin Franklin, Jean-Jacques Voltaire and their predecessors, Denis Diderot, Thomas Hobbes and St. Thomas More. They found in the ancient Greek and Roman texts ideas about observation, logic and experimentation to prove whether something was "true" i.e.: a fact or not true. The brilliant work done by Galileo concerning bodies in motion and gravity led to even more experimentation by Sir Isaac Newton who pioneered modern physics, or the way to describe the physical laws that govern everything in the universe.

The ideas of the Philosophes, though they were tailored to fit the world of Medieval Europe, were by no means completely original ideas. They, themselves had been taught by Aristotle, Plato, Diogenes, Pythagoras and Archimedes who had existed in a world (ancient Greece) where God did not create the world in seven days and Jesus Christ wouldn't arrive for at least another four hundred years. The Philosophes simply recognized the basic truths in the ideas of the ancient thinkers and then applied them to the context of medieval society.

The Philosophes were both idealists, and men of ideas. They were idealists because they wanted to make society better, which they believed would make mankind better. They were men of ideas because they all had different solutions for making that perfect society. Some, such as Rene Rousseau felt that government should be chosen by the consent of the governed, or to put it more simply, people should be able to choose their own rulers. Others, such as Hobbes and Locke, who borrowed heavily from Plato, distrusted democracies and felt that enlightened despots such as Frederick the Great of Prussia and later, Catherine the Great of Russia were the answers to society's evils. What else did the Philosophes have in common? With few exceptions, they were all members of the Society of Freemasons. The reason for this has much more to do with the political and legal realities of the time than any moral or philosophical connections with people who hammered and chiseled stones all day.

If the reader will recall, Europe in the 1700's was in the stages of tremendous social upheaval. The introduction of gunpowder and cannon had evolved over two hundred years into the introduction of the rifle and the foot soldier who, over time, replaced the armored mace-swinging knight on horseback. Kings no longer needed to reward their henchmen and thugs with land on which to support them. By the 1700's, most armies in Europe were outfitted with the latest technological advances in musket and cannon. The soldiers who carried and fired the muskets did not need a long and distinguished pedigree, or any more than a few weeks of training. They only had to be able to walk to where the battle was being fought, load the rifle and point it in the direction of the enemy and pull the trigger, reload and repeat the process until they were either victorious, dead or given permission to depart the battlefield in haste. To support these armies, kings needed money for food, more rifles, food and clothing. At the same time, the landholding classes began to feel the pinch as the king was more inclined to demand money in lieu of the traditional service of the landholder.

The rise of the intellectuals

Because of the new learning that had come about after the fall of Constantinople, the landholding classes more often than not sent their spoiled children with little to do on the estate to the new universities and colleges in England and Europe, hoping to give them an air of manners and respectability, as well to provide them with a way to bring an income to the family. Bureaucracies were beginning to form to manage the cities, taxes and trade. In the universities, new ideas were being taught as people began to rethink what had, for two thousand years, been considered, "knowledge." Sciences such as biology, astronomy, geography, chemistry and physics were all the rage in the upper class "snob havens" of Oxford and Cambridge in England and Yale and Harvard in the American colonies, as well as the universities that were springing up all over the Continent.

But, as the students and professors of the new learning began to question and rethink the areas of science and mathematics, it was inevitable that they would eventually begin to focus their ideas on the very governments that controlled every aspect of their lives. In the late Middle Ages, speaking about the government and the social order in any other than a highly praiseworthy fashion was a very risky enterprise. Those who would dare to question the authority and legitimacy of the social order and the power of the king, who had paid spies everywhere, needed to do it in a place where they could be certain that their ideas would never leave the room, under threat of some very serious penalties. Luckily there was one group of people who guarded their secrets to the death, literally.

Enter the Society of Freemasons

Such a climate as the political one of Europe in the late 1600's to early 1700's represented a nearly identical political and religious climate in which the Templars had found themselves in 1307. The aristocracy, feeling a sense of redundancy, as the kings of Europe appeared more dependent upon peasant soldiers than themselves, began to reassert their rights in the social order. As the Templars had once needed to go underground, so did the freethinking non-landholding Philosophes. They saw the Freemason's success at maintaining their secrets and knowledge and decided that such an organization was ideal for their purposes. This would make the common workmen of Europe the rather odd bedfellows of upper class society in the Age of Enlightenment.

The subsequent marriage of the workmen and the intellectuals would be known as the Society of Freemasons. In 1717, at a tavern known as the Goose and Gridiron in London, the marriage was performed between what were known as "operative" masons, or those of the working classes who made their living chiseling and building with stone, and "speculative" masons, those upper crust individuals of the leisure and intellectual classes who needed a place to discuss their ideas and philosophies where they would be free of the large ears of the crown and the threat being drawn and quartered, which usually accompanied the charge of treason.

Within six years, the organization had hundreds of members all over England who met in secret locations called lodges. According to the documentary, *Freemasonry Revealed,* they also had a, "written constitution filled with fantastic symbols, signs, tools, handclasps and even their own alphabet. They devised a hierarchy of novice masons, master masons and Grand Masters. They had 33 levels called degrees. Each one reached through a secret initiation and rewarded with a secret password that members swear never to utter outside a lodge under penalty of death."

And so, with their own secure place to meet, men like Rousseau and John Locke met and discussed their own ideas and the ideas of the earlier Philosophes such as Descartes, Hobbes and St. Thomas Moore. The ideas they discussed would make their way from England, across Europe and across the Atlantic Ocean as their fellow Freemasons; Samuel Adams, Paul Revere and George Washington would end the 1700's with revolutions in America and then a few years later, in France. In the 1800's, the Freemasons would be instrumental in the revolutions of South America and in bringing a divided Italy under the control of a single government. But, before they could accomplish their lofty goals, the Freemasons were going to need guns, cannon and thousands of men to rally to their cause; in other words, they were going to need money and a lot of it. Fortunately for the Freemasons, the Rothschild's financial star began to rise at roughly the same time as their own.

By the very nature of their organization as a "society with secrets," with a self-professed lack of central control, dogma, or doctrine, the Society of Freemasons were bound to attract some of the best and worst men in society who would use the anonymity and secrecy of the organization to cover up their agendas and their sometimes dark deeds. It wasn't long after the formation of what is known as Scottish Rite Freemasonry in England, that this very thing began to happen. With its membership of speculative masons drawing members from both the clergy and the nobility, The Scottish Rite Constitution written by Dr. John Anderson for the English Grand Lodge stated, ""A Mason is obliged by his tenure, to obey the Moral Law: and if he rightly understands the Art, he will never be a stupid atheist, nor an irreligious libertine..." However, in spite of Dr. Anderson's warning, both "stupid" atheists and irreligious libertines began to populate the lodges in Europe, England and America.

Adam Weishaupt, Mayer Rothschild and the Illuminati

What is known as the Illuminati movement began with a highly idealistic former Jewish scholar-of-moderate-means-turned-Jesuit-priest by the name of Adam Weishaupt. Weishaupt was born in Bavaria in modern day Germany. His father died at the age of 7, so he was raised by his godfather, a Baron, who happened to be not only wealthy, but also served on the local government council. Weishaupt was a thinking man, and a very intelligent one. He began reading the works of the Philosophes like Diderot and Voltaire, and he really liked what he read.

"Lastly, when the whole body of the Church should be sufficiently weakened and infidelity strong enough, the final blow (is) to be dealt by the sword of open, relentless persecution. A reign of terror (is) to be spread over the whole earth, and...continue while any Christian should be found obstinate enough to adhere to Christianity.

(Letter from Voltaire to Frederick the Great)

This particular letter, which, when taken out of context by many who cite it as evidence of a Rothschild-Illuminati-worldwide conspiracy, does makes the remarks of Voltaire sound rather alarming. However, at the time of Voltaire's writing, the Church was no less involved in its own "reign of terror" against Jews, Lutherans and other Protestant sects. Like his fellow speculative Freemasons, Weishaupt blamed the social structure of Europe, with the nobility and the clergy on top and everyone else at the bottom devoid of legal or economic rights, for all of society's ills. Weishaupt, like Voltaire, did not think, as some of the Philosophes did, that ridding the world of the nobility would solve society's problems. Weishaupt, disillusioned former Jesuit priest that he was, believed it was the Church, which gave legitimacy to the social system that needed to go. Logically, if the Church were destroyed (and ignorance and superstition along with it), then the aristocracy would not have a moral leg to stand upon and would soon follow or undergo some change of heart. Of course this drama would unfold during the course of the French Revolution a few decades after Voltaire penned his sentiments to King Frederick II. Many attribute the rise and the success of the Illuminati to his relationship with Mayer Rothschild.

The "noble savage" and his influence on political thought

Many of the Philosophes, to include Adam Weishaupt, Benjamin Franklin, Thomas Paine, Voltaire, etc. believed that man was a "noble savage" whereby, once rid of the corrupt social system of late medieval Europe, mankind would revert to their own basic nature of natural goodness, as it had in the days before civilizations had given themselves over to the rule of kings and despots. Evidence for this kind of thinking had come back to Europe in the tales of adventurers and sea captains who spoke of egalitarian societies in the Americas, in the South Pacific and in Africa. This philosophy was called "naturalism" and it was based on the idea of natural law, or the laws that were visible every day in science and nature.

Of course, there were different opinions on how to arrive at this "natural" state, and those differences in ideas would range and still do range across the spectrum between free market capitalism, socialism and communism as they would come to be known in the next centuries. However, for the time, the choices would be limited to either Voltaire's "enlightened despotism" or Rousseau's social "contract" between the populace and the government, from which to choose. These ideas are evident in the ideas of the American Revolution and the subsequent United States Constitution with a President and an elected body of representatives all held in check by the rule of law. Freemason George Washington expressed his own sympathies with the noble savage idea when he said, "That government that governs least, governs best."

The "Enlightened" Ones

With the encouragement of Meyer Rothschild, Weishaupt began to recruit like-minded men into his order, which he officially founded on May 1, 1776. He called the new order, the "Illuminati" or, the enlightened ones. Initially he structured his order after the Freemason model with levels of degrees. In order to advance to the higher levels of the Illuminati Order, members had to read from the writings of the Philosophes, pass a series of tests and give sufficient reason for hating the present social order, especially the Catholic Church. "Illuminists" at all grades were to apply themselves "to acquiring of interior and exterior perfection", a perfection which would, through the works of the Order, illuminate the entire world with reason and good deeds.

His recruiting efforts spread throughout Europe and England, and of course his ideas made their way across the Atlantic to place like Boston, Massachusetts and Philadelphia, Pennsylvania, where men like Benjamin Franklin began to incorporate these ideas into what they thought would be the perfect form of government, but that would come a little later in the idea of the American compromise known as the separation of Church and State.

For the time being, Adam Weishaupt and his revolutionary thinkers began to find themselves in political hot water. Their rapid expansion in membership as they began to recruit throughout Europe, and their ties to the Freemasons either as members of Freemason lodges or Illuminati lodges claiming to be Freemasons, left them open to their arch-enemies, the Society of Jesus (Jesuits) who held considerable political power in the Illuminati birthplace of Bavaria. Disillusioned by the course of events, four university professors in the lower degrees of the Order disclosed their secret knowledge to the local elector, charging that the sect posed a threat to Christianity, condoned epicurean pleasures, justified suicide, and taught that "the end justified the means" if it served a noble cause. In 1785, with police raids, public trials and banishments, the Illuminati Order was abolished.

Not only were the Illuminati in political "hot water" the very ideas of the Illuminati, the inherent goodness of man who had become corrupted by both Church and State, began to unravel in front of Weishaupt's eyes. The Order, so dedicated to the perfection of mankind, soon found itself immersed in the travails of bureaucracy and the imperfections of present-day human nature. "Spartacus" –Weishaupt's secret Illuminati identity, wrote to "Cato" in August 1783:

"I am deprived of help. Socrates, who would insist on having a position of trust amongst us, and is really a man of talent, of the right way of thinking, is certainly drunk. Augustus' reputation could not be worse. Alcibiades does nothing but sit all day long with the vintner's pretty wife and spends his whole time in sighing and pining with love…Tiberius attempted to ravish the wife of Democides, and her husband took them in the act…"

So disillusioned with his undertaking at times was Weishaupt that he wrote, in anticipation of the arrival of a prominent candidate for the membership in the Order, that the minerval (potential members) would balk at joining a society of "dissolute, immoral wretches, whoremasters, liars, bankrupts, braggarts and vain fools."

Seized correspondence of the Illuminati, exhibited by Barruel, indicates that a growing portion of Weishaupt's activity was expended in maintaining a semblance of control of some of the freewheeling Illuminists. In one letter, Spartacus told a provincial lodge director that a "worthy brother of the highest rank and order" has stolen jewelry from another member. Would the Director implore the Brother to return his loot to the rightful owner? In spite of his goal to "fit man by illumination for active virtue," even Weishaupt was caught up in the tragic comedy. "I am in danger of losing at once my honor and reputation," he wrote, "by which I have had long such influence." Weishaupt then revealed how he had gotten his sister-in-law pregnant. Attempts to secure and abortion failed and he was forced to consummate the marriage after she bore him a son (Conrad Geiger).

The Illuminati Legacy?

And so, the idealistic savior of mankind appears to have been a casualty of his own remedy or at least the victim of his own unrealistic notions of humanity. Weishaupt's organization, with its lofty and ambitious ideals, soon became a victim of its own success as members began to betray one another over petty squabbling and their own licentiousness, which, unfortunately for Weishaupt, probably was the reason some were drawn to the Illuminati Order in the first place. Adam Weisahaupt died in 1830 as Shakespeare's Hamlet once lamented, "All sound and fury, signifying nothing."

But is that really the Illuminati legacy that Weishaupt left behind? There were many who insisted that Illuminati actually went underground and that even today, the Illuminati, or a derivative thereof, are very active in controlling the world as a puppet master controls a marionette through the medium of international finance. Is that true? Does a secret organization still exist, hidden deep within the ranks of the Freemason Organization? Is it still following the Illuminati agenda of destroying the Church and Christianity? Are Illuminates still intent upon freeing mankind from the chains of ignorance and poverty, the by-products of our own inability to divorce ourselves from the old social order in favor of the "novus ordo seclorum" that is printed on the US one dollar bill?

Many people in the modern age, unfamiliar with the social, religious and political realities of late medieval Europe cite the stated goals of the Illuminati, which, when taken out of context, can appear quite conspiratorial, if not outright frightening in our own time. For example, the following appears on an internet website, regarding the Illuminati:

"As the name implies, those individuals who are members of the Illuminati possess the 'Light of Lucifer'. As far as they are concerned, only members of the human race who possess the 'Light of Lucifer' are truly enlightened and capable of governing. Denouncing God, Weishaupt and his followers considered themselves to be the cream of the intelligentsia - the only people with the mental capacity, the knowledge, the insight and understanding necessary to govern the world and bring it peace. Their avowed purpose and goal was the establishment of a "Novus Ordo Seclorum" - a New World Order, or One World Government."

As we have already discussed in a previous chapter, the "Light of Lucifer" reference, refers to many different things. Of course, it can refer to 'Old Scratch,' or, 'Beelzebub,' or, as we have seen, if we go back far enough it refers to Venus of the Greeks, Isis of the Egyptians and Astarte of King Solomon. However, this reference appears to be cut and pasted from Albert Pike's Morals and Dogma. The Illuminati, in fact were atheistic in their approach, which separated them from the Scottish rite form of Freemasonry. They would not have professed a belief in any deity, which was, according to them, the source of society's problems in the first place. As far as the Illuminati being formed from the cream of the intelligentsia, this would have been a very subjective label. As most of us know, anyone who agrees with us is considered intelligent. Anyone who disagrees is an idiot. By referring to themselves as intelligentsia, though I am not sure if that were ever the actual case, the Illuminati Order was simply trying to recruit like-minded individuals with the ability to "think outside" of the medieval box.

Looking for the Illuminati

Because this book is not about conspiracies, rather, it is an attempt to help the reader to understand the world a little better, it is not the author's intent to draw attention to what might have happened, rather, in the light of the serious investigator, it would serve the reader better to know what did happen. In that context, the reader can, as has already been stated, form his or her own judgments and if so disposed, to investigate events in other, more qualified sources. In that regard, we will continue on to investigate what did happen to the "Illuminati" after it was officially banned as a threat to social order in 1785.

If a person decides to look for something, say a lost remote control, a set of car keys or a missing person, logically, the single most important piece of information relative to the search is what the characteristics of the missing item or person actually are. In the search for the Illuminati, it would be important to note their characteristics before the search actually begins. First, the Illuminati were sworn atheists, which got them into trouble with their conservative counterparts in the Freemason lodges of England, though not necessarily in France and Bavaria. However, not all of the Order were sworn to atheism, rather, they were anti-Christian, which meant anti-Catholic Church. Second, the Illuminati, in order to remain out of the clutches of the Church and the local nobility whom they vowed to destroy, had to remain a secret society. We have already seen that when their status as a secret society was sacrificed in the name of recruitment, all kinds of trouble followed.

Last, and certainly not least, like any business enterprise or political campaign, no matter how lofty an idea may be, it is going to amount to very little to unless there is a sufficient amount of money to back it up. There are those who claim that Mayer Rothschild used Weishaupt's organization in order to establish secret connections for his son's banking enterprises in the political capitols of Milan, Paris, London and Frankfort. The subsequent disbanding of the organization before his sons were actually old enough to set up businesses in those cities goes a long way in disproving those theories, if, in fact the Illuminati Order ceased to exist in 1785.

As a matter of fact, the Rothschild's would not attain any of their legendary wealth or status until the first decade of the 1800's, but, the conspiracy fires are fueled by the fact that time and time again, organizations with the same characteristics as the defunct Illuminati were to reappear on the political or intellectual scene throughout the next two centuries. To add even more fuel to the conspiracy fire was the fact that the people and groups who shared the political philosophy of the Illuminati, such as the Jacobins who controlled France during the infamous Reign of Terror, where thousands of suspected loyalists were imprisoned or decapitated by Freemason Dr. Guillotine's, uh, Guillotine, were suspected of being of the Illuminati Order under a new name.

If the shoe fits...

In 1848, Karl Marx published his Communist Manifesto in London, the center of the Rothschild's, Freemason's and the world's power. Within the ideals of communism were the nearly identical ideas of the Illuminati, with an economic twist. Namely, the dissolution of the Church, the rule of the "intelligentsia" and a belief in the community of men provided they were provided with the "right" kind of leadership and education. Most importantly, the accusation made by the four university professors who exposed him to the Jesuits, that the Illuminati believed in the idea that "the end justifies the means," does sound a lot like a plagiarized version of Weishaupt's own Illuminati ideas. The subsequent actions taken by the London and New York financed communist revolutionaries in Russia does leave the door wide open to the accusation that the Western financed communist governments of the world share a lot of similarities with the Illuminati. May 1st or "May Day" the date in which the Illuminati were formed was also celebrated in the Soviet Union, though their revolution began in October. The red flags of the Communist states of Russian and

China are similar to the "red shield," the English translation of the Rothschild family name. It would be naive to believe that Illuminati "thinking" was completely abolished in 1785. And, if it was not, why do scholars not accuse Karl Marx of the plagiarism of Weishaupt's ideas about the "perfect" political order?

Freemasons, Rothschild money and the American Revolution

The marriage of Rothschild money and the revolutionary ideas of the Enlightenment began rather suspiciously, when in 1775, it looked as if there was going to be no reconciliation between the American Colonists and King George III. Oddly enough, at a time when emigration to America might seem a hazard to a person's health, a rather peculiar banker showed up in Philadelphia. His name was Haym Solomon. Solomon, like Mayer Rothschild, was a Jewish moneylender from Eastern Europe. He had somehow decided at the time of greatest tension to date, to immigrate to the colonies and open a shop in Philadelphia, where he specialized in bills of exchange for overseas trade.

A bill of exchange was basically a check that was issued by a moneylender, which could be redeemed in Europe. How did a Jew from Eastern Europe hold such sway in the financial world that his checks were good on both sides of the Atlantic? The same way he was able to negotiate loans from the Dutch for the American War effort. Haym Solomon had connections within European Jewish banking families, one of whom was of course Mayer Rothschild. We remember Mayer was, at the same time, responsible for paying the Hessian soldiers who were fighting the American colonists on loan from Prince William of Hesse to his cousin, King George III.

In 1781, the American Revolution and its Enlightenment ideals were on the verge of disaster due to a lack of ready cash. At the Battle of Yorktown, George Washington and the Continental Army was set to pounce on a surrounded British Army under Lord Cornwallis. Washington's forces blocked the British from escaping on land, while at sea the French fleet under Admiral Rochambeau blocked any relief for Cornwallis by the British Navy. It was at that time that George Washington was informed that the Americans had neither the money, nor the credit to press the attack on Cornwallis. It was at that point that Washington was heard to remark,

"Send for Haym Solomon." Haym Solomon saved the American Revolution with his loan of $20,000 to Washington and the Continental Army. Thanks to the quick and ready loan, the Americans were subsequently victorious at Yorktown, the final battle of the Revolutionary War.

Prince Hall and the loyal revolutionaries of Freemasonry

The Revolutionary War and the subsequent Independence of the United States leaves more questions open as to the involvement of the Freemasons on both sides of the Atlantic after the War. As we have seen, the Illuminati or, Enlightenment principles of Voltaire and Benjamin Franklin, both members of the 3 Muses (sisters) Lodge, which they often attended together during Franklin's time in France as U.S. Ambassador, were major influences on the United States Constitution, while the naturalism ideas of Sir Isaac Newton and John Locke heavily influenced Thomas Jefferson when he wrote the Declaration of Independence. George Washington, a 33rd degree Scottish Rite Freemason, was a former colonel in the British continental militia. His aide de camp, the famous Frenchman La Fayette, was also a Freemason, as was German drill instructor Baron Von Steubben, who gave the Continental Army its first taste of drill and order in the Prussian style. In fact, the list of Freemasons included Alexander Hamilton, future Secretary of the Treasury and most of Washington's general officers. With so many Freemasons involved in the Revolutionary War effort, a peculiar state of affairs during the war, as well as after independence, was to raise the question; how independent was the United States from Great Britain?

The question arises from the fact that during the American Revolution, a white officer in charge of a unit of black soldiers from Boston initiated a soldier by the name of Prince Hall, as well as a number of other black soldiers into the Masonic order. Curiously enough, the Masonic Order known as Prince Hall could not officially recruit members until 1784 when they were finally granted a charter from the Grand Lodge-in England.

It does seem somewhat curious, that one year after the Treaty of Versailles, in which the United States of America was initially recognized as a free and independent nation, that the Freemasons, who sacrificed so much for the Revolution, were still loyal to the Grand Lodge of England.

Furthermore, the Grand Master of the Grand Lodge of England is a member of the British Royal Family. It is indeed a curiosity that, in an organization that claims to have no head, or leadership, the Grand Lodge of England is responsible for granting charters to lodges around the world. It does raise the obvious question: Is the United States, with its powerful organization of Freemasons really an independent nation?

European Royalty and Freemasonry

Another rather intriguing question lay in the very real fact that beginning in 1798, Europe saw its monarchies toppled one by one, starting with Louis XVI by the Freemason order known as Jacobins (or Illuminati?). By the end of World War I, there were only a handful of monarchs left in Europe. Kaiser Wilhelm of Germany was kaput, the Holy Roman Hapsburgs of Austria were deposed, and Czar Nikolas of Russia along with his family had been murdered. Interestingly enough, the royal families who seemed to do quite well in the centuries of regicide, were the monarchies of England as well as those other countries such as the Netherlands and Scandinavia, who appeared to have either Masonic ties or direct involvement with the House of Rothschild. Was there a reason for this, or is it merely coincidence? Interestingly enough, the present head of the Grand Lodge of England is the Duke of Kent.

What is similarly interesting is the connection between the Crown, the Freemasons and the world of international banking. According to Des Griffin:

"The Rothschilds operate out of an area in the heart of London, England, the financial district, which is known as 'The City' or the 'Square Mile.' All major British banks have their main offices here, along with branch offices for 385 foreign banks, including 70 from the United States. It is here that you will find the Bank of England, the Stock Exchange, Lloyd's of London, the Baltic Exchange (shipping contracts), Fleet Street (home of publishing and newspaper interests), the London Commodity Exchange (to trade coffee, rubber, sugar and wool), and the London Metal Exchange. It is virtually the financial hub of the world.

Positioned on the north bank of the Thames River, covering an area of

677 acres or one square mile (known as the "wealthiest square mile on earth"), it has enjoyed special rights and privileges that enabled them to achieve a certain level of independence since 1191. In 1215, its citizens received a Charter from King John, granting them the right to annually elect a mayor (known as the Lord Mayor), a tradition that continues today."

Both E. C. Knuth, in his book *Empire of the City*, and Des Griffin, in his book *Descent into Slavery*, stated their belief that 'The City' is actually a sovereign state (much like the Vatican), and that since the establishment of the privately owned Bank of England in 1694, 'The City' has actually become the last word in the country's national affairs, with Prime Minister, Cabinet, and Parliament becoming only a front for the real power. According to Knuth, when the queen enters 'The City,' she is subservient to the Lord Mayor (under him, is a committee of 12-14 men, known as 'The Crown'), because this privately owned corporation is not subject to the Queen, or the Parliament.

Notwithstanding the "failed" Russian experiment with Communism, is there a mysterious organization that retained its Illuminati identity and still pursues the goals of a God-less society that is dominated by powerful elites who are blessed with the virtue and reason that is necessary to rule the world? Well, the simple answer is; what would be the point of that? As we have already seen, by the 1820's the Rothschild banking family controlled the currency of England, France, and the United States. By 1823, the very object of the Illuminati's wrath, the Catholic Church, had signed over its banking affairs to the Rothschild bankers. What the Illuminati set out to do, by political means, was much more easily accomplished by economics. This very fact was stated quite eloquently by the head of *M.A Rothschild and Sons* Bank in Frankfort, Amschel Mayer Rothschild (1773-1855) in 1838: "Permit me to issue and control the money of a nation, and I care not who makes its laws."

And so, finally, we have come to understand that within a society with secrets or a secret society, sometimes it is possible for secret societies to exist, such as the "defunct" Illuminati who remained protected within the Society of Freemasons with goals and purposes for which the society was supposedly never intended. We also saw that by the very nature of their secrecy, a fantastic change was wrought by these societies whose secrets made it possible for the world we live in to exist. But, we also have seen that a society with secrets also has the potential to attract the less noble minded and we need some kind of assurance that this kind of thing only happened in the past. Such a society could not, in the modern day, still be responsible for hiding secrets, especially the nefarious deeds of its members, could it? Before we begin to answer that very question, let us take a closer look at some secret societies from the past.

CHAPTER 18

SECRET SOCIETIES:

GETTING AWAY WITH MURDER

Masonic Connections

Human, or rather, recorded history seems to point to the fact that civilizations familiar with the art of masonry, or constructing buildings out of stone that is first quarried and then carved, seems to be the norm, rather than the exception. India, Cambodia, Thailand, China, Tibet, Nepal, and Japan in the East, and Egypt, Greece, Rome, and medieval Europe in the West, all are examples of civilizations whose skill in masonry is commonly known. In Central and South America, if the reader will recall, we discussed the civilizations at Caral in Peru, as well as the Mayan Civilization in Central America and Mexico. All of these cultures share the common similarity that they were experts at the construction of elaborate temples and pyramids.

Is there evidence then, such as the Freemasons claim that their society's mysteries originated during the time of Solomon, ancient Egypt or possibly before that? To which mysteries are they referring, the art of carving and building with stone, or is there another mystery, or mysteries that were also present in previous civilizations? Were the Native Americans also Freemasons by the same definition as the Freemason of Europe and the Middle East? Did they also conduct themselves as secret societies or societies with secrets?

The dictionary tells us that, "Freemasons are known by their "charitable works" and "secret rites. "We do not have any evidence that the societies in the countries of the Far East, Ancient Egypt, Greece, or Central and South America were known for their "charitable works." However, if we look a little closer at Biblical and historic texts, we can see that there is evidence of secret rites in all of these cultures. In the Middle East, Greece and Egypt were what was known as the "mystery cults." Their rites, initiations and actual practices of worship were known only to their members, which I suppose is how the term "mystery" ended up being a part of their name. Similarly as we are about to see, these same types of organizations existed in Central America and among the Native Americans prior to the arrival of the Europeans. The existence and similarity of these societies or cults, to modern Freemason societies is part of another mystery to some, but not those who accept the Book of Mormon as a factual account. Before we get into all that, let us first arrive at an agreement of terms. According to the dictionary, Freemasons practice secret rites. So, what is a "secret rite," or a rite, for that matter? The dictionary tells us that rites are: "ceremonial act (s): a solemn ceremony or procedure customary to a community, especially a religious group (*often used in the plural*)."

Therefore, a "secret rite" must be defined by the same definition, only, as the name implies, they are performed in secret. According to that definition every Christian, Muslim, Jew, Hindu, Buddhist, etc., who practices a ceremony that is shared with the members of their religious group practices rites. One example would be the Jewish bar mitzvah or the Muslim hajj. But these rites are not necessarily secret. The Freemasons and members of the LDS Church on the other hand, practice rites that are secret, such as temple marriages or baptisms for the dead in the case of the LDS Church. The initiation of members to the 3rd degree in Freemasonry was shown in a televised documentary, so it is not really secret anymore (unless they changed it). In the case of the rites of temple ceremonies where the LDS Church is concerned, these rites were meant to be secret until disaffected members of the LDS Church made them available to the public. The difference between the LDS Church, whose temple ceremonies have been made public, and the Society of Freemasons is the fact that the LDS Church does not promise to murder those who betray their ceremonies in rather a grisly fashion, rather, the LDS Church chooses to leave the final judgment of those people to God.

The Third Degree

Why then would the Freemasons, whom the 33rd degree Freemason Bill-Gates-owned Microsoft Encarta Dictionary claim to be charitable in their nature, be so occupied with murder to protect their secrets? Why would an organization so freely discuss the act of murder in its ceremonies? Do the Ten Commandments not say, "Thou shalt not kill?" Why does Solomon raise Hiram Abiff from the dead, a power supposedly only reserved for Jesus Christ? Which God do the Freemasons believe in, and what is their understanding of their relationship with the God they worship that they can institutionally ignore the commandments of the God of Israel? Is there a basis in murder and killing other human beings that goes back farther than most of us understand? Is this one of the mysteries of which the Freemasons claim knowledge that goes back to the dawn of man? Of course, it is not possible for the non-initiate to know the answers to any of these questions. We are therefore limited to the same scriptural references from which the Freemasons profess the origins of their secret rites, specifically, the Old Testament.

Cain and Abel: Murder for gain

The first murder, at least to those who practice the Jewish, Muslim and Christian faiths, occurred shortly after Adam and Eve were expelled from the Garden of Eden. It involved two of Adam's sons, Cain and Abel. According to the Old Testament:

"And Adam knew his wife; and she conceived, and bare Cain, and said, I have gotten a man from the Lord. And she again bare his brother, Abel. And Abel was a keeper of sheep, but Cain was a tiller of the ground. And in process of time, it came to pass, that Cain brought of the fruit of ground an offering unto the Lord. And Abel, he also brought of the firstlings of his flock and the fat thereof. And the Lord had respect unto Abel and to his offering. But unto Cain and his offering, he had not respect. And Cain was very wroth, and his countenance fell. And the Lord said unto Cain, Why art thou wroth? And why is thy countenance fallen? If thou does well, shalt thou not be accepted? And if thou doest not well, sin lieth at the door. And unto thee shall be his desire and thou shalt rule over him. And Cain talked with Abel his brother. And it came to pass, when they were in the field, that Cain rose up against Abel his brother, and slew him. And the Lord said unto Cain, Where is Abel they brother? And he said, I know not, am I my brother's keeper? (Genesis 5 1-9).

The murder of Abel by Cain is the first murder in the religious texts of the three Western religions. The murder of the younger, more capable brother is also seen in parallel in the teachings of Freemasonry. In the Chapel at Rosslyn, there are two mysterious columns. One is obviously well constructed and elaborately decorated, while the other is much simpler in its design. According to Masonic lore, the columns represent the works of a master and his apprentice.

According to the story associated with the columns, the master finished his column and left his apprentice to finish the second. Upon his return, the master discovered the work his apprentice had finished far exceeded that of his master. The master in turn, flew into a rage and slew his apprentice. It is certainly a striking similarity to the story of Cain and Abel. Those who saw the column of the apprentice would respect his work as the Lord respected the younger Abel's offering. On the other hand, those who saw the column of the master, like the elder Cain, would have no respect at all for his efforts. According to Freemason lore, the head of the apprentice appears on one of the corners of the chapel with a gash in his forehead where he was struck by his master and killed. He looks blankly across the chapel at his master, whose head is carved into another corner of the chapel. Did Cain also strike Abel in the head and create a mortal wound? The Old Testament account, wanting for detail, leaves it simply at the level of coincidence that the Freemason story only roughly parallels the story of Cain and Abel.

However, the Book of Moses in the *Doctrine and Covenants* gives a more detailed account of the incident described in the fourth book of Genesis. In the account, a pattern is laid down that involves Jesus Christ, lies, murder for profit and murder for oaths.

"And he gave unto them commandments, that they should worship the Lord their God, and should offer the firstlings of their flocks, for an offering unto the Lord. And Adam was obedient unto the commandments of the Lord. And after many days, an angel appeared unto Adam, saying: Why dost thou offer sacrifices unto the Lord? And Adam said: I know not, save the Lord commanded me. And then the angel spake, saying: This thing is the similitude of the sacrifice of the Only Begotten of the Father, which is full of grace and truth. Wherefore thou shalt doest all that thy do in the name of the Son and thou shalt repent and call upon the name of the Son

forevermore. And in that day the Holy Ghost fell upon Adam, which beareth record of the Father and the Son, saying: I am the Only Begotten of the Father from the beginning, henceforth and forever, that as thou hast fallen, thou may be redeemed, and all mankind, even as many as will. And in that day, Adam blessed God and was filled and began to prophecy concerning all the families of the earth, saying: Blessed be the name of God, for because of my transgression my eyes are opened, and in this life, I shall have joy, and again in the flesh I shall see God. And Eve, his wife, heard all these things and was glad, saying: Were it not for our transgressions we never should have had seed, and never should have known good and evil, and the joy of our redemption, and the Eternal life which God giveth unto all the obedient. And Adam and Eve blessed the name of God, and they made all things known unto their sons and daughters. And Satan came among them saying: I am also a son of God; and he commanded them, saying: Believe it not, and they believed it not, and they loved Satan more than God. And men began from that time forth to be carnal, sensual and devilish. And the Lord God called upon men by the Holy Ghost everywhere and commanded them that they should repent. And as many as believed in the Son, and repented of their sins should be saved; and as many as believed not and repented not, should be damned; and the words went forth from the mouth of God in a firm decree; wherefore they must be fulfilled. And Adam, and Eve his wife, ceased not to call upon God. And Adam knew Eve his wife, and she conceived and bare Cain, and said: I have gotten a man from the Lord; wherefore may he not reject his words. But behold, Cain hearkened not, saying: Who is the Lord that I shall know him? And she again conceived and bare his brother Abel. And Abel hearkened unto the voice of the Lord. And Abel was a keeper of sheep, but Cain was a tiller of the ground. And Cain loved Satan more than God. And Satan commanded him, saying: Make an offering unto the Lord. And in the process of time, it came to pass that Cain brought of the fruit of the ground and offering unto the Lord. And Abel, he also brought of the firstlings of his flock, and the fat thereof. And the Lord had respect unto Abel, and to his offering; But unto Cain, and to his offering, he had not respect. Now Satan knew this, and it pleased him. And Cain was very wroth and his countenance fell. And the Lord said unto Cain: Why art thou wroth, why is thy countenance fallen? If thou doest well, thou shall be accepted. And if thou doest not well, sin lieth at the door, and Satan desireth to have thee; and except thou shalt hearken unto my commandments, I will deliver thee up, and it shall be unto thee according to his desire. And thou shalt rule over him; for from this time forth thou shalt be the father of his lies; thou shalt be called Perdition; for thou was also before the world. And it shall be said in time to come-that these abominations were had from Cain; for he rejected the greater counsel which was had from God; and this is a cursing which I will put upon thee, except thou repent. And Cain was wroth, and listened not anymore to the voice of the Lord, nor to Abel his brother, who walked in holiness before the Lord. And Adam and his wife mourned before the Lord because of Cain and his brethren. And it came to pass that Cain took one of

his brother's daughters to wife, and they loved Satan more than God. And Satan said unto Cain: Swear unto me by thy throat, and if thou tell it, thou shalt die, and swear thy brethren by their heads, and by the living God, that they tell it not; for if they tell it, they shall surely die; and this that thy father may not know it; and this day I will deliver thy brother Abel into thine hands. And Satan swore unto Cain that he would do according to his commands. And all these things were done in secret. And Cain said: Truly I am Mahan, for I am master of this great secret, that I may murder and get gain. Wherefore, Cain was called Master Mahan, and he gloried in his wickedness. And Cain went into the field, and talked with Abel, his brother. And it came to pass that while they were in the field, Cain rose up against Abel, his brother, and slew him. And Cain gloried in what he had done, saying: surely I am free; surely the flocks of my brother falleth into my hands. And the Lord said unto Cain: Where is Abel, they brother? And he said: I know not. Am I my brother's keeper? (Moses 5:1-33)

In the more detailed version of the story of Cain and Abel, there are some obvious correlations to the oaths taken by modern Freemasons, particularly those who practice Scottish Rite Freemasonry. According to the documentary, *Freemasonry Revealed*, "In fact, the Masonic oath guarantees a gruesome death for those who reveal the secrets." One of the more popular oaths the Freemasons swear to, is that: "I do promise and swear under no less penalty than to have my breast torn open, my heart and vitals taken from thence and exposed to rot on the dunghill." And how does that correlate with the oath taken by Cain?

"And Satan said unto Cain: Swear unto me by thy throat, and if thou tell it, thou shalt die, and swear thy brethren by their heads, and by the living

God, that they tell it not; for if they tell it, they shall surely die; and this that thy father may not know it; and this day I will deliver they brother Abel into thine hands."(Moses 5:29)

Kevin McNeil Smith, editor of Freemasonry Watch tells us:

"According to Masonic ritual, if you break your oath, you will be murdered. That is the basis of the oath. Now, masons will say, 'This is a joke, we don't murder people anymore.' Well, punishments become more bizarre, from having your throat slit to having your chest opened perpendicular and your legs thrown over your shoulder and buried in the sand."

There are two important elements to remember here. Satan made Cain swear by his throat, and he made his brothers swear by their heads. Is it just a coincidence that the apprentice in Rosslyn Chapel has a gash on his forehead? Is it also a coincidence that the Freemasons perform a ceremony whereby Hiram Abiff is slashed in the throat and ultimately dies by having a mallet crush his skull? Next, the oath is taken and the murder is performed for the reason of the oath and to "get gain," or to take what rightfully belongs to someone else by murdering them.

It doesn't take much intelligence to know that the political history of mankind is the history of the murder of people or populations in order to take their possessions. Only, we do not refer to murder and theft on a massive scale by that name. Instead we refer to it as, "war," and the governments who engage in this activity create entire cultures around their enterprise in order to justify their actions and to entice their citizens to support and engage in the devilish activities of the government.

Whether a person believes in it or not, we have already seen from the civilizations of Assyria, Babylon, Egypt, Greece, Rome, Europe, England, Germany, Japan, China, Saudi Arabia, Israel, America and so on and so on, that the plan of Satan; to destroy people's freedom, to get men and women to kill their fellow human beings and to swear oaths to protect themselves from the truth is as common an attribute of mankind as the ability to walk upright. The great teachers of peace all found themselves the victims of Satan's conspiracy with men, from Jesus to Mahatma Gandhi to Dr. Martin Luther King.

On the other side of the coin, the most important message in this account, whether a person is Christian, Jewish, Muslim or whatever, it doesn't matter. All things on this earth must be done in the name of Jesus Christ and his simple gospel of faith, repentance, baptism and the gift of the Holy Ghost is the foundation of all human activities and all human knowledge. Whether or not a person believes in Jesus Christ as the Lord of this world is of no significance to God. His law is His law, it is in the Scriptures, and that is just the way things are. If a person chooses a different road in life, especially one full of mysteries and superstitions, oaths and secret societies, then that person will most likely become distracted from the real purpose of life and most likely end up in the clutches of evil, either they will suffer evil themselves or they will inflict evil on others.

There isn't anything mysterious nor complicated about anything Jesus taught and anyone who professes something different, such as hatred, intolerance, and the limitation of humans to have the freedom to choose their own path in life, no person, whether they be LDS, Freemason, Jewish, Muslim, Catholic or Protestant, is in synch with ideas of the God of Israel.

As we all know, the use of lies and half-truths is the favorite tool of politicians and anyone else who is up to some sort of malfeasance or other. Why, for instance, does the Old Testament not include the Books of Moses and Abraham, both of which serve as testaments of the mission of Jesus Christ? Who would be interested in keeping that information out of Holy Scriptures? As Adolf Hitler, one of history's biggest criminals said a lie becomes the truth if you keep telling it enough. So, along with a regimen of murder for the purpose of getting gain, those allied with the Dark Prince use lies to deceive good people into doing bad things. So, are the Freemasons themselves somehow allied with the Lord of the Flies? Our best indication would come from the eternal litmus test for judging between good and evil.

"And by their desires and their works, ye shall know them."

(Doctrine and Covenants 18:38)

Does not the Microsoft Encarta Dictionary tell us that the Freemasons are known for their "charitable works?" If that were completely true, then there would be no need for an oath. Keeping a donation to a local charity secret does not usually warrant death by slitting open someone's chest.

On a more philosophical level, the story of Cain and Abel is a story that reflects man's own ambitions and serves to set boundaries for what is acceptable and what is not in the realm of human endeavors. In the days before centralized governments, police forces and forensic investigations, the only way a man could be convicted of murder was if someone came forth and testified that they either saw the act (Thou shalt not bear false witness) or was aware that the perpetrator was responsible for the act. Suppose there are witnesses or accomplices, but they have taken the same oath to never reveal their dark secret upon penalty of death. How many prophets, teachers, kings, presidents, and everyday folks like you and I have fallen victim to these kinds of secret societies? If everyone belonged to such a society, then there would be no society, as we shall soon se

Secret Societies in the Americas

Conspiracies aside, our previous question of whether or not there is evidence of Freemasonry, in the form of secret societies in the Americas can be found in the Book of Mormon. If you will recall, the Jaredites, who came to the Americas after the confounding of human language at the Tower of Babel, left evidence in their record that they were plagued by secret societies. Moroni, whose own society was destroyed by these secret societies, comments upon the plight of the Jaredites by saying:

"And behold, it came to pass that they formed a secret combination, even as they of old; which combination is most abominable and wicked above all, in the sight of God; For the Lord worketh not in secret combinations, neither doth he will that man should shed blood, but in all things hath forbidden it, from the beginning of man. And whatsoever nation shall uphold such secret combinations, to get power and gain, until they shall spread over the nation, behold they shall be destroyed; for the Lord will not suffer that the blood of his saints, which shall be shed by them, shall always cry unto the ground for vengeance upon them and he avengeth them not. Wherefore the Lord commandeth you, when you shall see these things come among you that ye shall awake to your awful situation, because of this secret combination which shall be among you; or wo be unto it, because of the blood of them who have been slain, for they cry from

the dust for vengeance upon it, and also upon those who built it up." (Ether 8: 18, 19, 22-24)

Later, in the societies of the Lamanites and Nephites, there were also secret combinations that were actively involved in assassinations of kings, judges and prophets.

"But behold, Kishkumen, who had murdered Pahoran, did lay wait to destroy Helaman also; and he was upheld by his band, who had entered into a covenant that no one should know his wickedness. For there was one Gadianton, who was exceedingly expert in many words, and also in his craft, to carry on the secret work of murder and of robbery; therefore he became the leader of the band of Kishkumen. Therefore he did flatter them, and also Kishkumen, that if they would place him in the judgment seat-he would grant unto those who belonged to his band that they should be placed in power and authority among the people; therefore Kishkumen sought to destroy Helaman. And it came to pass that he met Kishkumen, and he gave unto him a sign; therefore Kishkumen made known unto him the object of his desire. Desiring that he might conduct him unto the judgment seat that he might murder Helaman. And when the servant of Helaman had known all the heart of Kishkumen, and how that it was his object to murder, and also that it was the object of all those who belonged to his band to murder, and to rob, and to gain power, (and this was their secret plan, and their combination) the servant of Helaman said unto Kishkumen: Let us go forth unto the judgment seat. Now this did please Kishkumen exceedingly, for he did suppose that he should accomplish his design; but behold, the servant of Helaman, as they were going forth unto the judgment-seat, did stab Kishkumen, even to the heart, that he fell dead without a groan. And he ran and told Helaman all the things which he had heard, and seen, and done. But behold, when Gadianton had found that Kishkumen did not return he feared lest he should be destroyed; therefore he caused that his band should follow him. And they took their flight out of the land, by a secret way, into the wilderness; and thus when Helaman sent forth to take them they could nowhere be found." (Helaman 2:3-5, 7-9, 11)

"And now behold, those murderers and plunderers were a band who had been formed by Kishkumen and Gadianton. And now it came to pass that there were many, even among the Nephites, of Gadianton's band. But behold, they were more numerous among the wicked part of the Lamanites.

And they were called Gadianton's robbers and murderers." (Helaman 6:18)

According to the Book of Mormon, the Kishkumen and Gadiantons were rewarded with fire when Jesus returned to teach the Nephites and Lamanites:

"And behold, the city of Laman, and the city of Josh, and the city of Gad, and the city of Kishkumen have I caused to be burned with fire, and the inhabitants thereof, because of their wickedness in casting out the prophets, and stoning those whom I did send to declare unto them concerning their wickedness and their abominations."
(3 Nephi 9:10)

Although these are just brief glimpses of the actual accounts that were translated by Joseph Smith, we can see in the Book of Mormon cultures of the Jaredites, Nephites and Lamanites, that secret societies were responsible for the murder of government leaders for the sole purposes of putting themselves in power. Just as importantly, they were responsible for the general degradation of both societies through lies, violence and general lasciviousness until the majority of each population relished in nothing more than hatred and bloodshed.

Native American Secret Societies and Masonic connections from the past

Today, many Native Americans belong to Masonic lodges and consider them a natural progression of their rites and practices as they observed them before the European conquest. In a talk given at the 2004 Annual Masonic Symposium in San Diego, Dennis Chornenky told members of the Masonic Brotherhood,

"In light of current scholarship, not to mention common sense, it is obviously absurd to claim that Native Americans practiced Freemasonry prior to the advent of European settlers. However, if seriously examined, there emerge notable parallels and similarities between Western initiatic rites and symbols and those of the Native Americans."

In his address, Mr. Chornenky describes some of these "notable parallels" but dismisses them out of hand as, "a testament to the traditional character of Freemasonry," whatever that means. Others however, may look at the examples he uses in his talk to arrive at different conclusions.

First, Mr. Chornenky cites the findings of Dr. J. Mason Spainhour of North Carolina, who addressed the Smithsonian Institution in 1925 regarding a Native American grave he had recently uncovered. Dr. Spainhour described the grave in the following way:

"The facts set forth will doubtless convince every Mason who will carefully read the account of this remarkable burial that the American Indians were in possession of at least some of the mysteries of our order, and that it was evidently the grave of Masons, and the three highest officers in a Masonic lodge. The grave was situated due east and west; an altar was erected in the center; the south, west, and east were occupied, the north was not; implements of authority were near each body. The difference in the quality of the beads, the tomahawks in one, two, and three pieces, and the difference in distance that the bodies were placed from the surface, indicate beyond doubt that these three persons had been buried by Masons, and those, too, that understood what they were doing. Will some learned Mason unravel this mystery, and inform the Masonic world how they obtained so much Masonic information?"

Mr. Chornenky, rather than addressing the odd coincidence that the three Native Americans were buried according to strict Masonic ritual, simply moves on to quote another example of Freemasonry as practiced in the Americas by citing a reprinted passage from *California Freemason* in 1956 which originally appeared in *Oregon Freemason* magazine:

"Here's a new slant on how American Indians may have actually had what was the forerunner of Freemasonry as we have it today. To accept this theory it is necessary to set aside the discovery of America by Columbus, and possibly even the claim that Leif Ericson came here looking for Minnesota ahead of all the others. Now comes the story that ancient Welsh bards have records of a Prince Madoc who was presumed to have been lost at sea in 1172. Five hundred years later a report came from America of two or three Indian tribes that spoke the Welsh tongue. About 1909 two Welsh miners, looking for gold in Arizona came across an Indian tribe rehearsing a Masonic ceremony in Welsh. The supposition is that Prince Madoc reached the Americas and taught the Welsh tongue and Welsh Freemasonry to the natives."

Again, Mr. Chornenky simply dismisses the account out-of-hand by saying: "Luckily, the academic caliber of the *California Freemason* magazine has improved substantially since 1956." Mr. Chornenky, whose credentials as the president of the Masonic Restoration Foundation qualify him to make final determinations about the accuracy of reports by eyewitnesses, scholars and researchers without further investigations, is able to dismiss the similarities between Native American burial rituals and accounts of Welsh speaking Indians performing Freemason ceremonies out of hand. However, even Dennis Chornenky does admit that the similarity between many initiation rites and societies of Native Americans and their belief in a "Great Spirit," and even cites the ghost dancers of the 1890's Indian uprising at Wounded Knee, who referred to their leader as "the Christ (the deliverer)."

He also cites a peculiar artifact in possession of the Pueblo Indians that is also known among Freemasons:

"Pertaining to the theme of center and circumference, there is a highly sophisticated calendar device of the Anasazi (contemporaries of the Aztec civilization), ancestors of the Pueblo Indians of today that bears a strikingly close resemblance to a certain Masonic symbol. The Sun Dagger calendar is close to one thousand years old and was first systematically studied by Anna Sofaer in 1977. It allowed the Anasazi to observe the harvesting and planting seasons and easily record time's passage. It likely served other more spiritual functions as well."

However, In spite of Mr. Chornenky's conclusions, there are fortunately others who have examined the issue of Freemasonry among the Native Americans and have come to conclusions that differ from the attitude that the similarities can be attributed to something other than the ... "traditional character of Freemasonry."

In his book, *Mormonism and Freemasonry*, author Cecil McGavin relates in further detail both the similarities of Freemasonry to religious rites practiced by Native Americans, as well as their familiarity with certain Masonic practices and customs. Quoting from Mackey's *Encyclopedia of Freemasonry*, McGavin writes:

"Among the many evidences of a former state of civilization among the aborigines of this country which seem to prove their origin from the races that inhabit the eastern hemisphere (Middle East), not the least remarkable is the existence of Fraternities bound by mystic ties, and claiming, like the Freemasons, to possess an esoteric knowledge, which they conceal from all but the initiated." (McGavin 159)

McGavin also cites Frank Cushing of the Smithsonian Institute, who studied the Pueblo Indians and relates that during his studies as an initiated member of the clan:

"The existence of twelve sacred orders, with their priests, their initiations, their sacred rites, as carefully guarded as the secrets of the ancient mysteries (Freemasonry) to which they bear great resemblance." (McGavin 160)

Furthermore, McGavin quotes Daniel G. Brinton in his book, *Myths of the New World*, as Brinton explains the secret societies of the Algonquin Indians who settled primarily in the Great Lakes region the following way:

"The priests formed secret societies of different degrees of illumination, only to be entered by those willing to undergo ordeals, whose secrets were not to be revealed under the severest penalties. The Algonquians (sic) had three such grades- The Waubino, the Meda, and the Jossakeed, the last being the highest. To this, no white man was ever admitted. All tribes appear to have been controlled by their secret societies." (McGavin 160)

Freemason Dr. James William Mitchell wrote in 1858 in his book, *The History of Freemasonry*, the final word on the topic of the knowledge of Freemasonry by the American Indians:

"It is true, that, if we believed there was reliable testimony that Freemasonry was in the possession of the Indians before the discovery of the continent by Columbus, it would become a subject of deep interest to inquire whether the aborigines sprang from the Lost Tribes of Israel; and this fact, being ascertained, then to determine whether, at any period, there was a commercial intercourse carried on between them and any other portion of the world; for, if in 1492, Masonry was known to the aborigines, the conclusion is irresistible, that they received it from an intercourse from some other nation or people, as they could not have brought that knowledge with them long before Masonry was instituted.

The religious ceremonies, but more especially their belief in one great spirit, one great first cause, one God, favors the idea that they were descended from the Jews...

To our subject, it is important that we ascertain, if possible, whether the American Indians, prior to the discovery of the continent by Columbus, knew Freemasonry. If it can be shown that Masonry was, at that time, known to the aborigines, it would prove to our mind, satisfactorily, either that the Indians came here since the building of the Jewish Temple; or that, if they emigrated to this country at any time anterior to the days of Solomon, other emigrants came among them afterward, for no man can show any reliable evidence that masonry existed in the world until it was instituted by King Solomon. No one, who does not jump to conclusions from mere chimeras of the brain, can for a moment suppose that Masonry was in possession of the Lost Tribes of Israel, and they, landing on this continent, perpetuated it down to the present day. As well we might suppose that it had been left here by Noah, or that it was instituted at the Tower of Babel, after language was confounded, with a view that, by this universal language, men might be able to recognize and hold communion with each other the world over. Each of these fanciful suppositions would drive us to another, more serious in its consequences, viz; that God failed to accomplish his designs, for the Bible tells us, that the whole Earth was submerged and that only Noah and his family were saved; and that sacred volume also informs us that the language of the Babylonians was confounded, that they might not hold communion one with another, but thereby be compelled to separate into tribes or nations, speaking the same tongue. But granting that Masonry did exist on this continent before its discovery by Columbus, would it not be quite as rational to suppose it was brought here immediately after the completion of Solomon's Temple?

The Bible tells us that the wise men of all nations visited Jerusalem, to behold the Temple, and learn the Wisdom of Solomon. But we cease these wild speculations, and come to the naked proposition-Were the aborigines in possession of Freemasonry when this continent was discovered by

Columbus? We answer, unhesitatingly, they were not; and though we cannot be expected to prove a negative we shall proceed to show upon what shallow proofs reliance is placed by those who maintain the opposite ground." (McGavin 161-162)

In his refutation, Dr. Mitchell cites the same evidence cited one hundred and forty years later by Dennis Chernosky, i.e.; that certain Native American tribes in the Northeast and the Southwest were conducting Masonic ceremonies in Welsh, this being attributed to a Prince Madoc, a Welsh nobleman who was supposedly blown off course in a storm and ended up in what is today the Northeastern United States. Mitchell explains the familiarization with Freemasonry that was evident in that the "Menominee and Iroquois may have learned their mysteries from the Welch Indians...or their knowledge of the mysteries might be traced to a more ancient source-even the same from which the Druids themselves derived them...

There is ample evidence, both anecdotal and physical that Masonic rituals were practiced in both North and South America and Masonic symbols were familiar to Native Americans. The familiarity and ease with which Native Americans have embraced Freemasonry in the light of the fact that those very men who possessed it were seeking to disenfranchise them from their land, or wipe them from existence altogether, is even more evidence that they saw something familiar in the craft.

It is more than obvious that no matter what evidence may be presented through historical and archeological research, the Freemasons will never acknowledge, at least publicly, that the indigenous peoples of the Americas were familiar with a society that dated at least as far back as the time of Solomon. Why would the Masons, as a group who claim to embrace all knowledge and wisdom, be as militant as to their attitudes towards the connection between Native Americans and Freemasonry? The answer is quite simple; if the Native Americans knew about Freemasonry, then they must have brought it with them, or learned it, as Dr. Mitchell states, after the time of Solomon. If they admit that, they must also admit or explain how the Book of Mormon, which is replete with the accounts of secret societies, either is or is not an accurate history. Because Mr. Chornenky's and Dr. Mitchell's accounts are both matters of public record and because we do not know what secrets the Freemason claim to have, we have no evidence that the Book of Mormon is not a part of the "secret" knowledge of the Freemasons and that the Church of Jesus Christ of Latter-day Saints is in possession, as Joseph Smith claimed, of degrees of knowledge of the Kingdom of Heaven in which even the Freemasons are not familiar.

Dark Secrets of the Modern Society

And so we have seen that societies such as the Freemasons, who protect their members and their secrets by oath, are advantageous during times of oppression, superstition and ignorance. We have also seen that the benefits of such societies can sometimes be outweighed by their ability to commit evil, secure in the knowledge that no one will reveal their works to the general public. We have also seen that the same society that claims to have existed since the very beginnings of man, shares suspicious parallels with the Biblical murder of Abel, the fall of Lucifer and the use of oaths and lies to protect its secrets. Therefore, we can conclude that the idea of the Freemasons as a secret society is sometimes good, but, because of human nature, can have a tendency towards evil works, which can then be covered up.

What happens when the men who, as in the case of the secret societies of the Gadiantons and Kishkumen in the Book of Mormon, place themselves in positions of power? What happens when they become the judges, and as Kevin McNeil of *Freemasonry Watch* asks, "How many members of the police department in the senior ranks are Masons? How many members of City Hall are Masons? Who gets awarded contracts?" Furthermore, what happens when the Freemasons decide to break the law, when in fact, they *are* the law? How is justice served then?

Broken oaths and secret murders

What follows are three examples of known incidents of Freemasonry gone wrong. The last incident, which will be covered in detail in the next chapter, relates to the relationship between the Latter-day Saint Church and the Society of Freemasons. There are a number of very obvious reasons for this. One is due to the fact that, by the Society of Freemason's failure to ever acknowledge their deeds, it becomes quite apparent that a society with secrets such as the Freemasons can get away with murder. Second, it also underlines the importance the Society of Freemasons places upon the spread of disinformation and the denouncement of the Church of Jesus Christ of Latter-day Saints.

Murder One: Captain William Morgan

Captain William Morgan was born in Virginia in 1774. In 1819, at the age of forty-five, he married Lucinda Pendleton who was sixteen years of age. He moved to Canada to where he became a distiller of whiskey. However, Morgan's still burned down, and he was reduced to poverty. Broke and in poor spirits, in 1826 he moved to Batavia New York where he attempted to join the local Batavia Freemason lodge. In spite of his apparent knowledge of the initiation ritual, Morgan was denied permission to visit the lodge. When a new lodge was proposed, the initial petition included his name but an objection was made and a new petition was submitted, absent the name of William Morgan. Later, it was learned that in 1825 he had in fact, received the New York Rite Royal Arch Degree at Le Roy, New York. Regardless, his name was never added to the list of the proposed new lodge.

Angered by the lodge's refusal to admit him as a member, Morgan approached David C. Miller, a local newspaper editor who, according to Masonic history, had also been refused advancement after receiving the first degree in Masonry. Miller agreed to assist Morgan in the publication of a book entitled *Illustrations of Masonry*. William Morgan made his and Miller's intentions of revealing the secret rites of the Freemasons publicly known. Shortly thereafter, the newspaper building burned down. Three Freemasons were subsequently indicted for the charge of arson and were sent to jail.

Following the indictment of the three Freemasons, Morgan was arrested for failing to pay a two-dollar debt. Editor David C. Miller paid his bail, but shortly thereafter Morgan was arrested again. Events following Morgan's second arrest are shadowy at best. According to the story, two unknown men showed up to the jail in the middle of the night, paid Morgan's bail, and the three rode out of town on a wagon. Morgan was never seen again. Morgan's body was never found. The identities of the two mysterious men who led him off to jail were never discovered, and therefore, there was neither indictment nor conviction for the disappearance and possible murder of William Morgan.

The news of the disappearance of Morgan spread throughout the U.S. as old flames against conspiratorial organizations, such as the Illuminati, who many suspected might still be hiding within the ranks of the Freemasons, surfaced again. There were many mysteries surrounding the disappearance of Morgan. For instance, some Freemasons claim he was seen in other parts of the country. Others claimed his body was dumped in Lake Ontario. Still others claim his remains were discovered in a box in 1881. In spite of all the mysteries regarding the final fate of William Morgan, the basic facts are the same: Morgan had been initiated into the order in 1825. He threatened to expose the secrets of the order. William Morgan disappeared never to be seen again and there were no indictments or convictions for his disappearance or murder.

Murder Two: God's Banker, the Freemasons, the mob and The Catholic Church

In 1982, a scandal of international proportions rocked the world of not only Freemasonry, but international finance and the Catholic Church as another Freemason who had threatened to break his oath, was found hanging by a rope under a bridge in London. The ensuing cover-up by London police would result in the opening of a virtual "can of worms" in a scandal that would name people like Henry Kissinger, George H.W. Bush, the Gambino crime family, the Vatican and members of the Freemason lodge in Italy known as "P2."

The murder of Roberto Calvi, who had come to be known as "God's banker" would highlight not only the corruption possible within the walls of a society with secrets, it would also support the notion of the ability that Freemason members of local police forces have to cover up the dark deeds of their own members. Finally, it would highlight a worldwide connection between Freemasonry, international financiers, the C.I.A., the mafia, politicians and the Catholic Church, a connection that some would allege then and now, that also led to the murder of Pope John Paul I in 1978. The list of events leading up to the death of the director of Banco Ambrosiano, Italy's second largest bank, read like a fiction thriller. However, for the sake of the reader, we will focus on the involvement of a Freemason Lodge gone wrong in the worst sense of the word.

The reason for the murder, as in the case of William Morgan, would turn out to be the threat of revealing both mafia and Freemason secrets. In the words of Luca Tescaroli, the Italian public prosecutor in charge of the investigation: "Calvi was murdered as a punishment for pocketing money that the Sicilian Mafia and the Camorra had asked him to launder. He threatened to tell everything." Furthermore, the subsequent cover-up by London police, the lack of evidence against the men indicted and the "mishandling" of evidence by police investigators are all the classical earmarks of a Freemason murder. They always seem to end with no evidence and no convictions.

The Vatican Bank and the Gambino crime family

Roberto Calvi's problems probably began when he joined forces with the Vatican Bank in the 1970's, which, at the time was being run by Michele Sindona, a banker who was in the money laundering business for the Gambino crime family's heroin smuggling operation. Both Sindona and Calvi were members of Propaganda Duet, or P2, a "mobbed up" Freemason Lodge which was headed by a former member of Benito Mussolini's fascists by the name of Licio Gelli.

In 1974, Michele Sindona wanted money from Calvi to prop up his failing Franklin Bank in New York, which Calvi refused to do to the extent that would satisfy the Gambino banker. In 1978, information "mysteriously" arrived at the Bank of Italy, Italy's official bank regulator, regarding certain improprieties at Calvi's own Banco Ambrosiano. That same year, newly elected Pope John Paul I ordered an investigation into the ties between the Vatican Bank, and the P2 Freemason Lodge, whose members included the mafia, police, political, intelligence and military officials, which was suspected of laundering heroin money through Banco Ambrosiano. After thirty-three days in office, Pope John Paul I died mysteriously of a heart attack, though it was later rumored that he had an adverse reaction to his heart "medication."

In June of 1982, Calvi warned Pope John Paul II of an impending collapse of Banco Ambrosiano, saying in a letter that the collapse would, "provoke a catastrophe of unimaginable proportions in which the Church will suffer the greatest damage." Two weeks later, Banco Ambrosiano collapsed when it was discovered that the Vatican Bank, under the directorship of mafia banker Michele Sindona had taken from 700 million to 1.5 billion dollars out of Banco Ambrosiano, leaving it virtually insolvent.

Shortly after Calvi's letter to the Pope, he disappeared and was not seen again until he was found hanging underneath Black friar's Bridge in London. When his body was discovered, Calvi had ten thousand dollars in various currencies stuffed in his pockets and an expensive watch on his wrist. In his pockets were rocks and bricks taken from a nearby construction site.

London Police officials immediately ruled Calvi's death a "suicide" and closed the case. It took twenty-five years of private investigations, a second coroner's report and a re-enactment of the "suicide" to convince officials in Italy and London to re-open the case. When the case was re-opened, London Police investigators admitted that mistakes had been made in the initial investigation. Specifically, according to Detective Superintendent Trevor Smith:

"There were various omissions by the original investigation. The first was in the handling of Roberto Calvi's body. The knot that was tied in the rope around his neck was untied, when the proper procedure was for it [the rope] to be cut and [the knot] preserved. Then when his body was taken to Waterloo Pier, the bricks and stones in his pockets were taken out. This should not have happened there, but at the mortuary. Also, when pictures were taken of his body his jacket was buttoned up and that should not have happened either. The post mortem was also very short and not at all of the type that would normally be carried out for a suspicious death. In cases like this, what we call a special post mortem should have been carried out, but this was not done." Superintendent Smith continued: "There was a rush to judgment that this death was suicide. The original pathologist, Professor Keith Simpson, was briefed that it was a suicide and he was not given any other options. He should have been given alternative theories about Roberto Calvi's death, but this was not done. He also revealed that the scaffolding under the bridge was never fingerprinted and that when police found Calvi's London flat after searching for two days they did not fingerprint that, either." A London coroner, presented with the City of London police evidence, recorded a verdict of suicide. (Standard Examiner)

The rush to judgment and the botched investigation on the part of the London police could not directly be tied to any "conspiracy." The fact was, according to Italian officials, Calvi had attempted suicide in his jail cell upon his arrest in 1981, though the family denied this and there is no independent verification outside of the Italian police that the suicide attempt ever took place. After his apparent "suicide" in 1982, Calvi's family, believing that he had been murdered, hired a private investigator to investigate the facts surrounding the banker's death. When the family of Roberto Calvi was finally able to bring the people suspected of the murder to trial in 2007, it was more than obvious that there was much more at stake than what the prosecution claimed was retribution for losing the mafia's money-a charge which would have been more aptly applied to Michele Sindona. What was apparent was that the mafia, the Vatican, the Freemasons of P2, and United States intelligence agencies had been using Banco Ambrosiano for the purposes of sending aid to the Polish Pope's allies in the Solidarity movement in Poland, laundering drug money, funding anti-communist activities in Italy and supplying money covertly to Reagan's Nicaraguan Contras in Central America, a fact that would come to light in 1987.

However, twenty five years after the fact, it was the opinion of most that the men who were ultimately responsible for ordering the murder: high officials in government, banking, intelligence and Freemasonry, fearing that Calvi would either blackmail them or go public, had ordered Calvi's death, and would never be brought to trial. According to the indictment, the five ordered Calvi's murder to prevent the banker "from using blackmail power against his political and institutional sponsors from the world of Masonry, belonging to the P2 lodge, or to the Institute for Religious Works (the Vatican Bank) with whom he had managed investments and financing with conspicuous sums of money, some of it coming from Cosa Nostra and public agencies". In 2002, Calvi's death was changed from suicide to strangulation. Before the second trial began, Calvi's personal secretary "jumped" to her death from the window of her office. Archbishop Paul Marcinkus, who had immunity as an employee of the Vatican, and was closely associated with Calvi, was found dead of "unknown causes" in his home in Phoenix, Arizona. When the evidence was presented at the trial, the presiding judge threw the case out for the lack of evidence.

And so, another Freemason, whom it was suspected might reveal their secret works, was dead and once again, there were no guilty verdicts announced. There was one telling aspect of the second investigation into Calvi's murder that serves as much of an indictment of the Freemasons as a guilty verdict itself. When the second investigation was conducted, the London police specifically stipulated that no Freemasons were allowed to be involved.

And so, just like the oath sworn by Cain who slew his brother and swore to keep his deed secret, we have seen two cases of men who have been killed for violating their Freemason oaths of secrecy. Freemason William Morgan, who threatened to publish the secrets of Freemasonry, disappeared in the early 1800's, a little over one hundred years after the first recorded meeting of Scottish Rite Freemasonry at the Goose and Gridiron in London. The second murder, for those who think that secret societies are a good thing was that of Roberto Calvi at Black friar's Bridge in London in 1982. The disappearance of William Morgan in upstate New York involved a man who liked to drink, a small Freemason lodge, some local ruffians, a small-time printer and rather inept, or corrupt police force. The murder of Freemason banker Roberto Calvi involved the Vatican, the mafia, a Freemason lodge whose membership included a (former) fascist leader, future Italian Prime Minister Silvio Berlusconi, prominent bankers, industrialists, intelligence, army and police officials, and of course, various mob crime families, all working to protect each other's secrets.

The times they have a' changed

During the trial, it was revealed that the Vatican was directing money from the mafia heroin trade (whether they were aware of it or not) to support the democracy movement in Poland. The Reagan Administration was using the same piggy bank (cocaine profits?) to fund their anti-communist activities in Central America. To put the frosting on the cake, the murder took place in London, the birthplace of Freemasonry. Was it all coincidence, or an arrogant show of the power of the new ruling classes? Have we traded in the power of the Church and the landowning descendents of thugs for, uh, the Church and corporate thugs? What is so new about that "world order?"

When the news of William Morgan's disappearance became public in 1826-27, the Freemason organization was nearly shut down in the United States, an anti-mason candidate nearly won the presidency and, for generations, the Freemasons were suspected of conspiracy after conspiracy. From 1982, when a similar half-hearted and botched investigation into the death of Roberto Calvi was undertaken, until 2007 when the actual trial took place, hardly anyone batted an uninterested eye. When scandal after scandal broke in the news media involving the Gambinos and John Gotti, Barry Seal's cocaine smuggling with the full protection of the DEA and CIA, Iran Contra, and the allegations of the Clinton's involvement in murder and cover-up in drug smuggling in Mena Arkansas, etc. very few people even cared and nobody mentioned the fact that the actors in the government were prominent Freemasons or the Skull and Bones.

Freemason Ronald Reagan, whose administration was discovered selling missiles to Iran, while at the same time supporting its enemy, Iraq, in a bitter war that cost hundreds of thousands of lives, suffered such insignificant political fallout that his vice-president and former CIA director, and Skull and Bones man, George H.W. Bush, was elected president in 1988. P2 Freemason Lodge member and "alleged" mafia associate, money launderer, and drug trafficker, Silvio Berlisconi was elected Prime Minister of Italy in 1994. Since then, we have seen Bilderberg (another secret society) members Bill and Hillary Clinton serve two terms in the White House. George Bush Jr. (Skull and Bones) served two terms as President to be followed by Prince Hall Freemason Barack Obama. From 1963, when John F. Kennedy was assassinated to the present day, a period of nearly fifty years, the Oval Office has been occupied for only four years (Jimmy Carter) by someone not connected to one or another organization that is connected to a secret society or Freemasonry.

The "disappearance" of William Morgan and the murder of Roberto Calvi have two things in common. They are both events that the Freemasons grudgingly admit involvement at one level or other. In each case, they cite the fact the Batavia New York Lodge and Propaganda Duet were "rogue" lodges over which the Masons have no real control. This is easy enough to believe if one is inclined to forget that the Grand Lodge of England, the leader of which is no less than the Duke of Kent, who is in line for the throne of England, grants Freemason Lodges charters. In any case, it is more than apparent that any society who swears an oath, such as the one sworn by Cain, his great-great-great grandson Lamech, the first to kill for an oath, the Gadiantons of the Book of Mormon, the Templars of Medieval Europe and the Freemasons of today. No matter how charitable and full of good will as they claim to be, they can, as well, ultimately become a liability to society, a threat to law and order and to civilization itself.

There is still one murder that even today, the Freemasons fail to acknowledge, though, in their secret circles, they probably count it, along with its cover-up, as their greatest deed since Jesus Christ was mercilessly beaten and put upon the cross. It is one that everybody knows about, but that nobody speaks of, because it was not only a dark day in the history of the Freemasons, it marked an equally dark day in the history of mankind. Even today there are many accepted facts about the Freemasons most prized murder. Because of the Freemason control of society and information, few of them are unfortunately, true. So let us put the facts into the spotlight about the day Freemasons were involved in and helped protect those who were indicted for the assassination of a United States Presidential Candidate, a General in the Illinois Militia, the Mayor of Nauvoo, Illinois, the Leader of the Latter-day Saint Church, and a man who many claim to have been a Prophet of God.

Chapter 19

The Kingdoms Meet

The Latter-day Saints and the Freemasons

As we have seen in the previous chapters, by the early 1820's, the banking interests of the Rothschilds and their allies had gained control of the currencies of the United States, England, and France. They had also taken control of the banking interests of the Catholic Church itself. From the exchanges of London, the banking families of Europe had control of the British Empire through the power of finance. Since the British were active in the trade of Europe, India, the Caribbean, the South Pacific, China, Africa, the Middle East, and North and South America, it doesn't take too much imagination to understand that the financiers, who provided capital and insurance for these overseas enterprises, were in control as well. No matter what diabolical plots may have been cooked up in the lodges of the Illuminati some fifty years earlier, it would have scarcely been possible to conceive then how thoroughly the overthrow of the power of the Catholic Church and the reigning monarchs and nobility of Europe was turning out to be.

It looked as if the new age of Enlightenment that had begun a hundred years before was finally coming to fruition. Religion especially, with the exception of some backwards countries like Spain and Russia, had taken a back seat to the new age of science and discovery. As a result, the men of science, logic and reason began to come out of their Freemason lodges and into the public light. Faculties at colleges, at least in England, Germany and Western Europe, were no longer dominated by clerics and their censure of ideas that were not considered orthodox. The new science brought new ideas about everything from chemistry to engineering as laboratories sprung up on college campuses and professors and students began to dissect and classify everything they could get their hands on. The new science brought new technology and new technology brought progress.

There were some however, who began to ask how far all the science and learning was going to go and where it was that the new science was taking mankind. In England, the *Romantic Movement* in literature attempted to keep the human race in contact with the forces of nature that it was trying so forcefully to tame. Mary Shelley wrote *Frankenstein,* which raised questions about how far science was going to take us, and whether or not there should be some limitations on the new 'religion' of the masses. Ordinary people for the most part, upon seeing the improvements science and reason added to their lives, favored the new learning. The technologically advanced British and other European countries were pushing their empires to the ends of the earth. Superior technology in sailing, shipbuilding, armaments and a surplus population meant there was plenty to do for everybody. The Society of Freemasons began to grow and prosper as sons and grandsons of the growing middle-classes started new lodges wherever the British, French, Dutch or American flags flew. The Freemasons began to shed their earlier stereotype as 'blue-bloods' who met secretly to discuss odd philosophies, and gained a new reputation as the vanguard of the educated middle-classes. The Freemasons were men who got things done.

Digging up Jesus

And so it was, in the 1820's when it looked like science and reason had taken hold, and religion was on its way to being an outdated tool that had long kept the poor and ignorant in line, that news began to spread in the newly formed United States of America about a young farm boy named Joseph Smith, Jr. who was making some really outlandish claims. Joseph Smith actually claimed to have been visited by no less than God the Father and Jesus Christ as a young boy, along with an angel with the odd name of "Moroni."

By the 1830's, the boy had reached adulthood and published a book that he claimed was a record of the inhabitants of the Americas written a thousand years before the Europeans arrived. His "golden bible" claimed that the Native Americans were descendants of the Jews and that Jesus

Christ had appeared after He was resurrected and had ministered to them. As more information would come to light, this new "Latter-day Saint" religion would make claims that went way beyond the day-to-day Christian belief systems. There would be links with Egypt as well as temples, rituals and talk of secret societies. As we shall see, the new religion made claims that seemed to out-Freemason the Freemasons. It all would have been dismissed as just another demented Yankee trying to make himself some extra money, but, as the LDS Missionaries began to travel to other countries to preach, it became apparent, to the surprise of many in the worlds of organized religion, governments and Freemasonry, that many people were paying attention to what the LDS Missionaries were saying. In other words, just when it appeared Jesus had finally been put to rest, the "Mormons" as they were called, had dug Him back up again.

The "new" ancient societies: Latter-day Saints and Freemasons

To better understand the religious aspects of the relationship between the Church of Jesus Christ of Latter-day Saints and The Society of Freemasons, it is imperative to understand that both belief systems date themselves back to the pre-Christian era. Specifically, they both trace their lineage back to the time of Adam and Eve. However, for the reader who is either skeptical or unfamiliar with the following information, please understand that these are belief systems. They are not meant to be taken as historical fact, unless the reader believes them to be so. For the skeptical reader, this information is important because as belief systems, there are many people, both Freemasons and members of the Church of Jesus Christ of Latter-day Saints, who in fact, believe the following to be true.

It may be the reader's inclination to exclaim at some point, "Eureka! Both organizations are descendants of Cain, and therefore of the devil," or, "One is the descendant of Cain, and one is the descendant of Adam's good son, Seth." I should caution the reader before actually doing so. In the previous chapter, we examined the danger of secret societies because they can literally get away with murder. We also discussed the danger of societies with secrets, because of their potential for evil deeds, such as getting away with murder. Of no less danger is the possibility that the reader will come away with an unclear understanding, which would be synonymous with a half-truth, which would be of little use to the reader, as something that is half true is also half of a lie. I would therefore further caution the reader once again, that this information is merely an overview, I am by no means an expert in either LDS theology or Freemasonry and I encourage the curious reader to investigate these matters in more authoritative works from more authoritative authors and sources than myself.

That being said; let us review briefly that Adam and Eve, after their transgression and expulsion from the Garden of Eden, repented. Adam was given the fullness of the Gospel of Jesus Christ and both orders of the Holy Priesthood by which God's work could be performed on earth. It was after Cain slew Abel that Cain took an oath, which he passed on to his brothers and thereby, they became a secret society, or a society with secrets, the most obvious secret being of course, murder for power and gain. Adam's son, Seth, on the other hand, carried with him and passed on to his descendants the Holy Priesthood, or the ability to do good works in God's name here on the earth and make those works binding in the worlds where God reigns supreme.

Furthermore, in the book of Abraham, we are led to understand that the Priesthood which was passed on through Seth to Enoch, Noah, Abraham, Moses and the Levites, was also present in Egypt. However, as Abraham explained and we discussed in an earlier chapter, the Priesthood of the Egyptians was not the Priesthood of Adam, Seth and so on, because the Egyptians as Canaanites were cursed by Noah as the descendants of Ham so that they could not hold the Priesthood. And so it was that the Egyptians were privy to many of the secrets, or "mysteries" of the Priesthood, but they did not perform their rituals with the authority that came directly from God. This issue, strange as it may seem to the present day reader, was a point of serious contention between Joseph Smith and the Society of Freemasons.

As we have seen from the Old Testament, the mystery cults of Astarte (Isis, Venus, and Lucifer) and Moloch, (Saturn, Baal) were brought to Solomon by his foreign wives, especially Phillo, the daughter of Pharaoh. As we have already said, the Egyptians and the Canaanites, through Ham, possessed a corrupted form of the Priesthood. Whereas some might say it was corrupted by the deceptions of Satan, others might say it was corrupted by the influence of contact with other cultures, time, loss of understanding, etc. However, there was a form of the Priesthood that was brought to

Solomon, and it differed enough from the Priesthood of the Levites, the keepers of the sacred ordinances, to such extent that Solomon's practices of worship were included in the Old Testament Book of Kings in a negative context, which we discussed earlier. Therefore, it is possible and likely that both the LDS Church and the Freemasons share many of the same belief systems and in some cases, rituals and ceremonies because of their associations with the Priesthood of Adam. As we shall see, it was the similarities that led some to accuse the leaders of the early church of borrowing Masonic rituals.

Also, because the Catholic Church defined exactly what Christianity was and was not, many of these rituals and mysteries of the legitimate Priesthood were left out because they had been confused with Judaism and the corrupted versions of the Egyptian and Canaanite Priesthoods. That lack of understanding on the part of the offshoots of the Catholic faith, or Protestant Churches, would lead to accusations of "devil worship" and many other bizarre accusations in the early days of the restored Church that were, and are, also applied to the Freemasons. In fact, many LDS members were also members of Masonic Lodges, a circumstance which has nothing to do with the Priesthood rather it has more to do with, well, circumstance. We will look into the particular circumstances of LDS participation in Freemasonry shortly, but, before we do that, and before I give the Catholicized Christian Churches and organizations ammunition to label both organizations "devil worshippers" as they are so often eager to do, it is important to re-examine the history of the Christian Church from the time of the Council of Nicaea down to the present day.

Back to the Beginning: the birth of Christianity

As we discussed in the chapters about the history of the ancient world, the Roman Emperor Constantine called the Council of Nicaea in 318. His purpose was political, as he himself was not a Christian at the time he called the Council. The purpose of the Council was to create universal or "Catholic" Church. The establishment of a religious hierarchy with its supreme base in Rome was meant to put an end to the squabbling that had gone on within the Church since the death of Christ. As we have seen, the Catholic Church filled the vacuum left by the collapse of the Roman Empire in the West, which occurred one hundred years later. To some extent, standardizing the Christian Church did put an end to the squabbling regarding doctrine, the nature of God, etc. The supreme Bishop in Rome had the final say in all matters and anyone who disagreed with the Church, or Pope, was declared a heretic and, depending on the person's circumstances, could suffer a rather unenviable fate. The system worked pretty well, and fostered much good in a world ruled by wandering tribes of people ruled by warlords who were always on the lookout for more land, money, peoples to conquer and so on.

When the Reformation began in the 1500's and the Bible began to be printed in languages other than Latin, any man who could afford a Bible could, provided he wasn't captured by the Church, become his (or her) own expert in theological matters. If the person could convince enough people that their version of theology was correct, or at least more correct than the doctrines of the Catholic Church, a religious movement began. For example, the Puritans who founded Plymouth Colony in Massachusetts were just one of the hundreds of movements that sprung out of the Protestant Reformation. The Amish, Lutherans from Germany who settled outside of the realms of English society in Pennsylvania, were another example of a religious movement that appeared after the Protestant Reformation

As the saying goes, "Old ways die hard," and there were two aspects of the new religions that determine even today, the answer to the question, "What religion are you?" With the exception of members of LDS Church, all Christian religions are classified as either Catholic or Protestant. Though there are many reasons for this, the simplest one is that the new churches that were formed as a result of the Protestant movement dared not stray too far from the organizational structure of the Catholic Church. They appointed cardinals, bishops, priests, deacons and the like. Church was held on Sunday in a big square building where the commoners and the nobility sat for an hour or two and listened to a church authority teach about the matters of God.

"Priestcraft"

The second way in which churches of the Reformation resembled the Catholic Church was the continuation of what the LDS Scriptures refer to as "priestcraft" or, the act of paying the clergy to keep up the church, preach sermons and counsel members as to the relationship between God and man. One sticking point for many of the Protestant reformers was the sale of "indulgences" by the Catholic Church, which basically meant that if a person sinned, they could buy forgiveness from a priest in the form of a donation to the Church. As a business idea, it was a grand scheme, but for persons who were sincere in their relationship with God, it was no less than blasphemy at its worst. Jesus himself had said, "Money is the root of all evil" and the Church had suddenly made evil the root of all money, sort of. However, the Reformation Churches, though they did away with things like indulgences, still held on to the idea of a professional clergy. After all, when a person's everlasting soul is on the line, religion can be a very lucrative business.

The Early Church

When Jesus Christ was alive, his occupation was not that of a preacher. Nobody paid him to go around and cure the sick, preach forgiveness and talk about how a person gets to Heaven. If the reader will recall, Jesus was a carpenter. After He was crucified, the early Christians met in private homes and talked about Jesus' teachings and read from whatever documents were available. They also took the sacrament. This was one reason non-Christians of being a "secret society" suspected them. It wasn't until over a hundred years had passed that the idea of worshipping in a building set aside for that purpose began to take hold. Of course this idea had come from the former Jews who made up the majority of early Christians who were used to worshipping in a synagogue. It was the natural order of things that a building such as a synagogue would have a rabbi, so a church must have what we call a priest.

The idea caught on throughout the Roman world and so, bigger cities, like Antioch, Corinth, Jerusalem and Rome, with larger populations, began to build larger churches and therefore needed larger staffs in which to care for the needs of their members and their buildings. Jewish rabbis and synagogues were supported by donations from their members, so it was common sense that the Christian priests should also supported by the contributions of their members. At some point in time, being a Christian priest went from being a voluntary position, as in the case of Jesus, to becoming a full time job.

When the Church of Jesus Christ of Latter-day Saints was established, it made the point that it was different from all existing Churches. In fact the Church calls itself "restored" because it was set up with basically the same organizational structure that Jesus instituted when He was on the earth. In other words, with the exception of administrational offices, and the salaries of employees of the Church, nobody gets paid to be a Latter-day Saint. In fact, quite the opposite is true. LDS members are expected to fill all offices from stake presidents, quorum leaders, relief society presidents, bishops, and Sunday school teachers to groundskeepers and janitors on a voluntary basis, in addition to their professional, student and family obligations. If that is not enough, members of the Latter-day Saint Church are expected to fulfill missions of eighteen months at their own expense, as well as pay ten per-cent of their income in tithing to the Church. The money paid in tithing goes into a fund for welfare programs, new buildings etc. etc.

I think that it is easy to see, that before we begin to discuss the relationship between Freemasons and the LDS Church, it is important to point out the attitudes of organized religion towards the early and present day LDS Church and the reason for their animosity, which has a lot to do with economics. In a nutshell, every person who converts to the Latter-day Saint faith is a threat to the livelihood of every priest, bishop or clergyman who makes his or her living from Christianity. In other words, if all Christians were to become Latter-day Saints, the professional clergy of every religion would have to find another way to make a living. Fortunately for the clergy of other Christian denominations, the Church of Jesus Christ of Latter-day Saints requires an enormous commitment in terms of conduct, time, and money. Most people are content to be religious on Sunday and pay someone else to worry about their souls, read the Bible, etc.

In addition to their assured income by keeping their flock close to home, there is plenty of money to be made by those clergymen who would 'stir up' their congregations to anger toward anyone who is not a member of their own congregation by pointing out differences or errors in the way of thinking of other religions or denominations as opposed to the correct one, which happens to be the one that the clergyman professes. Paranoia within the established Christian Churches of the world is not just limited to LDS members, although the LDS Church does seem to take the lion's share of the wrath of the "Christian Evangelists" who also make their accusations against Catholics, Jews, Jehovah's Witnesses, Muslims, Seventh Day Adventists, Freemasons and the like.

There are also non-clergy who have seen a way to make even more money by writing defamatory books, producing movies or developing websites in order to make false claims to simple-minded folks who don't bother to ask any questions. All of this works in the favor of those Christian organizations that depend on their livelihoods by keeping their "flocks" from straying too far from the fold and the money piling up on the collection plate. That being said, we can now discuss in more detail the somewhat strange relationship between the LDS Church and the Society of Freemasons that will ultimately culminate in the assassination of Joseph Smith in Carthage, Illinois in 1844.

As we shall see, as in the case of Jesus Christ who goaded the Pharisees, the Sadducees and the Romans two thousand years ago, as well as U.S. President John F. Kennedy in our time who goaded the mafia, the military, the intelligence communities, the bankers and the Freemasons, when we discuss the life of Joseph Smith who was a Prophet, the leader of the Latter-day Saint movement, the commander of the Nauvoo Legion, a Presidential Candidate, a teacher, a scholar, a father, a husband and a friend to thousands, the question, becomes not, "Who would want to kill Joseph Smith?" instead, in a rather tragic commentary on life and the people in the early history of the United States, the real question was, "Who didn't want to kill him?" At the end of the next chapter, the reader will hopefully not only understand why Joseph Smith was assassinated, but that his assassination and the sham investigations and trials that followed had all the earmarks of the disappearance of William Morgan twenty two years earlier and the murder of banker Roberto Calvi one hundred and thirty eight years later.

To begin, in spite of the detractors and the misinformation that is spread about the LDS Church, unlike the Freemasons, the Church of Jesus Christ of Latter-day Saints is not a society of secrets open only to initiates. Anyone and everyone are welcome to attend LDS meetings and social functions, provided they adhere to the Latter-day Saint standards of acceptable dress and behavior. There are no elaborate initiation ceremonies or re-enactments beyond a greeting and a welcome.

Anyone who agrees to take on the covenants of baptism, no matter what their sex, race, background or income is baptized and admitted into the Church as a full member. Non-members and members who are not living according to the gospel of Jesus Christ and the LDS Church requirements of chastity, obeying the Word of Wisdom, paying a full tithe, and dealing "squarely" with their fellow men (and women), are not allowed to enter temples for the sole reason that, as in the Temple of Solomon, the space within the Temple is the resting place for the Holy of Holies. No unclean or impure thing or person can enter there.

Finally, members of the LDS Church who do take oaths and covenants and enter the temple, and then later renege on their oaths do not have their throats cut, their chests slit open, their legs thrown over their shoulders nor are they buried at low tide, etc. Men and women are free to do as they choose, as was the original plan presented by Jesus Christ. If they choose to leave the Church, they are always welcomed back if they are so inclined at a later time. There are instances where, because of sin, members are excommunicated where adultery, crimes or murder are involved.

Two churches, two ideas

To further illustrate the differences between the Latter-day Saint Church and the Freemasons, it is important to remember the separate paths taken at the very foundations of these organizations by Adam, who was evicted from the Garden of Eden and his descendants. Please note; this is a simple recounting of what happened according to the scriptures. The devil, evil, negativity, bad karma, darkness, gingivitis, halitosis, can infiltrate any group of human beings. This is not necessarily a condemnation of Freemasonry, it is an attempt to point out some of the peculiarities between the two groups, one of which claims to have its foundations in the Beginning of the World with God the Father, and in his Only Begotten Son, Jesus Christ. The other claims a connection with "the Great Creator" or "Geometer" or "God" but never really specifies what, or who that God is and as we have seen, establishes connections with the same deities that were brought to the Temple of Solomon by his foreign wives.

In the first case, Adam and Eve repented of their sins and they developed a close personal relationship and love for their Creator and Jesus Christ, whereby Adam became the first head of the Church of Jesus Christ (of early day saints?). In opposition to Adam and the first Church of Jesus Christ, Satan began his own church with the idea of the secret society that was first seen on earth in the manifestation of the oath that Satan gave to Cain to kill his brother and neither reveal his deed or the oath. In turn, Cain's great grandson, Lamech, in the Book of Moses, killed a man for the sake of the oath and for no other reason.

"For Lamech, having entered into a covenant with Satan, after the manner of Cain, wherein he became Master Mahan, master of the great secret which was administered unto Cain by Satan; and Irad, the son of Enoch having known the secret, began to reveal it unto the sons of Adam; Wherefore Lamech, being angry, slew him, not like unto Cain, his brother Abel, for the sake of getting gain, but he slew him for the oath's sake." (Moses 5:49-50)

Furthermore, Lamech's son, Tubal Cain was an artificer in, "brass and iron." Brass was the metal from which the deity Moloch (Saturn, Baal) was constructed. According to accounts from the Romans, who saw the Carthaginians perform sacrifices to Moloch, a brass statue represented the god. It was heated from the bottom and children were thrown onto its outstretched arms and cooked alive. It was this same Moloch that Solomon constructed in his old age that was an abomination to the Lord.

Getting down to "brass tacks"

In relation to the building of the Temple of Solomon, as we have already seen, there are two Hirams that are mentioned in the Old Testament Book of Kings. One is Hiram, the king of Tyre and the other is Hiram, the widow's son, whom we can assume is the same Hiram Abiff who is murdered in the Freemason re-enactment of the initiation into the third degree of Freemasonry. Interestingly enough, neither of these two Hirams is specifically mentioned in the Bible as a mason or "stone squarer," as they are referred to in the Book of Kings. Instead, Hiram of Tyre, who is "fetched," by Solomon is a "widow's son of the tribe of Naphtali," as we have already seen, and not a mason, but, "cunning to work all works in brass," as was Lamech's son, Tubal-cain. Was Hiram, the widow's son, also proficient in the construction of statues, particularly that of Moloch?

That association of "artificers in brass" presents us with some immediate questions. If the Freemasons are known for cutting stone, why are their symbols not representation of stones? Why are their compass and square, as they are seen on their buildings, books and fancy tiepins always the color of brass? For a belief system so reliant upon the Old Testament and Solomon, why would they choose the one metal that is associated with the son of Lamech (Tubal-cain) who killed for an oath?

"And Zillah, she also bore Tubal-cain, an instructor of every artificer in brass and iron…"
(Genesis 4:2)

Why would the Freemasons choose a material that is associated with the Canaanite god, Moloch, or Baal a brass statue on which children were cooked alive, sometimes in front of their own parents? Why don't the masons use steel or iron representations, which is more practical for the stonemason, or gold and silver, which is much more visually appealing and noticeable? We will leave that for the conspiracy theorists and continue on with our inquiry.

The Holy Priesthood and LDS Organizations

As we discussed earlier, the Freemasons, Judaism, Christianity and The Church of Jesus Christ of Latter-day Saints are all organized around the concept of a particular priesthood. The LDS Church is founded upon two priesthoods orders, the lesser, or, Aaronic (Levitical) Priesthood and the greater, or, Melchezidek (High Priest) Priesthood, both of which, according to LDS beliefs, have been on the earth at certain times. Both of these priesthood orders have been taken from the earth for periods of time as well. The last time both priesthoods were on the earth was during the life of Jesus and John the Baptist. When Jesus Christ was resurrected, He took the Melchizedek and Aaronic Priesthoods with him, however, Jesus may have bestowed the Aaronic Priesthood, or the ability to baptize and confer the Holy Ghost, upon the Nephites and the Lamanites during his brief ministry in the New World following his resurrection. Regardless, both priesthoods were restored to the earth and Joseph Smith through the prophets Elias and Elijah and John the Baptist in the 1820's.

Adam possessed the Aaronic and Melchezidek Priesthood, as did Noah and of course, Melchezidek himself. The Aaronic Priesthood was bestowed upon Moses and the Levitical tribe of Israel. The Aaronic and Melchezidek priesthoods are not some secret fraternity. As we have seen, the Aaronic Priesthood is for the purposes of baptism by the direct authority of Jesus Christ and the conference of the Holy Ghost. At the age of twelve, worthy Latter-day Saint young men are conferred with the Aaronic Priesthood. The second Priesthood, the high priesthood or Melchezidek, is to seal on this earth what will stand in the world, or worlds to come. The Melchezidek Priesthood is usually conferred at the age of eighteen, or prior to undertaking a mission for the LDS Church. In order to facilitate such work as eternal marriages, the sealing of families and baptisms for people who lived when the fullness of the Gospel was not present upon the earth, temples were constructed in ancient times as they are being constructed throughout the world today.

Structurally, the Latter-day Saint Church is similar to that of the Church that Jesus instituted during his time in Israel. The leader of the Church of Jesus Christ of Latter-day Saints is known as either, "the Prophet," or as the President of the Church as he is the presiding Elder in the House of Israel. Below him are the Twelve Apostles, and below them, the Council of Seventies. Community churches are called wards, which usually contain around three hundred active members. Presiding over the ward is a bishop and two counselors. Below them are quorum presidents who preside over different levels of priesthood holders.

In the LDS Church, girls, young women and ladies all belong to similar organizations that are not centered upon the priesthood, but revolve around the personal development of the person and the strengthening of the family. Girls share the same Sunday School and other classes with young men, and are only segregated during priesthood meetings. Adult women are members of the Relief Society Organization. Children are selected as presiding members of their Sunday school classes and other organizations.

Above the ward is the stake, which consists of a number of wards, and is presided over by a Stake President, two counselors, a Relief Society President and so on. Each stake is a self-contained entity and takes direction directly from the President of the Church or the Twelve Apostles. As disappointing as it may be to conspiracy theorists and detractors of the

Church, the entire purpose of the organization of the Church is the spiritual and temporal care of its members. Priesthood meetings usually revolve around such mundane issues as a lesson about the life of Jesus, one of the prophets or virtues such as honesty, forgiveness and charity. There are also assignments for member assistance projects, the singing of songs and the ever-present jokes and theories as to why the ward's sports teams can't seem to win any games.

Not being a member of any Society of Freemasons, the author must profess ignorance beyond what is common knowledge as to the organizational structure of the Freemasons the purpose and the philosophy of the Freemasons. What is common knowledge is that the Masons are divided into lodges. They practice a form of self-imposed general segregation for blacks and whites. Women are not allowed to be members, although they have, in recent years, been given charters to form their own lodges in Europe and the United States. The head of the lodge is known as the Grand Mason and usually holds the order of the 32nd or 33rd degree, or Master Mason. According to the Freemasons themselves, Freemason lodges are not under any national or international authority. Their stated purpose is the work of charity, and as they say, "we can make good men better. We can't make bad men good." Freemasons of the Scottish Rite Order of Freemasonry accept members of all faiths, while other orders are Christian in their orientation. Since we have already covered the history of the Freemasons in detail in the previous chapters, let us continue with the relationship between the LDS Church and Freemasonry.

Joseph Smith and the Freemasons: the William Morgan connection

Some ill-informed detractors of the LDS Church cite Joseph Smith's relationship with Captain William Morgan, who, as we have seen, many believe to have been killed by the Freemasons in 1826 for publishing, or at least threatening to publish, the secrets of the Freemasons. These detractors use Joseph Smith's relationship with Morgan, and Captain Morgan's subsequent disappearance, for the repeated condemnations of secret societies throughout the Book of Mormon. Although amusing, these accusations are absurd once the facts are examined more closely.

There is no evidence whatsoever that Joseph Smith ever knew Captain William Morgan. Furthermore, Joseph Smith Sr., Joseph Smith's own father, was a Master Mason and a member of Lodge number 23 of Canandaigua New York. Joseph Smith's older brother Hyrum, who died with him in Carthage, Illinois, was a member of the Mount Moriah Lodge number 112 in Palmyra, New York. Joseph Smith Jr., having been raised in a Masonic family, at no time ever spoke publicly about the Freemasons in a negative context. At the time of Morgan's disappearance, Joseph Smith was not in possession of the Golden Plates from which he transcribed the Book of Mormon, though, according to his own testimony, he had been made aware of their location near the hill Cumorah. The only connection between William Morgan and Joseph Smith was the fact the Smith married Morgan's widow, Lucinda, many years after his disappearance. At her behest, Captain Morgan was the first baptism for the dead that was performed by the LDS Church in the Temple in Kirtland, Ohio.

So, with the misguided theories of a relationship between Joseph Smith, Jr. and the mysteriously vanished Captain William Morgan being nothing more than a testament to the fact that people will say anything to discredit Joseph Smith, while still others will be more than willing to believe them, the question still remains; what actually happened between the LDS Church and the Freemasons? More particularly, what happened between Joseph Smith and the Freemasons? And finally, who was responsible for Joseph Smith's assassination?

Joseph Smith, the "Mormons" and the Freemasons; a match made in heaven?

The formal relationship between Freemasons and the early LDS Church was, besides the fact that Joseph Smith's family were upstanding Freemasons, based on the simple fact that many of the early converts to the Church were already practicing Freemasons themselves. Church leader John C. Bennett, who used his Masonic ties in the Illinois State Legislature to influence the introduction of a town charter with broad powers delegated to the Saints, was also a practicing Freemason. Other prominent LDS Freemasons became adamant that Joseph Smith and Sydney Rigdon join the Society in 1840. Furthermore, the earliest missionary work done by the LDS Church was in working class communities on the eastern seaboard of the United States, where many converts were skilled carpenters, blacksmiths, wheelwrights, shipbuilders and masons, many of whom were also Freemasons. Subsequent missionary efforts in England, Ireland,

Scotland and Scandinavia attracted similar working class people with similar trades, which again included many Freemasons. The list of Freemasons who converted to the Latter-day Saint Church includes Brigham Young, Heber C. Kimball (grandfather of later LDS President Spencer W. Kimball) and many of the early church leaders.

However, in spite of the involvement of his father and his brother in Freemasonry, it wasn't until ten years after the publication of the Book of Mormon and the establishment of the Church of Jesus Christ of Latter-day Saints, at a time when the Saints were firmly lodged in Nauvoo, Illinois that Joseph Smith himself was encouraged to join the order by the Freemasons within the Church leadership. Many of them, seeing the apparent similarities between the Freemason beliefs and rituals and those of the restored Church of Jesus Christ, encouraged Joseph Smith to join the Illinois Lodge, to which he finally agreed. The Illinois Grand Master made him a "Master Mason on sight," In Joseph Smith's History of the Church, he writes in 1842:

(Tuesday, March 15) "I officiated as the grand chaplain at the installation of the Nauvoo Lodge of Freemasons, at the grove near the Temple. Grand Master Jonas, of Columbus being present, a large number of people assembled on the occasion. The day was exceedingly fine; all things were done in order, and universal satisfaction was manifested. In the evening, I received the first degree in Freemasonry in the Nauvoo Lodge, assembled in my general business office.

(Wednesday, March 16) I was with the Masonic Lodge and rose to the sublime degree.

Joseph Smith and the Church's prompt fall from Freemason "grace"

From that time in 1842, the relationship between the LDS Church and the Freemasons turned from sweet to sour. The issues at hand are complicated and hard to understand for the non-initiates of Freemasonry and non-members of the

LDS Church, but I will try to explain them in the simplest terms possible. The primary issue has to do with the subject of what are called "keys." The easiest way to understand the idea of the keys is in the scripture of Matthew where Jesus is speaking to Peter, James and John:

"And I will give unto thee the keys of the Kingdom of Heaven: and whatsoever ye shall bind on earth, shall be bound in Heaven." (Matthew 16:19)

Not being a member of the Freemasons, I do not know what importance the Freemasons place on these keys, nor how they are represented. Having never taken the LDS Temple endowments, I do not know exactly what these keys are but I am fairly sure they won't start a car or open a front door. However, for the uninitiated, the simplest explanation is that these keys are procedures or words that allow acts undertaken on earth to be recorded in worlds other than the one which we currently occupy. A person who is physically holding them, as in the case of Jesus and his disciples, can only pass them on. Author G.B. Arbaugh, in *Revelation in Mormonism* explains keys in the following way:

"Joseph preached: "The keys are certain signs and words by which the false spirits and personages may be detected from the true. Which cannot be revealed to the Elders till the Temple is completed...There are signs in heaven, earth and hell; the Elders must know them all, to be endowed with power, to finish their work and prevent imposition. The devil knows many signs, but does not know the sign of the Son of Man or Jesus." (p.191)

The issue of the keys is only important to our study when it comes to the issue of the number of keys and the specific purposes of the keys, which Joseph Smith claimed to possess. If the reader wishes to know more about them, they may simply inquire of the Freemason organization or contact the LDS Mission in their area.

The first keys were given to Joseph Smith and Oliver Cowdery on May 15, 1829, according to both Joseph Smith and Oliver Cowdery, who was then assisting Smith with the translation of the Golden Plates. According to Joseph Smith, the two prayed to the Lord regarding the issue of baptism and who had the authority to conduct it, an issue that they were then translating in the Book of Mormon. At that time, according to Oliver Cowdery "The voice of the Redeemer spake peace to us," (Joseph Smith History 1:71) and a heavenly messenger, John the Baptist, "came down clothed with glory." John the Baptist bestowed upon them the keys of the Aaronic Priesthood or, the power of repentance and baptism. (Joseph Smith History 1:69)

Later, the apostles Peter, James and John conferred upon Joseph Smith the Melchezidek (Hebrew for righteous priest) Priesthood, the same priesthood that Jesus had conferred upon them while he was on the earth. According to one of the LDS apostles, David B. Haight in an article in the LDS Ensign in November of 1980:

"On April 3, 1836, in the Kirtland Temple, the same heavenly beings that appeared to the Savior and his three apostles on the Temple Mount appeared and conferred additional priesthood authority and keys upon the Prophet Joseph Smith and Oliver Cowdery for the building up of the Church preparatory to the coming of Christ to rule and reign over the earth forever. Moses appeared and conferred the keys of the gathering of Israel. Elias restored the covenants and authority given to Abraham. Elijah appeared and restored the keys and power of turning the hearts of the children to the fathers and the fathers to the children."

So what benefit did Joseph Smith, who held all of the keys to the Kingdom of God, think his adoption of Freemasonry would have for himself and the members of his Church? In, *The Life of the Prophet Joseph*, Edward Tulledge explains it this way:

"He understood that masonry is the endless chain of brotherhood and priesthood, linking all the worlds-the heavens and the earths but he believed that this earth had lost much of its purpose, its light, its keys and its spirit, -its chief loss being the loss of revelation. For instance, his conception might be expressed in the statement that the Masonic Church on earth ought to be in constant communication with the Masonic Church in the heavens, notwithstanding its many nations, races, religions, civilizations and law-givers."

The very fact that Joseph Smith's views that the "Masonic Church" ought to maintain contact with races and civilizations that do not exist on the earth will be of extreme importance later on when we delve into the extraterrestrial phenomenon and why the Freemason organization is adamant that contact with these civilizations is only to be conducted within the realm of Freemasonry. For now, it is apparent from the chronology of subsequent events, that many of the claims made by detractors of

"Mormonism," who cite the similarities between LDS Temple rituals and Masonic rituals do not make sense. In other words, Joseph Smith received his "keys" as they are listed above in the Kirtland Temple in the year 1836, while he did not become initiated into Freemasonry until six years after that time. Other aspects of the LDS religion, concerning the foundations of the world, the nature of God and the purpose of the sun, stars and moon, which make up the Book of Abraham in the Pearl of Great Price, which also seem to share some similarities with Freemasonry, predate Joseph Smith's initiation into Freemasonry. Further, as Cecil McGavin states in *Mormons and Masonry*:

"It is a fact that Joseph Smith had in his possession the manuscript for the Book of Abraham for seven years before any of it appeared in print, yet the section which has the most to say about this subject was not printed until the very day he was admitted into Freemasonry. Furthermore, the Mormon Temple ceremony was revealed almost a year and a half before he joined the Masonic Lodge, yet he did not impart that information to his brethren until he had been a Mason for seven weeks."

Because of the institution of the Temple Ceremony and the revelation of the Book of Moses, the seemingly ideal relationship between Joseph Smith, the LDS Church and Illinois Freemasonry came to a screeching halt. The Illinois Freemasons, upon hearing the extent to which Joseph Smith, as a "sublime" member of the Society of Freemasons was adding to their ceremonies, were outraged and withdrew the membership of all lodges in Nauvoo. Freemason Arbaugh explains:

"On February 9, 1843, Joseph revealed three, "grand keys," for detecting the nature of a heavenly being, but left some keys unrevealed since he died before the temple was completed. Above seven weeks after he joined the lodge Joseph began to give instruction on the ancient order of the keys, washings, anointing, and endowments and it appears that twelve thousand Mormons went through those rites in Nauvoo. This Masonic ritual, it was explained, was revealed by an angel, and the Prophet only joined the lodge to see to what extent it had deteriorated from its Solomonic purity. Furthermore, there is best evidence for believing that Joseph taught that Masonic principles and practices operated among the gods as well as on earth. His followers were taught that there is a divine Masonry among the angels who hold the priesthood, by which they can deter those who do not belong to their order. Those who cannot give the signs correctly are supposed to be imposters."

J.H. Beadle in *Life in Utah; or the Mysteries and Crimes of Mormonism* writes:

"Some years after, however, the Mormons all became Masons, and so continued until they reached Nauvoo; there, Joseph Smith out-Masoned Solomon himself and declared that God had declared to him a great key-word, which had been lost, and that he would lead Masonry to far greater degrees, and not long after their charter was revoked by the Grand Lodge. How much of Masonry has survived in the Endowment, the writer will not pretend to say; but the Mormons are pleased to have the outside world connect the two and convey to the world that this is celestial Masonry."(p. 409)

It is more than apparent that, in the eyes of the Freemasons, Joseph Smith had overstepped his bounds. Initiating non-Freemasons in the temple ceremonies that even today Freemasons claim are their own ceremonies with some minor changes, would have violated the oath of secrecy taken by Freemasons of the Third Degree and would have warranted his death according to the Masonic Code. For the Masons, Joseph Smith's sins were further inflamed, because they believed that Smith began to classify them as followers of a corrupted Masonry, or as C.A. Larue writes in *The Foundation of Mormonism*:

"Smith denounced Masonry as an unholy institution of the Priesthood and proceeded to invent his Endowment rite which he called the true Masonry known to Seth and Solomon. He began to administer these rites in a brick store in a room he had prepared in Nauvoo."

Joseph Smith had violated his Masonic oaths, which, as we have already said, are taken with the understanding that revealing the secrets of the order is punishable by death. Shortly thereafter he understood that his time on earth had been cut short. The fourth President of the Church of Jesus Christ of Latter-day Saints, Wilford Woodruff, recalled his last meeting with Joseph Smith in the Church publication, *The Millennial Star* in 1889. President Woodruff was quoted from his address to the General

Conference of young men and women of the Church given nine years before he died:

"Before the close of this conference, there is a subject upon which I wish to bear my testimony...I am...the only one living in the flesh who was with Joseph Smith, the Prophet of God, when he gave to the Twelve Apostles their charge concerning the priesthood and the Kingdom of God; and as I myself shall soon pass away like other men, I want to leave my testimony to these Latter-day Saint(s).

"The Prophet Joseph, I am now satisfied, had a thorough presentiment that that was our last meeting we would hold together here in the flesh. We had our endowments; we had all the blessings sealed upon our heads that were ever given to the prophets or apostles on the face of the Earth. On that occasion, the Prophet Joseph rose up and said to us: "Brethren, I have desired to see this temple built. I shall never live to see it, but you will. I have sealed upon your heads all the keys of the Kingdom of God. I have sealed upon you every key, power, principle that God has revealed to me. Now, no matter where I go, or what I may do, the Kingdom rests upon you."

Chapter 20

Assassination and Masonic Machinations in Nauvoo

"You must conceal all crimes of your brother Masons...and should you be summoned as a witness against a brother Mason be always sure to shield him...It may be perjury to do this, it is true, but you're keeping your obligations."

(Ronayne: *Handbook of Masonry*, page 183)

In early 1844, Joseph Smith knew he was going to be assassinated for his crimes against Freemasonry. Throughout his life he had suffered and survived numerous vicious beatings for his claims and his beliefs. He had survived the 1838 Missouri War and the execution order given by the commander of the Missouri Militia, Sam Lucas. He had survived months of incarceration in a Missouri jail with no charges brought against him and no trial. In spite of his apparent good fortune or luck, Joseph Smith knew that once it was commonly perceived that he had revealed any of the secrets associated with Freemasonry that the very devil himself would not rest until his soul was removed from the earth. That is a simple fact. Given that he was not ill, and that, over the course of his life, he had accumulated many, many enemies, the awareness of his own impending doom would not count as a prophecy or a revelation. He had crossed the Freemasons and they would kill him for it. Thanks to the power and influence of the Freemasons, even Joseph Smith's death, like his life, was to be embroiled in lies and slander that remain to this day.

The Prophet, the Mayor, the General and the Candidate for President

To look at the particular details of the assassination of Joseph Smith without considering the overall picture of events that were taking place in Nauvoo, Illinois in the early 1840's, would leave the reader open to the same half-truths and lies that have surrounded Smiths's assassination ever since. Previously, we discussed the events surrounding the "Mormon War" in Missouri in 1837-38 and the migration west to the Salt Lake Valley following the assassination of Joseph Smith.

If the reader will recall, the Latter-day Saints moved to Nauvoo, Illinois fleeing the "Extermination Order" issued by Governor Boggs of Missouri and the subsequent violence and vigilante mobs that the order had encouraged. In the town of Nauvoo, they began to rebuild their lives, as well as a community in which they could worship as they were guaranteed by the Constitution of the United States. In his book, *Nauvoo*, Robert Bruce Flanders describes the general feeling about the Saints as they came to settle on the banks of the Missouri River:

"At first the Mormons were welcomed in Illinois, but the rapid growth of Nauvoo and of the Church, the sizable Nauvoo Legion, the unusual independence of the Nauvoo government, Mormon participation in Illinois politics, and Smith's candidacy for President of the United States, considered together with the aggressive, energetic, strident qualities which seemed to pervade Mormonism, all tended to leave an unquiet wake among their "gentile" neighbors. The Mormons were to use their own description, "a peculiar people," and not surprisingly aroused antagonism on a local, then regional, and finally on a national scale."

Furthermore, according to the *Encyclopedia of Mormonism*, the rapid growth in the population of Nauvoo, led to animosity as politicians in the state legislature vied for the "Mormon" vote:

"Nauvoo in 1844, gathering place for the Saints on the Mississippi River, contained elements of both greatness and dissension. Almost overnight, it grew from a village of religious refugees and new converts to the point where it rivaled Chicago as the largest city in Illinois. With

Democrats and Whigs both vying for the Mormon vote, Nauvoo was granted one of the most liberal city charters in the state, an independent military force, and a strong judicial system (see Nauvoo Charter). However, as in Missouri during the 1830s, natural rivalry with older citizens in neighboring towns like Carthage (the county seat) and Warsaw (the next largest port city) turned to jealousy and hatred as Nauvoo's economic and political power grew."

Due to continued fear of persecution of the Saints, Joseph Smith announced his candidacy for United States President stating in February of 1844:

"I would not have suffered my name to have been used by my friends on anywise as President of the United States, or candidate for that office, if I and my friends could have had the privilege of enjoying our religious and civil rights as American citizens, even those rights which the Constitution guarantees unto all her citizens alike. But this as a people we have been denied from the beginning. Persecution has rolled upon our heads from time to time, from portions of the United States, like peals of thunder, because of our religion; and no portion of this Government as yet has stepped forward for our relief. And in view of these things, I feel it to be my right and privilege to obtain what influence and power I can, lawfully, in the United States, for the protection of injured innocence" (*History of the Church,* 6:210-11)

Because of their treatment in Missouri and, what looked to be a renewed campaign of violence that would soon follow them to Illinois, Smith and other leaders in the Church had petitioned their representatives at the state and national levels with little or no effect. Arnold K. Garr, in a speech given at the Brigham Young University Campus tells the story of the events leading up to Joseph Smith's candidacy for President:

"Joseph's commitment to political work came out of the persecutions the members of The Church of Jesus Christ of Latter-day Saints experienced in Missouri. While confined in Liberty Jail in 1839, Joseph received a revelation that commanded him to take accounts of the persecution and suffering and "present them to the heads of government." In October, Joseph Smith, Sidney Rigdon, Elias Higbee and Porter Rockwell left Illinois to present petitions to the senators, representatives and the president. Rigdon became ill and didn't continue on the way. Joseph and Higbee went to the White House unannounced with letters of recommendation and met with President Martin Van Buren, who, treated them cruelly at first, but who ended by saying that he would reconsider their situation.

"For the next few months, Joseph met with members of Congress. He presented 491 petitions from members of the LDS Church for redress. The petitions ended up in the Judiciary Committee but never made it out to the floor of Congress. Joseph met a second time with Van Buren (although there is some confusion among historians about when this meeting took place). At this meeting, Van Buren told Joseph, "Your cause is just, but I cannot help you. If I help you I will lose the vote of the state of Missouri." This just infuriated Joseph Smith. On the way back to Illinois, Joseph Smith campaigned against Van Buren and predicted that Van Buren would never be elected to an office of trust ever again. That prediction came true, despite Van Buren being favored to win re-election.

"The motivation of going to Washington was to get redress for wrongs and to prevent future wrongs. Back in Illinois, Joseph worked with John C. Bennett to get a charter passed by the Illinois legislature to govern Nauvoo that would include some protection. The Nauvoo charter allowed the city to pass any laws that did not conflict with the U.S. Constitution or the laws of Illinois. It allowed for the creation of the Nauvoo Legion, which became the second largest military organization in the United States (second only to the U.S. Army). It created the University of Nauvoo. It also granted extensive judicial powers." (Garr)

The powers that had been granted by the Illinois Legislature, which basically allowed the Latter-day Saint community the right to defend itself against the vigilantes and mob incursions from inside and outside Illinois, was, ironically, to lead ultimately to the arrest and martyrdom of its leader. Notwithstanding the threats the Latter-day Saint community felt as growing hostility and violence from outside of the community, those same external forces were creating hostile influences and dissension from within the community as well. The catalyst was the issue of polygamy, with had been instituted by Smith upon the arrival of the Saints in Nauvoo. Polygamy or plural marriage was not popular with some of the Saints. It was the antagonism caused by the issue, along with the power that Smith held as commander of the Nauvoo Legion, President of the Church and Mayor of Nauvoo that some individual members saw as a despotic takeover of the Latter-day Saint Church.

William Law and the Nauvoo Expositor

Using the institution of plural marriage, which was highly unpopular outside of the Church as its battle cry, William Law, along with a group of like-minded Nauvoo businessmen, who were receiving encouragement and aid from outside of the community, went on the offensive. Law, who had been appointed to the First Presidency of the Church by Joseph Smith, accused Smith of trying to seduce his wife and coerce her into marrying him (Smith) while still maintaining her marriage to Law. Law was soon removed from his position in the First Presidency. William Law then began his now infamous publishing enterprise the newspaper entitled *The Nauvoo Expositor*.

In the *Expositor's* one and only edition, Law accused Smith of being a fallen prophet because of his introduction of polygamy, that his role as Mayor and head of the Church gave him too much power and, most inflammatory of all, Smith was using his position to coerce or force young women into plural marriages with himself. The majority of the content of the one and only issue of the *Nauvoo Expositor* constituted a personal attack on Joseph Smith. The writers of the paper railed against Joseph Smith on the issue of polygamy (specifically Smith's own), his accumulation of power and the business dealings of both he and his associates.

Along with the libelous claims that were printed, there were two "resolutions" published in the paper which would have caused immediate concern for the safety of the Saints. Specifically, in the recommendation and justification of vigilantism and mob violence, as well as the appearance that hostile outside influences appeared to be seeking to gain some kind of sympathy within Illinois for the disaster and the bloodshed in Missouri six years prior. The "Extermination Order" issued by the Missouri Governor was still in effect for which numerous arrest warrants for Joseph Smith had been issued. Up to that time, Smith and the town council had avoided these warrants, which, as subsequent actions would show, would have led to his murder, by demanding that all warrants be presented to the town council prior to their execution.

"Resolved 4th, That the hostile spirit and conduct manifested by Joseph Smith, and many of his associates towards Missouri and others inimical to his purposes, are decidedly at variance with the true spirit of Christianity, and should not be encouraged by any people, much less by those professing to be the ministers of the gospel of peace."

"Resolved 5th, that while we disapprobate mallicious persecutions and prosecutions, we hold that all church members are alike amenable to the laws of the land; and that we further discountenance any chicanery to screen them from the just demands of the same."

(*Nauvoo Expositor* June 8, 1844)

The reaction on the part of the Nauvoo Town council was to call a special meeting on the 9th of June, where two days of deliberations were undertaken in order to decide the fate of the newspaper. The council finally came to the conclusion that the paper was libelous and a "public nuisance." The paper therefore merited destruction according to Blackstone's legal canon. Mayor Joseph Smith made an entry into the minutes of the meeting, stating he "...would rather die tomorrow and have the thing smashed, than live and have it go on, for it was exciting the spirit of mobocracy among the people, and bringing death and destruction upon us."

Subsequently, the town Marshal was ordered to destroy the press. The Marshal complied and reported that the destruction of the press (it was smashed and thrown into the street) was carried out in a "peaceable manner," while Charles A. Foster, a co-owner, of the ill-fated *Expositor* claimed the deed was carried out by "hundreds of minions," who damaged the building considerably in their eagerness to destroy the printing press. The considerable damage was debatable since the building, according to local inhabitants, was used for years afterwards.

In a letter to Illinois Governor, Thomas Ford, Smith announced the opinions of the Nauvoo Town Council and explained their actions.

"In the investigation it appeared evident to the council that the proprietors were a set of unprincipled men, lawless, debouchees, counterfeiters, Bogus Makers, gamblers, peace disturbers, and that the grand object of said proprietors was to destroy our constitutional rights and chartered privileges; to overthrow all good and wholesome regulations in society; to strengthen themselves against the municipality; to fortify themselves against the church of which I am a member, and destroy all our religious rights and privileges, by libels, slanders, falsehoods, perjury & sticking at no corruption to accomplish their hellish purposes. and that said paper of itself was libelous of the deepest dye, and very injurious as a vehicle of defamation,—tending to corrupt the morals, and disturb the peace, tranquillity and happiness of the whole community, and especially that of Nauvoo."

Letter or no letter, as the word of the destruction of the printing press spread throughout the state of Illinois, the hostility towards the Latter-day Saint community at Nauvoo began to reach a boiling point. Threats from outside communities like Warsaw and Carthage began to reach the city. Thanks to the claims of co-editor Charles A. Foster, calls were made for Mayor Joseph Smith to be charged with inciting a riot and treason. In the *Warsaw Signal*, Editor Thomas C. Sharp wrote in an editorial:

"War and extermination is inevitable! Citizens ARISE, ONE and ALL!!!—Can you stand by, and suffer such INFERNAL DEVILS! To ROB men of their property and RIGHTS, without avenging them. We have no time for comment, every man will make his own. LET IT BE MADE WITH POWDER AND BALL!!!" (*Warsaw Signal*, June 12, 1844, p. 2.)

In light of such threats, Smith as mayor and commander of the town's forces, declared martial law and called out the Nauvoo Legion. Meanwhile, forces hostile to Smith and the LDS community filed charges against both Joseph and Hyrum Smith for inciting a riot. Subsequently, the brothers appeared in Nauvoo to answer the charges before a tribunal and were released. Later, they appeared in

Nauvoo before a non-LDS judge and were fully exonerated of the charges. A few days later however, Illinois Governor Thomas Ford, either through threats of mob violence or political pressure, insisted Joseph and Hyrum stand trial in Carthage, the county seat, where he guaranteed their safety. Joseph and Hyrum, understanding that they would never return from Carthage alive, initially fled West across the Mississippi. Their relatives that no harm would come to them convinced them, and so, they returned to Nauvoo and then ventured to Carthage to face the charges.

Treachery in Carthage

Once they reached Carthage, the Smiths found that they were no longer being charged solely with inciting a riot. A new charge had been filed against Joseph Smith, Commander of the Nauvoo Legion and Mayor of Nauvoo. The Smith brothers discovered upon their appearance in the Carthage court they were both to be tried for "treason" because Joseph had declared martial law. They were placed under arrest and moved to the Carthage jail, where, because of the heat, and the fear of violence from the mob, the jail keeper and his wife allowed them to be housed in their bedroom on the second floor.

The Illinois militia was on hand, suspiciously, according to one account published in modern times, "...in anticipation that such a warrant (for the arrest of Joseph and Hyrum) could not be served peaceably." Word was sent to Nauvoo, and the Nauvoo legion was put on alert." Since the Carthage militia was under the direct authority of the political leadership of Illinois, specifically Governor Ford, it is still a remarkable fact that they chose to assemble of their own volition and without orders. However, even more remarkable was the fact that Governor Ford chose to dismiss all but the most hostile elements of the militia while he himself, left the prisoners guarded by their worst enemies as he left Carthage for Nauvoo. According to Elder John Taylor, who was with the Smith brothers in the room that sultry afternoon and, who was shot five times during the attack that resulted in Hyrum and Joseph's death:

"The report of the governor having gone to Nauvoo without taking the prisoners along with him caused very unpleasant feelings, as we were apprised that we were left to the tender mercies of the

Carthage Greys, a company strictly mobocratic, and whom we knew to be our most deadly enemies; and their captain, Esquire (Robert F.) Smith, was a most unprincipled villain. Besides this, all the mob forces, comprising the governor's troops, were dismissed, with the exception of one or two companies, which the governor took with him to Nauvoo. The great part of the mob was liberated, the remainder was our guard."

In other words, the majority of the militia was dismissed to do as they pleased. As we have previously discussed, the Prophet Joseph Smith was thoroughly aware of the consequences and the fate that awaited him. He ventured to Carthage in the summer of 1844 knowing that most likely, he would not return. Like Jesus Christ, whose gospel he worked so hard to live and promote, he surrendered himself to the law and, like Jesus, was arrested on false charges, and was martyred as a testament to all, whether Latter-day Saint or not, that the works he had accomplished and the organization that he had founded at the behest of God the Father and Jesus Christ, was something that he could never deny. The basic truths of the gospel and the work that had to be accomplished before the end of this dispensation, or period of earth history, were more important to Joseph Smith than the brief existence of his own life. For many of us, who do not see a day-to-day connection with what we do in our lives and the overall picture of the universe, what Joseph Smith did was courageous and was above and beyond what many of us would consider ourselves capable. However, Joseph Smith, simply said, "I am going like a lamb to the slaughter; but I am calm as a summer's morning; I have a conscience void of offense towards God, and towards all men. I shall die innocent, and it shall yet be said of me — he was murdered in cold blood."

Assassination and cover-up; Freemason style

So, who really assassinated Joseph Smith? The answer to who was responsible is as simple as examining what happened in the aftermath of his death. Many lies have been formulated to cover up the shameful deeds of the cowards who assassinated Joseph Smith and his brother Hyrum while they were imprisoned in the Carthage Jail. Joseph Smith's own words, "murdered in cold blood," never made it into the "approved" history books. As we have seen in the cases of Morgan and Calvi, it was not just the lackeys who carried out the deed that ultimately escaped justice. The men sitting in high places that provided the setting and guaranteed the safety of the perpetrators were as much to blame for the infamous crime. Unfortunately, as in the previously discussed cases, those who were responsible, as well as those who were responsible for the orders to carry it out, would use the cover of Freemasonry to ensure that they would never be found guilty of the slaying of the Latter-day Saint Prophet.

No lie or half-truth can cover up the fact that Joseph Smith and his brother Hyrum were murdered inside a jail that was surrounded by a detachment of the Illinois State Militia. No lie or half-truth can cover up the fact that somehow a mob managed to get past the militia and the two jailhouse "guards." No one can deny the fact that the mob rushed unopposed to the second floor and began firing into the room while outside, the militia stood idly by until they saw an opportunity to put a bullet into the back of Hyrum Smith. Joseph, knowing there were Freemasons in the mob, either asked for their assistance, or, pointed out to all who were present, who his murderers were. In the few seconds before he was dispatched, with rounds of bullets from the mob striking him in the back and the militia firing from below, Joseph Smith cried out. "Oh Lord my God…" the beginning words of the Masonic distress call "…is there no help for a widow's son?"

The suspects

Who really killed the Prophet Joseph Smith? There were plenty of people who wanted to be rid of both him and the "Mormons" for good. First, there were the Missourians, who had already fought a running gun battle and who, with the help of the state militia, had defeated the "Mormons" quite handily. However, the execution order given by Major General Sam Lucas to kill Joseph Smith and the other church leaders had never been carried out. Joseph had spent months underground in a cell but with no charges ever brought forward and no hope of release, had finally managed to escape Missouri "justice."

Then of course, there was the assassination attempt against the man who had issued the Missouri Extermination Order. In 1842, as Lilburn Boggs sat in his chair in his living room, a blast of buckshot fired from his shotgun outside of his window, entered his face and chest. He almost died, but later recovered. Many, even to this day, suspected Joseph Smith's gun fighting bodyguard, Porter Rockwell of the deed, but, after being held for a year, Rockwell was released for lack of evidence. Certainly Governor Boggs and the good people of the State of Missouri had a motive to kill Joseph Smith.

There was also the irate publisher of the single edition *Nauvoo Expositor*, William Law, whose bitter hatred for Smith would follow him to the grave. William Law had been one of many Latter-day Saints who, seeing the changes in the Church, felt that Joseph Smith was taking it in the wrong direction. Law had not only lost his wife to Joseph Smith, but his printing press as well. There are many who claim that William Law was in the mob that stormed the jail that day, but there was never enough proof to convict him of complicity.

Next, there were the pro-slavery landowners in the North and South, who saw Smith's Presidential candidacy and the Latter-day Saint views on slavery as a threat to the peace and stability of the Union. Joseph Smith had presented a plan to eliminate slavery by 1850. According to Smith's plan, the government would purchase the slaves from their owners by using money from the sale of public land. (Garr)

Then, there were the various "Christian" churches with their preachers and evangelists who saw the "Mormons" with their "gold bible" as a threat to their livelihoods and their worldviews. To highlight this reality, one of the defendants in the subsequent murder trial was a Baptist preacher named "Colonel" Levi Williams. Others, like Williams, instigated their poorly educated congregations with wild tales of "Joe Smith" and the "Mormons" to hatred and sometimes, even murder. Along the same lines, we should also consider the less enlightened elements of the civil populations of Missouri and Illinois, who simply hated the Mormons as they hated Negroes, Jews, Catholics and anyone else who was "different."

Finally, there were the Freemasons, who felt that Joseph Smith had betrayed their oaths, insulted them and claimed to have revelations much greater than their own, which he had passed on to non-Freemason members of the Church in temple endowment ceremonies. The departure of Governor Thomas Ford from Carthage to Nauvoo after Governor Ford had agreed to meet with Smith the following day, left him open to suspicion. According to J.H Beadle in his book, *Life in Utah: Or the Mysteries and the Crimes of Mormonism,* Ford explains:

"Upon hearing of the assassination of the Smiths, I was sensible my command was at an end; that my destruction was meditated, as well as that of the Mormons; and that I could not reasonably confide longer in one party or the other. I am convinced that it was the expectation that the Mormons would assassinate me, on the supposition that I had planned the murder of the Smiths. Hence the conspirators committed their act while I was at Nauvoo." (112)

The Governor and his "alibi"

Governor Ford's actions were, to put it mildly, highly suspect from the beginning. From the time that Joseph and Hyrum, who had already been exonerated of the charge of inciting a riot, were ordered by the Governor that they must appear in again Carthage to face the same charge, to the time Ford left the Saint's worst enemies, the "Carthage Greys" outside of the jail to guard them, his actions are highly suspect. The fact that Governor Ford had Joseph Smith (and Hyrum) arrested for the laughable charge of treason because Smith had done his duty and declared martial law in response to outside threats of violence is also suspicious. Had Joseph Smith's epitaph in the national newspapers already been planted labeling Smith as a "traitor" once Ford's betrayal was complete?

After Joseph, Hyrum and the other members of the Nauvoo City Council had posted bail for their first charge and volunteered to stay in Carthage in order to meet with him the next day, Governor Ford, in spite of his promise to guarantee the Smith's safety, promptly left town. He traveled to Nauvoo, "to explain to the Mormons the severity of the charges against the Smiths, and to encourage them (the Saints) not to seek retaliation." Was it retaliation for a trumped up charge that would have taken a simple reading of the Nauvoo Charter, or the editorial from Sharp's *Warsaw Gazette* to dismiss? That doesn't seem likely. Considering subsequent events whereby the Illinois Militia allowed a "darkened face" mob to enter the jail and then open fire on the prisoners they were supposed to protect, the role of the Illinois Militia would logically be considered not suspect, but criminally negligent, if not just criminal. And what about Governor Ford? A skeptical person may even say that Governor Ford was looking for the perfect alibi. However, his alibi was far from perfect. For his benefit, let us just example the two possible scenarios that took place on June 27th, 1844.

In the first scenario, Governor Ford, as he claims, did not know that the mob would storm the jail and kill Joseph Smith that afternoon. So, there was no need for the governor to travel to Nauvoo surrounded by two companies of militia to protect him. He had assured Joseph and Hyrum that he would guarantee their safety. So, there was no need for the Governor to go to Nauvoo at all. If Governor Ford didn't know what was going to happen, considering the very real possibility of violence, the best place for Governor Ford to be, to ensure his own integrity and the integrity of his troops, as well as the welfare of his prisoners whose safety he had guaranteed, was in command of the situation in Carthage. Why would he feel the need to go to Nauvoo? Was it to tell the people there the news about the new "surprise" charge of treason? People had been coming and going from Smith's cell all day long. They would have explained to the people of Nauvoo what had happened.

On the other hand, let us assume the Governor did know that the mob was going to attack the jail. Where is the one place Governor Ford would not want to be if he had no intention of preventing what he knew was going to happen? It stands to reason that the last place he would want to be, like a mafia boss who has called in a hit, was at the scene of the murder where he could be implicated, or at the very least, have suspicions raised that would be hard to quell. So, where would be the best place if you knew that someone was going to be killed, and you didn't want to be implicated?

The best place to be in terms of an alibi is at the victim's house demonstrating your concern for the person about to be murdered. To ensure your own safety, in the very likely case you are considered to be an accomplice by the victim's relatives and loved ones, it doesn't hurt to have a hundred or so armed troops to protect you. Unfortunately, Governor Ford, nor any other high ranking official, was ever called to stand trial for the assassination of a Presidential Candidate, the Commander of the second largest military force outside of the US Army, the Mayor of Nauvoo and the leader and Prophet of the Church of Jesus Christ of Latter-day Saints.

The crime was, in fact, on equal footing with the assassination of Presidential Candidate Bobby Kennedy and Dr. Martin Luther King and represented one of the darkest days in the history of a country, which guarantees the right to worship as one pleases. Regardless of what a person thinks about the role Governor Ford played in the cold-blooded murder of Joseph Smith and his brother Hyrum, the resulting trials for the people indicted in the murders, to include their immediate admission into or advancement in the Masonic Lodges of Warsaw, Illinois in order to protect them from prosecution in a courtroom where no "Mormons" were allowed to sit in the jury, provides as much or more proof as to who was responsible for the murders of Joseph and Hyrum Smith as any eyewitness testimony.

Mock justice and Freemason protection in Illinois

The five men indicted for the murder were, Colonel Levi Williams, Jacob C. Davis, Captain Mark Aldrich, Thomas C. Sharp and William N. Grover. Cecil McGavin in *Mormonism and Masonry* writes:

"Nine men were indicted for the murder, four of whom figured prominently in the lodge at Warsaw. Upon these four culprits, the censorship of the lodge rested, yet their manner in treating this case was very different from their prejudiced treatment of the Nauvoo brethren (LDS Masons)...Aldrich had been a Mason for many years, while the other three seem to have been taken into the lodge at Warsaw after the Martyrdom or a short time before as a means of protecting them."(19)"

According to McGavin, the men indicted for the murders and their immediate inclusion into the Warsaw Lodge, did, in fact, raise a few eyebrows with the Grand Lodge of Illinois, especially after the brothers of the lodge, "elected Mark Aldrich who was holding the humble position of steward to the high office of Worshipful Master at the first opportunity at the same time he was under indictment for the murder of the Mormon leaders." (22) The acceptance of the petitions of Colonel Levi Williams and Jacob C. Davis to join the Warsaw Lodge while under indictment speaks volumes about the confidence the Freemasons felt in protecting their own from the Illinois justice system. John Montague answered the inquiry of the Grand Lodge. His reply to the Grand Lodge was this:

Author's note: The entire letter is included for the simple reason that its contents are hard to believe.

"Brother Lusk:-Sir, your letter of the 5th, inst., referring me to resolutions passed by the Grand Lodge, at the last regular communication-also making inquiry concerning the initiation of certain individuals into the lodge who were, at the time under indictment, duly received. At a regular meeting of the Lodge on 9th inst., I laid your letter before the Lodge for their consideration. On motion of Bro. C. Hay, the lodge requested me to answer that part of your letter making inquiry in relation to initiating, passing, and raising certain individuals under indictment. The facts were as follows:

At a regular meeting of the Lodge on 23 Sept. 1844, the petition of J.C. Davis was received, read, filed and ordered to lie over until the next regular meeting of the Lodge. Bro. Stephens and Aldrich (author's note: Aldrich was also under indictment) were appointed to a committee to inquire into the character and standing of the applicant. At a regular meeting of the lodge on the 21st of Oct. 1844, the committee reported favorable. On motion, the ballot was taken and found clear. On motion, Mr. Davis was introduced and initiated. At a regular meeting of the lodge on 4th Nov., 1844, at the request of Bro. Davis, to be passed on to the second degree-on motion, the ballot was taken and found clear. On motion, he was introduced and passed. At a regular meeting on the 18th of Nov.-on motion, he was introduced and raised to the sublime degree of Master Mason.

At a regular meeting of the lodge on 18th Nov., 1844, the petitions of T.C. Sharp and Levi Williams (both under indictment) were received, read, filed and ordered to lie over until the next regular meeting of the Lodge. Bros. Aldrich and Stephens were appointed a committee to inquire into the standing of the applicants. At a regular meeting of the lodge on the 16th of Dec., 1844, the ballots were taken separately for Messrs. Sharp and Williams and found clear. On motion, Mr. Williams was introduced and initiated. At an adjourned meeting of the lodge Feb. 18th., 1845, the ballot was taken to raise

Bro. Williams to the degree of Master Mason and found clear. And, at a regular meeting of the lodge on the 17th of March, 1845, on motion, Bro. Williams was introduced and raised to the sublime degree of Master Mason, agreeable to ancient form.

At a regular meeting of the lodge on the 16th of Dec., 1844, the ballot was taken to initiate Mr. Sharp, and found clear. On motion, he was introduced and initiated. At an adjourned meeting of the lodge on the 6th Jan., 1845, on motion, the ballot was to pass Bro. Sharp and found clear. At an adjourned meeting of the lodge on 9th Jan., 1845, on motion, Bro. Sharp was introduced and passed to the second degree.

We believed at the time we balloted for the candidates to be passed and raised, at adjourned meetings, we were not violating any of the ancient landmarks of the institution. We see the Grand Lodge recommend a different course. We are not disposed to violate any regulation of the Grand Lodge by which a subordinate lodge shall be governed.

At the time said petitions were presented, the fact of these individuals being under indictment for the murder of Joseph and Hyrum Smith, was referred to, and the question of the propriety of their admission fully discussed. It was admitted that those individuals were worthy members of society, and respected by their fellow citizens-no objection to their initiation therefore existed, except the fact of their afore-mentioned pending indictment. In relation to the matter, it was argued that an indictment was no evidence of a crime; in this instance, particularly, it was publicly known that the indictments against said applicants had been procured by the testimony of perjured witnesses who had been suborned by the Mormons, for the purpose of procuring indictments against prominent men of the country who had become obnoxious to them. The standing of those individuals in community had not been at all impaired by the indictment; on the contrary, they were regarded with even greater consideration than before, from the fact that they had been particularly selected as the victims of Mormon vengeance. The community regarded the proceedings against them as a persecution, rather than a prosecution, and the event of the final trial proved the correctness of the conclusion. Under these circumstances, it could not be considered that those individuals should be regarded in the light that persons ordinarily are, who are arraigned for a crime-besides this, Bro. Aldrich has held an honorable standing in the Fraternity for upwards of twenty years, was also under indictment for the same offense. There would therefore seem to be as equally good grounds for his suspension, as for rejecting the petitions of the individuals referred to. But to do this when there was no evidence of his guilt, would be to reverse the fundamental principle of the Order, and cast off a brother because he was in trouble. The action of the lodge in the case referred to, was not without due deliberation. If we have erred, we were not aware we were infringing any of the usages or regulations of our ancient and honorable Order. Yet, if we have erred, we do not dispose to shrink from any responsibility that may rest on our lodge, touching the subject under consideration. We hope the above will prove satisfactory to yourself and the most Worshipful Grand Master.

Very respectfully,

John Montague

Speaking to the "usages of our ancient and honorable order," three of the indicted initiates did not hide their deeds, or their feelings from the public, or as McGavin states:

"When Thomas C. Sharp, Jacob C. Davis, and Levi Williams fled from Carthage, they boasted that they had, "finished the leading men of the Mormon Church." Sharp published an account of the tragedy in the Warsaw Signal, again boasting that "If my influence helped to produce the state of feelings that resulted in the death of Joe Smith, why I am, in common with some hundred others guilty of not murder, but extra-judicial execution."

There were a number of options open to the Warsaw lodge when it came to the consideration of the petitions of the men under indictment for murder, the most politically expedient being to let the trial run its due course and then, upon their acquittals, initiate the men. The fact that they were initiated and then raised to various degrees within months of their initiations, along with John Montague's reply to the inquiry of the Grand lodge, that the indicted had achieved an even greater status in the community because the Mormons suspected them of being ringleaders in the murders, speaks volumes when it comes to the issue of what kind of justice the Smith family and the LDS Church could expect to receive in Illinois. Their actions also bear witness to the Warsaw lodge's own contempt for the due process of law and their faith in their ability as part of the Freemason Brotherhood to manipulate the Illinois legal system. The question then arises, were the men initiated in order to ensure their protection, or as a Cain-like reward for their complicity in the murder of two innocent men? No one will ever know the truth except the men of the Warsaw lodge.

When it came to the trial of newspaper editor, Thomas C. Sharp, Baptist preacher Colonel Levi Williams, Captain Mark Aldrich and Jacob C. Davis, only three witnesses came forth to testify against the defendants. According to McGavin in *Mormons and Freemasonry*:

> "It is said that the counsel for the defense argued that if the prisoners were guilty of murder, that he was also guilty; that it was the public opinion that the Smiths ought to be killed, and public opinion made the law; consequently it was not murder to kill them (20-21)."

"Of the many witnesses examined, nothing was said against the accused except by three persons. Two of them had joined the Mormon Church, hence their testimonies were said to be contradictory. The third witness was a girl named Eliza Jane Graham, who was a waitress at the Warsaw House. She had assisted in feeding the hungry mob when they fled to that place after the murder. She told the jury what the men said as they feasted, how they boasted of their foul deeds of bloodshed, and driven the Mormons from the state. In a very dramatic manner she impersonated some of the leaders of the gang, gesticulating wildly as she mimicked the angry mob (20)."

The court itself discredited the one witness who was allowed to testify that the accused had participated in the murders. According to McGavin:

> "The Jury was cautioned to disregard Miss Graham's testimony because her nervous and sensitive character had been powerfully influenced by the horrible tales of slaughter, having brooded constantly upon the death of the Mormons, she had come at last to

regard her own fancies as positive occurrences. Her testimony was interpreted to the jury as nothing more than her insane zeal, something to be discredited."

The jury was then instructed:

"If then the jury can make any supposition consistent with the facts, by which the murder might have been committed without the agency of the defendants, it will be their duty to make that supposition, and find the defendants not guilty...Loyal to their advisors the jury returned a verdict of "not guilty."

In the Atlantic Monthly in December of 1869, Colonel John Hay wrote about the sham trial:

"The case was closed. There was not a man in the jury, in the court, in the county, that did not know the defendants had done the murder. But it was not proven, and the verdict of not guilty was right in law...The elisors presented 99 men before twelve were found ignorant enough to act as jurors (McGavin 20-22)

Along with the men who actually stood trial, there were three other men who were also indicted by the court due to the fact that Joseph Smith, using a pepperbox pistol, had wounded them in trying to defend his brother, Dr. Willard Richards, and John Taylor. Their names were William Gallaher, who suffered a bullet wound to the face, William Voras, who was shot in the shoulder and John Wills, who was shot in the arm. These men, who bore the only evidence in the way of scars for the attack, could not be found to stand trial.

Just like the cases of William Morgan two decades earlier and Roberto Calvi, thirteen decades later, the lack of evidence, a sham investigation and, in the case of the Smith's murders, the immediate protection and reward of the murderers by their inclusion into the Masonic Brotherhood of the Warsaw Freemason Lodge while they were under indictment demonstrated the will and the ability of the Freemasons to carry out the murders of any who violated their oath, no matter who that might be.

Aftermath

The LDS Church, in the spirit of Christian brotherhood, does not hold the Society of Freemasons responsible for the deaths of Joseph and Hyrum Smith. The men who committed that dark deed have long since received their rewards and the Church prefers to leave the matter closed. On the other hand, the Freemason's attitudes towards the LDS Church have changed little over the nearly two centuries that have since passed. They can best be summed up in the words of Utah Grand Mason J.M. Orr in 1878:

"We say to the priests of the Latter-day Church, you cannot enter our lodge rooms-you surrender all to an unholy priesthood. You have heretofore sacrificed the sacred obligations of our beloved Order, and we believe you would do the same again. Stand aside; we want none of you. Such a wound as you gave Masonry in Nauvoo is not easily healed, and no Latter-day Saint is, or can become a member of our order or our jurisdiction."

Freemasons good? Freemasons bad?

The deaths of Captain William Morgan, Roberto Calvi and the LDS Prophet, Nauvoo Mayor and Presidential Candidate Joseph Smith, tragic as they were, and as compelling as they are as mysteries, are not the subject of this book. The subject of this book is information, or how we get it and who controls it. Each case has the commonality of an association with the Society of Freemasons. In each instance, the murdered or vanished victim, as in the case of Morgan, broke his oath. In each instance, there was either a shoddy or non-existent investigation by the police. In each instance the men who were charged with the murder were not the men who had the power to order it and then to conceal the deed.

Finally, in each case, the facts of the case had the following in common: The murdered men were involved with the Freemasons. They swore an oath of death if they revealed secrets. They revealed or threatened to reveal secrets and subsequently were murdered. In each trial, there was little or no mention of the Society of Freemasons, except as more of an afterthought. Instead, the facts of each case were distorted and obscured by information that was completely false, misleading or irrelevant.

The documentary *Freemasonry Revealed* is an attempt to show the Society of Freemasons in a favorable light by not delving too far into the facts their most infamous deeds. The deaths of Morgan and Calvi are mentioned but the facts are vague or downplayed. Morgan is portrayed as a, "troublemaker" and a "drunkard." In the same documentary, it is stated that Roberto Calvi "siphoned 1.5 billion dollars from Vatican accounts." That is not exactly true. As we saw, Michele Sindona, the mafia money launderer, wanted money to save the Franklin Bank in the U.S. and either forced or extorted the money from Calvi and when the bank closed anyway, Sindona turned Calvi in to bank regulators in Italy. The statement that Calvi "siphoned" off money without mentioning the facts makes it appear that he was some kind of crook whose death was due to the fact that he lost money for the mafia, and who subsequently killed him. In other words, in both cases the murder of a troublemaking drunkard and a "siphoner" of 1.5 billion dollars from the mafia almost seemed justified thanks to the misinformation provided to the public.

Interestingly enough, how does the documentary, *Freemasonry Revealed* in which the Grand Master of the Washington D.C. lodge openly jokes, "We know what happened at Roswell. We know who murdered JFK," treat the murder of Joseph Smith? The same murder where the Governor of Illinois left the Latter-day Saint leader in a jail cell to be guarded by a detachment of the Latter-day Saint's worst enemies? The same murder where eighty-seven jurors were questioned and dismissed before twelve could be found that were ignorant of the case? The same murder where those indicted for the murders were accepted to, and raised up in the Warsaw, Illinois Freemason Lodge while under indictment? Interestingly enough, the documentary *Freemasonry Revealed,* doesn't mention the Freemason's most infamous killing at all, even though there was as much or more evidence of Freemason involvement than either the Morgan or the Calvi case.

In each case, the common denominator seems to be that there has been no evidence, or at least enough to get any kind of conviction. In the rationale society of a world dominated by science and reason, everything depends on evidence. From a scientific theory to a new diet, a claim without evidence is just a theory. Who handles evidence? The police handle evidence, or, in the case of the Roberto

Calvi and Joseph Smith, they mishandled or destroyed the evidence. Witnesses wound up mysteriously dead or not admitted to testify. The accused or the conspirators used a Freemason lodge to secure their deeds by an oath of death. In the case of Morgan, he was released in the middle of the night to persons "unknown" to the jailer.

It goes without saying that the misinformation provided to the public regarding Joseph Smith and the Latter-day Saint Church goes far beyond the accusations of "drunkard and troublemaker" and "siphoner of funds." The non-LDS reader can simply recall what has already been read in this book as well as the "common knowledge" people have about Latter-day Saints in order to understand how deep the misinformation campaign has been and continues to be towards both Joseph Smith and the LDS Church. As we close this chapter in old history, let us recount some of the things we have learned from the last chapter. Specifically, that there are two major organizations in the United States, and in the world for that matter, Latter-day Saints and Freemasons, who both hold firmly to the belief that there are other worlds, other dimensions and other beings that exist within our universe. One of these organizations has people in positions of power all over the world. It is possible that this same organization, with its influence within the government, corporations, banking, military, police, intelligence community and the media that is capable of either hiding evidence or creating misinformation, or a "spin" of a topic in order to keep the public ignorant of facts they wish to conceal by simply concealing the evidence and then saying, "there is no evidence."

Are the Freemasons bad? Of course they are not. The Freemasons do much good in the world and the world of today would be a lot different, if not a lot worse, if it were not for them and the accomplishments and sacrifices they have made to contribute to the betterment of mankind. Are secret societies or "societies with secrets," bad? As we have seen, they certainly can be, and what is worse, they have a basic infrastructure that dates all the way back to the time of Adam, either literally, or, in a philosophical sense, that allows, in fact obliges, members to conceal any wicked deeds of their fellow members.

In fact, Joseph Smith, and who knows how many others, were killed for revealing, among other things, information about other worlds and other beings simply because the Freemasons regard that information as their own domain, handed down from the Mystery Cults of Egypt, Mesopotamia and Greece. So, thus armed with that knowledge, let us continue on our inquiry into the world of science, the nature of matter, and the discoveries that are changing our view of the universe in the very same way Galileo changed our view of the universe five hundred years ago.

PART 4

THE EXTRATERRESTRIAL QUESTION

Chapter 21

Homo Sapiens' Science

Stark realities

In order to proceed to the next part of this book, it is unfortunately necessary that we review a few basic concepts from the field of science. I use the term "unfortunately" for two reasons. First, I am assuming that some, if not most of the readers of this book will have little or no interest in science. That is most likely due to the fact that, when we think of science, thanks to the lack of importance we have placed on public education for the last fifty years, we usually think of some nutty science teacher in a white lab coat who told jokes that nobody understood. We also had the opinion in our public school education, that science was a "hard" subject and was only taken because it was one of the requirements that was necessary to graduate.

Science was left to the "brainy" kids who had no social life. Once we "not-so-brainy" kids finished with our basic, required courses (provided we passed), we turned our back on science as fast as we turned our backs on a plate of asparagus. At least that was my experience with science, and I am assuming it was probably yours. This leads us to reason number two of why I use the term "unfortunately." The second reason I use the term "unfortunately" is because I am, unfortunately, the one who is going to try to explain science to you. If you listen closely enough, you can almost hear the sound of scientists all the way back to Sir Isaac Newton and Galileo turning over in their graves.

In the last five hundred years, and more importantly, in the last one hundred years, we have gained so much knowledge in the field of science that through our endeavors, our own science has once again arrived at what some would call a crossroads of metaphysics, or what others would call proof of what religions have been saying for most of our recorded history. Through our scientific and mathematical endeavors, what we have come to know and understand about the universe has left us on the threshold of a newer and better understanding of who we are, and more importantly, what we, as human beings are capable of achieving in the positive realms of our own intellectual abilities.

Unfortunately, we, as human beings have a hard time adjusting to new realities, and we have seen that time and time again over the course of our history. For people living in the twentieth and twenty-first centuries, it seemed like once we became comfortable with one reality, such as the atomic bomb and the Cold War, another reality soon took its place in the form of even more powerful weapons, new enemies, and the introduction of the afternoon talk show. In the 1940's, we became accustomed to war, and then we had to become accustomed to peace. In the 1950's, we had war again, but not the kind of war where we fought to win. In the last half of the twentieth century, we had to live with the Cold War and the threat of nuclear annihilation just around the corner. Suddenly, the Cold War ended and terrorists with dishtowels on their heads became the new enemy.

The Science Gap

But, as dark and bleak as the picture of the world is as it is painted for us on the nightly news, in the fields of science, unbelievable strides have been taking place. Unfortunately, you don't know about them because the network programmers are afraid you will change the channel if they try to get too cerebral during the news hour or prime time. Regardless, while we were busy watching *Gilligan's Island* and *Happy Days*, scientists were giving us a greater understanding of the human mind, the earth's climate, the universe, and even of the very processes by which we were created (or evolved) than ever before. Most people aren't aware of our breakthroughs in science and the advances we have made in understanding the laws of the universe. Well, at least not until a new prescription hits the pharmacy or a new electronic product such as a cell phone or DVD player hits the shelves of the local electronics store or, we see a new type of weapon being used in our latest war. We have been quite comfortable leaving science to the guys in white lab coats, or the people we used to call "eggheads." Since the late

1700's we have hoped that they would come up with something that would solve all of our problems for us and not destroy the world in the process. Since then science has taken the place of religion on a worldwide scale.

Not unlike religion, science has been left to the "high priests" of research who populate our universities, corporate and government research centers. Also like religion, scientists are basically kept within a circle of like-minded individuals (other scientists) and when one of them does start to speak, they do so in such a way that only other scientists seem to have any idea of what it is they are talking about. Science is also similar to religion because there are some topics that a scientist will not discuss, ever. If they do make the mistake of discussing certain forbidden topics, scientists are quickly moved into the realm of "pseudo" scientist, which is the modern day equivalent to the medieval heretic. The scientific and academic communities and their funding sources shun these unfortunate and unwise souls. Their university tenure and their careers become things of the past. Finally, the last similarity between religion and science has to do with language. Because of the gap, or rather abyss that exists between the field of science and the rest of the world, the scientist of today, whenever he or she tries to explain something to us common folk, is basically conducting the sermon, or uh, lecture, in Latin to a congregation that speaks German or English.

If you watch most of the shows that deal with scientific topics on TV, like the History, Discovery and National Geographic channels, you will notice that there is hardly any science involved in them at all. The broadcast is usually reduced to talking about some topic the writer has written into the show to appeal to the viewer who is either nine years old, or has just taken a couple of hits from his or her bong. The science we see on television is meant more to give the viewer some shocking revelation that will keep the viewer interested, along with a "dumbed-down" rudimentary explanation of the vocabulary of the subject before the viewer changes the channel. This is known as the "Whoa, man" factor and rarely leads to any real understanding of the topic. However, the History, Discovery and National Geographic channels should be given credit for at least trying.

"Global warming" for example, is discussed in relation to emissions of what are called "greenhouse" gasses, which describes a warming effect of gases such as carbon monoxide, carbon dioxide, and fluorocarbons when they combine in the upper atmosphere and keep heat from escaping from the earth. But people today are too ignorant of science to understand what those gases are, where they come from and why they are harmful to the earth's climate. They are simply called "greenhouse" gases and they are labeled "bad" as the viewer looks at some melting glaciers in order to associate the greenhouse gasses with receding ice sheets. In fact, "greenhouse" gases aren't gases one would find in a greenhouse at all, yet the public is assumed to be so ignorant that the only way they will understand the theory of global warming is to compare the earth to a greenhouse, which is evidence of another problem between science and the general public.

The term "greenhouse," which most people could understand at the time it came out in the '60's and '70's, was the place the where scientists and other people grew their weed. People back then knew greenhouses got hot inside, which of course meant better weed. But today, weed is grown outside or under lights in the basement of overpriced suburban homes in order to make the mortgage payment. If the narrator of the show doesn't explain what a greenhouse is, many people may assume the term "greenhouse gas" involves gases that are in a house painted green, which also explains the drop in sales of green paint at the nation's hardware stores. It would have been easier for the writers of these shows if our public education system had explained to us what things like carbon monoxide and carbon dioxide are in the first place.

Another problem with the failure of our education system and its ability to teach science is in the relationship between science and government, or, more specifically, in the relationship between the cost of doing science and attracting government money to continue research. The best example, as laughable, or sad, as it is, is known as the LHC, which stands for Large Hadron Collider. It is a particle accelerator that sits in the town of Cern, Switzerland on the border between France and the land of Pippy Longstocking. In order to attract money for science in the United States, a scientist today has to demonstrate how his or her research can be used to kill or spy on people in order to attract the El Dorado of science; military funding. In Europe, where they are a bit more civilized and educated,

European taxpayers justified the multi-billion dollar accelerator because scientists explained that it was a way to understand the fundamental nature of matter.

Imagine trying to get money from an American politician using terms like, "the fundamental nature of matter." Imagine a senator from a place like Texas or Arkansas trying to justify funding for that kind of research to their voters. In order for Americans to understand what is going on with the Large Hadron Collider, the scientists have to use "dumbed down" terms like, "God particle" and "Anti-matter" which sounds like a Star Wars meets Ben Hur. It wasn't always like that. There was a time, when we all liked science.

Sputnik and the Quest for Science Superiority

In 1957, when Sputnik, the first Soviet Satellite was launched into orbit, the United States and the rest of the "free world" woke up to the fact that America, and the West, well, really it was just America, had fallen behind in science education. The public schools began to revamp their science curriculum and every school kid left high school with a basic understanding of things like electricity, the solar system, the atom and magnetism. Once the United States succeeded in landing men on the moon and beat the Russians in doing so, the political will to explore even further into the realms of science and space were all but forgotten. After all, TV shows like *Star Trek* and *Lost in Space* were much more interesting and they didn't require billions in taxpayer funding. As soon as the three networks (ABC, CBS, and NBC) stopped airing Apollo Missions, Congress began to question the wisdom of the space program and subsequently began to cut the budget for the National Aeronautic and Space Administration (NASA).

In the United States, big government contracts were being awarded for weapons systems and once again, humanity relegated its intellectual endeavors towards trying to kill each other off or control each other as efficiently as possible. The military and the scientific community became married in secret projects called "black projects" using the threat of the Soviet menace to keep their research and their programs from the rest of the world. For the average American, science had gotten so far out of the realm of everyday experience that, since nobody spoke the language of science anymore, nobody cared. So, that is where we are going to begin, with the language of science.

Now, before you, the reader, begin to tune out or start skipping ahead, let me say two things. First, the arguments I will make in the following chapters of this book will be pointless to the reader who has no understanding of the fundamentals of science. Second, please be assured, my own scientific education was less than stellar, and in any science class after junior high school, I was awarded 'D' grades only out of the charity of my teachers. My high school physics teacher once explained it to me this way: "I know you don't deserve to pass, but I know you will get it, someday." Therefore, I can assure the reader that there is very little chance of me going "over your head" as I explain the fundamentals of science in a way that even a "dummy" like me can understand. Hopefully, for the benefit of my high school physics teacher, I "got it" enough to explain it to you.

Our friend, the Atom

The first fundamental that we must understand when it comes to science, is of course, the atom. Now, please understand that nobody has ever actually seen an atom because it is so darn small. The only reason we know about atoms is because of very smart people who go all the way back to the ancient Greeks. They in fact, coined the word "atom" because they theorized that it was the smallest particle that made up matter that could not be divided into any smaller parts. Scientists in the late 1700's predicted that there were such things as atoms and then conducted experiments, the results of which supported the idea that there was a very tiny structure that was the basic building block of the universe. As it would turn out, they were right and wrong at the same time.

Okay, so we have the atom, and like any machine, the atom has parts and each of those parts has certain characteristics. First of all, picture in your mind, the big, blue earth. The earth is a round body made up of stuff like dirt and water. Around the earth, there is a smaller round body called the moon. If you have a picture in your head of the earth and there is something that looks like the moon going around it, congratulations, you have made the first step in understanding the atom. To be more specific, you are imagining the hydrogen atom, which makes up the majority of the matter in the universe. In fact, hydrogen atoms make up about twenty percent of you, who are made up of seventy per-cent water, known as H2O. H2O simply means one hydrogen atom has combined with two oxygen atoms a couple of billion times to make up most of your body.

Now, let's talk about size. Imagine that you are holding an apple and standing somewhere on the face of the earth. Now, blow up that apple in your mind to equal the size of the earth. The original apple would be the size of one atom in your earth-sized apple, so we are talking really, really small. Now, go back to that picture you had of the earth and the moon and let's start assigning names to things. The earth, is what we are going to call the "**nucleus**" of the atom, and the moon, we are going to call an "**electron**." Now, in your mind, do you see the earth, or nucleus? Do you see the moon, or electron? Great! What you see when you imagine the earth and the moon going around it, is the atom. An earth (nucleus) with no moon is not an atom. It is called a **hadron**. A moon (electron) with no earth is called a **lepton**. They must be together, like the Lone Ranger and Tonto or Batman and Robin to be called an atom. Now let's continue.

Protons and Neutrons

Look at the earth again in your mind. That nucleus, as we called it, is different than the earth. Just how is it different? Well, let's start by looking at the nucleus or hadron as something else. Let's say we will think of the nucleus or hadron as a bowl of fruit, specifically a bowl of red apples and orange oranges. Now I want you to think of those apples, which we would prefer to eat before we ate the oranges (oranges involve pealing and juice flying everywhere) in our nucleus or bowl of fruit. Those apples, which we prefer to eat, are positively charged, or in scientific terms, we give them a plus. But, with a positive, we must have a negative charge to balance things out and that negative charge is in the moon, or electron floating around it. **For every apple, or positive charge, we must have an electron**. Well, at least for now. So plus in the middle and minus floating around it, which we will call a grape since the moon would crush our bowl of fruit. So we have apples (+) and grapes (-) flying around them. So that is the atom, yes? Not quite, because we forgot our oranges, which we decided we weren't that excited about, so we will call them neutral because we will only eat them when the apples are gone, or if there are a lot of napkins lying around.

So, since scientists like to speak in their own complicated language, let's make scientific names for our fruit. We will start with our apples (+) and call them **protons** because we are pro-apple, right? As we are neutral about the oranges unless of course, we run out of apples, we will call the oranges, **neutrons.** This also works out quite handily when it comes to physics, because these are the same names physicists have given to these very small particles. They have given them these names, not only because Claude and Mary were already taken, but also because they reflect the electrical charge that each particle possesses. **A proton has a positive charge, or (+) while a neutron has no charge at all.**

So, before we move on, let us see if we understand. First, there is a teensy weensy bit of matter that makes up almost everything, from our shoes, to our fingers, to the sun itself. It is called an atom. Looking at it, the atom has two rather distinct parts. The bulky middle which is called the nucleus, and the things flying around outside the atom in a moon-like orbit, called electrons. Inside the atom are two types of particles that have a mass or weight and they are different from each other because they possess either an electrically positive charge that you could connect your red jumper cable to in order to start your infinitely tiny car, and another particle that has no charge at all, which, I suppose you could connect to the black jumper cable. Around the atom are negatively charged electrons, which correspond exactly in number to the number of protons, or positive charges in the nucleus. You may have some trouble connecting the black jumper cable to these, and I will explain that in a moment. So, if you look at an atom with your tiny microscope and count eight electrons, how many protons will be in the nucleus? If you guessed seven, you need to add one more to make an equal number and possibly invest in a new calculator. Now, there are some cases when the electrons differ in number than the protons and the number of neutrons is different than the number of protons, but to keep things simple, let's just stay with our perfect atom for now.

Enter the Quark

Looking at our perfect hydrogen atom, with one proton, one neutron and one electron zipping around, are we content with our understanding of the building blocks of all that we see around us? Well, hardly. The problem is with those crazy scientists. They can never just leave well enough alone, and no sooner did they discover what appeared to be the structure of the super small, they had to ask, "I wonder if there is anything inside the nucleus besides protons and neutrons?" With a little bit of investigation, they found something unusual about our positively charged protons and our no-charge neutrons. They found that inside the protons and the neutrons were even smaller particles they decided to call "**quarks**." Most likely they are called quarks because it sounded a lot like what their friends and relatives called them when they announced they wanted to find out what was inside the protons and neutrons of the atom's nucleus.

Fortunately for us, these "quarks" are pretty easy to figure out. For our basic purposes of understanding the inner workings of the atom, whether, a proton, or a neutron, there are thankfully only three quarks inside of each and they always come in easily identifiable packages. If we are looking at a **proton,** we will see **two quarks (+) on top** and **one quark (-)** on the bottom. If we are looking at a neutron, we will see the opposite or **one quark (+)** on top of **two quarks (-)**. Now, this is the really cool part about matter. In the simplest of explanations, each of the three quarks inside either the proton or neutron has one of two electrical charges based on their spin. The positive charge is +2/3 and the negative charge is -1/3. It is this arrangement in the neutron, which has two negative quarks, and one positive quark that gives it its "neutrality." And the proton with two positive quarks and one negative that gives the proton its positive charge.

Positive Protons and Neutral Neutrons

Another way to look at it this arrangement is to think of two "nuclear" families in the neighborhood called Nucleus Heights. We will call one family, the "positive" Protons and the other family the "neutral" Neutrons. Our first family, the "positive" Protons, is well liked in the neighborhood. Though a little "quarky," the two parents are always positive about everything. But, unlike their parents, the Proton's son, "negative" Ned, seems to put a damper on things whenever he can. However, the positive outlook of the parents, "positive" Pete and "positive" Pauline and their willingness to give Ned a smack every now and then, gives the Protons the appearance of being "positive" and willing to look on the bright side of any situation. On the other hand, next door to the "positive" Protons are the "neutral" Neutrons. As opposed to the Protons, the Neutrons just can't seem to get excited about anything. It isn't completely their fault. In fact the mother, "positive" Polly, is really positive about everything, but the father, "negative" Nathan, and their daughter, (equally) "negative" Nellie, cancel out their mother's positive outlook on life. And so, the "neutral" Neutrons are not as likely to get involved in community events, as are the "positive" Protons. We will come back to these quarky characters a little bit later, but for now, let's move on to a more enlightening topic.

The Lighter Side

What could be more enlightening, than, uh, light? If you will recall, the study of matter has led us to understand a lot about what is infinitely small. But the study of what makes up the two-day-old pizza sitting in your refrigerator was not the end-all of end-alls. There are things around us that don't seem to be made of matter at all, and it would not be fair to the giants of science, like Max Planck, Albert Einstein, Enrico Fermi and Bill Nye the Science Guy, to leave our understanding of the universe at the atom. The most obvious thing around us, that does not appear to be made up of what we understand as matter, is light.

For thousands of years, people have tried to figure out just exactly what light is, and until this century, thanks to Einstein and many others, we have a better understanding of what it is that allows us to be aware of what is going on in the world around us. The first thing we must rule out about light is of course, magic, although this may be hard to do. If I flip on a light switch, immediately the room is filled with light, as if it were magic. It would seem that light could be anywhere and everywhere at the same time. It appears to go around corners, into caves, and even comes out of flashlights. It can be made by the sun, lightning or by a campfire. But does light have limitations, and if it does have limitations, can it be more readily understood, or harnessed as energy?

We now know, as any school kid will tell you, there is a thing called, "the speed of light." If the kid is smart, he or she can tell you that the speed of light is 186,000 miles per second. Now, this seemingly trivial bit of information is very important, because if light has a speed limit it cannot be magic. In other words, I cannot stand on the moon, turn on my flashlight and instantly my friend, standing on the earth, will see my flashlight. It will actually take a fraction of a second, which my friend may barely even notice, but it shows us that light is not something that can be everywhere, all at once, in an instant. Knowing that, we then must ask ourselves, is light a bunch of really fast moving atoms? If they are, why don't they slow down when they reach the atmosphere of earth?

Quantum leap

Before we give ourselves a migraine re-inventing the wheel, let us just jump into the answers. What people like Max Planck, Einstein and others discovered was that there was no way, given the mathematics that we had in the early part of the century, to explain things like light. For some reason, thanks to a guy called Rene Descartes, a Philosophe who lived in the 1600's, who said anything associated with movement that cannot be described on a graph using mathematical equations, is merely the raving of a lunatic.

Since it was not possible to describe the movement of light on a graph, physicists had to invent a whole new math and even a way of thinking in order to describe light as well as the electrons that circle atoms, but more about that later. What they had to come up with was a mathematics that dealt not with a single point or answer, but with all possibilities of answers. Scoff if you must, but their new math, called **quantum mathematics** allowed us to break Germans codes in World War II, develop the atom and hydrogen bombs, gave us the microchip for our computers and allowed us to speak on hand-held cell phones. So, what exactly is quantum mathematics? I don't know, nor do I think anybody really knows, but I will give it a try in the simplest terms possible.

Do you remember our friend, the atom? Do you recall that around the atom, there is a small particle with a negative charge called an electron? Do you remember how we first used the analogy of the moon orbiting the earth and the earth was the nucleus and the moon was the electron? You do? Well, good, now, I want you to scrap all of that as we enter into the field of quantum mechanics and mathematics. The problem with the electron, which has about one percent of the mass of the infinitesimally small nucleus, is that physicists or we anyway, have never been able to find it. We have built entire fields, such as chemistry on the foundation that all substances, such as iron or oxygen, exist as collections of atoms that we can use to combine with other substances to create the chemicals that make up our world.

The reason that the science known as Chemistry is possible is based on the theory that electrons occupy different orbits around the nucleus. These orbits are, unlike the moon of our earlier model, called **electron shells**. In the outermost orbiting electron shell, electrons called "**valence**" (no relation to the fifties singer) **electrons** need an exact even number in order to lead contented, fulfilled lives. If there are an odd number, such as one as in the case of the hydrogen atom, the atom will find another atom with an odd number of electrons and share their outer electron shells, or they will actually steal that electron, leaving the hapless victim to the fate of what is known as an **ion** (As in I "oned" an electron and it was stolen). The reason it is an ion is because it has less electrons than the number of protons in its nucleus, so it is now out looking for an electron to make it whole again. Now, back to the light...

Because there was no way to actually see an electron, there had to be some way to find out where it was, so the mathematics people and the physics people came up with a theory, and a set of equations, to say not where the electron is, but, to point out all the possible places that it might be at any given time. Confused? Well, look at it in real terms. Do you know exactly where you are going to be at this time next week, next month, next year? Well, of course you can't know for sure, but you can take a look at your life, your habits, and even your health and make some predictions as to where you are going to be at some moment in the future, but you can never be exactly certain. It is the same way with **quantum physics**. The best that can be done to find our little negative friend, the electron, is to quantify such things as the atom he or she is a part of, it's connection to a molecule, it's physical state and so on and so forth. In other words, we can make rationale predictions through mathematical equations as to where that elusive little electron might be at a given time, and that is quantum mathematics, and it seems to work. So that, in a way, brings us back to our discussion about light.

As we have already decided, light cannot be an atom, because if it were, it would not be able to travel with such speed, and we would be able to, given the right equipment, freeze it solid, warm it to a liquid and then, if we were feeling saucy enough, boil it away as a gas. But we cannot do anything to light of that nature, so it, must be something else (but not magic). So, the physics people did what they do best with things they can't readily explain. They made up a theory.

Photons: Particles or Waves?

Physicists theorized that light is made of special particles called **photons**. So, you must be asking yourself, "A photon? Then it must be a little particle, like an atom?" And you would be half right in suggesting such a theory, as many people have. The only problem is that light demonstrates the characteristics of both a particle, like an atom but, to keep them scratching their bad hairdos, physicists also discovered that light seemed at times to act like a wave. Since we have not, as yet, talked about waves, let me make another of my over-simplistic analogies about waves.

The most popular waves that we know of are the ones that we see when we go to the beach. They seem to start as nothing farther out at sea and then, depending on the conditions of the day, waves seem to gain strength when they hit the beach. Again, depending upon the conditions they may be gentle and small or they may be strong and large. No matter what physical characteristics they possess, they have some things in common. First, they have **frequency,** which is the number of times a wave hits the beach in a period of time, say one minute. They also have size, big waves, a favorite of surfers, are more popular because of the opportunity the offer to "hang ten" from ten to twenty feet. Little waves are more popular with boaters and enthusiasts of rubber duckies.

Physicists did their own surfing of sorts, developing all kinds of experiments and no matter what they did, they could not get around the fact that the mysterious substance that made up light, or what they had dubbed "photons" acted as both waves and particles, depending on the experiment. That left them scratching their heads and messing up their hair even further until they came up with, you guessed it, quantum physics. With quantum physics, and its accompanying mathematics, amazing things are possible, such as describing how a particle can also be a wave and vice-versa.

To save us from another droll explanation of quantum physics, think about that wave that is hitting the beach. As we recall, it has height, in this case a lot of height, say fifteen feet so we can put a surfer into the picture. As the wave approaches the beach and the surfer gets up on the board, we see that the wave begins to curl on the top. As it curls above the seemingly curly and empty head of the surfer, what does it do? It breaks into millions of little pieces as gravity and the friction of the upcoming beach slow the wave and it breaks apart in the air. As the surfer wipes out and disappears, the little pieces of water join back together again with the water leaving the beach from the previous wave. There is a tremendous roar of water and air and somewhere the words, "gnarly, dude," ring out from the beach. In either form, as little particles, or as a solid wave, the force of impact on an object, such as our surfer, is still going to be the same where things like air resistance are not present. In a nutshell, this is what quantum physics does; it explains how that single wave can be broken into little pieces and still retains its characteristics of its original "wavy" self. Einstein dubbed these little pieces of wave "quanta" as he was studying light, and the rest, as they say, is history.

Quanta not only described the characteristics of light, it also described the little elusive particle that we have been talking about called the electron. We can't find it, because, if we did, we would change its very nature, as **Heisenberg** stated in his famous **"Uncertainty Theory"** which says, in simple terms, if you look at something, such as a particle or a wave, or a naughty child, just the fact that you are observing it will change its behavior. In other words, if you are conducting tests to show that light is a particle, it will act as a particle. If you are conducting tests to show that light is a wave, it will act as a wave. So, light as either a particle or a wave is very important when it comes to understanding not only our physical universe, but also our personal everyday lives as well, so let's talk about how light affects us personally.

The electromagnetic spectrum; wavelengths and frequency

Look at some object in the room, any object, it doesn't matter. If you were to describe that object, one of the things you would describe is the color of the object. So, what does light have to do with color? Light, with all its mysterious properties, amazing speed and mysterious photons is one of the most incredible things in the universe, though you may not know it by just looking at it. Now, the object you are looking at has a color because that object is absorbing every **wavelength** of light you see, except for the color you see. What? What is a wavelength and why is it being absorbed?

Do you remember the waves on the beach? When we say "wave length" we mean the distance between each wave of all the photons that are striking an object and then bouncing off the object for you to see. Confused, well think of it like this, before, we spoke about **frequency**, which is the number of times the waves hit the beach in a given time period. The length of the wave is the distance measured between the peaks of the waves at their highest point. On a windy day, the "wave lengths" will be shorter and the frequency of the waves will be faster than on a calm day.

If you are looking at your favorite hanging fern, you probably see a dark green, unless you have neglected to water it for a while. So, why do you see green? You see the color green because the plant is absorbing every other wavelength in the **electromagnetic spectrum** but the visible waves of the color green, which cannot pass through the chlorophyll in the plant and bounce back or are reflected back out, similar to an eighteen year old at a bar without a fake ID. Do you remember our old friend from junior high school science, **Mr. Roy G. Biv**? Or, red, orange, yellow green, blue, indigo and violet? These are the colors in the wavelengths of light in the electromagnetic spectrum that we can see. They are all traveling across space together but they strike objects at different speeds, like the waves on a beach on a windy day move faster than on a calm sunny day. The waves on the "Biv or blue side, are moving in slower and less frequent waves than the waves on the red or "Roy" side. The color 'green' in the middle of the spectrum cannot be absorbed by chlorophyll and so that is the color coming from your fern. It works that way for all objects, with two exceptions; they absorb all wavelengths of light except the color you see. Black reflects no light, so you see no color. White reflects all light, therefore when you see something that is white, you are actually looking at the electromagnetic spectrum in its original form.

However, these colors of what is called the spectrum of visible light are just a tiny fraction of what scientists refer to as the **electromagnetic spectrum**. If you go left of red, you will see light that is known as infrared. If you go further, you will get into things like microwaves and radio waves. If you go to the right of violet, you will get into wavelengths called ultraviolet light. Now, it is from our knowledge of non-visible light that we have things like cell phones, which use microwaves and fiber optic cables that converts magnetic signals into light, and then changes them back at their destination. All around you, the atmosphere is charged with light moving in wavelengths that you cannot see. The earth itself is bombarded with this same invisible energy from not only our star, the sun, but by stars spread throughout the galaxy, which is why we can see them at night.

How light allows us to see

So how does light allow us as human beings to see the world around us? We are able to see because the reflected light, say from your fern, sends you a signal at the "green" wavelength that is picked up by your eye, more specifically, the pupil, which gets bigger and smaller, in order to allow just the right amount of light into your eyeball. The cornea, or lens of your eye, focuses on the object, and, thus focused, your eye changes that light into a chemical signal, which is sent immediately from your eye to the back of your head, via a network of nerve cells. There the occipital lobe receives that chemical information and forwards it to the other parts of the brain to be analyzed. In other words, the color green, or any other color for that matter, does not actually "exist." They are simply coded messages sent back to you from any object in the form of light waves (or particles) that your eye picks up and then translates into a format that your brain can understand. In other words, what we call "seeing" is actually a much more complicated process of fast moving waves being changed into chemical signals that our brain can then interpret and make decisions about regarding our own environment.

Looking at your fern, your eyes, if they are in good working order, will detect the reflected color of green, and also, they will detect any other colors, such as darker areas, as well as lines. It is the lines and patterns that you see in objects that allow you to identify them. Camouflage, for instance, is merely the art of breaking up the lines we associate with an object, such as a person an animal or a Huffy 10-speed bike. Recognition of lines happens faster than you can be aware of, because you "see" a fern only after the information is received, changed into a chemical, transmitted to the back of your head (upside down) and then transmitted all over your brain. Your brain then analyzes the information it has stored regarding green things, decides you are looking at plant, recalls information you have about plants, and, lastly, makes you conscious of the fact you are looking at a plant called a fern. If you spend more time looking at the fern, you may recall you bought that fern from your favorite nursery where they always give you good advice and have reasonable prices.

Now, instead of your friendly fern, imagine that the object at which you are looking is a fast moving bus and it is heading right for you as you cross a busy street. Your will eyes pick up the reflected light and the lines of the bus and your brain will compare two quick "snapshots" of the image and immediately notice the lines of the object appear to be gaining in size and will direct your focus and attention on the moving object. This information is picked up, transmitted and monitored by the same process to your occipital lobe and sent via chemical and electrical signals all over your brain. Because the lines are getting bigger, your brain is aware that an object is getting closer to you. Instead of thinking that the bus is a pretty color of yellow, or white, if it is a metro job, the signals in your brain are also being transmitted to an area of the brain known as the **reptilian brain**, which is a simple mechanism that controls our four survival instincts. The reptilian brain can override any other portion of the brain, and does so the millisecond it receives the signal that there is a life-threatening threat. In this case it is a fast-moving bus that is heading in your direction.

The reptilian brain sends a signal to your legs to start moving quickly while at the same time it sends chemicals to your heart called adrenalin that makes it pump more blood and oxygen to your muscles in order to get them to move quickly and increase your strength. Once the bus has passed, and you are hopefully not pinned to the front, the reptilian brain disconnects and lets the other areas of the brain process the information that just happened, with the hopes that you will learn not to step in front of moving buses in the future.

Our rather drab explanation about ferns and buses is to help you understand that you don't actually "see" anything. What you see is a lot of reflected light in the form of waves that are changed into chemical signals. That is what makes up what we call, "reality." We should all be thankful we live in a reality where all objects give off light waves in the spectrum that we can see. Can you imagine what life would be like if there were large objects or life forms like bears that only gave off infrared, or microwaves? Were that the case, it may not be possible for us, or the world, or the universe as we know it to exist.

What is light?

If light is important, the next obvious question then, is, what makes light, light? Like everything else, light is very simple to understand. Do you remember our atom? Do you remember the electrons that orbit around the atom as what we came to understand as a quanta (neither wave nor particle)? If, you will recall, the electron occupies an orbit, which is also known as an energy state. If you, for example, want to go to the kitchen to get some cookies, you are going to need to use some energy. The farther you go, the more energy you will need. It is the same with electrons. If they move to an outer orbit, they need some outside energy to give them that little push. Photons can be one source of this energy. If the electron wants to move back from its outer shell, it must give off energy in the form of a single photon. **Simply put, light, or photons are created when one (or many) of those electrons loses energy by changing its place in the orbiting scheme around the nucleus of the atom.** The best example is to look at everyone's favorite light source, the sun. In a process that is so complicated that it would put the reader to sleep, or confuse to near insanity, I will criminally simplify the process in order to make it at least understandable to the non-science person. The sun is made up mostly of hydrogen atoms, which, as we will hopefully recall, is made of one electron going around a nucleus made up of one neutron and one proton. If we will also recall, atoms do not like an odd number of electrons, such as one electron in their outer shell. We also remember that when two hydrogen atoms meet, in order to get some stability in their outer shell, somebody has to lose an electron.

When the electron is taken from one of the hapless hydrogen atoms, the process of "stripping" the electron from its nucleus and energy state causes a photon, or one tiny particle of light to be emitted. What is left is an atom with two electrons, or helium, while inside the nucleus, the protons combine, converts to neutrons and positrons and zippity-doo-da, becomes a helium atom.[4] Of course, this process is much more complicated but it occurs billions and billions of times every second, so the sun is able to emit billions and billions of photons every second. As the filament decays, the electric current traveling through the filament in the bulb forces photons out of the filament, we can see this same process in fire as well as in many chemical processes. So, light, as wonderful and handy as it is, is a very simple thing to understand. When we see it, we are just seeing electrons floating from one atom to another, or changing the position of their orbit from an outer to an inner shell.

Forces

So, with our understanding of light and the atom, we are almost finished with our "basic science" discussion. I don't want to force the issue, but the last issue we need to discuss, or at least become familiar with are forces themselves. There are **four fundamental forces** that governing everything in the universe, so far as we know. To make things simpler, let's start where we started before, with the atom. Do you recall that inside the nucleus are protons and neutrons? They are particles made up of quarks and they carry a positive charge (proton) and no charge (neutron). So, what holds them together? The force that holds them together is also, coincidentally, the first force we are going to talk about. That force is called the **"strong force,"** or **"strong nuclear force."** Of course, scientists have come up with a name for the particles that possess the "strong force" and these particles are called, for obvious reasons, **"gluons."**

---

[4] "Zippidy-doo-da" is not the actual process by which hydrogen converts to helium. It is slightly more complicated but no less fun to learn about.

Gluons, like electrons are funny particles called "leptons" because they have almost no mass, but carry an electrical charge. Unlike their lepton counterpart, the electron, the strong force gluons are not to be trifled with. If you will recall the Japanese cities of Hiroshima, and Nagasaki, the explosions that caused them to be destroyed were the result of slamming the nuclei of an atom's protons, thereby smashing the field of force that held the atom together, the result of which was a blast and a man-made supercharged flash of light that had never been seen before on the planet. This process, called fusion, was the predecessor to fission, where the nucleus of an atom is stripped apart, whereby the disruption of the strong force causes a tremendously large chain reaction of free quarks and electrons smashing into other nuclei, lots of bright light, a mushroom cloud and tons of radioactive material to fly all over the place.

Accompanying the strong force is a force known by many names, all except Frank. The force that binds the electron to the atom is called the **electromagnetic force**, or the "**weak nuclear force**." The weak force is so called because it allows atoms to decay and lose their electrons. When this happens, as when an electron is stripped from an atom, or changes its place in the atom's orbits or outer shells, it creates a single photon of light.

The third force is called **magnetism**. We all have seen a teacher demonstrate magnetism by dropping iron filings on a magnet. They are arranged in a certain pattern and that pattern is called a "**magnetic field**." Magnetism is closely related to electricity or, electromagnetism and the weak force because electric currents create magnetism and electric currents are, in turn, created by magnetic fields and electric currents often emit photons.

Finally, there is the weakest of all forces and that is the force known as **gravity**. Gravity allows you to sit in your chair and read this book without floating up to the ceiling. Gravity is an attractive force that exists between all objects. The force of gravity one object exerts on other objects is determined by the mass, or weight of the object. When gravity exerts force on an object, it does so uniformly across a field whose strength can be calculated based upon the mass of the objects and the distance between them, thank you Sir Isaac Newton. Gravity allows the moon to orbit the earth, the earth to orbit the sun and the sun to orbit the galaxy. With the exception of the strong force, gravity has been the least understood force and scientists have been content with Sir Isaac Newton's laws for four hundred years because Newton described gravity with enough accuracy that we could use his equations to send men to the moon and to place satellites in what is known as geo-synchronous orbit.

Newton hypothesized that the force, which the earth exerts on the moon, is counteracted by the force that the moon exerts on the earth, which basically means that the moon is in a perpetual state of "falling" around the earth. Much like the apple that fell on Newton's apocryphal head. At the same time, the earth is in a limited way, "falling" around the moon. The force of the moon's gravity is strong enough to warp the shape of the earth, and affect the movement of fluids, like water, that creates tides. Similarly, the earth and the other planets are "falling" around the sun. Newton's rather basic understanding of gravity stood unchallenged for almost four hundred years until Dr. Albert Einstein began to rethink the problem.

Fields

Before we continue, since I have used the word "field" twice, I should explain what a field is, briefly. A field, although a convenient place for cows and sheep, is not exactly the same kind of field we are talking about when it comes to the forces of gravity and magnetism. Unlike a field full of cows and sheep, which always stays the same size and shape, a magnetic field can change, depending upon the force of the current flowing through it and the distance from an object to the field. As the electric current increases, the magnetic field increases, but decreases according to how far an object moves from the source of the magnetic or gravitational field. This is known as Planck's constant, and can be seen in an equation that looks a lot like $E=MC2$, but is not exactly the same, because you have to figure in the force of the current. Therefore, if I have an iron plate in my head, I am in less danger of an embarrassing moment the farther I stand away from a powerful electro-magnet. If I am orbiting the earth, I am in less danger of plummeting to my death the farther away I move from the earth.

If you are still confused about what a field is, go get your vacuum cleaner out of the closet. Take the head off so that you are holding the hose that connects to the body of the vacuum. Now, turn the vacuum cleaner on and put your hand over the hose. If it is a reasonably good machine, you will feel suction on your hand. If you pull your hand away from the hose, you will notice that at first, it is difficult to do, but as your hand gets farther and farther away from the end of the hose, the easier it is to pull away from it. What you are doing, in a way, is operating in a field. A magnetic or gravitational field operates in pretty much the same way.

In addition to gravitational fields, the earth, along with a number of other planets in our solar system have rotating magnetic fields. If you will recall the iron filing experiment you did with magnets in the second grade, you will remember that the "fields" created by the magnet had a North, or positive orientation and a South, or negative orientation. You will hopefully recall that if you put two North ends of a magnet close to one another, they would push away from each other. If you put a South end near a North end, they would attract to each other. Now, here is the fun part. If you were to put a string through the middle of the magnet and spin it around next to a wire with a light bulb on the other end, you would produce an electric current and the light would begin to glow. Your spinning magnet is known as a "dynamo" and is the reason your car doesn't have to run on a battery all the time. The spinning magnets create the car's electric current. Recent studies have shown that the earth's core, which is composed of liquid iron, creates that same kind of effect. As the earth spins, the iron in the core is both positively and negatively charged, thus creating a dynamo of significant proportions that creates a magnetic field around the earth. Now that we have had enough fun with magnetic fields, let's move on to gravitational fields.

Let's do the time warp again

As we have already pointed out, gravity is something we are all aware of, but few of us ever really understood until Sir Isaac Newton wrote the laws by which it governs large bodies, such as planets and stars. Beyond that, nobody really had an understanding of gravity until Dr. Albert Einstein came up with his **Special Theory of Relativity**. What Einstein understood about gravity was that, in simplest terms, gravity, or the force that large bodies exert on everything else, actually warps space and time. If that sounds a little confusing, let's think about it in these terms; if there were no gravity, space, as we know it, would be completely flat. What large bodies like the earth, moon, or the sun do is to create a kind of round three-dimensional hole in the otherwise flat fabric of space. Of course we cannot see the hole, or the fabric of space for that matter, but we can see that the moon follows a particular pattern as it orbits the earth and we can feel the effects of the hole if we jump up in the air.

In more simple terms, the warping of space and time by the earth's gravity creates something like an invisible gutter that your bowling ball lands in if you don't have much skill in bowling. With the moon as our bowling ball, the outer side of the gutter is created by the earth's gravitational pull; the moon can't jump past that on its own. The inner side of the gutter is created by the moon's gravitational pull on the earth. Instead of the forces of both bodies adding up and sending the moon slamming pell mell into the earth, the two forces, like two bullies getting ready to fight, can't get close enough to each other to land a blow because the force of one cancels out the forces of the other. So the moon is forced, literally to stay in its orbit, held there, like the bowling ball in the gutter, by the earth's gravity warping the space around it.

Einstein further predicted that not even light the "golden boy" of the universe can escape the effects of gravity. He predicted correctly that light would be bent during a lunar eclipse of the sun. What observers saw when they tested his theory during a lunar eclipse was that even though the moon covered the sun, the light from the sun was still visible on the outer perimeter of the moon because the light was being bent, or warped, by the moon's gravity. That simple idea that was thought out in Dr. Einstein's frizzy head opened up the world to a universe where nothing was constant.

If light could be bent by gravity, it could be slowed down. All of a sudden light, which was non-negotiable, became negotiable. If light was negotiable then time was negotiable. In fact, during the first space missions, it was shown that clocks in space actually slowed, compared to the clocks on earth, which confirmed another of Einstein's theories. As an object approaches the speed of light, time will begin to slow down relative to other, slower moving objects.

At the speed of light, time stops. In other words, it takes a photon eight minutes to reach us from its starting point at the sun. Eight minutes for us. For the photon, if the photon were to be conscious of time, and go so far as to be wearing a watch, the trip from the sun to the earth happened instantly without the second hand even moving. One second the photon was sitting on the surface of the sun, the next, it was bouncing off your fern (at least the green wavelength) and hitting you in the eye. To sum it all up, what Einstein did, was to put into mathematical form what the Greek Philosopher Plato wrote almost twenty five hundred years ago when he said, "Time is space with number." In other words, what Einstein proved was that time and space are parts of a whole. It is not possible to travel through time, without traveling through space, and vice versa until you reach the speed of light, then you can travel through space, but not through time.

You may say, "Aha, I got you there. I haven't moved from my chair for the past hour, so you are wrong. I have moved through time, but not space." And I would reply to you, that you are sitting on the earth, which is going around in a circle and is moving on an orbit through the solar system, which in turn is orbiting around the Milky Way, which in turn, is rocketing through the universe as the universe continues to expand. In the last hour of your "not moving," you have moved unbelievable distances in all three dimensions, but you just weren't aware of it, and that my friend, is Einstein's Theory of Relativity.

What does it all mean?

At this point, the reader may ask, "Why is any of this important?" The answer to that question, in the simplest terms possible, can most readily be answered by looking at any object in the room. Without the science that I have just described, that object is exactly what it appears to be. If it is a chair, it is a chair. If it is a picture, TV, a dog, or a burglar, they all are what you see them as. However, because of the work of scientists, we have been able to break these objects down to their component parts, and then, thanks to the work of theoretical physics and quantum theory, we have been able to break most objects down from their component parts to the basic building blocks of all matter. The result is that no matter what the object, you are actually looking at billions of atoms made up of electrical charges that are arranged together to form molecules of matter and that matter makes up the object you see which is possible because of the photons that are reflected and hitting your eyes at differing wavelengths. Whether it is wood from the chair, glass from the TV screen or steel from the burglar's gun, your surroundings are not what you imagine them to be.

If it is hard to imagine billions of atoms, think of the sky on a cold, clear night. Now take every star you can see and squash it down until they all fit into the object at which you are looking. Now, think of the three quarks inside each of the protons and neutrons inside the tiny atoms you squeezed into your object. They are spinning electrical charges. The spin of those electrical charges creates electricity, which creates magnetism, which creates an electromagnetic field that operates around each and every little nucleus that, in turn, keeps its electrons in a sort of orbiting field around the atoms. The entire object then, is a composite of magnetism, gravity and electricity held together at the nuclear level by the strong force. Now, that burglar doesn't look so frightening anymore, does he? (It would probably be best if you give him your watch and point out the places where you keep your valuable before we move on…)

Finally, the other forces in the universe are acting upon that object at which you are looking. The earth's gravity keeps it stationary. The light from the sun, or the light bulb in your room, is bombarding it with photons. While it is being bombarded with photons, it is sending a certain wavelength of light bouncing back into the room, which allows you to see it. Still further, the atoms in that object are being bombarded with subatomic particles from throughout the universe. And while you are looking at it, thanks to the weak force, it is slowly decaying back into the form of atoms from which it is originally composed and they, in turn will decay as they lose their electrons. But you are not aware of that process, unless you are looking at ice cream, because you are moving through time at precisely the speed that is necessary to perform the things you need to do, such as mature, reproduce, raise your young and die. If you could travel at the speed of light, you would see that process-taking place all around you instantly, but you can't, at least not yet. For now, the best you could possibly do would be to spend your life traveling in earth's orbit, which may actually allow you to slow time by a few weeks.

The Big Question; the Unified Field

The big question scientists who work in the field of theoretical or practical physics, have been trying to answer for the last one hundred years is the question of why the four forces have the values that they have. What if the strong force, was not quite so strong? What if the weak force was not quite so weak? What if gravity had been stronger or magnetism weaker? All physicists agree with the idea that if there were one tiny bit of difference in the four fundamental forces, the universe as we know it, could not exist. Everything had to be exactly as it is in order for us to be able to contemplate our own being.

With all of his brilliance and frizzy hair, the question of the Unified Field haunted Einstein throughout his life. Einstein, and many before and after him, tried to find a theory where all of the forces; strong, weak, magnetic and gravitational would be equal to each other. Physicists began to study the Big Bang as the possible point in time where the forces were, in fact, equal to one another, but in Einstein's lifetime, the theory known as the Unified Field eluded him and thousands of others. Thanks to their work however, today, we are fast closing in on an understanding of the Unified Field Theory and how it may be possible to equalize all the forces.

Once again, that takes us back to the LHC in Cern, Switzerland, where physicists are attempting to find out what is inside the atomic particles, like quarks or leptons (electrons) that we are fairly certain exist. At the Large Hadron Collider, scientists are trying to figure out what is inside the tiny particles that make up the atom. They are doing this, as the name says, by colliding them together at incredible speeds, after which, the scientists will pick up the pieces and see what came out. So why would this be such a big deal, and how could it change the future of mankind? Do you remember a few hundred years ago when Benjamin Franklin took his young son William out to fly a kite in a lightning storm? Franklin came up with the idea, probably from watching the key in his bottle glowing, that the amazing force inside the bottle might someday be used as a power source to make machines do work. Some two hundred and fifty years later, think of how much your own life has been made easier by electricity.

To be able to understand the processes and forces that make up all matter, would make the discovery of useable electricity seem about as important as the invention of the kerosene lamp. The knowledge gained in understanding how to harness and manipulate atomic particles would change the way we manufactured almost everything. In fact, we may someday be able to create our own artificial atoms. It would change the way we communicate and it would change the way we travel. Theoretically, it may even change us as human beings into beings who are more morally advanced, less susceptible to disease and capable of learning at much faster rates than ever before.

For, now, it is important that the reader understand that all this is happening at this very moment. But, as we shall soon see, there are many other things that are also happening and that have been happening for a long, long, time. As we shall also see, there is and has been, a complete and undeniable cover-up by people who like to keep secrets, and who think it is best to keep this information and information like it for themselves.

Chapter 22

Alien Science

Now that we are somewhat familiar with the science of the fundamental matter and the forces that apply to all matter in the universe, we can move forward and explore how non-earthly civilizations have used their knowledge of matter to manipulate the very forces that govern everything from the very large to the infinitely small, but not quite yet. In the last chapter, we basically covered scientific advancements in physics that brought us into the World War II era. From that time to the present, that basic and fundamental knowledge of the nature of matter has allowed us to progress in leaps and bounds toward an understanding of the very nature of life, energy, time and reality that is so astounding that many feel it is in the best interest of mankind as a whole, to keep it secret, cloaked in "black projects" and away from the peeping eyes of the public. In this chapter, we will discuss in a very simplified way, the advances we have made in the past few years about nature of matter and the universe that will allow us to at least begin to understand, what it is that these people and organizations are hiding.

For their eyes-only: the beginnings of the shadow government

The extraterrestrial phenomenon constitutes the biggest, most expensive and longest lasting deception ever told to the world by the United States government. It would almost be a joke, like in the *Naked Gun* movies, where the policeman stands with a megaphone in front of an obvious catastrophe shouting, "Nothing to see here!" if it were not for the people whose careers and lives have been destroyed and sometimes ended for telling the truth about their extraterrestrial encounters or experiences. The extraterrestrial cover-up may yet one day qualify as the funniest sham ever pulled on an entire population, however, for now, there aren't so many chuckles while the lack of acknowledgment continues to ruin lives and erodes the credibility of the U.S. while the intelligence, scientific and corporate communities continue to deny the presence of extraterrestrial beings at the same time they are reengineering their downed craft.

For the reader who is still under the impression that there are no intelligent life forms and no extraterrestrial visitors flying around us in craft that are way beyond our technological capabilities (at least for the moment), please stop reading now. There is no way you will have the intellectual capacity to understand what will follow in this book. There are plenty of books available that will get you "up to speed" on the issue if you are so inclined. If, after seeing the other published evidence, you are still convinced there are no extraterrestrials operating within our atmosphere, I can assure you that your government is proud of you and wishes it had more citizens with your cerebral capabilities. People with your mental capabilities are in high demand on news shows and talk radio, provided you possess the rudimentary reading skills to read a teleprompter. Bon voyage.

The rest of us are beyond the mental and intellectual insults flung at us by "spin" doctors and disinformation artists or, as they used to call them, "liars." We are more interested in issues such as: How do the extraterrestrial craft fly? What do they use for an engine? Are they able to travel faster than the speed of light? Do we have the technology to duplicate these craft? Finally, we will look into what is probably most important question of all: What are the extraterrestrial beings doing here? For the rest of this book, I will try to give, in as simple of terms as possible, answers to these questions based on our limited understanding of the physical properties of the universe we inhabit, based on my own rather feeble understanding of science, technical research and history.

For the reader who is not quite sure about the extraterrestrial issue, pay attention, as this is a very brief, "crash" course in extraterrestrial encounters and the responses and policies of the U.S. government. The reader who is interested, and who has little else to do in his or her spare time, may also find it interesting to research the names of the officials involved in the cover-up past and present and determine how many of them are members of the Society of Freemasons. I will point out some of the most obvious members of the Society of Freemasons who have been involved in the cover-up, but there are hundreds, if not thousands more who have, or have had access to this information over the course of the last sixty years.

So what do the Freemasons have to do with extraterrestrials? We discussed at the end of a previous chapter that extraterrestrials, and the idea of contacting them as "Masonic brothers," got Joseph Smith in a lot of trouble, in fact, it got him killed. The nice and handy thing about Freemasons is the simple fact that if their members, like Joseph Smith, Roberto Calvi and William Morgan, reveal any secrets or "classified information," they know they will be killed, so who better to trust with the secrets of the extraterrestrials? So, with the understanding that extraterrestrials are an issue that Freemasons and Latter-day Saints have always taken quite seriously, we will leave that alone for a while and move on to our quick review of extraterrestrial events and the actions of the government.

UFO's and Nuclear Weapons

Since the much-documented Roswell crash of at least one extraterrestrial craft in 1947, a campaign of denial and disinformation has been the official policy of the U.S. Government. Following the Roswell crash, 33rd degree Freemason and 33rd President of the United States, Harry S. Truman began one of three officially as well as publicly recognized projects in order to study the extraterrestrial phenomenon. Project "Sign" was the first. It had a brief lifespan of two years, and was ended in 1949. Following "Sign" the Air Force undertook project "Grudge" which may have suggested what the Air Force would have against anyone who filed UFO reports. Following an equally short tenure as the Air Force's answer to all the UFO sightings, Grudge didn't hold for long and was replaced in 1952 by Project Blue Book, which lasted until 1970, at which time the government closed the (blue) book on UFO's, citing the fact that there was no evidence to support any further research. The mission of these three projects was to investigate reports of "unidentified flying objects" by the public and to dismiss them out of hand as "swamp gas" "Venus" or "weather balloons," and show the public that their tax dollars were hard at work.

Of course, the real story was, as extraterrestrial encounters have been recorded throughout the history of mankind, the detonation of atomic weapons in the 1940's and hydrogen bombs in the 1950's and the interest these events seemed to spark in the extraterrestrials regarding the United States, the United Kingdom and the Soviet Union. At the time of the crash (es), Roswell Army Air Field was the home of the 509th Bomber Group, and had in its arsenal, a number of atomic weapons. Five years later while the U.S. was actively pursuing the world's first hydrogen bomb, in July of 1952, on consecutive weekends, extraterrestrial craft appeared on the radarscopes of operators at Washington National Airport, not far from the White House. Numerous eyewitnesses from military personnel to airline pilots and crews reported their presence. In spite of the hundreds of eyewitness accounts, and the thousands of calls that were coming in on Project Blue Book's telephone lines, the Air Force dismissed them as a "temperature inversion," and, to their credit, they did so with a straight face.

A few months later, during a NATO training exercise in the North Atlantic off the coasts of Denmark and Norway involving hundreds of ships, a thousand aircraft and tens of thousands of men, the extraterrestrials came back. A variety of very large silver, metallic objects were seen following the NATO fleet as it conducted exercises and flight operations. Of special interest to the extraterrestrial craft appeared to be the aircraft carrier *USS Franklin Delano Roosevelt*, which was carrying atomic weapons. A week later, reports of multiple extraterrestrial craft appeared to be "buzzing" Sweden, Denmark and Germany.

Following the events of the Washington D.C. "invasion" in the summer and the encounters in the North Atlantic and Europe in the fall of 1952, a think-tank known as the **Robertson Panel** met in January of 1953. Present were heads of the CIA as well as civilian and military experts such as Air Force Chief of Staff and Freemason, Nathan Twining. As a result of the meeting, the "UFO" phenomenon was about to find itself at a government-issue fork in the road. It was decided, first and foremost, that the UFO's could be used by foreign militaries to panic the public prior to an invasion (see War of the Worlds, 1937). It was also decided that the number of civilians reporting sightings were clogging up the information arteries of the Air Force. The best solution (fork U) was to use the media such as Freemason, Walt Disney's company along with the rest of the

Freemason controlled media as well as celebrities, astronomers and psychologists to ridicule people who reported sightings. General Twining then began to address the extraterrestrial phenomenon for what it really was (Fork A). He issued orders that the 4602nd Air Intelligence Squadron was to investigate only UFO reports that were deemed of "technical or strategic interest." All other reports were to be filed away as swamp gas or similar ludicrous explanations by project Blue Book.

The psychological operation part of Twining's plan or, "Fork U" worked. As people became fearful of ridicule for coming forward with stories about sightings and encounters, the number of reports dropped

significantly. Just to make sure all his bases were covered regarding Fork U, in December of 1953 the Air Force, Army and Navy made it punishable for any military serviceman to reveal classified information regarding extraterrestrials with a fine of ten thousand dollars and/or two years imprisonment. It can only be assumed that private contractors and other civilians were threatened with similar imprisonment, fines or worse, for disclosing classified secrets.

While the media, the scientific community and the government were waging an open campaign of psychological warfare against the American people, in this case, upon those who reported sightings, General Twining and his boys at the 4602nd Air Intelligence Squadron in "Fork A" of the operation were on the lookout for downed extraterrestrial craft they could bring back to the laboratory. There they could analyze it, gain intelligence from the craft's pilots, provided they were still alive, and try to reproduce any technology within the realm of our own scientific and engineering capabilities. The phrase used to describe their mission "of technical or strategic" interest is simply military jargon for grabbing as much science and technology as they could from the downed objects and converting it to our own military uses. As we shall see, they were quite successful.

One classic example of the influence of the intelligence gained from the sightings and recovery of extraterrestrial craft involved Clarence "Kelly" Johnson, the chief engineer of Lockheed's super-secret "Skunkworks." In December of 1953, Johnson saw a huge, almost bat shaped extraterrestrial craft near the California coast. He watched as it hovered for a few minutes and then accelerated away at speeds far beyond the capabilities of anything man-made. Johnson made drawings of the craft which today, most people would identify as a B-2 bomber. For the time being, Kelly Johnson, who was the chief engineer in a classified project to develop a secret high-speed reconnaissance aircraft, came up a few months later with the SR-71 Blackbird, a completely revolutionary aircraft in design, materials and flight characteristics.

Meanwhile, a considerable number of people in the government such as Admiral Roscoe Hillenkoetter, the first director of the CIA, Admiral James Forrestal, as well as other prominent professionals in the fields of science, industry, national policy and the military did not think that General Twining's "forking" of the American people in regards to extraterrestrials was either sound policy or acceptable in a democratic state. They formed the organization known as NICAP (National Investigations Committee on Aerial Phenomena). In 1960, in a letter to Congress that was subsequently reported in the New York Times, Admiral Hillenkoetter said:

"Behind the scenes, high-ranking Air Force officers are soberly concerned about UFOs. But through official secrecy and ridicule, many citizens are led to believe the unknown flying objects are nonsense

The Condon Report

In spite of statements like the one made by the first head of the Central Intelligence Agency, the lies and the disinformation spread by government agencies such as the Air Force, CIA and National Security Agency, as well as their friends in the media, were enough to keep interest in UFOs within the realm of fringe elements of society. In 1966, the U.S. Air Force convinced Robert J. Low of the University of Colorado to undertake an "objective" investigation into the UFO Phenomenon. Understandably, there was a considerable amount of reluctance on the part of scientist within the faculty, who were afraid of having their professional reputations tainted with an association to UFO research. Condon assured his reluctant colleagues in a memo put out to university faculty in 1966:

"Our study would be conducted almost entirely by non-believers who, though they couldn't possibly *prove* a negative result, could and probably would add an impressive body of thick evidence that there is no reality to the observations. The trick would be, I think, to describe the project so that, to the public, it would appear a totally objective study but, to the scientific community, would present the image of a group of non-believers trying their best to be objective but having an almost zero expectation of finding a saucer." Low also suggested that if the study focused less on "the physical reality of the saucer", and more on the "psychology and sociology of persons and groups who report seeing UFOs", then "the scientific community would get the message."

Understandably, the *Condon Report* failed to find any proof of extraterrestrial craft and was hailed in such publications as *Science* and *Time* Magazine, which also seemed eager to pick up on the aspect of the psychological profiles of the people who reported sighting of extraterrestrial craft. *Nature*, a well-respected scientific journal, voiced its opinion that the extraterrestrial question was better discussed in the fields of philosophy than of legitimate science. Among the final conclusions of the *Condon Report* was the statement that the UFO Phenomenon appeared to pose no threat to the security of the United States. Logically, if there was no threat, there was no reason for the Air Force to be concerned with any reports of sightings on an official or public level.

Back to Roswell

By 1987, many of the original witnesses who had been living in Roswell in 1947 were getting along in years. Too old to fear the government's threats to throw them in jail or kill them if they spoke about the crash, they finally began to come forward. Almost overnight, the frenzy that General Twining and his boys had attempted to quell suddenly erupted. But, by the late 1980's, seventeen years after Project Blue Book was officially closed, the people of the United States knew all too well the last place to report an extraterrestrial encounter was to their own government. Instead, thanks to the advent of cable television and advancements in home video cameras, there were plenty of producers and writers willing to use footage captured by civilians of extraterrestrial craft. Television shows and movies, such as Freemason Steven Spielberg's *Close*

Encounters of the Third Kind (1977) and *E.T.* (1981) which highlighted extraterrestrials, abductions and encounters, attracted millions of viewers.

Today, although though two sitting U.S. Presidents have confirmed UFO sightings, and one, Ronald Reagan stood in front of the UN General Assembly and spoke about "...a threat from another world..." and John F. Kennedy had been briefed while a member of Congress about the Roswell crash, the federal government or at least the part that likes to lie and keep secrets, still denies there are such things as extraterrestrial beings or spacecraft. Fortunately for them, there are enough simpletons in the general population who continue to buy the government's stories, that they feel no obligation to tell the truth. Then, to add to the confusion, there are those researchers who have made a living out of a game where they "catch" the government lying about extraterrestrials and make a documentary or write an article or book about the incident. These people were monumental in bringing to light the information that we have today. But now, by giving us information we already have (that the government won't tell us the truth about extraterrestrials), they actually help the government by keeping attention away from the fact that there are thousands of these craft sighted every year flying over our cities, possibly abducting our citizens and who knows what else. These researchers still focus on the questions of whether or not these extraterrestrials exist and the subsequent cover-up, instead of asking what it is these beings are doing here. These are the last questions the government wants anyone asking, so the game continues. Now that we finally have all of the preliminary information out of the way, let's jump into the exciting stuff, shall we?

The Science of Extraterrestrial Craft and the Unified Field

In the last chapter, we left off talking about what was once called the Unified Field Theory. It was a theory that said that, theoretically, at some point, possibly at the exact moment of the Big Bang, or before, all forces, i.e.; the weak force, which binds electrons to atoms, gravity, magnetism and the strong force, which binds protons and neutrons together in atoms, were exactly equal. Then, for some reason, they were no longer equal and that, in theory, was the cause of the Big Bang. It may seem a trivial point to the person on the street, but, as we said before, for physicists, theoretical or otherwise, the fact that each of the forces has just the exact amount of effect on matter, not a hair more, not a hair less, is what allows the universe to exist in the form that we know it. If, for example, gravity were slightly weaker, the earth, the sun, the galaxy and the universe would not look at all like they do. If the weak force, the electromagnetic force that binds electrons to atoms, were slightly stronger, the chemical process that allows DNA to replicate cells may have never taken place, or, it may have taken place in such a way that life as we know it could be completely different and unrecognizable to us.

"So, big deal," you might say, "Strong force, weak force, magnetism shmagnetism, who cares?" Well, a lot of people are beginning to care because of a number of reasons. Of course, one of them being these extraterrestrials who are flying around at incredible speeds and who are apparently capable of breaking all of the laws of physics as we know them and who never seem to get so much as a speeding ticket or splattered on the inside of their craft when they change direction at a few thousand miles an hour. For us, who live in a world that is using up its resources faster than they can be discovered or replaced, a world that is teetering on the brink of a global energy crisis that will shut off our machines within the next two decades, we have two choices. Figure out how they work, and

don't think the trusty corporation/government is going to help us there, or go back to the horse and buggy days. So, it is imperative to begin to understand just what it is we are talking about when it comes to these technologies.

Earlier we talked about the Large Hadron Collider, but we didn't really talk about what it is, or what it does. It is basically a large magnetic tube that is around fifteen miles around. Inside the LHC, the physicists of the world are conducting a number of experiments in order to answer the question, at what point were the four universal forces equal? There is a lot of hype surrounding the Large Hadron Collider regarding the production of what is called "anti-matter." Anti-matter is really just a sideshow to keep the simple-minded public interested in spending the billions and billions that have gone into the project. The production of anti-matter sounds like something straight out of a Star Wars sequel, so it is easy to sell to the larger public as a possible future weapon, which is how scientists keep their grants coming in.

To explain what is really happening at the LHC, along with the Star Wars sounding Anti-Matter project, is something that is much more fascinating, but something that the general public might be too bored or too confused, or even too scared about to want to spend money, especially billions of dollars, conducting experiments in pursuit of a theory that is really on the fringe, or string as it were. In order to explain these other kinds of experiments, it is necessary to say, "Hello," to our little friend, the atom once again.

The Universe on a String

If you will recall, we were looking at the atom in the last chapter. To refresh your memory, the atom has a nucleus (hadron) and at least one, all the way up to 238 electrons. Just to see if you were paying attention, if an atom has 238 electrons zipping around outside in some kind of orbit, how many protons does it have? If you said 238, you were paying attention and your name will be forwarded to Mensa for further consideration. Of course, there aren't always the exact numbers of protons and electrons but, for the sake of keeping things simple, let's just continue. Now, inside that nucleus, if you will recall, were the protons that have positive charges and neutrons, which have no charge at all. If you will also recall, inside the proton and the neutron are what scientists call, for lack of a better word, subatomic particles. The ones we talked about earlier were called quarks. As we said, quarks are easy to understand because there are almost always three of them together inside protons and neutrons. In a proton, there are two up, or positive quarks and one down or negative quark. In a neutron there is one positive up quark with two negative down quarks, which cancel out the charge, making our neutron neutral. We left off at that point in the last chapter, but it is here that we would like to resume our discussion.

Picture in your mind our nucleus or hadron, if you prefer to call it that. Inside the nucleus, we have three protons and three neutrons, just to keep things simple. How many quarks are present? If you said eighteen, you are correct, because each neutron has one up quark and two down quarks and vice versa for the protons. Now, not to complicate matters too much, let's just look at one proton, by peeling off the shell and looking at the quarks inside. Were you actually able to tear off the shell of your proton, you would see that the quarks are spinning, according to older theories and vibrating, according to the latest theories. As you will recall, quarks also have electrical charges. To keep things as simple as possible, let's leave our quarks spinning, or vibrating inside the proton, put the shell back on and back away from our nucleus.

As we are backing away, we see our protons and neutrons and between them are our old friends, the gluons, holding them together. Now gluons, electrons and a number of other subatomic particles are really, really small and, as we have said, we have never really been able to find them. That is what makes up the term "theoretical" in "theoretical physics." They are only particles associated with a theory. In the theory, these particles are what are called "leptons," and should not be confused with the subatomic particles that make up little Irish elves, called "lepertauns."

Mind you, there are a number of these other particles that are much, much smaller than the protons and neutrons that make up the atom, such as bosons, and meions and morons. Okay, so I made up the last one. Anyway, suffice it to say that there are much smaller atomic particles, like quarks, that are called subatomic particles. I am not sure if there are such things as sub-subatomic particles, but that is probably how theoretical physicists would classify leptons and bosons if they could say sub-subatomic five times after as many cocktails. Now, armed with your impeccable understanding of particle physics, let's go back to Geneva and the Large Hadron Collider (relax, the alien technology bit is coming).

What the scientists are doing at the Large Hadron Collider, is taking small subatomic particles, like gravitons or the particles that make up gravity, for example, and accelerating them in magnetic fields to almost the speed of light. Once they reach that speed, they will collide one graviton with another graviton traveling at the same speed in the opposite direction. The logic being that in order to find out what is in such a tiny particle, the best way is to smash it into another particle and see what flies out of the accident. They are looking for proof of their leptons, gluons and bosons. They are also looking for something else.

A little bit earlier, if you recall, while we were looking at the protons and neutrons in our nucleus, we were looking at the three fundamental particles of each called "quarks." If you will recall, the earliest theories said that the quarks were actually spinning rapidly inside the protons and neutrons like little tops. In the 1970's, a new theory emerged that sounded great, but like many new theories, was put on the back burner, along with the theoretical physicists like Michio Kaku who endorsed it. Then, in the 1990's, based on new discoveries, it emerged once again. The new theory that attempted to find a state of matter in which all forces are equal, became known as "String Theory" because it says that all particles such as electrons, quarks and what have you, are not single points of tiny matter carrying a single tiny charge. Instead, they are actually "strings" of energy that are vibrating at a certain frequency and it is the frequency of this vibration, along with the shape of the string itself, that makes up all the matter that we see around us.

For those of you who feel that I am just "stringing" you along, I am going to get to the extraterrestrial part in a minute or two, if you will just bear with me. Now, according to people like theoretical physicist Brian Greene and Michio Kaku, these strings of energy are actually vibrating at certain frequencies. Now, let's stop and think about that. We know that light moves in waves, or particles, and these waves are translated, depending on the frequency, or number of times they strike your pupil, into a signal in your brain that tells you the color is orange or blue. Sound, we also know, travels in waves and strikes your eardrum which vibrates with a particular frequency and, in a similar fashion the vibrations are translated into signals for your brain to interpret as the your dog barking or your kid telling you they just wrecked the car.

Now, look at an object. Look deep down into the object, whether living, or dead. Can you see the molecules of atoms glued together by shared electrons? Look even deeper. Can you see one atom? Look inside its nucleus. Can you see our quarks? Before, we saw them spinning. Now, think of them as little charges, like when you touch a doorknob after walking across a carpet. You should see two positive charges and one negative charge and they are stuck, I mean *stuck* together by the ultra-fast frequency at which they are vibrating. Now, slowly back away from your quark and back outside of the hadron.

Now, stop. If you were looking at one atom of say, uranium 235, you would be looking at over seven hundred quarks, each of them vibrating with a fantastic amount of energy. And that is just one hadron! Now think of the billions of hadrons, or atoms that make up just one gram of uranium. You are talking about some serious energy just vibrating away.

The object, at which you are looking, though its atoms are not as tightly packed as uranium, is still loaded with billions upon billions of atoms. Inside each one of which are any number of protons and neutrons and inside any one of them are three vibrating pieces of almost pure energy. Now, back all the way out and look at your object again. No matter what it is, whether it is your fern, your stereo, your chair, or that burglar, wait, he's still there? He may be planning on stealing this book, so you better hurry or ask him if he wants something to eat. Anyway no matter what it is you are looking at, what you mistake as "matter" is nothing more than billions and billions of very tightly packed electrically charged particles that are vibrating with so much energy that they are nearly impossible to tear apart, and should you try, you would get an explosion similar to the hydrogen bomb blasts of the 1950's.

Now, I am going to say this as simply as possible in the most basic and fundamental states of matter, quarks, bosons, gluons, etc. There is a fundamental geometry in the vibration of the particles. Geometry, you say. Let me explain. The only problem with Quantum Theory in general is that there are holes in the theory that seem to be able to work accurately enough to give us an understanding of matter and energy that allows us to produce microchips, carbon nanotubes and the like, but there are still holes in the theory. I mean literally, holes. The description of matter and energy only makes sense, if extra dimensions are added to the mathematics. Of course, I am not going to attempt to explain this any further, other than to say, that according to the theory, the only way we can find out where these little vibrating particles are is to incorporate ten, and possibly, eleven dimensions that co-exist with us, or vice-versa.

The Multi-Dimensional World

When I say dimensions, I would like to be able to leave it at that, but I know that you, the reader, are insatiably curious as to what I mean, or would like another good laugh as I try to explain to you the concept of dimensions as they relate to science. Simply put, think of a piece of paper, or get one out, and while you are doing so, grab yourself a pen or pencil. Got it? Okay, now draw one dot on the piece of paper. Finished? Good that one dot is one dimension. It is a single point in space. There is no up, down, back, forth, here, there, only that one dot. Now, if you draw a line of any size from that dot and stop, you have created two dimensions. If you hold your paper in front of you so that you are looking at the edge, you are looking at a two dimensional world. If you are holding your paper correctly, you cannot tell the size of the paper, only the length. In the two dimensional world, there is only here, there, and everywhere in between those two points. There is no up and there is no down. There is no front, or back. If you tried to see the back of your paper, you would have to rotate it in your two dimensional world and by doing so, you would only be aware of more lines connected by the points that we would call the edges. You would never be able to tell what lies beyond those lines in a two dimensional world.

Now, take the paper away from your eyes before you cut them and possibly blind yourself. Hold it flat in front of you again and bring the corners of any side of the paper together, but don't fold the paper. What you are looking at is a three dimensional world. You see length, width, height and depth. If you were still in your two-dimensional state, the part of the paper that was folded, with the exception of the part that is still somewhat flat in front of you, has disappeared. Now, flatten out the paper and find the line you drew between two points. Now, one more time, bring the corners of your paper together again and change from a two to three-dimensional world. Now, let me ask you a simple question. They say that the shortest distance between two points is a straight line. Now, look at your line in the three dimensional world. That fundamental rule we probably learned in Geometry is not true in the three dimensional world, is it? In the three dimensional world, the shortest distance between any two points on that line is found by folding the space between them together, right? This is something that we are just beginning to understand about the nature of space.

Now, think about yourself in the fourth dimension, or the dimension of time. In the fourth dimension, there is height, depth, width and length, but there is also the element of time included. For us, living in the third dimension, we can no more see the world of the fourth dimension than we could see the folded paper when we were in our two dimensional state. We can only theorize what the world would look like then, and in that state, there we can imagine that we would look more like one of those extended exposure photographs we see of cities at night where the car lights are stretched (us) while the objects around us that are moving more slowly (buildings, trees, college professors), seem to be moving, but are not the streaks of light that we appear to be. In the fourth dimension, we can only imagine that we, who have but a brief lifespan, appear as mere blips on the screen of life. For a being observing from the fourth dimension, the details of our birth, life and death would be as obvious to them as the size of house would be to us. As theoretical physicists theorize, there are even more dimensions, and to put it simply, an observer in each dimension is able to look into the lower dimension and see it as we would see the one, two and three dimensional worlds around us. Now, back to Geneva…

Anti-matter, Death Stars and light sabers aside, the scientists at the LHC are actively looking for those other dimensions. According to Brian Greene, they are smashing particles called "gravitons" or the particles that make up gravity (I assume because they are so void of mass and energy, they won't create a thermonuclear explosion as would the collision of a larger particle like the proton when the strong force is torn apart). What they are looking for in the collision is for some of the energy of the collision to disappear. Wait, you say, "They are waiting for *what* to disappear?" I knew that wouldn't be so easy.

Think about a horrific head-on collision between a remote controlled AMC Pacer and a Ford Pinto under lab conditions. In all the twisted metal, leaking radiator fluid and other grisly remnants of these engineering masterpieces, the investigators can't seem to find the sporty rear-view mirror that one of the crash-test engineers, claims was mounted securely on the door of the Pinto. The investigators then must do some simple physics and calculate the speed of the cars and add in their weight in order to determine how much force was involved in the collision. By doing their calculations, they would be able to determine that the missing mirror is lying exactly twenty five feet behind the Pacer, and given its spherical shape, rolled from that point to either ditch on the side of the road. Sure enough the mirror is found and the claims adjustor is able to inform the Pinto owner that his recovery of the mirror keeps the Pinto from being classified as a total loss.

But, what happens if the mirror is not found in the ditch? What happens if the head on collision of these "supercars" of the '70's is not as catastrophic as we had expected. Suppose the mirror, in fact, doesn't go anywhere. That means that at some point, the cars slowed down, but with no drivers, that would have been impossible. Somehow there was unexplained interference, in this case, the loss of energy during our collision. That means only one thing; our laws of physics broke down.

Much like the accident investigators at the scene of the collision, the scientists at the Hadron Collider are going to calculate the force of the collision between the two gravitons and, then calculate the force of the debris that flies out from the collision between the two particles. If, according to theoretical physicist Brian Greene, there is less energy from the collision and the subsequent spraying of subatomic particles than was involved in the collision itself, then there may be proof that their theories are correct. In other words, the only place those particles could have gone would be, according to the theory, to another dimension.

In other words, if I were standing in our two dimensional world and something, like our line disappeared (because you erased it), I couldn't see what was happening to the line, only that it was disappearing as a flat, pinkish object seemed to be pushing it out of existence. I could never comprehend what happened to it because I couldn't see anything that was "up." Another way to explain it is to think of a merry-go-round. Let's say that you are determined to take a picture of yourself but you have no friends and a timed camera. You set up the camera to take pictures at regular intervals. When you look at the pictures, you notice that you are in some of the pictures, but in others, you are on the opposite side of the merry-go-round. If our strings of energy are actually vibrating in and out of our dimension when the crash occurs, the ones that are outside of our dimension at the moment of impact cannot come back. This loss of energy would be the first evidence that our "quarky" friends are actually strings of energy that, as they vibrate within our three dimensional world, and create the light, the trees, the smog, and the person sitting next to you on the bus that takes you to work, are simultaneously vibrating in a number of other dimensions, and what those dimensions would look like, we can hardly even speculate.

A visit to another dimension

Do you remember when we talked about how lucky we are that light travels at 186,000 miles an hour? That magnetism is limited by an equation called the Planck's constant? That gravity is not stronger or weaker than it is? It is quite possible that in these dimensions to which we are connected, these values are not the same as they are in our own dimensions. That would explain why we could not enter them. It may even be possible that light does not travel in those dimensions at all, which would explain why we couldn't see them. In that kind of a scenario, should we be allowed, somehow, to cross into such a dimension, and look back to where we had come from, we might possibly see our world as a TV screen.

If we had stepped into the fourth dimension, we would be able to see all of time pass before our eyes, as we might look at our bowl of cereal on our breakfast table in the morning. If this is difficult to understand, think of yourself looking at the one and two-dimensional images you drew on your paper. If you will recall that time is not an element of the first and second dimensions, you can understand that you, observing from the third dimension, have observed everything that has happened and will happen in your one and two dimensional world, but it may be a boring way to spend an afternoon. If you are in the one and two-dimensional world, there is no time. You exist only as a single point in space in the first dimension, or a line from one place to another in the second. It may sound a little confusing, but it gets better, well actually it doesn't, just more confusing, but once you get this, the extraterrestrial stuff will be a cinch.

As you cross into the fifth dimension (and this is where quantum physics comes in) you begin to see not only your life as a single point in time and space, but you also begin to see all of the possibilities of the life you have lived. Remember when you began ditching piano lessons in favor of guitar lessons because you thought you were going to be the next Jimi Hendrix? In the fifth dimension, you will see what happened to you if you continued with your piano lessons. Maybe you would have been the next Beethoven, or maybe you would have had your fingers broken by an unappreciative instructor. Remember that time you were almost run over by a car when you crossed the street without looking? In the fifth dimension, you would be able to see what would have happened if you had not chosen to look at the last second and stepped back in time.

Continuing on into the sixth dimension, you would see the universe from the beginning at the Big Bang, all the way to the final seconds of the universe, whatever they might be. In the seventh dimension, you would be able to see the sixth dimension as a single point in time, and that would continue into the eighth, ninth, and tenth dimensions, until you could see all possible universes, and all possible outcomes, and it is in the upper dimensions where you would finally see what scientists, like Einstein, have been trying to find for the past sixty years. You would finally be able to see the universe, as it would be if gravity, magnetism, electromagnetism and the strong nuclear force were equal. If it sounds confusing, it is because it is. But there are enough people who have sorted out the mathematics and the physics to convince the governments of Switzerland and France to let them build a machine in their back yard in order to try to rip a hole in our dimension and see what, if anything, is on the other side.

Now, that I have dragged you, sometimes painfully, through another whole chapter without ever explaining anything to you about extraterrestrial technology, instead only teasing you with tidbits and then leading you through almost another whole chapter devoted to science, let me assure you, it is for your own good. Now, that you understand the fundamentals of atoms, vibrating strings, electromagnetism and the basic states of matter and dimensions, you have enough knowledge to venture forward into the exciting world of extraterrestrial technology.

Chapter 23

Extraterrestrial Science

Now, as promised, let us finally move on to the subject of extraterrestrial biological entities and their marvelous machines. In case you haven't seen the pattern yet, it is just not this author's "style" to give you information without some kind of a rational explanation as to the; who's, the where's, when's and finally the why's and the how's of the extraterrestrials for two reasons. We know, for instance who some of them are, who is interested in them, who has the power to keep them from the public and we know how and why they are doing it. We know where and when they have been seen in both scriptural and historical contexts. However, as to the where; as in where do they come from, there are many theories, but since we are talking about a number of different life forms, where they come from is probably as divergent as the number of individual species or beings, we, or at least the agencies and corporations who study them have seen. We have also looked at some *possible* reasons as to why they are here. Because of our advances in science and technology, as well as our work on the extraterrestrial craft that have been recovered by our military, we do in fact, know how some of these machines work. But to explain "how" without some kind of understanding of the fundamentals of physics, would make this little more believable than science fiction, rather than science fact, to the average reader. Secondly, by understanding a little bit more about the science of these craft, the reader will also hopefully become a little bit more educated about the field of science itself.

So, let us begin with the question of how these beings are able to travel in ways that seem to defy our fundamental understanding of physics, or at least the fundamental understanding of physics that we possessed until the latter part of the twentieth century. What we will see in this chapter is that some of the technology that we have discovered is not really so "new" at all. The Society of Freemasons and their predecessors have protected some of it for hundreds and possibly thousands of years. Other technologies, such as anti-gravity machines, have only come into our realm of understanding in the last two decades, at least as far as scientific research that is not being hidden under the cloak of military "black" projects.

As I am by no means an expert in any of these areas, what follows is a simple general overview. Many of the concepts here, to understand fully, would require years of study in the fields of physics and engineering in order for the reader to be fully able to understand them. I am only offering enough detail to keep the reader interested in the subject, which will hopefully encourage the reader to investigate this amazing field of science in books, magazines and through further individual study. Finally, there are probably many other methods of propulsion, or, ways of moving these vehicles, that we most likely are not aware of, or do not understand. What follows are the methods that we most definitely do understand and that our military and aerospace corporations are actually working with in the present.

The shape of things to come

The craft that have been photographed, or that have been seen since men first started taking note of these things some five thousand years ago in China, India and Mesopotamia, for the most part seem to have shapes that are similar in form. They appear to come in the classic round, "flying saucer" model, the cigar shaped, long cylindrical model and of course the triangular shaped model. What we now understand is that, as form follows function, the shape is determined first, by the type of engine that are used by some of these craft, or more accurately, propulsion system. It is that propulsion system that our scientists have, since the forties, been working to understand as they took apart crashed craft and tried to reproduce the parts inside. It seems that we now understand them well enough to be able to reproduce them for our own purposes.

In order to understand how these things work, we must review some of the information we covered earlier. You may recall that there are four basic forces in the universe. Well, as it turns out in the search for the Unified Field, as well as the search for how extraterrestrial vehicles work, scientists have discovered that all along, we have been operating on a few misconceptions. Before we continue, let me once again explain that I am writing for the common person to whom atomic theory and gravity may as well be the name of some rock band from the eighties. My explanations may be simplistic, but because this is all relatively "new" science, I believe they are at least as fundamentally accurate as possible at this time.

We are beginning to understand gravity, electromagnetism and magnetism are not as different as we once thought. Do you remember our discussion of fields? Quite possibly your hand is still smarting from the vacuum cleaner experiment we conducted earlier. If you will recall, a field is any place where force, such as magnetism, electricity or gravity are present. The interesting thing, as it turns out, is that people outside of the scientific mainstream like Nikola Tesla and Coral Castle builder, Ed Leedskalnin, had a much more advanced understanding of electromagnetism and gravitational fields than most of our most brilliant scientists. As we shall soon see, their understanding is what has led to our understanding of anti-gravity drives of extraterrestrial craft. But where did they get their understanding? We will talk more about that later.

Technology 1: Ferro-magnetic super fluids

What we do know now, thanks to the experiments conducted by physicist like Ning Li, of the United States, Giovanni Modanese of Italy and Eugene Potklinov of Russia and, most likely, U.S. and United Kingdom scientists, as well as scientists around the world who are working under the secret cover of "black" projects, is that there is something called a **gravito-magnetic** effect that occurs when, simply put, you create a spinning, or rotating magnetic field by accelerating a fluid full of tiny magnets around a circular donut-shaped container at unbelievably high speeds. This spinning of magnets in the fluid creates a magnetic field called a **vortex**, which is similar in its characteristics to a tornado. When a special fluid containing thousands of microscopic, magnetically charged metal fragments is rotated in a donut shaped cylinder at ultra high speeds, it creates a vortex with amazing properties. According to the research conducted by Eugene Potklinov, who conducted these experiments in Finland, they created a magnetic field that was *trillions* of times greater than expected. Such an intense magnetic field is able to defy gravity, well, in a way, along with a number of other startling effects that all seem to explain how extraterrestrial vehicles are able to perform right turns at ten thousand miles an hour without killing the crew.

Before we continue, and you get a "negative" feeling about my explanation, let us review the force called magnetism. Magnetism can come from many sources, such as electricity. As we all remember from Boy Scouts or science class, magnetism is also present in iron, such as in a magnetically charged compass needle. Also, magnetism is present in the earth, which is why we find the compass so handy in the first place. Now, just think about it. What happens when a positive magnet end meets another positive magnet end? They push each other away, correct? Now, what happens if the negative end of a magnet encounters a positive end of a magnet? They attract, yes? Now, just imagine what would happen if you were able to create an enormously powerful magnet like the one created in a super-fast spinning magnetic fluid that was created by Ming Lee, Potklinov and Modanese. Since the earth is surrounded by a weak magnetic field, and you with your super-duper magnet are able to create the opposite polarity of the earth's magnetic field, logically, you wouldn't have to worry about gravity anymore. You could just float wherever you want to go, at least in theory. There are some limitations, but it seems the aliens, and we Homo sapiens as of late, have got those limitations pretty much figured out as well.

Technology 2: John Hutchison and resonance technology

As we stated earlier, men outside the realm of established science have made most of the advances that have been made in the area of what is called "alien technology." People who have made breakthroughs in technology that involved energy and anti-gravity are, like physicist Ming Lee, inducted into the realm of military black projects where they and their work are not heard of again, or, members of the scientific field discredit them. Men like Nikola Tesla and Ed Leedskalnin lived before the intelligence community took over the scientific community, which is probably quite fortunate for them, as well as us. However, they were privy to knowledge, as we will soon see, that was way before their own time and slightly ahead of ours.

In the last chapter, we saw how, the Children of Israel were able to disintegrate the walls of Jericho using sound. Before we begin to discuss the work done by Tesla and the anomaly of Ed Leedskalnin's Coral Castle, we must first discuss what is known as the **Hutchison Effect**, which is named after John Hutchison, another self-made scientist. The Hutchison Effect says that all matter is vibrating at a certain frequency-we now call that **resonant frequency**. For example, think of the famous Ella Fitzgerald Memorex commercial from the 1970's where they replayed Ella's voice on a Memorex cassette. The reproduction on tape was able to shatter a crystal glass in the same manner as Ella's live voice.

What happens in the Memorex commercial is; at the atomic level when the sound waves hit the crystal glass, they vibrate the atoms in the crystal until they reach an appropriate frequency, the same frequency at which the subatomic structures called quarks are vibrating, which in turn, causes the atoms to separate far enough apart that the glass shatters. So, far, this explanation is just a theory, but it works well enough to explain the Hutchison Effect that it is the most practical theory available. In his time, Nikola Tesla did a famous experiment in an apartment building in New York using resonance frequency technology. In his first experiment, Tesla's resonance frequency machine began vibrating the building in which he was conducting his experiment so violently that it had to be destroyed before it brought the building crashing down.

What John Hutchison, along with Tesla and Ed Leedskalnin seemed to understand was that it is possible to vibrate any matter, provided it is done at the right frequency so that the atoms (or the quarks inside the atoms) begin to vibrate at the same frequency as the individual quarks within the matter. By doing this, it is possible to levitate an object, either because the gravitational field is also vibrating, or because the vibration of the atoms actually separates them far enough apart to make the force of gravity equal to 'zero' within the atoms.

The second obvious effect that would happen to certain materials being treated with resonant frequency would be to make it impossible for light to bounce off the object, at least within the same wavelength of the electromagnetic spectrum and, in some cases it would either seem to disappear, or it would change color. At this juncture, since I am not a physicist, to keep my foot from disappearing into my mouth, I will not venture to explain any further. Experiments have been done using sound waves to levitate things like frogs inside a vacuum chamber. John Hutchison inserted block of wood into solid piece of iron without changing the shape of the wood, and Nikola Tesla, as well as many others in our own time have demonstrated how to levitate objects using resonant frequency, so there is ample evidence the Hutchison Effect is in fact a reality.

The Philadelphia Experiment

During World War II, the U.S. Navy wanted to test this **resonance frequency theory** that was first proposed by Nikola Tesla. The Navy asked Dr. Albert Einstein if he would collaborate with them on a series of tests designed to make ships invisible using the same effect. What became known as the ***Philadelphia Experiment*** went tragically right as well as tragically wrong. Although no records of the experiment survived the US Navy's classification process other than a lot of terrifying stories, what actually happened in the simplest form of explanation was that the experiment did succeed in making the ship disappear. Three Tesla coils, which are basically superconductors of electricity, were placed on the front, back and main mast of the ship. When the generators began to power up, the ship began to rise out of the water and then it disappeared completely. It is after that the stories began to get very strange.

When the ship re-appeared, some say it appeared a few hundred miles south of its original location. Others say that the crew who were working on the deck suffered from burst blood vessels all over their bodies, including their eyes. The crewmen working below decks appeared to actually have been fused into the hull of the ship and died shortly thereafter. Some of the crew disappeared altogether. According to a local bar owner in Philadelphia, a few of the sailors, looking rather haggard and beat up, showed up at his bar and ordered beers. Afterwards, they walked through the back wall and were never seen again.

As evidence that the Philadelphia Experiment was in theory, at least possible, John Hutchison has levitated materials in the same manner as was accomplished in the Philadelphia Experiment.

Furthermore, John Hutchison's ability to fuse pieces of wood into solid blocks of iron, without changing the original shape of the wood, is fairly strong evidence that the stories of sailors actually fused into the hull of the ship are not simply the products of imagination.

Magnetic Super fluids, Resonance Technology and Extraterrestrial Craft

So, what does any of this have to do with extraterrestrial craft? If you have ever seen an extraterrestrial craft, or a photograph or movie of a craft that is actually flying, or heard or read reports of them, there appear to be some other unique features about them which allow observers to conclude, that they are using this same technology. Most sightings of extraterrestrial craft are described as being craft that are either extremely fast, or appear to be able to hover silently and then appear to either accelerate at unbelievable speeds, or, in some cases, just seem to vanish into thin air. In the **RAF Bentwaters** encounters of 1983, an Air Force serviceman approached a small extraterrestrial craft that was hovering in the woods near the base and reported feeling a strong electromagnetic current as he touched the side of the craft.

A craft that is floating on the earth's magnetic field will exhibit the same characteristics as a positively charged magnet floating in a positive magnetic field. Any craft able to repel the earth's magnetism will be able to move up, down, left right, stop and reverse direction at incredible speeds. Any craft using the technology to vibrate itself as in the Hutchison Effect, would be operating in a zero gravity environment. Zero gravity would mean that crews inside the craft would not be subject to things like centrifugal, or "g" forces (but better wear that seat belt just in case) and would allow them to make seemingly impossible maneuvers, as well as appear to disappear.

Based on what we know from the experiments done in the realm of legitimate research, as opposed to the secret projects conducted by the military and, from what we know about what is known as the Hutchison Effect, many of the characteristics of these craft are no longer as "unreal" as they were once thought to be. To reiterate, in a craft, that has a propulsion system that is based on what are called, ferro-magnetic super fluids, which can be more easily understood as magnetic particles rotating at super high speeds in a mixture of frictionless liquids, the movement of that craft near the earth is going to resemble the movement of two magnets of opposite charges that are held closely together.

Do you remember how, when you were playing around with magnetism in your sixth grade science class, the opposite ends of the magnets just would not stay together? If you have access to any UFO footage, such as can be found on the countless documentaries produced about sightings, you will notice that most of the craft are behaving the same way as your magnets did. They appear at times to be steady, but then at other times, they appear to be bouncing up and down in the same way a magnet would in the proximity of an oppositely charged magnet. The reason for this is simple. The earth's magnetic field that the craft is using to repel the force of gravity is not constant and in some places, those miniscule changes in the magnetic field affect the craft's position. Without going too far out of my league, the craft, especially in "hover" mode, is not creating massive amounts of magnetic force to keep its position steady. Much like a boat will rock up and down on the waves in choppy water until the engine is given enough gas to keep it moving forward and change its direction of momentum, so too do the hovering extraterrestrial craft ride on varying waves of the magnetic force above the earth's surface.

What is even more interesting is that these craft, producing such high amounts of electromagnetic energy, do something even more bizarre than fly at high speeds and hover noiselessly while abducting people, cows and other barnyard animals. It also appears, that when operating at such high levels of electromagnetism, they are actually able to produce the Hutchison, or Tesla, or Philadelphia effect. Because of their energy level, they also appear to actually vibrate at the molecular level. In other words, they are able to actually disappear, move from one place to another faster than the speed of light and, even more amazingly, as Einstein predicted, the occupants of the craft have no conscience knowledge that they are moving through time at a much slower speed than everything around them.

Does this sound familiar? How many alien abduction stories involve what is known as missing time? And to think that all this time the aliens had some secret knowledge whereby they could manipulate time! They were just stealing the ideas of Albert Einstein, who said the closer you get to the speed of light, the slower time passes. Does this mean that alien abductees are whisked away through the galaxy at super high speed while the aliens perform unthinkable experiments? We know now that it is not even necessary to go anywhere. Do you remember that Einstein said that gravity is simply a dent in the space-time continuum? Well, once you escape gravity by vibrating all of your subatomic particles at the right frequency, you must also, as the laws of physics go, escape time.

Otis Carr and his amazing "Aquamarine" flying saucer

A rather bizarre incident reportedly happened during the "UFO" encounters of the 1950's. While engineers such as Kelly Johnson at Lockheed's Skunkworks were using models of extraterrestrial craft as designs for military craft, one enterprising scientist, a self-proclaimed protégé of Nikola Tesla, Mr. Otis T. Carr, was building spacecraft for the civilian market. The story seems to coincide with the whole range of "out of this world" tales that came out of the 1950's, with one exception. Whether it is true or not, the account of a flight in one such craft seemed to coincide directly with the science of resonance technology, which in those days, was locked away with the rest of Nikola Tesla's papers. The account that was later told by engineer Ralph Ring, who claims to have actually flown in Carr's "flying saucer," describes the effects of this technology that, at the time, to which nobody outside of the military had access. According to Ralph Ring in an interview with the History Channel's UFO Hunters:

"We got on board and Carr said what we're going to do is we're going to vibrate this craft to that particular frequency; the color aquamarine. So they fired it up and this thing turned into this beautiful brilliant aquamarine. The whole craft inside lit up. And then he said, "Okay, that's it. Come on down to the de-briefing, that's the end of the experiment." The experiment lasted 15 seconds.

And he said, "What you did was you went down range ten miles and came back. You resonated here for about 5 to 10 seconds and for you it will probably equate to about fifteen minutes. He said, "Well, check your pockets." We had these little jumpsuits on and we emptied our pockets. There were stones and stick and grass and we piled it up. He said, "Where did that come from?"

The debris Ring allegedly found in his pocket was from an area ten miles from testing site. He asserts he did not have it before the testing of the craft.

We (Ring and his colleagues) said, well, how come we don't remember that, he (Carr) said, "The brain had reached its optimum capacity."

The "official" story is that Carr's operation was shut down and he was sentenced to 14 years in prison for defrauding investors in Oklahoma when he couldn't "reproduce" his spacecraft for the civilian market. Others claim that Carr was threatened by the U.S. intelligence and military agencies that were conducting the same research as Carr. Either way, Ralph Ring's tale does sound a little weird, but when comparing the story of the "aquamarine" aspect of the Carr's vibrating craft with descriptions of the sighting of an extraterrestrial craft during Operation Mainbrace in 1952, it doesn't sound so "far out."

"September 13--The Danish destroyer Willemoes, participating in the maneuvers, was north of Bornholm Island. During the night, Lieutenant Commander Schmidt Jensen and several members of the crew saw an unidentified object, triangular in shape, which moved at high speed toward the southeast. The object emitted a bluish glow. Commander Jensen estimated the speed at over 900 mph."

Robber Barons, Tesla, Coral Castle, Freemasons and UFO Technology

So, who was Nikola Tesla, the man who gave Otis Carr his inspiration? Who was Ed Leedskalnin? They were both men who may have given us our greatest understanding of the nature of matter and the world in which we have found ourselves today. It has taken science almost one hundred years to "catch up" to their understanding of electromagnetism and the fundamental states of matter, but, as we have seen, science is catching up and it is catching up fast. In fact it is catching up so fast that it is hard for the keepers of secrets to keep it all, well, secret.

Nikola Tesla and Ed Leedskalnin were born, raised and educated in Europe; Tesla in Serbia and Leedskalnin in Lithuania. They were also Freemasons. In the case of Nikola Tesla, his insights into electricity and magnetism were revolutionary, especially his idea that energy, which is provided by the universe, should be available to everyone for free. In the pursuit of a world where energy was available for free, Nikola Tesla basically pulled the world into the modern age. Well, at least until the men and the forces who saw Tesla's abilities as a way to make themselves even richer and more powerful, if you will pardon the phrase, "pulled the plug" on him. Among his many inventions and patents, Tesla is credited with the invention of alternating current, or AC as opposed to DC, and the radio. His work on radar allowed England to develop an early warning system without which they would have easily lost the Battle of Britain to the Nazis early in 1940.

Tesla's naiveté would be his undoing however, as he ran into the unscrupulous robber barons of the United States during of the early part of the twentieth century. Given a visa and hired to work for Thomas Edison upon his arrival in America, Edison told Tesla he would pay him $50,000 if he could make his electrical transformers run more efficiently. Tesla worked for months and finally developed a number of ways for Edison's generators to produce and conduct electricity more efficiently to the paying public. In the process, he patented a number of devices. When it all was finished, Tesla asked for his $50,000 dollars, to which Edison famously replied, "You don't understand the American sense of humor."

Needless to say, Tesla had less than congenial feelings for the inventor of the modern light bulb. He was forced to take a job digging ditches so that he would have enough money to continue with his work. His pet project, and one that was to be his ultimate undoing, was to invent a way to send electricity through the atmosphere, without the need of expensive wires. He envisioned a world where electricity would come to each household via an antenna in the backyard, just like television reception. None other than JP Morgan funded his project. It was dubbed the Wycliffe Tower and was near completion when Morgan asked Tesla, "Where do I put the meter?" When Tesla explained that the electricity was to be generated for free, Morgan immediately pulled the funding from his project and had Tesla labeled, in essence, a nut. It was at that point that Tesla was discredited in the scientific community. His patent for the radio was revoked and given to Marconi. Still, Tesla continued on with his work in the uses of electromagnetism. When he died, the United States Immigration Office seized all of his papers, research and experiments. Later they were turned over to the FBI, where they were locked away.

However, Tesla's ideas of the transmission of energy through the atmosphere did not die with him. In the 1950's and 1960's, government and military scientists began reviewing his papers and, as the world of science began to catch up with Tesla's ideas, his ideas began to seem more and more practical. One of Tesla's dreams, the idea of sending free energy into the ionosphere was seized on by the military and the Department of Energy and they began the HAARP project in Gakona, Alaska. There, high-energy microwaves are beamed into the ionosphere in experiments to see what the effects are upon the earth's magnetic field, and the ionosphere itself. Although the military potential of these microwaves has never been discussed, it is known that Tesla had conceived of a "death ray" that could knock planes out of the sky and kill enemy soldiers on the ground by the thousands. A sufficiently large electromagnetic pulse, or EMP deployed like a bomb over a target area from a satellite, would have the ability to knock out all communications, electronic components and even manipulate human brain waves, causing panic, hysteria or insanity in a population.

Nikolas Tesla, the consummate showman, was as famous during his time as any rock star, politician or movie actor of our time. Yet, after his death, thanks to the enemies he had created in the world of capitalism, he seemed to disappear from history until more recent times When it became apparent that oil was not going to last forever, his ideas concerning electromagnetism began to resurface among scientists, many of whom were either working under military contracts or were outside the established and therefore, accepted fields of science.

The mysterious Ed Leedskalnin

Our second virtually unknown subject of study was Ed Leedskalnin, a sickly, unassuming little man and Freemason who migrated to the United States in the 1920's. In one of history's greatest puzzles, Ed may have left us clues to the very nature of not only magnetism, but the very keys to unlock the nature and properties of the atom as well as the fundamentals of life itself. Ed literally left these clues in a pile of rocks, possibly in the hopes that someday science would correct its misconceptions (according to Ed) and then advance far enough so that the clues he left could be understood. Until recently, what we call "legitimate" science has ignored Ed Leedskalnin. Subsequently, his secrets may have remained undiscovered if it were not for the people who refused to give up trying to solve the mysteries he left behind. If not for their tenacity, the knowledge that he so stubbornly guarded may have passed us by like a warm Florida breeze.

At the time he was alive, not even great thinkers like Einstein, or possibly even Tesla himself would have been able to understand, nor agreed with Ed Leedskalnin's ideas. But today, with our ability to work with the very subatomic structures of the atom, we are able to understand the clues Ed Leedskalnin left in the massive limestone structures known as Coral Castle then, and Rock Gate Park, in modern day Homestead, Florida. As with the rest of the information in the book, this is merely a summary or overview in order to present the information necessary to support its premises. There is much more information in the work and research conducted by **Jeremy Stride** who seems to have solved the code left by the numbers carved into the rocks, seemingly at random, in different locations around Coral Castle, and another brilliant independent research named Jon Depew.

Jon Depew, who used Leedskalnin's book, *Magnetic Current* to decipher some of Leedskalnin's mysterious phrasing and codes, is continuing to do work with replicas of Leedskalnin's wheel and the interactions of magnetic vortexes, electrical currents and resonant frequency upon matter. For fear of either confusing or boring the reader, I will not delve too far into the realm of Jeremy Stride's use of prime numbers, the Golden Ratio nor the resonance frequency of atoms in a magnetic field. For the reader who is skeptical, as the reader should be because Coral Castle has appeared on shows like

Unsolved Mysteries and the popular 1970's TV show *In Search of*, there has been a tendency to associate Coral Castle with the mystical or some unexplained phenomenon and then ignore it. However, the clues left by Leedskalnin and re-discovered by Jon Depew regarding electromagnetic vortexes and the atom are presently being confirmed by scientists in such journals as *Science* magazine.

As a testament to Ed Leedskalnin's understanding of the nature of what he termed "magnetricity," which is what we today call electromagnetism, and the forces that make up matter, Ed Leedskalnin created Coral Castle with nothing more than simple tools and a basic wooden "A" frame crane with a block and tackle that wasn't even tall enough to move some of his largest blocks. At one point in his life, he actually moved the entire structure to Homestead, Florida without allowing anyone to see how he moved his large stones.

During his time, when people asked Freemason Ed Leedskalnin how he managed to move and carve limestone blocks singlehandedly that weighed an average of 14 tons and ranged all the way up to 30 tons, Ed would simply reply that he, "understood the secrets of the pyramids." As a Freemason, we can only assume that Ed Leedskalnin and Nikola Tesla would have had access to many "secrets" that were available to a society that traced its beginnings back to Ancient Egypt. Would that also include the understanding of electricity? Apparently, if we are to believe Leedskalnin, and he never gave us a reason not to, the Egyptians had not only an understanding of electricity, but the forces of electromagnetism and its effect on atomic structures, which Ed was able to demonstrate through his construction of Coral Castle.

Ed's Wheel

One of the most important clues to Ed's knowledge was a mysterious, yet simple wheel that was found in Ed's workshop after he died in 1951. The wheel resembles a potter's wheel in some respects. It is around three feet in diameter and has a sort of hollowed out interior that resembles the club on a deck of playing cards. It was theorized that this section was used to hold an object in place, possibly a pyramid, according to Jeremy Stride. The wheel sits flat, like a table top. Around the perimeter of the wheel are 24 four

V-shaped magnets that are evenly spaced throughout the perimeter of the wheel, protruding a few inches out of the side. Each V-shaped magnet carries a positive and negative charge on each end of the V. When placed together in the wheel, they are arranged so that there is an alternating magnetic current (remember Tesla?) that is created when the wheel is spun.

In deciphering a clue left on a wall at Coral Castle, researcher Jeremy Stride uses the numbers Ed Leedskalnin left, seemingly as an afterthought, to arrange the magnets in the proper position and in the proper sequence on the wheel. The numbers are 7 129 on one row and 6 105195 on the second row. By arranging these seemingly obscure numbers in the right order and figuring their correct places on a table of prime numbers (1, 2, 3,

5, 7, 11...), Jeremy Stride has come up with a brilliant theory that, oddly enough, exactly matches the arrangement of the rays of the sun in the Norman Hall room of the Freemason lodge in Philadelphia, which was built years before Leedskalnin came to America. According to Stride, the Freemasons themselves agree with his calculations. So, what do a few prime numbers have to do with alien technology?

Nature's simplest design

As with everything else in this book, it is not as simple as that. First, we must understand what Jon Depew, using a clue left by Leedskalnin on the cover of his book, *Magnetic Current*, has discovered regarding electromagnetism and the fundamental structures of the universe. According to Depew, it took him a long time to understand what the two strange looking symbols on the cover of Ed's book actually represented. The symbols themselves resemble two inverted "S" shapes or snakes that seem to mirror each other. The two symbols more accurately resemble mirror images of the "S" in the United States Constitution, which, at first glance look like "*f*'s." The left "S" shape begins, or ends with a small red portion at each end while the opposite has similar blue points at the beginning and end. The lines of each "S" do not touch instead, they appear to come closest as they come out of their bottom curl but then the spread apart as they move toward the top curl, where the opposite ends appear to be facing each other like two snakes about to strike, or the ear portions of a doctor's stethoscope. They look aesthetically pleasing and resemble the same designs available in artwork across cultures throughout the world. This is probably why Depew initially mistook them for designs the publishers had randomly placed on the book to make it more appealing, as if a book entitled *Magnetic Current* wasn't already appealing enough!

But then Depew realized that they were the key. At first, according to Depew, "I started laying out the two curve pattern on paper imagining them as magnetic currents and trying to show myself how they might run. At first I ran the two-curve pattern out in straight lines. After drawing them this way it didn't feel right, so I thought, I'm going to lay these patterns out until I find something that makes sense. That's when it all came together and I realized Ed Leedskalnin knew the secrets of what is known as, "Sacred Geometry." These two curved lines Ed left behind held his biggest secret, his "Sweet Sixteen" the magnetic currents of creation, known to the Ancients as the Flower of Life among other titles."

Ed's "Sweet Sixteen: The Golden Ratio

Among the puzzling clues Ed Leedskalnin left us, was the story he told about how he had been jilted in Lithuania by his sixteen year old girlfriend, or his "sweet sixteen." In the days before the term "jailbait" was invented, people didn't realize that the forty something Ed was not necessarily referring to a young lady. "Sweet Sixteen" he was referring to was not necessarily a girl, but a number, or more accurately, a ratio. Its value is 1.618 to 1 and it is more popularly known as the **golden ratio** or the **golden mean**. It can be seen in **Fibonacci sequences** as well as in nature in the form of the nautilus. It is one of the main mathematical formulas contained in the pyramids and was considered to be an almost sacred number to the ancient Greeks.

To put it simply, if you draw a rectangle where the shorter top is A and the long side is B, and you drop the shorter top line down to the side, if the remainder of your side B (that isn't covered by the line you just dropped down from the top) is equal to 1 compared to the side that is covered by line A which is equal to 1.6 or a little over one and a half times the length of what's left of your side, your rectangle has the Golden Ratio. What is so important about that? If you stand up, and drop your arms down to your side, you will notice roughly the same ratio between the top of your head and the tips of your fingers compared to the remainder of your body.

But what do some ancient Greeks who liked to play around with geometry, a reclusive Lithuanian, Nikola Tesla and John Hutchison have to do with the science of extraterrestrials? An article recently published in *World Science* gives us a better understanding of how our new science is actually old science.

"The researchers in the new study focused on the magnetic material cobalt niobate. It consists of linked magnetic atoms, which form chains like a very thin bar magnet, but only one atom wide. They are considered a useful model for describing magnetism at tiny scales in solid-state matter. When a magnetic field is applied to the chain at right angles to an aligned "spin" of its particles, the magnetic chain transforms into a new state called quantum critical, according to the physicists. This can be thought of as a quantum version of a fractal pattern, a pattern that looks the same at any scale. *By tuning the system the researchers found that the chain of atoms acts like a guitar string whose tension comes from interaction between the spins of the constituent particles.* "For these interactions we found a series," or "scale," of "resonant notes," said Radu Coldea of Oxford University, who led the research. "The first two notes show a perfect relationship with each other," added Coldea, principle author of a paper on the findings to appear in the Jan. 8 issue of the research journal *Science*.

The "pitch" of these notes, or their frequencies of vibration, is in a ratio of about 1.618, the same "golden ratio famous from art and architecture," he continued. If two numbers are related by the golden ratio, their sum is also related to the larger of them by the golden ratio. In other words, if A divided by B is that special number, then $A+B$ divided by A is the same number. Artists and architects have used the gold en ratio for centuries—for example, rectangles 1.618 times higher than they are wide—because it supposedly provides esthetically pleasing forms. The golden ratio is irrational, like pi, meaning its decimals go on forever.

In the "quantum uncertain" state of matter, the ratio "reflects a beautiful property of the quantum system – a hidden symmetry,"

Coldea said. It is "actually quite a special one called E8 by mathematicians and this is its first observation in a material." The findings dramatically illustrate how mathematical theories developed for particle physics may find application in science at the Nano scale—the scale of a few atoms—and ultimately in future technology, he added. "Such discoveries are leading physicists to speculate that the quantum, atomic- scale world may have its own under lying order," said Tennant. "Similar surprises may await researchers in other materials in the quantum critical state."

In other words, when a string of atoms that are held together and spinning according to their magnetic properties, are "zapped" from the side with neutrons, they vibrate at speeds of 1 to 1.618 and so on and so on. It's a really simple rule that even a child could understand. So what did Ed Leedskalnin know a hundred years ago that we are just beginning to understand now? Apparently, he had a pretty good understanding of how electromagnetism is the driving energy that makes up all matter in our universe, from the very small to the galaxies themselves.

According to Ed Leedskalnin, all matter is affected by this simple equation: + 0 -, where "0" is matter. The negative and positive forces of electromagnetism are in a constant state of rotation, which results in a rotating vortex, at either the scale of the very small, like the atom, in an extraterrestrial craft or the very large, like the earth, the sun and the galaxies themselves. This vortex affects the creation of matter and life itself, from babies in the womb, to plants and planets. The same principal has been handed down to us from past cultures, but we either have not been able to understand it, or, it has been hidden from us. We see it in the Judeo-Christian concept of good vs. evil, the Chinese Tao, Hindu Karma, etc. The basics of all matter are explained by John Depew (via Ed Leedskalnin) in the following way:

"Magnetic energy flows through each and everything here on earth, but each and everything allows different amounts of it and reacts differently due to the interactions and resistance of the magnets which make up that matter. Atoms hold all matter together and two individual magnetic currents hold all atoms together. Ed tells us atoms should be constructed as the Earth, with 2 separate magnetic poles. Two magnetic currents are the fabric of what is

holding together everything in our universe including the atoms themselves, this is what builds and holds an atom into a structure. The Ancients knew this fantastic secret as did Ed Leedskalnin and there is a ton of evidence."

Furthermore, in order to demonstrate that evidence, Jon Depew has arranged those basic "S" symbols left to us by Ed Leedskalnin in a lattice work that is present in places like Roslyn Chapel in Scotland, the opposing snakes on Babylonian temples, the intertwined rotating snakes of the modern medical symbol, Mayan Temples in Central America, Buddhist Monasteries and Hindu Shrines. Now that we understand what they are, rather than being just aesthetically pleasing pictures and symbols, we can now understand that they were instructions from the ancients to us, so that when the time came, we would be able to manipulate matter and energy in order fulfill our destiny. At least that was what they hoped…

Why should we be interested in the ideas of an obvious "crackpot" like Ed Leedskalnin? He also seemed to have a fairly good understanding of human nature. He didn't just come out and tell people what he knew. He knew if he told people, he would be considered crazy, like Nikola Tesla and people who report sightings of extraterrestrial craft. People don't just accept truth, especially truth that is simple and easy to understand, in other words, truth that is right in front of their eyes. Ed knew that people like a mystery. So, Ed Leedksalnin left us a grand puzzle to figure out for ourselves once the right people, with the right knowledge and the right motives decided to tackle his multi-megaton mystery.

To attract those people, he left the biggest clue that he knew would be sure to grab our attention. He left Coral Castle, where Ed was able move his multi-ton blocks like, "hydrogen balloons" as some teen-agers who snuck into the woods to watch him work, later reported. We are nearing the point of solving Ed's puzzle, but, there are some who claim the technology to move large blocks through the air, is nothing new at all. And didn't Ed himself say he knew how the Egyptians built the pyramids?

Bruce Cathie in his book, *The Bridge to Infinity* recounts an amazing story that he says originated in a German magazine. It tells the story of astonishing feats of levitation accomplished by priests in a monastery high in the Tibetan Himalayas. Here, in English translation, are excerpts from that German article:

A Swedish doctor, Dr. Jarl... studied at Oxford. During those times he became friends with a young Tibetan student. A couple of years later, it was 1939; Dr. Jarl made a journey to Egypt for the English Scientific Society. There he was seen by a messenger of his Tibetan friend, and urgently requested to come to Tibet to treat a high Lama. After Dr. Jarl got the leave he followed the messenger and arrived after a long journey by plane and Yak caravans, at the monastery, where the old Lama and his friend who was now holding a high position were now living.

One day his friend took him to a place in the neighborhood of the monastery and showed him a sloping meadow, which was surrounded in the North West by high cliffs. In one of the rock walls, at a height of about 250 metres was a big hole, which looked like the entrance to a cave. In front of this hole there was a platform on which the monks were building a rock wall. The only access to this platform was from the top of the cliff and the monks lowered themselves down with the help of ropes.

In the middle of the meadow, about 250 metres from the cliff, was a polished slab of rock with a bowl like cavity in the center. The bowl had a diameter of one metre and a depth of 15 centimeters. A block of stone was maneuvered into this cavity by Yak oxen. The block was one metre wide and one and one-half metres long (author's note: the golden ratio). Then 19 musical instruments were set in an arc of 90 degrees at a distance of 63 metres from the stone slab. The radius of 63 metres was measured out accurately. The musical instruments consisted of 13 drums and six trumpets.

Behind each instrument was a row of monks. When the stone was in position the monk behind the small drum gave a signal to start the concert. The small drum had a very sharp sound, and could be heard even with the other instruments making a terrible din. All the monks were singing and chanting a prayer, slowly increasing the tempo of this unbelievable noise. During the first four minutes nothing happened, then as the speed of the drumming, and the noise increased, the big stone block started to rock and sway, and suddenly it took off into the air with an increasing speed in the direction of the platform in front of the cave hole 250 metres high. After three minutes of ascent it landed on the platform.

Continuously they brought new blocks to the meadow, and the monks using this method, transported 5 to 6 blocks per hour on a parabolic flight track approximately 500 metres long and 250 metres high. From time to time a stone split, and the monks moved the split stones away. Quite an unbelievable task.

Dr. Jarl knew about the hurling of the stones. Tibetan experts like Linaver, Spalding and Huc had spoken about it, but they had never seen it. So Dr. Jarl was the first foreigner who had the opportunity to see this remarkable spectacle. Because he had the opinion in the beginning that he was the victim of mass-psychosis he made two films of the incident. The films showed exactly the same things that he had witnessed.

The English Society for which Dr. Jarl was working confiscated the two films and declared them classified.

It is our recent understanding of things like resonant frequency and the electromagnetic properties of matter that make stories like this one in the book of Ether, seem less the work of imagination and fantasy and more a testament of an ability to comprehend the nature of matter:

"For the brother of Jared said unto the mountain Zerin- Remove, and it was removed. And if he had not faith it would not have moved; wherefore thou workest after men have faith." (Ether 12:30)

Or this one, in the Old Testament Book of Joshua:

"So the people shouted when the priests blew with the trumpets; and it came to pass, when the people heard the sound of the trumpet, and the people shouted with a great shout, that the wall fell down flat, so that the people went up into the city, every man straight before him, and they took the city." (Joshua 6:20)

So, thanks to the dedication, sacrifice and hard work, of people like John Hutchison, Jeremy Stride, Jon Depew, Nikola Tesla and Ed Leedskalnin, what was once deemed a miracle, is now a source for our understanding. As things usually tend to progress, once a thing is understood, it can be used for good, or it can be used for evil. It can be used to free us, or it can be used to control us. In the future, the world of science will venture further into the exploration of electromagnetism and resonant frequency. They will conveniently "bump off" Ed Leedskalnin and Nikola Tesla, and replace their names with their own as the discoverers of these "new" technologies.

But as we do begin to understand, quantify, develop and implement these technologies, the beings that are watching us in our progression (as we may watch an ant nest take hold in our back yard), at some point, will see that we have undoubtedly reached what I will refer to as the "Babel Demarcation." At that point, we will force those who are watching us to make the decision that we were warned about in the Old Testament Book of Genesis. Will they say to themselves, as they did then that *"...the people is one, and they have all one language; and this they begin to do: and now nothing will be restrained from them, which they have imagined to do,"* and send us rocking back to the stone age, or will they allow us to join them as equals in our search for knowledge about the universe in which we live?

They, or somebody left us clues, but they are clues that are vague, like the massive stones at Coral Castle that Ed Leedskalnin was able to carve and move because he claimed he knew, "how the pyramids were built." They are so vague that they are easily misinterpreted, and what is worse, they are easily concealed by those who know about them, but don't feel anybody else has the right to their knowledge. Anybody who investigates these clues suffers the wrath of the "legitimate" scientific community. So, we must make one more trip back in time, back to the one civilization that served as a bridge between the modern age and the very, very ancient cultures that existed long before the Pharaohs of Egypt. We will talk about them in the last chapter of this book. But, for now, let us look at the testimonies of those who came forth to testify that our extraterrestrial visitors are real, and that all we have discussed so far, is in fact, our new reality.

Chapter 24

Extraterrestrial Encounters in the Scriptures

"And the Gods formed man from the dust of the ground, and took his spirit (that is, man's spirit), and put it into him; and breathed life into his nostrils the breath of life, and man became a living soul." (Abraham 5:7)

Every culture in the world, from Japan and China, to Europe and South America, has written texts that describe encounters with extraterrestrials from ancient times to the present. In Mesopotamia they were called "Anunaki," in China they are called, "wai-zing-ren," Japan, "uchuujin," in Spanish speaking Central and South America, "extranjero," "extraterrestra" and "aliengena." These countries speak of them openly and with a maturity that has yet to be realized in the Freemason dominated societies in the United States, Great Britain and Europe. Now that we have a basic understanding of elementary science and physics, let us once again, revisit the stories of extraterrestrial encounters in the Holy Scriptures.

EBE's NBE's and EBD's

The first aliens that were captured or recovered by the United States government were classified as "EBE's" which is the acronym for "Extraterrestrial Biological Entity." In fact, according to the information that came out of the Roswell crash, the alien that the government captured who lived for almost a year was actually named "Ebe" (ee-bee) by its Air Force captors. This information makes it imperative to ask the question; if it were necessary to classify a captured alien as "biological," are there beings the government knows about that are "Non-Biological Entities, or NBE's?" Are there beings that have crossed over from other dimensions beings that we would refer to as "Extra-Dimensional

Beings" or "EDB's?" Of course there are. The Bible and the other Holy Scriptures are full of them.

For the countries that follow the Judeo-Christian or Islamic traditions of the West and Middle East, the first verse in the Bible describes an extra-terrestrial being. With apologies to Erik von Daniken, who has done a lot of work on this subject, but who is classified as one of the "UFO Conspiracy Theorists" and whose information is not acceptable thought for the "mainstream," let us, for argument's sake, take Einstein's saying that "Everything is a miracle, or it isn't," and apply it to the texts of the Bible, the Book of Mormon and the Pearl of Great Price in the Doctrine and Covenants. We can then, in the spirit of Newton, Galileo and Einstein, match the information that is written in Holy Scriptures with the information that scientists, physicists, researchers, eyewitnesses and abductees have compiled about extraterrestrial visitors and see if there is actually something to see there

The language barrier

For the benefit of the reader, let me point out a few things about language. The term "UFO" or "extraterrestrial" did not exist in the vocabulary of the people of the ancient world. Although I know very little about ancient languages myself, I can assure the reader that no such term existed and if it did, over the years as empires flourished and then subsided and knowledge was passed from one language or culture to another, the translators of the original language would bear the burden of trying to convey the meaning of the words of the old language into the new.

As we have seen, the Holy Scriptures were translated from Hebrew, or Aramaic (Jesus' spoken language) into Greek, Latin and then into the languages of German, English, Spanish and so on. At the time the translation process was taking place in the last years of the Roman Empire, there had been an intellectual decline that had been taking place for the past five hundred years. Therefore, if there were words like "extraterrestrial" or some words that meant "beings from above" in the languages of the Hebrews, Syrians, Egyptians or Mesopotamians, the Latin speaking translators did not possess a word comparable to the original, so the translation was limited to the written and spoken language of the day. Hence, extraterrestrials become "angels" or "gods," and the term for space, other planets or other worlds (dimensions) becomes "heaven." While the languages may have changed, I hope the reader will keep in mind that the origin of the messengers or the methods they used should in no way be confused with the message they bore, which still retains the same meanings, promises and of course, consequences for not heeding the words of the messengers and the Word of God.

With this understood, and in the spirit of reason, let us begin in the Beginning, so to speak, in Genesis chapter one, verse one, where it says, *"In the beginning, God created the Heaven and the Earth."* There you have it, the first words of the first verse of the Bible tells us that we are not alone. But there is more. God, or the Gods, then created man out of the dust and later used one of Adam's ribs to create a woman. To ancient man, the miracle of life is itself relegated to the One God because they could not possibly understand how it was possible. In our time, because of the work of Crick and Watson in the 1950's, we understand DNA enough to be able to reproduce life through the process of cloning. In the first case, where God created man out of the dust, scientists are closing in on the processes that will allow us to understand how life began on our planet. Will this eliminate our need for God, or will it vouch for the need for what some refer to as "intelligent design?" I will leave it up to the theologians to argue about the nature of God, whether He is EBE, ENBE, or EDB, but the fact is, our own traditions are based on the idea that there is someone or something out there greater than us, and science is fast coming to grips with an understanding of how, at least, some of the beings we have known throughout history as "gods" or "angels" are able to do what they do. It is only what we do with that information that begins to cause problems.

Lot's visitors

Continuing on in the Old Testament book of Genesis, there are many descriptions of visitors and beings that are not "human" beings. For example, in the story of Sodom and Gomorrah, two "angels" arrive at Sodom and Gomorrah to visit Lot and tell him to flee before God destroys the city with "fire and brimstone." (Genesis 19:24) The city is then destroyed in an explosion, which turned Lot's wife into a "pillar of salt." The archeological evidence that has been uncovered at the ancient cities points to the Biblical version being accurate, that Sodom and Gomorrah were destroyed by a fire, a fire that has been explained as the result of an upwelling of natural gas that resulted from an ancient earthquake.

If two wicked cities were destroyed by God in a cataclysmic explosion, isn't that enough to frighten sinners from their wicked deeds? Why throw in the story about the angels? Especially angels who are able to move people and blind them? (Gen. 19:10-11) Furthermore, what was the true nature of the "angels?" If they were our classic extraterrestrial aliens, with big eyes and grey skin, wouldn't they have "freaked" people out? Could there be different kinds, possibly even a human-like race of extraterrestrials? With their advanced understanding of physics and technology, could these beings have the ability to manipulate light so that we see them as human in form?

Furthermore, could there be beings that don't fly around in space ships, but occupy another dimension and at times, cross over into ours? These beings we would have to consider not extraterrestrial but extra-dimensional? We could consider them "extraterrestrial extra-dimensional beings" but the acronyms are really starting to add up. Anyway, is there something about the appearance of the extra-dimensional beings that have been recorded in the Scriptures that may give us clues that the physical properties of the dimensions from which they come are completely different than our own?

In the Gospel of St. Matthew, after Jesus is laid to rest in the tomb, Mary Magdalene finds one of these beings resting on the stone that guarded the entrance to the tomb:

"In the end of the Sabbath, as it began to dawn toward the first day of the week, came Mary Magdalene and the other Mary to see the sepulchre. And behold, there was a great earthquake: for the angel of the Lord descended from Heaven, and came and rolled back the stone from the door, and rested upon it. His countenance was like lightning, and his raiment white as snow." (Matthew 28:1-3)

In the Gospel of St. Mark, the two women see a similar figure:

"And when they looked, they saw that the stone had been rolled away: for it was very great. And entering into the sepulchre, they

saw a young man sitting on the right side, clothed in a long white garment, and they were affrighted." (Mark 16:4-5)

In the Gospel of St. Luke, it is not one, but two men who address them:

"And they entered in and found not the body of the Lord Jesus. And it came to pass, as they were much perplexed thereabout, behold, two men stood by them in shining garments." (Luke 24:3-4)

Similarly, in the Gospel of St. John, there are also two men clothed in white:

"But Mary stood without the sepulchre weeping: and as she wept, she stooped down and looked into the sepulchre, And she seeth two angels in white sitting, the one at the head, and the other at the feet, where the body of Jesus had lain." (John 20:11-12)

The account in Matthew, as we will see, is the most consistent with accounts of "Heavenly" personages that will appear to Joseph Smith one thousand eight hundred years later. After He is crucified, Jesus appears three times in the scriptures. One time before He has ascended to heaven, and once again when He accompanies God to instruct the fourteen-year old Joseph Smith in the restoration of His last earthly church. The two times he appears following his crucifixion, according to the New Testament Book of John and the Book of Third Nephi in the Book of Mormon, He appears still bearing the marks of his crucifixion. It is also important to note that Jesus cautions Mary Magdalene, not to touch him, *"For I am not yet ascended to my father."* (John 20:17) Later that evening Jesus returns, and in order to convince his disciple, Thomas, that He has risen from the dead, Jesus lets Thomas and the rest of his disciples feel the wounds in his hands, side and feet. In America, He similarly allows the Nephites and Lamanites to examine his wounds, which tells us that he was somehow able to regain consciousness after he had died. However, immediately after his Resurrection, for some reason, Mary Magdalene was not allowed to touch him.

If the whole thing were simply a miracle, then touching Jesus wouldn't have been a problem, but, for probably the same reason that we avoid touching dead bodies because of the risk of disease, and because of Jewish Law, Jesus did not want Mary to touch him until He had seen God. Something happened to Jesus that cannot be medically explained at this point in time, but, if He was able to be revived and then was worried about disease, that is within the realm of explanation. How Jesus could continue on with his work after seeing God, in spite of the horrible wounds and the pain He endured, it is fairly certain that He was converted into something or a form of matter that we are not even close to understanding in our own time. This conversion of the matter that made up the body of Jesus allowed Him to cross between dimensions, but there was another property that these beings also seem to possess, that of actually emitting light.

In Joseph Smith's *History of the Church*, he describes his visitation by Jesus and God in the woods of upstate New York in the following way:

"…I saw a pillar of light exactly over my head, above the brightness of the sun which descended gradually until it fell upon me. It no sooner appeared than I found myself delivered from the enemy, which held me bound. When the light rested upon me, I saw two Personages, whose brightness and glory defy all description, standing above me in the air. One of them spake to me, calling me by name and said, pointing to the other-This is my Beloved Son. Hear Him!"

(Joseph Smith, History of the Church Vol. 1:15-17)

When the angel Moroni later visited Joseph Smith, he describes Moroni's physical characteristics in the following way:

"While I was thus in the act of calling upon God, I discovered a light appearing in my room, which continued to increase until the room was lighter than at noonday, when immediately a personage appeared at my bedside, standing in the air, for his feet did not touch the floor. He had on a robe of most exquisite whiteness. It was a whiteness beyond anything earthly I had ever seen; nor do I believe that any earthly thing could be made to appear so exceedingly white and brilliant. His hands were naked and his arms also, a little above the wrists; so also were his feet naked, as were his legs, a little above the ankles. His head and neck were also bare. I could discover that

he had no other clothing on but this robe as I could see into his bosom. Not only was his robe exceedingly white, but his whole being was glorious beyond description and his countenance truly like lightning. The room was exceedingly bright, but not so very bright as immediately around his person. When I first looked at him, I was afraid; but the fear soon left me."

(Book of Mormon: Testimony of the Prophet Joseph Smith.)

Based upon what we have seen in these passages, it appears that at least these "extraterrestrial" excuse me, "extra-dimensional" beings have undergone some kind of a transformation that allows them to cross into this dimension, and are not subject to the same physical laws by which we terrestrials are bound. They appear to cross over from some other place in a light of some sort, they themselves seem to exude light, and they are not subject to the laws of gravity. From what we do know about light at least as far as our own dimension is concerned, it is created from the process of electrons jumping from one atomic state to another. That is the only way that light in our universe can be created. If God and Jesus and their messengers are able to actually give off light, then the very substance of their beings must either be made up of atoms in which electrons are jumping to a lower state of energy, or the energy that they are emitting is actually exciting the electrons in the atoms around them to higher states of energy. When we see terms like, "…*his countenance was exceedingly white like lighting,*" as in Joseph Smith's description of the angel Moroni, and Mary Magdalene says, *His countenance was like lightning, and his raiment white as snow,"* or the description of God and Jesus Christ as, "*two personages whose brightness and glory defy all description,*" reported by Joseph Smith, we know from a scientific standpoint that these beings are not bound by the physical laws of this universe, or at least our dimension of this universe, however, either the matter which they occupy and the matter which surrounds them is subject to the laws of our universe, and is affected by their very presence.

There are many other accounts of contacts with the extraterrestrial "non-biological entities" we refer to as our God, Jesus Christ and His angels. In the *Book of Exodus*, *"...the skin of Moses' face shone,"* after speaking with God, which is the result of contact with extreme electromagnetic energy, or radiation. Further examples of the physical properties of these beings exist in the *Book of Ether*, when the brother of

Jared asks God to touch stones he has smelted in order to give them light for their journey across the ocean. The brother of Jared says to the Lord:

"And I know, oh Lord, that thou hast all power, and can do whatsoever thou wilt for the benefit of man; therefore touch these stones, Oh Lord with thy finger, and prepare them that they may shine in the darkness; and they shall shine forth unto us in the vessels which we have prepared, that we may have light while we shall cross the sea. And it came to pass that when the brother of Jared had said these words, behold, the Lord stretched forth his hand and touched the stones one by one with his finger. And the veil was taken from off the eyes of the brother of Jared, and he saw the finger of the Lord, and it was as the finger of a man, like unto flesh and blood; and the brother of Jared fell down before the Lord, for he was struck with fear." (Ether 3:4-6)

If we are to believe these accounts, we have seen that it is possible for these beings to exist in our dimension, and that they appear to leave physical evidence of their presence. Is the opposite then true; that beings in our dimension of space-time are able to cross over into the dimension from which our God comes? In the *Book of Moses*, God allows Enoch, one of the grandsons of Adam, to see the future of the human race, right up to the end of days. In order to do so, Enoch is required to undergo a physical change, which is described this way:

"And it came to pass that I turned and went upon the mount; and as I stood upon the mount, I beheld the heavens open and I was clothed with glory. And I saw the Lord; and he stood before my face, and he talked with me, even as a man talked one with another, face to face; and he said unto me: Look, and I will show thee the world for the space of many generations." (Moses 7:3-4)

What exactly it was that covered Enoch as he was "clothed with glory", we of course do not know. However, whatever it was allowed him to see the continuum of space-time or, "the heavens," open.

Whereby, he was not only able to speak with God, but was allowed to see the entire history of the world. This would only be possible, as we now know if it were somehow possible for Enoch to enter what is known as the fifth dimension.

The *Book of Moses* also tells us about an entire city that was so righteous, that it was "translated" piecemeal into the heavens.

"And the Lord called his people Zion, because they were of one heart and one mind, and dwelt in righteousness; and there was no poor among them. And Enoch continued his preaching in righteousness unto the people of God. And it came to pass in his days, that he built a city that was called the City of Holiness, even Zion. And it came to pass that Enoch talked with the Lord; and he said unto the Lord: Surely Zion shall dwell in safety forever. But the Lord said unto Enoch: Zion have I blessed, but the residue of the people have I cursed. And it came to pass that the Lord showed unto Enoch all the inhabitants of the earth; and he beheld, and lo, Zion, in process of time, was taken up into Heaven. And the Lord said unto Enoch: Behold mine abode forever."(Moses 7:18-21)

So far, we have seen many examples taken from the records that have been passed on to us, that the Beings we call our Gods and the universe in which we exist, are bound, as Dr. Stephen Hawking once conjectured, by physical laws such that they are noted in as much detail as the occurrences themselves. It would have saved a lot of space writing with a feather and ink, or pounding out marks on a sheet of metal to just say that Jesus rose from the dead, Moroni, God, and Jesus all wore white clothes when they appeared to Joseph Smith, God changed the stones of the Jaredites into lights because he is God, or Enoch was taken up by God and shown the history of the world. For the faithful, that would obviously be enough. However, that is not how these occurrences were recorded. Why? Whatever the reason, the writers of these accounts possibly could not understand the science that we understand today, therefore, what was a miracle to them, as Einstein said, is no longer such a miracle to us. Could it be possible that someone understood that in the last days of the world, that men would be convinced, not by tales of miracles, but by science and facts that are proven by testing and observation?

We all know about God and Jesus, but are there other beings that live and work with them? What about passages such as the Book of Genesis where it says in regard to the Tower of Babel:

"Go to, let us go down and there confound their language, that they may not understand one another's speech." (Genesis 11:7)

Who is the "us" that God is speaking to? Of course, the stock answer among the religious would be that the "us" God is speaking to is the angels. But if it is God, couldn't He just snap his fingers? Why does God need help, and, who are these angels? If they are God's helpers, do they exist in one form or many? Do they exist in the same dimension as God, or are some of his angels actually beings that reside in our dimension, but beings who come from other worlds. In the Book of Moses, we read:

"And worlds without number have I created; and I also created them for my own purpose; and by the Son I created them, which is mine only Begotten." (Moses 1:33)

It is interesting to note here that God does not say, "I created them for the same purpose that I created man." Instead he created them for His own purpose. Of course it would be ridiculous to try to speculate as to what purpose that would be. However, if we look at ourselves and ask why we create things, the most common answer would be that we create most things to use as tools to accomplish our tasks. We create fire to cook our food and give us light. We created points out of stone to kill more efficiently. We created plows to make growing food easier. We created iron, concrete and steel to use to build the world we see around us. Therefore, could God have made other beings that serve as his tools in order to oversee our progress, inspire us and, at times, to carry out His work?

The real question is not whether or not these beings exist, as we passed that milestone a long, long time ago. The real question is; what are these beings doing here? Are these the same beings or entities that fly around in highly advanced craft? Are there clues in the Bible? In the Book of Exodus, it says:

"And Mount Sinai was altogether on a smoke, because the Lord descended upon it in fire; and the smoke thereof ascended as the

smoke of a furnace, and the whole mount quaked greatly." (Exodus 19:18)

The Ten Commandments, or the ten laws that Moses received from the God of Israel, and which formed the backbone of Western jurisprudence for nearly two thousand years was given to Moses in the following manner:

"And the Lord said unto Moses, Lo, I come to thee in a thick cloud, that the people may hear when I speak with thee, and believe thee forever. And Moses told the words of the people unto the Lord." (Exodus 19:9)

After receiving the Ten Commandments, the Children of Israel were instructed to build a tabernacle as the resting place of the Ark of the Covenant, which held the sacred stone tablets. Once finished, according to Exodus:

"Then a cloud covered the tent of the congregation, and the glory of the Lord filled the tabernacle. And Moses was not able to enter into the tent of the congregation, because the cloud abode thereon, and the glory of the Lord filled the tabernacle. And when the cloud was taken up from the tabernacle, the children of Israel went on with their journeys: But if the cloud were not taken up, then they journeyed not till the day it were taken up. For the cloud of the Lord was upon the tabernacle by day and fire was on it by night, in the sight of all the House of Israel, throughout all their journeys." (Exodus 40: 34-38)

Cloud by day? Fire by night? In the days before electricity, the only thing that gave off light at night was fire, but we know now that electric lights or electricity itself gives off light. Is there any modern documented evidence that extraterrestrial craft have been photographed moving under the cover of clouds? Of course, there is plenty of photographic and videotaped evidence of mysterious clouds that seem to be moving in the same direction as the craft they are concealing. In some videos, the cloud in question seems to be moving in the opposite direction of the prevailing wind. It doesn't take too much of a stretch of the imagination, knowing what we will soon know about extra-terrestrial craft, that the description of a cloud that had fire on it at night, also matches the description of an extraterrestrial craft.

So what was the Ark of the Covenant? Was it a beacon, a transmitter, or a homing device? I will leave that to the reader's own imagination, or to the movies of Steven Spielberg. Suffice it to say, that this is a more rational, and easily understood explanation of what it was that regularly visited the Tabernacle, than our ancestors, or the people who translated these accounts could have understood. The Ark of the Covenant, whatever it was, obviously caused enough fear in the hearts of the Children of Israel that it was carried before them throughout their journeys, and the fear of it, or what it attracted, far outweighed the fear of the tribes and kingdoms they would come across when they re-entered Palestine.

Of course, the first city to feel the wrath of the Israelites was the city of Jericho. In the book of Joshua, we read that:

"Ye shall compass the city, all ye men of war, and go round about the city once. Thus shalt thou do six days. And seven priests shall bear before the ark, seven trumpets of ram's horns: and the seventh day ye shall compass the city seven times and the priests shall blow the trumpets. (Joshua 6:3-4)

"So the people shouted when the priests blew the trumpets: and it came to pass, when the people heard the sound of the trumpet, and the people shouted with a great shout, the wall fell down flat, so that the people went up into the city, every man straight before him, and they took the city."

It appears that the Israelites used resonance technology in their conquest of the city of Jericho. Modern archeology has verified that Jericho's walls did, in fact, collapse in an "earthquake." But are they the only ancient culture that was aware of the effect of sound and vibration upon solid structures? The Roman Army, when marching across stone bridges, gave the command for their men to walk, and not march, having learned the hard way that the sound waves produced by marching soldiers was capable of collapsing stone structures.

But still, the question remains. What are these being actually doing here? We have already seen that through their very presence, they have inspired us, and most likely assisted us to the greatest achievements in the history of the human race, as least as far as we know. But, if they are, in fact, here as servants of our own God, do they have one purpose that they have yet to accomplish? In Joseph Smith's History, he left us with an interesting clue.

For behold the day cometh that shall burn as an oven, and all the proud, yea, and all that do wickedly shall burn as stubble; for they that come shall burn them, saith the Lord of Hosts, that it shall leave them neither root nor branch." (Joseph Smith-History 1:37)

Chapter 25

The Disclosure Project

On May 9th, 2001, Dr. Stephen Greer organized a *National Press Club* Conference for what is known as the Disclosure Project. The purpose and design of the Disclosure Project is to bring forth individuals whose oaths of secrecy taken during their military service, especially regarding their knowledge of extraterrestrial craft and beings has expired. At the conference, many former military, intelligence and individuals employed by the government, spoke to the National Media of the United States as well as reporters from other countries. This is the single most important public announcement in the history of mankind, yet it was basically ignored by the corporate/government, and "spun" by corporate/government/media attack dogs. The following are their testimonies transcribed verbatim. As in the rest of the book, with the exception of the use of the term "UFO" as it is used by the witnesses, since we have already determined that these craft are not of terrestrial or, at least most are not of man-made origin, the misnomer, UFO or Unidentified Flying Object has been dropped and replaced with the correct description of "extraterrestrial craft."

Extraterrestrial Craft Encountered in Alaskan Air Space

John Callahan: Former FAA Head of Accidents and Investigations

"My name is John Callahan. I'm a retired FAA employee. I was the division manager for the Accidents Investigation Division in DC. About two years before I retired, I received a call from the Alaska region. The region wanted to know what to tell the media.

My question: "Tell the media what?"

He says, "About the UFO."

It went downhill from there. "What UFO?"

It turned out I told him what any government employee would do, to tell them it's under investigation. And then I had him send all that data to the FAA's tech center in Atlantic City. The next day, my, uh, immediate boss, service director Hali Safir and I went to Atlantic City. I just purchased a new video camera, and I videoed the event.

In Atlantic City, we had them play back, on the air, on the scope. You call a scope a plain view display, a PVD, exactly what the pilot seen or the controller seen. We timed it in with the voice tapes so we could hear exactly what the controller said and what he heard and we taped it. We came back the next day, briefed the administrator, Admiral Higgin on what happened. He wanted a five minute briefing. After we started the briefing, he wanted to know if he could see the video. We put the video on. He watched the video, the whole video.

The next day, he set up a meeting for me to give a dog and pony show to President Reagan's scientific staff and whoever they brought over, and to hand off all that data to them. That morning, in the FAA round room, it was either nine or ten o' clock, three men from Reagan's scientific staff, three CIA people, three FBI people and I don't remember who the other guys were, along with all the FAA experts that I had brought with me who could talk about the hardware, software, how it worked. We put on a dog and pony show. We let them watch the video. We had all the data there. We had all the computer printouts.

They got all excited over it. When it was all done, the CIA men, one of the CIA, men told all the people they were all sworn to secrecy, that this meeting never happened, and this event never happened. I asked him "Why?" I thought it was probably just a Stealth bomber at the time.

He said that this is the first time we have recorded radar data on a UFO, and these guys were getting all excited, they were drooling over all this data. I said, "What are you gonna tell the public about it?"

He says, "We don't tell the public about this, it would panic the public." He says, "We're gonna go back and study this."

I said, "Okay, if it's what you're gonna do." I've told about this report many times and I get funny looks from people. I have with me, the voice tapes of the controllers that were involved, the FAA original tapes. See, after we handed this stuff off to the president's staff, the FAA didn't know what to do with it. We don't separate UFO's from real traffic so it's not our problem, okay? I have a copy of the original, of the video that we took, which is rather interesting. And, once the thing was all over, the reports started coming into my office, but because it wasn't an FAA traffic problem, the FAA's report ended up on a table in my office and it stayed there until I retired, when one of the staffers packed up all my gear and helped move it to my house. Also in a box, I found just a few days ago, in my 1992 tax return, I have the target printouts from the computer data.

So, if you want to retrace…or, look at every target that was up there at the time, you can now reproduce this from this piece of paper here, and it's called the UFO incident, Japan 1648 that happened on November the 18th, 1986. I'm prepared to go to Congress to swear before congress that everything I've told you people and everything that is here is the truth, thank you."

Projects "Grudge" and "Blue Book"

Lt. Colonel Charles Brown: U.S. Air Force (Ret.)

"Good morning, I hope you'll pardon me, I'm a little bit nervous. My Name is Charles L. Brown. I'm a Lieutenant Colonel in the US Air Force, retired. Subsequently, seven years with the Foreign Service. I like the name "Charlie Brown." Gentleman by the name of Charles Schultz of great talent, sort of elevated the name if you will.

During World War II, I was a young farm boy from West Virginia; I got the patriotic bug, joined the US Army, ended up flying bombers in Europe and ended the war transport in the Pacific. Finished college in the summer, late summer of '49, recalled to active duty in the newly formed United States Air Force. I was assigned to an organization called "Office of Special Investigations." The Air Force, as most of you know, was formed in 1947. OSI as a central investigative agency for the Air Force formed in 1948, so everything I think was relatively new. Needless to say, starting in '47, UFO's were rather new. The Air Force Intelligence, er, Technical Intelligence Center was at Wright Patterson Air Force Base and I had my office in a building adjacent to it. And, our organization was the worldwide investigative agency for the Air Force for any unidentified flying objects. This lasted for about two years. The project name was known as *"Project Grudge."* It was the predecessor to a project known as *"Blue Book,"* which Ed Riopelle headed.

During my experience with it, I would collect, data, didn't collect it, it was sent in to my office. I analyzed it. As a pilot investigator, I was able to offer some bits of advice to the Air Technical Intelligence people. Now, you might visualize a massive office, but as I recall, we had a First

Lieutenant, a secretary and a Technical Sergeant. That was the essence of *Project Blue Book* when it started, or, *"Grudge."*

Blue Book then expanded somewhat. During the review as an analyst of these various documentary reports, if you will, or documents, I became clearly convinced that there was substance to what was being reported, in that we had ground visual, ground radar, airborne visual and airborne radar confirmation of some of these sightings. The individuals who made the sighting were everything from airline pilots, military pilots, police officers- some of the people that your lives depend upon on a daily basis. These are very reputable and credible people. I hope that the testimony here from very credible people will convince you of that and will further Steve Greer's Disclosure Project, in that pressure needs to be brought to bring this to the attention, not only of the Americans, but the people all over the planet. These vehicles have been seen and confirmed all over the planet. I am willing to sign a sworn statement, or testify to my judgment and to what I have observed. Such things do exist, please believe me, please believe those who follow me. Thank you."

Extraterrestrial Craft: radar contacts in Oregon and Michigan

Mr. Michael Smith: US Air Force-Radar Controller

"My name is Michael Smith. I was in the Air Force, a sergeant from 1967 to 1973. I was aircraft control and morning operator. While I was assigned to Klamath Falls, Oregon in early 1970, arrived at the radar site and they were watching a UFO on the radar that was hovering at about 80,000 feet. It sat there for about ten minutes and then slowly descended until it dropped off the radar, was gone for about five, ten minutes and then instantly reappeared at 80,000 feet, stationary. The next week with the radar, it was 200 miles away, stationary. It hovered there for about ten minutes and then it redid the whole cycle, twice more.

When I found out what the normal, what you normally do when you see a UFO, I was told that you notify NORAD, you don't necessarily write anything down, and you keep it to yourself, it's a need to know basis only. And, NORAD one night called me later in the year to let me know it was a heads up there was a UFO coming up the California coastline. I asked them what I should do about this, they said, "Nothing, don't write it down, just a heads up."

And in late 1972, while stationed at the 753rd radar squadron in Sioux St. Marie, Michigan, I received a couple panicky calls from police officers who were chasing three UFO's from Mackinaw Bridge up by I-75. So, I immediately checked the radar, confirmed that they were there, called

NORAD and they were concerned because they had two inbound B-52's going to Kinslow Air Force Base. So they diverted them 'cause they didn't want any proximity of the two.

And, that night, I answered many calls from the police department, sheriff's department and stuff. My standard response was, "There was nothing on radar." And, I will testify to this under oath to a congressional hearing. Thank you."

Extraterrestrial craft over Mexico City, a threat to public safety

Mr. Enrique Kolbeck: Senior Air Traffic Controller (Mexico City)

"Good morning, my name is Enrique Kolbeck. I am an air traffic controller. Sorry for my English, I am so scared. I am not accustomed to talking in front of a lot of people. I'm here because I'm being a witness and I'm going to try away on my work. I work in Mexico City. I was an air traffic controller at the International Airport of Mexico. I'm going to give an example about this sightings that we have in Mexico. For several years, and each year it happens a lot of times in my country, unfortunately.

For example, March 4^{th,} 1992, we detected 15 objects west side of Toluca airport. It was very close to the international airport, fifty miles more, or less. Then July 28th, 1994, we have almost a collision or something that we can name in that way. International flight, I mean domestic flight of I Mexico 129, commands by the pilot Ramundos Hernandez Rano that has a trash or something in his main landing gear in the right leg. That's occur at night at 10:30 more or less. Then in the next week, the same year, in the same moment, the Air Mexico Flight 904 has another almost collision that was reported for the pilot Capitan Corso. At 11:30 in the morning, we detect that object on the radar, suddenly, just for a moment.

Then, the next week, we have a lot of sightings reported by the pilots that gave us information about the weird traffic or something, brighting lights at different times. We detect some of them in that week. But September 15th of 1994, we have a detection of about five hours more or less on the new equipment that we believe that equipment was working in not a good way because it is not common that you have five hours of detection by the same object without movement. Well, we concurred with the technical persons of radar in our country that our radar system was working well and was very exciting.

We were surprised the next day we received information about apara(?) Hymie Manson who study these case about a sighting about a lot of people in the Metepec City a located point southeast of Toluca airport about a sighting of a big flying saucer, apparently fifty meters of diameter. Then, for a lot of people that left trash, or something, in the ground. Next sighting November 24, 1994, we have on service, officially our new radar system and after that moment, we have information very exactly about these sightings about the same time with the pilot's detections. That's why I'm here, we consider, in my country that this is very dangerous. We have a lot of more cases but I don't want to use more time than this. But it's very important that the people in the world knows this evidence and consider that it could be very dangerous for aeronautical situation, especially in my country. I don't know why in my country that occur frequently, but the point is, that happens and we consider dangerous, and we have unfortunately only one crash but we don't want to have another one. Thank you very much and I'm sorry for my English."

Underwater extraterrestrial craft over the Atlantic Ocean

Commander Graham Bethune: US Navy (Ret.)

"My name is Graham Bethune, I'm a retired Navy Commander, pilot. I've got a top secret clearance. Fifty years ago, February the tenth, 1951, I was flying from Keflavik, Iceland to Argentia, Newfoundland. It was at night, it was dark. About three hundred miles outside of Argentia, I saw a glow on the water, like approaching a city at night. As we approached this glow, it turned to a monstrous circle of white lights on the water. We watched this for a while, the lights went out. There was nothing on the water.

Next thing we saw was a yellow halo, small, much smaller than whatever it was launched from and that was fifteen miles away (motions towards his face quickly) shoo! Up to our altitude. Because of our trajectory, I disengaged the auto pilot, shoved the nose over, tried to go under this thing. At that times, heard a noise underneath, thought maybe it hit us. It was actually some of the crew member ducking. They collided and some of them were injured.

Then it appeared over to the right and moved out slowly and moved with us. It was still not at our altitude. We could see the shape of it. It had a dome we could see the, we could see the corona discharge. I went back aft, let the other pilot, Al Jones take my seat to see what the passenger's reaction was. Came back to the cockpit, told him not to report anything, simply because of what the psychiatrist had said to me. Maybe they would lock us up.

So, basically, the instruments in the cockpit, we had four or five failures. In the area of the magnetic compass, you know, the electromagnetic effect, direction finders and this type of thing. The craft was tracked by radar in excess of 1800 miles an hour. It never did get to our altitude. We had thirty one passengers, plus the psychiatrist and the crew member that all sighted this at different areas. When we landed at Argentia, Newfoundland, we were interrogated by the Air Force, an excellent interrogation, Captain Paulson. When we landed at the Naval Air Test Center her at Pawtuxet River, we were required by Navy Intelligence to make out individual reports (holds up document). Out of the National Archives I have the eighteen page official Navy and Air Force report. I've made up a report to straighten out the truth, there's a stack of books written this high that have written all this up. So the truth is here. I will testify, under oath, before congress that everything that I have said is true."

Underwater extraterrestrial craft near Alaska

Mr. Dan Willis: US Navy

"My name is Dan Willis; I was in the United States Navy. I held a top-secret crypto level 14 sensitive material handling security clearance. I worked in the code room at the Naval Communications Station in San Francisco. In 1969, I received a priority message from a ship near Alaska that was classified as secret. The ship reported, emerging out of the ocean, near port bow, a brightly glowing, reddish orange, elliptical object approximately seventy feet in diameter, emerged out of the water, shot into space traveling at about seven thousand miles per hour. This was tracked on ship's radar and substantiated. Years later, I worked at the Naval Electronic Engineering Center in San Diego for thirteen years. The co-worker who I worked with worked at the NORAD facility. When he first started working at the facility, he noticed objects going on the screens that track everything out in space and in the air. Objects going off the scale, doing right angle turns when he inquired, his older supervisor advised him that, quote, "It was just a visit from one of our little friends," and thought this was a little unusual. These statements are true. I'm willing to testify under oath before congress. Thank you."

Lockheed Skunkworks, Blackbirds and extraterrestrial craft over Las Vegas

Mr. Don Phillips: Lockheed Skunkworks/ CIA Contractor

"My name is Don Phillips; I was in the United States Air Force and have worked with certain Intelligence Agencies of the United States Government. Prior to my Air Force, prior to my joining the Air Force, I worked for the famous Lockheed Skunkworks and I was working for them when I was attending college and, I worked for them in the capacity as a design engineer. It was one of my proudest moments of my life to work with a man by the name of Kelly Johnson.

A lot of you might be familiar with that. It turns out that the models of aircraft that we were building, as you know, were all classified, were in the deep black and that I came in on the end of the U-2 project. My main project was known later as the SR-71. The SR-71 had a predecessor, it had a special model built for the CIA and that those models were one passenger, one pilot special aircraft, in order to get from one place to another very, very quickly. Now these SR-71's as we know them, the Blackbird, are still classified in a sense as far as the altitude that it flies at and also the speed records that it holds. I'm very proud to say that this aircraft played a big part in helping to end the Cold War.

The aircraft, the predecessor aircraft, there's strong evidence to suggest that perhaps these aircraft had a different role, once in the air. Each pilot, and I knew a few of them, each pilot had an assignment before they took off. They learned about the assignment immediately prior to take off and there's strong evidence to suggest there was a dual role in that they were monitoring some type of traffic to and from planet earth. This can be verified at a later point. This was...I'll jump into my military experience.

My first field assignment for the United States Air Force was at Las Vegas Air Force Station. And that was my first experience with Las Vegas and I couldn't understand why people were so excited about going to a place such as this, but I soon found out, about a year later. Nellis Air Force Base is located there; Nellis is a major training center for different types of special aircraft and fighter aircraft. One of the premier training sites for pilots all around the world. However, when I learned that my assignment was at a radar site fifty miles out of town, up near Mt. Charleston, I had no idea where I'd be so, finally, in the daylight, I was able to find the location and reported in 1965 for duty.

In 1966, early in the morning about one to two a.m., I was sleeping, I was staying there on base and our barracks were at about 8,000 feet. I heard a lot of commotion. You know, at that altitude, sound carries, sound carries tremendously. And I thought, well, it's early in the morning, it's summertime and there is a lot...it's very warm, and maybe I should get up and take a look. I didn't really want to, but I got up, took a look, walked up the main road near my office, which was the commander's office. I was on the commander's staff, Lt. Col. Charles Evans and I couldn't...who was making all this noise? Who's making all this noise at this time in the morning?

So when I got within about fifty yards of the five, four or five people that were standing there, one of them being the chief of security, they were looking up in the air, their heads were all looking in the same direction. I looked up to the West, Northwest, and to my amazement, there were lights flashing around the sky, moving at from anywhere, what seemed like 2,400 to 3,800 miles per hour. Now, the fact that we're taking an estimate from a distance, you know, we figure, well, this is quite something. However, we continue to watch these darting lights go across the sky and stop, absolutely stop, come to a dead stop and reverse at an acute angle their direction and then proceed on, they were traveling so fast that you could almost see a pattern left. If you are computer people and you move your mouse across the screen, you see a little bit of a tail. Well, that's the way these six or seven craft worked.

After five minutes of watching these things, they all seemed to group up to the west, northwest. Okay, they started to come in on a circle. But what I would like to point out is that where they were putting on their display in the north, northwest sky, just directly east of that is known as Area 51. Area 51 is a AEC name, okay, Atomic Energy Commission that was the old name for the Atomic Energy Commission. We knew it as the Groom Lake Flight Test Facility, in the Air Force. And, it was where we tested our aircraft after we got the prototype made from the Skunkworks.

So, here are these, let's get back to the circle in the sky, what they did was coalesce and started rotating in a circle and then they disappeared. Well, I thought, gee this is something we have to keep quiet. That was verified by the chief of security. But, we waited there and talked it over for a little bit and it seemed like, I think it was an hour, and then came the radar people from their scopes, which were at 10,000 plus feet. Came down for their dinner at two o' clock in the morning and the first person off the bus was a good friend of mine, Anthony Kassar. He said…he was white as a sheet and he says, "Did you see that?" And we all said, "Yeah, yeah, it was a nice display. What a show." He says, we documented them on radar." He says, "We didn't give 'em clearance." We just, it's a standing order, just let them fly through our radar beam. He says, "We documented, six to seven UFOs." Now we don't know who was guiding those, but we're certain they were intelligent and we don't know where they landed because they coalesced and disappeared. So, I will say, at this point, to keep it short, that I will testify under oath as to what I say is true, and I will do so before congress. Thank you."

Extraterrestrial craft: "Monkeying" with our missiles.

Robert Salas: Captain; US Air Force

"My name is Robert Salas. Contrary to what it says on the card, I was not a Lt. Colonel in the Air Force. I was in the Air Force on active duty after I graduated from the Air Force Academy in 1964 until 1971, and separated as a Captain. In March of 1967, I was stationed at Malfdom Air Force Base, Montana as a missile launch officer; Minuteman Missiles. On an early morning of March 16th, 1967, I got a call from my security guard, primary security guard upstairs. We had about six, as I recall, flight security airmen upstairs. I was downstairs, sixty feet underground, in a capsule, monitoring and controlling ten nuclear tipped Minuteman Missiles.

I got a call that morning that they were seeing strange lights flying in the sky. I disregarded that call. I told them to call me when something more significant happened. I got another call, subsequent to that call and this time it was a more intense tone in the guard's voice. It was very clearly very frightened. He said there was a bright glowing red object hovering outside the front gate. It was oval shaped. He had all the other guards out there with their weapons drawn. After that call, I woke up my commander who was on a rest period, Fred Mywald, a retired colonel now, and told him about the phone calls. As I was telling him about the phone calls, my weapons started going down, one after the other. They went into a "no-go" condition, a condition where they are unlaunchable. We lost somewhere between six and eight weapons that morning. Within minutes of having received that second phone call about a UFO hovering outside the front gate. Again that morning, after reporting it to the command post, we were informed that a similar, a very similar incident happened at Echo Flight. I was at Oscar Flight. They lost all ten of their weapons under similar circumstances, very similar circumstances where UFOs were sighted over the launch facilities. They had maintenance crews and security crews out there that had spent the night and they were reporting UFOs over those sites and the commander of that flight was Eric Carlson.

He also separated as a captain. The deputy commander was Walt Feigel, retired as a Lt. Colonel. We have those witnesses that I just mentioned, the names I just mentioned have spoken of this event before and they will back up this story. We also have documentation that I received through FOA requests from the Air Force, outlining the Echo Flight incident including in that documentation, a reference to UFOs. We have telexes covering this incident. In one telex it says "the fact that no apparent reason for the loss of ten missiles can be readily identified is cause for grave concern to this headquarters." This was from SAC headquarters.

So we've received, we've got those telexes. I've got about twelve witnesses that'll verify parts of this story, including a man who investigated the incident afterwards for the Air Force and you'll hear a little bit more about that from the next witness and also another guard that had witnessed a UFO at the same time period and another officer who retired a full colonel, who had other reports of UFOs. Ancillary to that, I've got the complete report on a Minot North Dakota incident that was at Minot North Dakota Air Force Base, which happened in August of 1966, very similar UFO sight over missile silos and also a UFO incident that was investigated by the Air Force immediately after our incident within a week. I am willing to testify to the truth of all these matters that I have spoken about in front of congress under oath. Thank you."

Extraterrestrials and more Minuteman Missile "Monkey Business"

Lt. Colonel Dwynne Arnesson: US Air Force (Ret.)

"Good morning, my name is Dwynne Arnesson, I served twenty six years as a communications electronics officer in the US Air Force, all over the world, including Vietnam. I was lucky to be selected to be commander of three different units in the Air Force. I held a top-secret "SCI PK" clearance and for those who know, it is slightly above top-secret. I retired in 1986 as a colonel at Wright Patterson Air Force Base in Ohio. I would like to relate about three different experiences, if you will, that relate to UFOs.

As a young lieutenant at Ramstein Air Force Base, Germany, back in the early sixties, I was in charge of the cryptographic center. I had a top-secret "crypto" clearance at that time and I can clearly recall seeing a message that went through my crypto center which said a UFO had crashed on the island of Spitsbergen, Norway and a team of scientists were coming to investigate it.

Going forward to the 1967 time frame, I was assigned to the 28th Air Division at Great Falls, Montana. I was the officer in charge of the communication center there. Also, I was the top secret control officer for the division. I had a crypto account. I was the account custodian and I also passed out nuclear launch authenticators. During that time, I can recall seeing a message come through that communication center which said basically what Bob has just got through talking about, that a UFO was seen near the missile silos and the missiles were deactivated. Coincidentally, my first, the person that Boeing sent to investigate the particular missile conditions, if you will, what made them shut down, was my first manager at Boeing, Mr. Bob Kaminski, who has since passed away. And, I can recall him on different occasions; he lived close to me in Auburn, Washington, that's where I'm from, and he said, "Arnie, those missiles were perfectly clean," that was the result. So, my last incident, as a commander in Kassel Air Force Station, Maine, I had contacts with the security police at Loring Air Force Base and they told about UFOs that were seen near the nuclear weapons storage areas on Loring Air Force Base, and I'll be glad to testify to Congress that this is absolutely the truth, thank you."

Extraterrestrials in D.C. and contact near the moon

Mr. Harland Bentley: US Army

"Good morning, my name is Harland Bentley. During 1957 and 1959 I was a PFC in the United States Army, stationed north of Washington DC on the Ajax Missile base close to Maryland. In May, this month, in 1958, about six a.m., I heard a noise outside that sounded like a pulsating transformer. I sat up in my bunk. I looked out the window, and saw a craft heading for the ground and crashed. Pieces broke off. That craft immediately took off again. So there's a lot more to that story but I've gotta speed this up.

Now, the next night, I was on radar duty. I get a call from the Gaithersburg missile base. He says, "Hey I've got twelve or fifteen UFOs outside fifty to a hundred feet above me. " So I asked him, "What does it sound like?" He took his pen mike off, held it out the window and said, "Here." And the sound was the same sound I had heard the previous morning, except a lot more of them. So I, my radar was on standby, so I immediately turned it on and got the blip just outside of the ground clutter. I marked it on my radar screen. And then, for a few minutes later, all of a sudden, they took off. As they took off, the sweep came around, hit the blip, when it came around, it hit it again. That blip was two thirds of the way off my radar scope. In order to get that far, at a constant velocity, was 17,000 miles an hour. That was my first incident.

Ten years later, by this time I had received a Bachelor of Science degree in electrical engineering and I was working in California. Now, I'm sorry that all I can say is I was somewhere in California working on a classified project that had nothing to do with my experience that I had there. As I was working, and it was like two or three in the morning, California time, I heard a Houston Astronaut communication link, "com-link." I didn't pay much attention to it until I heard the word "bogey." Course, my ears perked up immediately. An unidentified object of some sort, whether it's a craft, meteorite or whatever, was on a collision course with that module going in a loop around the moon. So basically, I listened for some time and then I stopped and went back to work. And then I heard, "There they go."

In the astronaut world, for some of you may or may not know this, there's a term called green turtle and used to be, I don't know if it is used today or not. It used to be, you are not allowed to use profanity over the net and the first person that does that, whoever hears it first and says, "Green turtle," that astronaut has to buy that man and his entire family a dinner at the most expensive place in Cape Canaveral. Well, to end this real quick, one of them said, "damn" the UFOs took off real quick and one of them said, "damn that was fast," and somebody yelled, "Green Turtle." And then he said another word, a synonym to "crap." And then, somebody else yelled, "Green Turtle!" And you could see him grit his teeth, because now he had to buy two expensive meals. And, my particular experience, I will testify before congress if necessary and explain exactly what happened, thank you."

Secret documents, extraterrestrial images and the shadow government

Mr. John Maynard: Defense Intelligence Agency (Ret.)

"My name is John Maynard. I'm retired Army. I retired as a Sergeant First Class. My entire year, twenty one years of service, I held a top-secret clearance, compartmentalized at times to as high as "TK," "Omni," "Crypto," and others. I had access to very, very sensitive documents. My testimony is basically two prong. One, I retired from DIA in 1980. When I was an administrator, when you take over an office, you take over everything, you sign for everything. I signed for well over two thousand documents. In order to sign and inventory those things, you have to read them. Not word for word, but basically, I went through every document to make sure it was complete. It was there if they told me, so that when I turned my charge over to the next person, those same documents were there.

So I got quite a good knowledge of what was going on in those documents, and believe me, there are many, many different references to UFOs. There were also MPIC pictures that shows it would target objects that were casing you out (?). Now I worked on the SALT 1 and SALT 2 areas for the office that I worked in, so we were taking pictures all the time for verification of nuclear disarmament and there were some objects in those pictures that didn't belong there. Te second prong to this whole thing is that a lot of people talk about conspiracies over a "shadow government."

I'm willing to testify before congress that these black operations do exist. I nearly became part of it, but I saw the light, I think, and I got out. And that's it. We have to disclose what we know, and I am willing to testify before congress under oath, or before any other organization, that what I witnessed was true."

Photograph images of extraterrestrial moon base

Sergeant Karl Wolf: U.S. Air Force

"Good morning. I was a precision electronics photographic repairman with a top secret crypto clearance in the United States Air Force. I was stationed at Langley Air Force Base in Virginia. In 1965, in mid-1965, I was loaned to the Lunar Orbiter Project at NASA on Langley Field. Dr. Colley was in charge of that project. They had problems with a piece of electronic equipment that was bottlenecking their production of photographs. I went to the facility and when I walked into the facility, there were scientists from all over the world. I was stunned, naturally, to see people at a NASA project from all over the world. It didn't make any sense to me, initially.

I was taken to the laboratory where the equipment was malfunctioning. I couldn't repair it in the dark. I asked if I could have it removed. An airman second class was in the dark room at that time. I was also an airman second class. I was interested how the whole process functioned, how the data got from the lunar orbiter. (I) asked the young man if he could describe the process to me. He did. About thirty minutes into the process, he said to me, in a very distressed way, "By the way, we've discovered a base on the back side of the moon." And, then he proceeded to put photographs down in front of me, and clearly in these photographs were structures, mushroom shaped buildings, circular buildings and towers. And at that point, I was very concerned because I knew we were working in compartmentalized security. He had breached security and I was actually frightened at that moment, and I did not question him any further. A few moments later, someone did come into the room. I worked there for three more days, and I remember going home and naively thinking, "I can't wait to hear about this on the evening news." And, here it is, more than thirty years later and I hope we hear about tonight. I will testify under oath before congress that what I'm saying is the truth."

"Doctored" NASA images

Ms. Donna Hare: NASA Employee

"Good morning everyone, my name is Donna Hare and I worked at Philco Ford Aerospace for, from 1967 to 1981. During that time, I was a designer, illustrator, and draftsman. I did the launch slides and landing slides, also projecting plotting boards, lunar maps for NASA. We were a contractor, but most of the time, I worked on site in building 8. I had the opportunity to do extra work during down time, which was between missions, and I walked into a photo lab which was the NASA lab across the hallway. I had a secret clearance, which is not that high, but, I was able to go into restricted areas, which this was. At the time, I was talking to one of the techs in there and he drew my attention to a photograph, a NASA photograph. It had a dot on it and I said, "What is that?" Well, he drew my attention to it and I said, "Is that a dot on the emulsion?" and he's smiling and he has his hands crossed and he said, "Round dots on the emulsion don't leave round shadows on the ground." And this was an aerial photograph of the, earth, I'm assuming the earth, because it had pine trees on it. And the shadows of the craft, or whatever it was, were in the same angle as the trees, and by its very nature, UFO. And, I wanted to clarify that, to a gentleman who was talking to me, means "unidentified," so I did not know what this was but I realized at this point that it's very secret, that it was kept secret, because I asked him, "What are you gonna do with this piece of information?" And he said, "We always airbrush these out before we sell them to the public."

Sort of pesky little creatures appearing on the photograph, they wanted to get rid of. After that, I decided I would ask questions to other people that work there, and I found that I had to ask them away from the site, not on site. A guard told me that he was asked to burn some photographs and not to look at them and there was another guard guarding him who was in green fatigues watching him burn the photographs. And he said that he was too tempted, that he looked at one and it was a picture of a UFO, and he was very descript…I can go into that later with anyone. He was immediately hit in the head, and he had a big gash in his forehead. He was knocked out. And he's terrified, so he would have to be protected.

Another incident I knew someone in quarantine with the Apollo Astronauts. He told me that the Apollo Astronauts saw craft on the moon when we landed. And, that is what he told me. And, he also was afraid, he said, the astronauts are told to keep this quiet. They are not allowed to talk about it. So, I do want to let you know that I worked out there for a number of years and I ran into this, so it's not something that everyone knows that works out there for a long time. My boss didn't know about it. Some people that sat right next to me didn't know about it. It's very strange because I don't know how they do it. They can let some people know about it and others not. I'm willing to testify before congress that what I'm saying is true and thank you very much.

Extraterrestrials in England

Mr. Larry Warren: US Air Force-Security Officer

"Good morning ladies and gentlemen and members of the press. My name is Larry Warren. Twenty years ago in 1980, I was a security specialist assigned to RAF Bentwaters, one of the British NATO Air Force Facilities in Southeast Anglia. I had a secret security clearance. I guarded our backline nuclear weapons that were stored there at the time, without the knowledge of the people of Great Britain. I went through a portion of a three night UFO event, where objects made incursions over our WSA, fired pencil thin beams of light into them adversely affected the ordinance, possibly. These objects were on the ground on two different nights. Potentially, there was another life-form seen. This is an unpopular truth. These events were of extreme defense significance to not only Her Majesty's Government, but this government as well, and they are still shrouded in secrecy. They are very complex, they are very vast. This is more about a human rights issue than just a UFO issue. Twenty years ago, this room would be empty. I see a turn in history. This is history in motion, but unfortunately, it is history with a security classification. I would be more than honored to swear under oath, that I experienced what I did, that I saw what I saw. Thank you."

In hot pursuit: chasing extraterrestrial craft, alien killed by Fort Dix security

Maj. George A. Filer, III: US Air Force (Ret.)

"Good morning, my name is George A. Filer the third. The reason I am here is because George Filer the fifth is in the hanger and will be born on Friday. I'm a retired intelligence office and flier with almost five thousand hours and, I didn't believe in UFOs until London Control called us in the winter of 1962 and asked us, would we chase one, and, we said, "sure."

So, we let down from 30,000 feet to a thousand feet where the UFO was hovering and we went into a steep dive. I actually exceeded the red line of the aircraft, so it's kind of dangerous chasing UFO's. In any case, I was able to get the UFO on the aircraft radar about forty miles and we could see the light out in the distance. And, as we closed, we kept on picking up this radar return. Point I'm mentioning, that the radar return was very distinct and solid, indicating it was some kind of metallic object. We got about a mile from the UFO and it kind of lit up in the sky and went off into space, very similar to what the shuttle looks like when it takes off.

Later on, I was working in intelligence in Vietnam. I briefed General Brown about UFOS when I was in 21st Air Force, McGuire Air Force Base. Briefed General Glowe about a UFO over Tehran, Iran in 1976 where two F-4's from the Iranian Air Force had taken off and tried to intercept the UFO and when they turned on their fire control systems, they immediately went out, all the electrical systems went out. The planes had to return to base. This was particularly significant because it was also picked up by satellites.

In 1978, on January 18th I was going into the base, every morning I did the briefing of the general staff, and I noticed that there were some lights off in the distance at the end of the runway, there. When I got into the command post, the senior master sergeant in charge said that there had been UFOs in the air all night, they were on radar, the tower had seen them, they had gotten aircraft reports and so on, and that one had landed, or crashed at Fort Dix. Fort Dix and McGuire are right together. This is kind of like the Roswell of the east.

But, in any case, an alien had come off the craft and had been shot by a military policeman and apparently was wounded and was heading for McGuire. So, for whatever reason, the aliens liked the Air Force better than the Army, perhaps because they were shooting at them. But in any case, our security police went out there and found him on the end of the runway, dead. And, they asked me to brief the General Staff, General Tom Sadler at the eight o' clock stand-up briefing and I said, "I don' think I want to do this. You know, General Sadler doesn't have a good sense of humor." And, I'm not sure I believed it, so I did some calls to the 438th command post and everybody had pretty much the same story. And, at eight o' clock that morning, just before I went on, I was going to brief this and I was very worried about it, they said, "Don't brief, it's too hot," so to speak. That's pretty much my story. I'm prepared to tell the story in front of Congress and it is the truth. Now, because of this, I stayed interested in UFOs, and I'm the Eastern Director of the Mutual UFO Network and between the National Reporting Center, and Pete Davenport of MUFON, we get one hundred reports a week on average of people from all over the United States that see these things regularly. Now if you start checking, they're out there and people are seeing them all the time. Now, these are highly qualified people who essentially give us the reports by email, thank you."

Recovered craft, captured aliens

Clifford Stone: US Army

"Morning ladies and gentlemen, my name's Clifford Stone. I was a Sergeant First Class, United States Army. I had a secret clearance with nuclear assurity. I could get the clearance I needed to do whatever it was necessary for me to do at the time on special operations, when I was called in on those. What I'm referring to here is that I was involved in situations where we actually did recoveries of crashed objects, crashed saucers, for lack of better term, degrees thereof. There were bodies that were involved with some of these crashes, although some were alive.

While we were doing all this, we were telling the American public there was nothing to it, we were telling the world there was nothing to it. I'd like to go into detail on some of the cases, the nuts and bolts cases, but, I will be available if you have any concerning my involvement in this. You can talk to Dr. Greer to arrange for me to get to talk to you. But, the whole situation is, we've set back, we've told the American people that there is no such thing as UFOs. I've been involved where we have recovered these objects. We know them to be of extraterrestrials.

In 1969, I had an event that happened to me, while I was stationed at Fort Lee, Virginia. We went to Indiantown Gap, Pennsylvania. That would be my first exposure to anytime we would be recovering an unidentified flying object. When we went there, we, there were people that were already in the facility. We were back up team. We were supposed to be NBC because there were so supposed to be nuclear materials on board this craft. Later on, most people that were involved were to be told that there was nothing on board, it was just a crash of one of our aircraft.

I know better because I was one of the people that approached it with a Geiger counter to get surface readings. I was the first person to go ahead and see that there were bodies on it. That would be the first of approximately twelve events, UFO crashes are not events that take place every day. They're rare. I know we're not alone in the universe. I know that the absence of evidence is not evidence of absence. It's evidence that has been denied to the American people. I stand before you today and Almighty God and I tell you this: If Congress calls me in, and says, "Will you testify in detail what you know?" I stand here today, prepared and ready to do just that. Governments must never lie to the people, for no reason. Thank you."

Terrestrial craft of extraterrestrial design

Mr. Mark McCandlish: US Air Force

"Good morning, my name is Mark McCandlish, and for the last twenty one years, I have worked as a conceptual artist for a variety of defense contractors. I've been involved in conceptual artwork and the production thereof for Rockwell on the X-30 program and also on the HYSTEB program, that's spelled, H-Y-S-T-B that's the Hypersonic Test Bed Program. During the course of my career, I've twice had a secret security clearance. In 1967, my father was stationed at Westover Air Force Base, the headquarters for Eighth Air Force Strategic Air Command. I witnessed and watched through a telescope a UFO which hovered over a nuclear weapons storage facility for approximately ten minutes and then departed with an acceleration approaching a bullet leaving a rifle barrel.

In 1988, in November, a college buddy of mine, an associate, by the name of Brad Sorenson, informed me that he had personally witnessed three flying saucers at a large hanger at Norton Air Force Base, during the course of an air show that was held on Saturday, November 12, 1988. I subsequently called my congressman from that district, this was congressman George E. Brown Jr. who, at the time was the chairman of the congressional committee on Space Science and Advanced Technology and actually assumed that since the presentation that Brad talked about was for top military brass and certain congressional individuals, that his office must have coordinated this with the local Air Force Office of Public Affairs.

A male staff member in Congressman Brown's office, not only confirmed the exhibit, but the fact there were three disks at the exhibit. These disks were hovering off the floor without any visible means of support. They were referred to as, "Alien Reproduction Vehicles," also nicknamed the "Fluxliner" because they use high voltage electricity. To keep things short, this is a diagram that I made based on a sketch that Brad Sorenson did for me in rough form, shortly after he had his sighting and subsequently cleaned that drawing up and made it much more accurate. That's the drawing that Dr. Greer's holding there now. Later on, I obtained photographs that were taken in 1967 by a military pilot, Harvey Williams, flying a C-47 for the Air Force at 12,000 feet, approximately twenty five miles southwest of Provo, Utah.

This particular vehicle matches the so called ARV in all proportions and respects in terms of the detail of the shape of the craft. This was photographed, as I say, in June of 1967. I later spoke to a gentleman by the name of Kent Sellen that I met at an air show at Edwards Air Force Base in 1992, the first unveiling publicly of the B-2 bomber. He indicated to me that in 1973, when he was a crew chief working on experimental aircraft at Edwards Air Force Base, that he had unintentionally wandered into an area where there was a classified aircraft, namely the ARV. He described it in detail and he added other details to the account concerning the configuration and the operation vehicle that Brad Sorenson was not aware of.

Subsequently, Brad Sorenson met with the famous aeronautical designer, Burt Rutan, gave him a copy of this blue print which you've just been shown. Mr. Rutan felt that it was a joke and put it on his wall as kind of a joke and a third party confirmed for me later that a Colonel Ray Walsh from Edwards Air Force Base was visiting Mr. Rutan, saw this blue print on the wall and registered quite a degree of shock and anger-wanted to know where the hell he got this blue print because there was in fact such a craft at that time, approximately 1994-95, in a hanger at Edwards Air Force base, North Base Complex at that time.

Subsequently, I've done a lot of research on this product, this vehicle. I've come across a number of declassified documents that show that the Air Force, as early as 1960 was wind tunnel testing flying saucer shapes up to Mach 20. And, I also have declassified NASA documents that show similar shapes, in fact this is the document here that more or less, details the wind tunnel testing up to Mach 20. This is the NASA document right here, that was declassified and shows a variety of spherical and lenticular shapes that were flight tested up to, or I should say, wind tunnel tested up to Mach 6. I subsequently obtained a copy of an inner office memo from Hercules Aerospace. It describes a particular type of science involving something called 0 point energy and scalar waves.

According to Brad Sorenson, this is the basis for the technology for these anti-gravity propulsion systems. This particular document here, describes six different meetings involving the Defense Intelligence Agency, and cooperative efforts with the Russian scientific community investigating what is called the fundamental enabling technology that was discovered by Nikolai Tesla in the early 1900's. Anyway, I could provide you much more detail at a later time and I am prepared to testify in detail concerning these events and their truthfulness before congress, thank you very much."

Not even the US President has the proper clearance:

Mr. Daniel Sheehan*:* Attorney

"Good morning, my name is Daniel Sheehan. I am an attorney serving as General Counsel to the Disclosure Project. I'm a 1967 graduate of Harvard College in American Government Studies and Constitutional Law and a graduate of Harvard Law School. And, I served as General Counsel and one of the co-counsels for the New York Times in the *Pentagon*

Papers case and was involved in briefing and arguing the case in front of the United States Supreme Court, giving permission to the New York Times, giving permission to publish the classified documents, the forty seven volumes of the Pentagon Papers. Subsequent to that time, I served as special counsel to the office of F. Lee Bailey as one of the trial counsels when we represented James McCord in the Watergate burglary. Got Mr. McCord to write the letter to Judge Sirica to reveal the Watergate burglar's relationship to the plumber's unit in the White House, at that time. Subsequent to my service in that case, I went back to Harvard to the Divinity School to study Judeo-Christian social ethics in public policy. Did my Masters work and PhD work there and became General Counsel for the United States Jesuit Headquarters in Washington DC, assigned to their Social Ministries Public Policy Office.

It was there, in 1976, or, 1977, that I was contacted by Ms. Marcia Smith, who was the director of the Science and Technology Division of the Congressional Research Service. She asked to meet with me and I met with her and, she informed me that President Carter, upon taking office in January of 1977, held a meeting with the Director of Central Intelligence, who was George Bush Sr. and demanded that the Director of Central Intelligence turn over to the President the classified information about unidentified flying objects and, the information that was in the United States Intelligence Community concerning the existence of extraterrestrial intelligence. This information was refused to the President of the United States by the Director of Central Intelligence, George Bush Sr.

The Director insisted that the President, in order to have access to this information, needed to have clearance, to contact the Congressional research service, to contact the United States House of Representatives Science and Technology Division, to have them undertake a process to declassify this information because the DCI suspected that the President was preparing to reveal this information to the American Public. The Congressional Research Service Science and Technology Division, under the directorship of Martha Smith was contacted by the House Science and Technology Committee and instructed to undertake a major investigation of the existence of extraterrestrial intelligence and the relationship of the UFO Phenomenon to this.

I was contacted by Miss Smith and asked, in my capacity as General Counsel to the United States Jesuit Headquarters National Social Ministry Office, to see if we could obtain access to the Vatican Library to obtain information that the Vatican had with regard to extraterrestrial intelligence and the phenomenon of UFOs. I pursued that with the permission of Father

William J. Davis, the Director of the National Office and we were refused access, as the United States Jesuit

Order, to information in the possession of the Vatican Library. When I reported this to Miss Smith, she then later, subsequently asked me to participate in a project which I can go into in some detail during the question and answer period, to individuals.

Pursuant to which I was given access to, as a Special Consultant to the United States Library of Congress Congressional Research Service to declassify portions of the Blue Book project of the Air Force. At that point, it was in 1977, approximately May of 1977, I went to the Madison Building of the United States Library of Congress. There was no one in the building at that time. It was brand new. I was directed to a basement office, where there were two guards at the door and a third sitting at the table, who took my identification, verified that I had been designated as a special consultant to the Congressional Research Service of the United States Library of Congress and was admitted to the room.

I thereupon found photographs, some dozen photographs of what is unquestionably an unidentified flying object on the ground that had crashed and plowed a furrow in a field of snow and was embedded in a bank, an embankment. There were United States Air Force personnel surrounding this craft, taking photographs of the craft and, one of the photographs, I could see that there was symbols on the side of the craft. So, I proceeded through the photographs and I found a close-up photograph of these symbols. I had been instructed that I was to take no notes. I had to leave my briefcase and all my identification outside of this room, but I brought with me a yellow pad. And, so what I did is, I opened up the yellow pad and refocused the overhead to the same size as the cardboard backing of the yellow pad, and I physically traced the copies of the symbols on the side of this craft, closed the yellow pad, put the microfiche back into the canister, reclosed the box that I had and I said, "It is time for me to leave." And I took this and proceeded to leave the office, at which point the security guard stopped me and one of them said, "What is that you have there Mr. Sheehan, at which point, I handed the yellow pad to him and he flipped through all the yellow pages, and never found the copy that I had.

So, I took that with me and brought it to the United States Jesuit Headquarters, had a meeting with the staff of Father William J. Davis, reported this to them, was authorized at that time by the United States Jesuit Headquarters to make a report to the National Council of Churches and, to request that the entire major 54 religious denominations of our country undertake a major study of extraterrestrial intelligence, which they declined to do.

I was subsequently asked to deliver a three hour closed door seminar to the top fifty scientists of the Jet Propulsion Laboratory of SETI, the Search for Extra Terrestrial Intelligence, which I did do in 1977. I am more than happy to testify under oath to these details to the United States Congress. I will be happy to meet with any members of the press at that time. You may also recall, I served as Chief Counsel to the Karen Silkwood Case. Which, we obtained the rulings of the Karen Silkwood case. I also served as Chief Counsel in the Iran-Contra Case. I was the first one to testify before the United States Congress of the off-the-shelf enterprise of Richard Secord and Albert Hakkein. I will be more than happy to share the details of what I believe to be the off-the-shelf enterprise and the secret government which is concealing this information from the American public. And, I am happy and proud to serve as General Counsel to the Disclosure Project. Thank you very much."

Dr. Werner von Braun the shadow government and the weaponization of space

Dr. Carol Rosin

"Good morning, my name is Carol Rosin. In 1974, after being a sixth grade school teacher, I was introduced to the late Dr. Werner Von Braun, who is the father of rocketry. In my first meeting with him, during that first three and a half hours, he said to me, "Carol, you vill stop the veoponization of space."

And I said, "You know, teachers don't stop until June."

He said, "No, you have to understand, this is February, and we have to prevent the weaponization of space because there is a lie being told to everyone. That the weaponization of space is first being based upon the evil empire, the Russians. "There are many enemies," he said, against who we are going to build this space based weapons system. The first of whom was the Russians, which was existing at that time. Then there would be terrorists, then there would be third world countries, now we call them "rogue nations," or "nations of concern." Then there would be asteroids. Then he would repeat to me, over and over, "and the last card, the last card, would be the extraterrestrial threat."

Well, at the time, I kind of laughed when he said asteroids and when he said extraterrestrials, I knew I wasn't gonna deal with that subject. And now, we hear on the news, just today, this week, that they've slid in another enemy, only this time, we are gonna protect our satellites. In other words, we have to have some reason to spend these trillions to waste these dollars on a space-based weapons system and they're all lies.

"This is a system," he told me, "That would never protect anyone."

Even back then he talked about suitcase bombs. He talked about a chemical, viral, bacterial, biological warfare these space based weapons would never protect us against. And then he told me, that in fact if you travel around the world, which I did after he died in 1977. I met with people in over a hundred countries who were friends. They didn't want to build space-based weapons. I became a space and missile defense consultant and I worked with people around the world. I became an advisor to the People's Republic of China. They don't want to build a space-based weapons system, and he told me back then that they didn't. He said, "Go to Russia, they're considered to be the enemy."

I got on a plane by myself. When I got to Russia, I had a list of people that I had read out of the newspaper. Chernenko was in office then. He was the only one I didn't get a chance to meet. They introduced me to everyone when I got there. And when I got back, I said, "Oh my Lord, this man is telling the truth."

There is no threat and I've been waiting until this day for twenty seven years, and I'm expecting the "spin" to happen, because he also explained to me that, as a military strategist, as a person who worked on the MX missile, which I did later, he said, "You will find that there's going to be a "spin" to find some enemy against whom we have to build space-based weapons and now, we should expect the spin because he said part of the formula for the intelligence community is, if they might have a weapon, then we do have to consider that they do have these weapons."

So now, they do have these weapons, so now we have to build these weapons systems. And that's the formula, except that it's all based on a lie, and we have witnesses here today that have shown you that these extraterrestrial beings, that these craft that have come here are not UFOs. They are identified flying objects and we know that they have beings in them. And we have witnesses here who have told you that they can shut down missile silos, they can stop a rocket going into space that's a test. We have witnesses here who have worked in the classified departments who have the courage to come forward here, to support what Werner Von Braun told me back in 1974 to 1977.

And, I will testify before the congress that when I founded the Institute for Security and Cooperation in Outer Space, which I shut down a few years ago because I didn't believe we had a chance with this huge, integrated, around the world complex weapons system, that we had any chance at all of transforming that war industry into a space industry that could provide benefits, like Dr. Greer has said…of global warming, we can end that situation and the energy crises. We can build now, non-polluting technologies. Werner Braun used to tell me that we can have cars, back then, that drove around off the ground. He described this to me, on beams, so that we had no pollution on this planet.

And we can solve the problems of the people on this planet and the other animals and the other cultures, on earth and in space. And we can end the arms race without dislocating the industry, jobs without disrupting the economy by transforming, Werner von Braun told me, the global industry into a cooperative space industry that will provide, he said, more jobs and profits on this planet than during any "hot" or "cold" wartime, more products and services that can be applied directly to solving the problems of this planet. And we can have a whole planet, now, that lives in peace on earth, with all the cultures on earth and with all the extraterrestrial cultures in space and these are words that Werner von Braun told me in 1974 and I will testify in congress under oath to everything I have said, and more, thank you."

Questions and answers

Dr. Stephen Greer: Director of the Disclosure Project

"Thank you very much, I would like to thank each of the witnesses and for your patience, we're running about fifteen minutes late and I do apologize for that. I want to emphasize all of these witnesses, each could speak from anywhere from two to five hours about what they have witnessed. We're trying to give you a snapshot. We have another four hundred of these witnesses. I have carried this burden for eight years. I'm now giving it to you the American people and the people of the world to take it forward. What I would like to do now, is open the audience for questions from the media. You may address them to me, or you may address them to the individual witness as you deem appropriate.

Question 1: (unclear) Mexican Newspaper

"I have three questions. I want to know if there are laws in this country that in some way allowed this kind of secrecy, or not, and then I wanted to know if there's a need to change any kind of law. The next one I want to ask you if you may, is, who is profiting from this secrecy that maintains in secret, the solution to the energy crises?"

Dr. Greer: Let me get to those quickly because we are short on time. First of all, I think initially there was an appropriate security apparatus in the '40's during the Truman, and also Eisenhower years, by the late Eisenhower years, we have a testimony from Brigadier General Stephen Lufkin, still a practicing attorney, that by the late Eisenhower years, that he had lost control of these projects, primarily because of the compartmentalization into the military-industrial complex-operative word, "industrial."

There are corporations, such as SAIC, Lockheed Martin, Northup Grumman and others that deal specifically with this issue, with advanced energy and propulsion systems connected to UFOs, and I think that what has happened, from the best we can tell from insiders that have briefed me for eight years, is that we have lost control of these projects from a Constitutional Law perspective because the infrastructure within the military intelligence and corporate channels is so well funded and so complex and labyrinthine. There are compartments within compartments within compartments and people who are in the Congress, and in fact, President Clinton when he made inquiries, were simply denied access as you heard earlier that President Carter was denied access.

On your other question, I would say that in terms of profiting from the status quo, Big Oil, there's certain geopolitical and financial infrastructures that would not welcome a definitive replacement to the fossil fuels. I will tell you, and we can prove this with other scientists who are ready to come forward that we already have a complete replacement for fossil fuels for any ionizing nuclear power plants. We don't need them, haven't needed them, probably since the time I was born. Now, of course, this is a major issue, we are talking a multi-trillion dollar global infrastructure change and so this does hit the alarm bells at the National Security Council economics area. However, what is more serious to the national security? Keeping the status quo, or letting ourselves go into a global ecosystem collapse and running out of fossil fuels and having massive rolling black outs, not just in California, but globally. We've got to do something about this and soon, and that's why we're advocating open hearings in the Congress."

Question 2: (unidentified)

"I just want to know if anyone in the UN is looking into this."

Dr. Greer: "I personally met with Boutros Boutros Ghali's wife, Alia Ghali, who said that her husband is quite concerned about this. This was in the 1990's. Since then, we know that there have been other people at the UN who've made inquiries. The problem is, the UN has no mandate to deal with this, it needs to be given a mandate from its constituent member nations. And I think that the public and the member nations need to ask the United Nations to get involved with this. This is an international peace issue and an international security issue and it should be taken up by the UN Security Council and, of course, we are recommending that as well."

Question 3: (unidentified)

"My question is actually to, my question is to Clifford Stone. You said that you had seen, a craft that had crashed, I wonder if you could describe what they look like."

Clifford Stone: "I could, but it would probably take a whole lot of time. The reason that I state that, when I got out in 1959, we had catalogued fifty-seven different species. You have individuals that look very much like you and myself who could walk among us and you wouldn't even notice the difference. Except for some of the things, that, they might be able to go ahead, even in a dark room, go ahead and touch an object and go and identify what color that object might be. They would have a heightened sense of smell, sight, hearing. The situation is that you have various types of what you call "grays." We didn't call them "grays" in the military, but you had at least three types of grays. You had some that were much taller than we were. Uh, the unique thing I would like to point out for the most part is that the entities that we did catalogue were in fact, humanoid. Now this created a situation with the scientific community was trying to figure out why that would be the case, because you would expect, if life evolved on other planets that they would take on some other type of being, so to speak, not necessarily be humanoid or bi-pedal such as we are. But, apparently, we got quite a few of the species out there that are quite humanoid in appearance and that creates a question that yet has to be answered by science.

Question 4: (unclear) UPI

"Could you address the vehicle, there's a drawing displayed. Why would this vehicle be on display at an air show? What is the power source that you are asserting is going to be very useful and how can you determine this vehicle is not something that is being developed by a government agency?

Dr. Greer: "This is an Alien Reproduction Vehicle and just to be clear, this means that it is based on anti-gravity and zero point energy propulsion systems. Those are the propulsion systems. They are being manufactured by a consortium of companies that include Lockheed Martin, Northup, SAIC and other corporations. They do have super luminal capacity, in other words, faster than the speed of light capacity. I think that Mr.

McCandlish and other witnesses that he's identified could go into more of the technical physics of it. I'm just a country doctor from Virginia I tell people, I mean really. But this is, actually the reason this is called Alien Reproduction Vehicle is that it's based on the study of extraterrestrial vehicles, but it is manufactured by human military intelligence, with aerospace contracting arrangements, and this is very important. It means that we, Homo sapiens have the capability to access this so-called zero point field of energy, which is the ambient field of energy from which all matter is fluxing and can access that energy and generate all the power we need to run this planet without fossil fuels or pollution."

Additional Question UPI

"Do you have any direct evidence though, that this, I mean we're talking about the same government that so appropriately named a snooper program, "Carnivore." I mean just because it's named Alien Reproduction Vehicle," considering the history and the questions that for such a long time about flying saucers, I mean, do you know, is there any reason for me to believe that this is actually derived from technology and you have witnesses that can attest to that? And how, a rocket engine doesn't translate into electricity, can you elaborate on that?

Dr. Greer: "The first part of your question, I would say that the testimony of witnesses we have, some of whom are here. Some are not here. In the briefing materials we have studied specifically extraterrestrial vehicles which have been retrieved. The breakthroughs in that research have led to applications that led to the building of this, and similar anti-gravity devices, and that this can be proven in open testimony before congress and that is exactly what we are calling for. We have the witnesses to establish this and they also have the documents that have the specific details of the propulsion systems. But this is not a jet internal combustion system at all. It's kicked in by an electric power source. It then accesses this ambient zero-point energy field that is responsible for all matter and energy existing. And, by special configurations and what have you, it causes a cancellation of mass inertia and an anti-gravity effect. And, this is a complex technical discussion, which is beyond the scope of this conference. But, we have materials in the briefing documents that we can provide you with references to people who have studied the anti-gravity effect as far back as certainly the 1950's. We have one witness who said that his family is connected to the RAND Corporation and that by the 1950's, more money had been spent on anti-gravity propulsion systems than the totality of the Manhattan Project. So, yes, we can establish those elements."

As a final footnote to the Disclosure Project Conference, one of the most important events in the history of the human race, of the few publications that even bothered to print the story, the Washington Post headline reads: *UFO Believers Sighted Here*...the final sentence of the article reads:

"Rough Draft appears once in a blue moon at washingtonpost.com. To get the story of the news conference directly from the organizers, go to www.disclosureproject.org. For a scientific approach to the question of extraterrestrial intelligence, try

In other words, don't listen to the truth, the Corporation/Government/Media lies are all you really need to know.

Chapter 26

Back to the Past, or the Future?

Now that we have seen the irrefutable evidence that we are not alone, and that the Corporation/Government insists on keeping this information and the technology for cheap renewable energy away from us, we really need to find out why. In order to begin to answer that question, we must first understand the history of the human race may not be at all what we have been taught. The influence of Freemasonry and the knowledge that was possessed by the Ancients seems to have eluded all but just a select number of people throughout the ages, such as Freemason Ed Leedskalnin who claimed to know how the Pyramids were built and who seemed certainly more familiar than most in the pre-nuclear age about the very structure of the atom. If he, being a Freemason, knew how the Pyramids were built, then there must be other Freemasons who are privy to this information as well. To put it simply, we came to our understanding of extraterrestrial technology, resonance, magnetism and electro-gravitics only to find that Nikola Tesla and Ed Leedskalnin had beaten us to it because they were Freemasons. If this technology came to the Freemasons from the Egyptians, where did they learn it?

For us non-Freemason simple folk, our only connection to the Egyptians lay in the writings of the ancient Greeks. The question is; how did the Greeks know so much about the Egyptians? We are left with a clue in the *Dialogues of Plato*, but I must warn the reader, that opening up the *Dialogues* means opening up a literal Pandora's Box when it comes to our understanding, or what we have thought we understood about our own history. In the modern world, much of this information comes to us in regurgitated forms as dry doctoral dissertations on one hand or as the "research" of one archeologist or other who entices people on research grant committees with tales of

Atlantis-but mysteriously they always seem to look for it in the last place they will ever find it. More about that later...

In Plato's *Dialogue of Critias*, we find an interesting discussion regarding the source of much of the information the Greeks possessed and subsequently passed on regarding the civilization Plato refers to as Atlantis. I have removed the section reference numbers for easier reading. I also will apologize beforehand because there will be some cases in the text where it will be necessary for me to jump in and explain a few things or summarize information to keep the reader focused on the important aspects of the dialogue. I prefer this method rather than assuming that the reader is lacking the capability to understand the story without my paraphrasing, which is why people still think that Atlantis is a myth. Instead, I would prefer that the reader read the words of Plato, and then, based upon Plato's arguments, come to a conclusion for his or her own self. That is the way the Greeks would have wanted it. So, let us roll up our togas and begin.

"And one of our fellow tribesmen--whether he really thought so at the time or whether he was paying a compliment to Critias-- declared that in his opinion Solon was not only the wisest of men in all else, but in poetry also he was of all poets the noblest. Whereat the old man (I remember the scene well) was highly pleased and said with a smile, "If only, Amynander, he had not taken up poetry as a by-play but had worked hard at it like others, and if he had completed the story he brought here from Egypt, instead of being forced to lay it aside owing to the seditions and all the other evils he found here on his return,-- why then, I say, neither Hesiod nor Homer nor any other poet would ever have proved more famous than he."

Author's note: Solon, the man of whom they are speaking, is none other than the Solon who wrote the Athenian Constitution, and, as the passage says, was considered one of the wisest men in Greek History. So, apart from him being a very wise man, what is important about Solon is not only what he related to his fellow countrymen, but also, where he, in fact, heard the story. Unfortunately, and this may be the source of confusion, or the source of confusing the general public by many modern scholars, Solon was not a contemporary of Plato, or Socrates. He had lived two hundred years before their time, but his knowledge and wisdom in all things had been kept as we would keep the writings of George Washington. Solon, like Washington, was the "father" of Athenian Democracy. Now, let us continue.

"In the Delta of Egypt," said Critias, "where, at its head, the stream of the Nile parts in two, there is a certain district called the Saitic. The chief city in this district is Sais--the home of King Amasis, --the founder of which, they say, is a goddess whose Egyptian name is Neith, and in Greek, as they assert, Athena. These people profess to be great lovers of Athens and in a measure akin to our people here. And Solon said that when he travelled there he was held in great esteem amongst them; moreover, when he was questioning such of their priests as were most versed in ancient lore about their early history, he discovered that neither he himself nor any other Greek knew anything at all, one might say, about such matters."

Author's note: As we continue, pay close attention to the Greek account of the first man and woman, a story of a great flood, which was survived by one man and his wife, and the story of a great cataclysm of fire that originated in space. Also notice the Egyptian opinion of the Greek understanding of history.

"And on one occasion, when he (Solon) wished to draw them on to discourse on ancient history, he attempted to tell them the most ancient of our traditions, concerning Phoroneus, who was said to be the first man, and Niobe; and he went on to tell the legend about Deucalion and Pyrrha after the Flood, and how they survived it, and to give the genealogy of their descendants; and by recounting the number of years occupied by the events mentioned he tried to calculate the periods of time. Whereupon one of the priests, a prodigiously old man, said, "O Solon, Solon, you Greeks are always children: there is not such a thing as an old Greek."

"And on hearing this he asked, "What mean you by this saying?" And the priest replied, "You are young in soul, every one of you. For therein you possess not a single belief that is ancient and derived from old tradition, nor yet one science that is hoary with age. And this is the cause thereof: There have been and there will be many

and divers destructions of mankind, of which the greatest are by fire and water, and lesser ones by countless other means.

For in truth the story that is told in your country as well as ours, how once upon a time Phaethon, son of Helios, yoked his father's chariot, and,
because he was unable to drive it along the course taken by his father, burnt up all that was upon the earth and himself perished by a thunderbolt,--that story, as it is told, has the fashion of a legend, but the truth of it lies in the occurrence of a shifting of the bodies in the heavens which move round the earth, and a destruction of the things on the earth by fierce fire, which recurs at long intervals."

The Egyptians told Solon that there "have been and will be many and divers destructions of mankind" in response to Solon's 'immature' tale of an Adam and Eve story along with Solon's story of what sounds like the Biblical flood. What could they have been referring to? As the story continues, Solon urges his Egyptian teachers to tell their story, at which they recount how Athena, the Goddess of Wisdom, chose the Greeks to live in the lands that they presently inhabit. Then they continue with an astonishing story that, as uncomplicated as it is to understand, seems to baffle us to this very day. This is the story of Atlantis.

The account of Atlantis

"Of the citizens, then, who lived 9000 years ago, I will declare to you briefly certain of their laws and the noblest of the deeds they performed: the full account in precise order and detail we shall go through later at our leisure, taking the actual writings...For it is related in our records how once upon a time your State stayed the course of a mighty host, which, starting from a distant point in the Atlantic ocean, was insolently advancing to attack the whole of Europe, and Asia to boot. For the ocean there was at that time navigable; for in front of the mouth which you Greeks call, as you say, 'the pillars of Heracles, there lay an island which was larger than Libya and Asia together; and it was possible for the travelers of that time to cross from it to the other islands, and from the islands to the whole of the continent over against them which encompasses that veritable ocean. For all that we have here, lying within the mouth of which we speak, is evidently a haven having a narrow entrance; but that yonder is a real ocean, and the land surrounding it may most *rightly be called, in the fullest and truest sense, a continent. Now in this island of Atlantis there existed a confederation of kings, of great and marvelous power, which held sway over all the island, and over many other islands also and parts of the continent; and, moreover, of the lands here within the Straits they ruled over Libya as far as Egypt, and over Europe as far as Tuscany.*

  So this host, being all gathered together, made an attempt one time to enslave by one single onslaught both your country and ours and the whole of the territory within the Straits. And then it was, Solon, that the manhood of your State showed itself conspicuous for valor and might in the sight of all the world. For it stood pre-eminent above all in gallantry and all warlike arts, and acting partly as leader of the Greeks, and partly standing alone by itself when deserted by all others, after encountering the deadliest perils, it defeated the invaders and reared a trophy; whereby it saved from slavery such as were not as yet enslaved, and all the rest of us who dwell within the bounds of Heracles it ungrudgingly set free.

  But at a later time there occurred portentous earthquakes and floods, and one grievous day and night befell them, when the whole body of your warriors was swallowed up by the earth, and the island of Atlantis in like manner was swallowed up by the sea and vanished; wherefore also the ocean at that spot has now become impassable and unsearchable, being blocked up by the shoal mud which the island created as it settled down." (Timaeus 24e-25d)

The Atlantis Cover-up?

For some reason, this very simple explanation of a continent and an advanced civilization that disappeared into the sea where the Azores Islands are today in the Atlantic Ocean, at exactly the same time period as the great cataclysmic flood that occurred 11,700 years ago when the ice sheets suddenly melted seems to be off-limits to "legitimate" archeological and scientific research. Either way, the Egyptians and the Greek philosophers, who were not known for their practical jokes, seem to be describing a civilization from a place they called Atlantis, which, at some undetermined point in time, invaded all of Africa and had begun an invasion of Europe, enslaving everyone along the way. Today, people who even mention Atlantis are ridiculed and discredited unless they propose some outlandish theory that Atlantis was the Island of Thira, which exploded around

1400 B.C.E., within the memory of Greek Civilization, or, even more outlandish, that Atlantis was the city of Troy, which was written about by the Greek poet Homer and which any Greek school child then or today could have explained was not Atlantis.

If the insults to our intelligence are not enough, by placing Atlantis where it absolutely was not, scholars resort to reducing the story of Atlantis to nothing more than a fanciful myth told in a whimsical fashion
as a sort of fairy tale. However, a person who studies Greek culture for any length of time will come to understand that the philosophers and mathematicians of Greece were anything but whimsical. Even when recounting the myth of Phaethon and Helios, the Egyptian priests scoffed at Solon for thinking that the Greek myth had any basis in fact. They simply dismissed the myth and looked for a scientific explanation to explain what caused the massive heat wave that scorched the earth. But still, "legitimate" science will simply explain the story of Atlantis away and say that there is no evidence. So, once again, we must ask, why the cover up?

Evidence of Atlantis: Tiahuanaco: a port city in the Andes

The statement that there is no evidence of a civilization that existed before the Holy Grail of Civilizations or Sumer and the Indus River Valley, is similar to the statement that there are no extraterrestrials. There is plenty of evidence for this civilization and it is scattered all over the world. One of the best examples of this culture that either was inclusive of Atlantis, or co-existed with them, is the city of **Tiahuanaco** in modern-day Bolivia. The city itself is full of so many mysteries that scientists prefer to ignore it, or offer some off-the-wall explanations regarding its existence and location. However, the facts of Tiahuanaco speak for themselves.

To be brief, since the anomalies found at city of Tiahuanaco are numerous and there are more qualified works about the city that the interested reader may consult, we will focus on the most obvious and relevant to our discussion. First, the perimeter of the city itself, or what is left of it, is scattered with stone blocks, many of which weigh in excess of 100 tons, and some in excess of 440 tons. These stone blocks were carved with a precision that we could only duplicate today with the use of lasers. Unlike the limestone used in the Pyramids and Ed Leedskalnin's Coral Castle, the stone blocks at

Tiahuanaco are composed of andesite granite, some of the hardest, densest and heaviest rock on the face of the earth. How the residents of Tiahuanaco were able to quarry, move, carve and place these massive granite slabs is still anyone's guess.

Second, the city itself is a massive port. According to R. Cedric Leonard, "Some of the docks and piers in this area are so large that hundreds of ships could dock comfortably; yet there is nothing "oceanic" near these docks except a pre-historic coastline indicated by chalky
deposits of ancient saltwater fossils. Lake Titicaca, languishing miles away, is nearly one hundred feet lower than the level of the ruined docks."

Third, carved on the granite slabs are pictures of animals that have been extinct in the Americas for at least ten thousand years, specifically, toxidons and elephants. Fourth, a large pyramid was erected in what archeologists call "The Temple Complex." Around the complex stand large granite walls with what appear to be hieroglyphic characters that have remained undeciphered to this day. Finally, as if this all was not intriguing enough, the geologic evidence, along with the 100 to 150 ton granite slabs that lay about, "like matchsticks," according to R. Cedric Leonard, are indications of a cataclysmic flood. How cataclysmic? The ocean port city of Tiahuanaco is over *two miles* above sea level.

Archeological taboo: backdating civilization

How can we explain a city two miles high in the Andes Mountains with pictures of animals on its walls that disappeared from the fossil record ten thousand years ago? One method is by calculating the tilt of the earth as it rotates on its axis in a motion similar to a spinning top, which completes a complete cycle every 41,000 years. Many ancient structures, such as the pyramids, were built according to specific alignments with celestial bodies. By calculating the earth's natural "wobble" it is possible to calculate when these structures were built.

Professor Arthur Posnansky, who studied Tiahuanaco for fifty years and completed a multi-volume work in 1945 entitled, Tiahuanaco: Cradle of American Man, concluded that, along with the evidence of animals that went extinct in what is called the

Pleistocene Extinction some 12,000 years ago, that the city itself dates back some 15,000 years. According to R. Cedric Leonard:

"There is only one solution that can satisfy all of the above mysteries regarding the ruins of Tiahuanaco. This is none other than the geological cataclysm, which affected the entire globe geologically and climatically, causing the Pleistocene extinction and the sinking of Atlantis. Thus, if Tiahuanaco was built before the end of the last Ice Age, then the depictions of the numerous Pleistocene animals (extinct for 12,000 years) are readily explainable. The other indications of the apparent age of the city (tilted seashore lines, lime deposits and silt) would then harmonize with the astronomical alignments built into the buildings. The evidence is strong it seems to me, that Prof. Posnansky's original conclusions were correct. Thus I think it likely that Tiahuanaco was originally built near sea level ca. 15,000 B.C. as an Atlantean seaport."

Hidden stream of knowledge, or one "kooky" theory?

In his discussion of the Freemasons, author Jim Marrs speaks about a "hidden stream of knowledge" that has been passed down from the Ancients. Could the simple explanation be that while they occupied Egypt, the people of Atlantis demonstrated their technology, which included flying machines, electricity and anti-gravity devices that they used to awe the local population and convince them that they were indeed, if not gods, then, at least people not to be trifled with? Once they realized the melting of the ice sheets destroyed their civilization, did they assume the role of the ruling priest classes in Egypt, and the Druids in Britain and France? Did they pass on their knowledge to their descendants, knowledge which was preserved long after their civilization was destroyed? This knowledge, if kept within their own bloodlines, would assure their continuing power as civilizations rose and fell.

Who knows? It certainly sounds like the stuff of a really good conspiracy theory, doesn't it? All we do know is that we only have the evidence that the Greeks left us in this story about the civilization of Atlantis, and the viciousness of the attacks committed by the granted, tenured and well-funded scholarly and Freemasonry connected community upon anyone who attempts to include Atlantis or extraterrestrials in the history of mankind, not to mention the

Latter-day Saints. Does it not seem odd, that in the age of our advanced technology, we are controlled by people who appeal to our basest of natures, or, as it says in Critias:

"...and when they (the gods) had thus settled them (their division of the earth), they reared us (mankind) up, even as herdsmen rear their flocks, to be their cattle and nurslings; only it was not our bodies that they constrained by bodily force, like shepherds guiding their flocks with stroke of staff, but they directed from the stern where the living creature is easiest to turn about, laying hold on the soul by persuasion, as by a rudder, according to their own disposition; and thus they drove and steered all the mortal kind." (Critias 109b-109c)

Being directed by our emotions is not all we have that was left to us by the remains of the civilization of Atlantis, or the extraterrestrials, or the Egyptian priest class. The Greeks in turn, passed on their understanding of geometry and through their understanding of geometry they left us an understanding of life itself. Do you remember when we were discussing the subatomic particles of the atom and the fundamental energy called quarks by "legitimate" science? These are basically the same thing as the rotating vortexes described by Jon Depew and Ed Leedskalnin and the whirling ether flux talked about by Dr. Paul Laviollette in his book *Genesis of the Cosmos*. Apparently, the Greeks also had the same understanding that we do today. In the following passage, Plato has already described the creation of man, first as spirit, and then as we will see, as matter.

"For this alone He suffered to remain uncloven, whereas He split the inner Revolution in six places into seven unequal circles, according to each of the intervals of the double and triple intervals, three double and three triple These two circles then He appointed to go in contrary directions; and of the seven circles into which He split the inner circle, He appointed three to revolve at an equal speed, the other four to go at speeds equal neither with each other nor with the speed of the aforesaid three, yet moving at speeds the ratios of which one to another are those of natural integers. (Timaeus 36d)

Modern scholars, who misunderstood their meanings because they stopped studying the Greeks about the same time they discovered the atom, thought that when they referred to the atom as "indivisible," they thought they were talking about the atom. It is apparent that the Greeks understood quarks, and their particular spins within the nucleus of the atom. If the reader will recall, modern theoretical physicists theorize that the structure of the strings vibrating within a quark follow a certain geometry. What follows may require a large dose of aspirin, but the reader will understand soon enough, that the Greeks understood what that geometry was that our theoretical theorists, well, theorize about today. In Timaeus 35a, Plato gives us a complete description of molecular chemistry and does so as follows:

"…and in the fashion which I shall now describe.
   Midway between the Being which is indivisible (the vibrating positively and negatively charged strings that make up the quark of the
atom according to Ed Leedskalnin and modern theoretical physicists) and remains always the same and the Being which is transient and divisible in bodies (the molecule), He blended a third form of Being compounded out of the twain (the atom), that is to say, out of the Same (quarks) and the Other (molecules); and in like manner He compounded it midway between that one of them which is indivisible and that one which is divisible in bodies. And He took the three of them, and blent them all together into one form, by forcing the Other into union with the Same, in spite of its being naturally difficult to mix."
   Plato then goes on to describe how man was created in time and how time and gravity are related:

".... Accordingly, seeing that that Model (man) is an eternal Living Creature, He set about making this Universe, so far as He could, of a like kind. But inasmuch as the nature of the Living Creature was eternal, this quality it was impossible to attach in its entirety to what is generated; wherefore He planned to make a movable image of Eternity, and, as He set in order the Heaven, of that Eternity which abides in unity He made an eternal image, moving according to number, even that which we have named Time. [37d]

For simultaneously with the construction of the Heaven He contrived the production of days and nights and months and years, which

existed not before the Heaven came into being. And these are all portions of Time; even as "Was" and "Shall be" are generated forms of Time, although we apply them wrongly, without noticing, to Eternal Being. For we say that it "is" or "was" or "will be," whereas, in truth of speech, "is" alone [37e]
is the appropriate term; "was" and "will be," on the other hand, are terms properly applicable to the Becoming which proceeds in Time, since both of these are motions; but it belongs not to that which is ever changeless in its uniformity to become either older or younger through time, nor ever to have become so, nor to be so now, nor to be about to be so hereafter, nor in general to be subject to any of the conditions which Becoming has attached to the things which move in the world of Sense, these being generated forms of Time, which imitates Eternity and circles round according to number. And besides these we make use of the following expressions,-- [38a]
I will spare the reader, offer some aspirin and recommend a thorough study of *The Dialogues*, so that the reader has the opportunity to see, through the discussions of pure philosophy, what marvelous intellectual insights the Greeks have to offer. What Plato is saying is that we beings were created in a dimension where time does not exist, and which had to be artificially created by creating the universe in order for us to exist in a world where it would not be possible for us to know what we would become, or rather, what it is that we really are. It is also important to remind the reader that the Greeks were the first major culture outside of the Levant to adopt the teachings of Jesus Christ.

So, the question still remains, why do we put so much stock in the words of the Greek Philosophers, yet dismiss the story of Atlantis as a fairy tale? The answer is simple. Like the beings Critias described earlier, we are led by those who, lead us by our "stern" or, our base instincts and as we ignore our own ability to think rationally. When "legitimate" scientists tell us there is no evidence that any civilization existed before the civilizations in Mesopotamia and the Indus River Valley, they appeal to our fear of ridicule, which they are so eager to do, in order to dissuade us as a child looking for Christmas presents on December twenty-third.

A kick in the Sphinx

However, in the 1990's, "legitimate" science got another kick in the pants when a man by the name of John Anthony West took a picture of the Sphinx that lies near the Pyramids on the Giza Plateau, covered its head with a post-it note and presented it to geologist Robert Schoch of Boston University. John Anthony West then asked Robert Schoch if he could determine, from the picture, what caused the erosion on the limestone structure. The geologist didn't hesitate and said it was caused by water erosion. In fact, the erosion on the limestone that makes up the Sphinx was caused by water, a lot of water. The problem, similar to the one at Tiahuanaco, is that it doesn't rain that much in Egypt.

Further studies by illegitimate or "pseudo" scientists, researchers Colin Reader and David Coxill theorized that the Sphinx predates the eras of the Dynasties of the Pharaohs. According to their hypothesis, the Sphinx and possibly the pyramids must have been built when the climate was much, much wetter. But, as they say, there wasn't any proof. So, the researchers began to look for proof, or a period of time when the climate may have been much different in Egypt than it is today. Using the same process that basically backtracks the earth's somewhat wobbly orbit, which was used to calculate the dates at Tiahuanaco, researchers like Graham Hancock and Robert Bauval were able to determine that around 10,500 B.C.E (the same time period given by the Greeks), the Constellation Orion was exactly lined up with the layout of the pyramids. At the same time in history, the Sphinx, originally carved, according to their theory, as a lion, faced East at the sunrise-into the constellation of Leo.

They further theorized that the portals of the pyramids, or windows in their sides, lie at the point where their dimensions create the Golden Mean of 1.618. In other words, if you take the length of a side of a pyramid and locate that hole, and use that as a point to divide the top half from the bottom, you come up with a line with a ratio of 1 to 1.618. It is this very ratio which was also the ratio seen on Ed Leedskalnin's magnetic levitating wheel and is also visible in the Pyramids surrounding the picture of Hyrum Abiff on the wall of the Norman Hall Freemason Lodge in Philadelphia, and in Plato's description of the Golden Mean, or Phi. Was this strange clue left by Ed Leedskalnin that also appears in the works of Plato, and on the sides of the Pyramids of Giza, a clue to something that was left for humans from the past? If so, it is the clue to what?

Dr. Laviolette, 2012, and the Galactic Superwave Theory

Around the world, in Tiahuanaco, Bolivia, Central America, Mexico, in the Pacific Islands of Nan Madol, Easter Island and at Stonehenge, there are massive carved stones that weigh in the hundreds of tons in some cases. Nobody has any idea as to how they were moved. Like the Pyramids, scholars give us theories about rollers and wedges, but in hundreds of years of theories, not one of them has yet demonstrated how the stones were moved in any practical fashion. In the Pacific Islands of Nan Madol, where massive granite slabs were stacked like logs in a log cabin, the natives have long insisted that the people who built the cities were "gods" who levitated the granite slabs through the air. If we go by the data we have gathered from modern scientists, who have studied the climate of earth by looking at ice cores that date back 250,000 years, we can come to some interesting conclusions.

The climate of the earth fluctuates significantly. Until 11,700 BC, a massive sheet of ice covered the earth, at least the Northern Hemisphere. For some reason, either due to a massive meteorite smashing into the earth, the lack of sunspots, or a massive wave of supercharged matter
being shoved across the solar system, the earth began to warm. When the earth warmed, the ice melted. When the ice melted, entire land masses disappeared under the rising oceans. This scientifically proven fact can do a lot to rationally explain how a story about a man building a boat and surviving the flood is present in nearly every culture on the planet. It can also explain how the story about an advanced civilization that lived, "beyond the Pillars of Hercules" could have sunk into the sea, and why the people from the Mediterranean could not venture out past the "sea of mud" that was left in the Atlantic. Did these ancient cultures, as well as the Maya try to warn us about some upcoming catastrophe?

The Superwave and the end of the world?

Astronomer and physicist Paul A. Laviollette has done vast amounts of research over the years regarding what he calls, "Super wave Theory." His theory was laughed at by "legitimate science" and, as we discussed earlier in the book, has resulted in Dr.

Laviollette being placed on a blacklist (or "black balled" to use Freemason terminology) by Cornell University's science journal.

However, independent researchers have found ample evidence such as deposits of microscopic cosmic debris that is only associated with meteorites, such as iridium, deposited in uniform intervals in layers of glacial ice. Dr. LaViolette's Super wave Theory in its most simple form, is the theory that, at regular intervals, the center of the galaxy emits a massive amount of electrically charged subatomic particles in powerful bursts. Those particles go careening through space and, when they strike our solar system, they act like a strong wind blowing across a Kansas farm.

When these subatomic particles come in contact with the dust, ice and debris orbiting the solar system outside the Kyper belt, the Super wave pushes that debris across the solar system and inevitably, it will cover the earth, which will cause immediate freezing. When the debris strikes the sun, it will create an effect like throwing gasoline on a fire-a really big fire. The subsequent heat, not to mention the massive amounts of radiation that will strike the earth, could have the catastrophic effects of not only melting all the ice on the earth, but actually heating the water in the oceans, which would cause it to expand and evaporate causing storms like we have never seen. Furthermore, the charged particles could completely disrupt the earth's magnetic field and cause a "pole shift" where the Earth's magnetic field actually flips upside down. In retrospect, Dr. LaViolette's "Superwave" doesn't sound so "super" at all.

Again, let us look at the words of the Latter-day Saint Prophet Joseph Smith, who appears to have had some idea that the earth was going to be literally scorched. In Joseph Smith's History, we read:

"For behold, the day shall come that shall burn as an oven, and all the proud, yea, and all that do wickedly shall burn as stubble…" (JS-H 1:37)

Without getting too far off the subject, the Mayans also predicted this same event, which happens in extreme cases every 26,000 years, or as Critias said, "…at long intervals." According to the Greeks as told to them by the Egyptians, this cataclysm, or something like it, has happened before. The Greeks mention the tale of Phaethon, son of Helios and his chariot causing a fire that consumed everything. The Greeks attribute the catastrophe to "shifting bodies around the earth," and though I am no expert in ancient Greek, it seems fairly clear that if they meant the planets, they would have said so. The only body we know of that shifts around the earth is the moon, and they knew the name of that also. So, we are left with one clue that the Greeks explain away as a legend. But the Egyptians priests, rational men that they were, say what really caused the catastrophe was some kind of cataclysm that originated in space.

The biggest secret of all: the coming cataclysm

Could it possibly be that the "Super wave" is already on its way here? Are the prophecies of the Maya, Nostradamus, Joseph Smith and countless others about to come true? Are we about to suffer a cataclysm that will leave most of us dead, and the rest of us starving to death? What if, for argument's sake, some people did know what was in store for us? What if there were some people who did communicate with the extraterrestrials? If *you* knew what was coming, wouldn't you try to do whatever you could to save your skin? Would *you* tell anyone? Even more importantly, do you think the Corporation/Government/Media is going to tell *you*?

In a world that is suffering from overpopulation, a shortage of resources and a huge gap between the 'haves' and the 'have nots,' wouldn't a global catastrophe be perfect the way to "prune the vineyard" as it says in the Bible? If we could save those who were "worth" saving, and leave the useless ones to suffer a grisly fate, wouldn't a cataclysm like
Noah's flood or a possible firestorm from space ultimately be good for mankind? You may even agree, provided you were not deemed to be one of the useless ones. There is one thing we can all be sure of. If the earth is about to be destroyed by fire as Joseph Smith, the Egyptians, Greeks, Mayans and Nostradamus said it was, you will not have any say about it because if you even mention it, you will be carried off to the "boobie hatch" of public opinion.

With this understanding that there was a great civilization that was possibly more advanced than we are today that fell victim to a global cataclysm and that information is right up at the top of the list of taboos for science and academia, the question of who would want to keep the information secret goes no farther than the list of the people who have been keeping it a secret for thousands of years. The list of who might wish to protect this secret is a rather short, but powerful one. In the first case, there is the religious community. No matter whether Christian, Jew, or Muslim, all believe that the world is exactly as old as the Bible, Koran, or Torah says that it is. It is that firm and unyielding piece of knowledge that have allowed them to keep power for the past few thousand years. It is also that firm and unyielding attitude that has been the cause of the loss of faith for so much of the world's population. Maybe, based on the evidence, the Holy Scriptures are inaccurate when it comes to the exact age of man and of civilization?

So, the religious community obviously has a stake in protecting that secret. But what about the academics, surely they are open to new ideas and thinking and would love to hear theories about the lost civilizations of Atlantis and the wonderful world that existed before the end of the last Ice Age. Wouldn't they? Oddly enough, for hundreds of years, while they were divorcing themselves from religion, the academic community has also been divorcing themselves from any talk about a civilization existing before Mesopotamia and the Indus River Valley. "There is no evidence," they have been saying. What they really mean, is that they are not going to look at any evidence, or comment on evidence that might get their tenure revoked and their grants denied. Ironically, it is these same academics that owe their very livelihoods to the writings of Plato and the world that he and the other Greeks created. They created a world of science by observation, reason based upon logic and conclusions based upon empirical evidence. They created academies that would later grow into colleges and universities. In other words, our academics borrowed, stole, plagiarized and regurgitated almost every aspect of the teachings of the Greek Philosophers, from science to mathematics and philosophy, but the story they told of Atlantis, they dismiss as, "a fairy tale," and say there is no evidence that such a place ever existed.

That leaves us with only one more powerful group, and it is a group who has adopted so many of the Greek ideals, that they seem to be almost Greek themselves. They are people who, like the Greeks, have symposiums where they discuss abstract ideas. They have meeting houses modeled on Greek architecture. They helped fashion a government based on the ideas of the democracy in Athens and the Republic in Rome. They sponsor Greek fraternities and sororities in our colleges and universities. They have an obsession with geometry and they speak, of the One God, the All-Seeing Eye and they claim to have origins in the Mystery Cults of Egypt. In the headquarters of Scottish Rite Freemasonry in Washington D.C. the same words that adorn the Temple of Athena on the Acropolis in Athens are carved into a marble seat: "Know thyself." Need I say more? The Society of Freemasons is protecting many secrets, the secret of magnetism, the force that governs the very structure of matter and energy. They are protecting the secret of extraterrestrial beings and the secret of lost civilizations and they have been doing so for the past twelve thousand years. The question still remains, "Why?" That, my friend, is really for you to decide.

We began this story in the ancient past and we have seen through our own story or history, that as much as things change, they always seem to stay the same. Why is that? The answer is quite simple. If we don't change, how can we expect anything else to change? If we really want to change the world, ourselves, etc. etc we need to not only understand who it is that we are, we also need to make sure that everyone else is on the same sheet of music. So, who are we? Are we random chance? Are we a throw of the evolutionary dice or a grand design thought up by some other species, or God, or something in between? Quite honestly, that is the real problem.

The question about conspiracies, Freemasons, "Mormons" and extraterrestrials should be the least of your worries. It is the ability to focus your fears worries and concerns on things that ultimately have little relevance to your life that allows others to have power over you. Jesus once said, roughly, 'Don't worry about someone else's shortcomings when you have enough shortcomings of your own.' If you want to fix the world, fix yourself. Once you are genuinely happy with what it is that you are, go out and help one other person. Then help another person. We all have different skills and abilities, so use them. Once you have made a
positive effort in your little world, then that little world can help somewhere else. It will set off a chain reaction that in no time will encompass the globe with kindness and understanding. You have to stop believing that someone else is going to fix the world for you. That is what got us where we are in the first place.

As we have seen, we are not alone in this universe. In fact, we are at such a low end of the evolutionary process compared to the beings that visit our planet on a regular basis, we still think in terms of killing each other off, while dozens, if not hundreds of species that could have finished us off in an afternoon surround us.

Why didn't they? Probably because they understand the universe and the way things work in different dimensions. To them, we are simply pigs with opposable digits. The universe, as we have seen, runs on positive and negative energy. Either way, time, my friends, is running out for the human race. Now that you know about the Deceptions of the Ages, will you be on the positive, or the negative side of the universal equation?

SOURCES

Chapter 2

- Hawking, Stephen. *A Brief History of Time*. New York, N.Y.: Bantam Dell Publishing Company, 1988. P.4. Print.
- Aquinas, Thomas Summa Theologica Book 1 Question 25 article 3
- Naymik, Mary. "Romney Lands in Cleveland." *Plain Dealer* (2007): n. pag. Web. 8 Jun 2010. <http://blog.cleveland.com/openers/2007/11/romney_lands
- Shirer, William. *The Rise and fall of the Third Reich*. Simon and Schuster, 1990. Print.
- Moore, Michael. *Fahrenheit 911* Lions Gate Entertainment, 2004
- GONSALVES, SEAN. "WAR ON TERRORISM HAS OILY UNDERCURRENT." *Seattle Post-Intelligencer* 03 September 2002, Print.
- Shennon, Bergmann, Philip, Lowell. "THREATS AND RESPONSES: THE HEARINGS; 9/11 Panel Is Said to Offer Harsh Review of Ashcroft." *New York Times* 13 April 2004, U.S.Print.
- Makow, Henry. "Jewish Lobby Vetoes Candidate Over 9-11 Views ." *Radical Press* 27 September 2008: n. pag. Web. 8 Jun 2010. <http://www.radicalpress.com/?p=1042>.
- *Phenomenon - The Lost Archives: American Midnight*. Dir. Jay Miracle. Perf. Dean Stockwell. Image Entertainment, 1999. DVD.
- *Freemasonry Revealed*. Dir. Gary Lang. Perf. Bridget Adamo, Geoff Ball, Barry Birnbe. Koch Vision, 2007. DVD.
- *Endgame: Blueprint for Global Enslavement*. Dir. Alex Jones. Perf. Alex Jones. Disinformation, 2007. DVD.

Chapter 3

- *Holy Bible LDS Edition of King James Bible*. Saints, The Church Of Jesus Christ Of Latter-Day. Salt Lake City: Church Of Latter-Day Saints, 2007. Print.
- *Ancient Mysteries: Who Wrote the Bible (2pc) [VHS]*. Dir. Lionel Friedberg. Perf. Rabbi David Wolpe Lecturer University of JudaismStephen J. Patterson Associate Professor of the New Testament Eden Theological Seminary Daniel L. Smith

Christopher: Professor of Hebrew Bible Loyal Marymount. A&E Home Video, 2007. DVD.
- *The National Geographic: The Gospel of Judas*. Dir. James Barrat. National Geographic Video, 2008. DVD.
- *Phenomenon - The Lost Archives - Noah's Ark Found?*. Dir. Douglas Snider. Perf. Dean Stockwell. Image Entertainment, 1999. DVD.
- *The Day The Universe Changed*. Dir. Richard Reisz. Perf. James Burke. Ambrose Video Publishing Inc, 1985. Film.

Chapter 4

- Durant, Will. *Our Oriental Heritage - The Story Of Civilization, Part I*. New York, NY: Simon & Schuster, 1963. Print.
- Arrian. *The Campaigns of Alexander (Penguin Classics)*. Rev Ed ed. London: Penguin Classics, 1976. Print.
- Thucydides. *The Peloponnesian War*. 1st ed. New York: McGraw-Hill, 1982. Print.
- Homer. *The Iliad and The Odyssey*. boston: Wilder Publications, 2007. Print.
- *In the Footsteps of Alexander the Great (2pc)*. Dir. David Wallace. Perf. David Wood. Bbc Warner, 2005. DVD.
- Heines, Matthew. *My Year in Oman*. Vancouver: Trafford Publishing, 2005. Print.
- Homer. *The Iliad and The Odyssey*. Boston: Wilder Publications, 2007. Print.
- Herodotus. *Herodotus: The Persian War (Translations from Greek and Roman Authors)*. New York: Cambridge University Press, 1982. Print.
- Plato. *The Dialogues of Plato, Volume 1: Euthyphro, Apology, Crito, Meno, Gorgias, Menexenus (The Dialogues of Plato)*. ????. Reprint. New Haven: Yale University Press, 1989. Print.
- "BBC NEWS | Science/Nature | Age of ancient humans reassessed." *BBC NEWS | News Front Page*. N.p., n.d. Web. 21 Oct. 2009. <http://news.bbc.co.uk/2/hi/science

Chapter 5

- Plutarch. *Plutarch: Lives of Noble Grecians and Romans (Modern Library Series, Vol. 1)*. ?. Reprint. New York: Modern Library, 1992. Print.
- Homer. *The Iliad and The Odyssey*. boston: Wilder Publications, 2007. Print.
- *Ancient Rome: The Rise and Fall of an Empire*. Dir. Nick Green. Perf. Sean Pertwee, John Shrapnel, Peter Firth. BBC Worldwide/Discovery Channel, 2006. DVD.
- Thucydides. *The Peloponnesian War*. 1st ed. New York: McGraw-Hill, 1982. Print.
- Livy, Titus. *Livy: The Early History of Rome, Books I-V (Penguin Classics)*. Revised ed. London: Penguin Classics, 2002. Print.
- *The National Geographic: The Gospel of Judas*. Dir. James Barrat. Perf. Dr. Robert Shuller: Crystal Cathedral Dr. Craig Evans Acadia Divinity College Canada Dr. Elaine Pagels: Princeton University. National Geographic Video, 2008. DVD.
- *Decoding the Past: The Templar Code*. Dir. Geoffrey Madeja. Perf. Various. A&E (Ingr), 2005. DVD.
- Oerlemans, Johannes Hans Oerlemans (2005). "Extracting a Climate Signal from 169 Glacier Records". *Science* **308** (5722): 675–677. doi:10.1126/science.1107046. Retrieved 2009-12-25
- *The Day The Universe Changed*. Dir. Richard Reisz. Perf. James Burke. Ambrose Video Publishing Inc, 1985. Film.

Chapter 6

- *The History Channel Presents The Revolution*. Dir. Un Known. Perf. Bill Kurtis. A&Amp;E Home Video, 2002. Film.
- "The Rothschild Dynasty." *Bible Believers.Org.au*. N.p., n.d. Web. 19 Nov. 2009.
- Griffin, Des. *Descent into Slavery*. Colton, Oregon: Emissary Publications, 1994. Print.
- *Phenomenon - The Lost Archives - Monopoly Men*. Dir. Daniel Hopsicker. Perf. Dean Stockwell. Image Entertainment, 1999. DVD.

Chapter 7

- *The History Channel Presents The Revolution*. Dir. Un Known. Perf. Bill Kurtis. A&Amp;E Home Video, 2002. Film.
- *Phenomenon - The Lost Archives: American Midnight.* Dir. Jay Miracle. Perf. Dean Stockwell. Image Entertainment, 1999. DVD.
- *Endgame: Blueprint for Global Enslavement*. Dir. Alex Jones. Perf. Alex Jones. Disinformation, 2007. DVD.
- *The Day The Universe Changed*. Dir. Richard Reisz. Perf. James Burke. Ambrose Video Publishing Inc, 1985. Film.
- "The Rothschild Dynasty." *Bible Believers.Org.au*. N.p., n.d. Web. 19 Nov. 2009.
- *The Book of Mormon*. Salt Lake City: The Church Of Jesus Christ Of Latter-Day Saints, 1830. Print.
- *Phenomenon - The Lost Archives - Monopoly Men*. Dir. Daniel Hopsicker. Perf. Dean Stockwell. Image   Entertainment, 1999. DVD.
- Griffin, Des. *Descent into Slavery*. Colton, Oregon: Emissary Publications, 1994. Print.
- Smith, Joseph, and Jr. Smith.*History of the Church - Joseph Smith*. New York: Lds Book Club, 2003. Print.
- Report on the Bank, in Syrett, ed., *Papers*, 7:326-28
- Washington to Hamilton , February 16, 1791, in Syrett, ed. *Papers* 8:50-51
- Danzer, Gerald A.; J. Jorge Klor de Alva, Larry S. Krieger, Louis E Wilson, and Nancy Woloch. *The Americans*.
- Ratner, Sidney, James H. Soltow, and Richard Sylla. *The Evolution of the American Economy:*
- *Growth, Welfare, and Decision Making*. Fac Sub ed. New York: Macmillan Publishing Company, 1993. Print.
- Taylor, George Rogers.*Jackson Versus Biddle; The Struggle Over The Second Bank Of The United States (History - United States)*. Washington D.C.: Reprint Services Corp, 1949. Print.
- Thomas, Fleming(2003). The Louisiana Purchase. John Wiley & Sons, Inc., P:149

Chapter 8

- *Trail of Hope: The Story of the Mormon Trail.* Dir. Lee B. Groberg. Perf. Narrated by Hal Holbrook. Groberg Films, 1996. DVD.
- *History of the Church*, Vol. 4, pp. 535—541 Article of Fatith
- Katz, Irving (1968). *August Belmont; a political biography.* New York and London: Columbia University Press.
- Anderson, Richard L., *Clarifications of Bogg's 'Order' and Joseph Smith's Constitutionalism, Church History Regional Studies, Missouri,* ed. Arnold K. Garr and Clark V. Johnson, Department of Church History and Doctrine, Brigham Young University, 1994, pp. 27–70)
- Baugh, Alexander L., *A Call to Arms: The 1838 Mormon Defense of Northern Missouri,* BYU Studies, 2000.
- Cannon, Donald Q., and Lyndon W. Cook, eds., *The Far West Record: Minutes of the Church of Jesus Christ of Latter-day Saints, 1830–1844,* Salt Lake City, 1983.
- Corrill, John, *A Brief History of the Church of Jesus Christ of Latter-day Saints (Commonly Called Mormons),* St. Louis, 1839.
- *Document Containing the Correspondence, Orders &c. in Relation to the Disturbances with the Mormons; And the Evidence Given Before the Hon. Austin A. King, Judge of the Fifth Judicial Circuit of the State of Missouri, at the Court-House in Richmond, in a Criminal Court of Inquiry, Begun November 12, 1838, on the Trial of Joseph Smith, Jr., and Others, for High Treason and Other Crimes Against the State.* Fayette, Missouri, 1841,complete text.
- Foote, Warren, *The Autobiography of Warren Foote,* typescript in Harold B. Lee Library, Brigham Young University, Provo, Utah.
- Hamer, John, *Northeast of Eden: A Historical Atlas of Missouri's Mormon County,* Mirabile, Missouri, 2004.
- Hartley, William G., "Missouri's 1838 Extermination Order and the Mormons' Forced Removal to Illinois," *Mormon Historical Studies,* Spring 2001

- Jenkins, James H., *Casus Belli: Ten Factors That Contributed to the Outbreak of the 1838 'Mormon War' in Missouri*, Independence, Missouri: Blue and Grey Press, 1999.

- Jessee, Dean, *The Personal Writings of Joseph Smith,* Salt Lake City: Deseret Book, 1984.

- Johnson, Clark V., *Mormon Redress Petitions: Documents of the 1833–1838 Missouri Conflict,* Religious Studies Center, BYU, 1992.

- Journal History of the Church of Jesus Christ of Latter-day Saints, *LDS Church Archives, Salt Lake City.*

- Lee, John D., *Mormonism Unveiled: The Life and Confessions of John D. Lee and the Life of Brigham Young,* 1877.

- LeSueur, Stephen C., *The 1838 Mormon War in Missouri,* University of Missouri Press, 1990.

- McGee, Joseph H., *Story of the Grand River Country,* Gallatin, Missouri, 1909.

- Quinn, D. Michael, *The Mormon Hierarchy: Origins of Power*, Salt Lake City, 1994.

- Peck, Reed, *The Reed Peck Manuscript,* complete text.

- Rigdon, Sidney, *An Appeal to the American People: Being an Account of the Persecutions of the Church of Latter-day Saints; and of the Barbarities Inflicted on Them by the Inhabitants of the State of Missouri,* Cincinnati, 1840.

- Thorp, Joseph, *Early Days in the West Along the Missouri One Hundred Years Ago,* Liberty, Missouri, 1924.

- *The True Latter Day Saints' Herald,* Plano, Illinois.

- Van Wagoner, Richard S., *Sidney Rigdon: A Portrait of Religious Excess*, Salt Lake City, 1994.

Chapter 9

- Noyce, Robert . "Cinco de Mayo: A Mexican Holdiay with an American Twist." *Deseret News* [Slat Lake City] 27 Apr. 2004: na. Print.
- "The Rothschild Dynasty." *Bible Believers.Org.au*. N.p., n.d. Web. 19 Nov. 2009.
- Griffin, Des. *Descent into Slavery*. Colton, Oregon: Emissary Publications, 1994. Print.
- *Phenomenon - The Lost Archives - Monopoly Men*. Dir. Daniel Hopsicker. Perf. Dean Stockwell. Image Entertainment, 1999. DVD.

- Ferguson, Niall. *The House of Rothschild: The World's Banker: 1849-1999 [HOUSE OF ROTHSCHILD]*. London: Penguin Books, 2000. Print.
- Chernow, Ron. *The Warburgs*. New York: Random House, 1993
- Kuhn, Loeb & Co. *Kuhn, Loeb & Co. A Century of Investment Banking*. New York: Privately printed, 1967
- Kuhn, Loeb & Co. *Kuhn Loeb & Co. Investment Banking Through Four Generations*. New York: Privately printed, 1955
- Warburg, Paul M. *The Federal Reserve System*. New York: The Macmillan Company, 1930.
- During World War I, Max Warburg was appointed by Kaiser Wilhelm II to head the German Secret Service, where he served as chief financial adviser and strategic intelligence consultant.
  His brother Paul Warburg was the chief architect of the Federal Reserve Board in the United States.
  On December 12, 1918, the United States Naval Secret Service Report on Mr. Warburg was as follows:
  "WARBURG, PAUL: New York City. German, naturalized citizen, 1911. was decorated by the Kaiser in 1912, was vice chairman of the Federal Reserve Board. Handled large sums

furnished by Germany for Lenin and Trotsky. Has a brother who is leader of the espionage system of Germany."

This report, which must have been compiled much earlier, while the United States was at war with Germany, is not dated until December 12, 1918. AFTER the Armistice had been signed. Also, it does not contain the information that Paul Warburg resigned from the Federal Reserve Board in May, 1918, which indicates that it was compiled before May, 1918, when Paul Warburg would theoretically have been open to a charge of treason because of his brother's control of Germany's Secret Service. (Wikipedia)

- Cohen, Naomi Wiener. (1999). *Jacob H. Schiff: a Study in American Jewish Leadership.* Hanover, New Hampshire: University Press of New England.

- *Who* owns the Fed?." *SAPF Official Web Page*. N.p., n.d. Web. 12 Oct. 2009. <http://www.save-a-patriot.org/files/view/whofed.html
- "Board of Governors of the Federal Reserve System."*Board of Governors of the Federal Reserve System*. N.p., n.d. Web. 12 Oct. 2009. <http://www.federalreserve.gov
http://www.freemasonrywatch.org/
- "Freemasonry Watch - Is the Devil in the details? | Freemasons News | Freemason Information." *Freemasonry Watch - Is the Devil in the details? | Freemasons News | Freemason Information*. N.p., n.d. Web. 22 Oct. 2009. <http://www.freemasonrywatch.
- "Famous Freemasons." *Famous Freemasons*. N.p., n.d. Web. 10 Oct. 2009. <www.whale.to/b/33.html>.

Chapter 10

- Ferguson, Niall. *The House of Rothschild: The World's Banker: 1849-1999 [HOUSE OF ROTHSCHILD]*. London: Penguin Books, 2000. Print.
- *The Occult History of the Third Reich*. Dir. Dave Flitton. Perf. Patrick Allen. 1987. Eagle Rock Ent, 2004. DVD.
- "The Rothschild Dynasty." *Bible Believers.Org.au*. N.p., n.d. Web. 19 Nov. 2009.
- Griffin, Des. *Descent into Slavery*. Colton, Oregon: Emissary Publications, 1994. Print.

- Shirer, William. *The Rise and fall of the Third Reich*. Simon and Schuster, 1990. Print.
- "Freemasonry Watch - Is the Devil in the details? | Freemasons News | Freemason Information." *Freemasonry Watch - Is the Devil in the details? | Freemasons News | Freemason Information*. N.p., n.d. Web. 22 Oct. 2009. <http://www.freemasonrywatch.
- "Famous Freemasons." *Famous Freemasons*. N.p., n.d. Web. 10 Oct. 2009. <www.whale.to/b/33.html>.

Chapter 11

- Moore, William L.. "The Spalding Saga 2: Prequel to the Plates." *Solomon Spalding Home Page Search-the-site & Links*. N.p., n.d. Web. 13 Oct. 2009. <http://solomonspalding.com/SR
- Moore, William L.. "Spalding Research Project: Spalding Saga Intro." *Solomon Spalding Home Page Search-the-site & Links*. N.p., n.d. Web. 13 Oct. 2009. <http://solomonspalding.com/SR

Chapter 12

- Potter, George, and Richard Wellington. *Lehi in the Wilderness: 81 New Documented Evidences That the Book of Mormon Is a True History*. Springville: Cedar Fort, 2003. Print.
- Potter, George. *Nephi in the Promised Land*. Springville: Cedar Fort, Inc., 2009. Print.
- "Catastrophic ancient flood cooled the Earth | COSMOS magazine." *COSMOS magazine | The science of everything*. N.p., n.d. Web. 13 Jan. 2010. <http://www.cosmosmagazine.com/news/1864/catastrophic-ancient-flood-cooled-earth>.
- *The Book of Mormon*. Salt Lake City: The Church Of Jesus Christ Of Latter-Day Saints, 1830. Print.
- Potter, George. Did the Jaredites land in Peru? (2007) Bear River City, Utah. Website Article.

    www.nephiproject.com/.../April%202007%20Featured%20Article.doc

Chapter 13

- *The Book of Mormon*. Salt Lake City: The Church Of Jesus Christ Of Latter-Day Saints, 1830. Print.

- Knab, Timothy J., and Thelma D. Sullivan. *A Scattering of Jades: Stories, Poems, and Prayers of the Aztecs*. Tucson: University of Arizona Press, 2003. Print.

- Taylor, John *An examination into and an elucidation of the great principle of the mediation and atonement of Our Lord and Savior Jesus Christ.* Deseret New Company. (p.201) Salt Lake City. 1982 Print.

- Interview with Dr. Paul Laviollette. Coast to Coast A.M. June 21 2009

- Courlander, Harold. *The Fourth World of the Hopis: The Epic Story of the Hopi Indians as Preserved in Their Legends and Traditions*. na. Reprint. Albuquerque, NM: University of New Mexico Press, 1987. Print.

Chapter 14

- Wallace-Murphy, Tim . *The Templar Legacy & The Masonic Inheritance within Rosslyn Chapel*. Edinburgh: The Friends of Rosslyn, 0. Print.
- Ralls, Karen. *The Templars and the Grail: Knights of the Quest*. 1 ed. Wheaton, IL: Quest Books, 2003. Print.
- Butler, Alan, and Stephen Dafoe. *The Warriors and Bankers*. Baltimore: Ian Allan Ltd, 2006. Print.

- Hopkins, Marilyn, and Tim Wallace-Murphy. *Templars in America: From the Crusades to the New World*. San Francisco: Weiser Books, 2004. Print.
- *Les Dossiers Secrets d'Henri Lobineau* (1967), claim that hugh married catherine st clair
- Barry. "Modern-Day Knights Templar in the Holy Land - Part 1." *WATCH UNTO PRAYER*. N.p., n.d. Web. 14 Nov. 2009. <http://watch.pair.com/ritual.htm
- Odrowaz-Sypniewska, Margaret. "The Knights Templar." *The Knights Templar*. N.p., n.d. Web. 21 Nov. 2009. <www.angelfire.com/mi4/polcrt
- Smart, George. *The Knights Templar Chronology: Tracking History's Most Intriguing Monks*. -: Authorhouse, 2005. Print.
- *Decoding the Past: The Templar Code*. Dir. Geoffrey Madeja. Perf. Various. A&E (Ingr), 2005. DVD.
- *Freemasonry Revealed*. Dir. Gary Lang. Perf. Bridget Adamo, Geoff Ball, Barry Birnbe. Koch Vision, 2007.
- Martin, Sean. *The Knights Templar: The History and Myths of the Legendary Military Order*. First Trade Paper Edition ed. New York: Basic Books, 2004. Print.
- Shea, Lisa. " The Merovingian Kings - Mary Magdalene ." *Lisa Shea - Origami, Parakeets, Birding*. N.p., n.d. Web. 14 June 2010. <http://www.lisashea.com/hobbies
- Knight, Christopher, and Robert Lomas. *The Second Messiah: Templars, the Turin Shrowd, and the Great Secret of Freemasonry*. Gloucester, Maine: Fair Winds Press, 2001. Print.

Chapter 15

- "Templarhistory.com » Blog Archive » Philip IV – 1268 – 1314 ." *Templarhistory.com* . N.p., n.d. Web. 15 Jan. 2009. <http://blog.templarhistory.com/2010/03/philip-iv-1268-1314/>.
- Chamberlin, E. R.. *The Bad Popes*. New Ed ed. New York: Dorset, 2003. Print.
- Reardon, Wendy J.. *The Deaths of the Popes: Comprehensive Accounts, Including Funerals, Burial Places and Epitaphs*. Jefferson, N.C.: Mcfarland & Company, 2010. Print.

- *Mysteries of the Freemasons: The Beginning / America*. Dir. Pip Gilmore. Perf. Michael C. Hall. A&E Television Networks, 2006. DVD.
- *Decoding the Past: The Templar Code*. Dir. Geoffrey Madeja. Perf. Various. A&E (Ingr), 2005. DVD.
- Smart, George. *The Knights Templar Chronology: Tracking History's Most Intriguing Monks*. -: Authorhouse, 2005. Print.
- *Decoding the Past: The Templar Code*. Dir. Geoffrey Madeja. Perf. Various. A&E (Ingr), 2005. DVD.
- *Freemasonry Revealed*. Dir. Gary Lang. Perf. Bridget Adamo, Geoff Ball, Barry Birnbe. Koch Vision, 2007.
- Martin, Sean. *The Knights Templar: The History and Myths of the Legendary Military Order*. First Trade Paper Edition ed. New York: Basic Books, 2004. Print.
- Wallace-Murphy, Tim . *The Templar Legacy & The Masonic Inheritance within Rosslyn Chapel*. Edinburgh: The Friends of Rosslyn, 0. Print.
- Ralls, Karen. *The Templars and the Grail: Knights of the Quest*. 1 ed. Wheaton, IL: Quest Books, 2003. Print.
- Butler, Alan, and Stephen Dafoe. *The Warriors and Bankers*. Baltimore: Ian Allan Ltd, 2006. Print.
- Hopkins, Marilyn, and Tim Wallace-Murphy. *Templars in America: From the Crusades to the New World*. San Francisco: Weiser Books, 2004. Print.
- Odrowaz-Sypniewska, Margaret. "The Knights Templar." *The Knights Templar*. N.p., n.d. Web. 21 Nov. 2009. <www.angelfire.com/mi4/polcrt>
- *The Troubadours: An Introduction*, Simon Gaunt and Sarah Kay, edd. (Cambridge: Cambridge University Press), p. 112
- Crowley, Aleister; Mary. Desti, Leila. Waddell (2004)

Chapter 16

- Crowley, Aleister; Mary. Desti, Leila. Waddell (2004)
- David Shankbone (November 5, 2007). "Satanism: An interview with Church of Satan High Priest Peter Gilmore"
- *The Book of Mormon*. Salt Lake City: The Church Of Jesus Christ Of Latter-Day Saints, 1830. Print.

- *Doctrine and Covenants of the Church of Jesus Christ of Latter-day Saints*. 1897. Reprint. Salt Lake City: The Church Of Jesus Christ Of Latter-Day Saints, 1981. Print.
- *Holy Bible LDS Edition of King James Bible*. Saints, The Church Of Jesus Christ Of Latter-Day. Salt Lake City: Church Of Latter-Day Saints, 2007. Print.
-

Chapter 17

- Knight, Christopher, and Robert Lomas. *The Second Messiah: Templars, the Turin Shrowd, and the Great Secret of Freemasonry*. Gloucester, Maine: Fair Winds Press, 2001. Print.
- Geiger, Conrad. "American Atheists | Page Not Found."*American Atheists | Welcome*. N.p., n.d. Web. 15 Mar. 2009. <http://www.atheists.org/Atheism/roots/enlightenment
- SilverBearCafe.com, Johnny Silver Bear |. "The Illuminati and the House of Rothschild."*Red Ice Creations - Media for the Forefront - We Present, You Decide*. N.p., n.d. Web. 15 Nov. 2009. <http://www.redicecreations.com/sp
- Griffin, Des. *Descent into Slavery*. Colton, Oregon: Emissary Publications, 1994. Print.
- *Freemasonry Revealed*. Dir. Gary Lang. Perf. Bridget Adamo, Geoff Ball, Barry Birnbe. Koch Vision, 2007. DVD.
- *Mysteries of the Freemasons: The Beginning / America*. Dir. Pip Gilmore. Perf. Michael C. Hall. A&E Television Networks, 2006. DVD.

Chapter 18

- *Pearl of Great Price*. Salt Lake City: The Church Of Jesus Christ Of Latter-Day Saints, 1935. Print.
- *The Book of Mormon*. Salt Lake City: The Church Of Jesus Christ Of Latter-Day Saints, 1830. Print.
- *Holy Bible LDS Edition of King James Bible*. Saints, The Church Of Jesus Christ Of Latter-Day. Salt Lake City: Church Of Latter-Day Saints, 2007. Print.

- *Mysteries of the Freemasons: The Beginning / America*. Dir. Pip Gilmore. Perf. Michael C. Hall. A&E Television Networks, 2006. DVD.
- *Freemasonry Revealed*. Dir. Gary Lang. Perf. Bridget Adamo, Geoff Ball, Barry Birnbe. Koch Vision, 2007. DVD.
- McGavin, E. Cecil. *Mormonism and Masonry*. New York: Kessinger Publishing, Llc, 2004. Print.
- Chornenky, Dennis. *Freemasonry and Native American Traditions*. 2004 Annual California Masonic Symposium. http://www.freemasons-freemasonry.com/dennisfr.html
- The Morgan Affair." *Anti-Masonry: Points of View*. N.p., n.d. Web. 15 June 2010. <http://www.masonicinfo.com/morgan
- "Freemasonry Watch - Is the Devil in the details? | Freemasons News | Freemason Information." *Freemasonry Watch - Is the Devil in the details? | Freemasons News | Freemason Information*. N.p., n.d. Web. 15 Nov. 2009. <http://www.freemasonrywatch.o
- "SILENT WITNESS; The Mafia, the Vatican heavyweight, the 'suicide' of God's Banker 25 years ago.. the secrets that will be taken to the grave.(News)." <u>The Mirror (London, England)</u>. MGN Ltd. 2006.
- RICHARD GRAY. "Italian court to rule on 'God's banker'." <u>Scotland on Sunday</u>. Scotsman Publications. 2005.
- "BBC NEWS | Europe | Scandal-hit Vatican banker dies." *BBC NEWS | News Front Page*. N.p., n.d. Web. 16 June 2010. <http://news.bbc.co.uk/2/hi/europ
- "Will justice finally be served on killers of God's Banker? ; Roberto Calvi was found hanging from Blackfriars Bridge 25 years ago. Today a Rome court will resolve a murder that connected the Mafia and the Vatican." <u>The Evening Standard (London, England)</u>. McClatchy-Tribune Information Services. 2007.
- Mason indicted over murder of 'God's banker', The Independent, July 20, 2005
- Plea to Pope from 'God's banker' revealed as murder trial begins, The Times, October 6, 2005
- *Phenomenon - The Lost Archives: American Midnight*. Dir. Jay Miracle. Perf. Dean Stockwell. Image Entertainment, 1999. DVD.

- Helman, Scott . "Obama emphasizes his ability to effect change - The Boston Globe."*Boston.com*. N.p., 27 Dec. 2007. Web. 17 Nov. 2009. <http://www.boston.com/news/nation

Chapter 19

- *Doctrine and Covenants of the Church of Jesus Christ of Latter-day Saints*. 1897. Reprint. Salt Lake City: The Church Of Jesus Christ Of Latter-Day Saints, 1981. Print.
- *Holy Bible LDS Edition of King James Bible*. Saints, The Church Of Jesus Christ Of Latter-Day. Salt Lake City: Church Of Latter-Day Saints, 2007. Print.
- *The Book of Mormon*. Salt Lake City: The Church Of Jesus Christ Of Latter-Day Saints, 1830. Print.
- *Pearl of Great Price*. Salt Lake City: The Church Of Jesus Christ Of Latter-Day Saints, 1935. Print.
- McGavin, E. Cecil. *Mormonism and Masonry*. New York: Kessinger Publishing, Llc, 2004. Print.
- Chornenky, Dennis. *Freemasonry and Native American Traditions*. 2004 Annual California Masonic Symposium. http://www.freemasons-freemasonry.com/dennisfr.html
- The Morgan Affair." *Anti-Masonry: Points of View*. N.p., n.d. Web. 15 June 2010. <http://www.masonicinfo.com/morgan
- "Freemasonry Watch - Is the Devil in the details? | Freemasons News | Freemason Information." *Freemasonry Watch - Is the Devil in the details? | Freemasons News | Freemason Information*. N.p., n.d. Web. 15 Nov. 2009. <http://www.freemasonrywatch.o
- Beadle, J. H.. *Life In Utah; Or, The Mysteries And Crimes Of Mormonism*. New York: Blunt Press, 2008. Print.
- Rue, William Earl La. *The Foundations of Mormonism: A Study of the Fundamental Facts in the History and Doctrines of the Mormons from Original Sources*. Toronto: Nabu Press, 2010. Print.
- Tullidge, Edward William. *Life of Joseph the Prophet*. New York: General Books Llc, 2009. Print.
- Smith, Joseph, and Jr. Smith.*History of the Church - Joseph Smith*. New York: Lds Book Club, 2003. Print.

- Smith, Joseph, and Jr. Smith.*History of the Church - Joseph Smith*. New York: Lds Book Club, 2003. Print.

Chapter 20

- McGavin E.Cecil, *Mormonism and Masonry*. Second enlarged edition. Salt Lake City: Bookcraft Publishers, 1949. 20-22.
- Flanders, Robert. *Nauvoo: KINGDOM ON THE MISSISSIPPI*. Urbana: University of Illinois Press, 1975. Print.
- University, Brigham.*Encyclopedia of Mormonism*. New York, New York: MacMillan Publishing Company., 1992. Print.
- *History of the Church of Jesus Christ of Latter-day Saints (7 V. + Index)*. 2nd, rev. ed. Salt Lake City: Deseret Book Co., 1978. Print.
- Esplin, Ronald K. "Joseph Smith's Mission and Timetable: "God will Protect Me Until My Work Is Done.'" In The Prophet Joseph Smith: Essays on the Life and Mission of Joseph Smith, ed. L. Porter and S. Black, pp. 280-319. Salt Lake City, 1989.
- HC 6:519-631, esp. 561-622.
- Jessee, Dean C. "Return to Carthage: Writing the History of Joseph Smith's Martyrdom." Journal of Mormon History 8 (1981):3-19.
- Madsen, Truman G. Joseph Smith the Prophet, pp. 109-126, 174-83. Salt Lake City, 1989.
- Miller, David E., and Della S. Miller. Nauvoo: The City of Joseph, pp. 130-74. Salt Lake City, 1974.
- Oaks, Dallin H., and Marvin S. Hill. Carthage Conspiracy: The Trial of the Accused Assassins of Joseph Smith. Urbana, Ill., 1979.
- *Encyclopedia of Mormonism, Vol. 3, Martyrdom of Joseph and Hyrum Smith*
- "The Destruction of the "Nauvoo Expositor"—Proceedings of the Nauvoo City Council and Mayor".
- Beadle, J. H.. *Life In Utah; Or, The Mysteries And Crimes Of Mormonism*. New York: Blunt Press, 2008. Print.
- *Freemasonry Revealed*. Dir. Gary Lang. Perf. Bridget Adamo, Geoff Ball, Barry Birnbe. Koch Vision, 2007. DVD.

Chapter 21

- "Background: Atoms and Light Energy." *Imagine The Universe! Home Page*. N.p., n.d. Web. 18 June 2010. <http://imagine.gsfc.nasa.gov/docs/teachers/lessons/xray_spectra/background-atoms.html>.

Chapter 22

- Salla, Michael . "Exopolitics Journal vol-3-2." *Exopolitics Journal vol-3-2*. N.p., n.d. Web. 3 June 2010. <http://exopoliticsjournal.com/vol-3-2.htm#Salla>.
- "REPORT OF SCIENTIFIC ADVISORY PANEL ON UNIDENTIFIED FLYING OBJECTS CONVENED BY OFFICE OF SCIENTIFIC INTELLIGENCE, CIA January 14 - 18, 1953." *The Computer UFO Network*. N.p., n.d. Web. 21 Mar. 2010. <http://www.cufon.org/cufon/robertson
- Cohen, Jerry. "NICAP Disputes Condon Report (1/69)." *The Research of Jerry Cohen*. N.p., n.d. Web. 13 Nov. 2009. <http://www.cohenufo.org/nicapcondon.htm>.
- REPORT OF SCIENTIFIC ADVISORY PANEL ON UNIDENTIFIED FLYING OBJECTS CONVENED BY OFFICE OF SCIENTIFIC INTELLIGENCE, CIA January 14 - 18, 1953
- Denzler, Brenda (2003). *The Lure of the Edge: Scientific Passions, Religious Beliefs, and the Pursuit of UFOs*. University of California Press. ISBN 0-520-23905-9.p. 17
- "Archived UFO Case Files-UFO Casebook Files." *UFO Casebook, UFO Case files, UFO Photos, UFO Video, Aliens, UFO News, Magazine*. N.p., n.d. Web. 21 Mar. 2010. <http://www.ufocasebook.com/condon
- *UFO Hunters - Season 1 (Alien Engineering) (Steelbook)*. Dir. Bill Birns. Perf. Narrator James Lurie. A&E Home Video (New Releaset), 2008. DVD.

- Clark, Jerome, *The UFO Book: Encyclopedia of the Extraterrestrial*, Visible Ink, 1998, pp. 593-604
- Groleau, Rick. "NOVA | The Elegant Universe | Imagining Other Dimensions | PBS." *PBS*. N.p., n.d. Web. 14 Feb. 2010. <http://www.pbs.org/wgbh/nova/>
- http://www.youtube.com/watch?v=JkxieS-6WuA
- Extra spatial dimensions of String Theory http://pdf.aiaa.org/preview/1981/PV1981_1608.pdf
- Brian Greene The Universe on a String- http://www.youtube.com/watch?v=YtdE662eY_M&feature=related
- Alien Scientist John Hutchison-

  http://www.youtube.com/watch?v=uGC-

  ZuFr3Oo&feature=PlayList&p=D87EAE0AB19FE92B&playnext

  _from=PL&playnext=1&index=36

Chapter 23

- Alien Scientist ferro-magnetic superfluids gravito-magnetic effect http://www.youtube.com/watch?v=pJJ-4lnwrck
- Depew, Jon. "CORAL CASTLE CODE / JON DEPEW / FORMULA of ENERGY." *CORAL CASTLE CODE / JON DEPEW / FORMULA of ENERGY*. N.p., n.d. Web. 21 June 2010. <http://coralcastlecode.com>.
- Stride, Jeremy. "Code 144."*Code 144*. N.p., n.d. Web. 21 June 2010. <http://www.code144.com>.
- Cathie, Bruce L.. *The Bridge to Infinity: Harmonic 371244*. Revised ed. ?: America West Publishers, 1989. Print.

Chapter 24

- *UFO Hunters - Season 1 (Alien Engineering) (Steelbook)*. Dir. Bill Birns. Perf. Narrator James Lurie. A&E Home Video (New Releaset), 2008. DVD.

- *Phenomenon - The Lost Archives: H.A.A.R.P. - Holes in Heaven?*. Dir. Wendy Robbins. Perf. Dean Stockwell. Image Entertainment, 1999. DVD.
- "The Philadelphia Experiment." Nimoy, Leonard. *In Search of*. CBS. 17 Feb. 1977. Television.
- "Ralph Ring and Otis Carr."*Project Camelot*. N.p., 15 Aug. 2006. Web. 3 Dec. 2009. <www.projectcamelot.org/ralph_ring
- Clifford A. Pickover, *Strange Brains and Genius: The Secret Lives of Eccentric Scientists and Madmen*. HarperCollins, 1999. p.14
- ""Golden ratio" hints at hidden atomic symmetry."*World Science - Science News*. N.p., 7 Jan. 2010. Web. 21 Apr. 2010. <http://www.world-science.net/othernews/100107_goldenratio

Chapter 25

- Greer, Steven. "Search Results for "thedisclosureproject.org"."*Search Results for "thedisclosureproject.org"*. Dr. Steven Greer, 8 May 2001. Web. 21 June 2010. http://thedisclosureproject.org
- Joel Achenbach. "UFO Believers Sighted Here!." The Washington Post. Washington Post Newsweek Interactive Co. 2001.

Chapter 26

- Plato. "Perseus Digital Library."*Perseus Digital Library*. N.p., n.d. Web. 20 June 2010. http://www.perseus.tufts.eduhttp://www.perseus.tufts.edu/hopper/text?doc=Perseus:text:1999.01.0180:text%3DTim.:section%3D24e
- http://www.goldenageproject.org.uk/survey.php (Atlantis) Christian O' Brien
- Advanced Ancient Civilizations of Peru and Bolivia, ONLINE, the pre-Inca culture of Tiwanaku and Wiracochas.

- Bennett, Wendell, C., "Excavations at Tiahuanaco," *Anthropological Papers* of the American Museum of Natural History, Vol. xxxiv, Part III, 1934.

- Posnansky, Arthur, *El Gran Templo del Sol en los Andes: La Edad de Tihuanacu*, Bulletin No. 45 of the Geographic Society of La Paz, 1918.

- Posnansky, Arthur, *Tihuanacu, the Cradle of American Man*, Vols. I - II (Translated into English by James F. Sheaver), J. J. Augustin, Publ., New York, 1945; Vols. III - IV, Minister of Education, La Paz, Bolivia, 1957.
- http://www.atlantisquest.com/prehistcity.html
- Laviolette, Paul. "Sphinx Stargate:.. N.p., n.d. Web. 21 June 2010. <http://www.etheric.com>.

MORE GREAT BOOKS BY MATTHEW D. HEINES

My Year in Oman: An American Experience in Arabia During the War On Terror

Deceptions of the Ages: "Mormons" Freemasons and Extraterrestrials

Killing Time in Saudi Arabia 2004-2005

www.heinessight.com

Made in the USA
Charleston, SC
12 September 2014